After qualifying in medicine from Oxford, and then becoming a Fellow of the Royal College of Surgeons, the author has enjoyed a varied and rewarding surgical career.

A longstanding interest in history and in teaching medical students has made it clear that an understanding of the past and how advances in medicine and surgery have been achieved makes it easier to follow the rationale for present treatments. This learning process seems as valid for nations, politicians and despots, even individuals, as for medical students and doctors.

In memory of the last generation who spared no
effort to give this generation the best start in life.

For Rory, Henry, Esme, Lydia, Freya, Noah and Beatrix.

Jeremy Plewes

HISTORY IN 100 CHAPTERS

AUSTIN MACAULEY PUBLISHERS™

LONDON * CAMBRIDGE * NEW YORK * SHARJAH

Copyright © Jeremy Plewes 2023

The right of Jeremy Plewes to be identified as author of this work has been asserted by the author in accordance with sections 77 and 78 of the Copyright, Designs and Patents Act 1988.

All rights reserved. No part of this publication may be reproduced, stored in a retrieval system, or transmitted in any form or by any means, electronic, mechanical, photocopying, recording, or otherwise, without the prior permission of the publishers.

Any person who commits any unauthorised act in relation to this publication may be liable to criminal prosecution and civil claims for damages.

The story, experiences, and words are the author's alone.

A CIP catalogue record for this title is available from the British Library.

ISBN 9781398443495 (Paperback)
ISBN 9781398443501 (ePub e-book)

www.austinmacauley.com

First Published 2023
Austin Macauley Publishers Ltd®
1 Canada Square
Canary Wharf
London
E14 5AA

I am not a historian by any possible measure, but it is hoped that as an outsider, I have been able to highlight and explain important areas and connections. Needless to say, I have undoubtedly committed errors of both commission and omission, for which I can only crave the reader's indulgence. I owe considerable thanks to my ever-willing secretary, Kath Leckey, and considerable apologies to my long-suffering wife, Jenna. Thanks are also due to many helpful friends, including Juliet Horne, John Barnett, John Adams, and my informal English teacher, Geraldine Wall. John Leatherdale took the excellent cover photograph of Richard I outside the Houses of Parliament. I am particularly grateful to my digital wizard, Ben Plewes for advice and rescue when my electronic inadequacies have been exposed.

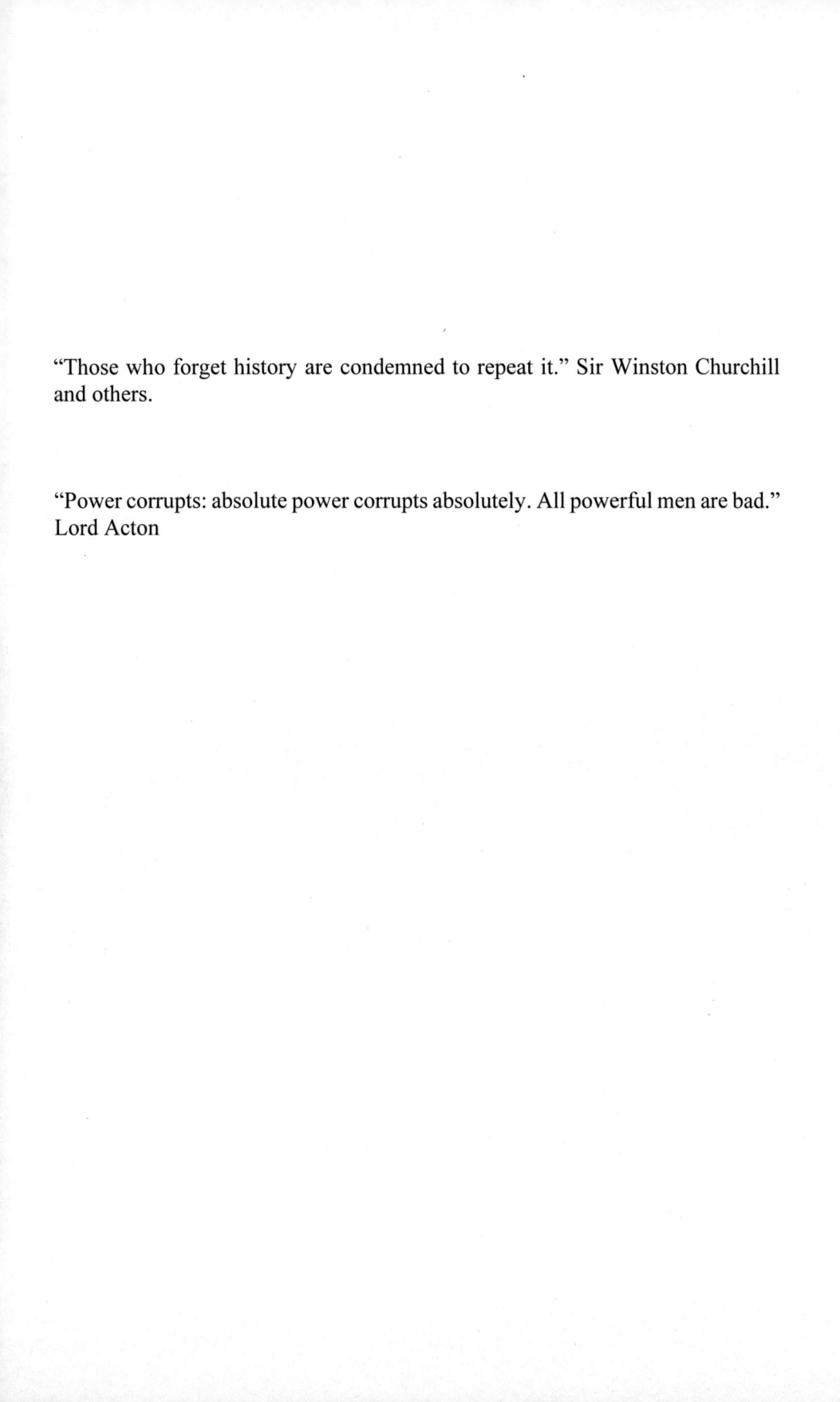

"Those who forget history are condemned to repeat it." Sir Winston Churchill and others.

"Power corrupts: absolute power corrupts absolutely. All powerful men are bad." Lord Acton

Table of Contents

Preface	15
Chapter 1: In the Beginning	18
Chapter 2: African Origins	25
Chapter 3: The Stone Age	31
Chapter 4: The Bronze Age	37
Chapter 5: The Early Iron Age	45
Chapter 6: Egypt	51
Chapter 7: The Indus Valley	57
Chapter 8: The Far East: Early China, Japan and Korea	61
Chapter 9: The Early Americas	68
Chapter 10: The Medes and Persians	73
Chapter 11: Agriculture and Technology	81
Chapter 12: Writing	86
Chapter 13: Ancient Greece	91
Chapter 14: Etruscans to Romans	98
Chapter 15: Roman Britain	105
Chapter 16: Rome and Christianity	110
Chapter 17: Societies, Religions and Christianity	116
Chapter 18: The Dark Ages	124
Chapter 19: Early Africa and Asia	131
Chapter 20: Arabia and Islam	137
Chapter 21: Early Islam and Arab Thinkers	144
Chapter 22: The Late Dark Ages in Britain And France	149
Chapter 23: The Vikings and Norsemen	155
Chapter 24: Russia – The Early Years	160

Chapter 25: The Norman Conquest of Britain	165
Chapter 26: Byzantine Empire	170
Chapter 27: Western Medieval Religion and the Crusades	176
Chapter 28: The Mongols	182
Chapter 29: England 1154–1485 – The Plantagenets	186
Chapter 30: Europe, 11th To 14th Centuries	195
Chapter 31: The Medieval Arab World	201
Chapter 32: Medieval Empires	206
Chapter 33: Early Maritime Exploration	214
Chapter 34: Exploration West from Europe	220
Chapter 35: Exploration East from Europe	225
Chapter 36: Printing	229
Chapter 37: Mapping	233
Chapter 38: The Tudors	238
Chapter 39: The Reformation	243
Chapter 40: The Renaissance	250
Chapter 41: Elizabeth I 1533–1603	256
Chapter 42: The Stuarts and Civil War	261
Chapter 43: Scotland, the Early Years	267
Chapter 44: Wales	272
Chapter 45: The Early Years of Ireland	276
Chapter 46: Early European Emigration to North America	283
Chapter 47: The Restoration	289
Chapter 48: The Enlightenment	294
Chapter 49: Early Finance and Banking	300
Chapter 50: The Scientific Age	307
Chapter 51: Colonisation of North and Central America	311
Chapter 52: Art Through the Ages	319
Chapter 53: Literature and Theatre	324
Chapter 54: Music	329
Chapter 55: Russia from 1584	335

Chapter 56: The House of Hanover	341
Chapter 57: The Second Great Age of Exploration	347
Chapter 58: Early Technology	353
Chapter 59: Slavery	357
Chapter 60: US Independence to Civil War	362
Chapter 61: The French Revolution	369
Chapter 62: Britain 1760–1810	376
Chapter 63: Emerging Africa, Japan, China and India	382
Chapter 64: The Industrial Revolution	388
Chapter 65: Development of Scientific Thought	393
Chapter 66: Europe after Napoleon	397
Chapter 67: Britain 1820–37	402
Chapter 68: Queen Victoria to 1865	406
Chapter 69: The Americas in the 19th Century	411
Chapter 70: Development of the British Empire	417
Chapter 71: Physics and Chemistry	426
Chapter 72: Development of Biology and Medicine	431
Chapter 73: Civil Engineering – Roads, Buildings and Canals	438
Chapter 74: Mechanical and Transport Engineering	444
Chapter 75: Astronomy and Navigation	449
Chapter 76: The Far East	453
Chapter 77: Britain 1865–1901	458
Chapter 78: The United Kingdom	463
Chapter 79: 19th Century France	471
Chapter 80: Germany	476
Chapter 81: USA 1865–1918	480
Chapter 82: Urbanisation	486
Chapter 83: Edwardian England 1901–14	491
Chapter 84: Empires	496
Chapter 85: Emancipation	501
Chapter 86: Legal Systems	507

Chapter 87: Electrical and Chemical Engineering	513
Chapter 88: Culture, 1600–1914	518
Chapter 89: La Belle Epoque – Development of Science	525
Chapter 90: Sleeping Eastern Giants – India and China	532
Chapter 91: World War 1	537
Chapter 92: Russian and Chinese Revolutions	542
Chapter 93: Brief World Overview of the 20th Century	548
Chapter 94: Energy	559
Chapter 95: Evolving Politics	564
Chapter 96: Climates and People	572
Chapter 97: Religion	577
Chapter 98: Warfare	584
Chapter 99: World Population	590
Chapter 100: Global Warming	595

Preface

The excuse for writing a book of history when tens of thousands already exist is simply that it often seems that historical periods are taught or studied in isolation, but also that many periods of history in different parts of the world do not appear on most school or university syllabi. Thus, both for exams and for the purpose of making appealing television programmes, considerable depth is often shown for different short periods that are felt to be 'interesting', without the inter-relationship between periods, or indeed the relationships with contemporary global events being discussed, but instead being minimised or even ignored.

The rationale for this book is therefore to provide an overview of history which is the study of what is important about the past, and to try and illustrate the general development and progress of humankind, whilst at the same time acting as a springboard for more detailed study of events and developments by the reader.

Any account is written from an individual point of view which is necessarily slanted according to the perceptions of the age and culture from which the writer views past events, and this particular account is written from the British, and indeed English-speaking, perspective. From a Chinese, African, Indian or Russian point of view, the world probably looks quite different. Both one's vantage point and cultural upbringing influence one's interpretations and conclusions, and thus colour the historical landscape. Objectivity is always difficult, but nevertheless attempts must be made to put national events in perspective with world development.

In pursuit of that, this account derives from many sources, and it is to be hoped that the end result is a reasonably balanced overview which will not prove too contentious. There is thus an emphasis on context and chronology, such that readers will be able arrive at their own understanding, and will also receive sufficient pointers to guide further reading in detail about subjects which interest them. It is also important to remember that our history was once someone else's present, and that there is a danger of judging the actions of the past with present attitudes and the advantage of our hindsight.

At the end of most chapters, I have indicated books for possible further reading, though usually limiting this to only one, or occasionally two. The books are not necessarily ones which I have used as major sources since a long list of all the works consulted might be scary or off-putting. The intention has been to choose interesting books about the period, which are both authoritative and provide a good read. One hundred books would however be an overload for most readers and the reader will doubtless choose from among those subjects or periods which have proved most interesting.

To obviate the need to buy hardback or other books, readers will often find that many of the suggested books are available very cheaply second-hand through various internet sites. It is also worth drawing attention to the Oxford University Press 'Very Short Introduction' series; these are both physically small and seldom much more than 100 pages; as there are now approaching 500 books in the series, most readers should be able to find some titles of interest. They are also an ideal pocket size for reading on buses or trains while commuting.

Chapters here are divided both by geography and by dates, and there may sometimes be a need to range back and forth through time to accommodate different areas and periods and the way the chapters have been arranged, but I hope this will not prove too cumbersome. Each chapter has been written to be relatively free-standing so allowing dipping into individual subjects if desired, though this does sometimes mean that there may be a small element of repetition where the same event or topic crops up under different chapter headings.

With regard to dates, there has been thought about whether to express dates in the time-honoured notation of BC and AD; since both of these abbreviations reference time to Christianity and the birth of Christ, it has been suggested that the abbreviations BCE and CE should be used to avoid offending those of non-Christian or other cultural backgrounds. It is reported that the Venerable Bede was the first to suggest this in the 8th century, and as it does not appear to have caught on through succeeding centuries, this book from a largely Christian and English-speaking world has stayed with the old terminology.

The past century has seen considerable developments in historical research which range from an increasing understanding of pre-history and archaeology thanks to techniques including radiocarbon dating, dendrochronology, ice core analysis and pollen analysis, to more recent advances, studies, finds of historical documents and most recently genetic studies by chromosome analysis. Research into ancient documents, some of which have appeared only quite recently, ranging from the Dead Sea Scrolls to medieval records, is also allowing a better understanding of all periods of history. Of necessity, many important people and events have had to be omitted and the selection of those that are included represent my own choice. Many people are mentioned, and their dates given, but time and space precludes much amplification of any individual details.

The intention of this book is therefore to stimulate interest and to encourage readers interest in distant historical periods. It is intended as a 'sighting shot' for the reader to get an overview of a period, country, event or trend, for which further reading will then be enjoyable and profitable. Clearly decisions have been made about which events are appropriate to be included and in how much detail, and I hope such decisions appear reasonable.

Numerous ways to pursue history in depth now exist, but for many people, and in particular for the younger generation, Wikipedia will often be a good starting point from which to fill in details that may have been omitted. I have also tried to provide short background descriptions or explanations for each event or person mentioned without assuming prior knowledge of them.

To reiterate, therefore, the book tries to show the complete jigsaw of history in miniature. Each event and development is seen in its temporal relationship to others across the world, and each individual happening may be studied and scrutinised individually later in greater detail, with its context better appreciated. I have purposely stopped one hundred years ago at the end of the First World War, and at the onset of a time when what we now call globalisation was starting to accelerate.

For the sake of completeness, there is a brief chapter in the form of an overview of the last 100 years, but there are already many more appropriate, easily available and detailed accounts of this often-contentious period, most of which still lies within the living memory of many. However, the last few chapters are an attempt to incorporate recent knowledge and bring matters up to date, thereby pulling together some of the threads and lessons from the rest of the book.

Jeremy Plewes
Withybed Green
October 2022

Chapter 1
In the Beginning

It must have been an awesome occurrence. The start of our world is thought to have resulted from what is called the 'Big Bang'. It was an almighty explosion, for which the nearest thing we can imagine would be to be situated at the centre of a vast nuclear explosion; temperatures and pressures would have been unimaginably immense and matter would have been hurled outwards, expanding in all directions with great rapidity.

The universe is still expanding, but since that early Big Bang, the matter that was generated and thrown outwards has gradually cooled, allowing clouds of subatomic particles to coalesce and to start forming atoms. Quite what existed before the Big Bang, and what in turn caused the Big Bang, is not just beyond the scope of this book, it is also not yet understood by physicists or astronomers, and indeed may never be.

After the Big Bang, the gradual cooling that followed allowed clouds of hydrogen to coalesce by gravity to form stars. Hydrogen is the simplest atom, comprising a nucleus, made up of a neutron with no charge, and a proton with a positive electrical charge; the atom is completed by a negatively charged electron, which used to be thought of as a small mini planet orbiting the nucleus, but now seems better regarded as a negatively charged cloud around the nucleus. With further cooling heavier atoms appeared as hydrogen atoms fused, building up the elements of the modern periodic table, which indicates both their affinities and their gradually increasing size, in numbers of neutrons, protons and electrons. The organisation of elements into the periodic table was first recognised in 1869 by the Russian chemist, Dmitri Mendeleev (1834–1907).

Over the billion years following the Big Bang, quasars (massive active galactic nuclei which emit electromagnetic energy) and galaxies came into being through the coalescence of matter. Stars appeared of which our sun is one; some of these stars had collections of matter thrown off them, which became planets and orbited their star as a result of gravitational attraction. It is thought that Earth was born and formed from our sun about four and a half billion years after the Big Bang. In turn, the moon separated off from Earth, and again thanks to gravity, now orbits Earth.

The way in which we understand all this is explained by the Swiss physicist Albert Einstein's (1879–1955) general theory of relativity published in 1905 and updated in 1917, and which in turn has been expanded and clarified by Lemaitre in 1927. Einstein thought that the universe was static, but Lemaitre (1894–1966), a Belgian priest and astronomer, first proposed the continuing expansion of the universe. This was confirmed mathematically by the American astronomer Edwin Hubble (1889–1953), after whom the Hubble space telescope is named. This continuing expansion is now generally accepted.

Gradual cooling of the universe continued. Around three and a half billion years ago, and ten billion years after Earth was initially formed, the earliest signs of life appeared. These early life forms are known as prokaryotes, and they arose from protobionts (literally meaning 'pre-life'), which are organic molecules surrounded by a membrane, in other words, a very primitive type of possible cell. About a billion years after this, and two and a half billion years ago, there is evidence of photosynthesis, which may be regarded as the earliest true form of life.

At this time, Earth was still very hot, and the surface of the planet was devoid of its present covering of gaseous oxygen. The atmosphere then is often described as a 'primordial soup'. The heat and the violent stormy and electrical climate produced many random chemical reactions, eventually leading to the chance production of nucleic acids, initially ribonucleic acids (RNA), and later deoxyribonucleic acid (DNA).

Attempts have been made to replicate this situation in the laboratory: Miller and Wrey at the University of Chicago in 1951, were the first to do so by cycling a mixture of water, hydrogen, methane and ammonia in an atmosphere of electrical sparks; this is the nearest that the laboratory can get to simulating 'primordial soup'. They found that under these conditions 10% of the carbon from methane and ammonia was converted to organic compounds, including amino acids. This stage in the start of evolution of life into a carbon-based from was not possible until Earth had cooled considerably.

From these simple beginnings, more organic molecules were formed, and then by a gradual process of accretion, protobionts followed. In turn, protobionts became more complicated, and gave rise to Archaea, which are the first true single cells possessing a membrane, but no nucleus. Archaea still exist and were initially discovered in harsh environments, although they have now been found widely dispersed throughout nature, including in soils and in the oceans. Alongside them, as sub-groups, are the two big classes of single-celled organisms, bacteria and eukaryotes (organisms with a membrane and a nucleus).

The first complex single cell organisms seem to have originated about one billion years ago when an archaeon engulfed, or fused with a bacterium. Bacteria subsequently became the mitochondria of later cells, producing the energy that the cell generates. Once this life was established, the photosynthesis that followed was probably the next vital development in the early appearance of life on the surface of the planet. Plants with photosynthetic ability extract carbon dioxide from the air, and return oxygen to the atmosphere after generating energy.

Over a very considerable period of time, photosynthesising plants brought the initially very low oxygen content of Earth's atmosphere up to its current level of 21% (the remaining gases in our air are 78% nitrogen and 1% of some rare gases). The way was thus paved for the evolutionary appearance of oxygen breathing, non-photosynthesising life, mainly single celled animals, which could then in turn start to evolve. Initially, most of these very primitive animals fed on equally primitive plant cells which were able to photosynthesise their energy from the basic materials of water, carbon dioxide, mineral salts and energy from sunlight.

Evolution has only been fully recognised since Charles Darwin (1809–1882) published his world changing book in 1859, though several earlier scientists were already edging towards thinking along these lines, including Cuvier, Humboldt, Lyell, Mantell, and Darwin's own grandfather Erasmus (chap 72). It was extremely controversial at that time in the 19th century and took a while to be accepted but is now firmly part of the explanation of our history, confirmed by the later discovery of DNA and how it works through the action of genes.

The salient points of Darwin's teaching are fourfold – firstly, the world, and the species on it evolve, with new ones coming into existence and old ones dying out all the time. Secondly this process is gradual and not noticeable to a single human generation; thirdly all creatures and plants have a common descent and ancestors; and fourth, natural selection controls the process, ensuring the 'survival of the fittest' (not a phrase that Darwin himself thought of or used); this contrasts with artificial selection, which people have practiced through selective breeding of plants and animals throughout previous generations.

Since then, evolution has continued apace, but it is remarkable to note that the early simple forms of life all relied on nucleic acids; and although life has now become extremely complex, the basic building blocks, and the continued development of life, all rests on deoxyribonucleic acid (DNA). Plants as well as animals continued to evolve, becoming increasingly complex. There have been many separate lines of plant evolution, and most plants that we are familiar with today have become very specialised and survive under certain fairly specific climatic conditions.

In turn, the animals that have evolved live off these plants (or off other animals), so that the animals we now find around us are also limited by climatic and other conditions. Many animals are highly specific about the plants or other life that they feed upon, and therefore the conditions under which many animals are found are a reflection of their food source.

Scientists classify animals into invertebrates and vertebrates. The invertebrates are amazingly diverse and include many simple forms of life, including all the insects. Many invertebrates live in the sea and provide a basic food source for the more complex vertebrate animals, including fish and other vertebrates. Vertebrates are so called because they have a backbone made up of segments with one vertebra in each segment, and the evolutionary tree has resulted in many branches, with surprisingly different forms of animals.

However, we must note at this stage that all animals, like all plants, rely on DNA as the code for the development and growth of each individual organism, and also as the code for passing on their structure and organisation to their offspring. For the vertebrates, we must note that two common features are evident throughout the animal kingdom: first, these creatures all have a backbone, and second, they all have four limbs made up from different body segments, indicating a distant common ancestor. The backbone and limbs of vertebrates have developed in many different ways to provide us with the richness and variety of difference that we see in the creatures around us, but the basic structural pattern has remained constant.

Driving the evolution of both animals and plants are a number of different mechanisms. Internally the existence of genetic mutations, which are chance alterations in nuclear DNA, give rise to major evolutionary possibilities. It must be remembered, however, that most mutations within animal or plant DNA will turn out to be potentially lethal to the organism, and therefore that branch of the evolutionary stock of the animal or plant will die out, slowly or rapidly. Sometimes the mutation will be relatively neutral, or even beneficial, in which case it may permit life to continue under different climatic conditions, or with greater competitive advantage.

This is a subject that we can now understand thanks to the discovery of DNA in 1869 by Friedrich Miescher (1844–1895), a Swiss biologist working on white blood cells at the University of Tubingen in Germany. Although this discovery came barely ten years after Charles Darwin's ground-breaking publication on evolution, full understanding of the microscopic workings of mutations was not possible until James Watson (b.1928), Francis Crick (1926–2004) and Rosalind Franklin (1920–1958) in Cambridge elucidated the molecular structure of DNA by 1963.

Other drivers of evolution are external to the animal, and include the competition between species, not forgetting the effect of man as a predator, and the movement of individual animals from different climatic areas to more or less favourable areas. In addition to this there are other drivers of evolution which can be large or small, and which may wipe out many whole species at a time, sometimes resulting in mass extinctions. These cataclysmic events can occur alone or as multiple interacting causes and were first postulated by Georges Cuvier (1769–1832). Cuvier was an important French naturalist who established extinction as a fact: he did not believe in evolution but thought that new creations occurred after each successive extinction due to catastrophe. In the last few hundred million years there have been some five or six truly major disasters which have each wiped out many or even most of the living species at the time.

Among the causes of catastrophe as drivers of evolution, we recognise the following:

1. Global cooling or warming.
2. Sea level changes resulting from the planet's temperature change.
3. Marine anoxia in the oceans, as oxygen is removed by excessive organic matter. Acidification also occurs in oceans and lakes and is caused by absorption of carbon dioxide producing carbonic acid; in addition sulphur dioxide from volcanic output also results in acidification due to the production of sulphurous acid.

4. Alterations in oceanic and atmospheric circulation.
5. Solar radiation causing mutations.
6. Volcanism causing huge dust clouds which obscure the sun producing a so-called 'nuclear winter'. Volcanism may also cause the extrusion of huge quantities of lava to engulf the landscape and form basalt rocks on cooling, two examples of which are recognised today as the Siberian Traps in northern Russia and the Deccan Traps in central India. As well as the floods of lava, considerable quantities of CO_2 are released by volcanism and ancient deposits of coal, oil and gas may be released and burnt.
7. Bolides (meteorites and other extra-terrestrial objects) striking Earth. These may leave surface scars of huge impact craters, such as the Chicxulub crater in Central America which is 180km in diameter and is estimated to have been caused by the impact of a meteorite measuring 10km in diameter.
8. Most recently, humans are proving to be a devastating changer of environment.

Although these catastrophes are impressive, they are probably only responsible for a minority of extinctions, and the majority of extinctions occur with much lesser changes of environment to which a species is unable to adapt. Throughout the ages there have been several episodes of mass extinction that we can identify, and which have arisen from disturbance or damage to Earth's crust. Three of the largest include the Great Oxygen Event 2.4 billion years ago whose cause is unknown and happened when an oxygen rich atmosphere killed many anaerobic species. The Permian-Triassic Event 250 million years ago is also known as the 'Great Dying', and is also of uncertain cause; and the meteor or asteroid causing the Chicxulub crater 66 million years ago which is thought to have wiped out all the land-based dinosaurs, are the other two massive events. The meteor collision is estimated to have caused an enormous tsunami up to 1,000ft high.

Earth itself is made up of a large core, which is about half the diameter of the planet, or 6,000km. The temperature in the core is extremely hot, due to the decay of radioactive elements, including uranium, but the core itself is mainly made up of iron and nickel. Around the core is a mantle, about 2,900km thick, which is much cooler, and outside the mantle is a crust that varies from 8–50km thick, mainly made of silicates, which is thinnest beneath the oceans.

The land masses we call continents are crusts effectively floating on this fluid mantle. In the wild variations of climate apparent as ice ages, the ice may build up to a thickness of several kilometres, principally in the polar icecaps. The weight of this enormous mass of ice depresses the floating continents on which it rests, and when much of the ice melts at the end of an ice age, there is a rebound of the underlying Earth's crust, causing the land to lift as well as a rebound rise in sea levels.

Earth's crust is in constant movement, a proposition first suggested by Alexander von Humboldt (1769–1859), and later formalised as a hypothesis put forward by Alfred Wegener (1880–1930), a German physicist and polar researcher, after he had compared maps of the opposing, and apparently matching, coastlines of Africa and South America. Movements are very slow in terms of human time, but the crustal motion generates events of enormous force. There are fractures in the crust which allow the plates of the crust to overlap and move above and below each other. In doing this, they generate what we experience on the surface as earthquakes, volcanic eruptions, and tsunamis if the movements are below the ocean. This whole process of moving crustal plates is known as continental drift and is a reflection of the enormous forces generated by the gigantic plates of Earth's crust that are moving around.

Continental drift has also influenced evolution, as is evident in the isolation of Australia and New Zealand, where the part of Earth's crust bearing these two countries has been divorced from other parts of Earth's crust for many millions of years, so that random evolutionary development of life has allowed very different flora and fauna to develop. As one can observe, there are no mammals in New Zealand (apart from one species of bat): there are no horses, elephants, lions or similar animals native to Australia, and similarly there are no marsupials or kangaroos elsewhere in the world. One can also observe that the animal life in North America is somewhat different from that in Europe and Asia, since recent evolution took different directions on these two continents at a time when there was no connecting land mass between them.

Of all living creatures that have ever existed, most are now extinct. We know them from the fossil record, where some of them have been preserved, but the fossil record as a whole gives us a picture of gradually increasing complexity and specialisation. Britain has only been a separate landmass from the main part of Europe for the last eight or nine thousand years, and so the time for separate evolutionary development has been minute. Even so, some species have become extinct in the British Isles, and others have developed in a way that is not found on the European mainland. Similar land bridges to that between Britain and the continent have existed elsewhere in the past, notably between Papua New Guinea and Australia, between India and Sri Lanka, between Italy, Sicily and Malta, and across the Bering Straits; as a consequence, some differences in flora and fauna are visible on each side of past land bridges.

From all this planetary cooling and crustal rearrangement, animals and plants have evolved in ever increasing forms of complexity. Humans have appeared and evolved only very recently in planetary terms. There is no absolute or precise cut-off in human evolution, and there have been very many different branches of evolutionary development. Over the last two to four million years, depending on where an arbitrary cut-off is placed in the continuous development of humans, we have arrived at our present form. During this time several different sub-species of human appeared, though all except one have become extinct, leaving Homo Sapiens alone to populate the planet over the last ten thousand years following the end of the most recent Ice Age.

Possible further reading:
The Great Extinctions by Norman MacLeod (Natural History Museum)
Life, an Unauthorised Biography by Richard Fortey (Harper Collins)

Chapter 2
African Origins

The onset of life emerged from all the chaos and chance outlined in chapter 1, first as organic matter, and then in turn as the appearance of single celled organisms. Later the advent of photosynthesis within these cells enabled the absorption of solar energy and gave rise to a gradually increasing variety of plant life. This plant life then spread across the land mass of the planet, providing a massive variety of basic foods on which evolving animal life could feed. Some of this animal life continued to be vegetarian, relying on plants for continuing sustenance, whilst other animals, both vertebrate and invertebrate, became carnivorous, feeding on the new profusion of animal life.

Amongst plant life, grass occupies a special place and first appears during the cretaceous era (145–66 million years ago) just before the extinction of the dinosaurs. The evolution of grass is a very important enabling event for two major reasons; first it allowed the subsequent evolution of grazing animals both large and small, and secondly it provided the precursor plants to appear bearing the seeds or grains which humans would later be able to domesticate and use in their transition from a foraging hunter-gatherer existence to an agricultural life.

Grass is unusual in that it grows from the base of the leaf, unlike most plants which grow from the new tip; thus when grass is cropped by grazing animals, it can rapidly regrow from the base – this allows good pasture to develop (and much later in our own time allows the development of lawns which regrow when mown.) It is noteworthy that there are over 50 cereal-producing edible grasses, of which more than half grow in the Fertile Crescent where they were available for stone age man to domesticate. In contrast there are only four varieties each native to Africa and America, and only a single one in Europe (oats).

In Africa, somewhere between two and four million years ago, our ancestors gradually evolved from their four-legged ape forefathers. Assumption of the erect posture was part of this evolutionary progress, and although the total benefit of the upright posture is a matter for speculation, clear advantages can be postulated. Using only the two hind legs for standing and walking leaves the two forelimbs free for other activities, including catching prey, or gathering food, and probably most important of all, using tools; it is also energy efficient.

It has further been suggested that in the savannah of Africa, with tall grass in most places, an upright posture would more easily allow distant vision to detect both possible prey and possible danger. What is lost by using only two limbs for locomotion, especially speed, is easily outweighed by the enormous gain in flexibility and prehension from the considerable adaptability of the forelimbs.

Early man was omnivorous, existing on a wide diet of plant and animal matter. A partial meat diet provides more calories, together with the advantage of being much less bulky than a plant diet; it also provides benefits in terms of storage and carrying food from place to place. It meant that early humans were able to spend less time foraging for nuts, seeds and berries, and had consequently more time to construct shelters, or to hunt, travel and explore.

Initially, in Africa, much of the meat in the human diet could have come from migrating animals, the herds of which were easily followed. A further advantage of a partially meat diet is that drying, and then storage of food, would have been much easier. There is evidence that early man hunted most available large animals, and the extinction of this megafauna (often before the last ice age), seems to coincide with the arrival of man the hunter and his skill at hunting these large animals in groups.

Africa, above all, provided a benign climate with plenty of food, caves to live in, seas and lakes, as well as the vast plains, full of plant foods, fish and animals. Early hominid fossils have been studied extensively and are of different types in Africa. Early stone tools have been found, together with other evidence of pre-historic habitation. Even fossilised footsteps have been found in the volcanic ash fall-out from around three and a half million years ago. Much of the recent initial research was done in the Great Rift Valley by the British archaeologist Louis Leakey (1903–1972), who was looking for evidence to confirm Charles Darwin's theory of evolution in the development of humans, as the valley seemed to be a place where early humanity might first have appeared.

The Rift Valley in Africa is a giant fault in Earth's crust in a situation where both climate and food supply together provided an ideal situation for early human development. Within the Rift Valley, which lies in Tanzania, the Olduvai Gorge has been a prolific source of evidence about man's early evolution with much of the early work there being pioneered by Dr Leakey from Cambridge. The Red Sea, lying to the north-east of Africa, is also a large rift valley and a big scar in Earth's crust. These two rifts appear to have been formed eight to ten million years ago by continental drift separation.

The earliest human remains found in Africa date to somewhat later, about three and a half million years ago: when the partial skeleton of a creature, since named 'Lucy', was discovered by the American anthropologist Dr Donald Johanson (b. 1943) also in the Great Rift Valley some sixty years ago. Since then, archaeology has given us a much better idea of the early evolution of mankind, and several different lines, or species, of humans have now been found and are known to have evolved.

One such line, Homo Erectus is apparent about three hundred thousand years ago, and another species of hominid called Neanderthal Man also evolved in Africa. The Neanderthals were bigger and heavier than modern humans, and even had bigger brains, but they died out just before, or at the onset of the last ice age, for unknown reasons. There is a little evidence of some interbreeding between Neanderthals and Homo Sapiens with some neanderthal genes persisting in a few populations of modern humans. Traces of various other human species have been found, both in Africa and in Asia, indicating that these early humans migrated out of Africa.

However, most of these hominids died out, and a single late line of Homo Sapiens persists through to the present day, having first appeared about eighty to seventy thousand years ago. There is a 'pinch point' found by DNA analysis about sixty thousand years ago, when the population of Homo Sapiens dropped to only a few thousand individuals. Even fewer of these individuals are our ancestors in a direct line and it has been suggested that only a single early woman from that time may be the direct ancestor of all presently living people – accordingly, she has been named 'mitochondrial Eve' since the female line can be traced genetically through mitochondrial DNA, while the male line is traced through the nuclear Y chromosome.

Once Homo Sapiens had evolved, migration out of Africa became possible, although due to geography and continental drift there were only three feasible ways for African creatures to leave that continent. The first of these is across the Straits of Gibraltar, but the Straits are 14km wide, and it seems unlikely that early man was ever able to negotiate this expanse of water. In the distant past, perhaps six million years ago, and long before hominids were around, there was a land bridge between Morocco and southern Spain, and the Mediterranean as we know it did not exist, but consisted of a series of land-locked, highly salty lakes, lying below sea level like the Dead Sea.

When sea levels rose some five or six million years ago, the land bridge was breached and the Mediterranean basin was flooded from the Atlantic leaving Africa fully cut off from Europe and Asia). The second possible way for humans to have left Africa is from the northeast across the Sinai desert. The third way would be to have crossed the isthmus of sea at the southern end of the Red Sea. At the end of the Ice Age with much of Earth's water locked up in the polar icecap, the sea level here would have been much lower and this Red Sea crossing would have been much shorter and easier, though still a considerable barrier for early humans; but the evidence indicates that this was probably the route by which early humans left Africa and spread east along the coast towards Asia.

The vagaries of the ice ages have undoubtedly influenced the various possibilities of human evolution. Frequent covering of the northern latitudes of Earth by great sheets of ice and the adjacent barren plains of arctic tundra, have severely limited the areas in which man could live. Before the onset of the last ice age, and in an inter-glacial period, Homo Sapiens had left Africa and migrated along the shores of India and Asia and up rivers, where fishing, hunting and gathering provided plentiful food and a benign climate.

Humans reached Australia fifty to sixty thousand years ago, when sea levels were very low and island hopping was possible from the Malaysian peninsula along the island chain east through Borneo and New Guinea to reach Northern Australia. It took much longer to colonise the remote Polynesian Islands and required considerable long-distance sea-faring ability; New Zealand was not reached until very recently, less than a thousand years ago.

It is possible that man spread along eastern Asian coastlines and over the Bering Straits into Alaska, and North America before the last ice age, though there may have been a pause in human migration on the northeast coast of Asia until the end of the ice age. It is also possible that this spread was halted further east on the northwest coast of America by the ice age, and that for a period of several thousand years, humans lived in ice age 'refuges'. These refuges were areas of relatively benign climate surrounded by glacial icecaps, either in the coastal region of present British Columbia and Alaska, or further east on the slopes and plains on the east side of the Rocky Mountains.

From there, it would have been a relatively easy migration later, when the ice sheet had receded, for humans to diverge in three directions: to the north east for those humans who would become the Eskimos, to the south east for other humans who would become the ancestors of North American plains Indians, and to the south along either side of the coastal mountain chain of north, central, and then south America, to populate Central and South America as the great civilisations of central America and northern South America.

The ice ages that have had such a great influence on man's evolution and subsequent migrations, are quite variable and cause enormous changes in climate, and in the height of sea level over the planet. At one stage of the last glacial maximum sea levels are estimated to have been three to four hundred feet lower than at present due to the water locked up as ice at the poles. The genesis of ice ages results from many factors which affect planetary temperature including:

- Intermittent increases in the atmospheric 'greenhouse gases', mainly the levels of carbon dioxide and methane.
- Changes in Earth's orbit which oscillates on an oval path; this oscillation is known as the Milankovitch Cycle after the Serbian physicist Milutin Milankovitch (1879–1958).
- The movement of tectonic plates on the crust of Earth altering the relative amounts of land to sea.
- Variations in the sun's activity and therefore changing heat radiation from the sun.
- Large meteorites causing immense dust clouds and 'nuclear winters'.
- Super-volcanoes have also caused nuclear winters: the last such eruption in recent history was that of Tambora in Indonesia in 1815, which year then came to be described as "the year without a summer", because the volcanic ash circling Earth cut out so much of the sun's rays.

The last ice age, which spans the period roughly from about twenty-five thousand years to twelve thousand years ago, had its glacial maximum around 20,000 BC and left a marked local effect on British geography. Because sea levels were so low, due to all the water locked up in ice at the Poles, there was a wide land bridge between Britain and Europe, and a further land bridge between Ireland and Britain. At the last Glacial Maximum, about twenty thousand years ago, the ice sheet from the North Pole extended as far as southern Britain, where the land became barren desert tundra.

Our current climate is now much more benign as we live in an interglacial period. When the polar cap receded, the land bridge to Europe persisted for a few millennia until further warming and gradual rising of the sea level cut Britain off from the continent around 8,000 BC. It is suggested that a giant tsunami originating close to Norway helped complete the process of flooding the land bridge.

As we have previously seen, humans are not thought to have migrated out of Africa across the Straits of Gibraltar. The second route out of Africa lies at the north-eastern end of the continent, where migration across the northern Nile Basin would have been possible. Humans would have found it difficult to get to this area because of the northern African desert lying between central Africa and this route out of Africa, but there is some evidence that humans achieved this migration and came to live in the Middle East in the last inter-glacial period, however these humans then appear to have died out by the start of the last ice age.

The third possible route out of Africa is across the Straits at the southernmost tip of the Red Sea, which avoids the need for migration across the desert belt of Africa. It appears this was the most recent route taken by a few migrants, before the last Ice Age. These humans multiplied and spread east along coasts, and up rivers into the interior, as the start of waves of migration which have since peopled the world. These few individuals are the ancestors of all present living humans outside Africa. In other words, these early people, possibly no more than a thousand, then multiplied exponentially to reach the present world population of over seven billion.

We have been greatly helped in understanding human spread by the recent ability to study DNA in present populations. This new science has allowed populations of people to be traced back through their ancestors and through either the male or female line. This is possible because the DNA of cytoplasmic mitochondria within cells is only transmitted through the female line, whilst nuclear DNA in the Y chromosome of men is only transmitted through the male line. Using this recent technology, it is now possible to say that most humans originated, and are the direct descendants of a very few early people, indeed possibly a single female, previously noted as 'mitochondrial Eve'.

Thanks to mutations altering the DNA through the generations, it is also possible to give good estimates of when and where specific populations of modern people originated. This DNA evidence has added greatly to our knowledge of ancient peoples, which was previously limited to the archaeology of their burials, monuments, painting, pottery and to the carbon dating of their artefacts.

This present understanding contrasts with the work of Archbishop and Primate of All Ireland, James Ussher (1581–1656), who calculated in 1650 that the origin of Earth occurred on 4004 BC. He arrived at this figure by tracing the generations back in the Bible to Adam and Eve, estimating the time span of each generation. Following this early intellectual attempt to estimate the start of history without any direct evidence, the Age of Enlightenment (chapter 48) produced a lot of evidence and knowledge by naturalists studying pre-historic life, events and fossils. Layered findings in caves demonstrated the succeeding historical eras, with the different cave layers demonstrating different fauna and flora: in this way it then became clear that both Earth itself, and life upon it, were very much older than the biblical account suggested.

Corroborating evidence comes from three important recent scientific developments: firstly carbon dating which measures the remaining amount of radioactive carbon14 in organic remnants since it was incorporated in a plant or animal: this is a technique invented by Willard F Libby at the University of Chicago in 1949, for which he later received a Nobel Prize. Secondly dendrochronology, the measurable pattern of tree ring growth which is now possible to assess back through time for at least 8,000 years, thanks to the discovery of some very long-lived trees and to other even older trees preserved in anoxic bogs, the tree ring growth also gives a temporal pattern of climatic variation.

Thirdly, sequential information is available from drilled ice cores in Greenland and the Arctic and Antarctic going back many millennia, and carrying contemporary evidence from dust particles, spores and such-like which settled to the ground after being caught up in rain or snow.

Possible further reading:
Out of Eden by Stephen Oppenheimer (Constable and Robinson)
The Ancestors Tale by Richard Dawkins (Houghton Mifflin)

Chapter 3
The Stone Age

The period prior to the last Ice Age is known as the Stone Age from the tools those early humans fashioned to do their different work and tasks. At various times different tribes, or populations of early people, devised differing and characteristic tools which have since been used to name and study these populations and their geographic and chronological extents. Any human population existing before the use of metal is known as Stone Age and might therefore include other hominids, including Neanderthals, who lived within the last two to three million years.

When the planet warmed up after the last ice age, a huge amount of the planet's water remained locked up in the polar ice caps, and as a result the land bridge between Britain and Europe still allowed migration of animals and humans. At this time the River Rhine poured out of northern Europe into a land area we now know as the North Sea, and then ran south through the Straits of Dover, where it cut a very wide gorge, leaving chalk cliffs, which are still visible today on either side of the English Channel.

At the time of the last glacial maximum, 20,000 years ago, the sea level was around 100 metres lower than at present, but as the ice locked up in the poles gradually melted, the land bridge between Britain and the continent, and between Britain and Ireland, slowly flooded again. This geological accident leaving Ireland and Britain separate from Europe has been a potent influence on the development and subsequent history of the peoples inhabiting these islands as part of Europe, but at the same time separate from it.

Once the ice receded at the end of the last Ice Age exposing bare ground again, the first life to return consisted of mosses, lichens, ferns and grasses. Soil gradually built up with cold-tolerant trees (birch, willow, aspen, pine and juniper), beginning the transformation of the land to scrubby forest, which in turn thickened up with hardwoods including oak and ash; the whole process took several millennia. After a further cold spell of a thousand years from 10,800 to 9,600BC the warming resumed allowing migration across from Europe to England initially, and then farther north to Scotland after 8,500 BC.

Most of these migrating people would have been nomadic hunter-gatherers, travelling north in the summer and south again for the winter. Gough's Cave in the Cheddar Gorge in England shows signs of both animal and human habitation back as far as 12,500BC, but much of the human activity in the south of Britain at this time could have been as summer camps for hunting.

After about 9,000 BC the receding ice cap and a period of relatively stable climate, allowed colonisation of the land, and people slowly progressed from the hunter gatherer Stone Age into becoming early farmers of both crops and animals. The period between 7,000 and 3,000 BC is known as the Holocene Optimum and was a much warmer interlude before some cooling set in once more. It is worth remarking that a further short period of warmth occurred between 800 and 1300 AD when the Vikings were able to establish colonies on coastal Greenland, and further west discovered the coast of North America, which they named Vinland because of the vines they found there. This was then followed by a much colder period known as the Little Ice Age, between 1400 and 1800 AD, when weather and winters became much more severe, and when life in Greenland became much more marginal and difficult.

The oldest Stone Age settlement found in Europe is on the banks of the Danube in Serbia at Lepenski Vir and was a planned central settlement with satellite villages dating from as far back as 9,500 BC. It was discovered in 1960 but was inadequately studied because of impending flooding by a hydro-electric scheme; although much of the site was transferred the remains were fragile and a lot of artefacts and architectural detail has been lost.

The Stone Age people who came to Britain after the last ice age were resourceful and inventive. But even before then, early cave art has been found in Europe dating from around 30,000 years ago, long before the last Ice Age. Cave art from the same time period is also known in the southern Sahara, which was not desert at that time, and further cave drawings are present in northern Australia from this time, where the early Stone Age Aboriginal people created fascinating pictures. Cave paintings are mainly of contemporary animals.

There seems to have been a cognitive revolution with a sharp increase in human thinking ability before the last Ice Age which cannot be tied in to any clear evolutionary anatomical or physiological development, but which prepared Stone Age people for the rapid development of civilisation that accelerated after the Ice Age ended.

The techniques for making and firing pottery appeared soon after the Ice Age, and pottery fragments and figurines (carved figures, usually female and produced possibly as fertility objects) are known from as long ago as 8,000 BC in Japan, and 6,000 BC in Britain. In the same way that stone age populations have been studied and classified by their tools, so pottery been used to define and differentiate more recent groups of people. Britain was eventually cut off from the continent by flooding of the land bridge due to rising sea levels around 6,000 BC: this process was possibly completed by the Storegga Slide, a giant under-sea landslide just west of the Norwegian coast, causing a huge tsunami which has left identifiable debris as far as 80km inland in Scotland; the contemporary effect on human and animal life would have been devastating.

Farming, and the early deforestation required to produce land to farm, is known from 6,500 BC onwards which falls in the middle of the Holocene Optimum, when the climate was warmer and as a result there must have been a lot of wildlife for hunting. A visit to any local British museum will allow you to see many artefacts from this Stone Age period. Flint arrow heads used for hunting are numerous, and larger flints were shaped as cutting and scraping tools for butchering animal carcasses. Other animal products were used in different ways; deer antlers were used as picks for scraping and loosening earth, and there is evidence for the use of woven baskets for carrying, wooden hurdles were used as fencing, or laid as paths across boggy areas, hides and furs for clothing were vital.

The first known community temple is at Gobeki-Tepe in Anatolia, Southern Turkey, and appears to have been built by hunter-gatherers (because there is no sign of nearby habitation) in about 9,500 BC. Farming also originated in the Anatolia region of Central Turkey when cereals were first domesticated and where summers in ancient times would have been dry and winters would have been wet. The wild grasses from which seeds were gathered were ideal for domestication, as the seeds were large and drought resistant. Barley and wheat were cultivated in the Middle East from around 10,000 BC in the valleys of the Tigris and Euphrates Rivers, known as the Fertile Crescent.

Rather later, millet and rice were being cultivated in China from around 6,000 BC, while at the same time maize was being cultivated in Central America. Thus, there is evidence for the synchronous and independent start of farming with domestication and selective breeding of the indigenous plants and animals across the world: in the Fertile Crescent with wheat, barley, peas, sheep and goats coming from Anatolia close by; in China with rice, millet, ducks and pigs; in Asia and India with chickens and cows; in North and Central America with maize, beans and turkeys; and in South America with potatoes and llamas. Horses were probably first domesticated in the central steppe region of Kazakhstan around the same period.

Once cultivation of crops was established, humans no longer needed to lead a migratory life following the availability of wild plants or animals, though there was undoubtedly a lot of hunting for wild animals alongside the early domestication and breeding of animals for food and skins. In this way, during the millennia after the last ice age, the early Stone Age hunters gradually changed their lifestyle from the rather insecure hunting and gathering of previous generations, to become more static farmers. In Europe some communities lived on the edge of lakes in huts known as pile dwellings or stilt houses ('crannogs' in Scotland), where fish would have made an important contribution to their diet, and the surrounding water would have conferred a degree of safety.

In addition to the domestication of animals for food, it seems likely that dogs were amongst the earliest animals to be domesticated, well before the last Ice Age, to provide labour, probably from strains of wolf. Wolves would have been relatively easy to domesticate because they possess a pack mentality and would have integrated well into the 'human pack', where they became very valuable in assisting early man to hunt, and also to herd the other domesticated animals. Herd animals were probably domesticated around this same time, though there is actually evidence for earlier controlled herding of reindeer in Lapland 20,000 years ago.

Clear evidence of social organisation amongst Stone Age people can be inferred from the large, ancient and well-preserved temple monuments they have left behind in Malta. The enormous stone circles at Avebury, Callanish, Brodgar, and Stonehenge in Britain, and the megalithic temples in Malta, all bear testament to their technical skills and interests, and also to the considerable social organisation which would have been needed to complete such vast monuments with very primitive tools, all in the fourth millennium BC.

Lesser evidence of stone age culture is frequently to be seen in the British countryside, on the western coast of France, Iberia and across the plains of Europe. Tombs, present as tumuli, mark the burials of Stone Age people throughout Europe. Some tombs were the site of many burials and can be seen as chambered tombs. Once again, many of these are present along the west coasts of Britain, Ireland and France, as well as in Spain and Portugal. In addition to this, single standing stones, or megaliths, are dotted around the British and French countryside.

Further to the east in Europe, the steppes show evidence of elaborate social organisation in burial mounds known as kurgans. The relatively similar design and construction of these Stone Age monuments indicates that Neolithic man was capable of travelling considerable distances, both by water and on land to trade and interact with other tribes and settlements. The monuments along the Atlantic coasts of France, Britain and Ireland, confirm the ability of ancient peoples to travel and trade. There is further evidence of Stone Age travel from the presence of axe heads and jewellery hundreds of miles from their source of origin.

Much evidence of early people no longer exists because the wood and plant materials that they used for their huts and other purposes has usually rotted away. Figurines and small carvings offer insights into Neolithic thoughts and priorities, but as writing was yet to develop, we have to infer most of what we understand about Stone Age culture from the tools, monuments and occasional stone buildings that have come down to us. A further source of information comes from middens; these are the rubbish tips of Neolithic man, which contain particularly the food residues that were of no use, including bones and seashells; pollen analysis on plant remains can also provide valuable insights. Cave drawings and megalithic decorations point us to important aspects of Neolithic culture.

The most decorated megalithic tomb in Europe, dating to around 3,800 BC, is on the small island of Gavrinis in the western French Bay of Morbihan. This megalithic tomb is a long passage grave, and the carvings are very similar to another very large passage grave at New Grange in Central Ireland. These passage graves were all aligned so that at the mid-winter solstice, when the sun is at its nadir, the passage was lit by the early morning sun shining down the passage into the central tomb chamber. There is a third equally impressive and large passage grave, at Maes Howe in the Orkney Islands.

It has been suggested – and it seems to fit well with the figures and information that we have – that technological advances, including farming, occurred when populations and their density reached a certain size, thereby perpetuating knowledge and skills and allowing cross-fertilisation and development of ideas.

The building of stone circles began around 3,200 BC and there are more than a thousand of them known in the British Isles, though many are small and relatively insignificant by comparison with Stonehenge. The enormous task of building of these stone circles can be gauged from the fact that the Sarsen stones at Stonehenge were brought from the Marlborough Downs, 30km away, and weighed around 25 tonnes each, others came from the Prescelly Mountains even further away in South Wales. The manpower required for this task would have been immense. There is evidence of celestial alignment in the stone circles, and they are thought in some way to have astronomical significance, though this is far from fully understood.

The favourable climate of the Holocene optimum existing between 7,000 and 3,000 BC must have been a great boon to the early settlers. By about 2,000 BC much of Europe had already been partially deforested for use as building materials and as firewood. In Britain even forests on the higher areas like Dartmoor and Exmoor, were being cleared to provide arable space for farming communities. To this day, small settlements of up to a dozen Stone Age huts can still be seen on Dartmoor, together with somewhat later evidence of field boundaries.

Once the trees were cleared from these areas, there would have been some years of reasonable cultivation, but after this time there were no tree roots left to help draw moisture from the soil, so the water drained downwards into the subsoil, making an impermeable layer which became sodden and too acid for earthworms, and where bacterial decomposition did not occur due to anoxia. On the flatter peaks, the sodden ground gradually turned into peat bogs, and in all probability the small hamlets gradually became untenable because of the lack of reasonable land for farming. However, the acidic and anaerobic conditions of these boggy areas have resulted in peat formation and some remarkably well-preserved archaeological finds have been discovered within the peat.

The invention of the wheel seems to date from around 2,500 BC and would have been used with early carts. In North America, where the wheel did not appear, the American Indians used small drawn platforms without wheels, called travois. Some of these technological inventions were undoubtedly conceived in several places at once, but in Europe other technology spread outwards from the fertile crescent of Mesopotamia. Carbon dating of early European Neolithic sites shows the gradual fanning out of advances in farming and technology from the Middle East at a rate that seems to correspond to about 18km every generation, or 25 years.

It is, however, quite likely that the generational interval in those times would have been nearer 20, or even 15 years, rather than the postulated 25. In the meantime, the fertile crescent in the Middle East had fallen victim to change in climate and over-use of the land, so it had become desertified by comparison with the previously lush days of 2,000 BC. Mesopotamia (the Fertile Crescent, that land around and between the two great rivers Euphrates and Tigris,) is often quoted as the birthplace of civilisation. Recent years, however, have shown a similar progress of Neolithic people towards farming and living in villages, to have occurred in other places as well.

Thus, Egypt around 3,100 BC, and the Indus Valley in India around 2,500 BC, are now recognised as at least partly independent areas where first farming, and subsequently civilisation, evolved. The Minoan civilisation in Crete and southern Greece and Turkey, around 2,000 BC, may also have been a moderately independent area for this evolution.

China, cut off by mountain ranges from the rest of the world, was going through the same process around 1500 BC. Early civilisation started much later in America, both in Central and Southern America, and in the centre of what is now the United States, this was probably in part due to the lack of draft animals for load carrying, and in part because the wheel did not appear in the Americas. In isolated parts of the world pockets of Stone Age culture have continued to exist up to the 20th century, such as the natives of New Guinea, the Ainu Tribe in Northern Japan, and the Eskimos in Northern Canada.

The world's oldest continually settled community is probably Jericho in Mesopotamia, founded possibly as far back as 10,000 BC in a venerable area which can claim the first writing and literature, together with the first numeracy, accounting, astronomy, architecture and brewing, as well as the appearance of early monotheistic religion.

Possible further reading:
Home by Francis Pryor (Penguin)
Europe Between the Oceans by Barry Cunliffe (Yale University Press)

Chapter 4
The Bronze Age

It was a huge step forward when people first discovered metal. Copper and gold were the first to be found; beaten copper has been found from Anatolia in central Turkey dating from 7,000BC. Smelting and other uses of the metal did not occur until about 4,000BC. But even at this time these metals were predominantly decorative rather than useful. It was not until the secret of making bronze was discovered that the early use of metal allowed valuable improvements in tool and weapon making which would lift humans out of the Stone Age.

Before the Bronze Age, there was a brief period, sometimes referred to as the Copper Age, because copper was the first metal to be smelted from ore in Anatolia. At about the same time, lead was discovered and makes its first appearance in the archaeological record as a necklace of lead beads. Lead has a low melting point and can therefore be produced easily from its sulphide ore, called galena, in an ordinary household hearth or fire. With the discovery and use of metal humans were able to progress to a new and higher level of control over their environment and the production of food.

Bronze is an alloy, predominantly of copper with 10–12% tin: although later it was discovered that the addition of lead formed an even harder alloy, and lead bronze can be more easily cast and beaten to the shapes required. Copper has a melting point of almost 1100°C, but tin becomes liquid at only 230°C, and by combining both metals together bronze with 40% tin melts at 720°C. Bronze is usually made with a tin content between 7–25%, later when lead came to be added this made an even harder alloy.

Interestingly, early mined deposits of copper were not found close to settlements, or to tin deposits, so transport to other centres, often over long distances, must have been undertaken to a site where artisans could then smelt, cast, beat and manufacture items.

The Bronze Age is generally recognised as lasting from about 2,500 BC to 1,500 BC or a little later. After copper was discovered around 7,000 BC in the Taurus mountains of central Turkey, beaten copper from the same region then appeared a little later. Later still smelting was introduced around 4,000 BC with bronze becoming available in Mesopotamia from a thousand years after this, around 3,000 BC. From Mesopotamia bronze spread by trade along market routes, and its spread across Europe was slow, but it reached Egypt soon after 2,000 BC, Greece by about 1,050 BC, and Britain around 750 BC.

Wherever it became available, it provided a great leap forward in tools for animal and plant husbandry, digging and ploughing, but also in its availability for use as weapons. Bronze swords and daggers were clearly highly prized throughout the Bronze Age since they represented an enormous practical improvement on the Stone Age weapons in use before that time. The earliest metal daggers found with burials are copper, but bronze appears soon afterwards. Unfortunately, much of our evidence from burials has been lost to grave robbers looking for gold, metal jewellery and artefacts through the centuries. Tin bronze was particularly prized for the additional toughness and sharpness it gave to weapons: and as such it fuelled the development of warfare in the Bronze Age.

It is not known how tin-based bronze first came to be made, since although it contains about 10% tin, tin does not occur in the same geographic regions as copper. The principal sources of tin which were used in early times, are in the mountains of western Asia, northern Portugal and Cornwall. There is historical evidence for a considerable trade in tin from Cornwall, where trade by sea with Europe commenced as long ago as 3,000 BC.

For geological reasons, copper is often found in large seams in the form of its sulphate and carbonate salts. Ancient copper mines have been found, and there are wonderful workings to be seen on the Great Orme in North Wales. The seams are irregular with alternately very narrow and very wide passages. The mine was only recently discovered, as it had been protected through use as a rubbish tip from Roman times onwards. The mine itself was easily apparent once the Roman rubbish and other rubble was cleared away.

Early mining of metals was difficult and dangerous and was accomplished either by hacking away at the seams with stone tools, or with bone implements such as antlers. Open cast mining would have been straight forward but in underground shafts there were limitations by two constraints, firstly the availability of light (although candles could be taken down a mine they were smoky and difficult to work by), secondly there was a problem with the amount of air available, and as sometimes the metal ore was often mined by lighting fires to crack the rock, this second constraint would have been the availability of enough air.

Once the initial seams of copper carbonates, present naturally as malachite and azurite, were used up, there were often associated seams of copper sulphides present, which appeared far less glamorous or attractive as a dull grey, but it was discovered that these sulphides in turn could be smelted down to provide copper, and if combined with arsenic during the smelting process they would improve the strength and the ability of the finished bronze to take a sharp edge. Arsenic is of course poisonous, involving the nervous system and leading to peripheral neuritis and also causing dermatitis, so there is likely to have been a considerable morbidity amongst copper miners and smelters making arsenical bronze.

It might be thought that the development of the early city states, often at war with each other, would have occurred on the open plains of Europe, but in fact early city states first appear on the relatively peaceful island of Crete where those two important conditions of benign climate and fertile soil produced a peaceful and cultured society, powered by their agricultural surplus and ability to trade. Because of the mountainous terrain of Greece and Turkey, the many scattered islands of the Aegean Sea, including Crete, represented a relatively easy trade route for early seafaring people. The islands of the Aegean were not inhabited early on because of their rocky nature and relatively poor soil that did not easily support agriculture or permanent settlement. However, these mountainous small islands in the Aegean were relatively rich in other desirable metal ores, including lead and silver, and this led to extensive Mediterranean trade; model boats made of lead have been found on the Island of Naxos, dating to 2,800 BC.

Our knowledge of the Bronze Age is much better than the customs and events of the Stone Age simply because various forms of writing came into existence contemporaneously with the early Bronze Age. This has provided a much better record of happenings and timings, and we can relegate the Stone Age, where there was no writing but only pictograms and cave art left for us, to pre-history. History itself may be said to start with the Bronze Age simply because at this time we start to have those good records to study, although recent research suggests that Stone Age man may have used a fairly standard system of pictographs across Europe for many years before writing was devised, and this may yield much information in the future with deeper study.

During the Bronze Age, which was climatically very favourable, the land on the steppes in northern Europe became less productive. Kurgens are large burial mounds found across eastern and northern Europe and the horsemen of this kurgen-building civilisation spread westwards, with hill forts springing up along the plains of the lower Danube, Bulgaria and Macedonia. As they migrated further into eastern Europe these kurgen builders brought with them horses, strong new arsenical bronze battle axes, and the technology of using two-piece moulds to make bronze tools and weapons. Their customs included burial of a chieftain with ritual sacrifice of his immediate family and servants.

Some of the earliest bronze artefacts have come from south-eastern Europe, where the change from Stone Age to Bronze Age culture started, spreading gradually west across the continent. Initially, the production of bronze was probably a closely guarded secret since it would have conferred great advantages on those people who could use it for hunting and warfare. In south-eastern Europe, on the plains between the Caspian Sea and the Black Sea, the final traces of a Bronze Age people are apparent in their large kurgens, some of which disgorged huge quantities of gold, silver and copper ornaments when they were first excavated in the 18th and 19th centuries, but unfortunately many of these artefacts have been lost to grave robbers.

Along with the jewellery and weapons, miniature representations of two and four wheeled carts have been found. One more interesting constituent of jewellery to emerge at this time is amber, which is a fossil tree resin largely found around the Baltic Sea. That amber jewellery should be found hundreds of kilometres from its natural source is an indication of the amount and distance of travel and trade between tribes and villages in early times.

All these Bronze Age developments were happening at a time when Stone Age populations were probably relatively static. Early civilisation came into existence on the premise of the land's exploitation by man, and with the presumption that natural resources were infinite, and pollution could be ignored. The transition to the first civilisation is generally recognised as commencing in Mesopotamia around 3,500 BC. It was followed fairly rapidly by a similar civilisation in Egypt, commencing around 3,100 BC. At the same time, Malta in the middle of the Mediterranean Sea, was the site of impressive Stone Age Megalithic temples.

We have no writings or pictures from this civilisation, but Malta's early people seem to have incurred some sudden natural catastrophe. The temples themselves date to around 2800 BC and habitation ceased quite suddenly in about 2,000 BC. It has been suggested that invasion by Bronze Age warriors with superior weapons is one possible explanation. It does seem, however, that Malta may have provided some of the early seeds of Megalithic Stone Age civilisations in Europe, which in due course gave way to the new world of the Bronze Age.

Early Bronze Sumerian culture produced the first potter's wheel, the invention of glass, as well as casting in bronze, all soon after the year 3,000 BC. Intense cultivation was possible in the Fertile Crescent soil of regular floods; barley, wheat and millet were all grown. The Sumerians also recorded frequent war between their city states from 3,300 BC to 2,400 BC. They are known to have had slave markets, possibly as a by-product of wars and the taking of prisoners.

Early village societies would have had to spend most of the daylight hours in farming activities to generate enough food for subsistence. It was only when the climate was favourable, and soils were also fertile, that the need to produce food ceased to occupy all of the daylight hours. Under these circumstances talented artisans were then free to spend some time making clay figurines, smelting metal, or producing jewellery from bone, shells or metal. At the same time the new affluence allowed rulers to pay for a standing army.

In addition to the use of bronze in tool and weapon making, and thanks to the onset of writing that coincides with the coming of the Bronze Age, six geographically separate centres can be identified where civilisation blossomed independently early on, seemingly due to climatic and geological circumstances, but also due to the relatively well organised nature of their Stone Age predecessors.

- First, in the Fertile Crescent in Mesopotamia, annual river flooding of the Tigris and Euphrates had built up a very rich soil, where the cultivation of crops would have been straightforward without incurring depletion of the ground. Irrigation systems were dug to cope with the hot dry summer months, and it was an early centre of dense population in small villages. In southern Mesopotamia, before the two rivers, Tigris and Euphrates join, in this area called Sumer, important early centres of population have been identified here. Large temples existed before 3,000 BC in such places as Uruk (called Erech in the Bible).

Much pre-Bronze Age pottery has been found here, and this pottery appears to be a very early example of a mass-produced product in which a pottery wheel was used for the first time, rather than the older and more simple method of coiling long thin sausages of clay around to build up a tall vessel. The Sumerian population continues through to about 2,000 BC, and for the first time their writing has come down to us in the form of pictograms, many of which are lists of staple foods and of accounts: they are the ledgers and accounting of the time which provide a mass of information.

- Second, civilisation in Egypt follows soon by 3,000 BC. Again, this was aided by the rich soil from the annual Nile flooding, and by man-made irrigation systems, which provided rich consistent crops. Possibly knowledge spread by travel from Sumeria.
- Third, human organisation in the Indus valley, on the western side of India, is apparent from 2,500 BC with early well-planned towns along the Indus valley.
- Fourth and much further east in China, civilisation appears around 1,500 BC along the Yellow River Valley, once again emphasising the importance of fresh water in allowing the emergence of farming, irrigation and transport to facilitate civilisation.
- Fifth, and undoubtedly completely independently, early civilisation in the Americas appears around 1,500 BC. Some early humans probably crossed the Bering Straits from northern Asia before the last Ice Age when there was still a land bridge, but the spread of people across the continent with the development of civilisation by the Inuit in the North, the plains Indians in present United States and Canada, and the great stone monument building tribes of Central and South America seems to have come much later. These early civilisations in the Americas all comprised Stone Age peoples.
- A sixth centre of human development occurred in Australia which early man somehow also managed to reach before the last Ice Age, but this culture persisted into the 20th century as the Stone Age Aboriginal population.

Apart from the evolution of human tool making, the Bronze Age brought writing. Early written information comes to us from the Old Testament books of the Bible, through which Archbishop Ussher counted the generations backwards to Adam and Eve, reaching an estimate of the birth of the world with Adam and Eve in 4,004 BC, though of course this estimate really marks the time when the Stone Age was eclipsed by the onset of the Bronze Age. Now that writing is present in the Bronze Age, we have the accounts of both the bible and the story of Gilgamesh (who was a real person, a ruler at Uruk in Mesopotamia), around 2,000 BC.

The story includes the description of a great flood, which we are also familiar with from the Old Testament. The flood is said to have wiped out mankind except for Noah's family and animals, and it is easy to see how a particularly disastrous year, when the Tigris and Euphrates both over-ran their banks and flooded much of Mesopotamia could have led to the legend of Noah. It might have seemed that the flooding extended to the boundaries of the known world. Flooding have been catastrophic to a multitude of simple villagers; repopulation and restoration of farming and homes would have been very difficult and time consuming, and doubtless many would have perished in the flooding or starved in its aftermath.

The Bronze Age also brings definitive evidence of worship of the supernatural and from the time of Mesopotamia onwards many artefacts have been found confirming the importance and worship of gods. Doubtless the existence of these gods allowed early peoples to rationalise their hopes and fears, and to explain to their satisfaction what must have been the many puzzling features of the natural world around them. The existence of large temples that begin to appear around this time show the concentration of religious activity in the early cities.

By 2,300 BC many gods had appeared, each one often patronising a specific activity. Some gods were needed in order to explain the human cycles of birth, life and death, and to reassure the living that there was an afterlife where worldly cares and problems could finally be escaped. The Sumerians had many Gods but three main ones; Anu, Father of the Gods; Enlil, Lord of the Air, and Enki, God of Wisdom; they also recognised Sheol, a place of darkness, which we might see as a precursor of Hell.

Much of the art that has survived from those early times is in the form of figurines and drawings with the themes of fertility, the animal world, and of course war (from the victor's point of view). In time, these themes are translated onto the decoration of pots, particularly in Greece, which give a rich view into the daily lives and culture of ancient peoples.

Gold jewellery, usually from graves, has been found and dated back as far as 4,500 BC before the Bronze Age. Gold would have been particularly valuable to ancient peoples as it does not tarnish and is relatively soft and easily worked. When found in a grave it is often a sign of a high-status individual because of its relative scarcity. Despite the fact that earliest civilisation is known to have originated in Mesopotamia and Egypt, and despite the fact that both of these civilisations valued gold as a metal from which wonderful jewellery could be made, the earliest gold mining and gold work comes from the mainland of Europe in the mountains. It seems that once copper smelting had been discovered, gold working was quick to follow.

The quantities of gold mined would have been small, but the ability to smelt and produce sheets or castings in gold would have followed naturally from the technology discovered in using copper. Because it was a scarce commodity gold must have had great importance to be buried with its owner. The act of burial of such items also implies that the society would have been able to replace the gold, by exchange and barter, for further items of jewellery, relatively easily. It is likely that many objects were passed down from one generation to the next, but the most personal items were often buried with their original owner.

With the coming of Bronze Age, technology and the advent of writing, there also came an increase in social organisation and trade. Another factor needs to be considered in the facilitation of trade, and that is the ability of wind and water to encourage the use of boats for trading. By the time of the early Greek and Egyptian civilisations at the end of the second millennium, much water transport involved using oars since favourable winds were not always reliable; the passage from the Mediterranean to the Black Sea in particular could be difficult if winds and tides were contrary. It is not surprising that an early centre of trade and settlement grew up on the maritime trade route between these two seas around 3,000 BC. Similarly, a city state called Troy, grew to a large size on the west coast of Turkey south of the passage through to the Black Sea.

The Greek writer Homer set out from Troy around 2,800 BC, and his tales, immortalised in the Odyssey and the Iliad, give us an excellent insight into the technology, and the ability to travel, in those far off times. Troy was later famously sacked by the Greeks and levelled to the ground in 1,184 BC, in a war caused by the abduction of a princess of exceptional beauty from Sparta, whom we know as Helen of Troy. The sacking of Troy, in which all the population was slain and the city walls destroyed, resulted thousands of years later in an amazing series of finds when the site was finally identified in 1822, after decades of argument, by a Scot, Charles Maclaren (1782–1866). An English archaeologist, Frank Calvert (1828–1908) first started excavations which were later taken up by the German archaeologist Heinrich Schleimann (1822–1890) from 1868 onwards.

Towards the end of the Bronze Age, there seems to have been a natural catastrophe around the eastern Mediterranean and western Asia. Populations were severely affected. Mycenaean cities were attacked, burnt and deserted by their peoples. The Hittites were driven south from the Anatolian Plain by drought, which also caused northern Persian towns to be abandoned. Disastrous floods occurred in Hungary, and in North Africa Libyan refugees tried to migrate to Egypt. This was all probably the result of three causes: firstly, a burgeoning human population which became greater than the land could support with the contemporary methods of farming; secondly, a severe worldwide change in weather, causing alpine glaciers and northern cold adapted forests to extend further south; and thirdly, there is evidence from tree ring and ice-core analyses from various sites, that indicates a massive eruption of the volcano Hekla on Iceland in about 1104 BC.

It seems likely that this eruption threw so much ash into the atmosphere that it worsened an already deteriorating climate, such that literally a Dark Age settled over the eastern Mediterranean and Europe. It is interesting to compare this period with the later Dark Ages in Britain and Europe after the Romans left, which has traditionally been ascribed to the collapse of civilised life once the influence of the Rome was withdrawn; however written accounts from across the world at that time show that there was another climatic disaster around the year

535 AD, which may also have resulted from a massive volcanic explosion, this time from Krakatoa in Indonesia, casting a huge pall of volcanic ash into the atmosphere, partially blocking out the sun and again causing crop failures and starvation across the world for several years and once again contributing to a Dark Age.

During the Bronze Age, many of the advances in civilisation, both technical and philosophical, occurred around Mesopotamia. Similar and parallel changes appear to have occurred in China, India and Egypt around the same time or a little later with different technical, philosophical and societal changes developing in each location. In the mid Bronze Age a new empire appeared in Mesopotamia, that of Babylon. The whole of Mesopotamia was unified, and the name of Hammurabi is particularly remembered as one of Babylon's early kings who left behind a major reputation as a law maker following his reign from 1790–1760 BC. His code of law was inscribed on stone steles and placed in the courtyards of temples for public consumption, the laws dealt with many questions in some 282 articles.

The Babylonians continued to develop science and technology accumulating astronomical measurements, so that by 1,000 BC the path of the sun and some of the planets was known with remarkable accuracy. Babylonian mathematics were advanced and have passed down to us as the sexagesimal system of Sumer, so that even today we still divide circles into 360 degrees, days into 24 hours, hours into 60 minutes, and minutes into 60 seconds. Eventually most of this Babylonian heritage would succumb to warfare and fragmentation.

The Hittites coming south from Turkey, and the separation of Assyria and Babylonia, usher in the early start of the Iron Age, along with a new wave of migrations into the Middle East around the 13th and 12th centuries BC, covered next in chapter.

Possible further reading:
Europe Between the Oceans 9000 BC–AD 1000 by Barry Cunliffe (Yale University Press)

Chapter 5
The Early Iron Age

The Iron Age is ushered in by the earliest experiments with smelting and fashioning iron tools which came about in Armenia and Turkey before 1000 BC. The Hittite Kingdom, which came to be around 1600 BC in central Turkey was unusually successful in warfare, and it seems probable that some of their local dominance was due to their iron weaponry. It is not entirely clear what caused the ultimate downfall of the Hittite civilisation, but their way of life and their cities were destroyed around 1200 BC by a catastrophe and destruction that struck the eastern end of the Mediterranean.

This catastrophe, known as the Bronze Age Collapse, affected all the other nations or developing kingdoms around the eastern end of the Mediterranean, including those of Mycenae, Babylonia and Egypt; there was a period of severe drought, and possibly the eruption of Hekla in Iceland (chapter 4) also contributed to this collapse of kingdoms and communities, starting a period of three or four centuries of a Dark Age. The absence of much in the way of written records has meant that we still have little concrete evidence for what happened.

The secret of iron and its smelting, casting and fashioning, escaped before or amid, all the destruction, and slowly spread to neighbouring Europe. Iron swords and weapons were much tougher than the bronze blades which were their precursors, so this new technology was taken up with enthusiasm by surrounding cultures and kingdoms. Even at this stage of human social development it is apparent that warfare and its technology has become the dominant force which will continue to drive the development of civilisation over succeeding millennia. Soon after the start of the first millennium BC, horses, and with them a little later, chariots, appeared in the Middle East from central Asia adding a further dimension to warfare, horses having been initially domesticated in central Asia during the fourth millennium BC.

Through this Dark Age around the Aegean Sea after 1100 BC, probably in part due to the destruction of the great Mycenaean centres by earthquakes and volcanism which caused the resultant collapse of many of the early Greek city states, the region was open for invaders called Aryans who came from the north. The picture is confusing for several hundred years, until the Phoenician traders (of whom more later) were followed by what we know as the Classical Greek civilisation which became re-established around Greece, Crete, the Aegean islands, and the western coast of Turkey.

Some of the turmoil of this Dark Age has come down to us in the classic writings by Homer of the *Iliad* and the *Odyssey*. Greek civilisation at this time remained a largely Bronze Age technology, despite the spread of the Iron Age around the eastern Mediterranean at the time. The Egypt of this period around 1000 BC, was not as monolithic as it appeared in later times, and it suffered from raids by the Phoenicians, as well as migrant peoples from the north and further east. An independent kingdom was also emerging to the south of Egypt (modern Sudan), later becoming Upper Egypt.

Through the later part of the second millennium BC, Bronze Age Greece, known as Mycenaean Greece after its best-known remains at Mycenae, was beginning to coalesce from a mass of small city states, including those of Athens, Sparta and Pylos, from which splendid archaeological riches have survived through to modern times. Ancient Greece was at its zenith in the 14th and 15th centuries BC, when expansionist warfare characterised much of Greek history, including war with Egypt.

One of the enduring legends that has come down to us is of the siege of Troy, which occurred about 1184 BC, lasted ten years and concluded with the destruction of Troy in such a complete fashion that its very location was not rediscovered until the late 19th century. Classical Greece emerged and coalesced around the 18th century BC.

The Dark Age transition from the Bronze to the Iron Age was characterised by much warfare between small kingdoms and townships around the Middle East. The period from around 1200–700 BC is a confused one. Farming was increasingly producing more wealth and stability close to areas in the desert to the south and the steppes to the north, which did not enjoy such favourable agriculture conditions. If anyone has doubt about the level of raiding and warfare between the small states in existence at that time, then reading the accounts in the Old Testament of the Bible provide a vivid illustration of the amount of jealousy, raiding, fighting and conquest that was happening in the region.

No doubt much of this was the consequence of relatively underprivileged and technologically unsophisticated peoples from the more marginal areas to the East migrating into the more stable kingdoms around the eastern Mediterranean and Mesopotamia in the hopes of finding a better life. Peaceful developments at this time include increasing sophistication in pottery and its decoration as well as early coinage.

At this stage, we need to consider the Phoenicians, whose history relates that they arrived in Tyre on the eastern coast of the Mediterranean around 2,700 BC; their origin is unclear and although they established city states, or harbour states, along Greek lines, they were a Semitic people, apparently from the region of Palestine, or possibly from the Red Sea region a little further south. The coastal plain of the eastern Mediterranean here is narrow and cut off from the rest of the continent by mountains on the east, the agricultural land is relatively poor. As a consequence of these circumstances of geography, the Phoenicians expanded seawards becoming a great maritime, exploring and trading nation.

They founded colonies as far away as Cadiz, just beyond the western entrance to the Mediterranean, which was known, with the Rock of Gibraltar in the north and the lesser Avila Mons on the south shore of the Mediterranean in ancient times, as the Pillars of Hercules, from where they explored the Atlantic coasts of Africa to the south, and Europe to the north. The name of Phoenicia refers to the purple dye obtained from a sea snail of the genus murex which is time consuming and therefore costly to produce, and has become known as royal or imperial purple, and adopted as such first by the Greeks and then the Romans. After a millennium or more of trading, the harbour cities of Tyre and Sidon were sacked by the Assyrians, and the Phoenicians retreated to their other settlements around the Mediterranean, notably Carthage in what is now Tunisia.

There is evidence that the Phoenicians traded as far north from the western end of the Mediterranean as Cornwall, for precious supplies of tin and silver; the tin was needed to make bronze and the silver mainly for jewellery; they also explored to the south along the west coast of Africa. Following the foundation of Carthage in the year 814 BC, the colony expanded, coming to exceed the size of the eastern Mediterranean settlements and including the southern half of Sardinia and much of southern Spain.

The Phoenicians were the first people to devise an alphabet and sounds which later evolved into Greek and then Latin (chapter 14). They continued to prosper, with much of their late history being absorbed by trade, piracy and disputes with Rome, until finally Rome lost patience and sacked Carthage, their capital, in 146 BC during the third and last Punic War, after which it became a Roman province and we hear no more of the Phoenicians in history.

There is great importance and information in the migrations and writings of the Jewish people, whose definitive history is set down in the Jewish Torah and the Old Testament of the Christian Bible. The early Jews were a Semitic people, nomads from Arabia, who migrated initially into the rich lands of the Fertile Crescent from their less hospitable homeland. The word 'Hebrew' means 'wanderer' and reflects the self-perceived picture of the tribes who settled around the Middle East in the second millennium BC. One of these tribes migrated, or was deported, into Egypt where they became the first people to establish the practice of monotheism. Their beliefs were codified in the Ten Commandments which Moses was given by God and brought down from the mountain.

Later, Moses led his tribe out of Egypt, and after years of wandering they finally settled in what has become known as the Holy Land, or Palestine. In later times this Semitic and Hebrew civilisation would produce first Jesus Christ, and then, 600 years later, Mohammed, two individuals whose beliefs and preaching would have an immense effect on the subsequent development of human civilisation. The word Semitic derives from the assumption that the Semitic people were descended from Shem, one of the three sons of Noah. The Bible gives details of the early prophets, who codified the worship of a single universal God, emphasising justice and punishment for sin, but mercy and forgiveness for sinners who repent. The Bible is consistently critical of social injustice, and the frequent hypocrisy of the ruling of priestly officials. After the times of the early prophets, Israel was overrun by the Assyrians in 722 BC, and the ten tribes of Israel were assimilated, enslaved or deported. The tribe of Judah managed to last longer in Jerusalem, until a Babylonian army destroyed the city and temple in 587 BC.

The Assyrian empire that conquered Babylon in 729 BC, and Israel later, was unusual in that it comprised a large unified empire ruled from Nineveh in northern Mesopotamia, with the installation of governors to rule its provinces, rather than creating subservient native princely vassals with many little kingdoms. Further Assyrian conquest continued to include Lower Egypt, Cyprus, Cilicia and Syria. After this, much of the Near East was ruled under a standardised system of government and law. Men were conscripted into the army, and populations were deported and scattered around the region, breaking up the previous tribal system. The Assyrian King Ashurbanipal (668–626 BC) established a magnificent library of stone tablets all over ancient Mesopotamia laying down his laws and leaving us valuable knowledge of the ideas and life of these times.

The combination of conscription into a large standing army which was well trained, and the provision of iron weapons and siege artillery, formed an unstoppable weapon of conquest for the time. The Assyrian empire depended on constant new conquest and capture of slaves and riches; only in this way was it possible to keep the royal family and the elite in the very extreme and costly luxury in which they lived. The conquests were short-lived however, and once Ashurbanipal died, the over-large Assyrian empire could not be sustained and slowly began to crumble. Barbarian invaders from the north, known as Scythians, contributed to the Assyrian downfall when they appeared on horseback, fighting with sophisticated bows and arrows.

Attacks by the Medes from the Persian mountains, along with Babylonians and Scythians, saw the major Assyrian cities of Nineveh and Nimrud destroyed. Following this Mesopotamia's supremacy was re-established with Babylon as its magnificent capital, though this was only short lived due to invasion in 539 BC by the Persians.

At the same time in western Europe and Britain, more primitive smaller settlements of people were coalescing into early tribes. This process was also happening all across the central belt of Europe between the 13th and the 8th centuries BC, to produce a civilisation which we know from their culture and burial practices, and which has come to be called Celtic. After living in small villages in the early first millennium BC these people erected defensive settlements with palisades, and also built hill forts still seen throughout Britain and Europe.

The first half of the first millennium BC was characterised by deterioration of the climate, which became colder and wetter and must have been much less hospitable both for farming and for living. Ancient salt mines in Austria and Switzerland have provided valuable preservation of artefacts from that time. Although Britain had long been separated from the continent by the North Sea, the English Channel remained relatively narrow and trade appears to have flourished with the European mainland.

The Celts appear during this transition period between the Bronze and early Iron Age when the ice sheet and glaciers had receded some ten to twelve thousand years previously, and the land bridge between the British Isles and the continent had disappeared five thousand years previously. Forests had been partially cleared and agriculture had developed. The pressure of population had increased, and the Celts had gradually radiated outwards from their homelands in central and northern Europe into lands that were often more favourable for human occupation. Territorial competition had led to the building of early hill forts and palisaded settlements, so that by the time of the first written accounts of Britain at the time of the first Roman incursion in 55 BC, Julius Caesar found a thriving society with a well-developed priestly caste of Druids, and some early proto-urban settlements.

Grave goods were both local pottery and bronze work, and were combined with items clearly imported from far away, showing the extent of trade with neighbouring European cultures. Celtic art, using bronze and often lavish amounts of gold, was concentrated in the area around the Rhine at that time. Graves and burial goods tell us that the place of women in Celtic society was often as prominent as that of the men. The Celts had trading settlements on the trans-Alpine routes and had expanded both south and west with a huge incursion into northern Italy during the 4th century BC. Many people from this early wave of Celtic migrants settled in the Po Valley in northern Italy, but a substantial number continued southward in 386 BC, defeating the Romans and then occupying Rome which was sacked, burned and ransomed.

Content with their ransom of a thousand pounds of gold, the Celts withdrew: many settled in northern Italy, others became mercenaries in the Roman army. Chronic low-grade warfare continued between Celts and Romans in northern Italy over the next century or two, with a massive battle in Etruria in 225 BC which the Romans won, and then continued on to capture Mediolanum (Milan), then the Celtic capital.

Another Celtic force had expanded into Macedonia and the Balkans, and into northern Greece, where Apollo's sanctuary at Delphi offered the prospects of immense booty to invaders. This Celtic movement ran out of steam early in the 3rd century BC, but in the meantime settlement by Celts in the Iberian Peninsula, northern France and the British Isles continued much more peacefully. The Celts were gradually subdued by Rome with northern Italy south of the Alps (known as Cisalpine Gaul) being conquered early in the 2nd century BC, and the Iberian Peninsula rather later, following years of resistance, in 133 BC. The southernmost part of Gaul then stood as a strategic barrier between Italy and Spain at the end of the 2nd century BC. The Celts of Narbonensis, then often called Gauls by the Romans, had been subdued and were under Roman control.

Eventually, it became imperative for the major part of Gaul to be subdued, and the Gallic Wars followed from 58 BC, in which Julius Caesar gradually overcame these remaining Celts, also leaving us his detailed autobiographical war diaries. The final battle came with the Siege of Alesia (present day Alise-Saintes in France) in which Caesar besieged and finally defeated a large force of Celts under the command of Vercingetorix in 52 BC, who was taken to Rome for a ceremonial victory parade and later executed. The Celts are further considered in chapter 18.

By the end of the first millennium BC, bronze remained a very useful additional material, which unlike iron does not rust, but the Iron Age was firmly established, and the future alignments of civilisation in Europe then depended on the use of iron and its development through succeeding centuries by different nations. Finally the 20th century ushered in a transition into the Age of Synthetics encompassing many different and sophisticated man-made products, including other metals, glass fibre, plastics, and most recently carbon fibre.

Possible further reading:
The Celts, First Masters of Europe by Christine Eluere (Thames and Hudson)
The Phoenicians by Donald Harden (Penguin)

Chapter 6
Egypt

We saw earlier that Egypt was one of the main centres where civilisation appears to have evolved spontaneously and independently. At the time of the last glacial maximum, around 20,000BC, the Sahara was a green fertile land supporting a large ecology of grazing animals, including antelope, buffalo and elephant, together with their predators, including lions. Archaeological remains in the Sahara include ancient settlement sites, stone circles, graves and a lot of rock paintings in caves, depicting animals and people. The paintings have survived remarkably well thanks to the drying out of the Sahara since that time, and bear testament to the flourishing population living and practicing early farming in stone age villages across the Sahara, the evidence also shows that there was a stone age population in this region 40,000 years ago before the last Ice Age.

Once the Ice Age passed, the climate changed and the Sahara dried out gradually becoming decertified, and thus presenting a near impenetrable barrier to humans between northern and southern Africa, with desert stretching from one side of the continent to the other. The big exception to this was the valley of the River Nile, which remained green thanks to the river itself, and its annual flooding, which often permitted two crops each year. In the early years before 10,000 BC and in addition to the regular annual floods, Egypt appears to have been inundated by intermittent huge floods, probably brought on by the altered climate following at the end of the Ice Age.

These floods are felt by some to be the basis of the ancient legends, firstly of Noah and the Ark, and secondly, of the lost continent of Atlantis. The lost continent is now felt to be a mythical story rather than a definitive piece of land submerged when sea levels rose, since scientific exploration of our world beneath the oceans has now become possible and undersea mapping has revealed no large subterranean land mass which would correspond to the legend.

By 8,000 BC, the geography of Egypt had become much as we see it today, namely a long narrow strip of land 50km wide, stretching 1,000km from south to north along the Nile River, and fanning out at its northern end into a large and steadily growing delta. In due course this delta region would become known as Lower Egypt, whilst the more southerly reaches of the Nile became known as Upper Egypt. Early Egypt was developing roughly at the same time as the civilisation in Mesopotamia, with both of these areas being dependent upon large rivers which flooded each year, bringing new fertile silt and life to the early farmers.

There was undoubtedly some interchange between the two regions, and because the Sumerian civilisation in Mesopotamia appeared a little earlier, Egypt would have often benefited from its experience and example. We know most about the early Egyptian civilisation because of the enormous richness of the excavated remains, predominantly in tombs, but also because of the considerable legacy of early pictographic writing, in the form of hieroglyphs which the Egyptians have left in their tombs.

Because of the Egyptian geography, dictated by the River Nile, civilisation started in small Stone Age villages, where people used flint tools and made rough pottery. In addition to cereal crops, animals were farmed, and both fish and waterfowl provided by the river were hunted: the early Egyptians knew how to make boats out of papyrus, and their farming was aided by the reinvigoration of the soil from Nile flooding each year. Much of Egypt's early history has been lost in the repeated flooding and annual deposition of silt, but also by the buildings of each generation being placed on top of the previous one.

Early Egyptian writing has, however, bequeathed a lot of information to us, so that we know from the written record that King Menes of Upper Egypt first united both Upper and Lower Egypt around 3,100 BC, starting what is known as the Archaic Period which lasted to 2,890 BC and comprised the First Dynasty. Menes' capital city was moved from Abydos in Lower Egypt to Memphis in the Nile delta, with Abydos remaining the major religious centre. Thereafter, the nation of Egypt remained united and passed through some twenty royal dynasties over the next two millennia.

Egyptian history is divided into three periods of stability, known as the Old, Middle and New Kingdoms, with two unstable periods of about a century each between them. During these intermediate eras there were problems with both weak government internally, and threats externally, though on each occasion Egypt came together as a nation once more under a Pharaoh who restored the ruling lineage, together with the religious beliefs and social functioning of previous generations. It is interesting to compare this with China where after periods of unrest and civil disturbance the ruling class then also placed importance on restoring the previous social structure and customs. The first two dynasties initiated by King Menes led into to the Old Kingdom period which lasted from about 2,700 BC for the next five hundred years.

It was the Old Kingdom which constructed many of the pyramids which have lasted down to the present day. From this period the name of Imhotep has survived. He was both an architect and a healer or physician, together with being a notable close advisor to the King: he was responsible for the construction of the first pyramid at Saqqara.

With the end of the period known as The Old Kingdom came a century known as the First Intermediate Period, of which we know very little due to internal power struggles and the absence of buildings, monuments and records throughout the time it lasted, which included the 7th to 11th dynasties (2181–2055), with a high point for Egypt at the end of this period. The exact cause of the disruption is not clear, but it appears that internal warring between families over the succession to the throne, severely weakened the central governing structure of the country. Eventually, however, stability was restored, and in 2,040 BC the Middle Kingdom or the 'Period of Reunification' commenced.

Upper and Lower Egypt were united again under a strong pharaoh of the 11th Dynasty who ruled for half a century, thus establishing the stability of the Middle Kingdom, which lasted for four hundred years through the 11th and 12th dynasties of which the last pharaoh was a woman, Queen Sobekneferu. Egypt then declined through the rather weak reigns of the kings of the 13th dynasty, probably because of problems with inheritance and dynastic continuity with inter-family power struggles, which came to a head in the Second Intermediate Period of internal strife, when there were some sixty rulers within about 150 years, and which lasted for a century or more from 1,650 to 1,550 BC.

This century was characterised by the invasion of Asiatic people called the Hyksos, who came from the north-east, conquering Egypt and setting up the 15th and 16th dynasties. In keeping with their Asian origin, the Hyksos brought with them improvements in bronze technology in the form of better battle axes, together with the composite bow: they also brought horses and chariots, both of which probably conferred overwhelming advantage in terms of warfare and invasion, quite apart from controlling the local Egyptian population.

The 17th dynasty began with internal revolt in Egypt, and gradually the Hyksos, who had mainly colonised Lower Egypt, were defeated and their rulers driven out under the apparent command and direction of Egyptians from Thebes in Upper Egypt. In this way the Second Intermediate Period of instability ended and the New Kingdom was ushered in around 1,550 BC, following which it lasted for five hundred years.

The New Kingdom included the 18th dynasty, of which Amenhotep IV was the most august Pharaoh ruling between 1,353–1,334 BC. He had been left a mighty empire, a powerful army and a very well stocked treasury by his father Tuthmosis. The Kingdom at that time enjoyed peace and great prosperity, with temple complexes being built at Luxor and Carnac outside Thebes. Amenhotep became fanatical about the worship of the sun and suppressed other religions, whilst also changing his name to Akhenaton. He built a new capital to celebrate his worship of the single god Aten, or the sun disc, and lived there with his great royal wife Nefertiti.

His preoccupation with religion resulted in lax supervision of Egypt's control over its vassal kingdoms to the north-east, but once his successor, the ten-year-old Tutankhamun, came to the throne the old gods were restored to their temples, together with control over the lesser kingdoms, and the economy gradually recovered. Tutankhamun's magnificent death mask made at the end of his ten-year reign is often pictured, and is credited with a big upsurge in present day interest in ancient Egypt when it was discovered in 1922.

Following Tutankhamun, Rameses I came to power as the founder of the 19th dynasty. He was succeeded by his son Rameses II, who occupied the throne for an unusually long period of 67 year and fought the Hittites in a critical Battle at Kadesh. The New Kingdom had re-established stability and seen Egypt establish its most powerful and widest extent, but the period saw war with the Hittite Empire (originating in what is now Turkey), in which an army under the Hittite King Muwattallis, came to fight the Pharaoh Rameses II at the Battle of Kadesh. This battle in 1,274 BC, between the Hittites and the Egyptians, took place next to the Orontes River on the modern border between Syria and Lebanon.

It was a large battle both in terms of importance and in terms of the numbers of troops involved. Extensive numbers of warriors mounted in chariots on each side engaged each other. Neither side was a clear winner by the end of the day, though the Egyptians may well have been spared defeat by running out of time when darkness fell at the end of the day: the ultimate outcome resulted in a peace treaty with each side claiming victory. The battle did however establish the Hittites as equals of the Egyptians and prevent further Egyptian military adventures northwards; Rameses later married a Hittite princess to cement relationships between the two kingdoms.

Ramses III ruled as Pharaoh from 1,186–1,155 BC, and this long reign was a time of gradual decline in Egypt, both politically and economically. His reign included invasions from Libya, and also by a force identified as the 'Sea Peoples', who may have been Phoenician or Greek. This was a time when natural disasters struck Egypt in the form of poor harvests and labour unrest due to the resulting high price of wheat, which may in turn have been due to the eruption of Hekla. This volcano in southern Iceland is known to have erupted in 1,104 BC and around 1,000 BC; evidence from tree rings and ice cores indicate an eighteen-year period of global cooling and poor plant growth, which would have been responsible for poor harvests.

The period of the New Kingdom was succeeded by the so called Third Intermediate Period, which lasted some four hundred years to 664 BC, and included the 21st to 25th dynasties, and was a time of gradual decline, although internally Egypt remained unchanged in terms of its religion and social structure. A brief period followed over the next three hundred years which included the 26th to 31st dynasties, with continuing social stability. Thereafter there was a period of some three centuries in which Egypt was ruled by the Ptolemys, who originated from Greece, but adopted Egyptian traditions.

Egypt had been conquered by Alexander the Great in 332 BC, who founded the city of Alexandria in the delta region which he named after himself, and which became a very prosperous capital of the Egyptian kingdom of the Ptolemys. The first Ptolemy was a Macedonian Greek general under Alexander who succeeded to become ruler of Egypt when Alexander died in 323 BC leaving his successor Ptolemys ruling Egypt for the next three centuries and turning the country into a Hellenistic kingdom and a great centre of Greek culture.

In 48 BC, Roman civil war pitted Julius Caesar against Pompey, his original colleague in ruling Rome. Egypt became involved in Rome's civil war (chapter 14) because after losing the battle of Pharsalus in central Greece, Pompey fled to Egypt, only to be pursued by Caesar, who promptly took sides in the then current Egyptian civil war between Cleopatra, as regent for the child pharaoh, and the rest of the Ptolemy family. Caesar defeated the pharaoh's forces at the Battle of the Nile in 47 BC, and made Cleopatra ruler of Egypt. Thereafter, Egypt became a province of Rome, and was later formally annexed into the Roman Empire under Octavian, Caesar's nephew, in 30 BC.

By aligning herself with Caesar, Cleopatra consolidated her power and they had a son together, but after Caesar's assassination in 44 BC, she sided with Mark Anthony against Caesar's legal heir, Octavian. With Mark Anthony, Cleopatra had twins, and then another son, but the struggle with Rome continued, culminating in a sea battle between Octavian's Rome against Mark Anthony at Actium off the Greek coast in the Ionian Sea in 31 AD.

After losing this battle, Mark Anthony and Cleopatra retreated to Alexandria where they were besieged, and both then committed suicide. Octavian was then able to bring peace to Rome ending the civil war; following this Egypt acted as an important exporter and source of grain for Rome. Egypt was thereafter ruled by a Roman governor appointed by the Emperor, becoming gradually Christianised and boasting Alexandria as one of the great Christian centres, renowned for its learning and its library. Octavian was proclaimed Augustus and Roman Emperor by the Senate in 27 BC, and thus commenced the Pax Romana, the longest period of peace ever seen in Europe, lasting two centuries to 208 AD with only minor infringements of war and rebellion.

Matters changed little in Egypt until in 619 AD the Persian Empire conquered and annexed the country from the Romans, thereby making it part of the Sassanian Empire of Persia. This lasted only for a short period of twenty years, at the end of which time, and following the death of Mohammed in 632 AD, an Arab army besieged and conquered Alexandria in 641 AD. Fighting with the Byzantine Empire occupied the next five years, but in 646 AD Muslim conquest of Egypt was complete. The Muslim conquest spread further across Northern Africa reaching Carthage, in modern Tunisia around 700 AD, and crossing the Straits of Gibraltar to Spain in 711 AD. The north African littoral including Egypt has stayed largely Muslim ever since.

Summary of Egyptian dynasties:

I and II Dynasties,	3150–2686 BC (Union of Upper and Lower Egypt 3100 BC)
The Old Kingdom, III to VI Dynasties	2686–2181 BC
1st Intermediate Period, VII-XI Dynasties	2181–2061 BC
Middle Kingdom, XI-XIV Dynasties	2061–1690 BC
2nd Intermediate Period, XV-XVIII Dynasties	1690–1549 BC
New Kingdom, XVIII-XX Dynasties	1549–1077 BC
3rd Intermediate Period, XXI-XXV Dynasties	1069–653 BC
Late Period, XVI-XXXI Dynasties	653–332 BC

Possible further reading:
The Egyptians by John Ruffle (Cornell University Press)

Chapter 7
The Indus Valley

In early times, four great river civilisations grew up, including those on the Euphrates, the Nile and the Yellow River. The fourth great river runs through what is now Pakistan, where the mighty Indus River carries rainfall and snow melt from the Himalayan Mountains south to the sea. This north-westerly part of the Indian sub-continent was relatively well insulated from the rest of the world in pre-historic times by its geography: the Himalayan Mountains to the north, the Indian Ocean to the west, and the Thar Desert to the east and south, all of which were big disincentives to trade and migration.

Early stone age farming probably came to the Indus valley around 6,000 BC, which is somewhat later than comparable farming in Mesopotamia. As in Mesopotamia and Egypt, the Indus River probably played a large part in producing a fertile agricultural plain and thus potentiating farming. The river with its many tributaries also provided a natural highway for trade and communication. There is evidence of ancient coastal connections with Mesopotamia along the shores of the Arabian Sea. Irrigation systems from the Indus River were devised for the farming of wheat, barley, fruit and pulses. Pottery was made using a wheel; sheep and goats were domesticated. Land transport started early using bullocks and carts.

Civilisation seems to have arisen independently in this region, and many centres showing early towns have now been identified. Five early cities of perhaps 20–30,000 people have been identified, together with many smaller ones, but the two best known and most investigated are Harappa and Mohenjo-Daro. These two cities, and others in the Indus valley, came into being in the middle of the 3rd millennium BC from a coalescence of the many small villages existing in the area before that time. Passageways between houses in the cities were clearly planned and laid out from the outset according to an organised, geometrical grid-type layout, with internal roads and drains running north-south and east-west. The buildings were all constructed of mud bricks of a standard size, there being no local stone.

Each city or town was fortified and boasted civic buildings and granaries to store the year's harvest, together with cisterns for water storage. The houses were often two storeys high, and in the two big cities a central palace stood on an elevated site. The whole compact city was surrounded by double walls, but no other evidence of defensive warfare, indicating a time of relative peace.

The Stone Age culture here morphed into the Bronze Age around 3,000 BC, and then persisted for at least a thousand years, from around 2,500 BC to 1,500 BC, thanks to mineral imports from mountains in Afghanistan to the north where there were rich deposits of copper, tin, gold and silver. There is little of evidence of writing, though pictographs were made, some of which have been found, but these pictographs are few in number and are not fully deciphered or understood yet. A similar, but less advanced and later civilisation, was beginning to coalesce on the eastern side of the sub-continent, along the course of India's other major river, the Ganges, where the region produced the first cotton for which there is historical evidence. Rice appears to have become the mainstay of the staple diet initially in the Ganges Valley, though it is not clear whether it was indigenous, or whether it came from China and South-East Asia in the first instance, perhaps spreading subsequently to the Indus valley in the west.

The Indus civilisation declined after 1,500 BC and seems to have ended around 750 BC, at a time which coincides with the migration, or invasion, of a race called Aryans migrating from the north. It is possible that this Aryan invasion was either coincidental with, or was facilitated by, deforestation in the mountains and consequent devastating floods. Although the native Indus civilisation gradually crumbled, the incoming Aryans, who were warriors and nomads of a Bronze Age culture, settled and integrated with the Indus Valley people. The Aryan culture was less advanced than that of the Indus Valley, and the scanty pictographs disappear, not to emerge again until around 500 BC.

The Aryans did bring with them three profound additions to the way of life in the Indus Valley. The first of these was their concept of religion, which involved many gods that we learn about from the Rig-Veda, a collection of religious hymns or chants performed during sacrifice and written down for the first time by 1,000 BC (chapter 17). The second import was the introduction of horses, mainly for the elite, and the third addition was the caste system, which initially had three divisions, a warrior aristocracy, priestly Brahmins, and the large majority of ordinary peasant farmers. Later categories included farmers, merchants and artisans and a further category of non-Aryans, or native Indus Valley people emerged, who were labelled "unclean" and known as Dalits. This caste system was subsequently greatly elaborated and has controlled the structure of Indian society down to very recent times.

Halfway through the 1st millennium BC, the basic text of Hinduism appeared, called the Bhagavad Gita, or 'The Hymn of The Lord'. Religious teaching enjoyed great popularity at this time, and in addition to Buddhism, Jainism became widespread following the teachings of Mahavira Nataputta and a series of teachers. Nataputta was a contemporary of the Buddha who preached absolute non-violence towards all living creatures and the renunciation of earthly pleasures and possessions.

Whilst the Indus Valley civilisation was in slow decline, the Ganges Valley society seems to have been steadily rising so that by the 7th century BC this represented the most populous and influential area of Indian life. By this time northern India had become organised into some sixteen different kingdoms, written texts became available again, and although altered over the years, these provide increasing evidence of how people lived. In the middle of the 1st millennium BC India's population has been estimated at around 25 million people, or a quarter of the whole population of the world then.

Classical Hinduism came into being at that time, and one of the world's earliest religions, Buddhism, also began here (chapter 17). The Buddha was born in the early 6th century BC. He was a prince of the warrior class called Siddhartha Gautama (chapter 17). He found his privileged life unsatisfying and became an aesthete for seven years, which also proved unsatisfying. He then began to teach an ethical doctrine of austerity, involving discipline and meditation. One of the reasons for his popularity was probably that he felt equality was owed to women, as well as to those of lower castes. Eventually, the rival faith of Hinduism would come to number more supporters throughout India, though Buddhism would spread through the rest of Asia, and its followers through Eastern Asia would become more numerous overall.

The sixteen different states that existed in northern India in the middle of the 1st millennium BC were quite volatile, and improved agriculture at that time led directly to the emergence of cities and the coalescence of the smaller kingdoms into larger ones through warfare. Alexander the Great made a journey of conquest (334–323 BC) which included annexing all the land around the Indus River, though this was lost again some thirty years later. After Alexander's death in 323 BC the empire fragmented, and a Mauryan King named Chandragupta from a relatively small and unknown tribe moved to fill the political void in the Indus Valley in 321 BC, eventually building a very large state which included both the Indus and Ganges valleys, together with Afghanistan.

The Mauryan dynasty lasted 135 years culminating with Chandragupta's grandson Ashoka (304–232 BC), who was a remarkable man and was the first indigenous ruler to conquer and unify all the small Indian states and princedoms; he has a strong claim to be regarded as the father of modern India. After a particularly bloody battle during the conquest of Kalinga state, in which 100,000 people are said to have died and many more were displaced or enslaved, he converted to Buddhism and its code of non-violence, resolving to rule by moral authority alone. Ashoka thought that the non-violent Buddhist philosophy could become a cultural cement for political unity across all his conquered states. The following Mauryan years were prosperous, improving both agriculture and trade.

Further migrations into the region came initially from the Greeks, and then later from nomadic Scythian tribes displaced or migrating south from central Asia; we know about these tribes and their customs from the earlier travel writings of the Greek historian Herodotus (484–425 BC). Also at this time the old trade routes, both by sea and overland to the west, became busy once again. Eventually by the 4th century AD, a native dynasty of the Gupta family rose to power and ruled for the next two centuries, until they faced severe disruption by yet further nomadic incursions of Asiatic tribes coming from the north.

Warfare between these tribes and states continued, and gradually temple Hinduism prevailed over Buddhism with the ruling elite becoming predominantly Hindu and acting as patrons to the temples with gifts of riches. Somewhat later Islam came to India through Arabic traders some decades after the death of Mohammed. Early in the 8th century AD, Arab armies conquered Sind, an area on both east and west banks of the river Indus (modern Pakistan with Karachi to the west of the Indus estuary).

This geographical situation then remained fairly constant for the unusually long period of the next three centuries, up to the early 11th century when further waves of Islamic migration from the north and west led to a Turkic sultanate being established in Delhi. The conversion of many high-ranking Mongol officials to Islam helped the success of the sultanate, spreading Muslim rule and religion throughout the region. Muslim invasion also extended across to the Ganges valley in the east but did not penetrate into the south of India where Hindu society survived largely untouched.

Possible further reading:
Histories of Nations by Peter Furtado (Thames and Hudson)
A History of India by Peter Robb (Palgrave)

Chapter 8
The Far East: Early China, Japan and Korea

For most of the last several millennia, these nations have developed in isolation, in part because of their geographical situation, but also due to the self-imposed separateness of the ruling elites. The prehistoric archaeology of China includes traces of both Homo Erectus and Homo Neanderthalensis almost half a million years ago, before dying out. Early Homo sapiens appears after the last Ice Age and would have migrated from Africa around the coasts of Arabia, India and South-East Asia, and then up the eastern Chinese coast. The three great rivers of China, the Yellow River (Huang He) in the north, the Yangtze in the middle, and the Hsi in the south, have also acted as important conduits for migration, settlement and communication through the ages. Initially, small villages grew up from the sixth millennium BC, particularly around the head waters of the Yellow River in the north, where millet was the principal crop, while rice was the main crop along the Yangtze River.

The names of early Chinese rulers from the second millennium have come down to us from records made on tortoise shells and oracle bones, which were ox shoulder blades heated in a fire until they cracked; the extent and direction of the cracking was then deciphered by the emperor to predict the future. The reading of these oracles by the emperor was a most important ancient Chinese ritual, at a time when the country was made up of a multitude of small fiefdoms run by warrior landlords, and overall control of the nation had yet to be achieved.

When records start to appear at the beginning of the second millennium BC, known as the Longshan period, northern China comprised a large number of small warring states, during a period since labelled the 'Ten Thousand Kingdoms'. Around 1,700 BC one of the war leaders, who had the military advantage of early chariots, was able to impose control on most of the country bordering the Yellow River. This was the founding of the Shang Kingdom or Dynasty, which was later enlarged by further conquest.

The Shang Dynasty lasted for the next several hundred years, and saw the onset of literacy and the use of bronze, together with technically and artistically wonderful pottery. Even during this very early dynastic period, the Chinese people were divided into a small, very rich ruling class, and a very large and very poor, peasant class, who farmed predominantly millet, rice and some domesticated animals (ducks, chickens and pigs), and produced the basis of wealth on which the whole country lived. Agriculture only came much later to mid and southern China.

Ritual ancestor worship was combined with belief in the need to bury their elite with sufficient grave goods that they could enjoy the luxury in death to which they had become accustomed in life, including the service of slaves placed with the dead person by human sacrifice. These customs are surprisingly similar to some other cultures across the world at the same time and have provided much archaeological information about early Chinese life. The same concern with the afterlife was either not displayed by the peasants, or, more likely, was simply unachievable. Literacy came to be with scribes and archivists recording life, and even the currency was standardised.

Bronze casting during the second millennium BC reached a peak of artistry and technical excellence using a bronze alloy made from copper, lead and tin, but was restricted to factories owned by the emperor. Technically everything belonged to the Emperor with peasants effectively being slaves, the nobility and bureaucrats had tenure which they passed to the next generation, so that social mobility was non-existent.

Available records show that a small number of very influential civil servants supervised work in the royal factories where bronze and pottery was made, and where shield makers, flag makers, carpenters, jade cutters and archivists all worked under strict supervision. Detailed early accounting and book-keeping confirm that millet was the basis of the staple diet, with wheat and rice also beginning to be grown; cattle, sheep, pigs, horses and water buffalo were domesticated and used for food and transport, as well as for sacrifice.

The Shang Dynasty was finally overthrown around 1150 BC, and supplanted by another tribe, or clan, called the Chou, from the western headwater region of the Yellow River. But the social organisation and elaborate government developed by the Shang was preserved and consolidated. Bronze working, decorative pottery, and ancestor burial rites, were also further developed and refined under the Chou, whose dynasty lasted to around 700 BC, when a Barbarian invasion from the extreme west, in other words the central Asian Steppes, drove the Chou east along the Yellow River.

In the second half of the first millennium BC, societal organisation began to be questioned by itinerant teachers moving around the country, who were known as 'legalists'. These teachers continued discussions through the centuries and spawned the most famous of all Chinese thinkers, Confucius, who was born a little before 500 BC. His thinking, and interpretations of his thinking, shaped China's attitudes for the next two millennia until he was bitterly attacked by the first post-Confucian Chinese state when the Communist party came to rule in the 20th century. The legalists thought that the power to make laws should replace oracles and ritual observances as principles for the organisation of society, and also that there should be a single set of laws, or code of conduct, for both the rich and the poor.

Confucius opposed these principles and wanted to strengthen the different principles of personal integrity and selfless service to the community, together with respect for elders; he believed that in the past there had been a mythical age when each person knew his place in society, did his duty, and lived according to his allotted station. This perception of an unchanging society, with support for prevailing institutions, was undoubtedly very influential in helping to preserve China with a fairly static social hierarchy for the following two millennia, but it was quite contrary to Marxist-Leninist principles.

Confucius postulated four principles for behaviour and good government in society – documentation, conduct, loyalty, and faithfulness. He and his followers attached more importance to the lessons and wisdom of history, and to the maintenance of good law and order, rather than to any theological questions or musings about a supernatural being. This attitude undoubtedly accounts for much of the difference between the development of Chinese society compared to the western Abrahamic cultures of the Jewish, Christian and Muslim traditions.

The next period, from 400 to 200 BC, is known as the 'Period of the Warring States', which is self-explanatory about the tensions of the time. At the end of this 'Period of the Warring States', little wars escalated, and finally China came to be a single great nation, ruled by a dynasty called the Ch'in (from which the name China derives) in 223 BC. The Ch'in superiority derived from an army numbering over half a million. Although the dynasty lasted only decades, the level of organisation achieved many societal changes and improvements. Under the 'Warring States' each of the states had built its own defensive wall against tribal invaders to the north; now the new dynasty sent at least half a million peasants and convicts to build linking walls so completing 2,400km (1,500 miles) of the Great Wall of China.

Apart from the Great Wall, the other great project which had started some time earlier was the building of the Grand Canal which had been begun in 486 BC, and would eventually run north and south to join the Yangtze and Yellow rivers, thus providing an enormous benefit for trade and the transfer of food; the canal could only have been made in a country with continuous, autocratic and complete government direction, but despite this completion was only finally achieved a millennium after its start in 611 AD.

At the same time, under the Ch'in currency, weights and measures were standardised and all non-official weapons were confiscated. In 21 BC, a purge was instituted known as 'Burning Books and Burying Scholars', when history books in particular, together with Confucian scholars in general, were targeted, with the object of suppressing intellectual thought and discussion, obliterating history, and thereby unifying political and social opinion (perhaps we can recognise similarities with present attitudes).

The Chinese nation continued to develop through the rest of the first millennium BC, with the Yellow River culture providing a continuing basis for the organisation of society. The way in which Chinese society was organised in those times has been perpetuated almost up to the present day, with preservation of the institutions and strata of society through the next two thousand years of history, this has assured the continuity of institutions, and the preservation of a small ruling and royal elite, alongside a massive peasantry. The Chinese aristocracy long enjoyed this very unequal monopoly of wealth, with reverence for ancestors and great importance being attached to preparation for the afterlife.

An idea gradually came to prominence through the first millennium AD that there was a god superior to the ancestral gods of the dynasty, and from this superior god followed a mandate to rule the country. This mandate gradually produced the hierarchy of ministers who ruled the country and oversaw the production of goods, while all land still belonged to the Emperor, who had a parallel civil service of overseers and scribes. Iron tools and weapons had appeared quite late at around 500 BC. Early Chinese weapons included mainly bows, arrows, and bronze axes; the Chinese invented the crossbow around 200 BC, but although this is a powerful and accurate weapon, its value is somewhat negated by the very lengthy time required for reloading. As time passed, armour and horses also came into use for warriors, along with chariots.

The Ch'in, or Qin, dynasty gave way to the Han dynasty in 206 BC after a rebel coup deposed the Qin. The succeeding period is generally seen as a golden age and persisted through to 220 AD with a small blip in the middle. Thereafter different dynasties came to power, but this made little difference to the labouring masses of Chinese people. Internal warfare waxed and waned over the years, sometimes resulting in changes of dynasty; the biggest change came in the 13th century when the Mongols conquered China, which they then ruled, largely using the governmental structures and civil servants which they found in place. Kublai Khan (grandson of Genghis Khan, chapter 28) pronounced the founding of Mongol rule in 1271 as the Yuan Dynasty, but eventually, palace rivalries and Mongol in-fighting led to the demise of the dynasty in 1368, when it was over-run and supplanted by the Ming Dynasty.

However, during the Yuan Dynasty, a civil servant called Wang Zhen (1290–1333) is remembered for trying to produce movable wooden type for printing; the venture failed because wood proved insufficiently hard-wearing (quite apart from the need to store 10,000 separate Chinese characters against the 26 letters needed for the western alphabet). Wang Zhen was also responsible for devising, improving and recording agricultural machinery. The next three hundred years were a time of relative stability under Ming rule, which was undoubtedly aided by a large standing army and navy. It was a time when artistic and technological endeavour was greatly refined, with the dynasty becoming known in the present art world as the zenith of China's achievements.

It has been suggested that through the centuries China produced four great inventions which have been of widespread benefit and application to all mankind: these are the compass, invented in the 2nd century BC but only finding a practical application in maritime navigation about a thousand years later: paper produced in the last century BC: woodblock printing, which was devised in the 3rd century AD: and gunpowder, which appeared in the 9th century AD.

In 1404, the Ming Emperor decided that it would be fitting to set down a written record of all knowledge, so 2,000 scholars were put to work and eventually produced an encyclopaedia of 4,000 volumes. In 1421 the Emperor decided that his nation would display its might, magnificence and technical skills to the rest of the world, so large fleets of trading junks were constructed and dispatched to carry messages and gifts demonstrating Chinese superiority in different directions, and to invite the visited nations to become vassals of China. Several voyages were made and the enormous junks were the largest ocean-going vessels seen up to that time. The largest junks displaced up to 1,500 tons (compare this with Christopher Columbus's contemporary little fleet of three ships each displacing about one tenth of this), and numbered almost four hundred vessels in several different fleets; they visited India, Arabia, Africa, possibly also Australia and the Americas, all at a time before Europeans had discovered the Americas or rounded the Cape of Good Hope.

After their return, at the end of the seventh voyage, lightning caused the destruction by fire of the newly rebuilt Forbidden City, seat of the Emperor and of government; this was interpreted as divine disapproval so the voyages were stopped, and China turned back inward and isolationist, shunning the countries visited by the fleets. Early trade with Portuguese and Dutch merchants began later with a hesitant start and some reluctance from the Chinese in the second half of the 16th century.

---oOo---

Japan is separated from the Asian mainland by 200km of sea, and dominated by mountains. It has been subjected through the centuries to volcanism, earthquakes and stormy weather. Not surprisingly this gave rise to belief in spirits of nature, or kami, who were thought by Japanese Shinto followers to control all aspects of daily life; Shinto involves an attention to ritual in order to connect with the past. In the very early days in Japan a hunter-gatherer society existed from at least 40,000 BC, equipped with stone age technology and gradually coalescing into small tribes or clans. The Bronze Age came to Japan from China sometime around the middle of the last millennium BC, and the Iron Age around the middle of the first millennium AD along with Buddhism. Chinese writing and art appeared at about the same time, but then developed somewhat differently to the mainland.

Through the early centuries AD, the many clans gradually came together as they fought over territory, so that by the 8th century Japan was united under a single Emperor, with the capital at Kyoto, where it remained up to the second half of the 19th century. The Emperor remained notionally in power over the country, but there was constant jostling for control between the various clans, especially between the two most powerful clans, Minamoto and Taira, who kept strong private armies outside the influence of the Emperor.

Civil war erupted on several occasions with the warring clans under chiefs, or shoguns, effectively running the country and the emperor rubber-stamping their actions. In 1274 and again in 1281, the nation's samurai warriors came together to repel Mongol invasions by a larger force, which they managed on each occasion, aided on the second occasion by a typhoon (called a kamikaze) destroying the invading Mongol ships.

Amongst the continuing petty conflicts, a full-blooded civil war broke out again at the end of the 15th century over the imperial succession, while in the 16th century European traders with firearms and catholic missionaries arrived to complicate the internal struggles. In 1594, and again a few years later the general and politician Hideyoshi, unified Japan and then invaded Korea, with the intention of continuing on into China, but on both occasions he was stopped and forced to retreat. His successor Tokugawa Ieyasu seized power when Hideyoshi died soon after his second invasion debacle. A new shogunate was then established which was to rule Japan from the very early 17th century up to the time of the Meiji restoration in 1868 when the Emperor's power was restored over the whole country (chapter 76).

---oOo---

Korea and its ancient history is barely apparent through the mists of time prior to 1,000 BC. The Stone Age continued up to this time, and then the Bronze Age arrived from the mainland, lasting until the middle of the first millennium BC, when the Iron Age dawned, again from neighbouring China. Despite this, legend has it that the old kingdom of Korea, called Gojoseon, was founded at the end of the third millennium in 2,333 BC, and is recorded in a collection of historical tales compiled and finally down written in ancient Chinese, though not until at least a thousand years later. The Old Kingdom broke up in the 2nd century BC into three separate smaller kingdoms, the most northerly of which included Manchuria on the mainland; these kingdoms were then intermittently at war with each other for several hundred years.

At the end of the 7th century AD, the three kingdoms were united under a single ruler from the central kingdom of Sill, whose dynasty lasted for some two and a half centuries, before the country fragmented again into three kingdoms after another period of civil war. Mongol invasions in the 13th century from 1231 onwards, finally took over the government by 1259, following several campaigns which resulted in great numbers of civilian deaths and privations. The Mongols ruled for some eighty years in a system closely resembling ancient China with its dynasties, and often reinforced by inter-marriage between the Mongol Emperor's family and Korean princesses.

Mongol control gradually broke down in the second half of the 14th century, and following a coup in 1388, the Mongols were expelled and a new dynasty was established by General Yi Seong-gye, the Joseon dynasty, which was to last and rule Korea until 1910. At the end of the 16th century Korea destroyed the Japanese navy when an invasion was attempted. During this period the civil service, social systems and economic systems were all reformed and the Korean alphabet, known as Hangul, was created in the 15th century.

Overall, however, Korean culture did not modernise or adapt as incoming European influence arrived, so that the nation was ill-equipped to cope with foreign powers and treaties (including the Catholic church), from the 18th century onwards, with the result of increasing isolationism.

Main Chinese dynasties:

Shang Dynasty	1600–1046 BC
Zhou Dynasty	1046–256 BC
Chin (Qin) Dynasty	221–206 BC
Han Dynasty	206 BC–220 AD
Jin Dynasty	265–420
Tang Dynasty	618–907
Yuan Dynasty	1271–1368 (Mongols)
Ming Dynasty	1368–1644
Qing Dynasty	1644–1912 (Manchu)

Possible further reading:
The Silk Roads by Peter Frankopan (Bloomsbury Paperbacks)
A History of China by JAG Roberts (Palgrave Macmillan)

Chapter 9
The Early Americas

The evidence tells us that the Americas were the last great continents to be peopled by humans. Traces of human habitation in both South and North America do not extend back for more than about 50,000 years. Until recently controversy revolved around whether the early humans came to the Americas before or after the last Ice Age. However, during the last Ice Age, when sea levels were much lower than at present, it seems clear that early humans migrated across the Bering Straits while there was a land bridge, and before sea levels rose again.

At the time of the Ice Age, northern Canada was partly covered by ice, but one large ice sheet covered the northern and western coastal Rocky Mountains, and another large ice sheet covered north-eastern Canada, extending over Hudson's Bay; there was a corridor between these two not covered with ice and snow. It would therefore have been theoretically possible for humans to have travelled south along this corridor, even though it extended for hundreds of miles of barren tundra and would have been a most inhospitable land for stone age hunter-gatherers trying to garner a living.

At the last glacial maximum, some 20,000 years ago, this corridor between the two ice sheets did not exist, but it gradually opened later. At the same time, a coastal route for migration along the south side of Beringia (the name for the land bridge that we now know as the Bering Straits) would also have been possible. Recent analysis of DNA data by Steven Oppenheimer and others suggests that humans did indeed enter North America prior to the last Ice Age. Some of these people migrated even further and set up small populations in Central America, and probably later still in South America.

The evidence also suggests that some of these early people became marooned, as it were, in Beringia, in an Ice Age 'refuge'. The climate had closed behind them, and the ice sheet barred their way forwards. They were able to exist by fishing and hunting, but only a small number would have survived through the Ice Age to continue their migration into North America, around 12,000 years ago. Thus, there have possibly been two human migrations into North America, one before the last Ice Age, and one immediately afterwards.

Once there, people fanned out in three rough directions, firstly east along the northern reaches of Canada, developing further into the Eskimo nation; secondly, migrating broadly southeast, to give rise to the different tribes of plains Indians in North America; and thirdly, south towards Central America along either side of the Rocky Mountain chain, and on to form the various tribes of Central and South America, many of which evolved into the impressive civilisations in the Andes.

From the Andes, on the west of South America, humans have migrated east to the interior, but traces of their occupation have proved very scanty because they lived alongside rivers and in forests and jungle where remnants of their life has mostly decayed away. It is those humans who settled in the Andes who have left us most evidence of their civilisation, with stone buildings and monuments. The plains Indians of North America hunted the native animals of the time, which included mammoth, caribou, bison and wild horses. Traces of their stone arrowheads and tools have been found, dating as far back as 9,500 BC. The change in climate, which occurred following 8,000 BC, together with over-hunting, resulted in some of these species becoming extinct, but bison survived living on the grassland prairies, and came to be the staple hunted animal of the North American Indians.

In the meantime, the Eskimos spread across the northern regions of Canada, fishing, and hunting mainly whales and seals. They developed harpoons with bone tips, rather than stone tips, and kayak boats made from skins. Kayak remains have been found as far east as western Greenland, dating from around 2,000 BC.

Further south on the North American plains, coastal dwelling humans found plentiful food in rivers and lakes, and initially continued with a hunter-gatherer diet, including plants, seeds and nuts. Later, agriculture was introduced, and maize and beans in particular were domesticated and grown. These Indians tended to live in wood-framed huts covered with deer skins, bark or woven mats. Even further south, in New Mexico and Mexico. where the climate is much warmer and drier, cave dwelling provided shelter, and also a rich source of archaeological remains for the present generation to excavate. Around 3,000 BC the Indian tribes living south of the Great Lakes had discovered copper and how to work it by cold hammering. Simple pottery has been discovered dating from around 2,500 BC.

Central America has bequeathed us the remains of the Olmec civilisation. As far as we know they did not have writing, and their civilisation, dating from about 1,500 BC, is known by their statues and buildings. They founded urban settlements on the Gulf coast of Mexico and built ceremonial centres in what is now Southern Mexico, extending into Honduras and Guatemala. Their agriculture involved drained terraced fields that were irrigated and in which they grew maize and beans amongst other food. Chickens were reared, and both freshwater and sea food was also available. They constructed early earth pyramids, which were later faced with stone.

The largest early Olmec centre, San Lorenzo, flourished from around 1,250–950 BC. A system of reservoirs and underground pipes conserved water, and a large monument was built on an earth mound at the centre of the complex. Large carved stone heads were made from rock brought from the mountains up to 50 miles away, but these stone heads were defaced and buried around 900 BC when the Olmec civilisation seems to have deserted San Lorenzo for reasons unknown. A new complex was built close to the coast at La Venta and situated on an island three miles long. A stone pyramid was built, and evidence of working in jade and serpentine is present. It seems likely that human sacrifice was practised.

The forest-living jaguar played an important part in their religious and cultural beliefs, and other Olmec gods have been identified, most of them related to animals in the local ecology. The Olmec remained the most advanced civilisation in Central America, and indeed in North and South America, up to the 6th century BC, but their settlements were gradually abandoned, and the civilisation disappeared sometime after 500 BC without leaving much trace apart from their buildings, and without leaving any clues as to why they faded out.

Further south, on the Pacific coast of what is now Peru, the Chavin also worshipped a jaguar god, and were the first great civilisation in South America, where they lived in the Peruvian Andes from about 900–200 BC. Like the Aztecs and other civilisations who followed, the Chavin were astonishing workers in enormous blocks of stone, which they were able to trim and fit together without mortar. They too had no writing, but the monuments that have been found indicate their worship of a jaguar god in temples made of large stones, minutely jointed together. They lived in the mountains, where today the main crops are potatoes, maize and agave, and it seems likely that even in prehistoric times this constituted a lot of their food, as well as fishing.

It is possible that the combination of fertile soil, together with sufficient warmth to allow three or even four crops a year as agriculture developed, were an important component of this sudden burst of civilisation in Central America. The later South American civilisations, including the Maya of Central America, and the Aztecs of South America, probably owe much of their religious beliefs and stone technology to the Olmecs and Chavin before them.

The Mayan sites of cities and temples are all located in tropical rain forests, where climate, disease, animals, and insects all posed considerable problems for human settlement. The Maya managed to sustain large populations with Stone Age agricultural techniques and impressive Stone Age buildings over many centuries. The Mayan civilisation rose initially in the Yucatan peninsula from the 3rd century BC, reaching its apogee between 600 and 900 AD, when great stone buildings were produced as well as pottery. Religion was central to their way of life, which included human sacrifice.

The Maya were an advanced civilisation in astronomical terms, and had a very well developed calendar. They erected monuments every twenty years to celebrate the passing of time, and the last of these is dated at 920 AD. Mayan civilisation achieved a lot of specialisation, but despite this, they never discovered the wheel, the plough, or the ability to use arches in their stone buildings. The largest Mayan city may have had up to 40,000 inhabitants, with a surrounding population of agricultural workers in villages amounting to ten times that number.

The Mayan civilisation gradually declined after 900 AD, and by the Middle Ages the remaining Mayan civilisation was a shadow of its former self. Although the Spanish invaders are sometimes blamed for this collapse, the Mayan civilisation was already largely eclipsed, and falling into profound disarray by the time the Spaniards arrived in South America.

Apart from the Maya, the other civilisation that the Spanish found in South America were the Aztecs, who appeared around 1350 AD, and overthrew the Toltec tribe of central Mexico who were living there. The Aztec empire expanded rapidly over a couple of hundred years to cover the whole of central Mexico, and further south into the Andes of South America. The Aztecs were warriors, who took tribute from other tribes or nations. Their capital, Tenochtitlan was built on Lake Texcoco, on a group of islands connected to the mainland by a large causeway, and is the present site of Mexico City.

It probably had about a hundred thousand inhabitants by the year 1500, and was filled with temples and pyramids, all of which derived from the faiths and skills of previous civilisations and conquerors. The Spanish soldiers who first saw this city in 1521, two years after the start of Herman Cortez' conquest of Mexico, were amazed by its magnificence, which seemed to exceed most European cities of that time. The Aztecs had no writing, but were very skilled farmers, despite not having ploughs or carts.

The Spaniards were also shocked by the human sacrifice necessary for the Aztec religion; we are told that 20,000 victims were sacrificed at the dedication of the Great Pyramid of Tenochtitlan. The sacrifices were provided from prisoners taken in battle and led to the Aztecs being feared by their subject tribes, from whom they demanded tribute, both human and in the form of precious artefacts.

Further south, the Spaniards found an Inca civilisation which had arisen in the 20th century in Peru. Like the Aztecs, they were a warlike culture, who assumed the skills and beliefs of previous civilisations, so that by 1600 the Inca empire extended from Ecuador in the north to central Chile in the south. Their administration and government must have been exemplary, and involved 16,000km (10,000 miles) of roads, along which runners took messages since there were no draft animals to speed transport in South America. These messages were memorised, because the Inca also had no writing, but they did have a form of record keeping called quipus, made from multiple strings with beads and used to keep tallies of crops, taxes and property; there was a special caste of hereditary keepers with the task of maintaining accounts, and coding and decoding messages.

The Inca organisation appears to have been a form of dictatorship, with a single despot, king or emperor, at its head, who controlled the population, which was organised into small groups from which agricultural produce and labour were owed to the centre. Rigid control was exercised over the individual and there was no commerce. Gold, silver and copper mining resulted in a wealth of personal and communal ornamentation. The Inca worshipped the sun. Our knowledge of both Aztecs and Incas is fairly detailed as a result of information given to the Spaniards after their conquest.

It will be appreciated that all the early American civilisations were very different from those in Asia or Europe. They were especially limited by the inability to move beyond Stone Age technology, apart from using precious metals as ornamentation, but also because their agriculture required human labour exclusively. The absence of the wheel and draft animals constituted a further barrier to progress, though arguably the jungle and mountain terrain was not fertile ground in which emergence of wheeled transport could flourish. Little culture or technology has passed from early American civilisations into the mainstream of present world usage. The Bronze and Iron Ages never came to the early Americas until the rude shock of advanced European civilisation burst upon them in the 16th century in a most unequal contest against their lands and culture.

Possible further reading:
The First American by C. W. Ceram (New American Library)

Chapter 10
The Medes and Persians

After 1,000 BC, a series of major human realignments started with Aryan tribes in the mountains east of the Mesopotamian plain. The Aryans (from whom we get the modern word Iran) were horse-taming nomads living in the fertile mountains and valleys of what is now Iran. They had existed for many generations paying tribute of horses to their Assyrian overlords on their western border, whose superiority in warfare was at least partly due to their skilful use of cavalry. In the 6th century BC, one of these Aryan tribes, known as the Medes, became increasingly resentful of the customs of their Assyrian overlords, and as oppression became more severe, episodic rebellions broke out.

In 615 BC, King Cyaxares (625–585 BC) united the Medes with other Aryan tribes, first driving back the Scythians to the north, and then defeating the Assyrians to the west, their possession of chariots against opposing foot soldiery was a considerable advantage. Three years later the Medes were sufficiently strong to besiege and lay waste the great Assyrian and Mesopotamian city of Nineveh; within a further four years Assyria itself had disintegrated. The Medes then spread further west across what we know as modern Syria and Turkey, and the next Median king, Astyages (who had a long reign from 585–550 BC), made conquests to the north and east, setting up his capital at Ecbatana in the mountains to the east of Mesopotamia, which lay on the Khorasan highway, a trading route pre-dating the Silk Road, and already serving as a vital route for both armies and merchants.

Astyages was warned in dreams of his future downfall, together with that of his kingdom, by prophets, or magi, who followed the Median religion of Zoroaster. Beliefs in Zoroaster were part of the start of major realignments between Assyria, Babylon, Persia and Egypt, during which time Assyria and Persia increased their ability to exert power whilst Babylon and Egypt declined in power. Zoroastrianism had arisen some time previously amongst the nomadic pastoral tribes and told of Zoroaster, who was enlightened at the age of 30 by a supreme being called Ahura Mazda. Ahura, meaning light, and Mazda meaning wisdom, became the ancient religion of Persia.

This enlightenment came to Zoroaster while he was fetching water for a sacred ritual; he was the first person to believe in a single deity, and in a constant battle between good and evil. Zoroaster taught of the holiness of fire, and that just as fire would consume everything, so everything had been generated from fire in the first place. His priests were known as magi, from which comes the word magic. He is said to have been killed at an altar in Balkh (in modern Afghanistan) during a holy Persian war in 583 BC.

Meanwhile, to the south of Ecbatana, the ancient mountain kingdom of Anshan was becoming more powerful and was the centre of an evolving Persia. In this kingdom the story tells of Astyages daughter, a Median princess who had been married by treaty to the Persian King, and who gave birth to a princely son named Cyrus. Prophecies of doom given by the magi, that the child would result in his downfall, resulted in a fearful Astyages ordering that the baby be exposed, in other words requiring that his followers made sure that the child would not survive.

However, the child was swapped with another infant and Cyrus survived and was brought up deep in the mountains and is next heard of succeeding to the throne of Persia in 559 BC. Astyages, still on the Median throne, came south with an army to prevent further prophecies being fulfilled, and a three-year war ensued. It was a rather protracted campaign, possibly including a lot of guerrilla warfare, but the outcome was that a large Median army was overcome by a much smaller Persian one. Unusually for those times, Astyages was not executed, but Cyrus was able to unite the nomadic tribes of both north and south, becoming king of the Medes and Persians and taking over Astyages capital at Ecbatana.

Cyrus did not wait to consolidate his position, but instead set off to the west through the unresisting remnants of Assyria into what is now Turkey. He pushed all the way to the Mediterranean, conquering the kingdom of Lydia and its King, Croesus, who has gone down in history as possessing unimaginable and indecent wealth. Indeed, it may have been rumours of this wealth that drew Cyrus in this direction. Croesus, famed even to modern times for this fabulous wealth, was also spared execution, although his treasury was fully plundered.

At the end of this six-year campaign, Cyrus had thus consolidated the central territories of the Medes and Persians and extended his rule throughout present day Turkey. The Persians who had only been a small mountain kingdom previously, had now become the largest and most powerful empire yet seen on Earth in the space of less than a hundred years.

In the following years, Cyrus turned his attention to the east, towards the Hindu Kush and the lands at the head of the Indus River, which we know today as Pakistan and Afghanistan. He had an enlightened policy, which at the same time was clearly one of considerable self-interest. His troops were disciplined, and instead of the usual mayhem of terror, rape and pillage, the land he conquered was annexed and the natives were incorporated relatively willingly into the Persian Empire, providing both monetary riches and troops for his army. There are similarities here with the middle years of the Roman Empire, when the inhabitants of conquered territories were allowed to become Roman citizens.

Despite Cyrus' light touch in ruling, and allowing some self-determination and religious toleration, there were some rebellious episodes and Cyrus himself was killed in battle at the age of 70 in 529 BC, leaving his Achaemenid, or

Persian empire to his two sons, Cambyses, and Bardiya. Of the two, the elder Cambyses was favoured to take over from his father, whilst Bardiya had been given the governorship of the eastern provinces of Bactia. In a most unusual move, Cambyses had been married to his two sisters, thereby preserving with absolute purity the regal blood line and at the same time ensuring that no rival noble families would have any claim on the throne by means of a bloodline.

Bardiya schemed, possibly intending a coup that would install himself as king, whilst his brother was preparing to conquer lands to the south of Persia, including what we know today as Egypt, Libya and Ethiopia. Rebellion by Bardiya came from the eastern region of Persia whilst Cambyses was still in Egypt waiting to be crowned Pharaoh after the conquest of Egypt; the Egyptians were not to rule themselves again for the next two and a half millennia until they achieved independence finally in the 20th century. While he was returning to Persia Bardiya openly claimed the throne and was hailed as king throughout the eastern provinces.

In the meantime, Cambyses, on the way home from Egypt, sustained an accidental thigh wound from his sword and Bardiya's scheming was rendered unnecessary when he suddenly died leaving behind him a reputation as a ruthless, unpredictable, rapacious and untrustworthy ruler of the Persian home territory, and an equally arrogant and unreasonable ruler of his conquered territories, who remembered him as the inventor of indiscriminate carnage. Three months later Bardiya was crowned and married one of his surviving sisters, who by now was the widow of Cambyses.

Following Cambyses death, the royal army was without a leader, but did possess a number of ambitious young officers, and when Bardiya confiscated the land and possessions of Cambyses closest colleagues he ensured that a conspiracy to overthrow him became inevitable. Seven high ranking young officers must have realised that a speedy coup offered them the best chance of getting rid of Bardiya and installing someone sympathetic on the throne. One of these young officers, named Darius, was a distant blood relation of Cyrus, and seemed to have had a better claim to the throne than the other six. They rode fast, and in a small party, along the Khorasan highway to intercept Bardiya before he could reach the capital at Ecbatana. Although Bardiya had an army with him, it seems that none of his troops were suspicious of the seven officers loyal to Cambyses, and they were easily able to bluff their way into the fortress where Bardiya was staying, and then into the royal presence, where Bardiya was quickly murdered.

The seven high-ranking conspirators had decided amongst themselves that Darius was the one among them who should become the next, and third king, of the Achaemenid empire. His claims of blood ties and of sanctification by the Zoroastrian god, Ahura Mazda, was rapidly proclaimed, and new discipline imposed on the Empire. But at the same time, rebellion broke out in Babylon to the east. This was the city reputed to be the wealthiest in the world, where another pretender had appeared claiming the kingship of its ancient nation, Elam.

Babylon's riches derived from its antiquity and its situation in the Mesopotamian plain surrounded by rich and irrigated agricultural lands. It had very large fortified city walls. It was at that time known as the city of hanging gardens, and gross opulence in its use of gold, silver and jewellery, both in its buildings and in the adornment of its people.

Darius quickly took his newly acquired army east to Babylon, where two decades previously Cyrus had annexed the city, and had been sympathetic towards its population and its rulers, together with its enormous population for those days, of a quarter of a million people. Darius turned out to be less forgiving, but initially he was welcomed into the city as an overlord should be, but then the ranks of royalty and nobility were simply purged to crush any remaining traces of the rebellion before he returned to central Persia.

Whilst Darius was sacking Babylon, rebellion was brewing for him in the Persian capital of Ecbatana. After further battles he purged all the suspect aristocracy in the capital. Darius then allowed subservient tribes to retain their individuality, and even their aristocracy and their kings, so underlining his boast that he was King of Kings. He built a new capital at Persepolis, with the intention firstly of centralising and organising the governments of all the kingdoms of which he was now king, and secondly to regularise the finances of an empire which had rather fragmented under Cambyses, losing the tribute and levies that should have come to the Persian capital.

We move now to Ancient Greece, divided at the time of the Persian Empire into city states around the Ionian Sea and the southern region of the Peloponnese including Sparta, and connected with the mainland of Greece only by a narrow land bridge. Sparta had developed separately, and according to the ideas of a thinker named Lycurgus who lived in the 9th century BC. Details of his existence are sparse, but the system of living which he is said to have proposed, and which doubtless became altered and exaggerated with the passage of time, was a very egalitarian society. It is also the source of the adjective 'spartan' that we use to denote living a life of minimal comforts and considerable devotion to an ideal of the greater good.

All Spartans were meant to adopt a similar lifestyle, with unremitting discipline in times of both peace and war. All male citizens were therefore dedicated soldiers, and the everyday work of growing food, building homes and other duties, was done by slaves. The Spartan army therefore had come to be recognised by its enemies as truly terrifying in its discipline and capacity against the often hurriedly assembled ranks of opposition. Spartans went into battle in ranks of precision, wearing uniform polished bronze shields and cloaks the colour of blood: their helmets carried horsehair crests the colour of blood running from side to side.

The Spartans had been at war with the Athenians for some time, but in 510 BC a Spartan army had liberated Athens from its effective dictator, a man called Hippias who ruled Athens from 527–510 BC. Traditional Athenian politics, where a tyrant was underpinned by the wealthy and influential, collapsed after this, and Cleisthenes (c.570–495 BC) had proposed a new form of government in 507 BC, namely democracy, from demos the people and krathos the power. An uprising followed, but was quashed, and Spartans were expelled from the city.

Cleisthenes reorganised the tribes and allegiances of both the city and the rural dwelling Greeks, and gradually democracy prevailed in Athens. Athenian ambassadors sent to the royal court in Persia were anxious to establish an alliance with the Persian Empire as a way of protecting themselves in future against any possible further war or invasion from Sparta. In the meantime, Athens, vassal to its notional overlords the Persians, had magnified a small quarrel and mounted an expedition across the Ionian Sea against Sardis, from where the governor of Lydia ruled his province.

Sardis is situated some miles inland, and as the small force of Greeks returned to their ships they were intercepted and decimated by rapidly mobilised Persian cavalry. A rather depleted band of Athenians managed to board their ships and sail home. This defeat divided the Ionian city states, including Athens, and set them squabbling against each other. The Persian response was to destroy all the Greek seafaring settlements on the eastern side of the Ionian Sea, notably Miletus, in 493 BC.

Against this background, the Athenians elected a young Themistocles (524–459 BC) to be their head of state, and a wily old, but militarily proficient, Miltiades (550–489 BC) to be one of their generals. The Persians at Darius' insistence extended their military campaign north across the Hellespont and into Macedonia and Thrace, where Alexander, King of Macedonia, recognised that resistance would only result in massacres of his people, and therefore bowed to the Persians. Persian emissaries sent to Greece and Sparta were killed, gestures of severe defiance.

In 490 BC, with the Greeks thus divided, Darius and a large army crossed the Aegean Sea to Greece subduing any islanders on the way. The armada landed in Euboea and sacked the city of Eretria. The Persians then re-embarked and sailed round the eastern coast of Attica to threaten the city of Athens. Instead of fighting behind their defensive walls the Athenians mobilised a small army and marched east to meet the much larger Persian invasion force. They blocked the two roads leading to Athens from the Plain of Marathon, and waited, hoping that Spartan reinforcements might join them.

Despite the overwhelming odds against the Athenians, both in terms of numbers and armaments and lacking cavalry and bows and arrows, the Athenians advanced against the Persian army. The Athenians were well encased in armour, and the Persians lightly clad, relying on their bows and arrows, and unable to use their cavalry because of the Athenian choice of ground. It took only a short while for the terrified Persians to turn and run from the heavily armoured Athenians wielding extremely long and deadly spears. Some of the Persians were also drowned in a big marsh stretching across the bay and across their line of retreat. The Persian fleet hurriedly set to sea with the surviving Persian foot soldiers.

The tired Athenians turned and retraced their initial march to Athens, twenty-six miles away, where they arrived by the evening; they had been preceded by a soldier messenger who ran back to Athens with the news only to collapse and die once he had passed on the great tidings; this feat is of course commemorated in our modern day Olympic long-distance race of the marathon. Only 192 Athenians died, and a huge burial mound was erected on the edge of the Plain of Marathon in their honour. This small number compares with the reported number of more than six thousand dead Persians.

Meanwhile, in Egypt, the demand for ever increasing quantities of grain to be sent to Persia had finally provoked rebellion. Preparations were made for a military expedition, but before it could be implemented Darius died at the age of 65 after a reign of 36 years. He was succeeded by Xerxes (518–465 BC), the most able of his many sons. A campaign in Egypt was brief and successful, and when Xerxes returned to his capital there was further discussion of punishing the Athenians in particular, and the Greeks in general. Intelligence from Greece, and prophecies from the magi, indicated that a land invasion across the Hellespont and through Thessaly and Macedonia would be propitious.

Anticipating this, the Athenians were preparing for war, but were also fearful of a further invasion by sea, and rapidly commenced the building of a war fleet. The Persians assembled a fleet from all their vassal states, amounting to well over a thousand vessels, and in addition Xerxes assembled a mighty army, which possibly numbered around two hundred and fifty thousand. He then embarked on a leisurely land-based invasion in 480 BC, marching through Turkey, across the Hellespont, and through Thrace and Thessaly.

Against this, the Greeks sent their navy north, and an army of around ten thousand men, with a small Spartan contingent of three hundred warriors, prepared to defend Greece against the invaders by blocking the very narrow route through a gorge at Thermopylae. The Persians stayed in camp, living off the land and the supplies they had brought with them, but they left matters to run rather too late in the year, and early autumn storms destroyed or disabled some two to three hundred Persian ships, whilst the Greek forces readied themselves in the pass at Thermopylae. After some days the Persians found a local Greek traitor who showed ten thousand of their best troops a way around the back of the mountain to approach the pass from the other end.

Leonidas, the commander of the Spartan band of some three hundred warriors, had sent the rest of the Greek troops back in the direction of Athens to fight another day, and the Spartans joined battle against the Persians knowing that they would be annihilated. Their sacrifice in the prolonged battle of Thermopylae which lasted for three days is commemorated in the epitaph, *"Go tell the Spartans, stranger passing by, that here, obedient to their laws, we lie."*

Back in Athens, families were evacuated to the east coast of the Peloponnese whilst the men prepared for a siege. Athens itself was evacuated except for the Acropolis, and the Persians, after laying waste to the countryside and firing the crops and hamlets that they passed, took over Athens. Any remaining people, including the priests in the temple, were massacred. The rest of the massive Persian navy followed a little behind the troops. The Athenians on the island of Salamis off Athens, had received an ambiguous forecast of the future from the Oracle at Delphi, which said that *"you will be the death of many a mother's son between the seedtime and the harvest of the grain"*.

By this time the Persian campaign had been so protracted that autumn was drawing on, and winter gales were in the offing. The Persians felt they had trapped the Greek fleet in the isthmus between Salamis and the mainland. A great sea battle then ensued in 480 BC, with Xerxes himself sitting on a throne on the mainland cliffs opposite the island, and able to watch events unfold, but unable to alter the strategy or tactics of his navy, and only able to witness a decisive Athenian victory against his fleet. A further major battle followed at Plataea where the Persians were once again routed a year later, and after yet another sea battle at Mycale a defeated Xerxes returned to the centre of his empire, where the Babylonians were in revolt. From then on, he gave up any ambitions of extending the Persian Empire across the Hellespont and into Europe; he was assassinated by a member of his court in 465 BC.

Macedonia, north of Greece, had now been united into a single state by King Amyntas III who ruled from 393–370 BC, keeping the Illyrians to the northwest, and the Thracians to the east, at bay, as well as the Greeks. His youngest son Philip, came to the throne in 359 BC and was relatively successful militarily in securing the Macedonian borders, aided by some judicious marriages with the neighbouring states. He joined the Delphic League, which antagonised Athens and resulted in a declaration of war, and then won a battle at Chaeronea in 338 BC, leading to an Athenian defeat by a Macedonian army which included Philip's son, eighteen-year-old Alexander commanding a substantial body of troops.

Two years later, Philip was assassinated and Alexander took over the throne and the whole army. The Greek city of Thebes rebelled only to be crushed and destroyed by the new twenty-year-old king; the inhabitants were either massacred or sold into slavery. By 334 BC, two years after coming to the throne Alexander set out on his conquests. He crossed into Asia to complete his father's ambition and ensure that the Persians would not be able to invade across the Hellespont into Europe again. He met the Persians under Darius, defeating them at the battle of Pinarus in south-eastern Turkey, where half of Darius' army was destroyed. The Persian naval base at Tyre was then destroyed after a long siege, leaving Alexander in control of Syria and Palestine, and able to occupy Egypt founding a new city there, the first of about twenty which bear his name to this day.

Darius had managed to raise another army in Babylon; Alexander confronted him at Gaugamela on the Tigris with a much smaller force, but nevertheless emerged victorious. Alexander continued east, plundering cities and eventually destroying the Persian capital of Persepolis. The relentless march east continued to the boundary of the Persian empire in Sogdiana, present day northern Afghanistan, while Darius was assassinated by one of his provincial governors. Alexander next turned south reaching the mouth of the

Indus River; he wished to conquer Northern India as far east as the Ganges, but his troops refused to go further without actually mutinying; they had been living, marching and fighting battles for eight years and 17,000 miles (27,000km).

The return journey to Babylon took two more years with Alexander still intent on fusing Macedonians and Persians with many other smaller tribes and also planning the conquest of Arabia, but he died in Babylon, probably of malaria, just before his 33rd birthday. As he left no formal heir his empire did not survive his death and was broken up by a series of civil wars between his generals, who divided the lands, with Egypt going to the Ptolemies, Asia to the Seleucids, India to Chandragupta (chapter 7), and leaving Alexander's Macedonian successors unable to hold the world's largest empire together. Apart from destroying the Persian Empire, Alexander had however, left a considerable legacy in terms of the spread of Greek culture, resulting in a new Hellenistic civilisation, and a fearsome reputation as a military leader.

Possible further reading:
Persian Fire by Tom Holland (Abacus paperback)

Chapter 11
Agriculture and Technology

Since the Stone Age, the two major drivers of civilisation have been agriculture, which permits reliable feeding of large groups of people, and technology, as humans moved from the Bronze through into the Iron Age, and became able to develop instruments, machines and weapons. Initially these instruments were largely directed either to agriculture or to warfare, though later developments, particularly in the last few centuries, have permitted much more sophisticated and much wider uses.

Early Stone Age man's existence is known as a 'hunter-gatherer' existence. Gradually there were changes towards what has been called 'proto-farming' with early attempts at domestication of both plants and animals. Many attempts have been made to classify human development and the early US anthropologist, Lewis Morgan (1818–1881), divided the history of human civilisation into five eras. The first of these he called the Savage Era, roughly corresponding to the Stone Age or Neolithic period in which man had fire, early pottery, bows, arrows, and spears, and energy came from human muscle power.

Following this, he called the second period the Barbaric Period: which roughly corresponds to the Bronze Age, in which plants and animals were domesticated, metal working started, and energy for some tasks, notably ploughing, started using animals. The third era he named the stage of Civilisation, which corresponds with the Iron Age onwards, when technology became much more sophisticated, plant energy was used (wood, coal, oil and gas), and writing and alphabetic symbols appeared.

After these preceding three periods, which can be seen as encompassing all of civilisation up to the present, we can add two more stages by subdividing the last stage into three so that stage four, possibly called Mediaeval, becomes a period in which there is extensive use of natural energy, starting with the fairly primitive use of water power and wind power, and which is followed by the much more extensive use of coal, gas and oil, moving on to steam engines and then the internal combustion engine. Finally, we move to the present era where wind, water and naturally occurring energy are once again used extensively, and where man's ingenuity taps further energy sources, including solar, tidal and nuclear power, using advanced technology.

To return to the Stone Age, tools have been found dating back before the last Ice Age, which show that humans hunted with bows and arrows, slings and spears, and butchered their prey with sharpened stone implements. Pottery and tools have been discovered from 25,000 years ago, and even a primitive form of flute made from a hollow vulture bone from the same time. Following the last Ice Age, the climate improved, proto-farming communities gradually evolved independently into early farming communities, not only in Mesopotamia, but also in China, the Sahel region of sub-Saharan Africa, the Indus and Nile Valleys, and in North and South America.

The early dry climate after the Ice Age favoured plants which put their energy into the annual production of seeds and died off each year, rather than plants which put their energy into producing wood and surviving from year to year. Seeds would germinate and grow again the following year, but they could also be gathered and stored as food. Initially seeds would have been gathered for food, but it would have quickly become apparent that with a little help, the early farmers could sow the seeds on favourable soil to produce an easily gathered crop later. Eight early founder crops sown by the first farmers have been identified in the Middle East, of which the two most important were emmer and einkorn wheat, other founder crops included barley, peas, lentils, chickpeas and flax.

In China, founder crops of rice and millet were important, whilst in North America teosinte was selectively bred to produce maize: in South America the founder crops included potatoes, tomatoes, squash and beans. Each of these plants produced valuable food for early humans, and by selecting the seeds from the biggest and strongest specimens for re-seeding the following year, this early selective breeding gradually produced better and more rewarding crops. The earliest wine harvests from grapes appear to have been made along the southern shores of the Black Sea where vines were indigenous and flourished in a climate which was perfect for them from the 6th millennium BC onwards.

At the same time, certain animals were also being domesticated and selectively bred, notably sheep, goats, ducks and pigs. Social organisation would have accompanied, and indeed been responsible for, this gradual progress in the domestication of plants and animals. In Ireland, at Ceide Fields, stone walls were used to divide the land and contain the crops of different plants or animals: these are the oldest known agricultural fields in Europe, and were created where pine and birch forests had been cleared to make way for farming. These Stone Age people lived around 3,500BC, or to put it another way, only some 200 to 250 human generations of twenty-five years each, before the present time.

By comparison, plants and animals with an inter-generational interval of only a year or two can complete up to five or six thousand generations in the same period of time, so that careful selective breeding can have a much more rapid evolutionary effect. Energy production throughout this Savage Era was limited to what people could achieve purely using their own muscle power.

In Lewis Morgan's second era, the Barbaric Period, starting at the beginning of the Bronze Age, perhaps 150 human generations ago between 2,000 and 1,000 BC, very little foraging was occurring in more advanced societies as most food was being obtained by farming of both plants and animals, and societies were becoming static. As farming gradually became more efficient, surplus production was available, such that not all the population need to be involved in the daily struggle and search for food, this in turn allowed the differentiation of roles within society, where non-farmers could become specialist metalworkers, potters, jewellery makers and such like.

An additional benefit of a food surplus allowing specialist artisans to appear, brings with it the possibility of trade, either in food itself, or in other prized objects, including everything from weapons to jewellery; this in turn encouraged the development of transport, exploration and distant trade links. Another occupation was also made possible by this food surplus, namely that of warrior; the Sumerians in Mesopotamia were the first to have sufficient surplus food supplies, not only to feed their urban population, but also to allow the recruitment and training of a standing army, which in turn made their likelihood of success in warfare much higher.

In time, this Sumerian army would have cavalry with mounted warriors, although most of their horse-borne soldiery was in chariots. Horses were initially domesticated in Central Asia some 2,000 years earlier, where the indigenous tribes fought on horseback, and were very proficient with bows and arrows when mounted.

Although we think of selective breeding back to the beginning of the Iron Age, with plants or animals in mind, it can also apply to humans. Two hundred generations are seldom enough to make a significant difference to human evolution, which is why ancient Greek and Roman statues portray subjects who do not differ significantly from modern Europeans. Over the last two hundred generations warfare has been a potent cause of intermingling of human genes. In olden times, this happened in two ways, firstly through rape and pillage by a victorious army or society, which introduced the victors' male genes into the conquered population, and secondly, by the extensive practice of taking much of the conquered male population into slavery, so introducing their genes eventually into the home population.

More recently, travel, settlement and colonisation have all played a part in spreading human genes more uniformly around the world. During this Barbaric Period energy was harnessed principally by using wind and water power; mills for grinding wheat have existed since very early times around the Mediterranean, though human power still supplied much energy, often by the use of slaves.

Localised development of agricultural improvements occurred throughout the world, and it is thanks to trade and travel that these improvements came to be rapidly accepted in areas far away from their region of origin. Areas with similar climates and natural features came to use, and to a certain extent control, features of flooding and irrigation, thus the Nile and Indus and Yellow River valleys relied heavily on the annual floods and fertile silt brought down with the water. More barren areas developed schemes for irrigation with the early use of dams in southern Arabia for instance, where the natural rainfall was insufficient for the production of good crops.

In some areas, a method known as shifting cultivation was practised, where the land was cleared and crops were then grown intensively for a few years.

Often this was done by fire to produce the clearance, giving rise to the name of 'slash and burn', or 'fire stick' farming. Ultimately the soil became exhausted, and the village moved on, leaving behind the exhausted soil, and clearing another area in the forest for domestic cultivation, with the old area reverting to primeval forest.

Unfortunately, there are areas in the world where this is still practised, either to harvest the virgin timber of the South American rain forest without replanting, or to produce vast plantations of oil producing palm trees, as in Indonesia. In the late 18th and early 19th centuries enormous amounts of wood were required to build British warships and merchant navy ships, much of which came from the newly settled eastern side of Canada. The building of one large warship required the timber from some 4,000 oak trees, with the masts being a particular sourcing problem since this needed very straight pine trunks of 100 feet in length, and a width at the base of three foot (30 metres by 1 metre).

All pine trees in eastern Canada were reserved for the Crown so that the navy would have sufficient timber for masts and spars. By about 1850, the loggers who were harvesting suitable trees, and who had started felling trees on the shores of the St Lawrence River, had reached Hudson's Bay, taking out only the biggest and best, thereby selectively breeding for smaller, weaker trees in the future.

In more settled areas of the world, the farming practice of crop rotation was rapidly appreciated. This allows the soil to rest for a while, and for vegetable mulch to rebuild the nitrogen stocks of the soil. It also improves the structure of the soil and helps prevent the build-up of damaging bacteria or insects that would occur if a single crop was to be repeatedly grown. In early European times a two-field crop system was practised, allowing half the land to lie to fallow each year. By early medieval times, a three-field rotation had been introduced, rotating one field of cereal with a second of lentils, beans or peas which have nitrogen fixing bacteria in their roots and leaving the third field fallow: this system was immediately attractive as two-thirds of the available land is used productively instead of only half.

By the early 16th century, a British landowner and prominent politician Charles 'Turnip' Townshend (1674–1738) who was Foreign Secretary for a decade, championed four-crop rotation, comprising wheat, turnips and barley, with clover as the crop for the fallow year: clover is a plant which also has nitrogen fixing bacteria in its root nodules, which further increases the efficiency of soil replenishment. Since those times, and thanks to the Industrial Revolution, we have come even further; nitrogen replenishment through the 19th century was largely achieved by the importation of huge amounts of bird guano (which also contains high proportions of phosphate and potassium) mainly from isolated South Pacific islands, though in the 20th century land fertilisation became achieved by using industrially synthesised nitrogenous chemicals. Pesticides to control the unwanted effects of single crop growing are also part of modern farming.

Throughout the Bronze Age, much of the technology available for agricultural use was primitive. Most everyday tools, including ploughs, were made of wood, albeit sometimes with metal tips, early versions of the plough did not have wheels; they were drawn by oxen, as horses were too expensive for farm use and did not appear until many centuries later. Wagons had solid wooden wheels, which were covered with 'tyres' of leather attached to the wood by copper nails, once again they were drawn by oxen. Harvesting for a long time was by human labour, with farmers harvesting grain by hand with sickles, and then threshing the wheat or barley on a stone floor with wooden flails to separate the seed from the chaff.

All of this was obviously tedious and back-breaking work; the Romans refined their agricultural system using an organisation of manors, often with tenant farmers, who used largely slave labour. The Romans, and the Greeks before them, started a drive towards specialist food production with an individual estate or manor usually producing a single crop such as grain, grapes or olive oil. We can judge their efficiency from the fact that the larger estates produced over 20,000 litres of wine or 750 bushels of wheat; a bushel is an old measure of volume rather than weight, measuring eight gallons (36 litres or 64 pounds).

It was not until the Middle Ages, only a few hundred years ago, that further major improvements started, with the introduction of the wheeled plough, draft horses, and the use of lime to replenish and restore the soil pH and nitrogen fertilisers.

The civilised era continues to develop with the widespread use of powered machinery providing the energy. Lewis Morgan's fourth era starts in mediaeval times and accelerates with the Industrial Revolution bringing a huge increase in farming productivity. It was a time that also brought with it great spreading of species around the world as people explored between the continents taking with them plants and animals to places where they had never grown or lived before. Citrus fruits were brought to Europe from the east and Africa, maize, potatoes, tomatoes and tobacco came from the Americas, rice from Asia. Some imports caused immense damage, such as the rabbits taken to Australia, and the rats and goats left to devastate native wildlife on small islands in the world's oceans.

The fifth era is our modern time where science is rapidly enlarging both our agricultural and energy technology, hopefully with better understanding and appreciation of the possible problems as well as the more obvious advantages, and is covered later in chapters 64, 94 and 95.

Possible further reading:
The Birth of Europe by Michael Andrews (BBC Books)

Chapter 12
Writing

Writing presupposes the power of speech and the formation of language, which can then be recorded. It is very uncertain when Homo Sapiens acquired speech and indeed how this came about. Several theories have been advanced, one of which suggests that the advent of speech came as a result of an increase in brain size and power many millennia ago, but bearing in mind the utterances of our closest cousins, chimpanzees and gorillas, an American physiologist, Jared Diamond has suggested quite plausibly that a change in the anatomy of the human larynx between 50,000 and 100,000 years ago could have been a major enhancing factor allowing early man to develop speech.

Once this major step forward had occurred and speech and communication had become routine amongst humans, it naturally followed that some means of recording this speech should follow. The recording of stories and information has become increasingly important as society has developed. There are recurring symbols in cave paintings over 20,000 years old, whose meaning has not been deciphered, but which probably represent the earliest human records.

When the Bronze Age came, hieroglyphs were developed; they have been found in Sumeria, Egypt and Crete: each of these systems of hieroglyphs being somewhat different. The glyphs have gradually developed, starting with a hieroglyph to represent a whole word, which meant composing and learning an enormous vocabulary for a scribe. Rather later, the glyph came to represent a single syllable, which could then be incorporated in a word. This then developed into the alphabet that we have today, from which many tens of thousands of words can be made up.

It used to be thought that the hieroglyphs found in caves used by early man were random jottings with meanings personal to the artist or tribe who created them; however, Genevieve von Petzinger, a contemporary Canadian scientist, has analysed thousands of markings in caves across Europe and has found that the shapes comprise only some 32 different symbols, which in turn remained constant through thousands of years; their meanings have yet to be deciphered.

The world's oldest known writing system is as yet undeciphered, and is known as proto-Elamite. It has been found in modern day Iran, just east of Mesopotamia, where so many other early aspects of civilisation developed. In Mesopotamia we know that that the Sumerians developed a recording system around 3,000 BC for making lists and doing accounts. This developed into writing which was widely in use through Mesopotamia around 1,200 BC.

It is likely that a relatively small number of scribes and of the population were able to use the system which was quite complicated, and which represents a half-way stage between hieroglyphs and what we would recognise as modern writing. A similar, but different, system appears to have evolved in Egypt at about the same time, using different hieroglyphs. By contrast with all this, the early civilisation in the Indus Valley had a working hieroglyphic system around 3,500 BC.

Independently, written documents appeared, and are still available and decipherable, from the ancient Shang dynasty in China, dating between 1200–1000 BC. Only a little after this the Mayan civilisation in Central America had developed a recording system by 300 BC, but this appears to have remained undeveloped for the next millennium at least, until there is evidence of the Olmec civilisation having written records.

Several systems of writing seem to have developed in the Middle East in the first millennium BC, and a further recording system known as proto-Canaanite developed at the end of the Bronze Age to become the Phoenician system of recording in the subsequent Iron Age, again about 1200 BC. This Phoenician system then developed in two distinct and different directions, one of which gave rise to an Aramaic alphabet, which we know as Hebrew and which is also a precursor of modern Arabic script, and the other which gave rise to the Greek alphabet, which is still recognisable today. Phoenician and Greek languages use the same letters and in the same order: they gave rise to several later languages, including Gothic, Cyrillic and modern Hebrew.

With trade, the Phoenicians rapidly spread their alphabetic system of writing around the Mediterranean along the north coast of Africa and into southern Europe. It is interesting that the Greeks who followed them initially wrote from right to left and then, for some unknown reason, changed to the European system we use today progressing from left to right. At the same time all writing systems have started at the top of a tablet or page and then worked downwards. The Greek writing system was copied and the Greek alphabet was modified around 500 BC by the Romans into what we know as Latin, which remained remarkably constant for the next millennium, though the Greek alphabet survived and persisted in Greece itself.

Writing and Latin came to Britain with the Roman Legions in 43 AD. It must have been used extensively for Roman recording, and for letters and accounts travelling backwards and forwards through the Empire, but it does not seem there was much enthusiasm for it amongst the native Britons, so that widespread use of Latin only came much later with Saint Augustine, who came to Britain at the end of the 6th century in 597. Saint Augustine (d. 604) was Prior of a Benedictine Monastery in Rome when he was chosen by Pope Gregory to lead a mission to Christianise King Ethelbert of Kent (560–616), in which he succeeded. After the Roman Legions had left, eastern Britain had become settled with largely pagan Anglo-Saxon tribes, whilst western Britain and Ireland had remained Christian, but developed in isolation from Rome for the next two centuries.

By this time, the use of writing allowed the storage of people's memories and history. The collapse of Rome led to a loss of Latin across much of Europe, where its use declined, whilst that of Arabic and Persian increased. The increase in use of Arabic in particular, was aided by the rapid spread of Islam from the 7th century onwards, along the coast of North African and up into the Iberian Peninsula. At the same time, the Indo-Arabic numeric system spread through the Islamic world. By the 11th century AD, Cordoba in southern Spain had become not only a big intellectual centre of Arab thought, but also possessed the world's largest library of the time.

By the 14th century, the Islamic Golden Age was waning, and the use of Arabic and Persian was declining, whilst at the same time Greek started to enjoy a resurgence, followed a little later by a considerable increase in the use of Latin. The high point of writing came in the early years of mediaeval times with illuminated manuscripts painstakingly executed by monks working in monastic foundations in the years before printing was invented.

Numerical systems have evolved slowly and in parallel with writing systems. Numbering systems may well be older than other forms of writing and have been known from ancient tallies kept as notches on wood or stone for at least 40,000 years. Clay tokens were used for the same purpose in early Mesopotamia. Abstract numerals however, do not appear until almost 3,000 BC, and even then they must have been difficult to keep track of. The Sumerians had different systems for recording numbers of different objects; thus, depending on whether you were counting animals, cheese, grain, land or time, there was a different measuring system for each.

The sexagesimal system arrived in old Babylon around 1,950 BC and has a counting base of sixty. It is the result of this that we still count minutes and seconds in sixties, and that we also count the degrees in a circle as a multiple of sixty, and the angles in a triangle also as a multiple of sixty. As a large number sixty is divisible into many more fractions than the decimal base number of ten. The concept of zero challenged the ancient world, but ancient Egyptian numerals were used on a base of 10 and included a symbol for zero, although the Greeks did not have or use such a concept.

A numerical system using a base of twelve finds favour with some mathematicians, and some primitive communities have been happy with a system based on four fingers with each finger having three joints or knuckles; however, the ordinary western citizen is now most comfortable with the decimal system. A scheme produced in Paris at the time of the Revolution to divide days, hours and minutes into tens and hundreds never caught on!

It may seem natural that with ten fingers and ten toes we should devise a counting system that resolves around a base of ten. Initially this could be done by simply counting pebbles into piles, or by threading pebbles, beads or shells on a string. From this idea came the Abacus as early as 1,000 BC, with ten beads to each row. The Greeks, and then the Romans, developed their own particular varieties of Abacus.

Similar devices are known from ancient China, Japan and India. In America the Mayans and the Aztecs developed a not dissimilar system, counting knotted strings on a rope using a base of twenty. For denoting numerals in everyday use today is easy thanks to Indo-Arabic numerals; this new system of numerals was brought to Europe from Muslim north Africa by an Italian mathematician from Pisa called Leonardo Fibonacci (1175–1250). Statues and monuments still often use the Roman notational system of numerals, which for large numbers is logical but can be extremely ponderous. It is however still used on buildings and statues to give a semblance of gravity and learning.

So we still live today with the decimal system pioneered by the Romans which seems reasonably natural to us. It is flexible, useful and easy to use on an everyday level. Another system is already becoming widespread thanks to computers, which is the binary system, with the simple choice between 0 and 1. The use of this system will continue to expand with the expansion of digital technology and machines, but for the great majority of us our everyday life will continue to be transacted in numbers from the decimal system, expressed in Arabic numerals.

Early writing materials were chosen for their permanence, which is exemplified by the Ten Commandments, which Moses brought down from the mountain inscribed in stone, and by the stone steles of Hammurabi recording the law in public places. Because permanent writing on stone is time consuming and tedious, much early writing has been found on clay tablets, where the writing can be done quickly, and then the clay can be left to bake into hardness in the sun, or it can be fired to make the writing permanent.

The word paper is derived from papyrus, an early paper made from the pith of reeds. The pith is extracted, flattened and glued together to make a thin flat surface which can be of any dimension required, and in early times when there was a considerable amount to be recorded, it would be made into scrolls. Papyrus is fairly exclusive to Egypt and was not made in other parts of the world, so that a lot of it was exported and in consequence became quite costly.

In Europe, vellum (from the Latin vitulinum meaning made from calf skin) was developed for writing or printing. It is made by cleaning, bleaching and then stretching calf skin on a frame. The finished preparation is known as parchment or, when fine quality, vellum. To this day British Acts of Parliament are still recorded on vellum as it will last for more than a thousand years where paper can only be relied on to last half that time.

Through medieval times in Europe, paper was made from linen, cotton and rags, commencing around the 12th century, but deriving from a method invented in China during the 2nd century AD. It was only very recently in 1840 that a German inventor, Friedrich Keller (1816–1895), invented a mechanical pulping machine to simplify and speed the process. At about the same time a Canadian, Charles Ferrerty (1821–1892), developed a way of making paper from wood pulp. Ferrerty lived in Nova Scotia, where his father owned a wood mill, and where supplies of timber are profuse. (To this day Canada produces 21% of the world's wood pulp, and the United States 16%.)

The history of ink used for writing on vellum or paper was discovered independently in many different regions. The Chinese used plant dyes as long ago as 2,300 BC. Indian ink, used from 400 BC, was made from burnt bones, tar, pitch and solvents. The Romans used iron salts mixed with tannin from nuts on trees, such as walnuts, oak apples, together with a thickener; when first used on paper this ink is blue/ black but fades to a dull brown with time. None of these inks turned out to be suitable for printing presses when they were developed in the 15th century in Europe, and a new ink was devised consisting of soot, turpentine and walnut oil.

Literacy was reasonably widespread in Europe under the Romans with both slaves and women often attending school and learning to read, but then through the Dark Ages this ability quickly withered away and became limited to churchmen and monastic establishments. Gradually through the Middle Ages the literacy rate started to climb again to a level of about 40% in 1800, then really improved once publicly financed education commenced, which in England followed an act of Parliament in 1870. In the 20th century literacy rates in many parts of the world have been slow to catch up, particularly in those countries where female school attendance is either not encouraged or is felt to be unnecessary.

Writing on paper was the first great invention for the transfer of knowledge after the oral tradition of ancient times; the second great method of transferring knowledge came with the invention of printing in the 15th century (chapter 36), while we are only just getting to grips with the third great method of knowledge transfer and recording in the digital revolution at the end of the 20th century.

Possible further reading:
The Story of Writing by Donald Jackson (Barrie and Jenkins Ltd)

Chapter 13
Ancient Greece

We have seen the development of civilisation around the eastern end of the Mediterranean and in the Middle East. The Sumerians, and then the Babylonians, produced complex and long-lived civilisations and empires in Mesopotamia, whilst the Hittites, who discovered iron, developed in their own way on the Anatolian Plain of central Turkey. At the same time small inter-related, but independent, city states were growing up around the eastern Mediterranean and the Aegean Sea. The terrain was mountainous and less than a quarter of the land area was suitable for farming, it is therefore not surprising that there was early development of fishing and sea-faring trade.

At the same time as the centres of population were developing around the Aegean Sea, a people known from the Bible as the Canaanites moved into what is now Lebanon. Again, their early civilisation was limited to a narrow strip of land between mountains and the sea, and in consequence fishing and trade by sea became their way of life. These people, known as the Phoenicians, developed ports on the eastern coast of the Mediterranean at the end of the 2nd millennium BC, which remained independent city states. The talents of these city states in using the sea developed into a culture of merchants and mercenaries. They traded in all sorts of goods, but the cedar trees of Lebanon were particularly prized for the construction of ships and large buildings throughout the Mediterranean. They developed warships and trading vessels with both oars and sails.

Early vessels, known as pentecontors, had a single row of oars on each side, often twenty-five in number, but as time passed ships with two and three banks of oars were produced, known as biremes and triremes, from the Greek remus, an oar. The ships had a single square sail and were therefore only able to sail before the wind and needed to use their oars when they had to progress into the wind. This type of sail contrasts with the lateen sail developed around the coast of Arabia, and on the River Nile in Egypt, which is triangular and allows a little progress up-wind, but is still inefficient compared with modern fore and aft sails, that have only really developed in the last couple of centuries.

The Phoenicians established a large outpost, or colony, at Carthage (modern Tunis) with an impressive harbour to shelter their merchant ships and warships, having an entrance measuring only 22 metres wide that could be securely closed by chains against foreign invading vessels; the city is reputed to have had a population of 200,000 inhabitants by 500 BC.

While the Phoenicians were developing their cities along the eastern Mediterranean coast, other migrating tribes from further north had established a Bronze Age civilisation on Crete which gradually expanded to the Greek mainland and Aegean Islands forming city states similar to those of the Phoenicians, and with its main centre at Knossos, one of four palaces on Crete. Later mythical writings about this Minoan civilisation relate that Minos, King of Crete, was the son of Zeus and the goddess Europa; together their union produced a bull-headed son, called the Minotaur, who was imprisoned in a labyrinth, where he was fed young boys and girls given to the Cretans as tribute.

Eventually, this monster was killed by one of his intended victims called Theseus. This Minoan civilisation ended abruptly about 1,400 BC leaving little evidence of the causative catastrophe, for which suggestions have ranged from earthquake and volcanism to invasion by the Mycenaeans who become the next people to inhabit Crete and establish their own city states around the Aegean Sea, of which Mycenae and Tiryns in the Peloponnese are left as the best preserved remains.

Following the destruction of Knossos, the Mycenaeans became more outward looking even attacking Troy at the entrance to the Black Sea, which according to legend, withstood a ten-year siege until it fell and was destroyed in 1,184 BC. Some decades later attacks by Dorians from the north over-ran the Mycenaeans, both on the mainland and on Crete and we hear no more of Mycenae, but intercity raiding and warfare remained common.

At this time, and with the Phoenicians spread around the Mediterranean, the Greek civilisation started to grow around the Aegean Sea during a period often referred to as the Greek Dark Ages. Gradually, order and cooperation were achieved, however the small Greek city states frequently still warred with each other, and it was this rivalry and failure to act in concert, which led to the eventual downfall of Ancient Greece centuries later.

Initially, the Greek city states steadily grew more prosperous from about 1,000 BC. They had iron weapons and tools, and their early society was very autocratic, which fuelled rebellions and warfare, so that around 500 BC new governments came into being which differed from the previous city states. Athens became the capital of Attica on the mainland of Greece, whilst Corinth on the isthmus between mainland Greece and the Peloponnese was governed by an oligarchy, or government of leading families. The state of Sparta itself stayed unchanged and was largely ruled by a militaristic race of Dorians, where all young men were expected to become warriors. (Much of the routine work and farming in Sparta was done by slaves, thus freeing the ruling population to pursue their warrior lifestyle.)

The Dark Age lightens in the early years of the first millennium BC at a time when the Phoenicians brought writing to Greece and good records commence. Cooperation between cities is evidenced by the Greeks coming together for the first Olympic games in 776 BC. The games were put on between city states in honour of Zeus, whose huge statue at Olympia was deemed one of the seven wonders of the ancient world (women were included in the games for the first two hundred years).

The games continued until they were suppressed by the Romans in 394 AD; they were restarted at the end of the 19th century by the French Baron Pierre de Coubertin (1863–1937), with the first modern games being held in Athens in 1896. The Greeks shared many characteristics with the Phoenicians before them; they were excellent seafarers living in small self-governing maritime communities. They were individualistic, enquiring and suspicious of authority as well as being competitive, humorous and appreciative of excellence, beauty and enjoyment.

Around the time of the 34th games in the 6th century BC, a Greek oligarch named Draco was charged with producing a written legal code to replace the existing nebulous oral code of conduct. Draco's penalties for misconduct often specified the death penalty for even minor offences, giving rise to our modern adjective 'draconian'. Just over a century later, the chief magistrate of Athens, Solon (638–559 BC), was charged with revising Draco's code of conduct and produced a more balanced and reasonable set of laws, which then served as the basis for Greek behaviour with alterations and fine tuning through the years.

The golden years of classical Greece comprised the 5th and 4th centuries BC, spawning a multitude of writers, philosophers and artists, many of whom came from the Ionian communities of western Turkey, including the great contemporary centre of Miletus. One of these first scholars was Thales (624–548 BC), a widely travelled merchant familiar with Egyptian learning of the time; he was the first to understand eclipses and to suggest that the moon shone by reflecting light from the sun. Among the philosophers, Socrates (469–399 BC) left no writings, preferring to teach by question and answer, but with much of his philosophy being recorded by his pupil, Plato (427–347 BC).

The dialogues of Socrates, as recorded by Plato in his book *The Republic*, comprise the first published philosophical text to set out a basic plan for a society directed towards achieving an ethical goal. Plato's pupil Aristotle (384–322 BC) wrote 170 scholarly works of which about a third have survived and are still studied today, he was also tutor to the teenage Alexander the Great. Also a pupil of Socrates was Xenophon (431–354 BC) who wrote down some of Socrates dialogues as well as being an innovative military commander and recording history.

The Greeks built municipal theatres, and again some of their plays by Aeschylus (524–455 BC), Sophocles (497–406 BC), Euripides (480–406 BC) and Aristophanes (446–386 BC), have survived for us to enjoy and marvel at, with Aristophanes being the first playwright to produce comedy, and to judge by these Greek plays human nature does not seem to have changed during the last two millennia! On other fronts, Herodotus (484–430 BC) is usually regarded as the world's first true historian who travelled and wrote extensively about the Greco-Persian wars and was closely followed by Thucydides (460–400 BC), who wrote about the Peloponnesian wars, and Xenophon (430–354 BC).

Hippocrates (469–399 BC) is regarded as the Father of Medicine, whose oath is still respected by modern qualifying young doctors. Other revered early scientists and mathematicians include Thales, Pythagoras (580–500 BC), Euclid (340–270 BC) who built on Thales early understanding of mathematics, and Archimedes (287–212 BC) who devised early machinery, both civil and military, in addition to formulating his famous principle. The sculptor, architect and artist Phidias (480–430 BC) designed and built the Parthenon, which is still a major tourist attraction today.

Greek religion developed over the ages from precursor religions, so that the Greeks had many gods. They had no holy books but have left us a mass of literature by writers and poets, including Homer, who lived in the early part of the first millennium BC, and Hesiod, who wrote around 700 BC about the activities of the Greek gods who were very humanoid in their feelings and failings. The Greeks believed in trying to foretell the future, both by sacrifices of animals, and by consulting oracles. The oracles were special priestesses, trained in trance-like meditation, who would answer difficult and important questions. The priestesses probably realised that their ability to foretell the future was limited and very fallible, and therefore often the oracle handed down an ambiguous answer: one of the best known of these occurred when Croesus of Lydia asked the oracle at Delphi what would happen if he invaded Persia. The oracle told him that he would destroy a mighty empire. Croesus then went to war expecting to be victorious, and in due course his own empire, rather than that of the Persians, was destroyed.

Thanks to much Greek writings of poetry and history which have survived, we have an excellent understanding of the Greek way of life and civilisation. Initially, Greek social structure divided people into two categories, citizens or slaves. Somewhat later Solon established four classes of citizen, ranked by their ability to produce wheat, wine or oil. To belong to the top class it was necessary to produce at least 750 bushels of wheat, or 20,000 litres of wine or oil each year, whilst the second class (known as Horsemen) only needed to produce 450 bushels of wheat or 12,000 litres of wine or oil (a bushel is a volume measure amounting to eight gallons, 36 litres, or 80 pounds).

The third rank of citizens known as Hoplites, consisted of those producing 300 bushels of wheat or 8,000 litres of wine or oil. Any farmers falling below this productive capacity were called Thetes, or daily labourers. In warfare the Horsemen became cavalry, the Hoplites provided infantry, and the Thetes are presumed to have been the rowers on the biremes or triremes along with slaves. In the early days of Greece up to 25% of the population may have been slaves captured in war and were predominantly female as the men had either died in battle, or had subsequently been executed. In later years, captured men tended to be kept as slaves rather than slaughtered after battle.

Greek houses were primitive and built of stone, or sundried bricks, without windows. Food consisted of peas, beans, onions, bread, cheese, olives and figs together with meat and fish. The dress for both sexes was a chiton not dissimilar to the later Roman toga, which gave cover from the neck to the ankles, and was usually made of wool. A cloak or cape would be worn in addition in cold weather. The Greeks established many colonies of small city states around the Mediterranean, including some in western Italy and Sicily, as well as on the coasts of Spain, France and North Africa. Colonies were also established around the Black Sea, particularly on its western shores, where the climate was benign and farmland was very productive.

Apart from their language and culture, we remember the Ancient Greeks for the Peloponnesian Wars in the 4th century BC. But before this the northern shores of the Aegean Sea, Macedonia and Thrace, and the eastern coast of the Aegean Sea, modern Turkey, were controlled by the Persians. The small Ionian city states revolted against Persia in 490 BC with support from mainland Greeks. War between the two nations continued over the next 20 years, and in 480 BC Xerxes I of Persia (518–465 BC) advanced into Greece where his very large army was held at Thermopylae by a much smaller force of Greek warriors including a legendary band of 300 Spartans, all of whom died and were remembered later in the epitaph, *"Go tell the Spartans, stranger passing by, that here, obedient to their laws, we lie"*.

Defeat only came after three days of fierce fighting following which Xerxes advanced on to Athens, to which he laid waste, but was then defeated in a great sea battle at Salamis by the Greeks, who destroyed the Persian fleet. Without ships to bring supplies, Xerxes retreated hurriedly back to Persia. Athens seems to have been rather overconfident about its military capability thereafter and initiated the first of the Peloponnesian wars in 460 AD. Throughout these wars Athens commanded an alliance of northern states known as the Delian League against the league of Peloponnesian states with Sparta at its head.

Initially, the Athenians defeated the Spartan navy, but then proceeded to sail up the Nile to take the battle to the Persian garrisons in Egypt. The Athenians were heavily defeated, and in consequence had to make peace with Sparta. After this, and with the Persian experience in mind, the Greek commander Pericles (495–429 BC), ruler of Athens at its peak, oversaw the building of two defensive walls from the city for six miles either side of a two hundred metre strip of land along the route to their port of Piraeus, called the Long Walls.

The second Peloponnesian War started in 431 BC, when Athens went to war with Sparta, Corinth and their allies. The result was disastrous for Athens as the Spartans sacked the surrounding country, while the Athenians retreated behind the Long Walls protecting the passage to their port, only to have plague break out and claim the lives of a third of the population. Some of Athens' allies defected to Sparta, and the war continued intermittently for the next ten years when peace was finally declared, only to be broken again in 413 BC, with Sparta eventually gaining the upper hand, after the disastrous loss of the Athenian fleet in battle while it had been trying to help its Sicilian allies.

The war continued with Athens again making some gains before matters took a turn for the worse once more, with a further major setback at sea for Athens following which the city was starved into submission, its Long Walls were destroyed and all its overseas colonies lost. Athenian power was ended, though the influence of its art and culture would persist.

From 404 BC, Sparta led Greece, but its inflexible militaristic rule led to rebellion amongst the other members of the Peloponnesian League and gradually Greece slipped into anarchy, becoming an easy target for the Persians. In 338 BC Philip II of Macedonia crushed the final alliance of Greek city states, and the whole of Greece was then absorbed into the Macedonian empire. Philip was assassinated in 336 BC after a reign of 23 years and succeeded by his son Alexander the Great (chapter 10). For a relatively brief time the Macedonians continued to spread Greek culture further around the eastern Mediterranean.

The Mediterranean was the essential focus for bringing together and developing the Greek civilisation from a Mesopotamian start, melding Persian and Egyptian influences with Phoenician maritime technology. This allowed exploitation of the North African littoral which was at that time much richer and lusher than today, with well-watered farmland and much woodland. Eventually the Greeks succumbed to Rome and were incorporated into the Roman Empire through the series of conflicts known as the Macedonian Wars.

The first of these was a series of indecisive skirmishes between 214 BC and 205 BC. The second Macedonian War between Macedon and Rome from 200–196 BC left Greece intact, while the third, or Seleucid War from 192–188 BC, was against the Persians and left Rome as the major power in the eastern Mediterranean. In the third Macedonian War, 172–168 BC, Rome finally took over Greece and Macedonia, and in the final conflict of the fourth Macedonian War Roman patience had at last disappeared, such that the Greek city of Corinth was razed to the ground in the same year of 146 BC when the Romans also obliterated Carthage, from then on Greece became just part of the unstoppable Roman Empire.

From the Greeks we have inherited a list of the seven wonders of the world as they were seen in the 4th and 3rd centuries BC. These were the Great Pyramid of Giza built around 2580 BC, the Hanging Gardens of Babylon built by Nebuchadnezzar in the 6th century BC, the Temple of Artemis at Ephesus and the statue of Zeus at Olympia, both 5th century, the Mausoleum at Halicarnasssus (tomb of Mausoleus, a local governor 350 BC), the Colossus of Rhodes, a 33m high statue to the Sun God Helios, and the lighthouse at Alexandria – all have since been destroyed except for the Great Pyramid of Giza.

Where previous peoples had simply made war and achieved conquests, the Phoenicians and the Greeks used the sea to trade and found colonies (albeit while still fighting amongst themselves). From 500 BC we have been bequeathed great and profuse amounts of written material comprising the start of philosophy, great drama, travelogues and accounts of warfare and political struggles, not to mention a superb architectural and archaeological record. The Greeks, rather than nations before them, or the Romans and others following after them, were the people who set Europe on the course it would follow over the succeeding two and a half millennia.

Possible further reading:
The Ancient Greeks by Edith Hall (Penguin (Vintage))
Taken at the Flood – The Roman Conquest of Greece by Robin Waterfield (Oxford University Press)

Chapter 14
Etruscans to Romans

The history of Ancient Rome properly starts with Etruria, which corresponds to present north-western Italy, including the region of Tuscany, which gets its name from the Etruscans. The area extends from Rome, north almost as far as the Alps, and from the western seaboard to the Apennine Mountains in the centre of Italy. The pre-history of the Etruscans is very vague, but they probably developed into a loose civilisation from tribes that inhabited the region since very early times. Etruria comprised twelve city states, loosely bonded together, and ruled by an aristocratic ruling cast of kingly priests.

Unusually, in the early world, women had equal rights with men. The twelve city states sent delegates each year to an annual meeting at the Sanctuary of Voltumna, north of Rome, to discuss political, religious and military affairs. Etruria was rich in metals, especially iron, which helped their early economy. They seemed to have been preoccupied with death; funeral rites are the main content of the few Etruscan writings that have survived. They built roads and sewers, and their architecture included arches, domes and vaults, which were all later adopted by the Romans.

It was the Etruscans who first founded Rome in about 600 BC, but did not venture further south because of the Greek colonies in coastal southern Italy. In 509 BC Rome rebelled against the Etruscans whose king, Tarquinius Superbus, was a murderous and very autocratic ruler, later dying in exile. 509 BC is therefore seen as the date when the Romans established their independence, though it took them another 300 years to bring the rest of Italy under one rule. A little later in 474 BC the Etruscan fleet was defeated by the Syracusans (Phoenicians from Syracuse) in the south, and northern Etruria was invaded by Celts migrating from central Europe. A further battle took place between Rome and the Etruscans at Veii, north-west of Rome, in 396 BC, and civil war between the various Etruscan city states followed.

At the same time as Etruria was being transformed into the early Roman state, the Persian Empire in the east was beginning to expand towards the Mediterranean. Greek cities along the coast of Asia Minor (modern day western Turkey) were annexed. In an early battle at the city of Sardis in 498 BC the Persians were defeated by Greeks from Athens, leading their King, Darius, to vow revenge on Athens in particular, and the Greeks in general.

In 492 BC, once he had raised a very large new army and fleet, Darius returned, landing at Eretria, north of Athens, and started advancing south. Darius with his large army was defeated again by a much smaller Athenian force at Marathon from where a messenger was dispatched with the news to Athens; he was just able to announce the victory before collapsing and dying. The modern Olympic 26-mile race commemorates this epic feat from Marathon to Athens, a distance of 26 miles.

After Darius' death, his son Xerxes again advanced on Greece, and this time the Persian land campaign on Greek soil was successful. The Persians were eventually defeated by a superior Greek fleet which was less than half the size of the Persian fleet (chapter13). Athenian defence was all possible thanks to riches derived from the wealthy silver mines of Laurium, south-east of Athens.

Once the stage was set with the weakening of the Greeks and the Etruscans, together with the defeat of the Persians, this provided an opportunity for a new and vigorous Rome to start expanding. The villages on the Roman hills of Palatine, Capitoline and Quirinal had coalesced to form early Rome as a trading centre, where the main north-south coast road forded the River Tiber. But Rome at the time prized the valuable metals that the Etruscans mined at Veii, some 15km north along the coast. Frequent wars between the two cities took place before Veii finally became part of the early Roman territory.

In subsequent generations, the Romans came to believe in a legend about themselves, that Rome was founded by two brothers, Romulus and Remus, who were deserted in infancy. The pair were said to have been found and suckled by a she-wolf, growing up to found the city; they were thought to be the sons of the god Mars, and to have been set adrift in baskets on the River Tiber. They were rescued and reared by the she-wolf, and in the legend Romulus later killed Remus before founding Rome in 753 BC.

In the early days of the Roman Republic after Tarquinius was exiled, the Republic comprised a two-tier class system between the upper-class Patricians, and the much lower and larger class of Plebeians, with one powerful consul from each class to enact the decisions of the senate. Rome had a complicated set of organisations and assemblies, including magistrates, consuls and the Senate, which in theory allowed all citizens to have their voices heard and to participate in decision making. There were, of course, two big exceptions to this involvement of all citizens, the first of these is the slave population who had no voice, but this is hardly surprising when one considers that many slaves were foreigners who had been captured in battle and would probably not have been sympathetic to Rome's values and intentions. The second is women, but although they did not have a vote, Rome's women were often highly influential, particularly if they came from the Patrician minority.

It is interesting to reflect that slavery in Europe lasted two millennia after the Romans, and the slave trade itself was not abolished between Africa and America (and within America) until the 19th century; indeed, slavery is not yet abolished from all countries of the world (chapter 59). Emancipation of women has taken even longer, and only really came to be meaningful from the beginning of the 20th century onwards.

The early Roman Republic from 400 BC onwards imposed conscription for male property owners, who served sixteen years in the infantry, or ten years in the cavalry. The legions were unable to stop an early wave of migrating Celts who settled in the Po valley in the early 4th century and then swept south to occupy and the sack Rome itself in 386 BC. After several months, the city was ransomed for a huge quantity of gold and the Celts returned north. Conscription turned out to be much too onerous a commitment as serving soldiers were unable to maintain their properties or farms back in Italy, and although it eventually allowed the Roman legions to become an immensely strong fighting force, it was not sustainable in the long term, but it did allow Rome to consolidate its mastery, and eventually dominate the whole of the Italian peninsula and the other Italian tribes.

It also allowed Rome to triumph in the three Punic wars, between Carthage (the Phoenicians) and Rome, which ended with the destruction of Carthage in 146 BC. Thereafter, the Roman army became increasingly professional, and indeed it needed to be a professional army, as the empire became more far flung, and remote areas became more troublesome, time consuming and difficult to administer.

Members of the Senate were elected by the upper-class Patricians: Tribunes were elected as spokesmen of the Plebeians: finally, after the distribution of wealth and land had become more and more extreme, one Tribune, Tiberius Gracchus in 133 BC, demanded that land should be appropriated and given to those who had none. Gracchus was murdered, starting a hundred years of rebellions, civil war and riots, during which the strongest men ruled. Among them Sulla (138–70 BC) is remembered for finally annexing Etruria, and was followed by other military dictators.

A Roman general called Marius (157–86 BC) was elected Consul (an annual appointment) for five years running, and subdued Gaul and North Africa. In 59 BC the nephew of Marius' wife, Julius Caesar, was elected Consul. He spent the next seven years conquering the whole of Gaul, which comprised most of France and some of western Germany as we know it today, leaving us his contemporary diaries, both autobiographical and acutely observational.

His long campaign allowed him to amass immense riches from booty and tribute, whilst avoiding the corruption, murder and general violence that had come to plague Rome at this time. Because of the domestic troubles Julius Caesar eventually came home and brought his legions into Rome across the Rubicon River. Previously the army had never been allowed into Rome, and from this occasion we have our modern expression "to cross the Rubicon", which means that there can be no turning back from a previously forbidden action.

Julius Caesar was a great general: after a relatively brief time in Rome he fought a long campaign to subdue Spain, followed by a military campaign in Egypt, where he became lover to Cleopatra, the last of the Ptolomies to rule Egypt, and fathered a son by her. He followed this with a campaign in North Africa, and then once more in Spain. Whilst in Egypt, he had been shown a way of reorganising the calendar by Alexandrian scholars, and decreed later that this should be adopted: thus, we now have what is called the Julian Calendar of 365 days divided into twelve months each year, with an extra day put in every fourth year to keep the calendar constant.

The Romans have also bequeathed us the naming of the days of the week after the planets as they knew them, with themes being more obviously related to modern language if we consider their French equivalents starting with the day of the sun (Dimanche) when God abolished darkness, Lundi, day of the moon, Mardi, day of Mars, Mercredi, day of Mercury, Jeudi, day of Jupiter, Vendredi, day of Venus and Samedi, day of Saturn.

Julius Caesar seized control of Rome becoming dictator in 54 BC. He was himself murdered ten years later in 44 BC because Romans feared he was becoming so powerful that he would make himself Emperor, but ironically his death resulted in yet further instability, such that ultimately the first Emperor had to be appointed by the Senate in 29 BC, ending Roman civil war and the age of the Roman Republic. The new Emperor was Octavian, Caesar's great-nephew, who had been adopted as his official heir and successor, in a way that Romans were allowed to do in preference to allowing succession to run on through the bloodline.

After Caesar's murder in 44 BC, chaos had continued in Rome, with several generals vying for high office. Shortly before Caesar was murdered, another general called Mark Anthony had tried to take control of Egypt, even marrying Cleopatra in Caesar's absence. Caesar pursued Anthony and his army to Egypt, where the naval battle of Actium off Alexandria in 31 BC was instrumental in Anthony's final defeat. Anthony and Cleopatra both committed suicide following this defeat, and as a result Egypt was formally annexed as a Roman province. Civil war flared in Rome between 33–30 BC, with many of the contenders for high office either being defeated in battle or murdered.

Octavian had spent this time developing his military skills in far flung corners of the Empire and emerged from all the bloodletting with his reputation largely untainted, in consequence he was elected Emperor in 27 BC, taking the name of Augustus. He had a long rule, dying in 14 AD, and for the following four hundred years Rome was ruled by an Emperor. Octavian ushered in a huge and steady programme which saw the building of infrastructure including public roads, temples and theatres. Unfortunately, Augustus was followed by a bloodline of three arbitrary, incompetent and debauched successors, Tiberius, Claudius and Nero.

Roman technology, including the invention of cement for building, bridges and aqueducts, was a key factor in the steady extension of the Empire. For these works the Romans used mainly slave labour, which made it possible to keep a very large standing army, of up to 750,000 men, to control the outlying Empire. The army was organised into legions, each with 5,000 infantrymen and 300 cavalry, the infantry being plebs or commoners, and the cavalry being aristocrats, all of whom were citizens of Rome.

Discipline was very tight, and it was this excellent cohesion which allowed this highly disciplined force to overcome the numerous but often poorly organised, ill-disciplined, and indeed chaotic, opposing tribes that the Romans gradually subdued. Apart from its military achievement, Rome also produced writers, poets, and dramatists of note, with Virgil (70–19 BC) who wrote the epic poem The Aeneid, Catullus (84–54 BC), Horace (65 BC–8 AD) and Ovid (43 BC–18 AD), whose lifetime coincided closely with Augustus.

The River Rhone, flowing down to the Mediterranean in southern France, was a well-travelled route for both commerce and invasion of the Mediterranean coastline from central Europe. Roman hold on the coastal settlements here was continually being challenged in a series of epic battles. Fabius, back in 121 BC, had defeated and killed one hundred thousand barbarians two hundred miles north of the Mediterranean, where the rivers Rhone and Isere join.

Later, in 105 BC, a hoard of Germanic Teutons and other Barbarians poured down the Rhone valley again intending to head for Rome. A hundred thousand legionaries were killed in the ensuing battle, following which Gaius Marius, the most famous Roman general of his day, fought the invaders at Aix-en-Provence, and this time the roles were reversed with a hundred thousand Barbarians killed and a similar number taken to Rome as prisoners and slaves.

In 54 BC, Caesar had been elected dictator and had accepted absolute power. Many Patricians and Plebeians viewed this ending of the Republic and the conversion to dictatorship as profoundly wrong, but after his murder in the Senate in 44 BC, the die was cast, and eighty emperors, or dictators, followed his rule. Roman civil war had changed the Republic into a dictatorial Empire, with the monarch being the Emperor. As already noted, Octavian was appointed by the Senate in 29 BC, following a period of great instability. He added to Caesar's conquest of Gaul with annexation of Egypt and was then awarded the title of Augustus. Thus began two hundred years of Roman supremacy and peace known as the Pax Romana, which lasted to 180 AD.

During this period, Rome allowed no other nations to make war, although it fought many wars itself. Amongst Augustus' adversaries, and the rebellions he had to cope with, must be included the Jews, with Jerusalem occupied by Rome in 65 BC. Rebellion followed, with the Jewish Temple being destroyed eventually in 70 AD. Rome subsequently rebuilt a temple to Jupiter, but then with further rebellions, Jerusalem was destroyed again.

The Empire reached its height under the Emperor Trajan in 117 AD, when it had expanded vastly to include all the shores of the Mediterranean, Mesopotamia, all of Spain, Gaul and Britain, but excluding most of Germany. The Roman road system stretched as far as the corners of Britain, the Caspian Sea, Egypt and Spain. Most of this territory still belonged to Rome when the Emperor Theodosius died in 395 AD, but at this time Rome's power was declining fast, and in that year the Empire was divided by agreement into a Western and an Eastern Empire.

The borders of the Empire were attacked, and Rome was now too stretched to defend these borders adequately. The attacking tribes were pushed further into the Eastern empire, in particular by Asian nomads coming behind them. The Empire collapsed as its defensive systems failed to hold, and its treasures were lost to looters. Rome itself was attacked and looted by the Visigoths under their Chief, Alaric, in 410 AD, and was finally sacked by the Vandals in 455 AD.

The Vandals were a Germanic tribe from present day Denmark and northern Germany, who were excellent seamen and who migrated down the English Channel and around the coast of France and Spain to invade and settle along the southern shores of the Mediterranean, where they made Carthage the centre of their new settled area. They invaded Gaul, Spain and Africa in addition to Italy, and by 455 their fleet controlled the Mediterranean. They sacked Rome and took the emperor hostage, causing immense destruction, so that the word 'vandal' now applies to a person who destroys property or possessions mindlessly.

After capturing Rome, the Vandals made war on the Eastern Empire (Byzantium), but their base at Carthage was in turn captured by the Eastern Empire, and then destroyed in 533 AD. Subsequently the Vandals rapidly fragmented and were incorporated into other tribes and states around the southern Mediterranean, and we hear no more of them as a force in history.

We see that Rome and its Empire followed the small Greek Empire, the larger Macedonian Empire established briefly by Philip II, and his son Alexander the Great, and the small settlements of Etruria. The Romans were able to integrate Greek, Macedonian and Etruscan cultures and technology into the immense land area of the late Empire. The Romans were not only excellent engineers, as reflected in their roads, bridges, aqueducts and public buildings, but they also possessed an immense gift for organisation. Their system was flawed, and two immense problems contributed to their eventual downfall. The first of these was the reliance on slave labour, often by slaves captured in battle, though later on the value of being a Roman citizen came to be appreciated, and non-Romans were allowed to become citizens.

The second major problem was the rapid growth of the centre of the empire around Rome itself, which came to have a million citizens at its peak, whilst at the same time having to rely on the import of food and materials from great distances, and from areas inhabited by conquered and resentful peoples. Long supply lines through unfriendly regions, with unreliable transport, have always been a problem for conquering nations.

Gibbon, who wrote his famous *Decline and Fall of the Roman Empire*, published initially in 1776, lists four principle causes of decline operating over a period of more than a thousand years as follows: his first cause is "the injuries of time and nature", in other words, cultural decay and alteration, which must include the transition from republican government to the imperial state. Secondly, there were many hostile attacks from barbarians and Christians; the Romans were unlucky to have come to eminence and built their empire in a period when many tribes in Europe were becoming restless and were outliving the capacity of their native homelands to support their populations.

Thirdly, 'the use and abuse of materials'; by this Gibbon refers to the valuables and art which the Romans produced, first and foremost amongst which were clearly items of gold and silver, but also expensive household and public articles, including glass, china, marble and such like, which were envied and prized by peoples without their own capability to create such items. Fourthly, the domestic quarrels of the Romans, public disorder and riots were frequent; powerful citizens often went armed, and some powerful families, even churches, were fortified for protection; this all produced a culture of quarrelsome activity, even if much of the time it was contained just below the surface.

Whilst the Romans were by nature cruel and not afraid of torture and maltreating their prisoners, together with the enforcement of slavery and summary executions, their culture has left us other areas of great and enduring value. We tend to forget the cruelty, the amazing number of arbitrary deaths and torture, and remember instead the writers, the dramatists and the poets. The Romans themselves did not achieve any important agricultural advances, but they were very organised in their trade and transport systems, including their trade in slaves, both to the north and to the east. The Roman legal system produced great bodies of precedent, but the law itself was not codified until after the collapse of Rome in 410 AD, when the emperor Justinian of the Eastern and Byzantine Empire, who ruled from 527–565, codified Roman law around 540 into a system that remains the basis of law in many western European countries to this day.

Overall, we have seen how the Romans became independent from the Etruscans in 509 BC, and in the succeeding 600 years built the Roman Empire to its greatest extent under the Emperor Trajan in 117 AD, when it covered all the shores of the Mediterranean and the Black Sea, together with all of Spain, France and most of Britain – a total of over six million square kilometres with a population about sixty million people. The next three hundred years were those of decline, but in the meantime the Emperor Constantine built a new city on the site of Byzantium (324–330 AD), then known as Constantinople, and now known to us as Istanbul. After the sack of Rome by the Vandals, Constantinople reached its peak under Justinian. In addition to codifying Roman law, Justinian replaced Latin by Greek, and instituted a campaign to promote Orthodox Christianity by punishing heretics and closing the Athenian schools.

Rome's great legacies to the world included its organisational skills, the disciplinary example of its legions and the lessons derived from running a huge empire. In addition, Roman engineers set standards that lasted for hundreds of years in public roads, water supply and sewers. Roman law, as codified by Justinian, still forms the basis of much of everyday law in Europe.

Possible further reading:
Europe Between the Oceans by Barry Cunliffe (Yale University Press)

Chapter 15
Roman Britain

We have seen in chapter 3 that during the last Ice Age the ice sheet covering northern Europe extended far south over most of Britain. Southern Britain, free of the ice sheet, was bare tundra. Because of the diminished sea levels, Ireland and Britain were still attached to the continent by wide land bridges. There would not have been any inhabitants of the British Isles at this time. As the Ice Age receded and southern Britain and Ireland became warmer, some intrepid humans migrated across the land bridges to populate the southern parts of the British Isles. Sea levels gradually rose with the melt water from the ice sheet so that by 8,000 BC, Ireland was separated from mainland Europe, and fifteen hundred years later, around 6,500 BC, Britain also became an island.

The land gradually became able to support plants across the Arctic tundra with the initial trees being birch, poplar and pine, which tolerate long cold winters well. Oak moved in from warmer southern regions around 6,000 BC. The hunter gatherers came across the land bridge after 12,500 BC, possibly using the region for summer camps from which to hunt. Humans were able to move back into northern Britain and Scotland permanently around 8,500 BC. For the next six millennia we have to piece together the living patterns on the British Isles from the evidence that archaeologists have found in places of human settlement.

The British Isles lived in rumour amongst the peoples of the Mediterranean, where some maps indicate mysterious islands at the end of the world, known as the Cassiteritides, or the Tin Islands (the naturally occurring ore of tin was then called Cassiterite). The trade in tin, which was made into ingots by smelting, seems to have commenced around 2,500 BC. Phoenicians, amongst others, traded across the Channel from Brittany to Devon and Cornwall. There would have been a willing market across into the hinterland of Europe, where the tin was needed to make bronze.

Alternatively, the Phoenicians would have returned to the Mediterranean, coast-hopping along the French and Spanish coasts past Cadiz in southern Spain, which was one of their large trading ports. This trade continued for the next 2,500 years without, as far as we are aware, any evidence of significant warfare or inland incursions by the traders. In the meantime, the local tribes of Celts were growing and were beginning to make hill forts for inter-tribal protection, which we see from about 1,000 BC onwards. We know of the Celts from Greek, and more importantly Roman writings, because many enlisted in the Roman army.

The Celts were a group of tribes, rather than a nation, who evolved out of the bronze age tribes in central Europe between the 13th and 8th centuries BC when their tumuli and forts start to appear, and their swords change from bronze to iron. The hill forts were constructed with immense earth ramparts and ditches, and a wooden stockade on top, and were probably erected as protection against internal tribal warfare. Farming and hunting would have continued outside these hill forts. This situation continued until Caesar's first visit to Britain in 55 BC.

Caesar invaded Britain twice at the end of a ten-year-long campaign to subdue the Celts in France, or the Gauls as he called them. The first time he came to Britain, his fleet and troops landed in the Medway, and left behind Richborough Fort, the massive external walls of which are largely still intact. His second visit to Britain came a year later, when he landed further up the Thames, near the site of London in 54 BC: once again this was only a temporary fact-finding incursion rather than a proper invasion. Trade probably increased after these visits with increased export of tin from Cornwall, and with both Romans and native Britons being much more aware of the trade possibilities across the narrow English Channel.

It was almost a hundred years later, when Claudius was expanding the Roman Empire, that a true invasion took place in 43 AD. The native Britons were disorganised at that time and were not in any state to resist the highly trained Roman legions that Claudius brought, so the Romans encountered a Britain of several different tribes, which in turn were divided into communities often scattered around Iron Age hill forts. The best remaining example of these hill forts is that of Maiden Castle in Dorset, which covers an area of 46 acres. The great ditches and palisades, which were designed to withstand spears, arrows and slings, were easily overwhelmed by the Roman legions with war machines. Colchester north of the Thames, which was the capital of the Catuvellauni tribe, was also rapidly overcome, and King Cunobeline (Shakespeare's Cymbeline) and his sons died together with their armies.

But a surviving son, Caractacus, retreated into the hills and resisted the Romans for a further eight years before the Romans carried out a three-pronged attack, the first occupying the central lowland area of Britain, with a dependent kingdom on either side, the 2nd centred on Chichester in Sussex, and the third attacking the land of the Iceni in Norfolk and Suffolk. The early siting of London was confirmed because of its position as the lowest crossing point of the Thames by ford. It took the Romans five years initially to occupy and pacify all the lowland area south-east of a line running from the Dorset coast to the Yorkshire Wolds, and another 30 years to subdue the areas beyond this, notably including the fertile plain of the lower Severn Valley, and a large triangle of wooded land and forests in the north-west Midlands. A fortress at Gloucester became the main Roman base for controlling the Severn Valley, and at Chester to control the northern Midlands.

The Celts emerge from the mists of prehistory as a cultural conglomeration rather than an ethnic race and were scattered across northern Europe, living an agricultural life as farmers and artisans, rather than living in cities like the

Greeks, Romans and Egyptians of the time. Many were driven north and west by Caesar amongst others, later becoming concentrated on the western fringes of Europe. The Romans struggled to control them as evidenced by Hadrian's wall in Northern Britain, begun in 122 AD, and the Antonine wall begun later in 142 AD. It is useful to distinguish the Celts from the Anglo-Saxons who came to Britain as a later migratory wave, occupying much of eastern England.

Caesar refers to a priestly class of Celtic Druids, noting their use of a war trumpet called a carynx. The Celts and Druids were polytheistic like the Romans, and within the British Isles were also known as Hibernii, Picti, Scoti and Caledonii. Most recently from the mid-15th century the Celts have undergone a cultural resurrection as a distinguishing feature from the population of central England, aided by the fictional 'Poem of Ossian', published by James Macpherson in 1760, who also named and popularised Fingal's Cave. The Welsh eisteddfods and their presiding Arch-Druids were reinvented in the 1860s.

In the middle of their pacification campaign in AD 59, the Romans marched on Anglesey, where there was a powerful concentration of Druids, the Celtic priesthood who were a unifying and symbolic force behind the British resistance. The Romans wanted to impose their own society and order, and the Druids were easily beaten by the legion sent to subdue them. But the conquest of southern Britain had been too rapid, and Roman settlers and officials had taxed and extorted from the natives so much that the Britons were extremely alienated and quite unable to see the value of the Roman civilisation.

When Prascutagus, the client king of the Iceni in East Anglia, died, the Roman government took over his kingdom instead of allowing a native Briton successor to do so. This acted as the spark for an explosion of discontent, and Prascutagus' widow, Boudicca, led an armed rebellion in Essex while the legion was absent up north in Anglesey. Colchester, London and St Albans, all important Roman settlements, were sacked and tens of thousands of settlers and supporters were massacred. The Roman legion sent to relieve Colchester was also routed.

Eventually, the Romans regrouped, and despite being outnumbered were able to defeat the native British forces. No British written history is available from that period, and the contemporary Roman writings of Tacitus and Cassius Dio do not agree as to whether, after this defeat, Boudicca committed suicide or simply fell ill and died, possibly of wounds. After this episode the Romans extended strict territorial control to the north but were never able to control Scotland. Initially defeat was admitted with the building of Hadrian's Wall starting in 122 AD from coast to coast at the narrowest point in England, but fourteen years after its completion in 142 AD the shorter Antonine Wall was built between the Forth and Clyde estuaries in Scotland. This second wall, 100 miles (160km) further north, was deserted only twenty years later due to the difficulties of subduing the very hilly border country, and thereafter the frontier of the Roman Empire remained at Hadrian's Wall until shortly before the Roman withdrawal in 410 AD.

During the Roman occupation, trade increased enormously. British imports included coinage, pottery, olive oil, wine, glass and jewellery together with assorted fish from the Mediterranean. Exports back to the continent have left less traceable evidence, but included metals, silver, gold, tin, lead, iron and copper, and probably also some agricultural produce. Much of the imports would have been needed to support the large military and settler-based settlements in the islands. The Roman provincial government looked after both the administration of the province of Britain, and the necessary taxation system to raise money.

The earliest Roman capital in Britain was Colchester for a while, but was soon shifted to London with its better river access. An extensive network of roads was built, many of which form the continuing trunk road network of modern Britain. All these changes resulted in considerable improvements in lifestyle for the average British farmer or small-holder, though despite this, life would still have been tough and unforgiving. Agriculture became more organised, and Roman technology, both in building and mining, contributed to the advance of society.

The initial invasion of Britain by Claudius included outlawing the Druids, whom Claudius felt were such a threat to Roman rule that he sent a legion north to Anglesey to get rid of them. Although the Romans had been anxious to destroy the native religions (about which we know very little because of the lack of written Druid records), the Romans themselves still practised very eclectic religion, worshipping all manner of things, and prophesying all manner of different beliefs. Sacrifice was important, and each household and clan sacrificed to its own preferred god with special rituals at important times.

Following Augustus, who died in 14 AD, the Roman Emperor held the office of chief priest (Pontifex Maximus) during the next two centuries, and this imperial cult continued for two or three hundred years. Christianity spread slowly in Britain, as indeed elsewhere in Europe, and local Roman governors tried to persuade early Christians to adopt the practice of sacrifice and renounce their faith of the small Christian religion which was spreading simply by word of mouth. One reason for Christian popularity may have been its egalitarian attitudes, commending it to the downtrodden British natives, together with the promise of an afterlife that appeared stronger than a similar promise by the Druids.

The Emperor Nero (37–68 AD) persecuted Christians during his reign and intermittent persecution continued through the next two centuries. Some martyrdoms occurred, with the majority of English saints being natives of the south of the country, particularly Devon and Cornwall, but by the end of the 2nd century AD Christianity had spread widely across Europe and official persecution ended, though throughout the Roman Empire a hotchpotch of religions, and the ability of an individual to worship whatever gods he or she wished, remained intact.

It was Constantine who continued to preside over freedom of worship during his later reign (306–337). He had a vision of the cross in the sky before the battle of Milvian Bridge outside Rome in 312 in which he was victorious in the civil war against the previous Emperor Maxentius, and it was this victory which was taken as a sign of the Christian god's favour which made him declare Christianity as the official religion of the empire. His successor, Theodosius the First (379–395) followed Constantine in confirming Christianity as the official religion of the Empire.

Earlier, the Roman Empire though the 3rd century AD had become an unruly and almost ungovernable place. The twenty-year reign (284–305) of Diocletian as Emperor ended this anarchic period. Diocletian was elected Emperor by the Roman army and realised that a large part of the problem was the sheer size and consequent ungovernability of the empire, he therefore reformed the army, the provincial administration, and divided the old large provinces into many smaller ones.

Diocletian created the Tetrarchy for the rule of four equal provincial ruling governors and split the empire into East and West, with capitals at Byzantium (Constantinople) and Rome. It was in Diocletian's reign that several official episodes of Christian persecution were instigated, and in one of these a member of his praetorian guard refused to disavow his Christianity with the result that he was martyred and executed; he was subsequently sanctified by the church and as St George he became the patron saint of England, the slaying of the dragon refers to a previous act in his life.

In 212 AD, the Emperor Caracalla had granted Roman citizenship to all free inhabitants of the Empire. Over the succeeding hundred years much of the population became Roman citizens, though clearly slaves were excluded from citizenship. The emperors from 312 onwards were all Christian, and this must have helped spread Christianity. In 410 the Goths sacked Rome and the legions, including those in Britain, were all suddenly recalled to the centre of the Empire to try and restore the authority of Roman Government after this appalling catastrophe for the Romans.

Throughout the 2nd, 3rd and 4th centuries, the Romans had spread the rule of Roman law, and the native population of Britain rapidly adopted this as a unified system across the country. To this day, Britain lives on a legal system introduced, codified and providing sound law to all citizens, by the Romans This is in contrast to some areas of Europe, where almost 2,000 years later Napoleon would introduce a legal system to replace Roman law. Overall, the legacy of three hundred and fifty years of Roman rule to Britain comprised this legal system, an excellent road network, increased trade and technology, and with all these advances, an increase in the general prosperity of the average citizen.

Possible further reading:
Roman Britain by Malcolm Todd (Fontana paperback)
The Conquest of Gaul by Caesar (Penguin Classics)

Chapter 16
Rome and Christianity

Rome and its empire is the most important antecedent influence for modern Europe along with ancient Greece. In terms of politics, the law and religion, the ways of Rome have left a profound impression upon Europe and the way it evolved through the subsequent two millennia. Many of our present fundamental concepts and ways of doing things can be traced back to Roman foundations. It is true that the Romans conquered and built upon the Greek civilisation that preceded them, but Roman customs and values are more easily seen as akin to our societal customs than are those of Athens. Rome can be seen as the cradle of both Europe and Christianity.

In the centuries before Christ, Rome gloried in being a republic with political balances and counter checks. This was in part a reaction to the multiple small warring kingdoms and tribes that existed around the Mediterranean at that time. It was the discipline and subjugation of the individual to the rule of the people as a whole, that allowed Rome to conquer other smaller tribes and grow until the empire included all the shores around the Mediterranean. The Republic of Rome lasted for several hundred years from 509 BC through to the moment when Julius Caesar became dictator in 45 BC.

A Roman general and statesman called Gaius Marius (157–86 BC) was elected Consul (an annual appointment) five years running, and subdued Gaul and North Africa. In 59 BC, the nephew of Marius' wife, Julius Caesar, was elected Consul. He spent the next seven years conquering Gaul, which comprised most of modern France and some of western Germany. This long campaign allowed him to amass riches from booty and tribute, whilst avoiding the corruption, murder and general violence that had come to plague Rome at this time.

Julius Caesar was a great general: after his relatively brief time in Rome he fought a long campaign to subdue Spain, followed by an intervention in Egypt, where he became lover to the Egyptian ruler Cleopatra (69–30 BC) and fathered a son by her, he followed this with a campaign in North Africa, and then once again in Spain. Whilst in Egypt he was shown a way of organising the calendar by Alexandrian thinkers, and decreed later that this should be adopted. This resulted in what was called the Julian Calendar of 365 days in twelve months each year, with an extra day put in every fourth year, to accommodate the additional quarter day needed to fit with Earth's orbit (even this is not quite accurate, and in 1582 Pope Gregory XIII made a further adjustment so that we now live by the Gregorian calendar which is accurate to within one day in three thousand years).

From 60 BC, three Roman senators Crassus, Pompey and Caesar had effectively ruled Rome through an informal political alliance. After Crassus died in battle against rebelling Parthians in 53 BC, Pompey realigned his political thinking with the majority of the senate and against Caesar, resulting in the senate ordering Caesar to relinquish his military command and return to Rome since the conquest of Gaul had been concluded. There was a specific long-standing tradition not to bring an army south across the River Rubicon, the boundary between Gaul and Italy, to Rome, but because of domestic unrest Julius Caesar returned to Italy, bringing his legion into Rome across the Rubicon River.

From this occasion, we have our modern expression "to cross the Rubicon", which means that there can be no turning back from a forbidden decision. Inevitably, this led to civil war between the factions supporting Caesar and Pompey, who fled from Italy. The two met in battle at Dyrrachium in 48 BC in modern Albania, with Pompey winning this first battle, but in a second battle at Pharsalus in central Greece the outnumbered army of Caesar prevailed and Pompey fled again, this time to seek sanctuary in Egypt, though he was then assassinated leaving Caesar effectively in control of Rome where he governed as dictator for the next five years, during which time he had an affair with Cleopatra and fathered a child with her. Many politicians gradually became afraid that Caesar had become far too powerful, dictatorial and dismissive of the senate, and this led to a plot that resulted in Caesar's murder in 44 BC.

Caesar had adopted his great nephew Octavian as his successor in a way that Romans were allowed to do in preference to allowing successions to run on through the direct blood line. Chaos continued in Rome for the fifteen years after Caesar's murder with several generals vying for high office, although a triumvirate of Octavian, Lepidus and Mark Anthony ruled as a three man dictatorship for two full five year terms, although Lepidus was overthrown in 36 BC and exiled.

Subsequently, Octavian fell out with Anthony whom he pursued with his army, to Egypt where the naval battle of Actium in 31 BC was instrumental in Anthony's final defeat. Anthony had married Cleopatra, the Egyptian ruler, and they both committed suicide following this defeat: the overall result was that Egypt was then annexed as a Roman province. Unstable conditions persisted and finally civil war flared again in Rome between 33–30 BC, during which many of the contenders for high office were either defeated in battle or murdered.

Octavian, who had been developing his military skills in the far-flung corners of the Empire, emerged from all the bloodletting largely untainted, and was elected Emperor in 27 BC being voted the name of Augustus by the Senate. He had a long rule, dying in 14 AD, and for the next four hundred years Rome was ruled by an Emperor with the absolute power of a dictator.

In this way, Rome lurched from its earlier idealistic republican days, through a civil war, to a dictatorial or monarchical political system. Each of these political systems has major drawbacks: the republican system has checks and balances, which are useful safeguards, but which do not always allow far sighted inspirational improvements and re-organisation; by contrast, an emperor is able to command and organise far sighted projects, but without any built-in checks and balances, so that large blunders are also possible.

An emperor can be arbitrary, vindictive and can act outside the law; four of Augustus' family ruled as emperors following him and displayed these characteristics in greater or lesser degree; Tiberius (ruled 14–37 AD), Caligula (ruled 37–41 AD), Claudius (ruled 41–54 AD) who conquered Britain from 43 AD onwards, and Nero (ruled 54–68 AD). There then followed a period when several emperors ruled very briefly and were murdered before stability returned in 98 AD with four twenty year reigns of Trajan, Hadrian, Antoninus and Marcus Aurelius who died in 170.

Rome had no formal religion at this stage, there was no single creed or dogma, and there were no priests. There was a multitude of gods, often personal to families or communities, and the Emperor held the additional post of Pontifex Maximus, or High Priest responsible for rituals and ceremonies to appease the gods in general. There was a mass of small cults worshipping many different deities or belief systems, and the Romans enjoyed a mixture of Greek mythology together with other rites and festivals. The Roman December festival of Saturnalia is still with us as Christians adopted it for Christmas. Freedom of worship was well tolerated, and politics and religion were often rolled into one overall system of conduct. There was a preoccupation with death, and there was also a hope for an afterlife.

Around this time, most tribes and populations had a belief in the afterlife, though the manner of this afterlife and the way in which it was thought to be achieved varied widely. We know most about it from the Egyptian perspective, and the provisions which they made to ensure their good treatment following death, though this provision seems to have been largely made for the Pharaohs and a few of the upper classes, and it is likely that the average Egyptian was not so optimistic about the provision and prospects for an afterlife.

Rome was a tolerant place as far as worship was concerned, and as long as the belief of an organisation did not threaten the civil state, Romans were free to worship as they wished. The big exception to this was the Jews, whose beliefs included a strict proscription against marrying outside the faith. The Jewish tribe came together following the exile of 587 BC. At that time Babylonian conquerors of Jerusalem and the Jewish homeland took away many Jews as slaves, and destroyed the temple. These actions were seen as a punishment of Judea for its sins, so that a new beginning was possible with deliverance of the Jews back to Jerusalem, where the temple could be rebuilt. The experience brought the Jews together as a nation.

This Jewish nation, and its diaspora, was unique at that time in having and worshipping a single God, and in having a weekly focus where the sacred texts would be read, explained and discussed, with their promise for the future. The first five books of the Christian Old Testament reflect this faith and its moral basis.

Almost fifty years after the exile, Babylon was overthrown by the Persians, and some Jews were able to return to Jerusalem and to rebuild the temple. Jewish independence from Syria came after a revolt of the Maccabees in 164 BC, who were a group of rebel Jewish warriors, and thereafter the Romans allowed independence until 63 BC, when Pompey (106–48 BC) liberated some middle eastern cities and then imposed Roman rule over what was named the Roman province of Syria. The independent period of the Jewish state had been difficult with a succession of arbitrary kings and priests, who were challenged by the orthodox Pharisees, who felt that the Jewish state was losing its way.

The Ten commandments, given to Moses on the top of Mount Sinai around 1300 BC, formed the essential basis at first for the Jewish religion, and following that for Christianity. The existence of ten such distinct and unequivocal rules for moral conduct and daily life have undoubtedly been a major factor in preserving both the Jewish faith and Christianity through the ages.

Into this world of Jewish certainty and opaque Roman gods and other cults, was born Jesus Christ, around 4–6 BC at a time when the Jews were divided between many different sects and beliefs. We know very little of Jesus' early life, and indeed our knowledge of his later life is limited to a few weeks, when he was actively teaching and preaching around Galilee in the time that led up to him being charged with blasphemy before a Jewish Court. The atmosphere at that time was febrile and violent, and Jesus was not a Roman citizen. It was therefore open to the Roman Governor, Pontius Pilate, to avoid further trouble and violence by ignoring Roman law to allow Jesus' conviction and crucifixion although blasphemy was not normally a capital offence.

Following the crucifixion adherence to the new Christianity gradually increased, and provided people kept clear of trouble and controversy, the Roman system was such that Christianity was tolerated, in the same way that many other small sects and cults were allowed to exist. Where evangelism and aggressive proselytization occurred, then violence could break out and some became martyrs to their faiths.

Christianity remained a largely urban phenomenon through the next three hundred years, but in the country peasants and less educated people stuck to the old deities. It is estimated that by the year 300 AD Christians may have comprised about 10% of the population of the Empire. Before this, persecutions by the Emperors Decius (ruled 249–251) and Valerian (ruled 253–261), directed that the old gods should be worshipped and sacrificed to. But persecutions faded, and Christianity continued to promise both a moral way of life according to the Ten Commandments, and a promise of salvation and an afterlife.

Another era of persecution followed under the Emperor Diocletian in 303 AD. Constantius, who followed Diocletian (ruled 284–305), only ruled as Emperor for a year, and died at York in Britain in 306 AD: his son, Constantine (ruled 306–337) was with him at the time, and was hailed as emperor by the army in York. A period of trouble and civil war followed, and it was only finally in 324 that Constantine was able to reunite the Empire under himself as a single ruler.

During these eighteen years, Constantine had built up a powerful army on the borders of the Empire using local recruits. He had been able to stabilise the gold currency, and restore a monetary economy rather than allowing payment of taxes in kind. Constantine did not indulge in persecution, and seems to have started life worshipping the sun god, but in 312 AD, following a vision of the cross in the sky, he ordered his soldiers waiting for battle to put on their shields the Christian symbol of the cross. The battle was won, and Constantine attributed this to divine intervention by the Christian god and thereafter allowed Christians all the toleration and property that other religions took for granted.

Constantine formally declared himself Christian in 324 AD, and called an ecumenical council, the Council of Nicea (modern Iznik in northwest Turkey), which met for the first time in 325, with three hundred bishops attending and Constantine presiding. The main task of this Council was to agree the Church response to a new heresy called Arianism, whose founder Arius said that Jesus was not divine like God. The question was settled against Arius' beliefs, and the Church therefore was able to take on the Imperial purple of Constantine.

The Arian belief (distinct from Aryan) died out by the 7th century. However, the main achievement at Nicea was to unite most of Christianity in a common belief which we know as the Nicean Creed, and which remains a fundamental summary of Christian faith to this day: the small number of dissenting delegates from across the Roman world were banished at the end of the council thereby ending the argument in the typical fashion of a dictator.

Constantine's sons were brought up as Christians, and although Constantine himself had presided over a decaying and fractious Empire up to the time of his death in 337, he had made the fateful break with classical Rome and in favour of the developing Christian Europe. One of his later decisions was to found a city to rival Rome at the entrance to the Black Sea on the western shore of the Bosphorus. Constantinople would remain a Christian capital for the next thousand years, until it was conquered by the Ottomans in 1453, and transformed into an Islamic stronghold.

In the early 4th century, there was a devastating famine in China causing a huge migration of people westwards into the Asian steppes in about 350–360 where a tribe known as the Huns had established dominance. The domino effect spread west to eastern Europe where Roman attempts to halt the flood of tribes were heavily defeated at the Battle of Adrianople in northern Greece with the Emperor Valens amongst the dead. This battle in 378 AD is often seen as the beginning of the decline of the Western Roman Empire with Valens, after his death in 395, being succeeded by Theodosius under whom the decline of the empire proceeded steadily.

Theodosius (347–395) was the last emperor to rule both East and West and had fought the Goths in the Balkans unsuccessfully. He had two sons who were both very young when he died and who ruled through regents. The eldest, Arcadius (377–408), was bequeathed the Eastern Empire to rule, while the younger, Honorius (384–423). became nominal ruler of the Western Empire while still an infant. The combination of dividing the empire, together with the fact that both boys grew up with poor tutelage to become weak and indecisive adults, with scheming and divisive ministers, provided the early death knell for the Empire from which it never recovered.

Theodosius II (401–450), the son of Arcadius, was declared co-emperor at the age of one; his regency ended when he was 15 and about a decade later he established the University of Constantinople and a Commission to collect and classify all previous laws, which would later form the basis for Justinian to codify the law.

The western Roman Empire continued in a much-reduced form following the sacking of Rome by the Visigoths in 410, and loss of North Africa to the Vandals in 439. The Huns continued to harry the Roman Empire in the Balkans and through northern Europe, notably under Attila (403–456). Attila himself whose name has gone down in history as the personification of barbarism was finally defeated at the end of a long and devastating campaign through northern France, at the battle of the Catalonian Plains near Chalons in France in 451. Attila himself died, probably as a result of a very drunken marriage feast two years later, and without his strong personal autocratic control the fighting and political ability of the Huns disintegrated.

Later, the Vandals sacked and plundered Rome in 455, and as decline continued a Roman soldier, probably of German barbaric descent, called Odoacer (433–493), became emperor in 476; the end of the western Roman empire is usually dated from the end of his reign a few years later. Nominally emperors continued to be appointed, often after fighting or murdering their way to the seat of power, but this power, and the empire's borders were steadily diminishing. Divisions and Christological debates continued to divide the western or Roman church. A further major setback came in the 7th century with the spread of Muslim armies through Egypt and across North Africa, reaching the Straits of Gibraltar in about 700, while at the same time the Roman province of Syria was also lost to the Muslim armies.

The Eastern Empire continued, ruling from Constantinople which had been founded in 300 and which was ruled by separate Emperors until it became the Byzantine Empire under Heraclius, managed to last for the next millennium until its fall in 1453 (chapter 26).

Possible further reading:
AD 410, the Year that Shook Rome by Sam Moorhead and David Stuttard (British Museum)
Attila the Hun by John Man (Bantam Books)

Chapter 17
Societies, Religions and Christianity

Early societies developed through the middle of the Stone Age across the world. From about 10,000 BC, at the end of the last Ice Age, we see increasingly frequent practices, many of which apply to most societies regardless of whereabouts in the world they develop.

The first common practice is that early societies built and have left behind monuments, which we can still see today as stone circles, standing stones, dolmens and burial mounds. Most of these seem to have had religious significance and are evidence of early societies' clearly developed religious faiths. The second common theme seems to have been the development of ceremonies which we know, not from the societies themselves, but from more advanced societies subduing and taking over more primitive ones; in the case of Britain, we have Roman reports of the Druids, with their ceremonies and temples.

The third common element of really early societies is the existence of cave paintings, of which the most impressive examples are those in the Sahara, in the aboriginal Northern Territories of Australia, and in the French and Spanish caves of Lascaux, Chauvet and Altamira.

The fourth common development, which appears to have occurred independently across the world, is that of sacrifice, which was not always a part of early societies, but the sacrifice of living creatures to the gods was quite common. Some societies went as far as to practice human sacrifice, either on special occasions, such as the dedication of temples, or in order to placate the gods if circumstances of weather and climate appeared to indicate the displeasure of the gods. Sometimes it seems that when human sacrifice occurred, it was with a certain degree of cynicism as the sacrificial victims were either captured prisoners or slaves.

In China and on the steppes of Asia, the sacrificial victims, who were often slaves or family, were felt to be a necessary accompaniment to the next world with their dead ruler, who would need a familiar and faithful retinue of servants. This last custom would obviously have been distressing and disruptive to some societies, and the Chinese in particular came up with the ingenious alternative solution of providing the ruler with an accompaniment of servants and warriors made especially for the purpose, such as the well-known Terracotta Warriors of Xian. Even Christianity starts with the ultimate sacrificial offering.

The fifth common element in many early religious systems of belief seems to have been the conviction that there was an afterlife. This belief, and the measures taken to indulge it, were many and various, but it seems that early man across the world was unwilling to accept that a single life on this Earth was all that was granted to an individual. The soul was postulated to be the repository of this continuing existence, and the soul did not require body, heart or brain to continue.

The Druids, in particular, felt that the soul was eternal, and transferred to another body after death of the current body: this is said to be one reason why Druidic and ancient British warriors were happy to die in battle since they believed that their souls would continue in existence in another body; the same seems to be true for modern Islamic jihadi fighters who are promised admission to paradise when killed in battle (jihad). These beliefs have been taken on and crystallised in Jewish, Christian, Muslim and Hindu thought to this day.

Because of all these preoccupations with death and life after death, many early societies developed funerary rituals, of which we can still find signs. These include the Stone Age long barrows, and the Bronze Age circular mounds, which are common around the British Isles, Brittany, Iberia, Scandinavia and eastern Europe. In these cultures, it was common for the dead individual to be buried with grave goods of a personal nature relating to his or her stature in society, rather than needing the accompaniment of any sacrificial victims. The grave goods, and sometimes paintings which were buried with the dead, have given us huge information about early societies from the Egyptians onwards.

Central European burial mounds, or kurgens, in particular have provided an enormous amount of information about the customs and living habits of early people. Radiocarbon dating tells us that barrows and burials mounds first appeared in Portugal around 4,500 BC, rapidly spreading northwards around coastal areas of western Europe and Britain.

Gradually, there was a trend from the early multi-theistic religions to monotheism which seems to have started in the Jewish faith at a time when worship and religious beliefs across Europe were very fragmented and individualistic, varying enormously from tribe to tribe. In central Europe the Celts were people living in a series of loose knit communities; we know them best from two well preserved archaeological sites, Halstatt in Austria, and La Tene on Lake Neuchâtel in what is now Switzerland. These two cultures are recognised by their highly distinctive pottery which became widespread across Europe, including Spain, Portugal and the south-eastern part of the British Isles.

Between about 500 BC and the Roman invasion of Britain in 55 BC, there was considerable Celtic migration, predominantly westwards. British archaeological sites have furnished much evidence of their pottery. Some of those who migrated would have settled in Britain and contributed to the melting pot of religions, though in Britain at this time culture and religion was dominated by the Druids, and centred on Anglesey, where little trace remains thanks to determined Roman obliteration. The Druids were the intellectuals of the migrating Celtic masses, and they acted in many capacities, including that of priests, doctors, bards and law makers. We owe our scant knowledge of them to Julius Caesar and other Roman writers who visited the British Islands in those early years.

The five hundred years before the birth of Christ was a period of philosophical ferment in which many individuals from different cultures and unconnected geographical backgrounds were driven to explore the meaning of life and the vicissitudes of the natural world, and to consider whether a god or gods might explain the mysteries of human existence together with apparently arbitrary natural events. These people were attempting to pursue rational enquiry and observation of nature to explain the workings of the world, and they include the ancient Greek philosophers; Socrates did not leave any writings, but his dialogues were recorded by his pupil Plato in the writings known as *The Republic*, which is a vision of an ideal society.

So many individuals, and so much discussion occurred looking for the meaning of human existence through the middle years of the last millennium BC that the German philosopher Karl Jasper (1883–1969) has suggested that the period should be called the Axial Age, since it appears to have been a time when preachers and early philosophers sprang up across the world apparently quite independently of each other in India, China, Persia, Greece and Judea, but with teachings which were all very different.

Much of human history in Europe before the coming of Christianity, and before the Greek and Roman empires, was the history of the Jews which was written down in books and known to Jews as the Torah, and to Christians as the Old Testament. These books were subsequently diffused across the European world, and indeed further by Christian missionaries initially, and later more widely following the invention of printing. The Jews were the first people to produce this abstract idea of a single God, and also the first to forbid representation of God by images, either as pictures or as sculpture.

Interestingly, the second commandment which Moses brought down from the mountain where the commandments had been given to him by God, includes the instruction that "thou shalt not make any graven image…"; and while Jews and Muslims obey this edict it has never really been observed by Christians since the early Christian centuries.

The origin of the Jewish religion comes from the Semitic and nomadic people of Arabia, which is a barren and desertified area, where early population increase produced pressure for northward migration to the fertile crescent of Mesopotamia. From the Old Testament we hear the accounts of Abraham, Isaac and Jacob, dating from around 1,800 BC. Abraham settled in Canaan, where his descendants became known as Hebrews, a word which means 'wanderer'. This Hebrew tribe comprised largely farmers, and one group of them migrated, or were deported, to Egypt where Joseph, the son of Jacob, became an important administrator in the Pharaoh's service.

Later in the story of this Jewish group appears the figure of Moses, who led the enslaved Jews out of Egypt into the desert, or wilderness. It must have taken an extraordinary capacity of leadership firstly to persuade the Jewish slaves to leave Egypt, and secondly, to hold them together in the subsequent years of wandering in the desert. The biblical account goes on to tell the story of the founding of the Law, when Moses communicated with God at the top of a mountain and brought back to his people the Ten Commandments inscribed in stone. To this day, these ten unequivocal instructions probably provide the best simple overall prescription for the morals of community life. Moses also brought down from the mountain a further 613 precepts or minor commandments; 365 of these are positive, or things to do, matching the number of days of the year, while 248 are negative prohibitions said to match the number of bones in the human body; modern day adherence to these precepts varies with different strands of Jewish thinking (since there is no mention of these 613 precepts until a thousand years after the time Moses there must be some doubt about where they originated and at what time).

Once the Jews had returned and settled in Palestine, the tribe was challenged by the Philistines, who were probably another Hebrew tribe, and the first Hebrew King appears around 1,000 BC. Saul is this first King who reigned over the Jews and commenced the tradition of appointing prophets. He was succeeded by his son David, who lives on in the Biblical account with Jesus a thousand years later counting himself of the House of David, and one of a continuing line of major prophets.

The Jewish authorities and the prophets continued to develop the monotheistic worship of Yahweh or God. There were weekly meetings, with interpretations of the teachings, and increasingly rigid enforcement of the Laws of Moses. The Jews tended to segregate themselves in towns with an increasing emphasis on the behavioural code which became gradually more strict. Jews were not allowed to marry outside their faith, while the faith itself, and adherents to it, brought the promise of a stable future in return. The Old Testament God called Yahweh, with an emphasis on punishment, persisted and only gradually morphed into a more gentle religion that included the promise of forgiveness for those who repented their sins after Christ's crucifixion.

This austere Old Testament approach to religion needed priests and arbitrators who would interpret and enforce the Law, and in the 1st century BC the Pharisees emerged as a reforming strain of priests teaching not only strict adherence to the old Law, but also a belief in the resurrection of the dead and a divine last judgement.

All these developments took place predominantly in Judea, which up till then had been under Roman control, but with the Romans appointing a Jewish King. Herod the Great (74–4BC) was appointed by the Roman Senate in 37 BC, but his reputation rapidly became damaged by the imposition of heavy taxes, and by the 'massacre of the innocents', an event, when he, as King of Judea, ordered the killing of all male infants, amongst whom was supposed to have been born a Jewish Messiah. When Herod died the Kingdom of Judea was divided in 4 BC between his three sons, which was an unsatisfactory arrangement, and in 26 AD Pontius Pilate, a Roman, was appointed Governor. The province was simmering with revolt and discontent, both against Roman rule and also with different organised groups of Jews, including the Pharisees and Sadducees.

The recent discovery and reading of the Dead Sea Scrolls (found in 1947 and dated to the 1st century BC), is interesting in that it promises faithful Jews much that was also to be offered by early Christianity. The Dead Sea Scrolls looked forward to a last deliverance which would follow the collapse of religious faith, and would be announced by the coming of a messiah.

Into this febrile climate Jesus was born in around 4–6 BC, in a country where many people were awaiting the coming of a messiah who would lead them to a military or religious victory, or both, and which would result in a great and glorious future for Jerusalem. The latest in the line of Jewish prophets was called John, who preached the coming of the Messiah, and importantly, baptised Jesus along with many others. Jesus' ministry commenced soon afterwards, by which time he was in his early 30s.

We have no information about Jesus early life, but it is likely that his time of preaching resulted from years of thought and maturing among the unsettled Jewish community of the time. Jesus was perceived by the ruling Jewish class of the time, including the Pharisees and the Sadducees, to be one of many threats to the community and he was therefore charged with blasphemy before a Jewish court. Following pressure from the Jewish authorities, the law was ignored (since blasphemy was not a capital offence at that time, and Jesus was not a Roman citizen) but as Pontius Pilate was trying to avoid further trouble and unrest, he washed his hands of the matter and allowed Jesus' crucifixion to proceed to placate the crowd.

Following his death, Jesus' disciples believed that he had risen from the dead and ascended into Heaven, and that the disciples themselves had received a divine gift of power at Pentecost some weeks later. The continuing story of the advance of Christianity is told in the New Testament, but it is remarkable that amongst all the competing ideas of religion and philosophy at that time the particular message of Jesus Christ should have caught on rapidly and spread across the Roman world within the next 50 years. The most important preacher of this message was Paul, who was originally a Pharisee and a persecutor of Jesus and his apostles.

Paul was converted by the new ideas and went on a series of missionary voyages throughout the eastern Mediterranean, where he continued to preach the possible imminent end of the world, with redemption and judgement at the end by God, with Jesus sitting next to Him. This idea was unacceptable to orthodox Jews, and Christianity diverged away from mainstream Jewish thought. Much of the Christian Church then evolved in other parts of the Roman Empire, including Greece and southern Turkey, and rather later throughout the rest of the Empire. There was a culmination of unrest with a great Jewish uprising in 66 AD, when extremists became the majority in Judea, and then took over Jerusalem.

A considerable military battle followed, resulting at the end in storming and burning of the Temple in Jerusalem by the Romans. Unrest continued to simmer, and events at Masada in 73 AD, when a whole community committed mass suicide, may have been the last stand of the Jewish extremists against the Romans. The Romans continued to try to suppress Jewish extremism, and the Emperor Hadrian made Jerusalem an Italian colony, which Jews could only enter once a year. The Jews were by now widely dispersed, but the longing for a Jewish homeland survived undimmed though the centuries until Israel was established in Palestine after the second World War, almost two millennia later.

Further east in India a wide spectrum of laws and attitudes to daily morality was coalescing into the Hindu religion from the stone age Vedic religion from two principal sources; firstly Shruti, or revealed texts, and secondly Smriti or remembered texts, but Hindu religion lacks a unifying doctrine, revelation, or book of authority. The Rig Veda was written down about 1,000 BC from previous oral traditions and there are three other slightly later texts, animal sacrifice is involved together with the idea of the cycle of life, escape from which can be achieved by observing the proper obligations and duties.

In Hindu religion, the concept of God rests with the individual. Yoga and meditation are used as a method of achieving the goals of life, of which there are four; firstly Dharma, righteousness or ethical living; secondly Artha, livelihood or wealth; thirdly Kama, or pleasure, and fourth, Moksha, liberation from the constant cycle of death and reincarnation. In addition people are felt to belong to one of four basic classes; priests or brahmins, warriors, merchants and finally manual labourers, meaning peasants.

Also in India, sometime in the 6th and 5th centuries BC lived the Buddha, Siddhartha Gautama, who was an itinerant teacher preaching a middle way between asceticism and excessive luxury, but recognising equality for women (chapter 7). He came to his way of life after trying regimes of luxury and aestheticism in turn and finding that neither satisfied him. Once again there is an emphasis on moral living and an ambition to escape a cycle of presumed life, death and reincarnation.

Buddhism is currently the world's fourth largest religion after Christianity, Islam and Hinduism. In India, some 80% of the population is Hindu with a further 14% being Muslim since partition in 1947, and Buddhism now represents less than 1% of the population, although it is more numerous in other countries. At the time of partition about a quarter of the population of India was Muslim; during partition as Pakistan was divided off into a separate Muslim country considerable violence resulted in an estimated 10 million deaths from the ensuing chaos.

As well as the large Hindu, Muslim and Buddhist populations there are many smaller sects including Tibetan Buddhism with the Dalai Lama at its head; the current Dalai Lama is the 74th in a line which commenced some 2,000 years ago with early Tibetan rulers and is not a direct descendant in this line into which each Dalai Lama is chosen as a young child and is regarded as a reincarnation of the individual occupying the position.

In China, Confucius lived from 551–479 BC (chapter 8). He was a teacher who taught moral behaviour in the form of five virtues, humaneness, righteousness or justice, propriety, knowledge and integrity. He believed women should be subordinate to men, either as fathers, husbands or sons in contrast to the view of Buddha, in addition he strongly supported ancestor veneration in a society which often included ancestor worship. In olden times, many Chinese believed in folk religions and spirits, often in addition to the three large groups of followers of Confucius, Buddha and Taoism. Taoism does not believe in a person or thing, but is rather a way of life orientated to appreciating the natural order and organisation of the world and to keeping one's actions and behaviour in sympathy with the rhythm of nature.

Since China suffered through the extremely turbulent decades up to the 1950s it has become a single party state which is officially atheist with members of the ruling communist party forbidden to practice any specific religion, though viewed from outside many would feel that Chinese Communism is effectively a religion with considerable intolerance of any departure from the Party line of thought; there are echoes here of the official thinking of first the wider Christian faith, and later narrower Catholic beliefs.

The early 7th century saw Mohammed's dreams and subsequent teaching, with devout Muslims believing that the dreams were direct communication and instructions from God, also a monotheistic being named Allah. Much later and with the spread of European culture in the 16th and 17th centuries many missionaries, both Catholic and Protestant, came to preach in eastern countries resulting in the considerable mix of religions now present across the world, a mixture into which the Muslim religion had contributed Mohammed's ideas a millennium after Confucius and Buddha (chapter 20).

It seems to be a common feature of all religions, that once established, and once the founder has died, its adherents start to develop different interpretations of what the true belief should be and what the founder really meant. This is often argued over vehemently, and results in the setting up of different sects or branches of the religion. In the case of Christianity, the religion became accepted across the Roman empire within some three hundred years of the crucifixion, by which time resources were being put into rich buildings and Christ was being seen as a warrior leading Roman legions. The emphasis was placed on faith to follow the perceived path, rather than pursuing rational thought or reasoning derived from Jesus's original teachings.

These struggles over doctrinal correctness came to a head in the 4th and 5th centuries AD as different churches had developed different versions of the faith. Ecumenical councils were convened by the reigning Roman emperors to try and agree a standardised version of the faith; thus councils were held in Nicaea in 325, Constantinople in 381, Ephesus in 431, Chalcedon in 451 and Constantinople again in 553. Agreement was far from unanimous, and a doctrine emerged that was as much political as religious, with a new order of bishops backed by the emperor and the state, and an ideology that the church and bishops alone had the right to determine truth, thus destroying the tradition of rational thought inherited from classical times.

Islam has displayed similar divisive tendencies with considerable violence between different branches of followers starting in the very early days after

Mohammed's death, and with fragmentation into many different followings, usually with great antagonism between them, not infrequently involving assassinations and massacres (once more we find similarities with Russian, Chinese and other communist states pogroms, purges and assassinations of those deemed annoying or unacceptable to the regime).

During the early years of Christianity, the Old Testament message of retribution and punishment gave way to a doctrine of love and forgiveness, apart from the episode of Constantine going into battle with Christ on his side, and on his soldiers' shields. Thus religion developed in Western Europe, however despite this doctrine of love the following centuries produced many wars of religion, including the dramatic spread of Islam in the 8th century and the resulting crusades in later centuries.

It was to be many centuries later in the 13th century that Thomas Aquinas would start the enlightenment with the reintroduction of Aristotle's thinking and rationality. This would lead in turn to further fragmentation of belief and faith leading to Martin Luther's break from Rome in the early 16th century and the steadily increasing division and fragmentation of Catholicism and Protestantism (chapters 36 and 47).

Possible further reading:
Millennium by Tom Holland (Abacus)

Chapter 18
The Dark Ages

There have been Dark Ages alluded to at various different times and places in history. In the British and European context, the Dark Ages are usually understood to commence with the sack of Rome and the withdrawal of the legions from Britain and other far-flung corners of the empire to Rome in 410 ADS, and to end in Britain with the emergence of the country from the Dark Ages in the 9th century around the reign of Alfred (877–899), although Roman grip on the provinces and territories had been slipping for several decades before this. The darkness referred to characterises both an intellectual and civilised state from which the inhabitants of the British Isles reverted to a relatively barbarous state, as well as referring to a sharp downturn in the climate.

There is an implied lack of learning with inability of most of the population to read, write or record events of daily life and history; an era in which religion relapsed from the Christianity imported by the Romans and retreated to the western fringes of the British Isles.

It was a time when the original inhabitants of the British Isles, the Celtic speaking Britons, whose traces today we localise to the western coastal areas, including Cornwall, Wales, the west coast of Scotland, and the Western Isles, as well as the western coast of Ireland, were descendants of those Celts who had migrated into Britain in the Neolithic and Bronze ages.

Into this relatively backward, but Iron Age Celtic-speaking Britain, had come the first Roman exploration of Julius Caesar in 55–54 BC. The time was not right for the Romans, and after a short period of observation and investigation, they left again. Later as the Roman Empire expanded the Romans returned with the intention of subduing the population and settling in 43 AD; for almost the next four hundred years they introduced the British to the benefits of formal civilisation, including reading, writing, business and finance (with coinage), the rule of Roman law, and in general the benefits of a regulated and static society. During this period through to 410 AD, Britain remained a fairly prosperous province of the Roman Empire, with relatively little interference from Rome itself.

During this period in Europe in the 3rd century AD, the Franks and the Alemanni were two large conglomerations of tribes living on the east bank of the River Rhine with the Celts living further to the east on the River Danube. Because of population pressures in middle Europe these tribes were constantly subjected to migratory pressures from the eastern steppes pushing them westward and eventually the Franks crossed the River Rhine into Roman ruled territory in 256. As Roman rule deteriorated the resulting Frankish Kingdom was finally recognised by Rome around 357, eventually becoming Roman allies after the collapse of 410.

There is a period of some two hundred years commencing around 375 and referred to as the Period of Barbarian Invasions, or the Migration Period, with each name implying a rather different genesis of events; the period coincides with, or perhaps is the result of, the decline of the Western Roman Empire. It starts with the arrival in Europe of the Huns who previously had been nomadic pastoralists in the Caucasus and Central Asia in war bands of up to 20,000 complete with their families of women and children and included not just the Huns, but others referred to in contemporary accounts as Goths, Vandals, Slavs, Bulgars and Alemanni.

The reason for this pressure on the tribes to migrate has been attributed to a multitude of causes including population pressure (perhaps better called famine or harvest failures), climatic deterioration, reinforcement of the great wall of China forcing the tribes west instead of east, and diminished political and military control of a declining Roman Empire. This period of tribal migration and population redistribution around Europe is mainly concluded when the Lombards conquer and occupy northern Italy in 568.

All the northern Franks were united by Clovis (465–511), who was possibly a previous Roman commander and the son of Merovech, thus commencing the Merovingian dynasty, which would rule the Franks for the next two centuries. Clovis established his capital in Paris where it has remained ever since, so firmly setting up a prototype of the France we know today. He married a Burgundian princess who eventually persuaded him to be baptised into the Christian church in 496. With the withdrawal of the Romans south in 410 the Merovingians moved to consolidate the situation in Francia ultimately coalescing under Clovis.

In Britain, the civil administration gradually collapsed, and the country was thrown back on its own local resources in hundreds of different settlements that possessed no clear central direction. There followed a period when waves of invaders from the continent arrived to settle and exploit the land, which was relatively uncrowded compared to the continental Europe they left, the Britons were driven west and possibly reused the old Iron Age hillforts. Very recent DNA analysis indicates that the newcomers assimilated into the native population and that a supposed exodus to the 'Celtic fringes' of the country has probably been exaggerated.

First Anglo Saxons, then Vikings, and finally Normans after 1066 all moved across the North Sea to settle; the actual numbers of immigrating Normans after the conquest, and their input into the British gene pool, appears to have been quite small with only a relatively small number of Norman nobles achieving the conquest of the British Isles. There is only poor information available for the first hundred years following the Roman departure of 410, although we know that flickers of Roman culture and civilisation were kept alight by small monastic communities, principally around the western coasts of the British Isles, and also in Brittany.

Into this 5th century vacuum appears the legendary King Arthur, possibly a surviving Romano-British leader whose real life was probably dedicated to uniting the British against the early migrating and invading Anglo Saxons from the Continent. This is in great contrast to the story which has been romanticised in history as the Knights of the Round Table and the quest for a Holy Grail. Around Arthur's time in the 5th century, the Celtic inhabitants of Britain were being driven west by the Anglo Saxon newcomers and some information about these early years after the Roman departure comes to us in a biography of St Germanus, a Frankish bishop who visited Britain first in 429 and again in 447; and in St Patrick's 'Confessions'.

Patrick, now the patron saint of Ireland, was a Roman Briton taken in slavery to Ireland at the age of 16 by pirates, but who was subsequently freed or escaped returning to Britain in 415 for a few years before returning as a priest to Ireland to teach Christianity to the native Celts. Details about his life are very vague, but he is thought possibly to have ended his life as primate of Ireland.

A shadowy war leader called Vortigern is the dominant British figure through the first half of the 5th century, though he was not King of the Britons. He was in part responsible for Anglo Saxon migration as he maintained his power using Anglo Saxon mercenaries whom he had imported across the Channel. Population movements during the Dark Ages all started with the Germanic tribes, Goths, Visigoths and West Goths, moving west into the Roman Empire, and indeed towards Rome itself. They were part of the chain of dominoes that started with the Huns, who were Asiatic nomads coming out of the Eastern Steppes, and expanding in all directions.

Alaric the Goth (370–410) sacked Rome in 410, despite the Empire racing to bring frontier legions back to defend the motherland. There was a hiatus before the Germanic tribes moved in. The Huns, a nomadic east European people, displaced the Goths and Visigoths, who in turn displaced the Anglo Saxons, and then the Belgae, all migrating westward. Rome was approached by Attila the Hun in 444, and a huge battle to contain the Huns' advance took place at Catalonian Plains in north-eastern France in 451. The combined Roman and Germanic tribes defeated the Huns in this battle at Troyes in northern France.

The last Roman Emperor of the western Roman Empire, Romulus Augustulus, was defeated in 476 by the Ostrogoth Odoacer, and this landmark event is thus often seen as the beginning of the European Middle Ages and of more significance than the sack of Rome in 410. Odoacer established an Ostrogoth kingdom in Italy which in turn was destroyed by the Byzantine Emperor Justinian in 493, and then the Ostrogoth King Theodoric (454–526) moved to set up the Roman capital in Ravenna on the northeast Italian coast. By 527 the Emperor Justinian in Constantinople attempted to restore the Roman Empire, and among other achievements built the huge church we know as Hagia Sophia in Istanbul (Constantinople).

The Franks held on in northern France and the Low Countries and Clovis was baptised and received into the Christian Church in 496. In the meantime, European trade and contacts were reduced as the invading Huns separated east from west. This constituted a formative age in Europe, when early societies were evolving into feudal monarchies, interrupted by these frequent Barbarian incursions. At the same time in Britain there was some semblance of order and continuing agriculture in small communities across the country. Solitary monks were spawned by the chaos and called Stylites.

In Italy, a monk named Benedict (480–547) had written out his rules for prayer and work under 73 different chapter headings; these rules became the foundation of western monasticism. Benedict founded a monastery at Monte Cassino in southern Italy, but his rules for monastic life were intended for use by solitary monks or by small individual communities and it was only centuries later that the Benedictine order came into being.

Around about 535 there was a huge climatic disaster. We know that the climate worsened, the days remained dark, and the sun was barely seen and gave no heat or light to ripen crops. Frosts came early in the autumn and persisted late in the spring. This change of climate was very sudden and is chronicled in contemporary accounts in the northern hemisphere from as far away as China and Japan, as well in European accounts. Famine was rife, and disease very prevalent. This abrupt climatic downturn has been confirmed by evidence from tree ring studies (dendrochronology) in both Europe and North and South America, and in ice cores from Greenland, which show that large quantities of dust and silt settled out during this time. The evidence points to 542 as being the coldest year in the previous 1500 years.

The cause of this darkening of the atmosphere is now ascribed to a massive volcanic eruption liberating huge quantities of volcanic debris into the atmosphere, which then took several years to settle out and allow a return to more normal climatic conditions (although recent work indicates the severe changes may have taken decades, rather than years, to recover). Such a catastrophic climatic change could only have worsened the already precarious state of the population, subject as it already was to famine and disease.

It is understandable that under these circumstances, people's priority would have been to continue trying to grow crops and animals for food rather than to spend time writing and recording. To add to people's woes in these adverse times Rome was hit by the Plague of Justinian, probably the Black Death, which arrived in Britain three years later to further decimate the population.

During the 6th and 7th centuries, the British Isles fragmented into a mass of small kingdoms, often reusing the old Iron Age hillforts where local warlords or princes held out. In England these small very localised kingdoms gradually coalesced into three larger and four smaller kingdoms, giving rise to a period consequently known as the Heptarchy. Of these kingdoms the three large ones have persisted in various forms, known as Northumbria, Mercia and Wessex, and four smaller ones also persist through the ages in recognisable form as East Anglia, Essex, Kent and Sussex.

The early Saxon settlements were established in the middle of the 5th century, and at the beginning of the 6th century a great king appears in Norfolk and Suffolk called Radwald, who was acclaimed King of the East Angles. At about the same time another king called Cerdic appears in the south of England as a Saxon leader who is said to have conquered some of the south coast by 495. The battle of Mons Badonicus at an uncertain site, is dated to 500, when King Arthur is reputed to have led a native British alliance to victory over the Saxons. During the 6th century, small kingdoms appear to have coalesced and fragmented again, so that gradually the Britons were driven out of southern England, leaving the Saxons in control.

At this time, Scotland was inhabited by a tribe known as the Picts, who were a late Iron Age and early mediaeval race living in the north and east; DNA studies indicate that they had a Celtic origin. They left their mark on the landscape with the brochs that they constructed for defence against the raiding Vikings. The Picts were the descendants, and probably the same tribe, as the Caledonii mentioned by Roman writers, from whom we hear that they raided south of the border, first across Hadrian's wall, and later across the Antonine wall, which had been built in the years following 142.

The Picts merged with the Gaelic tribes of Dal Riata to form Alba, or Scotland, according to the Venerable Bede, a monk who lived from 672–735 at Monkwearmouth monastery at the mouth of the River Tyne. He was a great scholar, historian, chronicler and translator. Much of our knowledge of this period and previous years we owe to his unflagging industry, although the fact that he was writing centuries later than much of what he was writing about, must throw some doubt on his accuracy. The Picts and the Gaelic tribes had similar societies and cultures, which in turn were quite similar to that of southern England. Their life was agricultural with some fishing; urban society in Scotland did not appear until much later, about 1200 (Chapter 43, Scotland).

The kingdom of Dal Riata on the west coast of Scotland also extended to the northeast coast of Ireland in County Antrim, with the kingdom reaching its apogee around 600. Soon after that it was conquered by the kingdom of Northumbria, and its independence ended altogether in the Viking era with the merger of Dal Riata and the rest of the Picts to form Alba, or Scotland.

The writings and chronicles of the monasteries which survived the Viking raids, notably at Iona and on the west Irish coast, give us their history and accounts of their daily lives. Much of the travel between those isolated communities was made by boat as overland journeys were long and arduous. The boats of the Picts and Dal Riata, were known as currachs; small craft of less than twenty feet in length with a hide covering stretched on a wooden frame, and much more primitive than contemporary Viking craft. Even the sea voyage from Scotland to Ireland would have been a considerable undertaking in such a frail boat, and most travel was probably restricted to the fair weather summer months.

During the 7th century, the power of Mercia in the English Midlands grew steadily, at the expense of its neighbouring kingdoms. The Saxon Cerdic ruled the kingdom of Wessex from 519–534 and his descendants gradually came to control much of the south of England, with this kingdom gradually absorbing most of England, though its true core remained in Dorset, Wiltshire and Hampshire, with Winchester as its regular royal base. The most notable monarch during this time was Cadwalla (685–688), followed by Ine (688–726), who seems to have had a significant influence on Saxon development. His legal code is the earliest following the Romans to survive, thanks to King Alfred, who updated and promoted it.

Through the 8th century, boundaries continued to change, and Mercia became predominant among the three large kingdoms. In the mid-8th century a dyke had been built to mark the frontier between Mercia and the Welsh tribes beyond. The dyke may have been more a boundary than a defence and the work was continued by King Offa (ruled 757–796), after whom it is now named. It would have been a considerable task both to build and then control this 200–mile (320km) barrier, and it seems likely that it was built as a border warning rather than a defensive structure, but nevertheless it indicates the considerable power and resources of manpower available to Offa.

During the Anglo-Saxon migration and settlement, much of Christianity had been destroyed and neglected. In 597, Augustine, a Roman prior, was sent to Britain by Pope Gregory the Great (540–604, remembered for Gregorian chant) at the request of King Aethelbert of Kent (560–616) to convert his people to Christianity. Augustine became the first archbishop of Canterbury, dying in 604 and controlling religious policy throughout England, from where his monks were able to convert Sussex, Wessex and East Anglia.

At the Synod of Whitby, convened by the King of Northumbria in 664, rival Celtic Christians from the monastery of Iona, accepted the authority of Rome, which Augustine had brought them and agreed to adopt the date of Easter set by Rome, and thenceforth England adhered to the Roman doctrine and not the Celtic one. Much of the history of this period we owe to the Venerable Bede, who wrote "The Ecclesiastical History of the English People" detailing his own times, along with the history of the previous era since the Roman departure in 410.

Viking attacks on the British coastline commenced in 793, killing many monks at the monastery of Lindisfarne in the northeast. Viking prowess with sea exploration owed its accomplishments to the technical perfection of their longboats, which had both oars and sails, as well as to their excellent navigational skills. Initially they appeared simply to be raiders and may have chosen the life of piracy because of adverse climatic conditions in Scandinavia. For the first half of the 9th century, raiding was their modus vivendi, but after 850 many stayed to settle and take over the eastern part of England which became known as known as the Danelaw. They added to the cultural and ethnic melting pot of Britain.

In addition to explorations around the British coast, they also raided the western French coast, around into the Mediterranean as well as making long sea voyages to the Shetland and Faroe Islands, Iceland, Greenland and even as far as Newfoundland in the year 1,000 which they named Vinland. A different group of Vikings migrated south and east from Scandinavia through the Baltic Sea, and by river to the Black Sea, reaching Constantinople where the Byzantine Emperor later recruited them as elite troops (the Varangian Guard). After all these upheavals and population movements western European thought emerged from the dark Ages as Christian rather than Greek or roman.

In the second half of the 9th century, Wessex continued to defend Christianity against the Vikings, and in 871 King Alfred (849–899) inflicted the first decisive defeat on a Viking army. Some years later the Vikings accepted conversion to Christianity, but at the same time appeared determined to stay in the British Isles. Alfred gradually increased his power, becoming the chief of the English kings, so that when he died in 899 he was the sole King of Wessex, and the worst period of Viking raiding was over; his descendants would rule a united country.

To achieve this, Alfred had founded a series of local strongholds, or burghs, as part of his national system of defence. His changes set the pattern for later urbanisation and many towns then initiated still survive and prosper today. Alfred was responsible for the rejuvenation of the English cultural and intellectual heritage; the shire structures were put in place, and boundaries were established which lasted for the next millennium.

The next reign of Alfred's son, Edward the Elder (874–924), was a time of warfare, containment of the Vikings and stabilisation of the country, so it was to be Alfred's grandson, Athelstan (894–939), who would continue to develop and lay down the principles on which the British Isles would develop in succeeding centuries.

Incomplete list of early English monarchs:

King Arthur	probably died 500
Cerdic	ruled 519–534
Aethelbert of Kent	ruled 560–616
Radwald of East Anglia	ruled 599–624
Cadwalla,	ruled 685–688
Ine	ruled 688–726
Offa, King of Mercia	died 796 after a 39–year reign
Egbert, King of Wessex	771–839, ruled 802–839
Alfred, King of England	849–899, ruled from 871–899

Possible further reading:
In search of the Dark Ages by Michael Wood (BBC paperback)
Catastrophe by David Keys (Arrow paperback)
AD 410, The Year that Shook Rome by Sam Moorhead and David Stuttard (British Museum Press)

Chapter 19
Early Africa and Asia

We have already seen that man evolved largely in Africa, and then some early humans migrated out of Africa before the last Ice Age, though other closely related branches of homo have been found and seem to have evolved in other parts of the world before dying out. The climate in the Ice Age was very different to that experienced today, and the equatorial belt across Africa, which now includes the Sahara Desert, was much more temperate, comprising savannah and scrub. Early man lived and hunted in this broad belt of land and has left behind many cave drawings which show the richness of the culture in those early years.

Following the Ice Age, the climate gradually became warmer, and this change, combined with overgrazing by pastoralists, gradually produced the present desert band across Africa which effectively divides northern Africa from southern Africa, so that the north and south have largely developed separately. This extensive swathe of country stretching in a band up to 1,000 km wide from north to south across Africa, and over 5,000 km from east to west coast is known as the Sahel. Domestication of plants and animals here is known from about 5,000 BC with nomadic tribes grazing their flocks through the region. With climatic warming in the two millennia after 4,000 BC, the region became far less habitable and many of the peoples migrated south to more hospitable and productive regions.

If we go back to the beginnings of civilisation in Africa, it is possible to distinguish three different racial groups. The first of these is known as the Hamitic people, who were of Caucasian ancestry deriving from the population of the Middle East, Mesopotamia and Egypt. The second group comprise the ancestors of modern bushmen living south of the Sahara; and the third, or negroid group, were those who became dominant in the central forests and in west Africa. All of these three early peoples exploited Stone Age technology. The negroid population increased in the grasslands between the desert and the equatorial forests south of it.

The first independent African kingdom was that of Kush in the southern reaches of the Nile, where it interfaced with Egypt and was populated by Hamitic people. The Nubian Kingdom on the southern Nile had been absorbed into Egypt, and a Sudanese kingdom to the south of this broke free of Egypt to emerge as the independent kingdom of Kush. By 730 BC Kush was strong enough to conquer Egypt, and several of its kings ruled as Pharaohs until an Assyrian invasion in about 674 BC destroyed the Kush dynasty and its control of Egypt, driving the Kush back south to their capital of Meroe, just north of present day Khartoum, on the middle Nile. They took with them however, the bronze and iron technologies existing in Egypt at that time.

Much later, in about 300 AD, Kush was overthrown by the Ethiopians, who were still trading with the classical Mediterranean world. Ethiopia was converted to Christianity by Copts during the 4th century, but then became isolated. The Copts were a Christian church founded by St Mark not long after the crucifixion in about 42 AD; they subsequently broke away from the main body of the Roman Church at the Council of Chalcedon in 451 AD over disagreements about the exact nature of Christ. Christianity across northern Africa along the Mediterranean coast, was rather weak despite the conversion of the Roman Empire to Christianity. Trade continued along the east coast of Africa, particularly with Arabia and India by sea.

Following this time, and with the Phoenicians vanishing from the scene, interchange with southern Africa became very scanty because of a lack of any Atlantic coastal trade, but also because of the increasing barrier imposed by the Sahel desert belt stretching across the centre of Africa, from modern day Mauritania in the west, to Egypt and Sudan in the east. Camels were introduced into Africa from Asia for transport around 200 AD, but by then the desert had become an almost impassable barrier between north and south.

The continuing development of culture and populations in southern Africa through the first millennium AD, shows the gradual spread of iron technology, which was then used in agriculture. The hunter gatherer bushmen tribes were displaced by farmers and herdsmen moving south, but although their use of iron technology was helpful in clearing forests, it did not extend to the introduction or use of the plough. This lack of an adequate instrument to till the land was perhaps due to the absence of a suitable animal to provide the necessary muscle power.

The enormous area of southern Africa failed to develop in the way that other areas in the world were progressing at this time, and this appears to be partly due to the limitations imposed by geography, climate and disease south of the Sahara.

Bronze, and then iron, technology was probably introduced along the shores of the Mediterranean by the Phoenicians. Some of this technology spread either directly south by land, or alternatively, was spread later by Phoenician sea-going traders, who left the Straits of Gibraltar and continued south around what is now the coast of Morocco and further. We know at this time the Phoenicians were capable sailing beyond the Straits of Gibraltar because they also voyaged north to trade as far away as Cornwall for tin and copper.

In southern Africa, some early iron-using communities are known in association with crop and livestock domestication, but this technology did not spread to the far south where nomadic hunter gatherers with stone tools persisted up to the time of the first European explorations two millennia later and have left very early Stone Age cave paintings.

Northern Africa developed as a series of littoral communities and in antiquity was very fertile. As Rome expanded and urbanised, the north coast of Africa became the bread basket of Italy and Sicily, providing a large and vital supply of grain to Rome and Italy which were no longer capable of growing enough for their own increasing populations. It was subject to the explorations in turn, of the Phoenicians, the Greeks, and then the Romans. Since much of the land and its crops was so prized warfare was not uncommon.

Egypt, on the eastern side of north Africa, developed separately thanks to the unusual benefit and agriculture conferred on it by the River Nile, because this too was a very rich developing farming community, annexed by the Romans in 30 BC for its grain harvests. Thanks to the Greeks, Romans and Egyptians we have written sources for the development of northern Africa, colonised as it was by these three civilisations in turn. During the last millennium BC the inhabitants were largely nomadic pastoralists who tended flocks and raised some cereals. They were displaced firstly by the incoming Phoenicians who founded Carthage (present day Tunis), almost a thousand years before Christ.

The Greeks followed with their trade and sea-based economy, and then in the 3rd century BC Rome challenged the supremacy of Carthage and colonised the south shore of the Mediterranean in order to produce the wheat that was needed to feed the considerable and still growing population back in Rome. Rome later extended its dominion into Egypt, which became a Roman province in 30 BC.

Carthage and the Phoenicians in the 3rd century BC were a source of great annoyance to the Romans. The Phoenicians were very skilled sailors and ship builders, and occupied Sicily, Corsica and Sardinia as well as Carthage and the southern shores of the Mediterranean. Eventually with newly developed naval skills, the Romans were able to defeat Carthage in the prolonged First Punic War (264–241 BC), driving the Carthaginians out of Sicily, Corsica and Sardinia in turn. In the Second Punic War (218–201 BC) the Carthaginians fought back and invaded Rome from the north with their General, Hannibal, bringing his army, including war elephants, from Spain over the Alps and into Italy.

In this second Punic War, there were two great victories for Hannibal at Lake Trasimene in Northern Italy in 217 BC, and then at Cannae on the eastern coast further south in 216 BC. Despite these great victories, Hannibal did not possess sufficient troops to carry on and conquer Rome itself, and after much fighting across the Italian peninsula over a period of fifteen years he was finally defeated at the Battle of Zama after retreating to North Africa close to Carthage in 202 BC, which ended the war.

Subsequently, Cato (234–149 BC), the distinguished Roman senator and historian, began agitating in the middle of the next century that Carthage should be destroyed. By then, Spain was largely under the control of Rome, together with most of southern France, so that all the northern shores of the Mediterranean from Gibraltar through to the Dardanelles, were under Roman rule. The Third Punic War, intended by the Romans to teach the Carthaginians a real lesson, started in 149 BC, and three years later the city was not just simply destroyed, but was razed to the ground with all its inhabitants being either slaughtered or sold into slavery. The site was cleared, and a new Roman province created. The

Romans named this province Africa, and it included what we know today as Tunisia, Libya and part of Algeria. It was to be a vital source of food imports to the Roman Empire for the next few hundred years.

Apart from the coastal regions, African civilisations arose south of the Sahara in Ghana (modern Senegal), Hausa to the east of the Niger River and around Lake Chad, and much further to the south, Zimbabwe; details are sparse and shadowy due to lack of recorded history. Stone Age settlements in west Africa are shown in the prehistoric cave art of the western Sahara and much later there was a flourishing trade in gold, copper, salt and slaves by the 6th and 7th centuries AD, sent north from the preliterate Empire of Mali. All these civilisations were radically altered when Muslims from Arabia swept across the north of Africa in the 8th and 9th centuries AD, then spilling down the west coast of Africa to tap the valuable trade from the gold and salt mines, together with the trade in slaves.

Arabic Islam had started to spread westwards across North Africa around 640 AD following the death of Mohammed, with Carthage being taken at the end of the century, and an Arab army crossing the Straits of Gibraltar to Spain in 711 AD. Thus the northern coastal countries of Africa, together with the eastern lands south of the Sahara as far as modern Ghana became Islamic by the end of the first millennium.

The period from the millennium to 1500 saw continuing spread of Islam across Africa alongside the establishment of organised states in much of the continent. It is from the writings of Muslim travellers that we owe much of our historical information about preliterate Africa, because kingdoms along the north coast, and in west Africa had become Muslim by the end of the first millennium, some three or four centuries after Mohammed died, and after the Muslim armies spread rapidly across the north of the continent. Several large loose civilisations had grown up long before this, and Ghana (modern day Senegal) was an important early kingdom, or empire, from the 8th century on, trading gold, salt and slaves north across the Sahara.

This trade across the Sahara had grown gradually since the 6th century providing wealth and the reverse transfer of metal technology and Muslim faith that slowly improved the overall standards of the early African empires. Initially, it seems that prisoners taken, as the empires waxed and waned fighting each other, were simply killed, until it became apparent around the millennium that they were a valuable commodity to trade alongside the gold and salt. The ancient kingdom of Ghana collapsed over the 12th and 13th centuries, to be replaced by the Mali Empire centred on the middle reaches of the River Niger, which was a recognisable entity from about 1230, again existing on the prosperity of trans-Saharan trade, and including the important Islamic centre of Timbuktu with impressive Muslim libraries and teaching.

Mali was in turn conquered by Morocco some centuries later. Islam spread south around the western end of the Saharan in the 11th century with Timbuktu becoming an important Islamic site and university in the 15th century as well as being at the crossroads of African trade, which had built up with the spread of

Islam. Many tribal agglomerations coalesced and then broke up during the two millennia from about 500 BC up to mediaeval times with constant warfare and raiding, sometimes throwing up powerful and charismatic tribal chiefs who were able to control large areas. The Ashanti empire appeared on the coast around 1700 to become an important trading and colonial land, gradually morphing into present day Ghana, which has no relationship, either geographically or politically to the ancient empire of the same name.

On the other side of the continent, journeying south along the eastern African coast, a string of trading posts grew up, exchanging not only gold and slaves to the north, but also ivory and spices. The coastal trade was carried on northwards to Arabia, Egypt and as far as India. The gold came from Zimbabwe, which was a thriving centre of the Shona tribe from the 11th to the 15th century; the gold was carried to the port of Kilwa Kisiwani (in modern day Tanzania) for shipping north. Great Zimbabwe, the remains of a stone citadel and surrounding town, was already in ruins when the first historical mention of it comes from a Portuguese sailor in 1531.

---oOo---

Much further to the east, and also fairly isolated geographically, similar kingdoms and empires were waxing and waning in Southeast Asia. These kingdoms were ethnically and religiously diverse with autocratic rulers and were never restricted by European-type parliaments or inclusive governments. They were land based with minimal coastal trade, though the great rivers were used as highways for travel and trade. They tended to incorporate conquered people into their societies without recourse to slavery. They boasted the largest capital cities of their time, certainly larger than contemporary European major urban sites, and they were centres of arts, craft and culture.

The Khmer empire (no connection to the murderous modern regime calling itself Khmer Rouge) is the best known, extending across present day Thailand, Cambodia, Laos, Vietnam and Myanmar, details have come to us from temple carvings and inscriptions in Sanskrit, as well as accounts from Indian and Chinese travellers. The empire is known from the early 7th century, but formally existed from 802, when King Jayavarman II declared himself supreme ruler of the world. Buddhism was the prevailing religion with numerous extensive temples, including the celebrated complex at Angkor Wat.

Rice farming and fishing sustained most of the population with well organised irrigation systems. Inter-tribal warfare was endemic, but the empire also suffered from severe clouds of volcanic ash falling on the land in the 9th century, and invasion by the Mongols at the end of the 13th century. It collapsed during the 15th and 16th centuries for unknown reasons, though the Black Death may have played a large part in this.

Other Asian empires are covered with China in chapter 8, the Mongols in chapter 28 and the Mughals in chapter 61.

Possible further reading:
The Lost Kingdoms of Africa by Gus Casely-Hayford (BBC Paperback)

Chapter 20
Arabia and Islam

When modern humans first left Africa, they would have done so either across the Straits at the southern end of the Red Sea at a time when sea levels were very low and the sea crossing would have been short, or across the land bridge at the northern end of the Red Sea where the Suez Canal now lies. The vast bulk of the Arabian Peninsula is desert inland, and these early people would have lived and migrated along the coast, particularly the south coast of the peninsula through what is now Yemen and Oman. The migration would have continued slowly, but some people would have set up coastal communities and stayed to subsist on fishing and coastal agriculture. Inland, much of the peninsula became inhabited by nomadic tribes grazing their flocks of sheep and camels between oases.

In the first half of the first millennium AD, Rome was at the zenith of its powers until, starting in 410 when the legions were recalled from the frontier regions including Britain, through to 475 when Romulus Augustulus, the last western Emperor of Rome, abandoned imperial Roman pretentions to the incoming Barbarians. The western Roman Empire and Church simply crumbled while that of Byzantium was left to sustain the continuing antagonism and warfare with Persia, which had been grumbling on for the previous five centuries, and which had severely bled the Roman Empire financially.

East of Byzantium, the Persian Empire had been feuding with their Roman neighbours to the west for the previous half century, whilst in between the two lay Mesopotamia, the Syrian desert and the inhospitable Arabian Peninsula comprising largely desert. Up till then the Arabs had been happy to live in this inhospitable buffer zone, frequently raiding to the east or west. Arabia remained important to the Romans to the west and the Persians to the east because of the trade routes to India, and even as far as China.

Because of the desert and raiding Arab tribes, and despite the difficulties of navigating treacherous reefs in the Persian Gulf and the Red Sea on either side of the Arabian Peninsula, not to mention frequent activity by pirates, much trade from India came by sea and was transferred at Aden to be taken north along the coast of the Red Sea through Mecca by caravan. This all meant relative wealth for Yemen on the south coast of Arabia, and the Yemeni Arabs were acknowledged as the leading and wealthiest Arab tribe through the early centuries AD. Apart from merchant caravans their livelihood came from raiding each other, as well as the frontier regions of the Roman and Persian empires to the west and east.

Yemen in particular, came to support a large urban community that traded along the coast, across to Africa, and as far away as India. A large and isolated community built up with stone temples and palaces, and with irrigation systems coming from dams and reservoirs in the hills. The great dam at Marib collapsed in 540 under the pressure of a major flood. The irrigation system that it fed through hundreds of miles of canals supplied a complex of 24,000 acres and a population of perhaps forty thousand people. The collapse of the dam appears related to the chaotic climate of the middle 6th century, which was also manifest as the European Dark Ages.

In addition, plague affected Yemen at this time, and the Koran tells us that large numbers of people were forced to leave the area due to the loss of irrigated agricultural land; two tribes migrated north to the Medina oasis. Thereafter Yemen, which had been the largest centre of civilisation in Arabia, diminished enormously. Inland centres had been increasing in importance, including Medina and Mecca, where there was an important shrine called the Ka'aba (a large black meteoric stone) guarded by the Quraysh tribe. Trade caravans passed through these centres, accounting for their continuing wealth and vitality.

Within the Christian church, Nestorius (386–450), Archbishop of Constantinople, who promoted a new interpretation of the incarnation, had been condemned by fellow Christians at the Council of Ephesus in 431, following which he and many of his followers were persecuted, many fleeing to Persia where they were welcomed. Only a few years later Eutyches (380–456), a fellow Constantinople cleric holding opposing views to Nestorius, was condemned by the Council of Chalcedon for advocating a different version of Christ's divinity, whilst the Orthodox Church believed that Jesus was part divine and part human.

Eutyches' teaching converted many Christians to the 'monophysite' way of thinking, believing that Christ and God were essentially one single individual, rather than two separate entities. At the same time in Arabia the Arabs along the border with the Byzantine Empire were stirred into a state of semi rebellion and anarchy against their Byzantine neighbours, while the Arabs along the Euphrates River were fomenting discontent against their Persian overlords.

Into this climatic and religious turmoil Mohammed was born, probably in 570, into the Quraysh tribe. All the period before the birth of Mohammed is known to Muslims as "The Ignorance", referring to religious ignorance rather than to the political and cultural attitudes of the time. Already the Arabian tribes were warring with each other, and fighting for survival in the unfriendly terrain of the Arabian Peninsula. The large black stone at Mecca, the Ka'aba, had been important to the Arabs for many years. There was worship of multiple gods by the Arabs, and there were also small Jewish and Christian communities dotted throughout Arabia.

Mohammed married a wealthy Qurayshi widow, whose riches derived from the mercantile caravans. Later in life, shortly after he became 40, he started receiving revelations in dreams. Mohammed was in the habit of retiring into the desert for a few days at a time to meditate. He would have been well aware of the fundamental beliefs and stories told by Jewish and Christian believers, many of whom lived scattered around the Arabian Peninsula. He would sleep in a cave, and one night dreamt that he was visited by the Archangel Gabriel who gave him instructions to preach and recite his faith.

Mohammed called his new teaching the Religion of Abraham, feeling that the revelations of Abraham had been distorted by the Israelites, and that Jesus had then been sent by God to restore the true faith. Subsequently he felt that Christian beliefs had, in turn, been adulterated so that God was now commanding Mohammed to restore the purity of his religion. The evolving Muslim religion drew significantly on pre-existing Jewish and Christian ideas with modifications and additions, often including many proscriptive instructions for the faithful.

Amongst the instructions from God in his dreams was the promise to all those who fell in battle against unbelievers, of immediate admission to Paradise: this promise to members of warring tribes has formed a potent incentive ever since for armed conflict against infidels for all subsequent generations of Muslims. After Mohammed started preaching his followers slowly grew in number but he managed to alienate the rest of the merchant class in Mecca, attracting their increasing persecution, and therefore he was forced to emigrate from Mecca to Medina three hundred miles away.

This migration known as the 'Hegira', occurred in June 622, and shortly afterwards occurs the date used for the beginning of the Muslim calendar and the Islamic era. In Medina, Mohammed organised his supporters into a community along with his Medina hosts.

Mohammed's convictions and beliefs were slowly taken up by the Arabs in central Arabia. For the last two or three years of his life most of the Arab tribes were paying tax to the Muslims in Medina. Mohammed died in 632 and was succeeded by his father-in-law Abu Bakr. The period which followed Mohammed's death is known as the 'Apostasy', during which time Muslim bands of Mohammed's followers raided and made war throughout the Arabian Peninsula, finally subjugating all the tribes of the peninsula so that Arabic political and religious power came to be concentrated together under the leadership of the new Muslim religion.

Once the tribes were subdued and united, the period of the Apostasy ended. Abu Bakr later achieved this submission of the Arab tribes in southern Arabia and southern Palestine over two years, and then the Arab expansion and conquest began. The causes of this vast aggression appear to have been partly the warlike attitude and traditional behaviour of the Arabs, who were now forbidden by the Faith from fighting each other, whilst at the same time, their traditional enemies, the Persians to the east and the Byzantine Emperor to the west, were weakened. Both Byzantium and the Persians, had abolished their local Arab dynasties of rulers, and were attempting to rule their frontier provinces directly.

In addition to this, the Roman Emperor Heraclius (575–641) in Constantinople had withdrawn subsidies formerly paid to the frontier tribes. As well as all this, both Persian and Byzantine empires were financially and morally weakened following three decades of war between them. It is not clear what instruction or incentive sparked off an internal conquest of Arabia, but during the second decade of his preaching Mohammed claimed that God, via the Archangel, now commanded Muslims to fight unbelievers. In 624 Mohammed, with a band of some 300 men, had set out to intercept a wealthy mercantile caravan coming from the north.

A much larger force came from Mecca to the south, and battle resulted at Bedr. Despite the numerical odds against them, Mohammed and his supporters triumphed. About a year later, a raiding band from Mecca set out to avenge the battle of Bedr and a further battle at Uaud ensued against greater numerical odds in which Mohammed was wounded. Despite the defeat at Uaud, Mohammed spent the next year raiding other tribes, thereby hoping to convince the tribes that it was better to ally themselves with him than with the remaining Quraysh tribe in Mecca.

One of Mohammed's dreams instructed him to recite in the name of the Lord, and for more than the next century, recitation of Mohammed's revelations and teachings were passed down from one generation to the next by word of mouth. Mohammed believed there was a single God whose message he was conveying to his people, and that although there had been prophets before him, of both Christian and Jewish faiths, he himself was the final prophet. In 630, his influence had become sufficiently strong that he was able to return to Mecca and destroy all the idols of other gods from the Ka'aba, leaving the black stone itself alone. Mohammed died in 632, but the Arab tradition of warfare persisted, though most if it was now externalised rather than occurring between the tribes.

Within two decades of Mohammed's death, Persia had been overrun, and Muslim forces were extending into India and modern Afghanistan. At the same time, Arab forces crossed into Egypt, occupying Alexandria in 643, and advancing along the northern African coast to reach the Straits of Gibraltar around 700. The Straits of Gibraltar were crossed in 711, with the southern part of Spain coming under Muslim rule thereafter. The conquest in the two centuries following Mohammed's death extended into the countries of the Middle East, including the ancient centre of worship at Jerusalem, and this expansion was due to missionary activity, as well as traders and the Arabic armies.

It has been suggested that the rapid advance of Muslim armies was expedited by the climatic conditions of the time as records show that the century before Mohammed's death was unusually cold with poor harvests and spread of the plague, following a rather slow and long recovery from the onset of the Dark Age; this could have been debilitating to urban populations while having less effect on small nomadic tribes who could have been much less susceptible to famine and epidemics of disease.

The Roman Empire was diminishing in strength, and Arabic coalesced into a single language and a single coinage as its strength and coherence developed fast. The Muslim faithful believed in the slaughter of infidel populations, including their domestic animals, thus purging and purifying the cities that they conquered.

Considering the rapid expansion of Islam through the 7th and 8th centuries, remarkably little was adequately documented. With previous civilisations we have documentary evidence that has come down to us from the Middle East, from Greece and from Rome. Only in the case of the Phoenicians do we have equally little contemporary writings to help us judge. It remains surprising that there is no real body of written contemporary evidence either about Mohammed and his lifetime, or about the Islamic expansion and conquests over the two centuries following Mohammed's death.

All that has been written about Mohammed, and the early days of Islam, was put down in writing well over a century later, and in accordance with Mohammed's instructions to recite, most of his teachings were passed from one generation to the next by word of mouth, though some contemporary collections of Mohammed's teachings do seem to have been written down. Contemporary Arabs have not left any good records of descriptions of their battles and victories, and even the Koran itself evolved and did not fully materialise in its final written form for some two hundred years after Mohammed's death. At that time, Muslim scholars attempted to collect and identify the sayings of the Prophet in order to record and organise these truths, sayings or 'Hadiths'. Muhammed Al-Bukhari (810–870) was a revered Persian Islamic scholar who travelled extensively throughout his life and collected hundreds of thousands of Hadiths but published only about 7,000 of them which he felt were adequately tested to be judged genuine. Many of the Hadiths were dismissed since the conclusion must have been that they had suffered the fate of 'chinese whispers', becoming multiply altered and evolving with time.

It remains remarkable that the conquests achieved by the Arabs through the 7th and 8th centuries, which imply considerable organisation and the centralisation of powers and direction, has left us with no good contemporary account or understanding of how this was achieved. In consequence we have no knowledge of how the different prongs of the Islamic invasion were coordinated, or indeed may have been totally separate entities.

When Mohammed died in 632, the old Arab warring tendencies came to the surface again. Mohammed was succeeded by Abu Bakr, one of his fathers-in-law (Mohammed had four wives), who was elected caliph, a post implying complete religious authority, but without the gift of prophesy. Abu Bakr died at the age of 61, only two years after Mohammed, but during this time imposed his authority on the Arabs by military campaigning to conquer neighbouring tribes, known as the Ridda Wars.

Following him in succession came another father-in-law of the Prophet called Umar who gave rise to the Umayyad caliphate later, his ten year caliphate ended with considerable Muslim extension north into the Byzantine empire, and the military conquest of much of the Persian empire; he was assassinated while leading prayers and is revered by present day Sunni Muslims. The next twelve years saw Mohammed's son-in-law Uthman succeed as caliph at the age of 67, under his leadership military conquests extended the empire into Persia (present day Iran) and Afghanistan until he was assassinated in 656.

Finally, another son-in-law, Ali Ibn Abi Talib became caliph and oversaw more military campaigns until he too was assassinated in 661. Between the four of them, these early caliphs guided Islam for the thirty years following Mohammed's death and are endorsed by the Sunni branch of the Muslim faith; they are known as the Rashidun caliphs. However, Ali is seen by Shia Muslims as the first true caliph to succeed Mohammed, because he was supposedly named by Mohammed as his successor: after his murder in 661 and a series of wars, the Islamic world divided in two, with the Umayyads (descendants of Umar) forming a second Caliphate, based in Damascus in Syria. Later, a third caliphate, the Abbasids who followed, was set up in Baghdad in 750 after an extensive civil war and after all the remaining Umayyads had been murdered; it lasted five centuries, up to the middle of the 13th century.

It seems that all religions have tended to fragment as each successive generation throws up individuals who wish to improve or modify the founding principles, or who simply wish to assume absolute power, and the Muslim religion has been no exception. The word Islam means submission to the will of Allah, and the initial years, first under Mohammed and then his close family, were concerned with channelling the energies of the warring tribes along a path of conquest together, but three of his four early successors succumbed to this warring tradition and were ultimately murdered.

The speed, and spread in extent, of the new empire under the early Caliphs' rule was remarkable. But these early years have left Islam with two major sects and more smaller ones. The divisions concern the succession to Mohammed, with Shias believing that the Caliph should be an Imam chosen by God and therefore a descendant of Mohammed, while Sunnis believe Caliphs should be elected by fellow Muslims.

Many early battles allowed the Muslim armies to forge north towards Iraq and Syria and two early victories were vital; the first of these was the Battle of the River Yarmouk in 636, just south of the sea of Galilee where the Roman Emperor's brother was heavily defeated by a smaller Arab army, thus putting an end to the Roman defences; while the second was the battle of Qadisiyyah, in the same year near the Euphrates River where the Persian army was decimated along with many nobles and high-ranking officers effectively allowing the Muslims to continue their progress towards conquering the Persian empire.

Islam spread along the coast of North Africa, took Carthage and arrived opposite Gibraltar in the early 8th century. In 711, an Arab commander, named Tariq, crossed to Gibraltar and advanced through southern Spain (Tariq is remembered in the name of Gibraltar, which means Jebel Tariq, jebel being the Arabic for mountain), which at that time was a Visigoth kingdom with its capital at Toledo. Twenty years later the Muslim armies had advanced deep into southern France, where their lines of supply had become over stretched and thinned over a considerable distance.

They were defeated by the defending Franks under Charles Martel (688–741, grandfather of Charlemagne) at the Battle of Tours in 732, and then pushed back into northern Spain, but left in possession of the whole of the Iberian Peninsula, then known as Al-Andalus (chapter 22). Muslim occupation of Spain and Portugal are the only two geographic areas where Muslim conquests have been reversed as the crusades failed to return the Middle East to Christianity in later centuries.

On the eastern front the Arab armies were stopped at Constantinople, and in the mountains of Azerbaijan in the Caucasus; the Islamic Empire would stop at these barriers. The Arabs had been lucky in expanding into lands where people were dissatisfied and oppressed by their rulers; they were driven on by the certainty that they were doing the work of God, and by the promise of Mohammed that death in battle against infidels would result in the certainty of achieving Paradise.

Thus, the Caliphates of the Quraysh, the tribe into which Mohammed was born, had split off a dissident group known as Shiites, and the Umayyad caliphate had given way to a further group of dissidents, now known as Sunni. The further split occurred in 750, when a new Caliph, Abu Al Abas, seized power in Iraq at the Battle of the River Zab and murdered the last Umayyad Caliph and his close family and followers.

The Abbasid Caliphate then ruled the Arab world from Baghdad for the next five hundred years. Opposition was not tolerated, and many executions were seen. Baghdad became rich again, both on the commerce passing along the caravan routes, and from taxing the indigenous peoples in the newly conquered eastern Islamic Empire. Arabic became the predominant language of the Middle East for scholars and aristocrats.

Possible further reading:
In the Shadow of the Sword by Tom Holland (Abacus paperback)
The Great Arab Conquests by John Bagot Glubb (Quartet Books)

Chapter 21
Early Islam and Arab Thinkers

Mohammed died in 632 and his relatives by marriage or blood provided the four Caliphs of the Rashidun caliphate following his death, The first three of these caliphs were elected by a shura or council; only Ali, the 4th Caliph could claim a blood tie with Mohammed as his cousin, and in consequence Shia Muslims regard him as the only genuine Rashidun Caliph. Abu Bakr, the first caliph was a close companion of the Prophet but died only two years after him.

Umar, the second Caliph was also one of Mohammed's companions and was assassinated after a decade of successful military campaigning and battles. Uthman, the third Caliph who reigned from 644–656, was married to first one of the Prophet's daughters, and then to another daughter after she died; he was able to stabilise the Umayyad regime before he was assassinated. The 4th Rashidun Caliph, Ali lived through a period of instability and Muslim civil war before he too was assassinated in 661 after a five-year rule.

The next Caliph, Hasan, was a grandson of the Prophet and commenced the Umayyad Caliphate but abdicated after only a few months to be followed by Muawiya, the Governor of Syria, who then ruled for almost two decades. A second civil war from 680 to 692 followed his death in 680 after which four Caliphs ruled in quick succession until Abd al-Malik ibn Marwan became Caliph and ruled for a steadying twenty years through to 705.

A Berber revolt from 740–743 split the Caliphate and resulted both in the collapse of the weakened Umayyad Caliphate, and in a number of small states splintering off along the North African coast; one branch of the Umayyad family fled to Al-Andalus (modern Spain) where they managed to set up an independent Caliphate which survived for the next 300 years. The Umayyad tribe was defeated in battle in 750 and following this the rest of the tribe were sought out and murdered, with the Abbasid tribe taking over the Caliphate; they were descended from Abbas ibn Abd al Muttalib (568–653), an uncle of Mohammed (despite being only three years older than the prophet), from whom they took the name Abbasid.

Following the murder of the entire Umayyad clan in 750 (except for the small branch who escaped to set up Al-Andalus in Spain ruled by Caliph Abd al-Rahman I from 756–788), the Caliphs were drawn from the Abbasids, and the capital of Islam was moved to Baghdad and confirmed in the Sunni branch of the faith. Shia disaffection inevitably followed, but opposition was ruthlessly suppressed. Provincial administration became hereditary, and more powerful, while the Abbasid Caliphate at the centre exercised only loose control. This Sunni versus Shia division has persisted ever since with the majority Sunnis believing that the Caliph should be elected, while Shias believe the Caliph should be a direct descendant of the Prophet, and even within Shia ranks there are more subdivisions of thought and opinion.

Considerable wealth built up within the Abbasid Caliphate thanks to religious cohesion and relative peace. Trade and caravan routes became very active again. Many existing ideas of previous Jewish, Zoroastrian, Hindu, Greek and Christian cultures were assimilated into Arabic Muslim culture. This evolving Arabic culture took over from the previous Roman thinking with its continuing debt to the writers of Ancient Greece from before Roman times.

The Islamic Empire had extended further east into Persia and north-western India than any Greek or Roman influence, and it was therefore freshened and given new life by the assimilation of Zoroastrian and Hindu ideas from these other two ancient cultures. Literature, mainly from ancient Greece rather than from Roman times, was transcribed into Arabic, which became the current common language throughout southern Europe and the Middle East for a period of some three centuries. Schooling and literacy under the Abbasids were better than in contemporary Europe, and were available on a more widespread basis.

To look back a little, we need to return to Plato, philosopher and pupil of Socrates, the first major independent thinker of whom we are aware. He lived from 428–347 BC, and wrote his seminal work, 'Mathematica', during this time. In turn, Aristotle was a pupil of Plato, and became the teacher and tutor of Alexander the Great. Aristotle was also a philosopher and a great polymath who lived from 384–322 BC and continued to have an influence on Jewish and Islamic thinking through the early years of the first millennium and into the Middle Ages, together with a continuing influence on later Christian theology. He was known to early Islamic scholars as 'The First Teacher'.

A little later and separately, the Greek mathematician Euclid (330–270 BC) lived and wrote in Alexandria, providing an early and solid basis for mathematics, after the earlier writings of Pythagoras (570–495 BC). From the Roman culture, Galen of Pergamum was a Roman physician and philosopher (129–217 AD). His ideas on anatomy remained unchallenged until the time of Vesalius in 1543, and his concept of physiology and function in human and mammalian bodies was not challenged until Harvey described the circulation of the blood in 1628, though in both spheres of knowledge his teachings were suppositional and took no account of hard evidence or experiment; this lack of factual background would only give way more than a millennium later, to the evidence-based findings of the European enlightenment.

All of these early thinkers had a great influence on Arab thinking. The giants amongst them include Avicenna and Averroes. Avicenna was a physician, philosopher and chemist, living in Baghdad (980–1037) and reputed to have written over two hundred books in his life, some of which remain extant today. Averroes (1126–1198) was born and lived in Cordoba in Al-Andalus, studying and writing widely across many disciplines from philosophy to law, politics, medicine and astronomy. Arabic thought and teaching were widespread, with Avicenna moving around the eastern Muslim provinces beyond Baghdad.

Albucasis (936–1013), another noted physician and early surgeon, lived in Cordoba, and left a thirty volume encyclopaedia of contemporary medicine and surgery, including descriptions of surgical procedures and instruments which he devised to perform this surgery. Ibin Zuhr (1094–1162) was a physician and philosopher living in Seville who demonstrates the broad geographical spread and independence of Arab thinking.

During this early period of the Abbasid caliphates, Al-Andalus, or Islamic Iberia, lasted from 711 until 1492, when the European fight back against Muslim occupation was completed. The capital and intellectual powerhouse of Al-Andalus was at Cordoba; the rest of Spain was divided into provinces. Cordoba itself fell to Europeans in 1236, leaving only the province of Granada to succumb 250 years later. Under the Abbasid caliphate slavery was permitted.

Five Pillars of Sunni Islam for the conduct of the Faithful were advocated; firstly, Shahadah – the concept of "Muslim life" or that no other god should be tolerated; secondly Salah, or prayer, this was ordained to be performed five times a day. The third pillar is Zakat, concern for the needy, alongside the concept that 2.5% of one's income should be given to the poor or needy; Zakat was also interpreted as the generosity of freeing a slave. The fourth pillar specifies Sawru, or self-purification and fasting as exemplified by Ramadan. The final pillar is the Hajj, a pilgrimage to Mecca, which was to be attempted at least once in a lifetime by all Muslims.

The Abbasid caliphate lasted from 750 to 1258, when the Mongols invaded and conquered Baghdad. Up until then this golden age of Islam was characterised by the development of artistic culture, including calligraphy, painting, glass, ceramics and carpets by artisans throughout the Islamic empire. Calligraphy concentrated on patterns rather than figures of animals or people, which some felt to be idolatrous, although in the early years of Islam there is quite frequent portrayal of animals or people.

The patterns often included Koranic verses. Because painting in early times, and still to the present day, tended to avoid people or animals, seeing this as forbidden by the Koran, art has been concentrated on botanical subjects and patterns and has since become known as Arabesque painting. Glass making became very sophisticated and continued the development of manufacturing and trading which had previously often been carried out by Jews. Glass making had been common through Persia, Syria and Egypt, but ended with the Mongol invasion of 1258–60, under Hulagu Khan, grandson of Genghis Khan, when most of the glassworkers were enslaved and repatriated to the Mongol empire.

Later, in 1400, the Mongol Emperor Timur captured and enslaved the remaining glassmakers who were taken to Samarkand, leaving the Middle East bereft of quality glass making for a while, but over the succeeding years the little kingdom of Venice moved to fill this production gap. Ceramics, including pottery and tiles, were developed in parallel with glassware, with which they share much in terms of manufacturing processes. The techniques of Roman Byzantium were further developed, and a lot of mosaics were used in grand buildings. Rugs and carpets have enjoyed a long tradition of manufacture in the Middle East, particularly in rural villages and small towns rather than in cities. Gold and silver work seems to have been prohibited by the Hadiths within the Muslim religion, particularly the wearing of gold rings.

Through the 13th and 14th centuries, Islam became suspicious of science and in consequence, madrassas concentrated all their teaching on the Koran. The decimal system, which had originated in India, spread into the Arab world where it was popularised, particularly by the Persian mathematician Al-Kwarizhra. It was later introduced into Europe in the 12th century by Peter Abelard, a French scholar and theologian (1079–1142). Islamic culture declined, particularly after the Mongol conquest of Baghdad in 1258 (chapter 28), and other factors came into play at this time; included in these was the destruction of madrassas by the Mongols to stop the teaching of the Koran, the stifling of independent thought, known as Ijtihad by the invaders, and of course the crusades. Genghis Khan had destroyed the eastern part of the Islamic Empire around 1222. Hulagu Khan, his grandson, then destroyed Baghdad in 1258, this destruction involved considerable massacres of people, together with destruction of libraries and major civic buildings and centres of learning.

The Dome of the Rock, also known as the Al Aqsa Mosque, on Temple Mount in Jerusalem, was the start of a new architectural tradition and was built in the early years of the Umayyad Caliphate, but the site had a long tradition of worship even before then. The Jews under King Solomon had initially built a temple there around the year 957 BC which was destroyed by the Babylonians in 580 BC. A second temple was built in 516 BC, but was again destroyed, this time by the Romans when they crushed a Jewish revolt after four years of rebellion in 70 AD.

Attempts at further rebuilding failed so that the site was next used in the early Umayyad caliphate in the middle 7th century when a large and impressive mosque was built, which has now become in recent years, a major bone of contention between the three large monotheistic religions. To the Jews initially, this was the place where Abraham offered the sacrifice of his son Isaac to God. The same implications were also taken on by Christians, who also believed that it was the site of the Temple of Solomon. It is the third holiest site in Islam after Mecca and Medina, and believed by Muslims to be the place where Mohammed was summoned one night and taken to heaven by the Archangel Gabriel, to converse and accept instructions from God for the Muslim faith.

Mohammed's night journey to heaven from Jerusalem is regarded as a miracle by Muslims. Mohammed is reputed to have travelled from his home on his holy equine steed, Buraq, from hundreds of miles away. He was taken to heaven by the archangel Gabriel and ascended in sequence up through the different layers of heaven until achieving the 7th heaven, where he was given commandments by God, which he then took back to the faithful waiting on Earth below. There is discussion amongst scholars as to whether this miracle is to be taken literally, or whether it is to be interpreted as one of Mohammed's dreams in which he was frequently given religious insights or instructions. Over succeeding centuries the Al Aqsa Mosque was alternately damaged and rebuilt such that the present structure was completed in 1033.

Islam has borrowed a lot from preceding Jewish and Christian thought and follows the habit of worship initiated by Mohammed in his own house at Medina, with a Mihrab, or alcove, in the wall of the building, indicating the direction of Mecca. While many cultural achievements were steadily developed, including Arab music, dance, singing and poetry, the missing elements appear to be theatre and the absence of figurative art. During the Golden Age of Islam, in the 9th and 10th centuries, there was a flowering of culture within the Islamic world, which at the same time sowed the seeds of its later gradual artistic deterioration.

Islam was different from the Jewish and Christian civilisations that had preceded it, in that state and religion were indivisible with political decisions being made by the high religious authority according to the precepts of the Islamic faith. In the early years Islam was still coming to terms with its Jewish and Christian predecessors and some contemporary observers looked upon their Muslim contemporaries as Jews, noting that they claimed to worship the single God of the Old Testament, while denying that Christ was the son of God. Others thought that Islam was simply a Christian heresy since great respect was given to Mary and the virgin birth. The other Islamic concept noted at the time was the emphasis given to spreading the word of the faith by the sword and by military conquest.

The recruitment of native peoples into positions of authority and responsibility within Islam, and the lack of adequate central control, resulted in slow fragmentation becoming inevitable across the whole Islamic world. Although the Mongol invasions of the 13th century and the sacking of Baghdad appeared at the time to be fatal blows to Islam, it has continued to grow, spreading into the Mongol culture after the 13th century and eastwards eventually to China. In the 15th and 16th centuries spread to the Far East across the Indian Ocean and to Malaysia and Indonesia would follow, but in spite of this expansion, nationalistic disunity and many different existing strands of the faith still prevail, particularly between Sunni and Shia, so that the unity of Islam remains only a distant dream.

Possible further reading:
Out of Arabia by Warwick Bell (East & West Publishing)

Chapter 22
The Late Dark Ages in Britain and France

The Late Dark Ages in Britain are considered to start in 849 with the birth of King Alfred at Wantage, when good records start to appear. It was at this time that the Vikings (chapter 23) first started to overwinter in England rather than simply raid through the summer months. At the young age of five Alfred had been taken to Rome by his father Aethelwulf, King of the West Saxons. There he had an audience with the Pope who consecrated Alfred as King, and as his spiritual son. Alfred was inspired by this with a sense of destiny and by the example of the ancient Roman culture and values. Thereafter his early years were concerned with learning the techniques and tactics of battle, which were to stand him in good stead in his later years.

The first major military engagement where we hear of Alfred was the Battle of Ashdown in 870, next to the Iron Age Ridgeway on the Berkshire Downs, where Alfred and his elder brother King Aethelred (847–871) faced and defeated a Viking army. Unfortunately, further battles were less successful for Alfred and his brother; defeat was frequent over the next year, with Aethelred himself dying in 871. Alfred, as the youngest and the only other of Aethelwulf's five sons to have proved himself in battle, was then elected King of England at the age of 22.

The Viking battle victories continued, and by 876 the Danish Viking army, under King Guthrum, seemed determined to conquer Wessex. Guthrum raided through the south of England and across Dorset west as far as Exeter, returning to overwinter in Gloucester in 877. In New Year 878, Guthrum captured Chippenham, where Alfred had stores intended for his West Saxon army. It was at this time that Alfred had to retreat to the Somerset Levels, rallying his forces at Athelney, where they were protected by the surrounding marshes. Guthrum probably felt that he had Alfred bottled up in a tiny isolated stronghold with a very small and inadequate band of warriors.

In the spring of 878, a further Viking army, which had overwintered in South Wales, sailed across to the North Devon coast to threaten Alfred, but he faced this army in battle at Countisbury Hill and this second Viking force was decimated, leaving Alfred able to confront Guthrum on a single front. Guthrum by now was camped on Salisbury Plain, while Alfred was rallying men from across the south-west of England.

In May 878, Alfred and Guthrum met in battle below the Ridgeway at Edington. Guthrum's forces were badly beaten and he retreated to his fortress in Chippenham, where they were besieged for the next couple of weeks before surrendering. Surprisingly Alfred did not insist on humiliating or executing his old enemy, but eventually took him back to Athelney, where he was baptised into Christianity. Alfred clearly recognised that the Vikings were determined to stay and settle in Britain, and decided that having them on his side would be a better option than continuing indefinite war. After Edington and Athelney, the Viking army left Wessex, moving back to East Anglia.

A few years later, Alfred signed a treaty in which he recognised the partition of England between the north-eastern Danelaw and the south-western Wessex, where his rule was solid. Alfred proceeded to develop the farming and trading abilities of Wessex, laying the basis for a recovery of town life and trade, thereby increasing the wealth of all the community and the contribution of tax to the monarchy. Provincial towns were selected and planned with fortified ramparts according to Alfred's directions, becoming known as burghs. London itself was taken over by Alfred in 886 after he had been acknowledged by popular acclamation as King of all the English, and the London city walls were then repaired. Acknowledgment of his status as king was also given by the Pope at this time which must have been a big boost to his authority.

Alfred's other great contribution to Britain was to revive the educational system and literacy, which had existed mainly in monasteries before the Vikings came. Alfred felt that learning should be available in the vernacular tongue and arranged for the translation and dissemination of seminal books from Latin into Anglo-Saxon from his base in Winchester, thus restoring literacy and culture as well as introducing England's first native coinage.

It is a recognition of his abilities, both in battle, and as a statesman and organiser, that English history accords him the accolade 'Great': he is the only English monarch to enjoy this distinction. The fortified towns known as burghs were situated to sustain surrounding economic areas of countryside and farms; these burghs and the shire system which Alfred created, did not change, in terms of either boundaries or organisation, until the late 20th century.

Alfred died in 899 and was succeeded by his son Edward the Elder who was then 25. Edward also ruled from Winchester, then capital of Wessex, and captured the East Midlands and East Anglia from the Danes in 917, also becoming ruler of Mercia in 918, which comprised much of central England. He was Alfred's second son and is reputed to have been the first English monarch to have learnt reading and writing as a child (Alfred himself apparently learnt to read at the age of 12). Edward amalgamated Mercia, East Anglia and Sussex from Danish lands, joining them all together with Wessex. He died in battle in 924 whilst fighting a combined Welsh and Mercian rebellion.

Edward was succeeded by Aethelstan, Alfred's grandson who was born in 894. In 927 Aethelstan had conquered the last remaining Viking kingdom in Britain, that of York, making him the first ruler to control all England, thus establishing his position in history as the first King of England. Later Welsh and Scottish kings accepted his rule. With Offa and Alfred, he completes the trio of the three greatest Anglo-Saxon kings. Aethelstan never married and died in 939 having centralised the government authority and laws of England. His contemporaries recognised his success in battle, as well as his effectiveness as a monarch directing learning and religion throughout the country, in addition to cementing his grandfather's practical vision of a single well-organised nation.

He was succeeded by his half-brother Edmund (921–946) at the age of only 18, who then lost northern England back to the Vikings for a period: it was not retaken from the Vikings until 954. Edmund's short reign of just over six years was taken up with military problems in the north of England, but he was able to reconquer the Midlands and Northumbria which had each been retaken by the Vikings. Edmund's reign was one of several short reigns of the late 10th and early 11th centuries and culminated in his murder in 946, by an exiled thief whilst he was attending mass. Edmund was succeeded in turn by his brother Adred, who ruled from 946–955. Subsequently Edmund's sons ruled; Edwig from 955–957, and Edgar from 957–975.

Edgar was known as "the peaceable", despite regaining Northumbria and Mercia by force. Following Edgar, the several successions to the throne were all contested, and the kings of England included two Danish kings and one Norman, Edward the Martyr, who only ruled from 975 until he was murdered in 978 in rather unclear circumstances. He in turn, was succeeded by Aethelred II ('the Unready' 968–1016), who was only 10 years old when Edward was murdered. Aethelred ruled until 1016 but was insufficiently experienced to make much impact.

He is however credited for enacting a law in 997 which led to the formation of local bodies made up of twelve men (but no women) charged with publishing the names of wrongdoers in their district. This is sometimes seen as the beginning of the jury system. Aethelred's 2nd reign was interrupted by an invasion in 1013 by the Danish King, Sweyn Forkbeard (960–1014), who ruled for only six weeks before dying of natural causes, whereupon Aethelred returned from exile in Normandy to resume ruling for another two years until his death in 1016.

He was succeeded by Edmund II (993–1016), whose reign was cut short by five battles against the Danes, culminating in his death within six months of his accession to the throne. He was defeated by the Danish King Cnut (or Canute, 995–1035), Sweyn Forkbeard's son who then wore the crowns of both England and Denmark, where he spent much of his time campaigning in Norway and Sweden from 1016 until his death two decades later.

After Cnut's death in 1035, he was succeeded by his son, Harold Harefoot (1016–1040). At this time there was a lot of jockeying for the English throne, and the kingdom reverted to a dual kingship with Harold ruling north of the River Thames, and his half-brother, Harthr Cnut (1018–1042), the son of Cnut, ruling south of the Thames, although at the time Denmark was so unstable that Harthr Cnut spent most of his time in Denmark trying to subdue his rebellious subjects, and having insufficient military support to risk setting foot in England; he was only 17 when he came to the throne and was the last Scandinavian to sit on the English throne, which he managed for only two years before dying at a wedding, probably from a surfeit of alcohol.

The English throne was then occupied by Edward the Confessor, son of Aethelred and half-brother to Harthr Cnut, becoming the last Anglo-Saxon king of England (1003–1066). As his name indicates he was seen as a religious and unworldly man, whose 24-year reign was marred by a lack of monarchical power due to interference by his nobles, although basically his rule seems to have been benign. He died without an heir and his piety was recognised when he was canonised by the Pope a century later. Edward appears in the opening scene of the Bayeux tapestry sitting on his throne before the events of the Norman conquest start to unfold. He also built Westminster Abbey, the first impressive Norman church in England, though it would later be demolished and rebuilt as the edifice we know today, by Henry III in 1245.

On the continent, a similar picture of tribes coalescing had been occurring to form a recognisable early France, which had slowly disintegrated after the death of Clovis in 511, who made the mistake of dividing his kingdom between his four sons who squabbled over their respective territorial allocations. Later in time Charles Martel (668–741) ruled the Franks from 718 until his death after inheriting the position from his military aristocrat father. It took him four years to subdue all his competitors for the throne, who all felt that he was an inappropriate choice as he was illegitimate.

Martel is usually regarded as one of the great founding figures of Europe, with his claim resting on two great achievements; firstly he was a magnificent warrior and military tactician who overcame the Arabs. After the crossing of the straits of Gibraltar in 711 the advancing Muslim armies had forged north through the Iberian Peninsula, and up through mainland France, where they were met and defeated by Charles Martel at Tours in 732, a battle which is seen as finally preserving the integrity of Christian Europe.

Secondly, he was a major supporter of St Boniface (675–754), an English monk born in Crediton in Devon and sent by the Pope to convert the tribes of Germania to Christianity. Boniface was eventually martyred in Frisia (modern Holland) but is now the patron saint of Germany. Charles Martel, from his base in Frankia, spent much of his life on campaign subduing Allemande, Bavaria and Frisia. When he died in 741 his kingdom was divided between his two sons, Carloman and Pepin the Short (714–768). Carloman retired to a monastery and Pepin deposed the nominal Merovingian King, Childeric III, who was a rather ineffective figurehead, and in this way Pepin started the Carolingian dynasty, of which he was crowned ruler by the Pope. Pepin's reign was notable for reform of the law and building on the ecclesiastical reforms of St Boniface.

Pepin's son, Charlemagne (742–814), is the most famous of the early French kings. He expanded the Frankish empire to its greatest extent, and was crowned Emperor of the West by the Pope on Christmas Day 800. Charlemagne continued the consolidation of the Carolingian Empire by imposing a central system of government, and giving land instead of money to his nobles, administrators and army commanders. He was a great promoter of learning, monasteries and the arts, and was also largely undefeated in battle. He reformed weights and measures, dividing a pound of silver into 240 pennies, which tradition would continue in Britain for the next 1100 years.

When he died in 814, he was succeeded by his son, Louis the Pious (778–840), whose achievements included expelling the Muslims from the Northeastern corner of Spain, but after Louis' death smaller kingdoms splintered off again, and in 843 Charlemagne's grandsons, according to the customs of inheritance, split the empire into three, of which the western fragments soon succumbed to the Vikings. Charlemagne's grandsons were unable to control the Viking raids up the River Seine, and in 911 land in Normandy was ceded to the Viking Rollo (846–930) by the French King Charles III (known as Charles the Simple). Francia was unstable and fragmented at that time and Charles ruled from 898–922 before being deposed. The land that was granted in lieu of tribute was gradually expanded to become the Duchy of Normandy.

In 800, when Charlemagne was crowned Holy Roman Emperor by the Pope, his empire included France, the Low Countries, northern Italy and the northern Balkans, in addition to the northern half of Germany, so that Western Europe was ruled entirely by Christian kings with the exception still of most of the Iberian Peninsula. Due to the lack of firm central control, division of the Holy Roman Empire gradually increased.

When the last Carolingian King of Francia, the young Louis V (866–887), died after barely a year on the throne, it was clear that change was necessary. Over previous years the monarchy had been increasingly enfeebled while the nobility had become correspondingly stronger, with a general feeling that the monarchy should become elective instead of hereditary. Hugh Capet (941–996), who was very well connected throughout the nobility and had royal ancestry, ascended to the Frankish throne, restored firm government, and continued to keep his capital in Paris, from where his descendants would rule France for the next 800 years.

Timeline of English Monarchs to 1066:

Alfred the Great	849–899	Ruled 871–899
Edward the Elder	874–924	ruled 899–924
Aethelstan	895–939	ruled 924–939
Edmund I	921–940	ruled 939–946 (murdered)
Eadred	923–955	ruled 946–955
Eadwig	940–959	ruled 955–959
Edgar	943–975	ruled 959–975
Edward the Martyr	962–978	ruled 975–978 (murdered)
Aethelred the Unready	968–1016	ruled 978–1013
Sweyn Forkbeard	960–1016	ruled 1013–1014
Aethelred the Unready	968–1016	ruled 1014–1016 (2nd reign)
Edmund II (Ironside)	990–1016	ruled for seven months (murdered or died in battle)
Cnut (Canute)	995–1035	ruled 1016–1035
Harold Harefoot	1016–1040	ruled 1035–1040 (murdered)
Harthecnut	1018–1042	ruled 1040–1042
Edward the Confessor	1003–1066	ruled 1042–1066
Harold Godwinson	1022–1066	ruled for ten months in 1066 (died in battle)

Possible further reading:
The Formation of England by H P R Finberg (Paladin paperback)

Chapter 23
The Vikings and Norsemen

Writing and records came late to Scandinavia, so the evidence about early times comes from archaeology and petroglyphs, or runic stones. After the ice sheets receded, the area first became tundra and then taiga, or snow forest, an area of conifers and birch which existed across northern latitudes of North America and Eurasia. It was a place where nomadic tribespeople migrated north and south with the seasons following salmon in the rivers and reindeer on the land, a place where the bronze and iron ages also came late in time, and a place with which the Roman empire did not bother, though trade took some of their weapons, household items and coins were lost and found later in this remoteness.

Many small tribes lived loosely scattered across this vastness, an area of mountainous terrain but without any great barriers. It was subject to multiple early invasions by nomadic tribes from the east, which gradually crystallised into a recognisable pattern of states by around the year 1200, and then persisted as Norway, Sweden, Finland and Denmark to this day, albeit with frequent shifts of boundaries through the past millennium.

Norway is characterised as a land of mountains and forest, Sweden and Finland as forest, and Denmark as flat with many islands. The incoming ethnic groups can be traced back at least as far as 2,000 BC when the climate was relatively warm, but there was no writing available at the time, and the history of migration is therefore vague, though some information has been gleaned from runes on memorial stones throughout Scandinavia. Writing came to Scandinavia in Latin and with Christianity around 1100, before that time the law and history were committed to memory and used orally. In the 12th century, once writing became used, the old Norse sagas of exploration and heroic deeds were transcribed from oral legends into book form some centuries after the exploits which they commemorated.

The Slavs in this region of Eastern Europe spread outwards from the Carpathian Mountains, both to the east and to the south, into the Balkans and what we now know as Bulgaria. Bulgaria itself was converted to Christianity in 865 following the conversion of their ruler by the two missionary brothers Saint Cyril and Saint Methodius, who were sent as emissaries from the Orthodox Christian Church in Byzantium.

Saint Methodius lived from 815–885, and his younger brother Cyril from 827–869: he is remembered as the inventor of the Cyrillic alphabet, named after him, which allowed the development of written records for this part of Europe.

They were Byzantine Greeks who were declared by the Orthodox Church as 'equal-to-apostles'. They were responsible both for translating the Gospels, and for writing the first Slavic civil code, in addition to the Cyrillic alphabet. On one occasion they travelled with the holy relics of St Clement to see the Pope. St Clement was Bishop of Rome and Pope from 92–99 AD, he had been consecrated by St Peter himself and was later executed by the Emperor Trajan at a time of Christian persecution; his relics were very precious to the church.

The Vikings were probably an early offshoot of these Slavic tribes who migrated into Scandinavia and appeared in the Balkans around this time. Their expansion into the lands south of Scandinavia, both east and west, may in part be attributed to the general climatic downturn of the Dark Ages which probably would have made agriculture and self-sufficiency in Scandinavia very difficult.

Other possible reasons for the Viking expansion in the 9th century include the rise of Islam to the south, disrupting much of the trade with the Middle East and along the Silk Roads to China, together with the weak state of England and Francia as they emerged from the Dark Ages without any naval protection against the agile Viking longships. The Vikings may also have been assisted by the advent, in the 8th century, of iron swords and battle weapons, together with the first horses to be seen in Scandinavia which all helped their competitiveness as warriors.

The word Viking derives from Vik, meaning a small creek, bay or inlet; the defining Viking characteristic was their excellent seamanship and boat building. They built large longships, up to twenty metres in length, and holding as many as ninety men. These boats were open, of clinker build, i.e. using overlapping planks of wood fastened with rivets or bent over nails, and used a single sail to travel before the wind: when the wind was absent or adverse, then they were rowed. The boats came in two shapes, the one long, narrow, shallow, fast and used as a warship, and the second wider, deeper and used as a transport. They had no rudder and steering was effected using a large steering oar, 'steorbord' in old English and 'styribord' in ancient Norse, which has evolved into the English word starboard for the righthand side of a ship. Sails were made of wool or woven flax; ropes were strips of sealskin.

In these craft, the Vikings expanded from the Baltic Sea at the beginning of the 9th century. One group, the Swedish Vikings living in the forests around the Baltic Sea, in Finland and along the north German coast, spread through the northern rivers to found a city in the 9th century we now know as Novgorod, on the River Volkhov, and then forged on south along the rivers Dnieper, Dniester, Don and Volga, to Constantinople, where they were busy traders. A second group comprising Danish Vikings from the flat coastal plains and islands did most of the raiding throughout the Baltic, and along the western European coast, while a third group of Vikings from the mountains and forests of Norway, raided and settled on the east coast of Britain, later voyaging round to the west coast, the Hebrides, Shetland, Orkney and Faroe Islands, before ultimately colonising Iceland, and even later Greenland, which is a much longer sea journey. The Greenland colonies were only marginally viable and died out after a couple of hundred years leaving the coastline to be resettled by eastward migrating Eskimos from the Canadian arctic who still inhabit the region.

After short overland passages from the Baltic, it was straightforward for the Swedish Vikings to travel south along the rivers Volga, Don and Dnieper which drain the central European Plain into the Caspian Sea and the Black Sea. The rivers were vital to the founding and subsequent growth of Russia, both to allow export of goods to the south, but also to facilitate imports, including grain, wine, gold and silver; to pay for this the Vikings exported slaves, furs, amber and wood to be traded in the south. At first it seems these routes were used mainly for trade, but once the relative wealth of the southern lands was compared with the natural resources and the difficulties of agriculture in the northern lands, then piracy and looting may have seemed a more attractive and rewarding occupation than trading in furs, walrus ivory, slaves, timber, soapstone and jewellery of amber and jet.

The Vikings had no money system or coinage but brought back silver Islamic coins which were used initially as jewellery then gradually became local currency. Byzantium (Constantinople) at the outflow of the Black Sea was besieged by the Vikings who were then bought off by the prospect of settling in Byzantium and forming the Emperor's mercenary bodyguard, where they became known as Varangians, a word which translates as 'sworn companions', though they might more accurately be called mercenaries. The Byzantines knew these raiding northmen as a tribe they called the Rus, and part of their story will unfold later into the nation we know as Russia (chapter 24).

In the other direction, the second group of Danish Norsemen extended their raiding along the western coast of Europe from their homes in Denmark, south-west along the coast of the Low Countries, Holland, Belgium and the northern French coast; they in fact raided as far south as the Mediterranean and the Atlantic coast of Morocco, and more directly to the west, across to the coast of Britain. They were able to sail round the north of Scotland and terrorise the Shetland and Orkney Islands, then the Hebrides, raiding south to Ireland. The first raid on Britain's east coast was in 793, when the Vikings sacked Lindisfarne and its monastery, the first raids on Ireland came two years later.

In 866, after many years of sporadic raiding, York itself was captured by a Viking army, and in 871 they defeated the West Saxons at the battle of Ashdown in Berkshire, which shows how far south they had extended. At this time some Vikings were settling permanently in Britain, and in 886 King Alfred agreed the boundaries of Danelaw with the Viking King Guthrum. Danelaw was defined as the north-eastern part of Britain and became settled and ruled by the Vikings for several decades. Warring continued and boundaries shifted; King Eric Bloodaxe (885–954) was defeated and forced to leave York in 954.

In the meantime, the Vikings had also firmly established themselves in northern France in the area we know as Normandy, by sailing up the River Seine. They had also migrated and colonised far to the west, setting up colonies in Iceland in 870, and Greenland in 980. Further migration west occurred in the year 1000, when the Vikings landed in North America and established a short-lived colony in Newfoundland, and possibly even further south, where the mild climate they found and the vines that were growing, led them to christen the area 'Vinland'. It is not clear whether they were exploring west by intention, or whether they were blown west by unfortunate gales which drove them onto the North American coast. The Vikings founded a trading settlement on the east coast of Ireland in 840, which later became Dublin, and lived there for almost two centuries until the Irish King Brian Boru (941–1014) managed to unite the rest of the Irish kingdoms against them in 1014 and defeat them in battle.

To the Vikings we owe the Althing, the world's oldest national parliament, where democracy was established in Iceland in 930, with each man (but once again no women, and especially no slaves) having a vote on matters of the day in a gathering that met once year. Throughout Scandinavia, local parliaments existed at this time and were known as Things, in which all the population were involved with the exception of slaves (unfortunate individuals captured as part of the looting raids and piracy and taken back to Viking lands to provide agricultural and building labour).

If the slaves became surplus to local requirements, then they were shipped to the Mediterranean and sold, the practice only ceased at the end of the 12th century when it was forbidden by the newly introduced Christianity. Viking society comprised three simple classes, thralls or slaves with no significant rights, karls who were free peasants with varying amounts of personal wealth, and jarls or nobles; women of free status (karls and jarls) possessed a remarkable degree of equality for that time).

Where the Vikings settled, it was often because the indigenous people had tried to buy them off with bargains of land, which they hoped would establish a neutral buffer between themselves and the raiding Vikings and would remove the incentive for the piracy they suffered. In Normandy, the county of Rouen, was ceded to the Viking Rollo (846–930) in 911; this effectively marks the founding of Normandy as a definitive kingdom to which the Normans steadily added, and from which they would later move north across the Channel to southern England in 1066.

In southern England, King Sweyn of Denmark and his son Cnut (Canute) defeated and drove out the Anglo-Saxon King Aethelred (chapter 22). Sweyn did not live long after this, so that Cnut became king of the Danes, with British colonies after the death of Aethelred in 1016. Cnut then ruled Denmark, and eventually all of Britain, until his death in 1035, after which Harthacnut, his son, succeeded as regent, but was never crowned and only ruled for two years without establishing control over his kingdoms on either side of the North Sea, before he was deposed and exiled.

Harold Harefoot, his half-brother, ascended the throne, but only reigned for three years until he died in 1040, after which Harthacnut was invited to return and take up the throne. Harthacnut was not in good health and therefore asked his half-brother, and son of Aethelred, Edward (1003–1066), to return to England from exile in France, nominating him as his eventual successor. Harthacnut died two years later and Edward duly assumed the throne; he became known as

Edward the Confessor, implying a certain unworldliness and piety, indeed he was canonised and made a saint by the Pope just over a century after his death. It seems that he was in fact an effective ruler, though his death in 1066 ultimately resulted in Viking descendants from Normandy arriving in England to take over the English throne in 1066 in a violent upheaval which is remembered as one of the most important and formative dates in English history (chapter 25).

A little later in Scandinavian history the Kalmar Union was formed in 1397 with Norway, Denmark and Sweden sharing a single monarchy, but remaining autonomous nations (Kalmar is a strategic town on Sweden's east coast). It all ended in the Kalmar War of 1611–1613 when the Danes attempted to impose unity by force and failed. Before this the three countries had all become Protestant, adopting Lutheranism in the early 16th century. Scandinavia became embroiled in the thirty years war from 1618–1648 as Protestants fighting against the Catholic Holy Roman Empire. Although Denmark initially did well in the war, it was Sweden that eventually emerged dominant with the maximum extent of its power and territory by 1658.

Possible further reading:
The Hammer and the Cross by Robert Ferguson (Penguin)
Vikings, Life and Legend by Williams, Pentz and Wemhoff (British Museum publication)

Chapter 24
Russia – The Early Years

Russians date the beginning of their history to 862 AD. Before that, the Russian Steppe and the land east of Poland, was inhabited by co-existing tribes for whom little detail is available. These tribes included the Scythians, Slavs, Veps, and Votes. They lived in a fairly fertile area which covered eastern Europe as far east as the Urals, and south to include an area which today we know as Ukraine. East beyond the Urals a barren desertified region existed with the Himalayas to the south and Siberia to the north, containing vast areas of sub fertile land.

Tribes were dispersed, possibly often nomadic, and probably warred amongst themselves, but no adequate records exist for us to be certain. To the west this land extended not quite all the way to the Baltic, where it joined the eastern boundary of Lithuania, which was a larger and much stronger state in mediaeval times.

Legend has it that in those disorganised times the tribes all disagreed amongst themselves, often fighting, and that there was no single individual who was sufficiently charismatic to dominate or unite the land. Unusually therefore, the chiefs of the tribes resolved to invite a ruler to come from abroad. Envoys were sent to the Vikings in Sweden, and in 862 Rurik of Rus (830–879) and his two brothers journeyed to Novgorod to provide a new Prince and ruler. His two brothers unfortunately died quite soon, but their deaths do not seem to have been suspicious. Rurik then ruled from Novgorod until his death in 879. The Vikings (also known at this time in Constantinople as Varangians) inter-married with the Slavic tribes, and Rurik's descendants continued to rule the newly united nation of Russia for the next several centuries.

The information for these events comes from the Russian 'Primary Chronicle', but was only recorded by a monk called Nestor some two hundred years later, as Nestor died in 1114. Under the Rurik dynasty the Vikings raided south down the Dnieper River into the Black Sea and to Constantinople. A great raid by Oleg, son of Rurik, was planned to pillage Constantinople, and the Vikings besieged the city until a severe storm scattered their fleet and gave victory to the citizens of Constantinople. This victory was attributed to the Patriarch of the city, who had interceded constantly by prayer with the Virgin Mary to protect the city. The Vikings also attributed their defeat to this powerful Christian God, and this probably represents the initial impetus for Russia to adopt Orthodox Christianity. A later raid in 911 by Oleg was much more successful for the Russians.

During their exploration down The River Dnieper to the Black Sea, the Vikings passed a very strategic and impressive hill next to the river, and later Oleg, who ruled 882–912, seized this hill and made it his capital, calling it Kiev. In 911 Oleg had agreed a Treaty with Constantinople, allowing trade from Kiev and the north by Viking merchants who were then permitted to reside in Constantinople, and trade their furs, honey, wax and slaves. In return, they took home the manufactured products of Constantinople, which were rare and precious to the Russians of that time.

Christianity was formalised with the Rus in 988 under Grand Prince Vladimir, a descendent of Rurik, who ruled 980–1015. Envoys from the Greek, Roman and Islamic Churches had been invited to present their religions to Vladimir to see which would be the most appropriate for the Rus to adopt. The Rus were already impressed by the Greek Orthodox Church, and by the amazing Church of Hagia Sophia in Constantinople. They were also impressed that the Slavs, Saint Cyril and Saint Melodius, came from their part of the world and had previously devised a Slavic alphabet and system of writing, and thus the decision over which religion to adopt fell easily to Orthodox Christianity.

Vladimir married a Byzantine Princess, but he kept the Russian Church separate and always ready to do his bidding, so that much later after the fall of Constantinople in 1453, Russia was to become the bulwark of the Orthodox Church. Vladimir was sanctified after his death in 1015, but he appears to have been an optimist and appointed his twelve sons to rule equally over different parts of Russia. His supposition that the twelve sons would all agree and rule together in peace and harmony was probably doomed from the start, and Russian cohesion inevitably diminished.

This fragmentation of the Russian lands under many different princes made it subsequently ill-equipped to resist the invasions that came from east and west at the beginning of the 13th century. From the east came the Mongols under the command of a grandson of Genghis Khan, Khan Batu (chapter 28). The Mongols conquered most of Russia around Kiev between 1237 and 1240, razing towns to the ground and massacring all their inhabitants. This was enough to persuade the citizens of Kiev to try and hold out, but the Mongols fired the city massacring some 50,000 inhabitants. The invasion was temporarily halted by the death of Ogodei Khan, son of Genghis, in 1241, whereupon the Mongols withdrew to their eastern homeland to choose his successor. The Mongols also lacked the administrative backup to rule the enormous area of land they had conquered. Russia remained in thrall and paying tribute to the Mongols, but from the beginning of this period the name of Alexander Nevsky (1221–1263), Russian ruler and descendant of Rurik is venerated. Some three years after the Mongol invasion in 1240 he was able, at the age of only 19, to repel a Swedish army much larger than his own force, and a year later, when the Rus faced invasion by Teutonic knights and Estonian troops, he was again victorious against a larger force which was lured onto a frozen lake; when the ice gave way under the considerable weight of armoured knights and horses, the battle was effectively won and Alexander passed into Russian legend.

Alexander tolerated the Golden Hoard of the Mongols from the east and continued to pay tribute, recognising their superiority of numbers and the terrible massacres that they would unleash if they were opposed: he was made Supreme Russian Ruler in 1252, and was later sanctified.

Many of the Russian Princes cooperated with the Mongols, and the Ruler of the Principality of Moscow took on the task of collecting Mongol tribute from his neighbouring Princes, thus starting the expansion of the small village fort of Moscow, setting it on its path to its present size. Much of this early expansion came during the reign of Prince Ivan I (ruled 1325–1340).

Some decades later, the Mongol stranglehold and control of Russia was declining. By 1453 Christian Byzantium had fallen to the Turks, leaving Russia and Moscow as the defenders of the Christian Orthodox Church. The Grand Prince had been sufficiently astute to ally himself very strongly with the Church, taking the title, after the Mongols left, of 'Tsar' (a derivation of the ancient Roman title Caesar). Ivan II (1440–1505), also known as Ivan the Great, Grand Prince of Moscow, saw the full retreat of the Mongol hoards back eastwards. Ivan had faced the Mongols down and had refused to pay the usual tribute: both sides prepared for battle but the Mongols retreated only to return the following year when the Grand Khan and his army was suddenly attacked and defeated, following which the army and its organisation disintegrated.

Ivan's son Vasilyevich (1505–1533) succeeded him and consolidated the enormous territorial gains that Ivan had made during his reign. Moscow was now assuming pre-eminence and gradually imposing a national unity, both at home and in foreign relations. With the Mongols no longer dominating Russia, the succession line of the Prince of Moscow was continued through Ivan III and his successor Vasily III, with the warring Russian princedoms becoming integrated under Moscow's rule, either by force or by consent. All of these early rulers were still in direct descent from Rurik, and Ivan III is remembered for tripling the size of Russian lands during his reign, a trend that was to continue more slowly through the next few centuries.

In 1530, Ivan IV was born, later becoming known as Ivan the Terrible. He succeeded to the throne at the age of three when his father died, so that his mother ruled as regent in his name for the next five years until she was poisoned by political enemies. After this the growing Ivan witnessed murder and power struggles as family and nobles fought to gain political power. He married a Romanov princess, Anastasia, when he was seventeen, and they had six children, four of whom died in childhood. When Anastasia died in 1560, Ivan was overcome with grief and went into retreat in the country intending not to return to Moscow. He was however, begged to return by the Muscovites, who feared another power vacuum and period of uncertainty comparable to his years of minority.

Ivan agreed to return, but on the condition that he would be allowed to govern without any restrictions, in other words that he would be an absolute dictator. With this agreement, he was able to reorganise Russia into large administrative units governed on his behalf and at his direction. He created a secret police force, known as Oprichniki. This was the forerunner of the secret police, and was unleashed by Ivan against anyone suspected of contravening his will. More than four thousand of the nobility are said to have been murdered in the following years, with Ivan often participating in destructive bouts of torture and killing.

Ivan's rage came to a climax when he was told that the city leaders of Novgorod, then the second city of Russia, were planning to rebel. He took the Oprichniki and rode to Novgorod, where they first pillaged the monasteries and homes of the nobility in a scorched earth policy within a 50 miles radius around the city. He then built a wooden wall around Novgorod to prevent anyone escaping, and in the weeks that followed he and his men systematically slaughtered all the inhabitants – men, women and children – often after long episodes of torture. The death toll has been put at up to 60,000. A similar fate befell the town of Pskov a little later, and the rest of the Russian population quickly absorbed the lesson that opposition to Ivan was inadvisable, such that it melted away.

During this time of Ivan's terrible years, western Europe was facing the turmoil of the Reformation and the formation of early Protestant Churches, with considerable dissent and even some political murders, but the intolerance of the Catholic Church in Europe failed to hold back the Reformation in Northern Europe, whilst the corresponding reign of Ivan the Terrible did effectively manage to hold back any changes in Russia for a further couple of centuries. The Orthodox Church in Russia backed Ivan, probably in large part as a means of self-preservation.

Ivan murdered his son and heir during a quarrel in 1581 so that when he died three years later, his other son, a feeble-minded teenager called Fyodor, succeeded to the throne and Russia was again plunged into decades of chaos with no strong central control. In this weakened state, matters were made worse by invasions from Catholic Lithuania and Poland in the west, Sweden from the north, and Muslims coming from the south and east. By decimating the nobility Ivan had sent Russia down the path of centralised autocracy on which it has largely remained to the present day. Church property was confiscated, and Church influence diminished, laws and rights did not develop, and a middle class was not allowed.

Following Ivan's death in 1584, his simpleton son Fyodor had only notionally ascended to the throne, and a governing council took over the running of the state. A member of Ivan's Oprichniki, Boris Godunov (1551–1605), emerged to take over as the power behind the throne. Ivan had appointed a council of several members for this function, but Boris Godunov rapidly became the controlling force.

After the simple-minded Fyodor died in 1598, for the first time in 700 years, there was no blood successor to Ivan, and as a member of the governing council, Boris Godunov seized the throne declaring himself Tsar. His rule, although autocratic, was relatively benign and popular until he died in 1605, resulting in another decade of political instability, before restoration of a new line of Tsars was created (chapter 55).

Possible further reading:
The Wild East by Martin Sixsmith 16th (BBC Books)

Chapter 25
The Norman Conquest of Britain

1066 is a very big landmark in English history because it diverted Britain to become part of mainland Europe and away from its possible alternative Scandinavian destiny. It created a new feudal society, but it is interesting to recall that the Normans had been Vikings less than two centuries previously, and therefore a degree of a Scandinavian heritage remained in the British development via Normandy. The Norman Conquest was an interruption in the process of organising the country started by King Alfred in the late 9th century and was well underway in the reigns of his descendants, Aethelstan and Edward the Confessor.

That process, started by Alfred, was to organise the nation in both human and geographical terms to cope with the pressures of population growth and with threats of external aggression, although being an island Britain would not be subject to marauding foreign armies in the way that the rest of Europe would suffer through the second millennium. In this sense the conquest, coming almost 200 years after Alfred's accession to the throne in 870, was a cruel distraction from the internal organisation and relative peace enjoyed by Britain at that time. Alfred's reign had issued in a relatively stable and organised period up to the early 11th century, in which firstly the Danes were held to the north and east, secondly there was an upsurge in monasticism and learning, and thirdly, the shire structure and the government had bedded in well following Alfred and Athelstan's early organisation.

Unfortunately, Alfred's later descendants failed to govern firmly, including a king castigated by contemporaries and historians as Aethelred the Unready (966–1016; though 'unready' should probably be better translated as 'badly advised'), such that the Danish kings overthrew the English throne leaving the Danish Cnut (Canute 995–1035) to rule. In this way, Viking settlers in England were Saxonised, just as Viking rulers in France had become Normanised, since in both cases the settlers' numbers were small compared to the overall size of the native population, with mainly aristocrats and knights becoming colonisers apart from some of the soldiery.

Although England was relatively prosperous by contemporary standards, life in the 11th century was still primitive and uncertain by our modern expectations; about half of all children died in infancy or early childhood, and for those who survived overall life expectancy was just over 40, greater for men than women due to the toll of childbirth. Medical treatment was very primitive and overlaid with superstition, while famine could often threaten life if adverse weather resulted in poor harvests.

In Normandy, society was feudal, in other words land was held by a noble in exchange for providing military service and troops for the King. This had resulted in a skilled and disciplined army. Duke William's army was mounted on specially bred horses. Knights wore chainmail and fought with swords and lances, acting together in squadrons. They had cover by archers and communicated in battle by flag signalling of instructions. By contrast the Anglo-Saxons remained on foot, using a rather primitive defensive shield wall to fight from, which would appear to have been a relic derived from the Roman legions. Directly descended from Rollo, to whom Normandy had initially been granted, William the Bastard (1028–1087, later the Conqueror), grew up against this background with constant taunts from his opponents of his illegitimacy, and therefore of his lack of suitability as a contender for royal rank.

Edward, known as the Confessor, had grown up in the Norman court, and had been invited back to England after the death of the Danish Harold Harefoot to take the throne in 1042 (chapter 23), restoring the old Wessex royal line, at a time when William was still in his early teens. It is likely that Edward designated Duke William as his successor since he left no direct heir, and William understood this had the agreement of Earl Godwin's son Harold.

Earl Godwin of Wessex (1001–1053) had become a very powerful figure under King Cnut, with a daughter who became wife to Edward the Confessor, and three sons; Harold, Earl of East Anglia, and the earls of Middlesex and Northumberland. But when Edward the Confessor died on the 5th of January 1066, Harold, Earl of East Anglia, seized the throne in an effective coup, and was crowned within days. Harold had previously promised that the throne would pass to William, whose wife was a direct descendent of King Alfred. William had been out manoeuvred, but was still determined to fight for the throne. He was in France at the time, and therefore started constructing an invasion fleet.

At the same time, Harald Hardrada (1015–1066) of Norway also had a familial claim to the throne and assembled a fleet in Trondheim in Norway. Each of these two fleets took months to build and prepare, but in September Harald of Norway finally landed on the north-east coast of Britain and marched on York, where he defeated the Northumbrian army at the Battle of Fulford on September 20th. Harald had come south from Norway with favourable northerly winds, but the same winds had pinned Duke William down in France, so mercifully for King Harald Hardrada there was only a single enemy to deal with at this time.

King Harold marched north, achieving a remarkable 160 mile forced march in four days. The Vikings were caught by surprise, and battle was joined at Stamford Bridge outside York, where King Harold won the day, despite the fatigue of his army, and the Viking leader Harald Hardrada was killed.

In the meantime, the winds had finally changed, and William of Normandy landed on the south coast on the 28th of September and began raiding locally. King Harold returned to London, probably leaving most of his exhausted army in York, and then raised a fresh army before marching to Hastings, where he was numerically outnumbered. He met with William of Normandy at the Battle of Hastings, which was decisive, and is recorded in the Bayeux Tapestry, now on display at Caen in France. King Harold was struck in the eye by an arrow, and was badly weakened, he was later surrounded and killed.

Some days later, English church and secular leaders met Duke William at Little Berkhamsted, and surrendered the kingdom. William was crowned in Westminster Abbey on Christmas Day using the English coronation ceremony. This was a rapid and complete conquest and may be contrasted with the Norman conquest of Italy and Sicily which started in 999, and was only completed much later in 1130, when all the small Norman princedoms south of Rome were finally united after a gradual process of battle-won accretions.

The following twenty years saw a massive redistribution of wealth, as William rewarded his followers and himself with confiscated lands, becoming extremely wealthy through a policy of very harsh taxation alongside confiscation of property. Many English knights and landholders had died at the time of the conquest, some at the Battle of Stamford Bridge, and more at the later battles of Fulford and Hastings; their landholdings were redistributed amongst the nobles and men of William's 5,000 strong invading army.

Rebellions and resistance from the Anglo-Saxon and Danish settlers plagued William's attempts at control over the next few years to such an extent that he took an army to restore his authority over the north of England, spending Christmas 1069 in York. The campaign has become known as the 'Harrying of the North'; villages were burnt, crops were destroyed so that people were forced to flee or starve. Records indicate that more than half of the settlements were laid waste and probably the same proportion of the population died.

Following this, the Anglo-Saxon population had little choice but to accept their new ruler so that by 1075 William was in full control of the country. William brought with him architects and craftsman who built not just castles, but also cathedrals, and a Benedictine monk called Lanfranc (1010–1089) to be Archbishop of Canterbury. Lanfranc organised the country into seventeen dioceses and started the building of a magnificent cathedral in each one. In this way the conquest was emphasised as being both secular and religious. Norman expansion was impressive at this time with the contemporary conquest of Byzantine Italy being completed soon after Britain in 1071.

Life quietened down, but oppression and harsh taxation continued. Finally in 1085, after Christmas deliberations with his courtly advisors, William decided that he needed a good record of the current wealth of the country, principally so that he could optimise his taxation policy. Teams of government inspectors and scribes were sent across the whole country to record the holdings of land, livestock, and its worth across the nation. It was achieved in the remarkably short space of only nine months and became known to the general population as the Domesday Book, since firstly there was no appeal against any inaccuracies that the survey officers might have recorded, and secondly since it led to taxation levies comparable to those expected on the Day of Judgement, or the Day of Doom. In Domesday the outlines of society recorded are essentially what was set up by Alfred, Edward the Elder and Athelstan over the previous 200 years, together with the assessed wealth and value of each little community.

William needed funds to fight the French, the Bretons and to continue to try and subdue rebellious Welsh and Scots. The total population of the British Isles at this time was around half a million souls, largely rural. William never learned to speak English, and the majority of the population never learned to speak his Norman French, so the Anglo-Saxon culture was preserved and the Normans gradually became anglicised, though the country as a whole changed to a feudal system in which the emphasis was upon military lordship, depending for its foundation upon hard-working masses of agricultural peasants.

Amongst the landholding classes in both Britain and France, the culture of knighthood gradually became highly developed, leading to the development of chivalry and the legends and tales that extol it. William's rule was severe, his taxation was oppressive, and when he died in a riding accident the year after the Domesday Book was completed, he was not mourned by the general populace.

Among his nine children, he left legacies to three sons, Robert to inherit Normandy, William Rufus to inherit the English crown as William II, and his third son Henry was left part of the treasury, but no land (two daughters became nuns, two more married French nobility).

William Rufus (1056–1100) was also a harsh man. His brother Robert was seen as a more sympathetic person and was invited from France by the nobility to come and fight William for the crown, but William Rufus bought the loyalty of the English army by promising a relaxation of his father's severe rule, and in consequence Robert realised he would not be able to achieve enough support to gain the throne, and he therefore returned to France. Once he was safely back in France, William subsequently reneged on his promises and resumed his cruel and greedy ways, milking the British population to fill the treasury. He died in 1100 whilst out hunting from an arrow through the chest. This was passed off as an accident, but assassination is a more likely explanation. William Rufus had continued to have trouble controlling the Scots and the Welsh; he never married and left no children, nor was he mourned by the English population.

William Rufus was succeeded by his brother Henry (1068–1135), the English speaking third surviving son of William the Conqueror, who had married Margaret, daughter of the Scots king Malcolm III. His older brother Robert was still alive and was invited once again by the nobility to come and fight for the crown, but he could raise neither the money nor the army to do this. Henry therefore became King of England unopposed. He gave a Charter repealing William Rufus' laws, and restoring Edward the Confessor's laws, thus diminishing the power of the Barons.

Henry had a daughter called Matilda, but no sons. Thanks to the relaxation of laws and taxes, he enjoyed a peaceful reign until he died in 1135. Before his death Henry had extracted oaths from the nobility that he would be succeeded by his daughter Matilda, but when he died in 1135 the Barons reneged on their oaths and chose his nephew, Stephen, who was a grandson of William the Conqueror through William's daughter Adela. Matilda had two big disadvantages in the succession argument: firstly that she was a woman, and secondly that she was too anglicised. She had also married the French noble Geoffrey of Anjou, who was not popular with the Norman nobility.

King Stephen (1092–1154) was a weak man, compared with his predecessors. He never managed to control the rebellious nobility, and his 19 year reign from 1135 became known as 'The Anarchy' in consequence of the continuing claim of Matilda to the English throne, which had started with her attempt to take the throne, but her army was defeated at the Battle of the Standard outside Northallerton in 1138.

Low-level civil war followed with Matilda controlling much of south-west England, and Stephen controlling the south-east. Civil war continued for some years, and at one stage Matilda was besieged in Oxford, but managed to escape the siege on foot from the castle across the frozen River Thames. Later, Matilda's son Henry came from France to fight Stephen, but they met at Winchester and made peace. This treaty acknowledged Stephen as king and Henry was adopted as his son to succeed him when Stephen died.

In the meantime, powerful barons had been building castles and fortifying their properties, and the peace agreement had also agreed that the castles would be destroyed once Henry came to the throne. Stephen died soon after this in 1154, and Henry II was crowned as the first Plantagenet King of England. He turned out to be a harsh but effective ruler: he strengthened the Anglo-Saxon systems of justice, local government and taxation, strengthened the Royal Exchequer, and instituted travelling justices to enforce the law throughout the country.

Norman English rulers:

William I	ruled 1066–1087	son of Robert Duke of Normandy	lived 1028–1087
William II	ruled 1087–1100	son of William I	lived 1056–1100
Henry I	ruled 1100–1135	son of William I	lived 1068–1135
Stephen	ruled 1135–1154	son of Count of Normandy nephew of Henry I (period of Anarchy)	lived 1096–1154
Matilda	ruled six months in 1141	daughter of Henry I	lived 1102–1167

Possible further reading:
The Normans by Francois Neveux (Robinson Books)
Domesday by Michael Wood (BBC Publications)

Chapter 26
Byzantine Empire

The site of Byzantium has been inhabited since pre-historic times. Even in those ancient times it probably existed as a trading post since it was situated in a perfect position for seaborne trade passing between the Mediterranean and the Black Sea. The site is an important one on the Straits of the Bosphorus between Europe on the western side, and Asia on the eastern side. It was settled by the Greeks in the 7th century BC as they colonised around the shores of the Black Sea; in those days any trade between mainland Greece and the colonies on the shores of the Black Sea would have most easily gone by sea and would have had to pass through the Bosphorus.

In this, the Greeks were following the spread of the Phoenicians around the eastern end of the Mediterranean. Greek influence was at its zenith in the 5th century BC, and their impressive cultural achievements in history, philosophy and literature, date from that period. This was followed by war with Sparta, starting in 431 BC, and this Peloponnesian War ended in 404 BC with the defeat of Athens and the disbanding of its empire. Macedon followed as the next major power in Greece with King Philip, and in turn his son Alexander the Great, who ruled between them from 359–323 BC. Alexander's vast conquests were all dissipated by his warring generals and relatives following his death; into the vacuum of control that resulted came an expansion of the Roman Empire in the 2nd and 1st centuries BC, including absorption of Greece into the empire, where the inequalities of Rome with its immense wealth, expensive spectacles and games, corrupt politics and cruelty, provided a glaring contrast with the relative equality and culture of theatre, sport and politics found in ancient Greece.

The first two centuries after Christ saw Rome at the height of its powers and with a tendency to over-extend the Empire territorially. By the time Constantine became Emperor in 306 AD, barbarian incursions from the north and east were putting severe strains on the integrity of the very large Empire. By the early 5th century migrations of Goths, Vandals and Franks from the north continued to eat away at the edges of the Empire (the last pagan emperor, Julian, died in 363). The western half of the Roman Empire was deeply troubled and had insufficient wealth to resource the armies and legions needed to control the Barbarian invaders.

After Constantine came to power in 306, he managed to unite once more the eastern and western parts of the Roman Empire, and then proceeded to build a new imperial residence at Byzantium calling it New Rome. The local population called it Constantinople in his honour, and although there was a period of relative stability under Constantine, and under his son Constantius II, this interlude did not last. Constantine had converted to Christianity and had united the east and west halves of the empire by 324 AD. He convened the Council of Nicaea the following year to include all the bishops and other representatives of the Christian Church throughout the Empire in an attempt to achieve a consensus on Christian doctrine.

The Council of Nicaea, some three hundred years after the death of Christ, was an attempt to prevent a gradual drift away from the very early Christian doctrines. The Council sat for a month, with Constantine as an impartial non-voting chairman despite his great stature amongst the company. The Council agreed firstly, the nature of the Son of God and his relationship to God the Father, namely that they were equal both in stature and through time, while the opposing view of Arius (250–336), a priest from Alexandria, put God above his son.

Secondly, it produced and promulgated the Nicaean Creed, which is still used today. Thirdly, it agreed a lot of early canon law, regulating the behaviour of church members. Fourthly, it separated the date of Easter from the Jewish calendar and agreed a method of uniform determination for the future date and observance of Easter. It is interesting to note that four years before the Council of Nicaea, Constantine had declared Sunday to be an Empire wide day of rest in honour of the Son of God.

During the first two centuries after Christ, the size of the Roman Empire had stretched the resources necessary to pay for the legions. At its maximum Rome is thought to have had almost half a million men under arms scattered across the Empire, but particularly facing the Barbarian threats from the north and east. During these centuries politicians and landowners had gradually surrendered their power, and this had led to diminishing support for the Emperor. The Emperor himself through this period had become more autocratic, and the Senate had been forced to assume a diminished rubber-stamping function. It was all these pressures, together with the size of the Empire, that led to the appointment in 285 AD of a co-emperor to look after administration and tax in the eastern Empire.

Byzantium/Constantinople was the obvious geographical site for this centre of administration, but despite this, and despite the wealth of the Eastern Empire helping to fund the legions, Rome would be sacked by barbarians in 410 AD. The changes were all developing at the same time as Christianity was growing, leading up to the time when Constantine had declared Christianity as the official religion of the Empire. The Council of Nicaea was intended to consolidate this process, and the degree of agreement achieved at the Council is remarkable, though one must note that even at that time there were individuals striking out on pathways diverging from mainstream Christian thought.

By the 6th century, the Emperor Justinian (482–565) ruling from Constantinople was still trying, but failing, to reunite the eastern and western parts of the Roman Empire which had been slowly drifting apart. The eastern Empire, in which he was based, had greater resources and greater wealth, but the amount that he spent on the western problems and the army only weakened his own eastern Empire, despite the fact that he was able to end the rule of the Ostrogoths in Italy, and regain Africa from the Vandals. His reign included an episode of the plague, which killed hundreds of thousands of people and was an enormous disruption and disaster in every aspect of life. Justinian is however also remembered for the construction in 532 of the huge church of St Sofia in Constantinople (since converted into a mosque as Hagia Sophia, meaning Holy Wisdom, and not referring to a specific saint, in 1453 by the Ottomans).

At the later Council of Chalcedon in 451 called by the Emperor Marcian (392–457), the differences between the many emerging Christian sects were amplified. The Council had been called to try and define once again the precise relationship of Jesus Christ, God the Son, to that of God the Father. Since the Council of Nicaea, over a century previously, there had been a gradual drift in doctrine within separate Christian communities, with differences developing particularly in Egypt (the Coptic Church), Syria (the Monotheites) and Persia (the Nestorians).

There was also Jewish influence from outside, reflecting the fact that even in the 5th century some Christians saw their beliefs as simply development and progression of the basic Jewish faith. Thus, when Justinian, the 57th emperor, died in 565, there was divergence of the eastern and western halves of the Roman Empire. Justinian had maintained the integrity of the eastern part of the Roman Empire, but this would in future, gradually develop down a separate pathway from that of the western Holy Roman Empire. From this time forward the eastern Byzantine Empire, centred on Byzantium/Constantinople, continued to develop separately from the Holy Roman Empire after the early 7th century.

Because the Roman Empire and the rule of the Emperor existed in a deeply pious society, people regarded imperial control as an extension of the rule of God and Christianity in general. In this overall atmosphere faith was more important than reason, which had to take second place until the time of the enlightenment a millennium later. Classical Greek philosophy, learning and literature was however preserved, together with some earlier pagan thinking, to pass to later generations.

This eastern Empire, declared Greek-speaking in the early 7th century by the Emperor Heraclius (575–641 ruled from 610–641) and comprising Asia Minor, Syria and Egypt, remained wealthy and populous compared to the increasingly chaotic and Latin-speaking west. In addition to converting the Empire to speaking Greek as the official language, he reorganised the army to cope with the enlarged empire but had to face the early days of Islamic expansion after Mohammed's death. In the early 7th century aggression from Sassanid Persia was countered and checked, but by the mid-7th century and the early 8th century, attacks were coming from the newly founded and aggressive Islam.

Territories on the boundaries of the Byzantine Empire were gradually eaten away, but through the late 9th and 10th centuries the frontiers were pushed back once more, though this stretched the resources of the empire to such a degree that repelling the incursions proved impossible to maintain. To complicate matters, in 1071, central Anatolia was invaded by Turks from the steppes to the north, who proved impossible to dislodge.

By comparison with Islam where secular and religious powers were exercised by a single person or organisation, power in Byzantium through the centuries was still divided between the Emperor and his senate, and the Patriarch of Constantinople who crowned him: the whole edifice was also buttressed by a dispersed army of secret police feeding information back to the centre in Constantinople. The priesthood in the developing Orthodox Church remained compatible with marriage, unlike its western counterpart, and this helped integrate daily religion and attitudes within the population.

Since the Emperor Valerian had been captured and humiliated while campaigning in Syria in 260, the power of the Roman senate to appoint the Emperor had diminished while the influence of the army had increased and resulted in the appointment of Diocletian (344–311) who reformed the empire's administrative structures and separated military and civilian financial systems by sub-dividing provinces in order to ensure tighter control closer to the population. Diocletian had taken the decision to base himself in Constantinople in the Eastern Empire which was most threatened by the Persians at that time.

In this way, Byzantium/Constantinople came to be defined for the next millennium by Roman identity, Greek culture and Christian religion. As the centuries passed, and the Byzantine Church lost ground in the south to Muslims, it gained new adherents to the north, including south-eastern Europe and Russia. The Emperor Heraclius (575–641) tried hard through the early 7th century to keep the Persians at bay on the Empire's eastern boundaries, though the price paid in terms of the looting and sacking of cities along the borders was high: Syria, Palestine and Jerusalem were taken by the Persians. Peace was achieved between the Romans and Persians in 628 after the death of the Persian Emperor.

The Empire's integrity declined further after Heraclius' death in 641; two years later Alexandria fell to the Arabs in the early years of the advancing Muslim invasions. Following this a few years later North Africa, Cyprus and Armenia were all lost to Muslim expansion. The religion of the early Muslims was strongly influenced by the contemporary Christian thinking of impending apocalypse and by Jewish messianic fervour for holy war. The Muslims expanded easily into the power vacuum in Syria and Palestine left by the exhausted Roman and Persian empires, with the Persian empire conquered and ceasing to exist after 656.

Arab Muslim attacks from the south continued with several years of direct attacks on Constantinople between 673 and 678, but without Arab success. Through the 8th century there were some reverses, with the Arabs being forced back out of Turkey and the Roman Empire's boundaries were extended once more to include Syria, Mesopotamia and Armenia. The Arab conquests resulted in desperate reorganisation of the Roman army with great administrative changes and tactical abilities orientated towards guerrilla warfare. The Eastern Roman Empire emerged from the 7th century considerably smaller, but with the power of the emperor enhanced.

In the meantime, the eastern and western Christian Churches were growing further apart, often as a result of doctrinal disagreements: the most well-known of these was the emergence of Iconoclasm for a period in the mid-8th century. The Iconoclasts were acting on the belief that the Old Testament commandment, "thou shalt not make any graven images", forbade the depiction of God, or his prophets or disciples, in paintings, icons, sculpture, or by any other means. There may have been an element of spill over here from the Muslim attitude, where the depiction of God, the prophet, or other holy men is prohibited.

It is interesting to note that after Justinian II's rule, the Iconoclasts destroyed much art of the period following an edict by the Eastern Emperor forbidding the use of such images in worship. Overall, this was one of many doctrinal differences between the eastern and western Churches which resulted in a continuing slow drift apart. These doctrinal differences finally came to a head in the Great Schism of 1054 with the East and West Christian churches accusing each other of heresy. The four principal matters of disagreement were firstly the source of the Holy Spirit, secondly whether the bread used at holy communion should be leavened or unleavened, thirdly the Roman, or Western, Pope's claim to primacy over the Eastern Patriarch, and lastly the ranking of Constantinople amongst the five principal Christian sees of Rome, Constantinople, Antioch, Alexandria and Jerusalem. Views were entrenched and irreconcilable, and the representatives of the opposing delegations ended up excommunicating each other. The split is known as the East-West Schism and persisted until it was finally revoked in 1965.

A little later, the Roman Empire was defeated by the Turks in 1071, and from then on the Byzantine Empire was confined to the European side of the Bosphorus. In the early 12th century, and for a further hundred years, a new imperial dynasty was able to push back Norman invaders from Greece, and Nomadic invaders from southern Russia called Pechenegs, but the dynasty was unable to win back the area of Bulgaria or any Turkish land.

Through this time, two other major factors were at work, the first of these being the rise of Venice as a colonising sea power across the eastern Mediterranean, and the second being the sporadic appearance of European crusaders heading for the Holy Land, starting with the first crusade in 1095 (chapter 27). In the later 12th century crusades the European crusaders found themselves fighting against the armies of Saladin (1137–1193), who captured Jerusalem for Islam in 1187 at the battle of Hattin. Saladin was a Sunni Muslim much of whose success came from uniting all the different Muslim tribes under his leadership.

In 1204, Constantinople itself was sacked, and the emperor deposed, not by barbarians but by a crusader army on the 4th crusade, the Emperor was only finally restored to the throne in 1261 after an interregnum in which a crusader, Count Baldwin of Flanders, was put on the Emperor's throne. The crusaders looted, sold or removed much of the cities' art and holy relics. At this time, to the north of Constantinople, there existed a large area we now know as Russia and Ukraine, which had been gradually organising since the 9th century. The Slav people living there, together with the Vikings, traded with Constantinople and came to provide many of their mercenaries, known as Varangians by the citizens of Constantinople.

After the catastrophic sacking of Byzantium in 1204, the city and environs were reduced to a small Balkan state with over-lordship from Venice. Fighting continued, but in a generally fruitless succession of battles, until in 1347 plague struck, decimating the population. It was thus a much-weakened Byzantium in 1453 that was finally conquered by the Ottoman Turks under Mehmet II (1432–1481), the Ottoman Sultan, then aged only 21. It was the result of two months of siege and warfare by the Ottoman Turks who were victorious against the 80th emperor since Constantine took the city as his capital.

Mehmet symbolised his victory by converting the great Santa Sophia Church into a mosque with a throne on which he would sit within it. Thus the Byzantine Empire was changed by the Ottoman Turks into an Ottoman Empire, and the Turks set out to conquer the surrounding countries to the north, and the remaining Greek communities along the southern coast of the Black Sea to the east. The Venetians and their Empire were also conquered and subsumed by the Turks into the Ottoman Empire, along with Hungary, Cyprus, and eventually Crete.

The Ottomans were a small Turkic principality of religious Islamic warriors from Anatolia who gradually came to prominence and power from the end of the 13th century after the Mongols retreated eastwards. Their founder Osman had started the dynasty by managing to unite all the local tribes and ruled from 1299 to 1323 initiating a line of sultans which would stay in power until just after the Great War in the 20th century; the empire at its maximum took in most of the coast of North Africa, much of the Middle East, around the Black Sea, and the Balkans in the middle of the 16th century.

Possible further reading:
Byzantium by Peter Sarris (Oxford University Press)

Chapter 27
Western Medieval Religion and the Crusades

It is necessary to start with consideration of the development of the Jewish peoples from whom first Christianity arose, and later in turn, Islam. The Jews, or Hebrews, were a very cohesive people, tending to live, work and worship together rather than becoming dispersed throughout the bigger communities in which they resided. Judaism is known as far back as the Bronze Age in Mesopotamia and stood out from other contemporary religions in being monotheistic at a time when most other societies worshipped a plethora of gods.

Nothing was written down until the middle of the last millennium BC when the Tanakh originated containing the story of Abraham as the first Hebrew, although this record appears several centuries after the events it describes. The story continues and was appropriated later by Christianity where it became the Old Testament of the Bible, including the account of Moses who was saved from death as an infant despite the Pharoah's command to kill all new-born Jewish babies.

As an adult, Moses would be summoned to God on the top of a mountain and told first to lead the Jews out of their enslavement in Egypt, and then later be given the Ten Commandments by God as the ideal basis of daily conduct for people, a set of instructions which both Jews and Christians follow to this day. Moses lived towards the end of the second millennium BC.

The middle of the first millennium BC was a particularly fruitful time for philosophy to result in new religions, and propositions for new ways of thinking. At this time, while Socrates, Plato and Aristotle were teaching and trying to make sense of the world in Greece, other thinkers were pursuing the same quest in Asia (chapter 17). Hinduism was developing along several lines in India; Zoroaster, Buddha and Confucius were developing their own lines of thought, and many variants of these faiths would also develop subsequently out of the thinkers from this period.

Jewish identity was reinforced and cemented through the years by the suppression and persecution to which they have often been subjected through the centuries. Jewish life received a major setback in 586 BC when the first temple in Jerusalem was destroyed by the Romans following a series of rebellions. Leaders, or rabbis appeared, and eventually Jewish religious and civil law was set down in the Mishnah in 200 AD with further expansion in the Talmud in 500 AD. Harsh Roman treatment of the Jews resulted in steady emigration from

Palestine and Mesopotamia to the shores of the Mediterranean, where small but coherent Jewish communities developed.

Initially, in the century after the birth of Christ, many followers of Jesus had seen themselves as Jewish, but with minor differences, though St Paul talks of bringing gentiles to Christianity even in his early years of evangelism. These differences became accentuated as the years went by, so that by the time of the Council of Nicaea in 325, and then Chalcedon in 451 (chapter 17), separation of traditional Christianity from its Jewish roots was fully achieved. In the same way that Christianity persecuted pagan minorities, the Jews were a readily identifiable sub-group of communities who were often persecuted when rulers were searching for scapegoats.

The pattern has been repeated through the centuries, and across many different administrations and nations. The Jews have comprised small, culturally distinct minorities, who have often provided the banking and money-lending facilities for Christian and Muslim communities where early church leaders frowned on the lending of money at interest, indeed Islam still prohibits the charging of interest on loans; this has made the Jewish community who do not have such prohibitions and therefore can often provide financial services for others, easy scapegoats for financial and other disasters. The persecution has continued relentlessly up to the Holocaust perpetrated by Hitler in the mid-20th century, and in other jurisdictions even after this.

Following Jesus's crucifixion, the new religion of Christianity spread quickly through the Middle East. Much of the dissemination of the doctrine can be attributed to St Paul, who was sent by the early church on several journeys around the eastern Mediterranean, to describe Christ's work and build up support. He visited Rome and at one time survived a shipwreck. Christianity received a massive boost when it was declared the official religion of the Empire by Constantine in the early 4th century, but up to about 500 AD it was confined to the Roman Empire.

After Constantine aligned church and state together in the 4th century, the church prospered, but the tradition of Greek rationalism was stifled while the church acquired a licence to quash dissent. Faith was all that counted, with realism and rational discussion being put aside in favour of beliefs that were untestable and for which no rational evidence existed (for instance whether the communion bread should be leavened or not). The crusades exemplified the competing problems of praying and fighting because a crusader spilling blood was sanctified by the church. In this respect, the crusaders are to be compared with modern jihad, which is once again a holy war against infidels with much the same ground rules.

Spread of religion continued, and by 600 AD, the eastern Mediterranean was largely Christian. Earlier, St Anthony (251–356), regarded as the father of monks, had escaped from the Coptic church to the desert, living as a hermit in Egypt. In the early 6th Century St Benedict (480–543) set up a monastery at Monte Cassino, one of an eventual twelve which he founded in southern Italy, with the intention of providing a community where monks would both work and worship in a highly moral setting.

The Benedictine rules which survive him were based on a life of work and prayer and specified eight hours work, eight hours prayer and eight hours of leisure and sleep each day. The Benedictines were known as the Black Monks after the colour of their habits, and to differentiate them from the White Monks, or Cistercians, who broke away from the Benedictine Abbey of Cluny at the turn of the 11th and 12th centuries. Benedictine monasteries spread throughout western Europe becoming widespread in later mediaeval times.

By the middle of the first millennium, the power of the Christian Church as a whole was becoming more visible, and in the 5th century Pope Leo the Great (on the papal throne 440–461) enhanced the influence of the Church and provided the basis on which discussions at the Council of Chalcedon commenced, while at the same time the Emperor declared that Papal decisions should have the force of law. Leo took up the title Pontifex Maximus, a largely symbolic title that the Roman emperors had discarded, using it to augment his authority.

The other great pope of this era was Gregory the Great, who reigned from 590–604. He was a scholar, writer, administrator and a champion of missionary activity, which was reflected in his action to send Augustine to become the first archbishop of Canterbury in 597. At the same time, the political and military rule of Rome was steadily weakening, and this deterioration of control was not helped by the splitting of the Empire into eastern and western halves, and by the growth of Constantinople as an alternative centre of religious power. The Council of Nicaea in 325 had helped to strengthen and direct Christianity, but the Council of Chalcedon in 451 did not achieve a general consensus in doctrine and did not prevent the steady splintering of the Church.

Into this melting pot of incipient nations and religions came the teachings of Mohammed in the early 7th century. Unlike the Roman Empire, Islam combined political and religious thought as an indivisible philosophy. There was no division of thought or purpose as existed between the Roman Emperor and the Pope. Islam spread rapidly in the course of a hundred years, both around the Middle East and along the north coast of Africa and across the Straits of Gibraltar (whose name derives from Jebel Tariq, the Mount of Tariq, the Muslim general who started the conquest of the Iberian Peninsula).

Among other effects of the spread of Islam were the compounding of the doctrinal disagreements from the Council of Chalcedon, and the creation of geographical pockets of isolated Christianity. Thus, the Monotheites in Syria, Nestorians in Persia, and Copts in Egypt and Ethiopia, all became cut off from the rest of Christianity. These sects had not been able to accept the doctrines of the rest of the Church at the Council of Chalcedon in 451, and they now continued to develop down separate paths. Roman Byzantium continued to drift apart over matters that may now seem to us quite minor, including the very precise details of how the liturgy should be used.

The conversion of the Slavs by the Saints Methodius and Cyril in the 9th century, also contributed to this process, which culminated in a schism between the western Roman and the eastern Byzantine churches in 1054, with Rome and the papacy claiming absolute primacy over both eastern and western Churches, compared with a much looser confederation of autonomous eastern orthodox Churches; many other matters such as the choice of date for Easter were also contentious. The schism had elements of farce as the heads of each Church excommunicated the other over doctrinal questions. Although the next thousand years would see attempts at reconciliation, the eastern and western Churches continued to drift apart. In the meantime, the extension of Orthodox Christianity into Russia had made that nation a powerful buttress for the church as Byzantium crumbled through the centuries on a path to the fall of the Byzantine Empire to the Turks in 1453.

Mohammed's teaching did not go down well in Mecca during his lifetime, which was at that time the major trading centre in western Arabia. Accordingly, Mohammed and some two hundred of his followers were forced to migrate to Medina, three hundred miles to the north-east; this migration was precipitated in a hurry to avoid personal threats to Mohammed. The migration is known as the Hijra in Arabic, and its date on the 16th of July 622 is taken as the beginning of the Islamic year and of the Muslim calendar.

Mohammed died in 632; his successor, Abu Bakr, in extensive military campaigns, conquered Arabia and some of Palestine over the next two years. The next three Caliphs, all part of Mohammed's close-knit family, fought many battles extending the conquest by force into Mesopotamia, Syria and Asia Minor, together with Persia, and eventually as far away as Kabul in Afghanistan and into northern India. At the same time, Arab forces had advanced west along the northern coast of Africa through Egypt, reaching as far as the Straits of Gibraltar in 711.

The next few years saw extension of Muslim rule through southern and eastern Spain, and even across the Pyrenees as far north as Poitiers in central France. At this stage supply lines and communications were hopelessly stretched and the Muslim armies were defeated in battle by Charles Martel and retreated south to the Pyrenees (chapter 20).

The word Islam means surrender or "submission to the will of God". It continues a belief which commenced with the Jewish Old Testament prophets and extended through Christ as the last in a long line of prophets before Mohammed's coming. During the 8th, 9th and 10th centuries Muslim unity fragmented, accentuating Sunni and Shia differences with little further territorial expansion happening. By the early 10th century, religious fragmentation was such that three separate Caliphs in different geographical areas were claiming religious authority.

The steady territorial advance of Islam generated resentment in Christendom, resulting eventually in a backlash of military activity known as the Crusades, in which European warriors were recruited to fight to regain territory conquered by Muslims several centuries before, with Jerusalem and the Holy Land being the principal targets. The first crusade in 1096 resulted from a call by Pope Urban II to help defend the eastern Orthodox Church against the Turks, and to liberate Jerusalem, which was achieved.

Crusaders were generally wealthy aristocrats from across Europe who were granted religious protection of their families and wealth whilst they were abroad, they were also granted indulgences, particularly a reduced time to spend in purgatory atoning for their earthly sins. The church encouraged the crusades as a form of Holy Service, while turning a blind eye to the associated licence for fighting and pillaging; it led also to a new form of moral behaviour involving taking prisoners instead of killing enemy warriors, and then ransoming them, a profitable side-line to the looting. Courtly behaviour became part of the expected norm and was encouraged by the church, so that it evolved into what became known as chivalry (from the French chevalerie, or fighting on horseback).

The second crusade 50 years later in 1147, resulted from the loss of the city of Odessa to Muslim rule, and the third crusade in 1189 resulted in the loss of most of the Middle Eastern Crusader territory, including Jerusalem, to Saladin (1137–1193), the middle eastern Caliph and a fearsome warrior. Jerusalem had been conquered by the crusaders in the first crusade largely due to the Muslim armies, or fighting bands, not working together, indeed warring internally, and it was lost again because Saladin re-united the Muslim tribes to work together once more. Muslim warriors were named Saracens referring to Mohammed's claimed descent from Sarah, wife of Abraham.

The Crusades to the Holy Land which started in 1096 were continued by Pope Innocent III (1160–1216) who regarded the Muslim recapture of Jerusalem as divine retribution for the sins and loose morals of clergy and congregations alike. From the start of his reign in 1198 Innocent also attempted to bring the Cathar population of southern France back into the catholic fold by preaching and missionary activity. The Cathars were centred on Albi, and therefore also known as Albigensians; they were part of a Gnostic revival in southern France and northern Italy, following a Zoroastrian belief originating form Persia and the Balkans in the existence of two gods, one good and one evil (also seen as the good God of the New Testament and the evil God of the Old Testament respectively).

They believed in the basic Christian value of perfection, poverty and preaching with the men of their church being known as 'parfaits' and the women as 'parfaites'. Pope Innocent's legate was murdered in 1208 and in response he launched the Albigensian Crusade calling on knights and nobles from northern France to bring the Cathars to heel; those who did not come back into the church were classed as heretics of whom many thousands were then burnt at the stake in a twenty-year campaign; the total slaughter is estimated in the hundreds of thousands.

Further crusades to the Holy Land followed with the 9th and final crusade in 1271. During these years, other internal crusades within Europe were also launched against dissenters from the church. The best known of these is the Reconquista in Spain, where the Iberian Peninsula was gradually liberated from

Muslim control, but without external support. Over the course of three hundred years Christian rule in Spain moved steadily south, finally liberating the last Muslim stronghold of Granada in 1492. Other Crusades were also launched internally against perceived heretics such as the Cathars in southern France, and Slavs in the Baltic region.

Eventually, the Catholic Church found it easier to desist from grandiose schemes to liberate the Holy Land by crusade, and concentrated instead on troublesome individuals, usually labelled heretics, within Europe. The Inquisition came into being in the 12th century as a consequence of the Albigensian crusade but was formalised by Pope Gregory IX at the end of this time in 1229, and responsibility for its action was devolved to the Dominican order of monks, formally the Order of Preachers who followed Saint Dominic, a Castilian preacher. The order rapidly developed a fearsome reputation for dealing with individuals brave enough to step outside the confines of orthodox Catholic Christian doctrine. The Inquisition was not wonderfully successful and after a while the church gave up on large crusades to concentrate instead on selected prominent and 'dangerous' individuals.

This pattern of religious behaviour, or perhaps one should say the behaviour of religions, has followed the early disagreements seen in the Councils of Nicaea and Chalcedon, and has continued right up to the present time with all religions continuing to splinter and spin off new sects or subdivisions, and with new religions being invented.

With splinter groups, the new faith usually assumes many of the beliefs of its parent, but with a small changed item of belief which is deemed sufficiently important to justify the separation. This change to a new faith can usually be attributed to a single charismatic individual. The other distressing behaviour of religions has been the tendency for differences and disagreements to escalate into discrimination or persecution of small minorities, or even outright war if the two sides are of more comparable size.

Possible further reading:
The Crusades by Christopher Tyerman (Oxford University Press)

Chapter 28
The Mongols

The story of the Mongols and their influence on the world starts with Turkic tribes of Central Asian, people whose pre-history is unclear. Writing was not part of their culture, and little is known about them up to the end of the first millennium AD. Their homelands comprised a loose tribal confederation extending right across Asia, and related to China in the east, India and Persia to the south, and Byzantium to the south-west. Warring nomadic tribes existed across Central Asia, including the area which we know today as Mongolia. The land is poor and desert like, which necessitates the nomadic lifestyle to provide adequate grazing for animals.

Periodically through history, the tribes have come together and burst out into the territories of their neighbours, notably China in the early years. The Arabs invaded Transoxiana in 667, an area to the east of the Aral Sea. They started the breakup of the Turkic tribes but left the tribes with the legacy of writing before they were driven back westwards. No Turkic written records exist however until the 15th Century, and our knowledge of the affairs of Central Asia derive from reports in the histories of adjacent countries.

In the 10th century, the T'Ang dynasty collapsed in China, while in the west Islam was divided and was weakening. New domino pressure from the Central Asian Turkic tribes pushed outwards, and one Turkic clan we know as Seljuks moved into the lands of the north-eastern Caliphate of Islam. In the early 11th century the Seljuks, who were Sunni Muslims, crossed the Oxus River, occupying Syria, Palestine and attacking Byzantium. This presence of Islam in what was left of the Roman Empire was one contributing factor to the Crusades, and as Turkey, and to a lesser extent Syria, adjoined Europe, they then bore the brunt of attacking European Crusaders.

The Islamic culture was consolidated in Turkey and throughout the Middle East for the next several centuries, up to the present time. Islamic culture in medieval times relied on the presence of the military, which came under the authority of Islamic teachers and leaders: the army included many slaves. This was a great contrast with Christian Europe, where a non-religious bureaucracy governed, while religious authority came from the Church and the Pope, centred in Rome.

Thus, the Crusades came about in part as a response to Seljuk power because the Seljuks in Islam were more strict, more anti-Christian, and more obstructive to European pilgrims than their predecessors had been. Quite apart from the

Christian world resenting the Islamic occupation of Jerusalem and the Holy Land from which it had been displaced by force in the early days of Islamic conquest, anti-Islamic feeling gradually increased, and by 1100 the re-conquest of Spain from Islam was underway; Sicily had already been freed of Islam in the decades before this by the Norman King Roger I, and some of northern Spain somewhat earlier.

The first Crusade in 1099 captured Jerusalem from Islamic forces and established four Christian Latin states in the Middle East, including those of Jerusalem and Edessa, which provoked counter-attacks from Seljuk Islam. The Second Crusade is generally seen as a failure, as it was unable to recover the province of Edessa from Islam, but it did result in the expulsion of the Arabs from Lisbon. The Third Crusade came about in response to the re-capture of Jerusalem in 1187 by the Seljuk General, Saladin. The Crusade failed to recover Jerusalem, despite the participation in the Crusade of the German Emperor, the King of France and the English monarch King Richard I.

The 4th Crusade originated in Venice, but never got as far as the Holy Land; the army was diverted to Constantinople, capital of the Eastern Holy Roman Empire, which was sacked and recovered in 1204. Many smaller crusades met with a singular lack of success and a considerable loss of life, often from devout, but ill-equipped masses.

In Europe, contemporary times were marked by the crusading Knightly Orders, who went into battle with the blessing of the Pope: they included the Knights of St John of Jerusalem, the Knights Templar, the Spanish Knights of Calativa and Santiago, and in Germany the Teutonic Knights, with all of these church orders providing the base for the development of chivalry. Contrary to the teaching of the church, men joined the Crusades for plunder and riches, massacres were common, and were felt to be justified by the original expunging of Christianity from the Middle East, and by being against infidels with the blessing of the Pope. As an aside, at this stage, we should note the eastern expansion of Germany into Orthodox territory, thereby causing a deeper rift between the Latin and Orthodox, or eastern and western, branches of Christianity.

Into this rich brew of war and religion came the Mongols, who had hitherto waged war amongst themselves and with their neighbouring states, notably China, whom they had raided with varying degrees of success over the centuries, provoking the Chinese into extending and strengthening the Great Wall of China (sections of which were first built as far back as the 7th century BC), to try and keep them out.

The Mongols were united by Genghis Khan who has gone down in history as a highly successful, ferocious and brutal Emperor. He was born in Mongolia in 1162, and gradually fought his way to the top of the Mongolian hierarchy through a mixture of cajolery and brutality. Genghis Khan felt he had a divine mission to rule the world and under his leadership the Mongols burst out of Mongolia around 1218, sacking ancient cities and spreading to both east and west.

Mongol tactics of warfare relied on mounted light cavalry, using highly effective rapid-fire bows and arrows. Under Genghis Khan, the Mongols invaded northern China, crossing the Great Wall and pillaging the nation. Attention was then turned westwards, against Muslim states, creating a trail of razed cities and massacres through Central Asia and Iran, into the Caucasus and north onto the plains of Russia to the edges of Europe. The Great Khan died in 1227 and is buried in an unknown secret grave in Mongolia. Unlike many previous Kings and Emperors, he had seen to his succession and left the Empire divided amongst his four sons, who continued the push into Europe.

Northern Russian principalities fell in 1237, with Kiev being razed in 1240. Further south, Baghdad was captured and looted with massacres and the murder of the Caliph. Cairo was sacked. Later in the east one of Genghis Khan's grandsons, Kublai Khan, became Emperor of China by 1260 thus founding the Yuan Dynasty, and at the end of this period the Mongolian Empire was the largest land empire the world has ever seen, and included over one 5th of all the planet's land mass.

The Mongols never gave up their nomadic customs, and never lost touch with their cultural history, tending sheep, cattle and goats for the necessities of life, including milk, cheese, meat, furs and skins. They lived in large felted tent gers, with a central fire, and two distinct compartments, one for men and one for women. The gers were taken down frequently and moved in large ox-drawn wagons, so that new grazing could be found for the animal herds.

When the Mongols were united under Genghis Khan, ruling from his capital of Karakorum in Mongolia, the Great Khan saw his heavenly mission to rule the world confirmed; he got closer to it than anyone else in history through the exercise of terror and brutality, and the massacre of millions of unoffending people. The Empire at its largest included Central Asia, Persia, southern Russia and China, and extended from Germany in the west to Korea in the east. In the north it stretched from the Arctic to the Persian Gulf, though the Mongols were unable to conquer Japan or Java. Their highly effective war cavalry was fast and difficult to resist. Their skill shooting with bows and arrows from horseback was highly praised by their opponents. Each warrior took with him on campaign many spare horses, such that the army was never short of mounts or weaponry.

Western Europe was eventually saved by the death of another of Genghis Khan's grandsons, the Great Khan Mongke in 1259, following which his brother had to leave his western armies and return east to Mongolia to deal with the succession crisis so leaving a depleted military force in Syria which was defeated. Then the Empire was carved up between different descendants of Genghis Khan. In Persia the resulting dynasty lasted less than a century, while in Russia the Khanate, known as the Golden Hoard, lasted for the next two centuries.

In China, where Kublai Khan had officially proclaimed himself the first of the Mongol Yuan Dynasty in 1271 after a lot of in-fighting, rebellions by the peasants, starting in 1351, grew as a response to brutal suppression and high taxation. Finally, a strongman, Zhu Yuanzhang, emerged and gradually drove the

Mongols west across the Gobi Desert and back into Mongolia, even forcing them out of their capital, Karakoram. After almost four decades of fighting during which time many were killed or captured, the Yuan Dynasty was overthrown and the new Ming Dynasty was declared in 1388, re-enforcing the rigid social system of agricultural communities with a hierarchical structure including the governing elite; the Ming Dynasty would use this structure to rule for almost the next three centuries backed by a large standing army of over a million men.

In 1398, Timur Lang (Tamerlane or Timor the Lame) attacked and overcame Delhi and its sultanate. Timur was a direct descendant of Genghis Khan; he was reputedly lame because of a leg injury where he was wounded by an arrow as a young teenager. Timur ruled from Samarkand and conquered southern Russia in 1369, together with the old territories of Hulagu Khan, a grandson of Genghis. He followed these conquests by extending his rule into Persia, Mesopotamia, Afghanistan and Syria.

His warfare was as brutal as that of his grandfather; it has been calculated that over a period of ten years in northern India some 17 million people, or 5% of the world's population were killed. After sacking Delhi, he founded the Timurid Dynasty, but his successors were less single-minded and less ruthless so that northern India once more fragmented into little Muslim and Hindu kingdoms. After Timur's death, chaos followed for the next century until his descendant Babur came to power.

In the 16th century, Babur of Kabul (1483–1530) revived Islamic power in Northern India. He was descended from Genghis Khan seven generations previously, and Timur five generations before. He was remarkable in ascending the throne as a young man of twelve and being able to control the palace and army politics and intrigues of the time. His accession to the throne and subsequent rule through the early part of the 16th century is seen as the onset of the Mogul (Mughal or Mongol) empire in India with its Turko-Mongolian antecedents. Babur's second unusual distinction is that he left an autobiography detailing his campaigns and his years at the head of the empire, which has been invaluable to historians since. The Mogul Empire established by Babur lasted until the British came to rule India in the 19th century.

Thus, the divine mission to rule all the world was lost as the Mongol Empire and its rulers fragmented and started to make war amongst themselves. Several factors contributed to Mongol decline including the fact that their empire grew so large so rapidly that administration and control became ineffective; their military efforts were diluted by two unsuccessful attempts to invade Japan. Chinese peasants were brutally suppressed and taxed; national disasters, including Yellow River flooding, caused great loss of life and famine; but perhaps most importantly, disputed inheritance after Kublai Khan's death eventually led to internal divisions and fighting.

Possible further reading:
Genghis Khan by John Man (Bantam Books)
The Mongol Empire by John Man (Corgi Books)

Chapter 29
England 1154 – 1485 – The Plantagenets

Following the death of King Stephen in 1154, the throne passed to Henry II (1133–1189), son of Matilda and grandson of Henry I. He was crowned at the age of 21 and was to reign for 35 years. His father, Geoffrey of Anjou, was given to wearing a sprig of yellow broom, both in battle and at other times (yellow broom has the Latin name Planta Genista, hence Plantagenet). Henry's reign was a time of considerable consolidation for England. Henry pulled down many of the castles which individual barons had constructed, thereby making conflict between barons more difficult and encouraging peace throughout the country.

He also made a wise choice for his Chancellor of Thomas à Becket (1119–1170), who organised and regulated much of the kingdom, gradually controlling the strife between barons and the King. In addition to Britain, Henry's coronation as King of France and his Norman ancestry meant that Anjou, Normandy, Touraine, Aquitaine and Gascony, all in western France, came under his rule, creating an Angevin Empire. It was a combination of this Empire and a 35–year reign without any significant or expensive warfare which left Henry a very rich monarch.

In the 12th century, Ireland was still divided into four separate kingdoms, which were intermittently at war with each other (chapter 45). King Dermot of Leinster had lost his kingdom and turned to Henry for help. Henry provided effective backing and thus came to be acknowledged as King above all the Irish Kings; his claim to this title was subsequently endorsed by the Pope in 1172. Also in Henry's reign Wales was conquered, so that by the end of his reign all of the British Isles, save Scotland, were united under a single monarch. The French possessions that Henry had inherited were however destined to be lost in the next generation.

Because of problems of corruption and scandal within the Church, Henry had appointed the very reluctant non-churchman and successful secular chancellor Thomas à Becket (1120–1170), to be his Archbishop of Canterbury. At the time Becket predicted that because of the different needs of church and state his appointment would end in disagreement. Eight years later in 1170, disputes between Henry and Becket had escalated, and eventually when the Pope insisted that bishops should be appointed by the Church in Rome rather than by the English Monarch, Henry refused to accept this. Becket, as a newly converted pious churchman, sided with the Pope, thus exasperating Henry, who is famously said to have declared *"who will rid me of this turbulent priest?"*

Four of Henry's knights duly rode to Canterbury and murdered Becket in the cathedral. Eventually Henry came to show sorrow and do penance at the cathedral, but in the meantime, the four murderous knights had been given a sentence to fight in the Crusades. The whole episode made Henry's ambition of the monarchy controlling the church an impossibility.

Henry and his Queen, Eleanor of Aquitaine (1122–1204), had eight children, thus guaranteeing that there would be quarrels over the succession amongst them. John, almost the youngest, was bought off in the first instance by the grant of power and lands in Ireland. Richard, the Lionheart (1157–1199), came to the English throne in 1189 after much fighting at the age of 32 (he was the fourth son of Henry II, but the eldest son had become Archbishop of York, the second son became Count of Poitiers, and the third son died before his father).

Richard I was an outstanding warrior and had been given his first army command at the age of 16. He went on the Third Crusade, probably as penance for a Jewish massacre in which he took part. He lived in France and during his ten-year reign only spent six months in England. This was despite being born in Oxford, but underlines the fact that he did not speak English. He had no heirs, and because of his absence on Crusade, the Angevin Empire gradually disintegrated.

Much of the wealth that Henry II had accumulated was frittered away by Richard in crusading. When returning from the Crusades Richard was captured by the Duke of Austria and kept prisoner from 1192 for the next two years. He was traded on to the Holy Roman Emperor, Henry XI, and finally ransomed for 65,000 pounds of silver (this approximates to two or three times the annual income of the English crown at the time). Upon his return he tried to re-conquer Normandy. After some initial success he was shot in the shoulder by a crossbowman and died a few days later because the wound became gangrenous, providentially in the meantime he had declared his brother John to be his successor.

King John (1166–1216) came to the throne in 1199 at the age of 33, and was devoid of military success, such that he lost first the Duchy of Normandy, and then most of the remaining Angevin lands in France. Much of his reign was spent taxing his subjects to support his armed efforts to try and regain these French lands. On other fronts John was a good administrator, and increased the power and the role of local sergeants, bailiffs and coroners, who had only recently been introduced in 1194; this was costly, so during his reign there was much taxation alongside the costly loss of French territory. This produced considerable unrest amongst the barons, who resented both the taxation and John's failure to consult with his councillors, since he preferred the opinions of various cronies.

Unrest continued in Scotland and in Wales. Tension between John and his barons came to a headfirst in 1212, and again in 1214 when a final military campaign to try and recapture Normandy ended in failure. But in April 1215, when John had returned from campaigning in France, rebel barons disregarded their feudal ties to the monarch and marched on London. John met the rebel leaders at the Island of Runnymede, in the River Thames, just upstream from Windsor Castle.

The Archbishop of Canterbury mediated a Charter between John and the barons, now known as Magna Carta. This Great Charter not only addressed specific complaints of the barons, but also proposed deeper political reforms to protect the right of free men generally, as well as the Church. It is remembered as a reasoned process of justice and policy making, and the beginning of the end of arbitrary decisions by the monarch. It has never been repealed and remains on the Statute Books of England and Wales.

In practice, the monarch remained pretty much unconstrained and arbitrary through medieval times in England, but by the time of the English Civil War in the 17th century, it was of great significance for those ranged against the King and determined to show that the monarch was subject to the law in the same way as ordinary citizens. Later still, Magna Carta had an important influence on the early American colonists, and had a major input in formulating the United States Constitution. King John's reign has been succinctly summarised by Sir Winston Churchill, who said that *"...when the long tally is added, it will be seen that the British nation and the English-speaking world owe far more to the vices of John than to the labours of virtuous sovereigns."*

John died on campaign against his barons only a year after Magna Carta. He was succeeded by his son, Henry, who was only 9 when his father died. Henry III (1207–1272) was to become one of only a very small number of English monarchs to reign for 50 years or more. He inherited a difficult monarchy, with half of England in the hands of rebels, and most of Richard and John's French possessions already lost to France. After an early year of warfare against his barons and the French king's eldest son who had invaded to try and seize the throne, Henry emerged successful mainly because he was lucky through his early years to be advised, tutored and protected by a wily old mentor, Sir William Marshal (1147–1219) who had served previous monarchs for fifty years, and by the Earl of Kent and the Bishop of Winchester.

Baronial unrest continued with the king being unable to gain the upper hand until 1234, when several Great Councils restored peace. He married Eleanor of Provence in 1236, but after a period of relative peace, revolt surfaced again amongst the English barons, and in addition, from the English Church, as well as from the Welsh and the Scots. Money was short, and harvest failure from poor weather, all conspired against Henry who was confronted with a coup d'état in 1258. A more powerful Council and Parliament was appointed by the barons, but this failed to restore stability.

A period of civil war (known as the Second Baron's War) finally ended in 1267 after the Earl of Leicester (who had effectively ruled the country for the previous year) was defeated at the Battle of Evesham. Henry's son, Edward (1239–1307), became Steward of England, responsible for much of the day to day running of the Kingdom, but Edward left for a period on the 9th crusade, and only returned to England two years after Henry's death.

Henry's legacy, apart from losing most of his French possessions, was the rebuilding of Westminster Abbey around the shrine of Edward the Confessor (the only English king to be canonised) so that it would provide the location for his own tomb; the abbey was later given the status of a cathedral as a 'Royal Peculiar' (a church responsible directly to the monarch rather than to the bishop or diocese where it is located), thus saving it from the fate of most other English abbeys when they were dissolved by Henry VIII.

Edward I is remembered for reforming royal administration and the Common Law. He restored the royal authority which had been badly undermined during his father's reign. He made Parliament permanent, initiating an arrangement whereby two knights came from each county and two commoners from each borough. He was nicknamed 'Hammer of the Scots' because of his brutality north of the border. He expelled all the Jews in England by an edict which remained in force for a further 350 years.

Wales was incorporated into England during his reign in 1284, and was divided into counties, largely subject to English law. Edward built eight Welsh castles to subdue and control the Welsh, and in order to try to please the Welsh people he had his eldest son invested as Prince of Wales in 1301, when this son, the future Edward II, was 17. Despite his achievements, Edward I's son would start his reign under a large cloud of financial problems, political instability and an uncontrolled Scottish situation.

Edward II (1284–1327) came to the throne in 1307 and ruled for the next 20 years. He married Isabella, daughter of King Phillip IV of France. His reign was one of conflict between a pleasure-seeking monarch and his barons. The two decades of his reign were marked by incompetence, political intrigue and military defeat, notably in Scotland, where Robert the Bruce (Robert I of Scotland 1274–1329, chapter 43), defeated Edward's army at Bannockburn in 1314, while Edward was attempting to re-conquer Scotland. Continuing quarrels with the nobility resulted in Edward revoking all laws to limit the powers of the monarchy, such that he would no longer be subject to the will of Parliament.

In 1325, matters had risen to such a state that there was a plot to murder him, though this failed. Edward had refused to negotiate paying homage to the French King for possession of Gascony, and his wife Isabella was sent to France to negotiate. Whilst she was abroad, however, the situation turned round, Isabella and her son Edward (to become Edward III 1312–1377) raised an army to invade England from France; Edward II was unable to raise an army of his own to confront this threat and was captured in January 1327 and imprisoned in Kenilworth Castle. He abdicated shortly afterwards in favour of his son and died, probably murdered, in prison in September that year. His wife Isabella ruled as regent until Edward III came of age in 1330.

Edward III had been born in 1312 and was only 14 when his father died. Thanks to the coup by his mother Isabella, he came to the throne at the age of 14, but three years later he led a successful coup against his mother and her consort Roger Mortimer, Earl of March (1287–1330), who was the real power behind the throne, and who was then tried and executed. Edward then campaigned in Scotland for the first ten years of his reign. When he refused to pay homage to Philip VI of France (1293–1350), the French King confiscated Edward's lands in Aquitaine. For the first time in Europe since the days of the Roman Empire standing armies appeared in both countries.

Edward made up for the disasters of his father's reign, turning England into a strong military power, and overseeing developments in the law and in the evolution of Parliament. Once Scotland was subdued, Edward declared himself the authentic heir to the French throne, tracing his lineage back to William the Conqueror, thereby retaining his title to the Duchy of Normandy after becoming King of England. His claim to the French thrones was rebuffed under Salic law because his lineage included a female ancestor. This started a series of intermittent campaigns that became known as the Hundred Years War, lasting as they did from 1337 to 1453, more than one hundred years later.

Following Scottish successes, a small English army, led by Edward himself, routed a larger French force at the Battle of Crecy, following which the King moved on to lay siege to Calais. After besieging Calais for a whole year through to August 1347, the Black Death arrived from the Far East spreading throughout Europe and thence to England. Within a few months in the second half of 1349, the population of both countries was decimated.

The Black Death, or plague, is caused by a bacterium called Yersinia Pestis carried by rats. Around half of England's population of about six million people is thought to have died. The disease remained in small reservoirs in the population, and a second outbreak of plague occurred in 1361, killing a further 20% of the population: less serious outbreaks continued to occur over the next three hundred years. Edward did however find time during the epidemic to found the Order of the Garter as a prime order of chivalry for his faithful military campaign companions.

The end of Edward's fifty-year reign was characterised by military and political failure in marked contrast with his earlier successful years. Edward himself became ill over the last two or three years of his reign, and played a limited role in government, dying in 1377. Since his son, the Black Prince, had died a year earlier, Edward was succeeded by his ten-year-old grandson, who became Richard II (1367–1400), coming to the throne in 1377 at the age of ten.

The most immediate and important consequence of the Black Death was a shortage of farm labour, with the consequences of rising wages and food shortages. The King and landowners were sufficiently worried that that an Ordinance of Labour was passed, pegging wages at the level that existed before the plague. Enforcement of these measures caused severe resentment amongst the peasants, and resulted eventually in the Peasant's Revolt in 1381, early in Edward's reign. Another consequence of the plague was a loss of respect and confidence in the Church in general, and the clergy in particular.

Church teaching was that the plague was a consequence of immorality amongst the population, but as more clergy than ordinary people died, and as there was a lot of corruption within the Church with many priests deserting their parishes, this all led to anti-clerical feeling. Chapels and churches were built in thanksgiving by those who survived, indeed three Cambridge University Colleges were founded following the plague. This climate of anti-clericalism would continue to fester and grow slowly leading eventually to Henry VIII separating from the Catholic Church to form the Anglican Church.

During the early years of Richard II's reign, a series of Councils had taken decisions on his behalf, including in 1381 the need to suppress the Peasants Revolt which was caused by a combination of political tension, the Black Death and new high taxes needed to finance war with France in the early years of the Hundred Years War. Richard personally faced down a large demonstration during the revolt at the age of only fourteen after the Archbishop of Canterbury and the nation's Treasurer had been massacred by a mob, but a considerable number of executions, including that of the rebellion's leader, Wat Tyler, rapidly restored order.

By 1389, Richard had gained political control and ruled peacefully for the next eight years, but in 1397 he took his revenge on the nobility who had opposed him earlier, executing or exiling many of them. In 1399 Henry Bolingbroke, grandson of Edward III, who had been exiled, invaded England to claim the throne, there was little resistance, and Bolingbroke was able to depose Richard and was then crowned as Henry IV. Richard died in prison soon afterwards, probably murdered.

Henry Bolingbroke, now known as Henry IV, was Richard II's cousin and the first English monarch to be a native English speaker. He managed to bypass Richard's seven-year-old heir apparent, Edmund Mortimer. Surprisingly Edmund was well treated and brought up with the King's own children, John and Philippa. He survived Henry's reign to be set free from his restricted protective custody, and to be rehabilitated by Henry V. He was appointed to be the King's Lieutenant in Ireland, where he died of the plague in 1425. Henry IV's reign had been an unruly one with rebellions and warring; it is noted for a Welsh rebellion led unsuccessfully by Owain Glyndwr (1359–1415), the last native Welshman to hold the title of Prince of Wales, later immortalised by Shakespeare in his play Henry IV.

Henry V succeeded his father, imposing his will on the country, and reviving the Hundred Years War with France. His reign is noted for his famous victory at the Battle of Agincourt in 1415 against large numerical odds and attributed to the supremacy of the English and Welsh archers with their longbows, which saw him come close to conquering France. At the end of the military campaign in 1420 the Treaty of Troyes recognised Henry as the Regent and heir apparent to the French throne; he subsequently married the daughter of King Charles VI of France.

In England, his reign was generally peaceful, he promoted the use of the English language, both in government as well as being the first king to use English in his personal correspondence since the Norman conquest. Through the years 1417 to 1420 Henry had continued campaigning in France, gradually amassing more lands in a bitter and brutal campaign; after a brief spell in

England, he returned to France in 1421, but died on campaign, possibly of dysentery, the following year.

His son, the infant Henry VI (1421–1471), succeeded to the throne when less than a year old, becoming the youngest monarch in English history. A regency council governed in his name, and he was formally crowned in 1429, at the age of 7. When still less than a year old, he also succeeded to the title of King of France through the Treaty of Troyes, and was crowned at Notre Dame in Paris in 1431 aged 10. Since he came to the throne, England had been losing ground in the Hundred Years War, due to a lack of leadership, and the brief, but startling, military campaign of Joan of Arc (1412–1431); she is described as a simple peasant girl who saw a vision of the archangel and saints who instructed her to lead the French army into battle and to victory.

Her persistence was such that she managed to gain audience with the French king, Charles VII (1403–1461), whose troops were faring badly at the time. After a solemn religious assessment she was sent with troops to try and lift the six month old English siege of Orleans in 1431. Army morale turned around rapidly and the siege was lifted in only nine days, however barely a month later she was captured and turned over to the English army. After a religious assessment and trial by the English, she was found guilty on several counts and was burnt at the stake, but by this time the tide of war had turned in favour of the French.

On reaching the age of sixteen in 1437, Henry VI was declared of age and took control of the government and as a young king chose advisors who favoured peace in France; his marriage was arranged with Margaret of Anjou, the niece of King Charles VII, who took as a dowry the regions of Maine and Anjou from England. More French land was lost to the English over the next few years in attritional battles. Henry had a mental breakdown in 1453, initiating three decades of civil war between Henry's House of Lancaster (symbol a red rose) and the rival House of York (symbol a white rose), who each claimed the throne through their Plantagenet bloodline; with their different coloured rose emblems it is easy to see why these years of civil war are known as the Wars of the Roses.

With Henry's breakdown, the Duke of York, Richard Plantagenet, was appointed Protector of the Realm and it had been agreed that, as Duke of York, he would succeed to the throne on Henry VI's death, but within a few weeks of this agreement being achieved, and after some years of factional warfare in England, he was killed fighting at the battle of Wakefield against an army of Henry VI in 1460. Henry's recovery from his year of insanity had prolonged this internecine struggle, and it has been said that *"...if Henry's insanity was a tragedy, his recovery was a national disaster."*

Within a few weeks of Richard of York's death, his eldest surviving son was acclaimed as Edward IV; Henry VI at this time was still alive, but was subject to a second episode of madness, such that Edward assumed the throne. Later Henry was captured and held as a prisoner in the Tower of London. After further campaigning the Earl of Warwick, the most powerful baron at the time and known as the "Kingmaker", restored Henry VI to the throne in 1470, and forced

Edward IV into exile. Henry, by this time, was no longer capable of ruling effectively, and his second reign lasted less than six months.

However, the Earl of Warwick had overstretched his forces in France and could no longer protect Henry, thus giving Edward IV the assistance he needed to win back his throne with Warwick being killed at the Battle of Barnet in 1471. Edward IV had been King of England for almost ten years, from 1461 to 1470, when he was briefly overthrown. He was the first Yorkist King of England, and the ten years of his first reign were associated with the violence of the Wars of the Roses, with its constant fighting for supremacy between those supporting the House of Lancaster, and the opposing House of York.

After the Earl of Warwick was killed at the Battle of Barnet in April 1471 Edward was again victorious at the Battle of Tewkesbury in May 1471 when the forces of the House of Lancaster were decisively defeated; peace then ruled until his death in 1483. Henry VI died in 1471, or was possibly murdered when Edward IV returned to the throne; his legacy was the building of Eton College and King's College Cambridge.

The Lancastrians (red rose) had largely been wiped out in all the various battles and political manoeuvring. Edward had ten children by Elizabeth Woodville, unusually the widow of a very minor noble, together with several illegitimate offspring, thus ensuring that there would be persisting claims to the throne in subsequent years.

Edward V, his eldest son, succeeded to the throne at the age of 13 on his father's death in 1483, and was notionally king for three months. Edward and his younger brother the Duke of York, as young princes were confined to the Tower of London, ostensibly for their own protection, but then disappeared, presumed murdered; their deaths are attributed to Richard III, their uncle, who had been appointed Lord Protector when the young Edward notionally came to the throne. Having effectively taken the throne, either as a result of the murder of the two princes in the Tower, or as a consequence of their death by illness, Edward IV was therefore succeeded by his nephew as King Richard III. He was to be the last Plantagenet king and the last king from the House of York.

Two major rebellions occurred shortly after Richard's accession to the throne: the first of which was by the Duke of Buckingham, his first cousin, who was defeated and executed. The second rebellion was led by Henry Tudor, whose claim to the throne was somewhat tenuous coming through the female line and an illegitimate one at that, but he defeated Richard at the Battle of Bosworth Field, making him the last English King to die in battle only two years after his succession to the throne.

Following the battle, Richard's remains were unceremoniously buried in an unmarked grave, but came to light in Leicester five hundred years later beneath a modern car park and have now been ceremonially reinterred in Leicester Cathedral.

In his brief reign, Richard achieved some improvements for his subjects, including a Council of the North, a Court of Requests for poor people without legal representation (compare with modern legal aid), and the introduction of bail in 1484 to protect people prior to trial. He also founded the College of Arms, and lifted restrictions on the newly introduced printing and sale of books, together with ordering that laws and statutes should be translated from the pre-existing Norman French into English.

Plantagenet English kings:

Henry II	ruled 1154–1189	son of Matilda	1133–1189
Richard I	ruled 1189–1199	son of Henry II	1157–1199
John	ruled 1199–1216	son of Henry II	1166–1216
Henry III	ruled 1216–1272	son of John	1207–1272
Edward I	ruled 1272–1307	son of Henry III	1239–1307
Edward II	ruled 1307–1327	son of Edward I	1284–1327
Edward III	ruled 1327–1377	son of Edward II	1312–1377
Richard II	ruled 1377–1399	grandson of Edward III	1367–1399

House of Lancaster:

Henry IV	ruled 1399–1413	Grandson of Edward III	1367–1413
Henry V	ruled 1413–1422	son of Henry IV	1386–1422
Henry VI	ruled 1422–1471	son of Henry V	1421–1471

House of York:

| Edward IV | ruled 1461–70 and 1471–83 | Great grandson of Edward III | 1442–1483 |

House of Lancaster:

| Henry VI | briefly 1470–1471 | Son of Henry V | d. 1471 |

House of York:

Edward IV	again ruled 1471–1483	great grandson of Edward III	d. 1483
Edward V	ruled for three months	son Edward IV	1470–1483
Richard III	ruled 1483–1485	great grandson of Edward III	1452–1485

Possible further reading:
The Plantagenets by Dan Jones (William Collins)

Chapter 30
Europe, 11th to 14th Century

Developmentally, this was a vital period for Europe; markers and patterns were laid down geographically, culturally and socially, which provided seminal directions and precursors that Europe would follow as it developed in the following centuries. The Christian Church had already diverged along differing lines with eastern and western Popes holding court in Constantinople and Rome respectively. The Church had developed separately from the apparatus of government, in great contrast to the Islamic Empire, where state and religion developed as one, and where accordingly the apparatus of government grew out of Islamic beliefs.

Whilst the teachings of the Church were clearly important in European development, they were only one of many factors contributing to social structure, and to the development of mores of behaviour. The precepts of Christianity, especially the Ten Commandments, are relatively few and much more broadly based than the thousands of directives laid down in the Koran, or indeed the punitive and retributive teachings of the Old Testament. Due to these broad Christian principles there is much more latitude for discussion and division than there is in Islam (although our modern age bears testament to the fact that Islam is no more free from theological disputation than its Christian counterpart), but there is a major emphasis on faith in Christianity, with downplaying and intolerance towards logic.

There was surprise and disappointment when the second coming of the Messiah did not materialise at the time of the first millennium on the presumed anniversary of Christ's birth, or again thirty years later on the anniversary of his crucifixion. There were faint echoes of this at the turn of the second millennium.

Although European boundaries would continue to shift in the thousand years following the first millennium, much of Europe by the end of this time is already becoming recognisable to us as we look back from today's map. Nations continued to wax and wane, and some would disappear altogether during the second millennium. This was a time when riches and power were still concentrated in very few hands. It was, however, also a time when those few hands were being increasingly questioned and resented. The great mass of the population was still engaged in subsistence farming, frequently as serfs, with a tithe of their produce owed to their landowner, who was generally either a local baron or the Church.

The Church was getting steadily wealthier, and accumulating more and more land and riches through this period, in a process that would eventually end in England when Henry VIII decided to confiscate Church property and possessions in the Reformation. In Germany the break with the Papacy had come a few years earlier than the English reformation as a result of Martin Luther's questioning of articles of doctrine, especially the selling of indulgences.

Life was dangerous in many parts of Europe due to marauding armies engaged in battles to acquire more land, or bands of brigands simply raiding and stealing. At the lower end of the scale, bands of roaming outlaws were only interested in stealing enough food or valuables to continue their existence outside the law. Outlaws were people declared to be outside the law and therefore also outside the protection of the law, such that they might be killed by another person without the killing being regarded as murder.

It was a time when the common man needed protection against these hazards, since individuals on their own were in no position to resist much of the violence and lawlessness that was abroad. In this way a system grew up that we know as feudalism, in which the peasant (or common man) gave a tithe of his produce to his lord in exchange for protection in times of uncertainty. Under feudalism the land was productive, and with gradual improvement in selective breeding of plants and animals a surplus was often produced which allowed the peasantry a certain safety net, and a minor degree of independence, although the downturn in the climate during the 13th century gave rise to poor crops and episodes of famine.

It is necessary to compare this European state of development with the two other great organised blocks of population existing at that time. The first of these is China, which was extremely autocratic and hierarchical. Such a system has a lot of problems, but it also has some advantages, and if the Emperor at the top of the hierarchy is farsighted and benign, then there is a good basis for development of learning and the invention of ways for improving the lot of the population. Although Chinese society was very autocratic, many advances and great projects had taken place, of which one of the most impressive is the construction of the Grand Canal, some 1,776 km of north-south waterway, to allow the transport of rice grown in the south to the less productive north.

Cities and trades were already well developed in China at this time because an autocratic Emperor can direct the production of sufficient food and other essentials to keep some of the population employed solely in producing other desirable goods, including everything from basic clothing and pottery, to artistic items. Such a society may also have sufficient spare capacity and money to maintain and train a standing army, a luxury which previously existed in Europe in Roman times and then not again for a millennium, but also a luxury available to a state with internal peace, which needs to defend its external borders against raiders or invaders.

The other great empire at this time that was developmentally well ahead of Christian Europe, albeit on a different path, was that of Islam. As already noted, the bureaucracy of religion and state were melded together in Islam, and once again, in an area with stable external boundaries and internal peace, learning and scholarship can be commissioned and can flourish. Around the Mediterranean, the accumulated experience and scholarship of earlier ages had been concentrated through the first millennium in major centres, notably Alexandria, Baghdad, Damascus and Cordoba. Great centres of learning like this continued to develop through the early years of the second millennium.

With the Muslim expansion into Spain, and the majority of the Iberian Peninsula under a single unified government, it was also possible for scholarship, art and architecture to forge ahead. The great library at Cordoba boasted a collection of at least 400,000 books by the 13th century, while China had long possessed groups of scholars and scribes working under the direction of the Emperor. By comparison with these intellectual power houses of China and Islam, we find a Europe with only those roads the Romans left, no canals, and with the seats of learning confined to small monasteries proud to own libraries containing only a few dozen books. Some indication of the differential wealth and scholastic development percolated through to Europe across guarded national boundaries, along the Silk Road from China when travel through Islamic territory was permitted, and through seaborne Mediterranean trade.

Europe was beginning to develop the means of state administration, and, with the feudal system, kings granted land to their nobles in exchange for the right to demand military service, either to defend against rebellion, or to provide armies for land grabbing invasions of other countries. In Britain Alfred, Edward and Athelstan in the 10th century had started to provide the basis of a state bureaucracy, and William the Conqueror then commanded his great census of 1086, which became the Domesday Book: knowledge is power. The internal situation of most European countries, as in Britain, was still unstable, and the succession from one monarch to the next was never assured.

Individual nobles would still often rebel, and battles over monarchical succession could last for months or even years. Each change of monarch or autocrat would bring a new set of rules, a different system of taxation, together with personal difficulties for any barons who had supported the previous regime and made enemies for when a new regime arrived.

The early centuries of the second millennium were a time of great change in Europe, both for peaceful activities and for the development of warfare. Gunpowder, primitive cannon and siege engines appeared, using technology developed, but not used, in the Far East. The crossbow was invented, refining shooting distance and accuracy, though at the expanse of speed of reloading. Personal armour increased, both as chainmail and as plated armour, and this in turn led to the concept of the 'Just War', the chivalrous knight, and the peacetime practice of jousting and mock combat, though when unhorsed a knight in heavy armour was very vulnerable.

Standing armies of professional soldiers became common again for the first time since the Roman era, but most armies still comprised a large proportion of rapidly conscripted and untrained men, who still fought on foot, in contrast to their landed overlords on horseback. Then as now, and through the ages, war has been a great driver of innovation and invention, not just in new armaments, but in all aspects of technology and science, including communications, transport, medicine and surgery.

The population of Europe, which is estimated at around 40 million people at the turn of the millennium, grew steadily, only to be severely knocked back by the arrival of the Black Death in 1347, which killed about half the population. Prior to this date land under the plough had increased in proportion to the population to be fed, while the proportion of existing forest had gradually diminished. Some peasants came off the land and were hired as paid labourers, and wealthier families recruited paid house servants. The economic effects of fewer people producing food combined with a scarcity of labour was a severe change to the labour market. Some villages were abandoned after the Black Death when their population had been decimated adding to the drift of peasants off the land and to the towns.

To add to this was the climatic downturn in the mid-13th century which accentuated the difficulties of food production and left pockets of famine. All this emphasised the growing money economy which was gradually replacing the previous rural system of barter. In Britain markets were licensed in towns in exchange for a tax paid to the monarchy, and the peasantry could now find an outlet for their surplus produce in exchange for cash; this was a system with echoes of a modern poll tax, but for a market stall, so that if produce was bartered or no purchase was made then no contribution went to the exchequer.

Sometimes, these new town markets were associated with a monastery, and in these instances, the monastery also frequently provided a focus of learning for a lucky few, but European literacy rates were well below those in China or Islam. In that era, as in our own, education in the form of the ability to read and write, and therefore facilitating the acquisition of knowledge, often provided a route out of poverty; once again we see that knowledge is power. Although ancient seats of learning were present in Islamic centres before the millennium, such as Alexandria, Baghdad and Cordoba, the concept of such centres of learning came late to Europe and was usually associated with a religious foundation.

European universities came into being, first at Bologna in 1088, followed quickly by Paris, Oxford and Padua in the 12th century. By 1400, Europe possessed over fifty universities, where knowledge was not only taught but also questioned. The taught knowledge was largely in the form of theology, law, and philosophy or natural sciences: medicine made up a 4th discipline. Knowledge was disseminated from Islamic centres and translated from Arabic or Greek into Latin, which became the universal language of learning and communication across Europe. Ancient writings on philosophy and mathematics together with the medical writings of Aristotle, Galen and Hippocrates were translated from the Greek and slowly diffused through Europe, in this way learning from ancient times gradually percolated through Arabia and across Europe.

Contributions to the everyday technology of Europe came largely from the Islamic World, often via Arabic Spain (then known as Al-Andalus), rather than from the Far East. Notable exceptions to this were the use of numbers, including decimals, which came from India through Arabic Islam, and the technique of making both silk and paper, which had been used in China for over a thousand years before reaching Europe. Even so, most documents of importance were still being recorded on vellum (calf skin), which is tougher and has a lifetime that is longer than paper, so that even today all British Acts of Parliament are still written and preserved on vellum, and copies of Magna Carta from 1215 are still on display 800 years later.

The interchange of thought between Christendom and Islam, was much impaired at this time by the Crusades. Apart from the organised and well recorded attempts to recover the Holy Land, and other territory around the eastern Mediterranean for Christianity, there was a gradual uncoordinated thrust southward through the Iberian Peninsula to drive Islam south. Cordoba had become the most prominent seat of government and learning in the early 10th century, some 200 years after Islamic forces crossed the Straits of Gibraltar, but in 1013 it was recaptured by Christian forces after internal Arab strife and division resulted in the end of the Umayyad caliphate there.

Sometime later, Toledo was captured by Christian forces in 1085, and as with Cordoba, its treasures of art and learning suddenly became part of Christendom. The union of the monarchies of Aragon and Castile in Northern Spain, through a marriage alliance in 1479 between Ferdinand of Aragon and Isabella of Castile, expedited the final expulsion of Islam from the Iberian Peninsula. The last Muslim capital of Spain was Granada, which surrendered after a long siege by Catholic armies in 1492.

In the meantime, the western strip of the Iberian Peninsula, which we now know as Portugal, had remained largely separate. In pre-Roman time Portugal was settled by the Celts. Al-Andalus had been first conquered by the Romans in the 3rd century BC. Two Roman provinces, Lusitania and Galicia in the north, were particularly valued for their metal mines producing copper, tin, gold and silver, so the Romans had built roads, bridges and aqueducts to service the extraction of these minerals. When Rome collapsed in the early 5th century, Portugal was invaded by Germanic tribes, including Goths and Vandals along with much of the rest of the Iberian Peninsula. Rome withdrew her legions when the city was sacked in 410 and following this, a Dark Age ensued for the next four centuries.

In 429, Iberia had become a Visigoth kingdom, with its capital at Toledo. Three centuries later, when the Muslims invaded from the south, Portugal became a country under Islamic rule, but as Muslim territory gradually contracted three centuries later, the kingdoms of Galicia and Portugal emerged. In the middle of the 10th century north eastern Spain had still resisted Islamic expansion, and comprised the three kingdoms of Leon, Galicia and Castile: these were united under the generalship of a legendary Castilian nobleman known as El Cid meaning 'The Lord' (1040–1099), who won a series of battles against the Muslims, or Moors, starting the process of driving them back southwards, known as the Reconquista.

Galicia stayed with Spain, and Portugal was effectively born after the Battle of Sao Mamede in 1128 for independence of the county of Portugal, with victory going to Afonso (1106–1185), who thus became the first King of Portugal. Knights travelling to the Holy Land for the second crusade stopped in Portugal and helped to liberate the city of Lisbon from the Moors in 1147. In the south the Algarve region of Portugal was only finally regained from Islam a century later in 1249. The country has remained intact and unaltered since then apart from the years 1580–1640 when a Portuguese crisis of succession caused the region to be ruled from Spain, during which period the Portuguese Empire and world influence declined.

In northern Europe, the increased prosperity and trading opportunities facilitated the founding and rise of the Hanseatic League. This was initially a trading empire of North German seaports which grew up to foster commerce by agreeing common diplomatic, legal and trading practices starting in the late 12th century. At its height around 1450 it included Scandinavian and some English seaports making a maximum of 170 trading cities and seaports. The League had its own ships, and even an army to protect its trading interests, but it grew large and unwieldy and declined from the late 16th century onwards with internal disagreements, though it was not completely dismantled until the German Empire came into being in 1862.

The 11th to 14th centuries in Europe thus saw the coalescence of several areas of civilisation, which would then see gradual expansion and further organisation through succeeding centuries into forms that we still recognise today. In this way learning, markets, trade, the use of money and banking, all put down foundations which developed into the later European structures that we now live with.

Possible further reading:
The Birth of Europe by Michael Andrews (BBC Books)

Chapter 31
The Medieval Arab World

The first four Caliphs, or successors, after Mohammed's death in 632 were his relatives. Initially fathers-in-law, and then his son-in-law. We have seen that the last of these, Ali, the 4th caliph, cousin and son-in-law of Mohammed, was murdered in 661 following which the Islamic world split into the Umayyads in Damascus in Syria (taking their name from Umayya ibn And Shams) and the Abbasids in Baghdad (named from Abbas ibn Abdul Muttalib, the third caliph and uncle of Mohammed): this situation lasted until the middle of the 10th century some 300 years after Mohammed's death (chapter 19). Comment has already been made upon the rivalries and splits within Islam, and the generation of different distinct branches of the religion; of the two major branches, the name Shia means a follower of Ali, and a belief that the caliph should be a direct descendant or relative of Mohammed; the name Sunni refers to the sunnah, the tradition or custom, of appointing the most appropriate individual to be caliph.

After civil war and considerable fighting, in 750 the remaining members of the Umayyad sect (who would become Sunni) were murdered, but one grandson of the tenth and last caliph, Hisham ibn Abd al-Malik survived and fled from Damascus to Spain (a Visigoth kingdom up to the time of the initial Islamic invasion in 711), where he was able to establish a geographically discreet new Caliphate of Islam known as Al-Andalus (chapter 20). This Caliphate lasted from 756–1031, with its centre at Cordoba.

Somewhat earlier, the Arab armies had penetrated from the south, deep into France, where they were finally defeated by Charles Martel at the Battle of Tours in 732 (Chapter 22). Thereafter the Arabs withdrew back to the Iberian Peninsula with Al-Andalus comprising the southern three-quarters of the peninsula; no further moves to extend the empire north again were undertaken. Cordoba became a focus for learning and intellectual achievement, as well as being a large financial centre. It had a population peaking at half a million, almost twice modern numbers. Religious libraries, medical schools and universities drew inquisitive individuals from across the Muslim world at the height of its eminence in the second half of the 10th century.

Matters changed suddenly with the coming of a new ruler in 976, who was only ten years old and whose principal advisor, Almanzor (938–1002), and other regents squabbled resulting in much violence and murder within the caliphate; there followed increasingly strict Koranic teaching by Muslim clergy with objections to many of the books in the libraries, and most of the books on philosophy were burnt, sold or lost to pacify clerical objections. A period of civil strife followed, with destruction of buildings as well as books. Steady decline followed up until the time when the city was recaptured by Christians after a long siege in 1236.

Further to the east after Mohammed's death, Arab armies had invaded Syria and Iraq to the north, and conquered Jerusalem in 638. Meanwhile other Islamic armies had spread east as far as Kabul in 664, and the Hindu Kush to the north of India, around 710. There are reports of Arab forces even reaching China at about the same time as Arab expansion into Spain at the beginning of the 8th century. After the ebb and flow of distant fighting, the frontier of the Islamic world stabilised along the Caucasus Mountains and the River Oxus following Arab defeats in Azerbaijan, and in the Pamir Mountains (in modern Tajikistan) in 751. The boundaries of the Islamic Empire then remained fairly constant through the centuries after the initial astonishing speed and spread of Islam through North Africa to southern Spain, all of the Middle East, and as far as Northern India. The Persian Empire no longer existed, and the Byzantine Empire struggled to maintain control over their restricted lands.

Arguments, and often warfare, persisted within Islam with the various Caliphates being passed on by blood inheritance. The dissident group known as Shiites claimed that the right of interpreting the Koran should be limited to Mohammed's direct descendants. This claim first arose following the murder of the Caliph Ali, son-in-law of Mohammed, in 661 with the contention that Ali as a descendent of Mohammed had been divinely appointed as Imam and was incapable of sin and error. By contrast, the Umayyad Caliphs, known as Sunni, believed that the doctrinal Islamic authority passed from one caliph to the next without needing direct inheritance.

Perhaps because the Empire was so young, and because there was neither a civil service type bureaucracy, nor a religious library of records, there is very little archive material from the first two centuries of Islam. Part of this seems attributable to the break-up of administrative arrangements in the countries conquered by the Islamic expansion, so that in addition to a lack of records, the period was also accompanied by a considerable drop in commerce and population. Gradually a new ruling Arab elite mixed and integrated with local populations. In 749 a new Caliph, Abu-Al-Abbas, set out to restore the Caliphate to earlier orthodox ways. His name translates as "shedder of blood", and in 750 he executed the last Umayyad Caliph and murdered all his male relatives, thus beginning the Abbasid Caliphate which ruled the Arab world for the next two centuries. During this time, there was a flowering of learning and culture in the Baghdad capital to rival that being achieved Cordoba, where there were said to be 700 mosques at its zenith. Taxes had been raised allowing the Caliph and his court to live in a distinctly magnificent manner.

In the 9th century the Persian troops in the Baghdad Caliph's army became unreliable, and therefore slaves from Turkestan were recruited and known as Mamluks (an Arabic word which translates as property or slave), and this made the situation worse; the Mamluks mutinied and murdered the Caliph, al-

Mutawakkil, in Baghdad: this event in 861 is a landmark which ended the rule of Mohammed's family, and as the central despotic authority of the Empire gradually collapsed, control fragmented. A central purpose no longer seemed to exist across the Islamic world. A hundred years later, however, in 972, descendants of Ali, cousin of the Prophet and the 4th caliph, spearheaded a revolution in North Africa, calling themselves Fatimids and claiming descent from the Prophet's daughter, Fatima.

Thus, by the end of the 10th century Islam had already split into three different Caliphates, each representing a rival branch of the Prophet's family. The Abbasid Caliph in Baghdad had little power, the Fatimid Caliph ruled North Africa, Egypt and Syria, and the Umayyad Caliph controlled a discreet but wealthy and cultured state comprising the southern three-quarters of the Iberian Peninsula. For the previous three centuries, this Islamic world had prevented European trade with Africa, Asia or the Far East along the Silk Road, and Islamic sea power had controlled and blocked trade through the Mediterranean. Due to internal Islamic strife this blockade on land and by sea gradually relaxed, allowing increased European trade which brought with it increasing wealth, power and culture, and helped Europe to climb out of its Dark Age.

In the 11th century, nomadic horse-riding tribes from the Steppes of Asia came south and west into Northern Persia and Mesopotamia. Included amongst these tribes were the Seljuks who occupied Baghdad in 1055, displacing the Abbasid Caliph. The Seljuk armies continued to the west, defeating a Byzantine army and over-running Turkey to reach the Bosphorus after battle at Malazkirt in modern eastern Turkey in 1071. Initially, the Seljuks had been heathen, but their emperors had become Muslim. Christendom had been fighting against Muslim aggression along southern European boundaries in Spain, France, Italy, Sicily and Crete for the four centuries since the death of the Prophet. Initially the Byzantine Empire had formed a buffer in the east, but after the Battle of Malazkirt the Seljuks (Turko-Persian Sunni Muslims) had reached the Bosphorus, and Christianity was facing an Islamic threat from the east as well from the south.

This caused the Byzantine Emperor Alexios (1048–1118) to appeal to European rulers for help in the defence of Christendom. As a result, in 1095 Pope Urban II (1042–1099) preached the first Crusade; the message, imploring aid for the defence of Christendom and help in liberating what we now call Turkey, became confused with the seemingly desirable objective of re-imposing Christian rule over Jerusalem, the most significant Christian location.

The First Crusade did indeed capture Palestine and Jerusalem, but without liberating Turkey from the Seljuks so that the Crusaders came to occupy some of the Holy Land but without any land communication in between to Europe, and their primitive lines of supply by sea were unable to cope with this. The next two hundred years would be marked by no less than nine crusades (chapter 27) with the Crusaders capturing Jerusalem, massacring the Muslim inhabitants and holding the city for almost a century until it was regained by Muslim forces led by Saladin (1138–1193), the Arab Muslim ruler of Egypt and Syria, in 1187.

This reversal for the crusaders led to the Third Crusade from 1189–1192 which regained a lot of the lost ground but failed to retake Jerusalem. Surprisingly during this period trade between Europe and the Middle East flourished, and at the same time Arabic thought, innovations and culture spread to Europe, contributing in part to the beginning of the Renaissance (chapter 40), aided by translations of seminal works from Arabic into Latin.

Before the First Crusade of 1098, the North African Muslim Caliphate had included Sicily and some of Southern Italy. This was at the time of Norman expansion, and contemporaneous with the Norman invasion of Britain in 1066, Duke Roger of Normandy (first Count of Sicily, 1031–1101) regained southern Italy and Sicily for Christendom. Somewhat later his son, Roger II of Sicily (1095–1154), took war against Islam south, and over the course of some 15 years occupied much of the African coastline, including the section from Tunis to Tripoli, thus breaking the control of Islam over Mediterranean sea trade. By the time of his death he had been able to unite all the Norman possessions in southern Italy, in addition ruling all of Sicily and his North African conquests

In the 12th century tribes from Mongolia and Central Asia were pressing westward against the eastern extent of Islam. The Seljuks were in control of the Turkish peninsula, cutting off the supply lines between European Christendom and the territories taken in the First Crusade along the east coast of the Mediterranean including Jerusalem, the Lebanon and as far north as Antioch. This lack of land communication, or a decent supply route for the crusading armies, was the major cause of doom for the crusader armies and their ultimate lack of success.

From the time of the end of the First Crusade in 1099 until 1184, Christendom, mainly in the form of the Franks, had managed to defend their conquests in the Middle East as four largely independent and self-governing territories along the eastern shore of the Mediterranean, starting in the north with the Princedom of Antioch on the coast, and the County of Edessa inland to the east, the County of Tripoli (not to be confused with Tripoli in Libya) corresponding to some of modern Lebanon, and the Kingdom of Jerusalem extending south to the Gulf of Aqaba, but not including Damascus.

There had been enough crusaders to hold this area because the Seljuk Empire in modern Turkey was prone to much infighting, but the situation changed when Zengi (1085–1146), a Mamluk soldier of the Seljuks, started campaigning after being made Lord of Mosul, and then Aleppo. In 1144 he was able to conquer the County of Edessa, which was subsequently abandoned by the crusaders, but only two years later Zengi was murdered by his servants.

The reaction in Christendom to the loss of Edessa was one of startlement and reaction; Louis VII of France and Conrad II, Emperor of Germany responded with the second Crusade. The Seljuks were now largely in control of the Turkish Peninsula and were responsible for starting the process of conversion of its peoples from Christianity to Islam. The Seljuks allowed a moderate degree of local autonomy, such that Asia Minor was still a Confederation of Tribes, but the strength of the Empire was its military might, and the central regime which they set up incorporating local customs, survived the Caliphates to become the essence of Islamic society throughout the Middle East.

The local tribal administrations were run throughout the Middle East by religious leaders and teachers of Islam, thus providing at a devolved level a common cultural, political and social system. These local religious elites were the key factor in building homogeneity of Islam across different tribes, and this Seljuk pattern spread through the Arab world to be maintained under successive empires. However, by the 13th century the Seljuk regime was already weakening, and its financial strength was sapped by recurring crusades: the Arabs had already lost Sicily and southern Italy, while in Spain the re-conquest by Christians had begun.

Saladin, the first Sultan of Egypt and Syria (1137–1193), had declared the North African Fatimid Caliphate to be ended in 1161 when he seized power in Egypt. He then proceeded to recapture Jerusalem in 1187, which along with the loss of Edessa, helped provoke the Third Crusade of 1189. He was a great warrior and was able to defend Jerusalem against the Crusaders. Following this hostility towards Christianity with persecution of Christians grew. Saladin founded the Abbuyid dynasty following Sunni beliefs, which ruled The Levant, Egypt and the Red Sea Coast, until it was taken over by a coup from its palace guards of Turkish Mamluks. The Mamluks faced and destroyed the remaining Crusades, and the Caliphate remained in Cairo with the eclipse of Baghdad now being complete.

In addition to this, the Mamluks had faced the Mongol onslaught under the generalship of Genghis Khan at the end of the 12th century (Chapter 28). In 1258 Hulagu Khan (1218–1265), grandson of Genghis Khan, crossed the River Oxus to besiege Baghdad. The Caliph was summoned to surrender, but because of his refusal the city was stormed and sacked, and this last Abbasid Caliph was murdered. Subsequently the Mongol army was weakened and distracted by the death of the Great Khan in 1260, and this weakened Mongol army was then defeated by the Islamic Mamluks in battle near Nazareth.

The spread of Islam to the east had got as far as the western parts of what we now recognise as India and Pakistan, where many of the Arab soldiery had settled, then leading a peaceful and unwarlike existence until the 12th century, during which time Buddhism had declined and Islam became more deeply rooted. This peaceful existence was upset by new Muslim invaders in the 11th century, and then again at the end of the 12th century, thus establishing an area in the Ganges Valley and around Delhi where Islam persisted, ultimately necessitating the partition of the Indian subcontinent between largely Muslim Pakistan and Hindu India in 1947.

Possible further reading:
Great Arab Conquests by John Bagot Glubb (Quartet Books)

Chapter 32
Medieval Empires

Europe, Africa and Asia have seen many Empires ranging from the large Roman and Mongol Empires to much smaller ones. There has also been considerable variation in the time for which Empires have lasted. By their very nature they often start their creation under particularly charismatic and ambitious rulers and may or may not last long, depending on that individual ruler's arrangements for succession, which may be through a bloodline or may be to one or more further selected people. Often, empires have succumbed to warfare and competition between the heirs or successors of an earlier ruler.

In Europe two thousand years ago, the Roman Empire was at its peak during the reign of Trajan in the early years of the 2nd century AD (chapter 15). A little later in the 4th century a tribe of nomadic people called the Huns arrived at the eastern margins of Europe, and within the next 50 years established a very large, albeit short-lived, empire which encompassed much of the present Balkan countries and the Steppes between the Adriatic and Black Seas. Their leader Attila (406–453) rose to conquer an area including present day Ukraine and the Balkans. He even attempted to conquer Gaul, getting as far as Orleans before being defeated at the battle of the Catalonian Plains in 451 when his adversaries were an alliance of Romans and Visigoths.

After being repulsed, a further Battle of Nedao was fought in the northern Balkans between the Huns and other tribes that they had previously conquered. On this occasion also the Huns were defeated; this last battle was fought under the leadership of Attila's son Ellak, whose defeat in 454 saw the start of the collapse of the Hunnic Empire in which other tribes had also been subjected by the Huns. Several of the Barbarian invasions of the 5th century, including the Vandals' sacking of Rome in 410, can be traced to the displacement or migration of people from Eastern Europe including the Austrogoths, Visigoths, Vandals and Francs. In this way the Hunnic Empire only lasted from 370 to 469, and as the Huns did not possess writing it has left little trace in the annals of history.

During the same unstable years in the north Mediterranean lands of the 5th century, many settlers moved to the coastal lagoons around the north of the Adriatic Sea in modern north-eastern Italy and north-western Croatia. Thus the Republic of Venice came into existence, not just around Venice itself, but also along the coastal islands along the eastern Adriatic. The Republic and its little empire existed on sea power and merchant trading and remained united as a communal defence mechanism against the Lombards and the Byzantine Empire then controlling northern Italy. The first Duke of Venice was proclaimed in 697 and through the 8th century Venice became more important as a trading port with an increasing shipbuilding industry. Help with defence was sought from Charlemagne's son Pepin. This tactic backfired because Pepin came to lay siege to Venice, but without success as the swampy conditions around the lagoon proved both difficult for fighting and was also a reservoir of disease, from which Pepin himself died some months later.

Through the 9th century, Venice was recognised and the beginnings of the modern city were laid down with its maritime waterways. In the middle of the 9th century Venice mustered a fleet of sixty war galleys, each with two hundred soldiers, to try and assist the Byzantine Empire in driving Muslims from Crotone in southern Italy, though this venture failed. Later in Medieval times Venice participated in assisting the efforts of the first Crusade and also in subsequent Crusades.

The largest empire centre on the Mediterranean was that which the Muslims forged in the years following the death of Mohammed in 632 and extended along the eastern and southern shores of the Mediterranean leaving the countries and regions to the north populated with Christian rulers and incoming tribes from the north. The Muslim empire is covered in chapter 21.

By the 15th century Venice was in control of most of the Dalmatian coast along the eastern shore of the Adriatic Sea and is estimated to have had a navy of over three thousand ships, each with a complement of at least one hundred soldiers. Enclaves were established on some of the Greek Islands, including Crete and Cyprus. In the early part of the 16th century Venice allied itself with the Holy Roman Emperor and the King of Spain, but suffered defeat in battle in 1539. War followed with the Ottoman Empire in 1570, when Venice, Spain and the Pope together combined to form the Holy League with a navy of over two hundred war galleys, half of which were Venetian. Hostilities came to a head at the Battle of Lepanto in 1571 when the Holy League defeated the Ottoman Empire in a great sea battle. Thereafter, the Ottomans slowly declined.

Fighting continued through the 17th century, but plague hit Venice in 1630 killing one third of the population, but although the epidemic hit Venetian military and trade efforts hard, other Mediterranean nations were equally affected. Venice remained a power through the 17th and 18th centuries with many wars between the various neighbouring European nations, but the constant fighting, and the expense of maintaining its navy, continued to wear the city down and by the end of the 18th century Venice was unable to continue defending itself, and particularly unable to resist Napoleon's troops in 1814 when the city was looted before peace was achieved.

On the western coast of northern Italy the Republic of Genoa grew up, becoming an independent state between 1005–1797, which included Corsica through much of the second half of this period. Rather like Venice, Genoa also established colonies around the Aegean Sea and indeed into the Black Sea and around Crimea. War with Venice followed towards the end of the 14th century, and in the 15th century the Genoese explorer Christopher Columbus voyaged across the Atlantic to the New World.

Most of the Genoese colonies were annexed by the Ottoman Empire during the 15th century, and in the middle of the century Genoa rose in power as a consequence of its banking industry largely due to silver imports from the New World which helped to finance much of the warfare around Europe. Banking continued to be strategically important through the 16th century with a lot of the newly mined silver from the Americas going straight to Genoa. Subsequently Genoa entered the war of Austrian Succession in 1745 on the wrong side and had to surrender to Austria a year later. Eventually the Republic was occupied by Napoleon Bonaparte's army and its politics and nobility were overthrown. Following the Congress of Vienna in 1815 deciding European state boundaries Genoa was awarded to the Kingdom of Sardinia.

The Bulgarian Empire, between the Adriatic and Black Seas, came into being around the 6th and 7th centuries. To the north a Slavic people would evolve into Poland and Russia and persist in various geographical forms through the whole of the first two millennia. The first Slav state that appeared was Bulgaria, though most of the Bulgars were not Slavs but had their origins in the Hunnic tribes. Slavic influence and individuals were incorporated with the Bulgars and against Byzantium. Gradually the Bulgars themselves were diluted by Slavic blood and influence so that the Bulgarian Empire is felt to originate from 681 and was helped to persist by becoming Christian thanks to St Methodius and St Cyril (chapter 24).

The Empire reached its maximum size during the reign of Simeon the Great in the 10th century. Between 1018 and 1185 there was a period of constant warfare with the Byzantine Empire when the Bulgarian Empire was ruled by the Byzantines. Restoration of autonomy was achieved after a rebellion in 1185 and persisted until the Ottomans conquered the area in 1396, following which many of the country's intelligentsia and priest migrated to Serbia and adjacent states.

The Mongol Empire and its intrusion into Europe is covered in Chapter 28 with the Mongols withdrawing east after only some six decades in Europe from 1206–1271. The influence and changes they left in India where Mongol rule morphed into the Mughal, or Mogul, Empire were rather more long lived.

Although present day Lithuania is a small Baltic country with a population of less than three million people, the country enjoyed much greater influence and ground area in medieval times. Lithuania came into being in the first years of the 13th century under Mindaugas (1203–1263) the first Grand Duke of Lithuania, who subsequently became king. Mindaugas is seen as responsible for stopping the advance of the Mongols in the 13th century. Over the decade following his assassination in 1263 the next three successors to the title were also assassinated. During the 14th century Lithuania was the largest country in Europe, including parts of modern Poland, Russia, Belarus and Ukraine, and in 1569 formed a Polish Lithuanian commonwealth which was to last for the next two centuries until inroads were made upon it by its neighbours, notably Russia. The modern Republic was founded after the First World War, but occupied during the Second

World War first by the Soviet Union and then by Nazi Germany, with the Soviet Union reoccupying the nation at the end of the Second World War. Lithuania became independent again in 1990 as the Soviet Union began to disintegrate.

The Serbian Kingdom emerged from a number of small princedoms, and came into existence in 1217 with the coronation of Stefan Nemanjaic (1165–1228). Further territorial acquisitions followed, and aggressive attacks from the Byzantine Empire were repulsed. Many of these acquisitions were made by King Stefan Dusan (1308–1355), his annexations included territory as far south as the northern part of modern Greece. He established and proclaimed the Empire in 1346. Unfortunately his son and successor was less charismatic and the Empire was gradually lost after the death of a weak ruler in 1371.

The Safavid Empire lasted from 1501–1736. It has its roots in the early 7th century Muslim conquest of Iran which also resulted in the Safavid Dynasty and Empire becoming the bastion of Shia Islam. Much of the Empire, excluding the vastness of the Arabian Peninsula, derived from the Sassanian or Persian Empire which had existed from 224 AD until a couple of decades after the death of Mohammed in 632. In the way in which one empire has often succeeded and replaced another, the Parthian Empire was the initial conquered area abutting the eastern border of the Roman empire and dated as an empire from 247 BC until it was replaced by the Sassanian Empire in 224 AD, which in turn then lasted until was replaced and taken over by Islam in 651 AD.

The Sassanian Empire was at its maximum extent around 620 and gave rise to much of what we now know as Islamic culture before it was taken over by Islam in 651. The Safavids were a later indigenous Persian tribe who took over Persian lands, ruling from 1501–1722. This followed the decline of the Timurid Empire which had been brought into existence when Iran was conquered by the Mongols under Timur, or Tamerlane. Before Mongol rule the region had not existed as a single country, but rather had been ruled by a series of Arab Muslim Caliphs and Turkic Sultans.

The first Shah Ismail proclaimed Shia Islam as the official religion and provided a strong demarcation with the Ottoman Empire to the west and Sunni Uzbeks to the east. The dynasty lasted until 1736, after which time Persia (modern Iran), was weakened firstly by the Dutch East India Company, and secondly by Britain taking over much of the Empire's trade.

The Muslim Safavid Empire occupied much of the land that we now recognise as Iran. The empire arose to fill the void by the Mongol Il-Kahn when it collapsed and disintegrated in the middle of the 14th century. Shah Ismail, who conquered the Mongols, belonged to a mystical Sufi order of Muslims of which there were several dotted around western Asia between the Caspian Sea and the Persian Gulf. Although Shia in origin, there was general tolerance in the empire of Sunni Islam together with long established communities of Jews, Christians and Zoroastrians.

The Safavid beliefs were gradually spread and accepted and the movement became increasingly wealthy, powerful and militant. The Turkman rulers of western Persia attempted to suppress the sect, but in 1501 a young Shah Ismail defeated the Turkmans and captured the capital city Tabriz in northern Iran. He was crowned Shah of Iran and once crowned Shah he also claimed the divine right to rule based on Islamic authority and on a direct relationship to ancient Persian Kings. In this way the Islamic idea of rule through the Caliphate was allied to an idea of royalty dating back to the achievements of the earlier Achaemenid Empire, which held sway from 550–330 BC. The Safavids claimed direct descent from the Prophet and Ismail's successors would in turn also claim to be divinely appointed.

Ismail, who was hidden from view from the age of one when his father died, was educated by a well-known Shia theologian. At the age of 12 he was revealed to the world, and when he was 14 Messianic Sufi fighters won early battle campaigns against the weakened neighbouring rulers. He was undoubtedly an extremely charismatic leader and had an intense self-belief in his ability. Under his rule, and that of his successors, culture flourished, artisans developed great creative and technical skills. The Safavids combined their Islamic Shia faith with elements of pre-Islamic Persian language, stories and customs, which was to act as a basis for the subsequent development of the region, and somewhat later as the national identity for Iran.

Safavid warfare with its frontier neighbours, together with internal manoeuvrings, plotting and chaotic rivalries, continued through to the end of the 16th century until a powerful Shah managed to restore discipline and central authority. The seat of government and monarchy was transferred to Isfahan in 1598 and at the same time the army was organised and equipped with firearms and artillery from European advisors. Control was cemented by Shah Abbas I (1571–1629) when he eliminated all his male blood relatives. Vast and impressive urban construction was ordered to coincide with the official move to Isfahan in 1598 which year corresponded to the year 1,000 in the Islamic calendar. Trade with Europe and India expanded enormously. The Safavid Empire in its closing years displayed great magnificence in culture, architecture and building, which imposed never-ending demands upon a budget already under pressure from military expenditure.

In its weakening state, the Empire expelled Sufi Muslims from Isfahan and put pressure on Jews, Christians and Zoroastrians to convert to Islam. Included among those pressured to convert were Sunni Muslims, and internal rebellion at the beginning of the 18th century exacerbated the problem coming from internal revolts. In 1722 the Afghans conquered Faharabad and laid siege to Isfahan for seven months before the Shah capitulated. The Shah and his family were imprisoned and later murdered, Isfahan was plundered and many of its citizens died, while central government collapsed into anarchy. However, the Safavids had restored pride and trade to the Empire and taken it from its early feudal origins to the newly organised military, administrative and royal hierarchies which became famous across Europe and brought it into the early European orbit, both diplomatically and commercially.

Through the last four millennia, dozens of different states and empires have come and gone in land area of present Pakistan, India and southeast Asia. Some of these entities have survived for hundreds of years, while others have been conquered in their turn after quite short periods, but during their years they have produced dynasties of rulers who lived in luxurious conditions at the expense of the masses of poor peasants, and in some instances the contrasts between the top and bottom of society was a major factor in their decline. In the early part of this period such states or empires could be attributed to a charismatic individual or dynasty; in more recent years religions, including the Hindu or Muslim faiths have provided the impetus.

The Mughal Empire (a corruption of the word Mogul or Mongol) started with Babur who was descended from Timur (Timerlane), and at the time of his death in 1405 had conquered a large part of Central Asia extending as far west as the Persian Gulf. Timur in turn had been descended from Genghis Khan. Timur and his descendants built an empire comprising most of India and Afghanistan, which was extraordinarily powerful and wealthy. Initially Babur conquered Northern India around Delhi, but only survived for a further four years. After his death in 1530 he was succeeded by his son who ruled for a decade, but was then forced out by a highly talented warrior and administrator called Sher Shah, who introduced many economic and administrative innovations.

Babur's grandson, Akbar (1542–1605), succeeded to the throne in 1556 at the age of 12, but his precocious talents meant that he was able to take on much of the royal duties as statesman and warrior within a few years, and as he reigned for almost 50 years he had time to consolidate and extend the territorial domination of the Mughals, thus leaving to his successors more than twice the extent of the Empire that existed at the time of Babur's death. Although Akbar was Muslim, he incorporated both native Indians and Hindus into his government.

India's rich resources, including both land and gold, were able to support a large standing army and internal peace was furthered by a policy of toleration for all faiths, together with a taxation policy which did not penalise non-Muslims. Akbar's son Jahangir was able to extend further his territorial authority. His internal authority was somewhat challenged by two incidents, the first of these was the execution of Arjun, the fifth Guru of the Sikh religion, for subverting the emperor's authority, the second problem was caused by imprisoning a leading Muslim theologian who criticised Mughal policy of ignoring Sharia Law.

Shah Jahan (1592–1666) two generations later is remembered for building the Taj Mahal for his favourite wife who died in 1651. Shah Jahan also built several highly decorated and magnificent mosques. He was succeeded by Aurangzeb who reigned from 1658–1707 and who was more severe in his Muslim observances than previous Mughals. By the time of his death the Mughal Empire covered almost the whole of the Indian subcontinent, which in fact was close to the same size as it had been at the end of Akbar's reign, though warfare in southern and central India and in the northwest had weakened the Empire. The empire continued to be beset by internal problems and rebellions and consequently the British East India Company was easily able to extend its influence.

The empire staggered on in this state through the first half of the 19th century, when there was much conspicuous display of wealth by the small section of the population at the top of the numerous small fragmenting kingdoms. The whole edifice came to an end in 1858 after an incident named the 'Black Hole of Calcutta' in which over a hundred British East India Company men, women and children died of asphyxiation in a prison cell designed for only a handful of people, and the British Government felt obliged to intervene instituting direct rule and disbanding the East India company's private army.

The Khmer Empire in southeast Asia came into being around 800 AD and lasted until the 15th century and was extremely rich in its art, architecture and culture as is testified by the impressive remains at Angkor Wat and other sites. Its demise appears to have been due to a combination of many factors including deforestation to increase agricultural land, the Black Death and a degree of overpopulation, the arrival of Europeans was probably a final insult.

The Ethiopian empire, although not European, has had strong Christian and other ties through the Mediterranean to European fortunes. It was ruled by a dynasty whose members claimed to be of the biblical House of David with descent from King Solomon and the Queen of Sheba, and they replaced the previous dynasty in 1270. This Ethiopian dynasty ruled through until 1974 with a few short gaps and continued in the Orthodox Christian tradition in which amazing churches were hewn into the rock of the mountains. The dynasty governed most of Ethiopia through the Middles Ages, and aided by its desert-like climate and mountainous terrain, managed to stave off Italian, Ottoman and Egyptian invasion attempts.

In the late 19th century the country suffered from invasion during the 'Scramble for Africa' which ended with Italy recognising the independence of Ethiopia. Italy made up for this later by invading and holding the country during the Second World War for a short period, but independence was returned by the end of the war. The Emperor was finally deposed in 1974 by a Communist Marxist-Leninist military coup, when Emperor Haile Salassie was imprisoned and later died, while the country became a single party Communist state.

Empires in the New World such as the Mayas, Aztecs and Incas replaced each other at times, but also were subject to climatic events such as droughts until Europeans discovered the New World and sealed their fate.

In this way, we see that Empires will usually be formed by strong and often charismatic autocrats. Amalgamation with another state by marriage will often lead to the bride's territory being subsumed into that of her husband. The resulting new state or empire may lack the internal resources and manpower for independent rule, or the political, economic and military environment may be too hostile to allow the new empire to survive. When a new empire starts with a new dynasty, it will always fail because of the differing attitudes and quarrels that arise with each new generation. Children should be spared the plight of having to try and follow, or live up to the dreams, diktats and presumptions of their parents (usually their fathers), not to mention the competition and jealousies of their siblings. Succession problems arise and heirs may die prematurely; the second generation may not share the vision or dedication of their predecessors. Many children will not rival their parents in terms of ability or aptitude for government, a lesson which often seems overlooked by modern dictators trying to perpetuate a dynasty to follow themselves.

The above account serves to underline the predominant place of warfare in determining the evolution, growth and decay of nations and empires, initial growth is usually due to charismatic individuals and is seldom achieved without war. States and empires may fail from internal or external reasons; externally from invasion or military over-extension; internally the territory may remain intact, but the government may be overthrown by revolution or by internal coup d'état. Alternatively, the whole edifice may suffer from system failure and implode losing the capacity to govern effectively, as suggested by Gibbon in his masterly account of the decay of the Roman Empire (chapter 14).

Possible further reading:
Vanished Kingdoms by Norman Davies (Allen Lane)
Decline and Fall of the Roman Empire by Edward Gibbon (Saturn Books)

Chapter 33
Early Maritime Exploration

Early man chose to live by water when this was possible. Apart from being one of the necessities of life and providing food, fresh water and rivers allowed early local exploration when people decided to move. Water did not provide shelter, and early man frequently lived in caves, but would have selected his shelter to be as close as possible to drinking water. Later, exploring along rivers and coastal shores would have been one of the ways of exploring local surroundings as well as providing easy fishing. Dugout canoes, formed from a large hollowed out tree trunks, or a raft of several trees lashed together with vines, would have made an effective way of crossing rivers or short sea journeys, providing the weather was calm. Dugout canoes are still in use in certain primitive communities, and prehistoric examples have been found in bogs where preservation is favoured, since after the oxygen dissolved in the bog material is used up all the bacteria of decay die away and any organic material, plant or animal, within the bog is preserved.

It is known that maritime trade with ancient Britain commenced before 2,000 BC, and this would have been in boats made of planks sewn together, or possibly hide boats. The simplest hide boats, called coracles, are still used in parts of the world, including on isolated rivers in Britain, where they may occasionally be seen: these are small circular boats with a framework of bent wooden branches covered with hides and waterpropitch.

A variation on the coracle theme is the Eskimo kayak: once again this is a boat made of skins, usually sealskin, stretched on a frame, though clearly the seaworthiness and the manoeuvrability of the kayak is vastly superior to a coracle. Kayaks were developed to provide a waterborne base for fishing and sealing that were manoeuvrable, seaworthy and capable of travelling considerable distances; the Inuit used wooden frames in coastal areas where this was available, but further north the Aleuts and the Inuit used whalebone, the skins were sewn together with seal sinews.

In Polynesia, early man travelled using dugout canoes with outriggers to provide stability, and sails to speed travel compared with the use of paddles. The voyages made in this way gradually populated the Pacific Islands, and are a tribute to both the extraordinary seamanship of their sailors, and to their very considerable navigational ability where island hopping was not possible using line of sight travel. The spread through the islands progressed gradually eastwards, colonising nearly all the Pacific islands over a period of at least a thousand years, and finally arriving in New Zealand around 1350. Much earlier arrival occurred in Australia, when sea levels were lower and island hops shorter, this allowed the development of a land based indigenous people, while in New Zealand the Māori people arrived only three or four centuries before Europeans. This settling of Australia, and much later New Zealand, represent the final phase of peopling the world on all five continents (omitting Antarctica).

Construction of larger boats proceeded apace in different parts of the world, though undoubtedly there was occasional interchange of people, ideas and information. First in the Arabian seas, where interchange between the Mediterranean and Arabian Seas and the Indian Ocean, travel would have happened thanks to the trade along the coasts. Quite apart from this ease of coastal trading compared with the difficult and often dangerous inland routes, the transfer of bulky or heavy cargoes would have been easier by ship than by caravans of camels (notably referred to as 'the ship of the desert').

Mediterranean navigation and sailing had occurred from very early times. Even before the first millennium BC the Arabs and Phoenicians navigated and traded west out of the Mediterranean and along the coasts to the north and south; indeed, according to Herodotus the Phoenicians had circumnavigated Africa and were well aware that this was possible.

Well before the Roman invasion of Britain there was seaborne trade with Cornwall in southwest Britain for the tin, copper and lead mined there; these were needed to make bronze, and even after the advent of the Iron Age there was a demand for these metals: prehistoric wrecks have been found around the British Isles containing cargoes of copper, tin and lead ingots due to be shipped back to southern countries. Trade with the British Isles, principally for its valuable tin and copper, is well documented in Roman writings, but as far back as 330 BC the Greek, Pytheas, had sailed around Britain and into the North Sea. In the 2nd and 1st centuries BC, while expanding the Roman Empire, the Romans also journeyed as far north as the Baltic Sea, and south up the River Nile, as well as throughout the Mediterranean and Black Seas closer to home.

The evolution of ship building around the Arabian Sea was largely driven by the need to produce cargo-carrying boats of moderate size that could trade along the coast between Arabia and India, using the power of sail. They were able to use monsoon winds which reversed with the time of year, thus allowing a cycle of sailing in each direction twice in a year. These craft were not fitted with oars, and their sails were square. By contrast, the craft that were developed to navigate the Nile used triangular lateen sails, giving the ability to sail upwind in a limited way. On the Nile oars were also used so that on ceremonial and other occasions the condition and direction of the wind was not vital.

In the Mediterranean by contrast, warfare was a much more important determinant of the evolution of ship building. Initially the Phoenicians, but following them the Greeks and then the Romans (not to mention the many colonies of pirates), all required craft which were both manoeuvrable and could proceed with speed on any course regardless of wind direction. Thus the Greeks developed multi-oared warships, initially these had a single row of oars, up to twenty-five on each side, and were known as pentecQnters because of the fifty rowers. As time went by, a second bank of oars was mounted above the first, and ultimately a third bank of oars to produce a fast, manoeuvrable and potent offensive naval ship, known as a trireme, from the Latin remus, an oar. Apart from the need to be manoeuvrable in any direction, the other criterion for a naval vessel was the ability to sink ships on the opposing side, and to this end Greek naval vessels were the first to incorporate a reinforced protruding battering ram at waterline level in the bow, so that ramming opposing ships was an important element of battle tactics in attempting to sink opponents. Evolving from these Greek craft, Roman galleys were very similar, and again were largely powered by slaves.

Thanks to the interconnection across Europe between the northern end of the Black Sea and the Baltic Sea through the rivers of Russia, Viking boatbuilding had become quite advanced by the time of the 8th century. Viking ships were clinker-built of overlapping wooden planks fastened with wood or metal rivets; the ribs and bracing timbers were added later in the building process. The boats were sea-kindly with high prows and sterns, and because they had very shallow draft they were easy to sail up rivers and to beach, not requiring special harbour facilities. In addition to a square sail, a variable number of oars and oarsmen were carried. Wider cargo ships were built for trading where much of the space was given over to goods and possibly animals, so only three or four pairs of oars were mounted; for warships, where speed and manoeuvrability were highly important, there was provision for manning up to forty pairs of oars.

Smaller versions used a side oar as a rudder and would have carried trade around the Baltic Sea. Square sails were the main means of propulsion which allowed little progress upwind, but for direct progress, or in times of calm, rowing would have been preferable. The Vikings, being an egalitarian society, did not differentiate between those who rowed and those who performed other functions. Thus, on their raiding trips the warriors both rowed and raided. Gradually increasing distances were travelled on raids down the west coast of Europe, past the Low Countries along the coast of France. Raiding across the North Sea to the Orkney, Shetland and Scottish Hebridean Islands was easily achieved through the 9th century, with the first recorded Viking raid being on the English monastery on Holy Island at Lindisfarne on the northeast English coast in 793.

The climate was relatively mild in the 9th–12th centuries which probably allowed the gradual extension of the range of Viking exploration and raiding. Erik the Red (950–1003) was outlawed from Iceland for murder in the late 10th century, and left to found the first colony on the west coast of Greenland. Some years later Bjarni Herjolfsson whilst sailing west to Greenland was blown southwards off his course, and missed Greenland, coming to sight land on the North American coast. He was able to return to Greenland, but 15 years later Leif Erikson ('the Lucky', 970–1020), son of Erik the Red, made use of this finding and sailed west to explore the new land with a crew of 35.

He found rolling grasslands, forests full of game and rivers full of fish. His voyage is noted for the vines that he found, from which he named the country of his landfall Vinland. The presence of vines implies a landfall quite far south, though the site has never been identified; Vinland probably refers to New England, but the remains of a Viking colony has been found further north at the northern tip of Newfoundland (at L'Anse aux Meadows). Excavations of this site are consistent with settlement around the year 1000AD, though the site was abandoned after a few years.

In the meantime, Norse settlement on Iceland was thriving in coastal colonies, with a probable population of around 30,000 in the early 10th century. These early Icelanders have bequeathed to us the earliest known democratic parliament called the 'Althing' (a Scandinavian name for a community meeting), which met once a year and extended voting to all adult men and women, but excluded slaves. With changing climate, and deterioration in temperature and weather, the Viking colonies of Greenland collapsed in the 12th century and were replaced by the more cold adapted population of Inuit, who spread east from arctic northern Canada.

Through the first millennium AD, boat building in China had taken a somewhat different direction with junks designed purely for trade and the carriage of cargo, and not for warfare. Junks had been used for centuries, initially as river and canal craft, but sea-going versions were developed for ocean voyaging early in the first millennium; they were heavy sturdy craft using fully battened sails, which improved their sailing ability and were able to sail upwind at a slight angle, but as they had no keel this ability was very limited, leeboards and centreboards were developed to overcome this problem, and later adopted by the Dutch and the Portuguese.

When the Chinese felt that warfare was necessary at sea then the junks were used to carry troops rather than to fight on water. The early junks were used as cargo carriers on the Grand Canal, begun in stretches connecting lakes in the 5th century BC, and completed soon after 600 AD; this 1770km waterway allowed trade and supply between the fertile southern part of China and the less productive north. Junks were used for coastal trading in the monsoon winds which reversed direction twice a year, thereby allowing passage from China to India or Africa, with a return voyage later when the winds reversed.

In the early 15th century the first Ming Emperor constructed huge fleets to visit the known world from China. Hundreds of junks were constructed with the largest being over 140m in length and 50m in beam. Six fleets of these giant ships were to spread out over the Indian Ocean for the purposes of trade, but also to impress the rulers and populace of other nations with the Chinese superiority both in ships, but also in the crafted gifts and trade ware that they carried, and to invite other countries and tribes to acknowledge Chinese superiority and world leadership. The whole venture is well researched and recorded in Gavin Menzies book, *1421*. Menzies has produced evidence which suggests that the Chinese fleet visited not just India and the east coast of Africa, but also explored and traded with Arabia and upper Persian Gulf. Some ships appear to have gone even further and possibly made landfall on both the east and west coasts of South and North America, even to Australia, New Zealand and Antarctica, but these assertions are regarded with a degree of scepticism by many contemporary historians. Despite the shipbuilding and navigational talents of the Chinese and Japanese, exploration east across the Pacific did not occur at this time and it would be more than three centuries later before Chinese or Japanese ships crossed the Pacific to the east of them.

By comparison with Chinese ship building, European construction of vessels at this time was confined to much smaller vessels, though these were arguably more manoeuvrable and equally seaworthy. These early vessels appeared at the beginning of the 11th century and are known as cogs, they were up to 25 metres long with a beam of about one quarter of this. Like the Viking longboats they were built of overlapping clinker oak planks, but their build was more sturdy and substantial than longboats, and as a consequence they were slower, but capable of carrying more cargo; like the longboats these early craft used a single square sail, but had a steering oar at the rear. Through to the 16th century these vessels grew in size and sophistication with the acquisition firstly of a true sternpost carrying a rudder instead of a steering oar, and secondly acquiring a second or third mast with some fore-and-aft sails in addition to the square sails on the mainmast, so giving them the ability to sail upwind.

From the Chinese expeditions knowledge permeated through to the Mediterranean, and a map by the Venetian cartographer Zvane Pizzigomo dated 1425, includes the Caribbean coastline. Although maps were often updated rather than completely redrawn it seems likely that Columbus in 1492, Vasco da Gama in 1497, and Magellan in 1519, knew that there was land on the far western side of the Atlantic Ocean, although they thought the landfall would be the East Indies approached from the opposite direction, hence the naming of the West Indies.

At the time of this burst of exploration from Spain and Portugal, Bartholomew Diaz (1450–1500) followed the west coast of Africa south and rounded the Cape of Good Hope, though he did not get much further. Diaz was a Portuguese nobleman, whose exploration ended just east of the Cape of Good Hope due to dreadful conditions on board his ship, including scurvy, and the mutiny of his crew. His exploration, as with subsequent voyages, was encouraged and funded by the Portuguese King, Henry the Navigator (1394–1460).

Christopher Columbus (1451–1506) is famous as the first European to make landfall in the Bahamas in 1492 before moving on to the Islands of Cuba and Hispaniola. Under the auspices of the King of Portugal Amerigo Vespucci (1454–1512) explored southwards along the coast of South America, showing that the new continent extended much further south than originally thought; his name has been immortalised in the naming of the new continent by the German map maker Martin Waldseemuller (1470–1520) in a world map published in 1507. He was followed across the Atlantic by Ferdinand Magellan (1480–1521), who left from Cadiz in Spain in 1519, and took a much more southerly course, making landfall off South America on the coast of Brazil, and then following the coastline south. He did not round Cape Horn, but discovered the Straits a little further north where the wind and sea is more kindly than the conditions around Cape Horn.

Magellan continued his voyage of exploration northwards and west for a while, and then west across the Pacific to the Philippines, where he was killed in a native war, though his expedition was able to continue back to Spain, completing the first circumnavigation of the world. In the other direction Vasco da Gama (1460–1524) left Portugal in 1497 to round the Cape of Good Hope at the tip of Africa and then journey north along the east coast of Africa and across to India, which he reached in 1498. Also in about 1497 John Cabot, a Venetian explorer was sponsored by King Henry VII of England and sailed west across the North Atlantic Ocean, making three voyages with landfall at uncertain sites on the North American coast.

These seafaring voyages of discovery were followed by land exploration of the Americas, all in an attempt to reach the Indies, which were well known from those who had previously voyaged east. It had been frequently assumed that voyaging to the west would result in arrival at the East Indies, which indeed would have been the case, except that the huge continents of North and South America required to be crossed or circumnavigated first. In 1513 Vasco Nunez de Balbao (1474–1519), an early Spanish explorer and Governor, who established the first permanent settlement on the American mainland, crossed the Isthmus of Central America in Panama with a small land-based expedition.

A few years later, Hernan Cortez (1485–1547) conquered the Aztec civilisation in 1520 with only a small force of men, but with the enormous advantage of firearms. By 1540 the Spanish had fully traversed Mexico and reached the Gulf of California. In the meantime English and French explorers were discovering and mapping North America, whilst others, including the Dutch, unsuccessfully sought a north-west passage round the north of Canada and Alaska to attempt to get to China by travelling west from Europe.

All this exploration resulted in the five continents of the world becoming known in outline by the beginning of the 16th century, such that further water-borne exploration would gradually give way to land based exploration, and mapping would follow. Conquest, and usually unequal warfare with native peoples, would follow with resulting decimation of the population of native peoples through warfare and disease. The colonisation of North and South America and Australasia with predominantly Europeans inevitably followed over the next couple of centuries.

Possible further reading:
1421 by Gavin Menzies (Bantam Books)

Chapter 34
Exploration West from Europe

The first great age of European exploration dates from Christopher Columbus' epic voyage across the Atlantic from Spain, to landfall on the east coast of the Americas in 1492. The Florentine scholar Paolo Toscanelli (1397–1482) is reported to have met Chinese visitors at the Vatican in 1431, and then rather later, suggested to Columbus in 1474, that it should be possible to reach the Spice Islands from the other direction by sailing west across the Atlantic.

Columbus (1451–1506) was an Italian from Genoa who made four voyages across the Atlantic with the backing of the Spanish Monarchy and the Catholic Church, making his initial landfall on the Bahamas and moving on to Cuba, Hispaniola (present day French-speaking Haiti), and the Dominican Republic; he later became Governor of an infant settlement, but later still was dismissed from this post due to charges of brutality and financial irregularities. He was undoubtedly helped by having a compass, originally invented in China sometime around 200 BC, but appearing in Europe in the 14th century; it appears that the Chinese did not use it for navigation until the 11th century.

The Spanish went on to establish a large empire in the New World with colonies in Central and South America. The Portuguese were also expanding into the region and explored southwards along the west coast of Africa as well as beginning to colonise Brazil. These early voyages rapidly established knowledge of hitherto unknown and unexploited lands that were rich in gold, silver and spices. The mines were initially worked by South American natives, but as sugar plantations grew up more labour was required giving rise to the early slave trade from Africa where slave markets were already long established.

Early exploration was often motivated by trade, particularly as exemplified by spices. At the same time as themes of exploration there was also a search for plunder, best exemplified by the gold and silver brought back to Europe from South America; in addition early explorers brought Catholic missionaries to 'enlighten' the native population. Alongside these activities Europeans brought disease to the newly discovered continents including smallpox, measles and influenza, all of which had a devastating effect on populations which had previously not been exposed to these diseases and therefore had no natural immunity.

In some areas, up to three-quarters of the indigenous population is thought to have died from imported European diseases. This consequence of the meeting of populations previously isolated from each other, produced the same effect in

North, Central and South America. At the time of Columbus' landfall some of Central and South America was inhabited by relatively small tribal groups, but through the Andes on the west of South America, the Incas had established a large empire by conquest of other tribal groups (chapter 9).

The Incas had built a road system along the Andes, allowing trade and administrative travel throughout their large empire. They had also imposed a common language and spread agricultural techniques of terracing and irrigating the mountainous country, together with selective plant and animal breeding. The only surprise is that the wheel never appeared in the Aztec, Inca or other South American regions, so that trade, communications and administrative government remained generally slow and localised.

Much of Amazonia, on the east side of the Andean mountain chain, involved small populations existing on fishing, hunting and gathering in the jungle and along the banks of the Amazon and other rivers, where sustainable fixed agriculture had not evolved. Similarly in Mexico to the north, there were many small tribal groups, also existing at a hunter-gatherer level, but in southern Mexico the Aztec Empire had evolved, becoming really successful in the two or three centuries before Columbus arrived. The sophistication of the Aztec population was considerable, with their principal city of Tenochtitlan (modern Mexico City) being larger than any European city of the same period.

The other distinction of the Aztec civilisation (and to a lesser extent of the Inca) was their use of human sacrifice. This sacrifice was felt necessary to give strength to their warrior god, and many of their victims were acquired either by capture in war, or by exchange with surrounding tribal societies. In Central America there were in existence at the time, many small tribal societies with varying mixtures of hunter-gatherer and agricultural societies. The richness of the area included the production of copper, gold, silver and jade, as well as the production of pottery, leading the Spanish to give part of this region the name of Costa Rica ("rich land").

Christopher Columbus' initial voyage to the Americas, where he in fact made landfall on the Bahama islands rather than the mainland of the American continent, was followed by many others. The name of the West Indies perpetuates Columbus' and others belief that he had discovered the Spice Islands that we know as the East Indies, by circumnavigation westwards instead of eastwards. Once it became apparent that an entirely new continent had been found between Europe and the East Indies, rather than the Spice Islands themselves, the name 'New World' came to be applied to the Americas.

Spain and Portugal had been trying for years to increase seaborne trade beyond Europe and had agreed an initial treaty giving the Portuguese sole right of trade in the Gulf of Guinea, along the coast of West Africa. This was subsequently revised in the Treaty of Tordesillas in 1494 between Spain and Portugal, which divided the regions of influence between Portugal, predominantly to the east, and Spain predominantly to the west, of a given line of longitude (unspecified in those days, but around 45 degrees west of the Greenwich meridian).

A few years later, Portuguese naval ships heading south toward the Indian Ocean by way of the Cape of Good Hope, skirted farther west than usual in search of more favourable winds, thus inadvertently making landfall on the Brazilian mainland, which had hitherto been unknown. Soon afterwards Amerigo Vespucci (1454–1512), voyaging at the behest of King Manuel of Portugal, explored the east coast of Brazil far enough south to confirm the existence of continental South America. This newly discovered continent was duly named after him, and later this name of America was extended to take in North America.

Within a few years, another Portuguese explorer, Ferdinand Magellan (1480–1521), sailed to the tip of South America in 1519, and through the Straits which now bear his name, into the Pacific Ocean. Magellan traversed the Pacific, but was killed in a battle with natives in the Philippines. His diminished crew, however, sailed on, though with only sufficient crew to sail one of his initial five ships, and returned to Spain after a three year voyage, having made the first full circumnavigation of the globe.

When European explorers first set foot in the Caribbean Islands, there was already an indigenous population of native Stone Age people who had spread from the American mainland, probably south from Florida, but also north from South America, many centuries before. There seem to have been at least three separate waves of incomers who populated the islands at different times.

In Central America in 1519, following Columbus' early landfall in 1492, Spanish plunder and conquest followed with the arrival of Hernan Cortes (1485–1547). Spanish settlers had already begun to colonise the islands of the West Indies with their rich vegetation and favourable climate. Vasco Nunez de Balboa (1475–1519) had settled in Hispaniola (later Haiti) from Spain in 1500, and later explored across the isthmus of Panama becoming the first European to see the Pacific. His expedition had been the first to start a trend of settlement, founding a small colony and sowing crops. This knowledge had been available to Cortes, who left Cuba with a few hundred followers, landing in the Gulf of Mexico at Vera Cruz to the east of Tenochtitlan (Mexico City).

Cortes burnt his ships to ensure that his followers could not return, and marched inland onto the high Mexican plateau, where they were amazed by the wealth of the civilisation they found in terms, not only of gold and precious stones, but importantly, very favourable agricultural land. The invaders brought with them horses, guns, iron and steel, and were technologically well advanced beyond the Aztec civilisation they found, so that conquest of the Stone Age Aztec people was easily achieved by Cortes' small army. Their task was aided by a rumour amongst the Aztecs that Cortes himself could be an earthly incarnation of their god, though it still took several years for the Spaniards fully to pacify their new territory.

Mexico, together with Peru, had rich deposits of gold and silver, which acted as a magnet for Spanish settlement. Sugar, cocoa, indigo and cochineal were also sought-after exports to bring back to Europe. The Spanish brought with them missionaries to convert the natives, principally Franciscans, and later Jesuit monks. In Brazil, the Portuguese harvested hardwoods, and then established sugar plantations for which there was not a large enough native labour force to tend them, so that the African slave trade became necessary to provide labour. Gold was discovered close to Rio de Janeiro in the 1690s, provoking a gold rush with immigration from the mother country. Brazil itself then developed more slowly, and did not achieve political independence until 1889, though it achieved considerable devolved power in 1822, after the defeat of Napoleon.

Further south, Argentina had been subjugated by the Inca around 1480. Before that, there is evidence of crop irrigation in the north-western Andes in the first millennium BC, followed by a corn-based civilisation in the 1st century AD. Although metals had been smelted, particularly gold and silver, bronze technology was barely used before Europeans arrived. Forty-five urban settlements have been discovered and are known to have appeared by the 9th century. Inca rule did not last long as it was interrupted by European Invasion. Juan Diaz de Solis (1470–1516), sailing from Spain, explored the River Plate in 1526, and started a settlement on the site of the present Buenos Aires in 1536 under Pedro de Mendoza (1487–1537), a Spanish nobleman and explorer. This had to be abandoned five years later following native attacks.

A permanent colony was later established in 1580 as an outpost from Peru, and was soon followed by early Jesuit missions and a Jesuit founded university of Cordoba. Independence was achieved in 1816. On the west coast of South America, central Chile had been explored south as far as Santiago by 1536, but was destroyed in a native uprising ten years later. Once again settlement brought the evangelising Jesuits in the early 17th century; Chile was to achieve independence in 1818.

By contrast with Central and South America, North America was explored and colonised rather later by northern Europeans on account of the harsher and more difficult climate. Following the early transient settlement by the Vikings at L'Anse aux Meadows in northern Newfoundland around the millennium, no further transatlantic exploration and settlement occurred for the next 500 years. That early Viking colony only lasted a few decades, and reports of its difficulties and lack of success meant that no further attempts were made until John Cabot (1450–1499), a Venetian explorer, voyaged to North America in 1497 sponsored by the English King Henry VII. He discovered rich cod fishing grounds on the Grand Banks of Nova Scotia and Newfoundland, but no settlement resulted from his expedition.

A little later Giovanni Verrazano (1485–1528), an Italian citizen in the employ of the French King Francis, explored the North American coastline south almost as far Florida in the early years of the 16th century, but again no settlement resulted from this. French and English colonisation on the east coast also in the 16th century came to nothing until a French settlement at Port Royal in Nova Scotia in 1605 and Quebec City in 1608. Settlements further south in Virginia in 1607, the Pilgrim Fathers in Boston in 1620, and Dutch New Amsterdam in 1626 (later to become New York), provided the first successful colonies to be established in North America.

Most of the European settlers tended to be from protestant and non-conformist backgrounds, while the French colonies were small and catholic. Canada was explored from the east coast westwards using the St Lawrence and Ottawa Rivers, by trappers seeking valuable furs (previously mainly available from Northern Russia), and by entrepreneurs and naval representatives looking for prime timber for ship building, which was becoming increasingly scarce in Europe.

Jacques Cartier (1491–1557), a native of Brittany, and Samuel Champlain (1574–1635), an early French polymath and settler who founded Quebec City, later becoming the French Governor General, stand out as hardened explorers who exemplified the seasoned and tenacious qualities necessary to explore this difficult terrain in the early colonial years. It is interesting to note that Cartier avoided the awful effects of scurvy by using infusions of tree bark two hundred years before vitamin C was identified in citrus fruit by James Lind and eventually used by the British Navy.

Sir Francis Drake (1540–1596), a Devon-born British mariner deserves a mention here as an exemplar of those early buccaneering transatlantic voyagers. He circumnavigated the world twice, with his second circumnavigation taking three years from 1577 to 1580. Initially Drake was a pirate in the Caribbean preying on Spanish and Portuguese merchantmen with their cargoes of valuable gold and silver. He was sponsored covertly by Queen Elizabeth I, who took half his booty in return for the sponsorship, and in his early years Drake's pirated profits were more valuable than the whole of the rest of Great Britain's national income in each year. These exploits must have added to the Spanish decision to send an armada against Britain in 1588, where they were met by Drake commanding the British naval response (chapter 38).

Possible further reading:
The Four Voyages of Christopher Columbus by Alexander McKee, Souvenir Press

Chapter 35
Exploration East from Europe

Exploration and trading to the east originating in Europe came only marginally later than the expansion across the Atlantic. This is partly explained by the enormous distances involved, and the fact that to voyage eastward necessitated sailing south to the tip of Africa and rounding the Cape of Good Hope, before heading north again to India and the large Asian 'Spice Islands'. The overland Silk Road through the centre of Asia and the alternative coastal route around India and through Arabia, suddenly became much more dangerous and difficult following the fall of Constantinople to the Turks in 1453, thereafter the Muslim Ottoman Empire posed a considerable barrier to overland travellers.

Earlier, the writings and descriptions of the east by Marco Polo (1254–1324) had excited Europeans. Marco's father and uncle had travelled to China along the Silk Road, at around the time of his birth; they had met Kublai Khan, at that time the Chinese Emperor, and seem to have been recruited into his entourage to act as the Khan's envoys. They returned to Europe after many years of travelling and trading, and with an ability to speak the useful eastern languages. This first expedition had been so successful that Marco Polo's mother returned across Asia with her family, including Marco, in 1271. They used the Silk route and again travelled and traded extensively in the Far East.

The family returned in 1295 by sea along the coast of India and Arabia with goods and riches for sale, but following their return, Marco Polo as a Venetian citizen, was caught up in a war between Venice and Genoa, as he was thought to have provided funds for a Venetian ship. He was captured in battle, and spent eighteen months in prison, but this period of imprisonment provided the time for him to record his travels and experiences in the Far East, in a book which is subsequently thought to have inspired Christopher Columbus amongst others.

In the 16th century, it was the mercantile and naval ships of Europe which provided sailors with the ability to explore the world's oceans. The Vikings did not possess sufficiently large and robust craft to achieve this 500 years earlier, and although some Chinese and Arabian vessels could have undertaken the same voyages, it was the impetus of trade from Europe which started to interconnect the world, although China was coming out of isolation and the Ming Emperor had sent out Treasure Ships at the beginning of the 15th century (chapter 8). At this time Chinese paper currency was suffering from severe inflation, such that cargoes of silver arriving on Portuguese or Dutch ships were welcome additions to be traded into the economy.

In the 14th and 15th centuries European ships had developed called caravels, typically around 100 tons, with one to three masts, which carried square sails on the mainmast together with lateen sails on the mizzen mast as used around Arabia and in the Mediterranean, which made them much more manoeuvrable in all winds. These were thoroughly seaworthy vessels, and two of Christopher Columbus' small fleet, the Nina and the Pinta, were such vessels, while Columbus' third vessel and flagship was a larger carrack.

At the same time in Europe the Dutch had been developing specific ships for carrying cargo. The 'fluytschip' was designed with the single purpose of trade in mind, unlike the ships of other nations which could be fitted out either for cargo or for warfare, and in consequence were a compromise in design with the ability to carry larger crews and cannon. By making the fluyts beamier and flat bottomed, and by adopting masts with fore and aft sails on the bowsprit and mizzen mast the sailing ability as well as the cargo capacity was greatly increased. Using better blocks and winches, a smaller crew was needed with less on-board accommodation; the invention of a rudder mounted on the sternpost rather than a steering oar, completed the transition to a more effective and much cheaper cargo vessel, with the first of these ships being completed just as the 17th century was ushered in. By 1670 the Dutch merchant fleet accounted for half of all European shipping.

Following the 16th century after Vasco Da Gama's exploration of 1498, the Portuguese led the way in establishing trade with the East. This happened despite Da Gama's clearly abrasive and often brutal behaviour combined with an aggressive missionary zeal. His activities appear to have involved piracy when he was running short of supplies to trade, and gratuitous violence against local populations using his ship's cannons causing many deaths; on one occasion he sealed a ship full of Muslim pilgrims and set fire to it resulting in some four hundred deaths.

The Portuguese were quickly able to build up bases and trading posts around India with the major facility being established at Goa. Faith followed trade, and Franciscan monks soon arrived to try to bring Christianity to what was widely perceived as a very backward area. By 1557 the Dutch had established a base in Macao in China, for the purposes of Far Eastern trade. The Dutch also took over trading rights in the Molucca Islands to fulfil their long held ambitions in the spice trade.

The Portuguese dominated eastward exploration in the 16th century forming the first European overseas Empire. Goa on the west coast of India was taken on as an early base for both trade and missionary activity with extension to the Spice Islands and the Moluccan Islands in 1513; soon afterwards trading was established with Indonesia and onwards from there to Timor. In 1540 the Portuguese were the first European nation to establish trading with Japan and in 1557 they negotiated a trading post with some settlement in Macao on the Chinese mainland. Through the second half of the 16th century the Portuguese remained the predominant nation trading with the Far East after Spain ceded their trading rights in India and the Moluccas. Spain and Portugal were united for a period commencing in 1580, but eighty years of war with Spain and with the Dutch depleted the Portuguese treasury and in the early 17th century the Portuguese Empire in the Far East collapsed to be replaced by the Dutch.

The Portuguese presence and power in the Far East started to wane after the union of Portugal and Spain in 1580 by Spanish conquest (though this union would last less than a century). At the same time Arab nationalism along the East African coast was replacing the trading power of the Portuguese. The Dutch East India Company had been set up as a governmental body in 1602 to promote Far Eastern trade, and a period of fairly ruthless competition between Portuguese and Dutch followed through the 17th century, and up to the middle of the 18th century.

Abel Tasman (1603–1659) reached Tasmania (later named for him) in 1642 while working for the expanding Dutch East India Company. Dutch trade advantage and influence came to an end in 1741 at the Battle of Colachel in which the Dutch fought the Indian kingdom of Travancore, suffering a heavy defeat from which their Far Eastern influence never really recovered. The Dutch were at odds with Travancore, and war had broken out as a consequence of their need to maintain their trading advantage. Following the loss of the battle, Dutch influence went into steep decline, carrying with it decline in trade.

The vacuum was filled by the British, who had also established an East India Trading Company which had been granted a royal charter by Queen Elizabeth in 1602. It was a private company financed by shares subscribed to by aristocrats and wealthy merchants who saw visions of large future profits. Although it was intended that trade would be throughout the east, the majority of trade ended up being with India and China, and for the first hundred years of its existence this remained the focus of its activities, but from 1700 onwards the emphasis changed to the acquisition of land. In this way British influence gradually rose through the 18th century under the military leadership of Robert Clive (1725–1774), who was later ennobled and made extremely rich through his Indian ventures, which were often criticised since his administration was guilty of high taxes resulting in areas of famine.

The East India Company ran its own army and its military action ended with the subjugation of India and with the company in full administrative control of the sub-continent, such that in 1757 the company established its capital in Calcutta and appointed a Governor General. The rise in British influence and control was aided by the collapse of the Mogul Empire in 1707 on the death of the Emperor, Arun Aurangzeb, following which power throughout India was heavily subdivided among princedoms, thus weakening the region badly.

This situation lasted for the next hundred years with the East India Company providing de facto government until the Indian Mutiny in 1857 when local troops mutinied, an action that was brought to a head by the use of animal fat to grease new rifle ammunition; the fat was variously rumoured to be of beef origin, anathema to Hindus who hold the cow sacred, or alternatively pork fat which was religiously offensive to Muslims, though it appears that it was possibly neither of these, but simply malicious talk.

On top of high taxes, land reforms and maltreatment of Indians, the result was an eruption of rebellion and fighting, often very vicious, on each side. The rebellion included the incident known as the 'Black Hole of Calcutta', in which dozens of British prisoners, including women and children, were locked in a very small airless cell and by the following morning, some two-thirds of them had died of asphyxia. Public indignation in Britain was huge and in consequence of this event and of the rebellion, the British Government officially removed military powers from the East India Company, formally taking on the administration of India in 1858.

Possible further reading:
Conquerors by Roger Crowley (Faber and Faber)

Chapter 36
Printing

In prehistoric times, communication was oral, and history was also learnt and recorded orally. The first big step forward from this came with the invention of writing, which as we have seen previously evolved in different ways in early times, and in different places (chapter 12). Some writing and numbering appeared very early on and quite often involved pictograms rather than lettering. It was still the first major step forward as a means of recording either daily events, accounting or past happenings.

The second big step forward was the invention and refinement of printing in the 15th and 16th centuries. Writing had been slow and laborious in antiquity, and in Europe often involved the use of animal skins, usually calf or lamb and known as vellum. Paper was a Chinese invention, probably dating back at least two millennia, but it had been appropriated by the Arabs when they conquered Samarkand on the Silk Road, taking Chinese prisoners in the 8th century AD. Early paper was made from macerated linen rags.

Early books were all made by scribes or copyists transcribing a single copy at a time, and writing either on vellum or on paper. By the 12th and 13th century in Europe many scribes, who were often monks, would be gathered together and found working in one place, often a monastery. Some monks would have travelled around to write legal and other documents in different places, but once scribes came to work together, the resulting enterprise was called a scriptorium, and the scribes had become stationary; this is how they came to be called stationers, and why stationers and stationery is now the current term for many aspects of writing and publishing.

In the meantime, metalworkers had been used to making coins for many centuries by using a punch with a negative image on it to form a positive imprint on a metal blank. It would have been a small technical and intellectual step to use a similar negative punch to make a letter or pictogram. From this a mould could be made and a positive letter formed suitable for printing. The Chinese tried this idea centuries before it happened in Europe, but further development failed, probably because the baked clay or wood carrying the letters was too fragile and brittle to withstand repetitive use, but also because the Chinese system of writing, with at least ten thousand different symbols, was a major logistical problem. The Koreans had also tried this method using special hardwoods, but royal prohibition made this also a non-viable option. In the 13th century the Korean King Sejong (1397–1450) invented a new alphabet of 24 characters to try and overcome these problems, but the system was never developed or spread.

Johannes Gutenberg (1400–1468) in the German city of Mainz devised the first viable system of printing in the 1450s. It is possible that he got some of his ideas from Arab traders, whilst the necessary marriage with metal technology may have come from his father, who was a coiner. Gutenberg devised a system with individual metal letters mounted on a standard sized metal stem, which could be used by putting rows of letters together forming lines of print. Once a page of letters and words had been set up, it should have been a relatively simple matter to ink the standing letters and impress them onto a sheet of paper.

Unfortunately, vellum turned out to be insufficiently absorbent to cope with the inks used at that time, and therefore Gutenberg had to devise new oil based inks. Although the labour required to set up a page of print was quite slow, the printing process of running off hundreds of copies thereafter amounted to an enormous speeding up of the total process. The system was resilient and could accommodate different type faces and languages, and lasted reliably into the second half of the 20th century, when compositors were still setting pages of print, including newspapers, in this way.

Initially, the shapes of the letters simulated the old fashioned and long used monkish script, but in Italy a new type face was devised to mimic the handwriting of chancery lawyers. An Italian printer called Francesco Griffo (1450–1518) in Bologna devised this new script to be closer to everyday handwriting and therefore more easily read; it came to be known as 'italic'. The combination of the enormously increased productive volume of material that printers could turn out, together with the much diminished cost compared with individual hand produced copies, led to a huge increase in dissemination of printed knowledge, which then came to be known as texts, after the textiles from which the paper was made. It was a major facilitator of both the reformation and the renaissance.

Johannes Gutenberg (1400–1468), credited with inventing printing, is thought to have first worked with his new form of printing as early as 1439, but it was only in 1455 that 180 copies of his first printed volume appeared. It is not surprising that these first printed books were copies of the Bible. Together with the slowly increasing rate of literacy through medieval times, printing would now allow richer individuals, including parish priests, to own their personal copy of the Bible and to refer to it frequently. This in turn would generate understanding and questioning, which in previous times had been the province of a very few intellectuals, or members of religious orders. Ironically, the teething problems of the system eventually bankrupted Gutenberg and, as with other later seminal inventions, it was those who followed in developing the system who profited, rather than the original inventor.

In Britain, William Caxton (1415–1492) introduced a printing press in 1476. Caxton was remarkable in that he translated over a hundred foreign texts himself in order to publish them in printed form. Because these were the first widely available texts in English, he is credited with starting the standardisation of the English language which proceeded apace as more and more people had access to the printed word, both sacred and secular. Caxton was a polymath in an age when it was still possible to span many disciplines.

He was extensively travelled, both as a diplomat and merchant, becoming Governor of the Company of Merchant Adventurers of London in addition to his writing and printing interests. He was the first English printer and seller of secular books, of which we remember Chaucer's Canterbury Tales as the first and most well-known example. Geoffrey Chaucer (1343–1400) had already written his books and died before Caxton discovered them, but thanks to printing, and to Caxton, Chaucer is credited with making writing in the vernacular respectable at a time when Latin and French still prevailed. His influence is probably in part a consequence of his connection to the nobility and to Court circles through his father's standing; he was Clerk of the King's Works for a short period.

The advent of printing, and the thirst for knowledge, uncovered a thirst for reading in the native language of the individual. Thus, in the initial years following the advent of printing, the Bible predominated, followed by translations of seminal works from antiquity translated from Greek and Latin, and thus available to scholars. Early text books on the sciences, particularly of mathematics and astronomy, also became available in the reader's own language.

William Tyndale (1494–1536) produced the first Bible to be printed in English. In this way he followed John Wycliffe (1320–1384) who had translated the Bible into middle English at a time when copies could still be produced only by scribes (usually monks) laboriously copying the text in front of them. To produce a full copy of the Bible in this way would take each monk at least a year. Wycliffe was a deeply questioning thinker, who contributed to the rejection of much Catholic thinking in the pre-reformation and pre-printing years. He taught at Oxford and was Master of Balliol College in 1361, though later he incurred official displeasure for his views and was forced to move to the periphery of the seat of learning. Those who followed his teaching became known as 'lollards', and although Wycliffe had no official organisation behind him, he is often blamed for the peasants revolt in 1381, even though he did not approve of the revolt.

The term 'lollard' was a derogatory one for those without an academic background who followed Wycliffe's thinking; it probably derives from the Dutch word for someone who mutters. Wycliffe believed that the Catholic Church was corrupt, and that the Bible should be available in the vernacular tongue for all to study, and in these two beliefs he presages the Reformation. He died from a stroke in 1384, but his writings and his followers continued to upset the Church authorities, including the Pope, such that in 1428 the Pope ordered that he be posthumously executed by exhumation of his corpse and then burning it!

The genie had escaped from the bottle however, and with wide dispersal of the Bible and other sacred texts, the Church's attitudes became increasingly analysed and questioned. The most famous and influential person here is Martin Luther (1483–1546) in Germany, who had been writing for some time questioning the teachings of the Church. In 1517 Luther became incensed by the presence in his German town of Wittenberg of a Papal representative selling indulgences. These indulgences were being sold by the Pope to raise money for his project of rebuilding St Peter's Cathedral in Rome, which had stalled for lack of funds. An indulgence was the promise of passage straight to heaven after death without spending time in purgatory for sins committed during a lifetime. Thanks to printing, indulgences came pre-printed as forms certifying that the bearer was excused the severe penances of the Church, and could accumulate merit in heaven.

Luther saw this as a dishonest Papal way of raising money, for which no scriptural precedent existed; he was convinced that it was not possible for an individual to buy redemption without at the same time reforming their behaviour. He posted his 95 theses, or criticisms, on the door of his church, and sent copies to his bishop and his friends. He was probably not expecting the storm of interest and reaction which resulted. Such was the power of the newly available printed word that within weeks of Luther publishing them his theses rapidly became available all across Europe, and it is said that within three years there were 300,000 copies in circulation.

In this way, the Reformation was unleashed and it was now a small step for anyone in authority, or any individual with original thoughts, criticism or novel ideas, to have them printed so that the ideas could be shared and could influence others. The new printing allowed the wide spread of theses, polemics, pamphlets and news sheets, to multiply across Europe, in addition to the broad dissemination of ancient Greek and Latin texts, often translated from an intermediary Arabic source. In terms of the advance of society, the world of writing had gradually evolved through many attempts at expression, to an age of printing where knowledge had suddenly become very widely available.

The new age of the printed word would last from its birth at the end of the 15th century through to the 20th century, when the advent of radio and television would once again bring the importance of the spoken word back into prominence, only to be closely followed by the digital age with its amazing possibilities of access and recording of the printed word. The Reformation of church thinking would be quickly followed by the Renaissance of early scientific thinking, thanks to the advent of printing providing easy and open speedy access to information between clerics and scholars.

Possible further reading:
The Day the Universe Changed by James Burke (Little Brown & Co)

Chapter 37
Mapping

Pre-historic man had primitive maps, both of the land, and often of the stars, which were important for direction at night, or for religious reasons. Maps, even in ancient times, were an aerial view of the land and sea, with the relative positions and features outlined together with the distances between such features. Sometimes these maps were symbolic and pictorial rather than cartographically accurate. Ancient rock carvings have been discovered in France and Turkey, obviously containing important knowledge to preserve and pass from generation to generation on a recurring basis. Apart from this, early man would have drawn diagrams in the dust or sand to explain routes or locations to others within the tribe.

By the time we get to the middle of the first millennium BC, we find examples of Greek maps exemplified by those which accompanied the Iliad and the Odyssey of Homer. These maps were not drawn by Homer, and are later, fantastical, and not to scale. The distinction for the production of the first reasonable Greek maps belongs to Anaximandr (611–540 BC) a Greek philosopher from Miletus in Turkey, and pupil of Thales who drew maps of the world where it is represented as a round disc: in other words, he was showing a flat plate-like Earth, which was a necessary representational convention that may have contributed to early flat Earth thinking.

However, around the same time Pythagoras was teaching that Earth was a sphere, and further that it revolved around the sun. He thought, as did most Greeks, that Greece was the centre of the world with people and life in general becoming more savage and barbarian as one travelled outwards from Greece at the centre, which was understandable given his knowledge. Aristotle (384–322 BC) is credited with proving that Earth was a sphere using the following arguments: firstly, that a lunar eclipse always shows a circular shadow of Earth, secondly, that ships seem to sink as they move away from a viewer, and thirdly, that certain stars can only be seen from specific parts of Earth.

Later in 240 BC, Eratosthenes set out to measure the diameter of the world by observation and measurement. He knew there was a well at Syene (present day Aswan) on the Nile where the sun cast no shadow at midday on one day of the year, the summer solstice when the sun was directly overhead. He lived in Alexandria, where also at midday on the solstice, he measured the angle of the sun's shadow cast by a tower as 7.2°, which is one fiftieth of a circle of 360°. He then sent out trained surveyors to pace the distance from Alexandria to Syene which came to 5,000 stadia thus calculating Earth's circumference at 250,000 stadia.

The stadion was not a standardised measurement at that time so we cannot convert the distance precisely, but he was clearly very close to the actual distance of 24,900 km. This was a remarkable achievement considering that we now know that Earth is not a perfect sphere but a flattened ellipsoid, and that the sea bulges up and sinks down from the true theoretical spherical shape depending on the density, and hence the gravitational attraction, of the underlying rocks. He also divided Earth with theoretical meridians which we now call longitude, lines extending north to south from one pole to the other, and parallels, the east-west lines which we call latitude. In addition he recognised the existence of different temperature zones, with the tropics around the Equator, two temperate zones to the north and south, and two further cold zones, namely the Arctic and Antarctic.

Eratosthenes' theoretical basis was further developed by the Greek mathematician, astronomer and geographer Ptolemy (90–168 AD), who lived in Alexandria and published his studies in an eight volume atlas called Geographica, in which known towns and cities were given with their latitude and longitude. It was Ptolemy who commenced the convention that maps should have north at the top of the page and east on the right; his atlas used later inaccurate estimates of the size of Earth which made it nearly a third smaller, his maps stretch from the Canary Islands to China and from Shetland down to the coast of East Africa, indicating contemporary knowledge of these regions. Only late medieval copies of his atlas have survived with later, and probably unreliable amendments, while his latitudes were reasonable his longitudes were wildly inaccurate because of a lack of precise measurement of time at sea, a problem which would only be solved in much later in 1773 by John Harrison (chapter 57).

Some similar early maps of China have been found, which date from about 500 years before Christ, and which were used to illustrate different provinces and frontier boundaries, together with the sites of productive mines and forests. Chinese maps continued to become more detailed and more accurate with the passing of time, but without including any details of the greater world. By contrast, during the expansion of the Mongol Empire in the 13th century, the conquered lands were made to send maps of their territory to the central government, thus extending Mongol and Chinese knowledge with mapping of the world as far west as the eastern end of the Mediterranean.

In the 9th and 10th centuries AD and later, Arabic mapping developed further the ancient Greek atlases with detailed knowledge, but once again the area covered was mainly confined to the Mediterranean with northern Africa and western Asia. Throughout much of this time there was a tendency to copy and 'improve' the maps of previous generations, with only scanty regard to accompanying research on the ground to confirm the physical knowledge incorporated in the maps. This is of course the time when Christopher Columbus set out and sailed to America, but his logs include the admission that as long as eighteen years before he set out, Columbus had a map of the Americas; he had also studied Eratosthene's works, but had not believed the Greeks' calculation of Earth's dimensions and used a smaller figure, thus coming to the conclusion that he would arrive at the East Indies on the other side of the Atlantic Similarly, it would appear that Magellan in 1520 knew that the straits which now bear his name were present to the north of Cape Horn, so that he was able to quell a mutiny of his sailors who felt that he was lost.

Maps by the German cartographer Martin Waldseemuller (1470–1520) in 1507, and another German scholar and map maker Johann Schoner (1477–1547), dating from a few years before Magellan set sail, already showed the Americas and Pacific together with the Straits of Magellan. To go further back, a map of the world by Albertinius de Virga, a Venetian cartographer of the 15th century shows northern Australia in 1411 some 250 years before Abel Tasman (1603–1659) exploring for the Dutch East India Company sighted New Zealand and Tasmania, and 350 years before Captain James Cook, the first European, set foot on the continent (chapter 75).

It would seem that much of this knowledge may have been transferred to Europe, specifically to the trading centres like Venice by Chinese fleets that visited and traded in the early 15th century before the great voyages of European exploration (chapter 8).

In the 16th century, world maps gradually proliferated and at this time the problem of representing the surface of a sphere in three dimensions and reducing it to a two dimensional drawing became apparent. A Flemish cartographer and polymath called Gerard Mercator (1515–1594) provided a major breakthrough by allowing this representation of the spherical Earth to be transferred to a flat page. The process was helped much later in 1851 by the adoption of the Greenwich meridian as the zero base line from which degrees of longitude east or west through 180 degrees can be calculated, while at the same time degrees of latitude are assessed from the equator extending north or south through 90° to each pole.

Gradually, the importance of accurate surveying on the ground came to be realised, and maps improved through the centuries as land owners and then governments needed detailed maps for effective administration, security and collection of rents and taxes. Private surveyors took commissions to survey estates, counties and whole countries, and then to sell printed maps to the public. In the first place, measurements were made with cricket-pitch length chains or simply by pacing.

When theodolites were introduced in the 16th century as telescopes mounted on a tripod and attached to graduated circles to measure both horizontal and vertical angles, it became quicker and more accurate to measure angles rather than distances. Using triangulation observing all the angles in a network of triangles it was possible to cover whole countries with fixed points from which to fill in map details; the length of just one side of one triangle as the baseline needed to measured accurately and then the rest could be calculated by trigonometry.

From the late 18th century, most national mapping programmes became the responsibility of the military or colonial administrations as defence and colonial rule justified the expenditure. The Survey of India is one of the oldest mapping agencies in the world created in 1767 by the British East India Company to control and exploit its territory. This 'Great Trigonometrical Survey' was started in 1802 and took 50 years to complete including Mount Everest which was named after George Everest (1790–1876) by the Royal Geographical Society (George Everest, Chief Cartographer).

In Britain, the army mapped the Scottish Highlands following the Jacobite Rebellion of 1745 to facilitate control of remaining rebels. The army had also carried out a joint Anglo-French cross-channel triangulation scheme to connect the Greenwich and Paris observatories in order to synchronise their astronomical observations. As the prime meridian of zero longitude is arbitrary many countries chose their own initially; French maps continued to use the meridian centred on Paris even after the Greenwich meridian was adopted internationally in1884.

Because many national mapping agencies are, or have been, controlled by their armed forces the maps they produced have been kept secret so preventing them from use by enemy nations, but also preventing their use for economic development and for the good of the country. The British Ordnance Survey published its first map of Kent for open sale on 1801 at a scale of one inch to one mile (1:63,360) and the cover was then gradually extended across the country; in the second half of the 19th century work started on large scale mapping of towns and eventually rural areas at 1:1250 and 1:2500 scales which are still in use today after periodic updating and digitisation. The French national mapping organisation, Institut Geographique Nationale was founded in 1940 out of its previous military incarnation which had started in 1887.

A big boost to this surveying came with the mapping of previously unknown territories, particularly in the United States and Canada, with the US Geological Survey providing accurate continental mapping. Early mapping of America received a big boost after the Louisiana Purchase in 1803 in which a huge area of central North America was bought by the US government from France for around fifteen million dollars. The following year two young US army officers, Meriwether Lewis (1774–1809) and William Clark (1770–1834), were commissioned by President Jefferson to explore the area and find a suitable transcontinental route to the Pacific; the Lewis and Clark expedition took over two years and relied on a lot of help from trappers and Indian peoples with local knowledge.

In early times, travel was often minimal, and most people seldom left the village or town in which they grew up, except perhaps as army conscripts, or occasionally as travelling traders or merchants. Villages and towns were connected by tracks, and major cities sometimes by larger highways which were simply bigger and better tracks, or unmade roads. An early impetus for travel was the need to facilitate deployment of military might. The Romans were the first to construct durable straight highways for the primary purpose of deploying their troops. Roman roads also served the purposes of trade, and enabled messenger services.

In Europe, the extensive network of Roman roads persisted for a thousand years after the demise of the western Roman Empire without being significantly upgraded. This was in part because the short sections of roads which cut across a landowner's property did not produce any income and was simply an expense on the negative side of the balance sheet. Long distance transport of goods and people only really boomed in the early 19th century with the advent of canals and railways. Somewhat later at the end of the 19th century and the beginning of the early 20th century invention of the internal combustion engine and the coming of cars and trucks resulted in upgrading of the long existing tracks into proper tarmac roads (chapter 73). It was the need to provide suitable guides to the use of these railways and roads in particular, which gave rise to a rapid upsurge in accurate map making through the 19th century.

Surveying and mapping techniques have changed out of all recognition since the onset of the 20th century commencing with various attempts to use photography from balloons during the preceding fifty years, with the first aeroplane-mounted photography dating to 1909. Once again warfare provided the stimulus to develop this technology for reconnaissance of troop placements during the First World War. The Second World War saw even more sophisticated use and updating of aerial photography, which then developed into quicker and more accurate mapping in the post war years.

In the second half of the 20th century, satellite photography has rendered even aerial photography obsolete and has allowed one country to map another unobserved and without the first country's permission. The Global Positioning System (GPS) has rendered triangulation and ground situated trig points superfluous and is now available for any member of the public to use from a good smart phone. GPS is extremely accurate and shows Earth's surface to be constantly changing with sea levels rising and continental drift now capable of sequential mapping. Among many other changes this now demonstrates that the Greenwich Meridian is now 100m east of the original line still carefully marked on the ground at the observatory!

Possible further reading:
Mercator by Nicholas Crane (Phoenix Books)

Chapter 38
The Tudors

The Tudors span a period of English history from 1485 when Henry VII came to the throne, until the death of Elizabeth I in 1603. The origins of the Tudor period go back to 1420, when Henry V married Catherine de Valois, daughter of Charles VI of France (Catherine appears as Kate in Shakespeare's history play Henry V). Catherine's son with Henry V became Henry VI, but after Henry V died young Catherine re-married Owain Tudor, and in due course their son became Henry VII, the first Tudor monarch.

Henry VII's succession drew to a close the Wars of the Roses, when the noble houses of Lancaster and York, rival branches of the House of Plantagenet, fought fiercely for supremacy and the English throne (chapter 29). Edward IV had died in 1483 when his son and heir, Edward V, was still a child. Edward V and his younger brother were left in the care of their uncle in the Tower of London, from where they disappeared in circumstances that remain mysterious. Whether their uncle, Richard III, or Henry VII, should be blamed for their disappearance remains a subject for debate. They represented a threat to the reign of either monarch, but no good evidence exists to explain their disappearance and presumed murders.

Once Henry VII, a Lancastrian, came to the throne, he ended the Wars of the Roses in the most direct way by marrying Elizabeth of York, daughter of Edward IV and the sister of the two princes who had died in the Tower of London. Previously Elizabeth had been betrothed to marry Richard III, and one can only wonder at the contradictions and reversals of fortune that must have come into her mind at this time. Following the Battle of Bosworth Field in 1485 between the Houses of York and Lancaster, in which Henry Tudor won the crown from Richard III, he set about restoring the nation's finances, and the fiscal position of the monarchy.

Parliament was re-established and provided information and opinions from other segments of the populace than the nobility. Henry's reign saw national cohesion beginning to consolidate. Although financially prudent, he was also somewhat greedy, but his reign was characterised by political astuteness following the old adage of 'divide and rule' (attributed to Phillip II of Macedon, but undoubtedly known and followed by preceding rulers). Henry also followed the contemporary trend of European exploration of the Americas, directing his efforts towards North America. He commissioned the Venetian explorer John Cabot (1450–1500), in 1497, to explore North America. This led to the discovery of the great cod fishing grounds on the Grand Banks of Newfoundland, but not to any European settlement which had to wait until Jacques Cartier (1491–1557), on a commission from the French King, established the first North American settlement in 1530 on the shores of the St Lawrence River.

This settlement did not last, but was followed by further small colonies much later in Port Royal, Nova Scotia in 1605, Jamestown in 1607, Quebec in 1608, the Mayflower Pilgrims in Boston in 1620 and New Amsterdam (New York) in 1626. These early colonies survived by exporting back to the mother country furs, grain and tobacco. In Europe Henry VII pursued a somewhat cautious policy, but in 1501 arranged the marriage of his first son Arthur to Catherine of Aragon. Subsequently his daughter Mary was married to Louis XII of France, and Margaret to James IV of Scotland.

Although Henry's eldest son, Arthur Tudor (1486–1502) was married to Catherine of Aragon the daughter of the Spanish King in 1501 and settled at Ludlow Castle, Arthur died only five months later. Catherine was later to swear that the marriage was never consummated, thus under religious law the way was left clear for her to marry Arthur's younger brother, who would become Henry VIII (1491–1547) in 1509. He came to the throne of age 18, and is commonly remembered for his six marriages, the first of which was to Catherine of Aragon in 1509, the widow of his brother Arthur, once legal niceties had been sorted out following Catherine's sworn statement that her marriage to Arthur had never been consummated.

Unfortunately Henry and Catherine together were able to produce only one live child, a daughter who would become Mary I of England. This failure to produce a male heir started Henry VIII on his battle with the Church of Rome to divorce Catherine. Ironically the Pope had declared Henry 'Defender of the Faith' in 1521 for his support of the Catholic church in the first years of his reign, when he had personally written a refutation of Martin Luther's views. Cardinal Thomas Wolsey (1473–1530), Henry's clerical chancellor, had bargained some concessions from the Pope in 1518, but these were deemed insufficient and neither Henry nor his reforming advisors were satisfied. Nor would the Pope agree to Henry's divorce from Catherine of Aragon, and so after years of political argument, a law was passed making Henry VIII head of the Church of England.

As head of the church, Henry then gave himself permission for the divorce. Once separation from Rome had been passed as an Act of Supremacy by parliament in 1534, Henry proceeded to appropriate the income and assets of abbeys, monasteries and convents, most of which had been founded three to four centuries earlier, but some of which dated back well before the Norman Conquest. Some 10,000 monks and nuns were displaced and about a 5th of all property in England reverted from the church to Henry, who used it as gifts to his supporting nobles and aristocrats.

This led to uprisings across the country, and a major rebellion two years later in Yorkshire and Lincolnshire, which became known as the Pilgrimage of Grace when a gathering of demonstrators estimated at up to 40,000 people marched to Lincoln and occupied the Cathedral, where they demanded that Henry's dissolution of the monasteries cease. Under the threat of force most of the protestors dispersed, but over two hundred of the leaders were arrested and executed. The uprising failed to prevent the continuing dissolution of the monasteries over the next few years.

On the much smaller positive side, Henry completed the building of King's College in Cambridge which had been started by Henry VI a century earlier only to run out of funds; he also took over and completed the Oxford college of Christ Church which had been started by Cardinal Wolsey when he was Archbishop of York. Wolsey had been made a cardinal in 1515, but his failure to persuade the Pope to grant Henry the divorce he wanted, finally broke Henry's patience. Wolsey was made a scapegoat and was charged with treason in 1530; on the way south to be incarcerated in the Tower of London he fell ill and died, thus precluding any trial.

Henry retained his personal belief in the core teachings of the Catholic Church, despite the ongoing negotiations with Rome. He married his second wife, Anne Boleyn, in 1533. A daughter, Elizabeth, was born soon afterwards, who would eventually succeed to the throne. Arguments within the kingdom about loyalties to the Catholic Church in Rome persisted, but Henry was intolerant of dissent, and some religious leaders were executed around the time of the Pilgrimage of Grace. These should have included Cardinal Wolsey, who escaped execution as he died whilst being taken to the Tower of London; Thomas More, a leading theologian, who was sanctified by the Pope shortly afterwards; and Thomas Cromwell, who oversaw the dissolution of the monasteries before bringing Anne of Cleves from Holland as a possible marriage prospect for Henry: she turned out not to be the beauty that Henry was expecting and Cromwell's star plummeted. Henry's six wives are easily remembered with the short rhyme – divorced, beheaded, died; divorced, beheaded, survived. They are as follows:

Catherine of Aragon, 1485–1536, divorced, seven pregnancies, only ('Bloody') Mary I survived; Anne Boleyn, 1501–1536, beheaded on the grounds of adultery, mother of Elizabeth I; Jane Seymour, 1508–1537, died in childbirth of Edward VI; Anne of Cleves, 1515–1557, divorced and never remarried; Catherine Howard, 1523–1542, beheaded on grounds of treason and adultery, no issue; Catherine Parr, 1512–1548, survived Henry but then died in childbirth with her next husband.

Henry sustained a severe leg wound jousting in 1536 which never healed and resulted in chronic debilitating sepsis which must have been a considerable deterrent to his wives. He united Wales with England by Act of Parliament, and ended the privileges of the Welsh nobility, replacing them with members of Parliament. In 1540 a similar treaty acknowledged Henry as King of Ireland, and two years later there was a treaty with Scotland. In the meantime, he had promulgated the Divine Right of Kings, asserting that not only did the Catholic Church not have precedence over his rule, but that he, and he alone, possessed the Divine Right to rule, bestowed directly from God.

Henry may be held up as an illustration of the undesirability of monarchy as a system of government; it allows a single individual unreasonable and unbridled authority over his or her countrymen and women: the monarch has been thrown into the post by accident of birth, and may be prejudiced, capricious, ignorant, illogical, arbitrary and biased, without recourse for his or her subjects to get rid of their monarch.

When Henry died in 1547, he left a son, Edward VI aged nine, and a daughter Elizabeth aged fourteen, who would later succeed to the throne at the age of twenty-five after a turbulent adolescence of changing fortunes. The nine-year-old Edward should have seen a Council of Regions govern for him, but his uncle, the Duke of Somerset, declared himself Lord Protector, and assumed the reins of power. Somerset was financially incompetent and personally lavish, milking the Treasury. Rebellion ensued, and Somerset was arrested two years into Edward's reign; after being released initially he was subsequently rearrested, tried and executed for felony.

Edward died of tuberculosis at the age of 15 after only six years of notional rule. On his deathbed he was persuaded to name his half-sister Mary as his successor rather than Henry VIII's instructed choice of Protestant Lady Jane Grey, Henry VII's great granddaughter. Lady Jane Grey, aged 17 and catholic, and her patron, the Duke of Northumberland, faced a large rebellion to which they surrendered, and following which they were executed.

Mary I ('Bloody Mary'), who ruled from 1553 for five years, was an ardent Catholic, where her half-brother had been an equally ardent Protestant. She tried to return the kingdom to Catholicism, interpreting the Protestant faith as heresy and treason, and in consequence her reign is also known as the Counter-reformation. Famously she earned her posthumous epithet 'Bloody' by sending Archbishop Cranmer (1489–1556), who had worked hard to try and achieve Henry VIII's first divorce, to burn at the stake, alongside Bishop Hugh Latimer (1487–1555) Cambridge theologian and chaplain to Edward VI, and Nicholas Ridley (1500–1555) Bishop of London; in this way, and through a further 300 martyrs Mary deserved her epithet 'Bloody Mary'. Her rear-guard action failed however, largely due to the successful spread of Protestantism throughout northern Europe over the previous two decades. Her husband and later widower, Philip II (1527–1598) of Spain, was equally active and energetic in his pursuit of heresy and his encouragement of the Spanish Inquisition.

In 1558, the Scottish Queen (also called Mary) was betrothed to the French Dauphin. Mary (1542–1587) had been six weeks old when her father James V of Scotland died, she was brought up as a Catholic and lived most of her early life in France while regents ruled in her name. She married the French Dauphin, Francis II in 1559, but he died soon after thereby erasing French hopes of Scotland becoming part of France and possibly succeeding to the English throne in later years. French policy towards her protestant minority Huguenot population was repressive at that time and Mary had signed a document to say that Scotland would become part of France if she and Francis had no heirs. France in fact occupied Scotland but a Scottish army defeated the Fortress at

Leith, where the French were unable to reinforce their garrison due to the insolvency of the French Monarchy.

When Mary and Francis were betrothed, rioting broke out in Edinburgh. Scottish Protestants were concerned that France would invade to help their Scottish Catholic cousins, and this fear was compounded by the French seizure of Calais, which had been a small English enclave up till that time.

At the end of 1558, Bloody Mary became ill and rapidly died in England leaving a divided and fearful nation behind her. After the death of Bloody Mary, her namesake, Mary Queen of Scots initially lived as a widow in Scotland following the brief reign and the death of her first husband Francis II of France, and then the death of her second husband, Lord Darnley. She had made a brief claim on the English throne at the time of Elizabeth's succession, but was forced to abdicate the Scottish throne in favour of her infant son after being suspected of the murder of her second husband, Lord Darnley. She then fled south to England seeking protection from her cousin, Elizabeth I. As a catholic, her motives and plotting against Elizabeth were highly suspicious as she wished to see the protestant revolution reversed and after many years under arrest she was finally executed (chapter 41).

The five Tudor monarchs from 1485 to 1601 are:

Henry VII	1485–1509
Henry VIII	1509–1547
Edward VII	1547–1553
Mary I	1553–1558
Elizabeth I	1558–1603

Possible further reading:
What the Tudors and Stuarts Did for Us by Adam Hart-Davis (Pan MacMillan)
Tudor England by John Guy (Penguin)
The Tudors by Peter Ackroyd (Pan Books)

Chapter 39
The Reformation

In the millennium following the birth of Jesus, Christianity spread to most of Europe. As it spread different individuals placed different emphasis and interpretations on areas of the Gospels. The Jewish faith, from which Christianity sprang, shared the founding base which Jews call the Torah, and which Christianity knows as the Old Testament. Christianity was then further developed in the Biblical New Testament, which represents the narrative and ideas following from the life of Christ.

Thus, by the end of the first millennium AD, Christianity was widespread within Europe, although variations of emphasis persisted, and many of the old customs of pre-Christian religious thinking had been incorporated into Christian life. Popes and rulers have always been prone to emphasise aspects of Christianity (and other religions) that suited their particular purpose, and to neglect other aspects of religious thinking which were contrary to the interpretation they wished to project. Indeed, the general tenors of the Old and New Testaments are somewhat at variance with each other, and these different attitudes are often glossed over.

Throughout the first millennium, different popes and other church leaders had often developed Christianity along different lines. Great conferences, set up by rulers and emperors, not bishops or popes, had been held to try and agree basic theology, and had often proved unsuccessful. Notable amongst such developments are included the work of St Benedict in setting up a monastery in the 6th century, devoted to the moral life from which many ordinary men and women of the time appeared to have deviated.

The Council of Nicaea in 325 had helped clarify thinking and strengthened the Church, but later in 451, the Council of Chalcedon failed to achieve consensus, and the Church was already splitting into small sub-groups or sects. The Papacy was unable to maintain control or uniformity across the whole of the Christian Church, and the Eastern Church drifted away from Rome as the precursor of what we now know as the Orthodox Church.

In its early years, much Christian teaching was of retribution, hellfire and damnation. Much time was given to thought and discussion around the afterlife promised by other religions as well. Christianity disseminated the message of purgatory and heaven in the afterlife, depending on the individual's moral worth and life following the present earthly existence. The New Testament also carries a vision of the apocalypse: a time when a final day of reckoning would occur, and the souls of the dead, together with the behaviour of the living, would be judged by God.

Religion occupied an enormous aspect of peoples' lives during the first millennium, with the Church leading in the development of thought. There being no evidence for or against heaven or hell, or indeed for or against an afterlife at all, many superstitions grew up. One of these was that an apocalypse would come to pass with the advent of the millennium. One thousand is a nice round number, and throughout the 10th century there was steadily increasing conviction amongst many people that the world would come to an end on the last day of the millennium. This has been vividly and convincingly laid out on Tom Holland's book on the subject.

Needless to say, the world did not end on the last day of the first millennium, or even the first day of the second millennium. Apprehension continued for a while as it was then suggested that the date should perhaps have been 1,000 years after the crucifixion of Christ, rather than after his birth, but once again, the apocalypse failed to materialise. The Church continued to evolve, and Papal ambitions increased in terms of trying to control both states and individuals. It is interesting to note that the same phenomenon occurred to a much lesser extent at the end of the year 2,000, though this time including fears of a computer Armageddon as well as a religious one.

Christian thinkers became more rigid in their outlook, and although the Benedictine teaching order had been established in the early 6th century, new revolutionary thinkers appeared in the 13th century, including the Franciscan Order which followed the thinking of St Francis. Two Dominican Friars followed the preaching of St Dominic, who went to southern France to preach to heretics known as the Albigensians who lived around Albi in southern France. Both orders were missionary and believed in poverty, but the intellectual thrust of their argument was similar. This internal European Crusade against the Albigensians started in 1209 with the Papal bureaucracy allying itself with secular states against heresy.

This thinking would continue and intensify and, in due course, would lead to the continuing growth of Inquisitions under the Franciscans, but often with the principal inquisitors being the Dominicans. A very strict and assertive Pope, Boniface VIII, was elected in 1294. His rule gave rise to violent disagreements resulting in the kings of England and France dismissing his authority. Boniface was kidnapped and subsequently freed, but died soon afterwards. In 1309 the new pope who was French and conscious of the considerable undercurrent of Italian resentment, moved the Papacy to Avignon, where a lifestyle of magnificence and indulgence was also rapidly seen by many ordinary Christians as unwarranted decadence. The luxury in which the Pope and his Curia lived was at great variance with the lives of ordinary people who provided the everyday wealth needed to sustain the Papacy in such style.

Questions and dissatisfaction about the Catholic Church's conduct, and about disparities in wealth between those at the top and the great mass of peasants at the bottom, began to rumble around early in the second millennium. St Francis of Assisi (1181–1226) gave up a life of privilege to preach and minister amongst the sick and the needy. He rapidly attracted followers, and the Order of Franciscans (grey friars) was authorised by the Pope in 1210. The Dominican order (black friars) was founded by a Spanish priest,

St Dominic (1170–1221), and Dominicans also took vows of poverty, but with an emphasis on combating heresy and heretics. The Cathars were at the receiving end of this first aggressive anti-heresy campaign, which lasted for two decades from 1209 to 1229, with considerable military force. The Cathars believed in two Gods, one good and the other in effect 'Satan'. A Papally approved crusade was commenced against the Cathars in 1209 in an effort to crush their heretical dissent; many Cathar strongholds were destroyed and the focal town of Beziers itself was razed to the ground with all its inhabitants massacred. The Dominicans survived by begging and on charity, and their philosophy is often felt to have led on to the Papal-led Inquisition which was established in 1184 by the Pope.

Peter Waldo (1140–1218) a wealthy merchant from Lyon in southern France, is recognised as founder of the Waldensians. Once again, he advocated a life of radical poverty and preaching, combined with strong condemnation of Papal luxury and much of orthodox Catholic theology. Waldo also advocated strict adherence to difficult principles, and translated the Bible into the vernacular. Because of persecution Waldo's successors were driven underground and developed a system of secretive travelling and preaching. In due course some 200 years later, the Waldensians adopted Calvinist beliefs becoming a Protestant denomination as part of the Reformation.

Catholicism was not helped at this time by in-fighting amongst its internal hierarchy and by attempts of the French monarchy to hijack the Papacy. From 1309 to 1377 the King of France managed to dominate the Papacy after a French Pope was elected and refused to rule the church from the Vatican in Rome, a succession of French Popes then ruled the Church from Avignon. At the end of this time in 1378, the Pope returned to Rome. But this brought about other problems with both Rome and Avignon attempting to appoint their own candidates to the Papacy in a period known as the 'Great Schism'. This was finally ended after a lot of discussion and wrangling in 1417, with the official Pope being anointed in Rome where the office has stayed ever since.

The dissatisfaction with the wealth, laxity and immorality of the Church and its high officers, together with their drift away from the early principles of the Church, was crystallised by John Wycliffe and Jan Hus. Wycliffe (1320–1384) translated the Bible into the vernacular because, as he wrote, '……..*this bible is for the government of the people, for the people, and by the people*' (this was quoted much later in a speech by Abraham Lincoln). He lived and preached in Oxford, and was very disillusioned with Church teachings, arguing strongly for a return to scriptural principles. He felt that the Papacy, most of the monasteries, and many of the clergy, were immoral, and he put forward 18 propositions suggesting a return to the basic values of the Ten Commandments.

Although his writings and preaching were highly critical of much of Church orthodoxy, he was relatively low key, and managed to avoid significant persecution. His followers were known as 'Lollards'; the Lollard movement was a precursor to the full Protestant Reformation. Following Wycliffe came a Bohemian priest and teacher from Prague called Jan Hus (1369–1415). Following his studies and ordination Hus became Rector of the University of Prague in 1402, where he translated the works of Wycliffe, which were at that time banned. He tried to reform Church moral failings, and published a list of 45 propositions, including preaching against the indulgences offered by the Pope. Hus went through the ordeal of appearing before a protracted church council, before being burnt at the stake as a heretic, despite having been offered a promise of safe conduct from the council.

The Hussite Wars which followed lasted from 1419–1434 as most of the Czech and Bohemian population supported the reformist views of John Hus against the Catholic church. During this time the Pope sent five Catholic crusades against the Hussites, all of which were defeated and eventually a truce was arrived at.

Criticism of the Catholic church and Papacy was next expressed by Martin Luther (1483–1546), who was a German priest and professor, best known for his protestations about the selling of Papal indulgences. In 1517 a Dominican friar had come to Wittenberg in Saxony, where Luther was a priest, selling indulgences. In reaction to this Luther published 95 theses, or propositions, which he is famously said to have displayed on his church door. For this Luther was excommunicated. Public debate followed, and in turn led to church debate, and then Luther's appearance at a church council in 1521 (convened to address the questions of both Luther's writings and the more general problem of spreading Protestantism), known as the Diet, or Council, of Worms.

The Reformation is often dated to this particular event thanks to the existence of Gutenberg's printing press, although clearly discontent and criticism of church behaviour and teaching had been brewing for many years. Luther's friends had translated his ninety five theses from Latin into German, and in print form they spread rapidly across Europe. Martin Luther is also remembered both for translating the Latin Bible into the German vernacular, and for getting married, thus setting a precedent for clerical marriage in Protestant Churches.

Anti-Catholic and anti-papal feeling and preaching became widespread through the early years of the 16th century with different individuals leaving us with differing viewpoints of opposition to Catholicism, which coalesced into the Reformation. John Calvin (1509–1564), was a French cleric and prolific writer who continued to develop Christian theology from a protestant point of view. He left the Catholic church in 1530, continuing to write and preach as a minister in Geneva, where he was relatively safe from persecution. His works are seen as the basis for the present Reformed, Congregational and Presbyterian Churches across the world.

The three fundamental principles of Protestantism are firstly belief in the bible as the highest authority, and certainly higher than church tradition;

secondly comes the importance of faith, with good actions and good works stemming from faith, rather than being important on their own; and thirdly the right and duty to read the bible in the vernacular, together with involvement of the laity, and the great congregation of believers, in church affairs, rather than the issuance of instructions from high church authority, particularly the Vatican. John Knox (1513–1572) in Edinburgh was a clergyman who got entangled in the Catholic and Protestant violence reverberating around Scotland, England and France of Reformation times, and lived for a while in the relatively safe ambience of Geneva where he knew Calvin; he is widely regarded as the founder of the Presbyterian Church of Scotland.

Erasmus of Rotterdam (1466–1536) was a Dutch priest, teacher, writer and critic. He wrote extensively and prepared a new edition of the Latin and Greek New Testaments. He continued to emphasise the traditional faith, and was somewhat at odds with Luther's concepts, but he was dedicated to the reform of Catholic church abuses. In Switzerland Ulrich Zwingli (1484–1531) preached criticism of Catholicism and the need for reform, but he died in religious violence and only some of the Swiss cantons followed his teachings. Many of his ideas survive him both in Switzerland and in Reformed Churches across the world.

In England, throughout these turbulent and contentious times, Henry VIII (ruled 1509–1547) is known for precipitating the English Reformation by leaving the Catholic Church and establishing the Church of England. However, Henry continued to believe in most basic Catholic theology, especially the Divine Right of Kings, in other words he felt he had been appointed by God and not by the church, so that as monarch he enjoyed the Divine Right to be at the apex of both Church and State. He dissolved the Catholic monasteries and Church foundations, appropriating their wealth to himself (chapter 38).

Henry justified the dissolution of the monasteries by the extravagance of the Church, but was equally profligate with his own wealth once he had destroyed the monastic foundations and appropriated their belongings. He is remembered for his six wives, and for the Pope's refusal to grant annulment of his first marriage, to Catherine of Aragon. This seems to have been the last straw in Henry's dealings with the Catholic Church which followed a series of statutes which he introduced through the 1530s. In the three decades after 1536, the beliefs of the Church of England were set down with several different revisions through this time. The process was not helped by a wobble back towards Catholicism under Queen Mary's short reign in the middle of the period, but by 1563 the Thirty Nine Articles were agreed by a church Convocation under Matthew Parker, Archbishop of Canterbury (1504–1575). These articles setting out the basic tenets of the Anglican faith differentiated the faith from Catholicism on one side, and Calvinism on the other side. This all set the seal for future internecine strife between the large mass of English people who became Protestants under Henry, and a minority who clung stubbornly to the old Catholic faith.

With all this, secession from the Catholic church, and questioning of church belief and authority, it was inevitable that a backlash should follow. In response to all the criticisms of the Catholic Church a Spanish knight called Ignatius Loyola (1491–1556) was inspired to abandon his military life (following an injury) and take up strict Catholic values. Like others, he took vows of poverty, chastity and obedience, and in particular, obedience to the Pope and current Papal thinking. With some followers he established the Society of Jesus, known by the popular name Jesuits, which was approved by the Pope in 1540. This constituted the beginning of a fight back by the Catholic Church against Protestantism, known as the Counter Reformation.

The Papal Inquisition had been established at the end of the 12th century to combat the Albigensian heresy of the Cathars, but it had largely atrophied. The Spanish Inquisition had been established in 1478 by Ferdinand II of Aragon and Isabella of Castile and there were similar Roman and Portuguese Inquisitions established by the state rather than by the Papacy, which were initially intended to ensure orthodox beliefs among those who converted to Catholicism from Judaism or Islam. At the beginning of the 16th century the Inquisition was very active in pursuing heretics. A high rate of conviction was obtained, often by apparently cynical manipulation of rather poor evidence, and many suspect Catholics were burnt at the stake, the idea being that the heresy and the sin would be consumed by the fire and the deviant souls would thereby be purified. Much of the Inquisitions' energies in Spain and Portugal were turned on Jews and Catholics, rather than on Protestants of whom there were relatively few.

An Ecumenical Council was finally convened with great difficulty at Trento in Italy by Pope Paul III and met intermittently between 1545 and 1563. This Council of Trent considered designated heresies committed by Protestants who left the Catholic church, and also specified current church dogma and permitted beliefs about the Bible, mass and sin, amongst many other topics. In 1570, with no sign of success in rolling back the Protestant tide, Pope Pius V issued a papal bull which purported to depose Elizabeth I from the English throne and excommunicated her, thus fortifying the enmity between Protestant England and Catholic France, Italy and Spain. France was riven with wars of religion between 1562 and 1598 which can be seen as starting with a massacre of Protestants attending a service in a barn in 1562, when they were spotted by the Duke of Guise, who ordered the barn burnt down with all those in it.

Conflict really escalated on St Bartholomew's Day in 1572 in Paris, when many wealthy and aristocratic Protestant Huguenots (French protestants of the Reformed tradition) had gathered in the city to celebrate the wedding of the king's sister, but instead of celebrations most of them were massacred on the king's instructions. Many thousands died in mob violence that day in Paris, and later across France, thereby reinforcing interfaith mistrust, and the Protestant view of Catholicism as a religion of violence and treachery.

Many Huguenots migrated to Germany, Scandinavia and Britain as well as to the New World. French persecution of Huguenots only finally came to an end at the time of the French Revolution with the Declaration of the Rights of Man and the Citizen, in 1789.

Possible further reading:
The Reformation by Peter Marshall (A Very Short Introduction, Oxford University Press)

Chapter 40
The Renaissance

The name "Renaissance", literally rebirth, is used to describe a phenomenon of gradually increasing cultural awareness and achievement occurring roughly between the years 1400 and 1600. It occurred in Europe against a background of Christian culture rejuvenating the perceived values and characteristics of the classical Greco-Roman period, and indeed building on those achievements thanks to improvement in technology and understanding. Placement in Europe is important with its background of Christian culture and relative free thinking, compared with the restricting climates of Muslim (Moorish) civilisation in Arabia, Africa and Spain, and similarly restricting attitudes and control in China, both in past imperial times and under more recent governments. This climate of opinion and relative openness contrasts with the imposed Islamic restrictions of the Caliphate in the Arabic world, and the severe class restrictions imposed by the effective dictatorship of Imperial Chinese rule.

By contrast, restrictions imposed by the teachings of the Bible, and by the Medieval Papacy, were relatively lax and were also often only loosely enforced, or even ignored as exemplified by the lives of Wycliffe, Hus and Luther, though we must not forget the persecution and deaths of many early Protestant thinkers, indeed Wycliffe was persecuted even after his death, Luther was brought to court but escaped, and Hus was eventually burnt at the stake.

It is noteworthy that alongside the Renaissance came the development of the Reformation in Northern Europe, which again was the result of relatively loose thought control, and relatively better tolerated questioning and re-thinking of Christian precepts in Protestant communities. Both Reformation and Renaissance were accelerated by the discovery and rapid introduction of printing towards the end of the 15th century. With the introduction of printing, wider and more speedy dissemination of thinking was possible. It also acted as a spur to increasing literacy amongst many sections of the population who previously would have had little to gain from the ability to read or write.

In Renaissance times, the Classical period was seen in a blurred way through the romantic and optimistic mists of intervening centuries, but it inspired development in the arts, initially mainly religious in form, though increasingly secular, as the Church monopoly on education and culture gradually diminished. The first universities in Europe were founded in the late 11th century at Bologna and Salerno, where they had reputations respectively, for the study of law and medicine; Paris followed in 1100, Padua in 1222, and Oxford in 1250, at a time when there were no comparable institutions of higher learning in India, China or the Islamic world, where Islamic universities taught a very restricted religious curriculum.

It is not possible, or even sensible, to ascribe the lighting of the Renaissance torch to a single individual, or even to a small group of individuals. However, Thomas Aquinas (1225–1274) is often singled out at the beginning of the process, and indeed was canonised by the church after his death as a model thinker and teacher. He was born in Rome and became a Dominican friar, philosopher and theologian, who accepted many of Aristotle's ideas, and is held up as one of the Churches greatest thinking theologians. He defined four cardinal virtues, namely prudence, temperance, justice and virtue.

St Thomas Aquinas ranks with the other four great early Church thinkers who had a great influence on the development of Christianity over the centuries, St Ambrose (340–397) who was Archbishop of Milan, and left extensive writings; St Augustine (354–430), Bishop in North Africa, and later sent to England, again an extensive writer; third amongst these figures is St Jerome (342–420), not only an extensive writer but also an early translator of the Bible into Latin whilst living in the modern day region of the Balkans; and fourthly and somewhat later, Pope Gregory or St Gregory (540–604), who wrote extensively and had an unprecedented influence on the liturgy of both Catholic and Orthodox Churches. At the time of the Reformation John Calvin was an admirer of Gregory, declaring that he was the last good pope.

At the start of the Renaissance, Dante Alighieri (1265–1321) an Italian poet, was born in Florence and is often called either "the supreme poet" or alternatively "father of the Italian language". His poem *The Divine Comedy* is seen as a masterpiece of early thought and expression. His fellow writers, Francesco Petrarch (1304–1374) born in Arezzo, and Giovanni Boccaccio (1313–1375) from Florence, all helped to provide a sound literary base at the beginning of the Renaissance. Perhaps it is not surprising that the Renaissance started in Italy where there were constant reminders of past Greco-Roman classical civilisation, not only in the form of ruined temples and cities, but also buildings and Roman roads still in use a millennium or longer after their construction.

The start of the Renaissance was not just concentrated in Italy, but more specifically in Florence, where it was facilitated by social, political and civic peculiarities. These included the early introduction of banking and the commerce it generated, particularly under the influence of the banking family of Medici, whose first patriarch, Giovanni de Medici (1360–1492), appeared near Florence in the late 14th century, building a banking empire and fortune on the trade in wool and textiles; the wealth made by these early bankers and merchants also contributed to the Renaissance through their sponsorship of arts and culture.

A further influence was the migration of Greek scholars and ancient texts which occurred following the fall of Constantinople in 1453. Before this Europe had been using the seminal texts of ancient Greece and more recently of Arabia, but after 1453 scholars had available to them additional texts of Plato, Socrates,

Archimedes and many others, together with many of the works of the early Greek playwrights.

The peculiarities of Florence and the other Italian city states at that time may be put down to three major influences, firstly Christianity, secondly responsive government with citizen involvement, and thirdly the birth of capitalism as the city states were dedicated to commerce. This accounts for the rise of the banking family of the Medicis in Florence, of whom the most famous, and indeed the richest, was Lorenzo de Medici (1449–1492). Other important city states included Milan, Genoa, Pisa, Siena, Lucca and Cremona, which were all avid to accept all opportunities for commerce and banking, when northern European rulers of the time were often stifling it.

The city states prized their independence from the Holy Roman Emperor, who at the beginning of this period was a German. The impetus continued for two or three centuries until European trade with the rest of the world opened up to North America, the Indies and Africa, and Mediterranean trade consequently diminished in importance. This early capitalism and the fortunes made from it was vital in allowing patronage of the arts and artistic individuals by wealthy patrons.

The Black Death in 1347 must be mentioned as a further influence. As it raced across Europe the death toll was enormous, resulting in the population diminishing severely as a quarter to a half of the population succumbed to its ravages. This drop in population not only freed up a lot of land and boosted the prices of those agricultural producers who could still supply wanted goods, but it was also a great leveller of social structures which had come to be very rigid in previous centuries.

In the Renaissance, religion played an essential role. It was a time when both theological thinking and philosophy in general expanded beyond the boundaries and strait-jacket of previous eras. The Czech thinker and principal of Prague University, Jan Hus (1369–1415), gave rise to much early Protestant thought and was burnt at the stake in consequence of his perceived heresy within the Catholic church, however his writings inspired others, including Martin Luther (1483–1546) and John Knox (1513–1572). Girolamo Savonarola (1452–1498), a Dominican friar active in Florence, denounced clerical corruption and the exploitation of the poor. He preached about the wickedness of people with regard to what would be called consumerism today, or 'conspicuous consumption'. He preached poverty and prophesised the advent of retribution from God. Eventually, popular opinion turned against him and at the same time he was excommunicated, imprisoned, tortured and finally executed by burning. His followers, and the reforms and poverty that he advocated, eventually died away, and Florence returned to an era of conspicuous consumption and patronage once more. Further north Protestant thinking was developed by Huldrich Svingli (1484–1531) in Switzerland, by Erasmus of Rotterdam (1466–1536) a Dutch priest, and by Philip Melanchthon (1497–1560), who collaborated with Martin Luther.

In architecture, which all the population of Italy had become accustomed to taking for granted, the Renaissance saw the development of the ancient Greek and Roman styles. The emphasis was on symmetry, proportion and the geometry of buildings. Filippo Brunelleschi (1377–1446) was famed for completing Florence Cathedral, crowning it with a magnificent dome, a feat not just of design, but one which implies a considerable knowledge of mathematical and engineering principles. The return of the Papacy to Rome in 1377, from its 67 year sojourn in Avignon resulted in a spate of new church building, particularly around Rome at the end of the 14th century reaching its peak later in the restoration and completion of the Sistine Chapel in 1480.

Michelangelo (1475–1564) was an extraordinary and most talented polymath who excelled not just in architecture and design, but was also an artist who has never been bettered in sculpture, poetry or painting. He completed the dome of St Peter's around 1560. Andrea Palladio (1508–1580) was a Venetian architect who wrote widely, with his master work *The Four Books of Architecture* being frequently referred to over succeeding centuries. His style was very much in the Greek and Roman tradition, which spread to the rest of Europe and remains a well-recognised style known as Palladian through the centuries since his death, and influencing the early British architect, Inigo Jones (1573–1652) when it appeared in England towards the end of the reign of Elizabeth I.

In art, the Renaissance saw the development of increasing realism and technical sophistication. There was the realisation of perspective and how to achieve it. Giotto de Bondone (1266–1337), a talented painter and architect in Florence, is often seen as the first of the great Italian Renaissance artists. Lorenzo Ghiberti (1378–1455) also came from Florence and trained in sculpture and as a goldsmith: he is noted for the magnificent reliefs on the bronze doors of the Florence Baptistery which are still admired today. Sandro Botticelli (1445–1510) an Italian painter of the Florentine School, was patronised by the banker Lorenzo de Medici (1449–1492) and has left many stunning paintings.

These early architects were followed by two outstanding polymaths, first Leonardo da Vinci (1452–1519) who was truly a genius with painting, sculpture and architecture, but in addition wrote widely on anatomy, mathematics, music and engineering. A few years later, Michelangelo was an equally talented polymath encompassing sculpture, painting, architecture, literature and engineering; in the final years of his life he painted the ceiling of the Sistine Chapel in the Vatican. Raphaello Sanzio da Urbino (1483–1520), usually known simply as Raphael, excelled in painting and architecture, he worked mainly for the Vatican and had a large workshop from which many paintings were forthcoming which were only partly done by Raphael himself; despite dying young at 37, he still left a large legacy of work.

In literature, Dante (1265–1321) is sometimes credited as the father of the Renaissance, and even as 'Father of the Italian language'. He was closely followed by Petrarch (1304–1374) who grew up near Florence but moved to Avignon when his family followed Pope Clement V there in 1309. Giovanni Boccaccio (1313–1375) wrote a number of influential and much quoted books, and was unusual in writing in the contemporary Italian vernacular. These three are often known as the *'Three Fountains'* for their part in developing early Italian literature, while Niccolo Machiavelli (1469–1527) is also often quoted through the succeeding centuries; he grew up in Florence, and in addition to writing history and philosophy, was active in politics and diplomacy. His name has passed into everyday usage to describe unscrupulous politicians and their evil or immoral actions. Along with others he wrote drama, helping rediscover the ancient Greek poets, including Homer, Demosthenes and Thucydides. Later in the enlightenment are numbered some English writers; Edmund Spencer (1552–1599) remembered for *The Faerie Queene*; Sir Philip Sydney (1554–1586), one of Queen Elizabeth's courtiers and soldiers; and William Shakespeare (1564–1616), whose plays remain popular to this day.

In philosophy, the early enlightenment was powered by the rediscovery of the writings of the ancient Greeks, including Plato, Socrates, Aristotle and Archimedes, and of the ancient Latin writers Cicero, Livy, Seneca and others. In the early movement Rene Descartes (1596–1650) although born in France spent most of his adult life in Holland, he exercised great influence in early mathematics, as well as philosophy. Sir Thomas More (1478–1535), an English lawyer and philosopher who was counsellor to Henry VIII and Lord Chancellor of England from 1529 for three years, opposed the Protestant Reformation, and also refused to accept Henry as supreme head of the Anglican Church. Because of his opposition to Henry's marriage to Ann Boleyn More was convicted of treason and executed, for which he was later canonised by the Catholic church.

Music developed rapidly during the Enlightenment. Throughout the first millennium most Church music had been in the form of Gregorian chant introduced by Pope Gregory at the end of the 6th century. The invention of notation by Guido of Arezzo (992–1033, chapter 54) in Italy, allowed reproducible music to be performed at different ceremonies and in different places (chapter 54). Once printing became available the spread of music and its developments accelerated rapidly. Harmony developed and the early composers who wrote music which is still appreciated today, include Giovanni Palestrina (1525–1594) in Italy, who produced an enormous output while directing the Vatican choir; Orlande de Lassus (1530–1594) from Holland, and Tomas Luis de Victoria (1548–1611) in Spain, both spent a lot of their active lives working in Rome.

Thomas Tallis (1505–1585), William Byrd (1540–1623) and Orlando Gibbons (1583–1625), all became Gentlemen of the Chapel Royal in England where they composed a lot of music for their monarchs. The first opera, *Dafni*, appeared in Florence at the end of the 16th Century composed by Jacopo Corsi (1561–1602), and opera became really well established with Claudio Monteverdi (1567–1643), whose seminal opera *Orpheo* was first performed in 1607.

The Enlightenment also saw the first awakenings of science as we recognise it. Nicolaus Copernicus (1473–1543) taught that Earth revolved around the sun rather than vice versa. The Catholic Church was not happy with this doctrine, despite the fact that Aristotle had taught this two millennia previously, and despite the fact that it did not contradict anything in the Bible. His books were proscribed, with the Vatican not removing this proscription against Earth not being the centre of the universe until the 19th century. Galileo (1564–1642) would have a similar battle with the church a century later. In this way much of the Catholic Church's attitude to science slowed down the development of scientific thought and experiment in Catholic countries.

In more distant parts of the world from Europe, including Asia, Africa, China and the Islamic countries, the Renaissance did not ignite; this may be put down to four main contributing reasons. Firstly, there was no background Christian outlook, secondly printed books to spread knowledge had not yet appeared, thirdly there was no patronage from wealthy individuals, only from a single ruler, and fourth, much of thinking and attitudes was effectively censored.

Possible further reading:
The Renaissance by Jerry Brotton (A Very Short Introduction, Oxford University Press)
The Ascent of Man by Jacob Bronowski (Futura Publications)

Chapter 41
Elizabeth I 1533–1603

Elizabeth I, the last of the Tudors, came to the throne at the age of 25 in 1558 after a turbulent childhood in which her mother, Anne Boleyn, had been executed at her father's behest when she was only two and a half, and after which she was declared illegitimate. During her childhood her fortunes altered and reversed on several occasions. As the daughter of Henry VIII she was a Protestant, but not aggressively so, and she managed through her lifetime to steer a middle course between Catholic and Protestant interpretations of Christianity, despite many Catholic plots that followed her half-sister Bloody Mary's attempts to restore Catholicism as the national religion of England during her short reign. Despite this, under Elizabeth there was certainly some persecution and hounding of Catholics who must have lived in terror and constant fear of their lives, because they were seen as treasonous rather than heretical.

Early in her reign, the Archbishop of Canterbury, Matthew Parker (1504–1575), who had been chaplain to Elizabeth's mother, Anne Boleyn, was commissioned to codify the Anglican faith. He is one of the primary architects of the Anglican Church along with Thomas Cranmer (1489–1556), also briefly Archbishop of Canterbury before Parker for two years, until he was convicted of heresy and burnt at the stake under Catholic Bloody Mary. The third important innovator of the infant Anglican Church, was the London priest and writer Richard Hooker (1554–1600), who is remembered for steering a middle course between Catholic and Protestant doctrines.

Archbishop Parker refined the original ten articles, produced in 1536 to define the new Anglican Church after Henry VIII's excommunication in 1533, and finally produced his Thirty Nine Articles five years after Elizabeth came to the throne: these articles which define Anglican doctrine and practice were incorporated in the Church of England's Book of Common Prayer, where they remain to this day, and are commemorated in the thirty nine buttons that fasten the cassock of an Anglican priest. In the meantime, Protestantism had continued to grow across northern Europe, thanks in large part to the advent of the printing press in the previous century and the consequent relative ease with which ideas and books could now spread across borders and within borders.

In Scotland, John Knox (1514–1572) had been ordained as a Catholic priest, but subsequently came to align himself with the thinking of the itinerant Lutheran preacher, George Wishart (1513–1546), who was burnt at the stake in 1547 after a Catholic show trial in Scotland. Knox became a Protestant minister and spent some time in England in the service of Edward VI, following which he studied in Switzerland with John Calvin while Bloody Mary was on the throne. He returned to Scotland in 1559 after Mary's death, and the Presbyterian Church in Scotland was recognised the following year. In the meantime, Elizabeth repealed the laws against heresy. Although undoubtedly Protestant she continued to equivocate with Catholicism to such an extent that Papal dissatisfaction finally culminated in her excommunication in 1570, like her father before her.

The objective of achieving a strong and stable Protestant nation, including Wales, Scotland and Ireland, was undoubtedly Elizabeth's main aspiration during her reign, but it was closely followed by the need to prevent invasion by Catholic continental countries, and this required a strong navy which she gradually developed, building on the earlier start of her father. During her reign Elizabeth travelled extensively throughout the country visiting her nobles. This was seen as a considerable worry by those lords who were asked to accommodate and entertain her, often for weeks on end, with a court consisting of several hundred courtiers and general staff, the expense involved was considerable. The policy did have the advantage that she was seen and appreciated by the populace at large and was able to hear their views, thus enhancing her reputation, while also conserving her exchequer.

Elizabeth's other juggling act throughout her reign, apart from the domestic religious one, was with the Catholic nations of Europe, where intermittent threats of war with Spain, Portugal and France was a constant problem. By juggling marriage proposals and possible alliances Elizabeth managed to spin out her diplomacy without ever committing herself to marriage. She had many regal suitors from Europe, but steadfastly rebuffed them all, knowing that a foreign husband would bring problems relating to continental and Catholic countries, while an English husband would result in internal factionalism. She did however have a favourite in Lord Dudley, whom she made Earl of Leicester, but declined to marry, resulting in continuous tension at court.

She had extensive spy networks providing her with information on individuals across the kingdom, and indeed also abroad. Mary, Queen of Scots, was a constant thorn in Elizabeth's side. Mary, daughter of James V of Scotland, had succeeded to the Scottish throne when only six days old in 1542, and a regency council had ruled for her while she was brought up in Catholic France where she was married to the Dauphin, Francis II at the age of sixteen in 1559, shortly before he succeeded to the French throne (only to die of natural causes seventeen months later, thus removing any French hopes of Scotland becoming part of the French Kingdom, or of a future French king succeeding to the English throne).

French policy towards Protestants, including Huguenots, was very repressive and Mary had secretly signed a document stating that Scotland would become part of France if she and Francis had no heirs. France controlled Scotland only very briefly, holding the fortress at Leith, with the Scotch nobility and army capturing the fortress which could not be reinforced because of insolvency of the

French exchequer. She returned to Scotland as Queen in 1559 reigning for six months in 1567, but after the murder of her Scottish second husband, she was forced to abdicate in favour of her one year old son (who would become James VI of Scotland and James I of England), and fled to England, where Elizabeth kept her securely guarded in Sheffield castle.

In France, persecution of Protestant Huguenots continued and Scottish suspicion of French Catholicism also persisted. As a Catholic claimant to the English throne with strong French connections, Mary remained an embarrassment and a danger to Elizabeth, so that when she was caught overtly plotting against Elizabeth after years of confinement, she was finally condemned to death and executed in 1587.

Elizabeth's reign is also noteworthy for the calibre of England's seafarers. Notable amongst these were Sir John Hawkins (1532–1595) and Sir Francis Drake (1540–1596), who enjoyed royal authority for exploration in the New World with lucrative piracy against Spanish shipping returning from the Indies laden with gold and silver. They were also involved in the early trans-Atlantic slave trade. Elizabeth was a covert but willing partner in the not inconsiderable riches that this brought back to her country; following one such period of buccaneering, Drake voyaged down round the southern tip of South America and across the Pacific, to achieve the second circumnavigation of the world between 1577 and 1580: during this voyage he landed in California and claimed it for Britain; he was knighted by Elizabeth on his return.

In one year, the value of his piratical booty from attacking Spanish trade galleons was more valuable than the whole of the royal income from taxes. At the same time, Sir Walter Raleigh (1554–1618), was a prominent and leading advocate of colonisation in North America, obtaining his sovereign's permission to call the early colony Virginia after his Virgin Queen. In later years he got into a skirmish with a Spanish colony in South America which resulted in his arrest and imprisonment on his return; he was subsequently executed in deference to irate and outraged Spanish opinion.

The writer and prominent London cleric, Richard Hakluyt (1553–1616), was also heavily involved in promoting American colonisation in his book, *Discourse of Western Planting* in 1584 which suggested the opportunities available to the youth of England as well as the possibility of increasing the numbers of young Protestants; he was a prime advocate of early settlement (or 'planting') in Virginia.

The piracy, together with other reasons including religion, makes it understandable that by 1586 King Philip of Spain was building an armada to invade England and seize the throne; his claim to the English throne rested on his marriage to Mary Tudor, great grand-daughter of Henry VII. In April 1587 Drake sailed into Cadiz harbour in southern Spain and systematically destroyed much of Philip's battle fleet, reporting to his sovereign that he had "singed the King of Spain's beard". In 1588, after restoring his fleet of around 150 warships, Philip's Spanish armada finally sailed north with 18,000 soldiers as well as the ships' crews. Drake was reputedly playing bowls on Plymouth Hoe when the approaching armada was sighted and pointedly finished his game saying there would be plenty of time to put to sea to fight the Spanish ships after he finished his game.

The Spanish moored off Calais expecting to embark 30,000 more troops, but at that stage they were assaulted by a small fleet of more nimble English fire ships, which destroyed many of the slow moving cumbersome Spanish galleons while they were at anchor. The surviving vessels fled to the north with gale force winds behind them, and in a period of particularly inclement weather, many were wrecked as they attempted to round the north of Scotland and the west of Ireland in an attempt to get back to Spain. In the meantime, Elizabeth had ridden to Tilbury, where her army was gathered, to meet an expected invasion; once there, dressed in white and wearing silver armour, she gave a rousing speech to her troops.

This year of the Spanish Armada, 1588, marks a turning point in Elizabeth's reign, the nation had rallied and come together, internal plots had been suppressed, and external threats countered. Her spy masters were in control of the domestic troubles, and the final years of her reign were free of the need to pursue a great deal of activity in foreign relations. Campaigns in the Netherlands against the Spanish, and to subdue trouble in Ireland, did not disturb the domestic calm, though catholic Ireland had been a problem throughout her reign. Elizabeth's father, Henry VIII, had proclaimed Ireland to be part of England in 1534 so that it would not become an external threat or a base from which invasions against England could be launched; in 1541 the Irish Parliament had proclaimed Henry as their king.

The next several decades saw much fighting to try and subdue the island, which was a considerable drain on first Henry's, and then Elizabeth's, exchequer. Irish rebellions by the Earl of Desmond between 1569 and 1583, and by the O'Neills (known as the nine years war), from 1594 up to the time of Elizabeth's death were brutal and costly. Although subjugation of the island was achieved, conversion of its inhabitants to Protestantism failed and left a religious legacy which remains problematic to this day.

In an attempt to remedy the situation, Protestant colonies (known as 'plantations'), were imposed on large areas of the north and south, with protestant settlers being sent from England, and later Scotland, to take over confiscated lands, with the hope that new settlements might seed the new religion of Protestantism. This expensive attempt at social engineering failed, leaving a still divided and bitter Ireland.

The end years of her reign is noted for the flowering of English culture and its contribution to the Renaissance. Among playwrights William Shakespeare wrote poetry as well as almost forty plays which remain in current use to this day. Christopher Marlowe (1564–1593) also wrote poetry and half a dozen plays, but died, or was murdered, young in a fight. Other notable poets include Edmund Spenser (1552–1599) and Sir Philip Sidney (1554–1586).

Elizabeth died in 1603, apparently leaving a big question mark over the succession, but also bequeathing to her successor a not inconsiderable amount of debt. Behind the scenes in the last year or two of her life as she slowly declined, courtiers had been making advances to James VI of Scotland, seeing him as the most legitimate and appropriate choice for England's next ruler. Elizabeth's long-time trusted advisor, Lord Privy Seal and Secretary of State, William Cecil (1520–1598) ennobled as Lord Burghley, had previously negotiated with King James in secret since Elizabeth refused to discuss the matter during her lifetime, though shortly before she died one of her final statements is said to have been that "none but James VI of Scotland" should succeed her.

From the point of view of the transition, it was however probably just as well that the succession had been planned and literally swung into action at a few hours' notice. James himself was clearly aware that this would happen, and set out for London within hours of the news reaching him.

Possible further reading:
Elizabeth by John Guy (Penguin)

Chapter 42
The Stuarts and Civil War

When Elizabeth died in 1603 without an heir, there was a distinct paucity of claimants for the English throne. Both of Elizabeth's half siblings, Edward VI and Mary, had also died without issue, and the individual with the greatest claim to the English throne was James VI of Scotland (1566–1625). James came from the Stuart family who had ruled Scotland since 1371, and was therefore seen by Elizabeth on her deathbed, and long before this time by her close courtiers, as the obvious choice for the English throne. James had been expecting this translation from north of the border for a number of years, it was therefore no surprise that on hearing news of Elizabeth's death he headed rapidly for London, where he was proclaimed King of both Scotland and England.

The Stuarts as a family provided England with a century of poor kingship. James VI of Scotland on becoming James I of England and Scotland made a good start, firstly by stopping English piracy against Spain and thereby ending the chronic war with Spain, which had been a costly drain on finances, and secondly by declaring England, Scotland and Wales to be Great Britain and a United Kingdom. He was personally responsible for designing the flag incorporating the red saltire of St George for England, and the white saltire on a blue background of St Andrew's cross for Scotland, thus uniting the nations which he now took pains to call Great Britain.

Various versions of the flag were in use for the next two hundred years until 1801, when a royal proclamation united Great Britain and Ireland and the red saltire of St Patrick provided the final version. The third good thing James did on coming to the throne was to convene a conference at Hampton Court to reconstruct and codify practices of the Church of England; included in this was the commissioning, translation and publication of what is still referred to as the King James Bible, and the up-dating of the Book of Common Prayer.

James had been brought up a Protestant, despite his mother, Mary Queen of Scots, being Catholic. Early in his reign on the English throne a plot was hatched to kill him and many of his Parliamentarians, and then place James' young Catholic daughter Elizabeth, on the throne to restore England to Catholicism. The conspiracy in 1605, known as the Gunpowder Plot, involved placing many barrels of gunpowder in the cellars of the Houses of Parliament with the intention of igniting them during the royal opening of Parliament, thereby disposing of both the King and many Protestant Parliamentarians. One of the plotters warned his Catholic parliamentary friends to avoid attending the opening ceremony that day, and as a result a search on the night before the opening revealed Guy Fawkes, an ardent Catholic, with 36 barrels of gunpowder in the cellars under the Houses of Parliament. Fawkes and his co-plotters were tortured and executed, and the occasion has been commemorated ever since on November 5th with effigies of Guy Fawkes being burnt on top of a bonfire.

Since Henry VIII had broken away from the Catholic Church, the Church of England had still remained remarkably like the Church of Rome, and this had gradually resulted in the Puritan movement, whose followers felt that gaudy dressing, ornate churches and displays in general were inappropriate. Fashions slowly began to change with people beginning to wear plain dark clothes, shorter hair, and generally less ostentatious dress. This represented a divergence in the opposite direction from those Catholics who still wished for a return to the Church of Rome. In trying to steer an impartial middle course between Catholics and Puritans, James merely succeeded in alienating and persecuting both sides.

One answer by some of the first Puritans was to leave the country, and rather than emigrate to Protestant Europe, the first Puritans to emigrate westwards are known as the Pilgrim Fathers; they actually came from a Calvinist community in Holland to which they had previously emigrated in search of religious freedom but found it unsatisfactory. English investors supported the new colony at Plymouth, Massachusetts. One hundred Puritans sailed in a ship called the Mayflower to reach America; unfortunately they made landfall further north, and later in the season than intended. Thus, they endured a cold winter with a minimum of food so that many of these early Pilgrim Fathers died before self-sufficiency farming could supply their new little colony. The Pilgrims called their settlement New Plymouth, and the Mayflower steps in Boston commemorate their first landfall. Many more were to follow.

By the latter half of his twenty-two-year reign, James had already alienated Catholics, together with Puritans at the other end of the spectrum, of whom some 80,000 are estimated to have emigrated to America by the end of his reign, but he also antagonised his largely Protestant Parliament by insisting upon his Divine Right as King. In 1614 Parliament was dissolved, and James did not re-call it for the next seven years, raising money in other ways and relying on ruling by authority of the Divine Right of Kings At the same time he continued to squander money on the fashions and frivolities of life. It was during James' reign that personal taxation was introduced to raise money and as a consequence surnames became necessary to identify the King's subjects so they could be individually taxed; people often took the name of the town or village in which they lived, or their occupation for this purpose. Theatre, music and literature enjoyed an upsurge in their activity with royal sponsorship.

But during this time, James' eldest son Henry died of typhoid at the age of eighteen, and his younger brother Charles, now heir to the British throne was sent to Spain with the possibility of marrying the daughter of the Spanish King. The gulf between Protestant England and Catholic Spain proved too much, so nothing came of this, except that when Charles succeeded his father in 1625 he had become a connoisseur of art and fashion, but was singularly lacking in the crafts of diplomacy and government, both regarding his relationships with his subjects, and with foreign powers.

In Central Europe, the Thirty Years War broke out in 1618 with the Holy Roman Empire attempting to stem the flow of states and people to Protestantism. Although initially a religious war it gradually changed into a contest between France and the Habsburg Empire for control of Europe. It also included Huguenot rebellions in southern France where up to 250,000 people died, though this number is dwarfed by the estimated death toll throughout the whole thirty years of about eight million. Spain entered the war hoping to subdue its rebellious Protestant enclave in Holland, but the end result left the Dutch finally separated from Spain and enabled to commence their golden period of conquest and trade with the Far East. When the fighting ended with the Treaty of Westphalia in 1648, France and Sweden enjoyed enhanced power and the map of Europe was distinctly altered.

When James died in 1625, his son came to the throne as Charles I (1600–1649), and shortly afterwards married Henrietta Maria, the youngest daughter of the French King who was Catholic, which stoked up the anti-royalty feelings (the US state of Maryland is named for her). Charles demanded more money from Parliament, which was felt to be unreasonable, and led to a major confrontation resulting in 1628 in the Petition of Right, drawn up and ratified by both Houses of Parliament, which explained to Charles that he was not able to raise taxes without the will of Parliament, or imprison people without trial, or maintain a standing army. It is seen as being of equal importance to Magna Carta. This Petition served as the basis for later declarations of civil rights, including the American Declaration of Independence, and the British Petition of Rights, enacted late in the century in 1689.

Unfortunately, Charles lacked the ability to choose suitable advisors, or to listen and gauge the public mood. His decisions were often impetuous and ill-considered so that they led to further alienation of his subjects, especially MPs. In 1629 he dissolved Parliament intending personal rule with the help of his advisors, though his opponents labelled this subsequent period 'The Tyranny'. He did not recall Parliament for the next eleven years, and in consequence money rapidly ran short; when parliament was finally recalled in 1640 it proved unwilling to vote any funds for the monarch so Charles dissolved it after only three weeks with the result that it became known as the 'Short Parliament'. He was able to extend some levies and duties which were outside Parliamentary control, but finally, when national finances became dire, a new Parliament was reconvened and now four-fifths of MPs were against the King. This came to be known as the 'Long Parliament' as it lasted through the next two decades until the Restoration in 1660.

It was a much altered chamber reflecting the changing wealth over the previous century from the Church and land owning nobles, to a newly emergent middle class of merchants, professionals and civic dignitaries. Apart from financial difficulties, riots occurred in Scotland when Charles attempted to impose a new high church prayer book on the largely non-conformist Scots, while in England along with Archbishop William Laud (1573–1645), he persecuted puritans for not attending Anglican church services. Laud was eventually arrested, imprisoned in the Tower of London and later executed in 1645. In 1641 the Petition of Right was reinforced by parliament decreeing that control of the church, the law and the army should be by parliament and not by the monarch. Taxes were regularised and the King's personal prerogatives severely curtailed.

At the end of his tether, Charles unwisely tried personally to arrest five radical MPs by entering the Commons chamber with an armed guard, a move which failed and further alienated parliamentary opinion. With growing disquiet the royal family fled first to Hampton Court and then to Greenwich. Henrietta Maria then took her children and fled to France while Charles raised an army to try and quell the dissent by force, in this way making civil war inevitable.

The country became factionalised after 1642 with the division of arguments not only between King and Parliament, but also between Protestant and Catholic, north and south. Puritan activity increased, and life became not only more sober, but also more dangerous. Writer and poet John Milton (1608–1674) became a propagandist for Parliament. The Royalist supporters were known as Cavaliers, and continued to adhere to the regal fashion of wearing hair long and dressing well, whilst the Parliamentarians cut their hair short, dressed soberly and became known as Roundheads. The advantages from the start were on the Parliamentary side, particularly since Charles still had no readily accessible source of funds while Parliament still enjoyed the national revenue raised by taxes from the cities.

From a military point of view, the royalist supporters and their cavalry were better equipped and trained on horseback. Charles' Royalist army met the Roundhead parliamentarians with the first battle at Edge Hill in the English Midlands in October 1642 which gave no clear advantage to either side as the undisciplined royalist cavalry scattered in pursuing a fleeing enemy. The Parliamentary army returned to London, but Charles retreated to Oxford and established his base and court in one of the colleges, Christ Church, from where he would supervise the rest of the war.

The following year, the Edinburgh Assembly effectively joined the struggle on the Parliamentary side by providing a large army to join the Parliamentary forces which were now commanded by Oliver Cromwell (1599–1658), a Member of Parliament who had risen rapidly as a charismatic leader. Following previous repressive military campaigns of subjugation in Ireland, he had become the principal commander of the Parliamentary army. Ironically for a Puritan, Cromwell's family wealth had been amassed under Henry VIII, when his ancestor by marriage Thomas Cromwell, Henry's chief minister, took over monastic properties. Cromwell saw action in many of the battles and sieges of the Civil War over the next three years until Charles surrendered in May 1646 after escaping from his besieged base at Oxford.

It cannot have helped Charles' case when it became known that he had tried to solicit help from an Irish or French army in return for agreeing to bring

England back to Catholicism. Internal debates within the republican ranks pitted Cromwell against moderate Presbyterians, and against a group known as the Levellers, whose philosophy incorporated extended suffrage, equality under law, and religious tolerance; their importance flourished through the early years of the civil war, but waned rapidly after the execution of Charles.

Charles' arrest and confinement at Hampton Court Palace generated much discussion, but he escaped, only to be later recaptured and then kept in different locations until he was finally brought to trial in January 1649. Parliament itself was purged of almost three-quarters of its number, leaving just radicals from whom a commission was selected to try the King for treason. Charles' reply to the charges amounted to simply asserting that a King could not be tried by any jurisdiction as he enjoyed the Divine Right to rule and there was no one superior to him. Despite this, he was found guilty of treason and executed; the Commons now had supreme power. The House of Lords was abolished, and rule by a forty-strong Council of State with Cromwell as its lynchpin was instituted.

Cromwell then took part of his army to Ireland where there had been a Protestant massacre, and carried out reprisals in which thousands of Catholic Irish were massacred, had their lands confiscated, or were sent into slavery in America (during Cromwell's campaigns in Ireland between 1649 and 1653 some 200,000 Irish inhabitants are estimated to have died). At the same time the Scots had made overtures to Charles' son, now aged 18, who set out to invade England and install himself on the throne. Cromwell defeated Charles and his Scotch army at Worcester, and Charles escaped to France.

By 1653 Cromwell got tired of endless Parliamentary debate, he arbitrarily dissolved Parliament, and subsequently agreed to be named as 'Lord Protector'. He became in effect an autocratic King of Britain by another name. The army was kept on to enforce the rules of Puritanism, and it was probably this that contributed eventually to a movement for restoring the monarchy. Indeed, the crown was offered to Cromwell, who actually refused the title of King, though he did agree to be addressed as "Your Highness The Lord Protector". In 1655 Cromwell divided England into several military districts and introduced additional puritan measures, including execution as a punishment for adultery, and the closure of taverns, brothels and theatres. Such intolerant measures only helped fuel a backlash against puritanism, but the situation was short-lived as Cromwell died in September 1658.

Before he died, Cromwell had named his son Richard as his successor, but Richard was an ineffective person, and it was only eight months before what was left of Parliament voted to end the Protectorate. This left the country devoid of authority, and General George Monck (1608–1670), Cromwell's military commander in Scotland, eventually stepped into the breach as notional ruler, a man who was highly sensitive to the feelings in Parliament and in the wider country, concluding that to avoid anarchy only one person would fit the bill as head of state, namely the exiled Charles II. In 1660 the Declaration of Breda (the Dutch city where Charles lived in exile) was signed by Charles II in response to overtures from General Monck and was later ratified by Parliament; Charles agreed to pay off the army, accept the supremacy of Parliament, promote religious toleration, and offer a general pardon to all who had participated in the Civil War, which meant that all combatants on both sides could retain their property and expect religious tolerance.

For his services, Monck was given a peerage and a large pension. A warship was sent to Holland to bring Charles to London where he was enthusiastically welcomed and arrangements were made for his coronation; subsequently all legal documents and laws were backdated to 1649 as if he had succeeded his father at that time, and as if the Puritan years had barely existed; Cromwell's period in power had however ensured that in the future no British ruler or monarch would be able to ignore parliament.

Possible further reading:
Puritanism by Francis Bremer (Oxford University Press)
Civil War by Peter Ackroyd (Pan)
Stuart Britain by John Morrill (Oxford University Press)

Chapter 43
Scotland, the Early Years

There is no record of Scotland before the Roman invasion since, as with England and Ireland, writing was not known at that time, and although some cave drawings and hieroglyphs persist, there is no decipherable information. The last ice-age lasted from around 25,000 BC to 12,000 BC, during which time the whole of Scotland and most of England was covered with an extremely thick ice sheet. Finds of tools and burials indicate that early man lived in the British Isles during the last inter-glacial period, but these people must have migrated south with the onset of the last ice-age. So much water from Earth's oceans was tied up in the polar ice-caps during the ice-age that sea levels dropped somewhere between 300 and 400 feet (100m) around the globe.

The British Isles were joined to the rest of the Northern European continent by an extensive land bridge and was uninhabitable until the ice gradually started thawing starting around 9,000 BC. The land bridge between Britain and Ireland then disappeared, and this in turn was followed by flooding of the land bridge between continental Europe and Britain, which had become a shallow North Sea by about 6,500 BC. From then on there is evidence of settlement throughout the British Isles, with gradually increasing sophistication.

Sometime just before 2,000 BC, a huge storm shifted thousands of tons of sand to overwhelm a small coastal village on one of the Orkney Islands. The village remained buried and perfectly preserved, until four millennia later, in 1850, the sands shifted again to reveal the village of Skara Brae, with its houses constructed of drystone walls, internal cupboard-like structures and cooking hearths; the thatched roofs had rotted away. Somewhat later in this ancient time in Scotland, hill forts, or brochs, were also constructed: these would have been used both for protection of herds of domesticated animals against marauding bears and wolves, but also possibly as defence against other tribes.

Evidence from archaeological finds indicate that the Bronze Age came to Scotland around 2,000 BC, and the Iron Age around 700 BC. The buildings, and the monuments of standing stones and graves, indicate a Megalithic culture which extended from the Orkney and Shetland Islands south along the west coast of Britain and Ireland, including Cornwall, and along the west coast of France, especially Brittany down to the western Iberian coast. Farming appears to have been well developed in this Megalithic culture from before 3,000 BC. The hill forts and defended farmsteads appear rather later from around 700 BC, when the

Celtic language and culture was spreading into southern Scotland, and settlements were coalescing to an early system of kingdoms.

Following Caesar's Roman expeditions to the British Isles in 55 and 54 BC, written records become available. Caesar himself wrote extensively about his campaigns and battles. In his first expedition in 54 BC when the Romans came to Britain under Caesar they were not ready to penetrate very far into the country, but a century later in 43 AD under the Emperor Claudius, they returned and effectively conquered Britain as far north as the line between the Solway Firth and the estuary of the River Tyne, although this process took several years. Later in 122 AD a defensive wall stretching for 117km was built along this line over a six year period, which we know as Hadrian's wall after the emperor of the time.

Later still, and to the north of this, a further line of defence was constructed between the Firth of Clyde and the Firth of Forth, stretching for about 63km, and named again after the contemporary emperor, the Antonine Wall was started in 142 AD and took twelve years to build. However, the Romans were unable to hold the extensive area of rather wild country to the south between the walls, and within 20 years they had retreated south to its predecessor, Hadrian's Wall, The Romans named the country north of Hadrian's Wall, Caledonia, after the tribe who lived in southern Scotland, and whom they called Picti, because they painted or tattooed themselves.

The Picts were a late Iron Age race who lived in the north and east of Scotland and left their mark on the landscape with the round tower-like brochs that they constructed for defence. They were either descendants, or possibly the same tribe as the Caledonii mentioned by Roman writers, because they frequently raided south across the Antonine Wall and Hadrian's Wall. The early Picts and Caledonii had similar societies and culture, and this in turn was also similar to that of southern Britain in early times; their life was agricultural with additional fishing and hunting as urban society did not appear in Scotland until around 1200. The Picts later merged, at the end of the 9th century, with the Gaelic tribes of Dal Riata on the west coast to form Alba or Scotland, where they lived in a loose confederation, together with a small area of Northern Ireland corresponding roughly to County Antrim.

The origins of Dal Riata are lost in the mists of time, and it is unclear whether the initial migration came from Gaelic Northern Ireland northwards, or was the reverse. It is equally possible that a whole loose confederation of western tribes along the coast grew up with co-existing trade and other links simultaneously. Much of the travel in those early days was made by boat, as overland journeys were long and arduous. The boats of the Picts and Dal Riata were known as currachs (in Wales coracles), which were basically small craft of less than twenty feet in length, made with a hide covering stretched over a wooden frame, and which were much more primitive than later wooden Viking boats. The minimum 21km sea voyage from Scotland to Ireland, and between the Hebridean Islands in particular, would have been a considerable undertaking and probably restricted to the summer months in such craft.

Dal Riata reached its zenith at the end of the 6th century after which it was conquered in battles with Northumbria. Much of our information about those times comes from the Venerable Bede (672–735), an English monk who lived in Northumbria near the eastern end of Hadrian's wall, and who also tells us about St Columba (521–597), an Irish abbot who spread Christianity to Dal Riata, starting with the foundation of an abbey on the island of Iona, after he had been granted the island by a Gaelic king.

Dal Riata remained subservient to Northumbria from the 7th century, and in turn was a client kingdom of the Picti to the north. Internecine warfare between the various tribes of Dal Riata on the west coast continued for the next 200 years until the Vikings appeared early in the 9th century, raiding Iona the year after their first raid on Lindisfarne on the east coast in 793. By the end of the 9th century the Vikings controlled most of the west coast of Scotland, including the Inner Hebridean Islands.

Around the year 900, there was a coming together of the northern tribes, including the remnants of the Picts, Dal Riata, the Britons of Alt Clut (present day Strathclyde), and the Anglian kingdom of Bernicia, which approximates to present day Northumberland and Berwickshire. This new conglomeration became the Kingdom of Alba, first ruled by Kenneth MacAlpin (810–858), effectively the first king of Scotland though the first person to hold the title of King of Alba was Donald II who died in 900. He was succeeded by Constantine II, who had a long reign of nearly fifty years dying in 952 after consolidating the kingdom, and is often seen as Scotland's first real monarch. Battles with the kingdoms south of the border continued with the defeat of Northumbria in 1018. A little later this Gaelic kingdom was ruled over by Macbeth from 1040–1057, whose exploits have been immortalised by Shakespeare, though not always accurate historically.

The descendants of Kenneth MacAlpin, the first King of the united Scotland, which he ruled after conquering the Vikings in battle in 843, continued to rule until the last MacAlpin King, Malcolm II, died early in the 11th century. The succession passed via Malcolm II's daughter to his grandson Duncan I (1001–1040), who also appears in Shakespeare's play as the predecessor of Macbeth. Macbeth became king after Duncan was killed in battle in 1040. Macbeth's reign was largely peaceful, but he died in battle with Malcolm III after an invasion from England, including the Earl of Northumbria (Shakespeare's McDuff). Malcolm III (1031–1093) invaded England five times, and was finally killed in battle at Alnwick in Northumbria in 1093.

Malcolm was succeeded by his youngest son David I (1084–1153), a powerful man who had inherited several English titles and had a Norman upbringing. David's background allowed him to introduce many new ideas to Scotland; the three main ones being firstly the introduction of feudalism, secondly the use of coinage, and thirdly he patronised and founded many monasteries, including those established at Holyrood and Melrose. He also created the first Scottish burghs after the model of Alfred and Athelstan, fifteen in all, which helped in efficient tax raising.

After the death of David I, the succession eventually passed to Alexander II in 1214, who was the first king to control virtually all of Scotland, though he failed to secure the allegiance of the Lords of the Hebrides and Argyll, who still swore allegiance to Norway. David (1084–1153) and Alexander (1198–1249) are credited with modernising the Scotland of the times and bringing in the Norman influence that was already well established south of the border. Alexander's political and armed help to Henry III of England, together with his marriage to Henry's sister Joan, placed him in a strong political position and he attempted unsuccessfully to re-conquer Northumbria. Peace was finally declared and formalised in the Treaty of York in 1237, officially defining the border that still exists between England and Scotland.

A succession problem recurred in 1286, when Duncan's descendent, and Alexander II's son Alexander III, died leaving only an infant granddaughter, Margaret Maid of Norway. Margaret became notional Queen of Scots for four years, until she died on a sea crossing from Norway to Scotland with a view to her engagement and marriage to the future Edward II of England, who was six years old at the time. Edward I, on the English throne at the time, launched a series of forays into Scotland, at the invitation of bishops concerned at the prospect of civil war between the two main claimants for the Scottish throne, John Balliol and Robert the Bruce. As the price for his endorsement of Balliol, Edward insisted on homage from, and superiority to, Balliol (1249–1314), who was not willing to accede to this.

Thus Edward was provided with an excuse to invade Scotland where he was eventually defeated by William Wallace (1270–1305) commanding the Scots army at the Battle of Stirling Bridge in 1297. The Scottish Wars of Independence were to continue for over fifty years more and only ended in 1357. Edward I continued the fight against the outnumbered and technically inferior Scottish army. William Wallace was captured and executed, but the wars continued with Robert the Bruce (1274–1329 grandson of the first Robert Bruce and a direct descendent of David I) fighting after a period of hiding in exile. After the death of Edward I, Bruce fought against his son Edward II, and at the battle of Bannockburn in 1314, the Scots scored a resounding victory, finally taking Berwick in 1318.

Following this in 1320, the Declaration of Arbroath was addressed to the Pope by Scottish nobles asserting Scotland's status as an independent country and its right to use military force if or when attacked. The Declaration was intended to overturn Edward I's claim to overlordship of Scotland in 1305 and secure the rescinding of Robert the Bruce's excommunication in 1306. The Pope exhorted the English to respect the demands in the document, but matters dragged on for years. In 1328 Edward III signed a peace treaty renouncing English claims to Scotland, but this only lasted for about five years.

Scotland remained intact as a nation recognised by the signing of the Treaty of Berwick in 1357, under which the captured Scottish King, David II, son of Robert the Bruce, was released by the English in exchange for a large ransom. The Treaty also agreed that Edward III would be named as David's successor, though when the time came this aspect was ignored. David II died without an heir, and his nephew, Robert II (1316–1390), ascended to the throne in 1371 starting the House of Stuart. The Stuarts were to rule Scotland for the next three centuries, and nine kings ruled without too many familial squabbles, although James I (1394–1437) who fought with Henry V in France, was captured in France and his relatives had to govern the country until he was ransomed from France.

He proved to be a spendthrift king who failed to pay his ransom of £40,000 and ran up debts spending lavishly on his Court, but he did assist in the founding of Scotland's first university at St Andrews in 1410 by Augustinian clergy under Papal blessing. This was followed by the founding of Glasgow University in James II reign in 1451. James III regained Orkney and Shetland from Denmark as part of his wife's dowry when he married. In the next generation James IV was Scotland's first Renaissance king and very cultured; he founded Aberdeen University and the Royal College of Surgeons in Edinburgh. His marriage to the daughter of Henry VII in England importantly allowed eventual union of the thrones of Scotland and England under his grandson James VI.

The Scottish Reformation came later than that in England when Mary I, daughter of James V, was on the throne: there were executions and many Protestants were burnt at the stake, but John Knox (1513–1572) escaped to preach Protestantism, and against Mary I. Knox was a product of St Andrew's University and one of the leaders of the Protestant Reformation who is generally seen as the founder of the Presbyterian Church in Scotland. While in exile on the continent he met John Calvin (1509–1564), and out of this experience drafted a new order of service for the new Presbyterian Church in Scotland. He was a powerful preacher on many subjects, including calling for the execution of Catholic Mary, Queen of Scots, who was eventually beheaded at the order of Queen Elizabeth in 1587.

The Protestant movement in Scotland was known as the 'Lords of Congregation', and was responsible for attacking Catholic Churches, sometimes with the aid of French troops. Eventually the Scots renounced allegiance to the Pope, and the Scottish parliament formally adopted Protestantism giving rise to the Church of Scotland (familiarly known as 'the Kirk'). James VI was born in 1566 and became King of Scotland when his Catholic mother, Mary, was forced to abdicate so that he could ascend the throne at the age of 15. In 1603 at the age of 37 he would succeed Elizabeth as James I of England, and in due course this would lead to the formal Act of Union between England and Scotland 1707.

Possible further reading:
Scotland by Rab Houston (Oxford University Press)

Chapter 44
Wales

The early history of Wales is not different from that of the rest of the British Isles, with people arriving around 30,000 BC before the last Ice Age, which eventually covered all of Wales, together with most of England. Human habitation reappears around ten thousand years ago after the ice sheet had receded north, allowing vegetation to appear. At that time the land bridge between Europe and the British Isles was still present, and the country was slowly populated with Celts migrating from their heartland in north eastern Europe, probably not as a great wave but rather as a steady trickle through the years.

There was a short Copper Age and then the Bronze Age commences in Wales about 2,500 BC. An extensive copper mine from that period has been found on the North Wales coast on the Great Orme, which has been preserved by virtue of its use as a Roman rubbish tip; this was recently cleared away, to reveal the Bronze Age copper mine beneath. Chamber burial tombs and other megalithic remains are present from the beginning of this period, and hill forts around Wales date from a thousand years later.

Much of what is preserved exists around the periphery of the country and in Anglesey, rather than in the mountainous central area where agriculture, and therefore settlement, has always been marginal. The Iron Age came to Wales about 700 BC, but writing and written history only appears once the Romans have come, though prior to this markings on stones and graves testify to cultural connections all along the west coast of the British Isles, France and Iberia.

Following the Roman invasion of Britain in AD 43, the Roman legions moved into Wales about five years later, and the Roman army then maintained control of the country along with the rest of Britain. The first three decades of Roman occupation were difficult due to the resistance put up by the native Celts who lived as five main tribal groupings in the south, north and east, with the centre of Druidic activity occurring on Anglesey. The tribes were not united in their resistance to the invaders, but much of the resistance is attributed to the charisma of Caractacus, Chief of the Silures, in south-eastern Wales, and the inspiration for Shakespeare's Cymbeline. In 61 AD the Romans sent a legion to Anglesey to stamp out the Druids and the resistance they were causing, which they did successfully, but while the legion was absent from the south, rebellion flared in East Anglia when the remaining Roman administration refused to recognise Boudicca (or Boadicea) as the legitimate heir to the Kingdom of the Icenii when her husband, Prasutagus, died.

The tribes under Boudicca rebelled, sacking the Roman bases of Colchester and London and causing tens of thousands of deaths among the Roman legion not on campaign in Wales, and also among the civilian population. They then moved on to St Albans which was also sacked and destroyed. The IX Legion returned urgently from Anglesey and after a short period of regrouping met Boudicca and the tribes at an unidentified battle site in the Midlands, where the tribes were severely defeated, and Boudicca was either killed or committed suicide.

The Romans prized the conquest of Wales for the availability of metals, including gold, copper and lead, all of which were mined. Fortresses and legionary strongholds were built in the northeast of Wales at Chester and the southeast at Caerleon. Towards the end of the Roman occupation the legions in Britain were commanded by Magnus Maximus who later briefly became the Western Roman Emperor in 383. When the legions were withdrawn from Wales and northern Britain in 383 to reinforce the troops on the frontiers of Gaul and Germania, Maximus is credited with leaving behind British descendants, who may have founded kingly dynasties in Wales, though definite confirmation of this is lacking. Maximus was proclaimed Emperor by his troops, ruling over Britain, Gaul, Spain and Africa, but in attempting to retake Eastern Roman territory in modern day Croatia he was eventually defeated by Theodosius and then executed in 388.

The early Welsh language is known as Brythonic and absorbed a fair amount of Latin during the 350 year occupation, along with a certain amount of Roman customs and culture. In the following 300 years transition to the early Welsh language occurred, while the Roman towns were largely deserted in favour of small hill forts and earth-mound castles. During this time after the final departure of the Romans in the early 5th century Wales became divided into several small localised kingdoms, where some of the Kings were sufficiently powerful to be named by the title of Rex Britannorum: this title implied power and tribute from the Breton Celtic communities along the west coast of Scotland, Wales, Cornwall and even Brittany.

None of these leaders possessed enough power to unite Wales fully, so internal struggles and fighting extended through the Dark Ages in much the same way as internal struggles in England and Ireland with Picts coming from the north, Saxons and Jutes from the east, and even raiders and settlers from Ireland. One of the English rulers of the time was Offa, King of Mercia, who ruled for the unusually long period of 39 years from 757–796, and built an enormous north-south dyke which bears his name to try and keep out raiders from east Wales.

The Dark Ages are now sometimes referred to as the Early Christian Age or the Heroic Age, it has also been called the Age of Saints, and indeed across the British Isles many monasteries were founded which emphasises this point. St David was a charismatic preacher and the founder of churches and monasteries and became the patron saint of Wales dying about 590. He established a monastery, probably on the site of the present cathedral in Pembrokeshire; he is the only national saint of the British Isles to have been born in the country of which he is patron. Several centuries later the Normans would change the Celtic church in Wales by appointing bishops to the major centres of Llandaff, St David's, Bangor and St Asaph, and at the same time forbidding the clergy to marry.

Traditionally in Wales, the rules of inheritance saw possessions and land divided equally between all the male heirs, thus steadily diluting and diminishing the size of already small kingdoms. Viking raiding around the coast from the north in the 9th century onwards did not help matters, because this meant that Wales was caught in a pincer situation, with the Normans pushing west from England following the Conquest. Halley's Comet was seen across England and Wales in 1066, the year of the Norman invasion and is recorded in the Bayeux Tapestry; it was generally interpreted as a malign omen. To aid control of Wales, though not to occupy the country, William the Conqueror created earldoms along the border at Chester, Shrewsbury and Hereford, with the hope of providing a belt of protection to thank some of his grateful nobles with their retainers and war bands.

This warring situation persisted with raiding between the kingdoms, and across into England until the reign of Henry III, when Llewellyn ap Gruffudd and his brother Owain, signed a treaty with Henry in 1247 at Woodstock Palace. The treaty did not last, and the English and Welsh were at war again a decade later. A little later, in the Treaty of Montgomery in 1267, Llewellyn was acknowledged as Prince of Wales by Henry III. After further fighting in 1277, Edward I, who had been on the English throne since 1272, brought a large army to subdue North Wales.

After a short period of peace, Welsh revolt spread in consequence of English oppression and the large amounts of tribute demanded. Llewellyn was killed in battle at the end of the year, thus ending the line of native Princes of Wales, and in this way Wales came directly under English administration, though formal annexation was delayed until the second part of Henry VIII's reign. Edward passed the Statute of Rhuddlan in 1284 which restricted Welsh lawsuits at a time when he had already surrounded Wales with a ring of large and powerful castles.

Plague came to Europe in 1347, and to Wales two years later when about a third of the population is thought to have perished. Richard I of England was captured and murdered by Henry Bolingbroke who seized the throne on becoming Henry IV and imposed draconian taxation on the Welsh. As a consequence a number of rebellions against English rule happened, of which Owain Glyndwr's revolt in 1400 and subsequent years is best known. Glyndwr (1359–1415) defeated several English forces, and for a few years controlled most of Wales. The first ever Welsh Parliament met under his control at Machynlleth in 1404. Henry IV achieved pacification of Wales and the rebellion finally died out around 1414, though Glyndwr himself vanished and was never captured; his ultimate fate is not known, but he appears in Shakespeare's Henry IV part I.

The rebellion had a long-term effect on Wales because of the great damage to property and crops, together with significant loss of life, leaving few men to farm and provide food for the population. Any coexistence with England had been shattered. As a result of his rebellion the English parliament passed the Penal Laws against Wales, which forbade Welshmen from carrying arms, holding official offices, or even living in towns. It took two or three generations for Welsh life to return to a semblance of normality.

In the middle years of the 15th century, Welsh soldiers were recruited for the English army, with the prominence and importance of Welsh archers in Henry V's victory at the Battle of Agincourt forming a significant part of the plot in Shakespeare's play. Eventually when Henry Tudor (Henry VII) with Welsh ancestry and brought up in Pembroke Castle, defeated Richard III at the Battle of Bosworth, his army contained many Welsh soldiers. After Henry VII died, his son Henry VIII, passed a 'Laws in Wales' Act (1535–1542) which absorbed Wales into England, abolishing both the Welsh legal system and the Welsh language from any official role: it did however allow members from Wales to represent Welsh constituencies in the English Parliament. The lack of a royal court in Wales with its attendant nobles and officialdom, together with very little urban life or commerce kept Wales from fully enjoying the benefit of the reforms and also slowed future development.

Still in Henry VIII's reign, Wales followed England into the new Anglican Church. William Morgan, Bishop of Llandaff and St Asaph (1545–1604) produced the first translation of the Bible into Welsh, which in turn aided the gradual spread of literacy. The legal distinctions between England and Wales were also abolished by the end of Henry VIII's reign. English became the official language of politics, commerce and the law, with Catholicism being repressed during the reign of Elizabeth such that when the Civil War came Welsh gentry and ordinary people were strongly supportive of the crown. Because of this Wales sided with the Royalist, rather than the Parliamentarian side, in the Civil War; this was despite Oliver Cromwell's Welsh inclinations and his conviction that Wales needed a new start with puritanism.

At this time, most of the population still spoke Welsh, while the only schooling available was in English. A minister of the Church of England, Griffith Jones (1684–1761) started teaching in Welsh. The teaching was largely Biblical, but was responsible for creating a fairly literate population with a good knowledge of the Christian scriptures: for this reason he is often thought to have been the precursor of Methodist ideas and teaching in Wales, which would become a major force after his death.

In 1707, Wales officially became part of Great Britain, and then in 1801 part of the United Kingdom.

Possible further reading:
The Story of Wales by Jon Gower (Penguin)

Chapter 45
The Early Years of Ireland

The first traces of human activity appear in Ireland around 8,000 BC. These early settlers were European Celts who may have come by sea across small distances between Europe, Britain and Ireland, or alternatively they may have migrated earlier when a land bridge still existed between Britain and Ireland. The land bridge to Ireland closed somewhere around 8,000 BC, and the land bridge between Britain and Europe closed somewhat later around 6,500 BC, but leaving a large island in the middle of the North Sea referred to as Doggerland, now the shallow Dogger Bank.

The early forests that had grown up following the gradually receding ice cap northwards were slowly cleared by these early Celts, both for use as firewood and as building wood. Most importantly they were cleared for agriculture, and the earliest field systems known in Europe are still visible at Ceide Fields in County Mayo in north-west Ireland. These fields with their ancient stone walls, scattered tombs and dwellings, indicate a reasonable level of sophistication of the society living there. Grazing by cattle and sheep, together with the cropping of cereals, bear witness to the evolution of dependable techniques for providing Stone Age man with his necessary food.

These early farmers were Celts from the same stock that have left their traces throughout western Europe: their descendants were destined to preserve what we now call Celtic culture, language and customs on the western fringes of Europe. Particularly during the Dark Ages in the middle of the first millennium AD, Christian Celtic settlements would be instrumental in keeping language and culture alive during otherwise dark and troublesome times. Irish trade with Wales, Cornwall, Normandy and even further south, would provide enrichment of the Celtic genes, and towards the end of the first millennium AD, Viking raiding and looting would also contribute to the Celtic gene pool.

Ireland first appears on maps of the classical world around the 4th century BC when Mediterranean peoples, from the Phoenicians onwards, came to Ireland and Cornwall, in search of tin and other metals. Tin was necessary for making bronze, but gold and silver (found in grave goods) was equally prized for making jewellery and items of high status, Trade continued during the Roman era as evidenced by findings of Roman coins and other artefacts at Irish sites.

From contemporary Roman accounts, we know that butter, cattle and Irish wolfhounds were traded for wine, gold and manufactured goods, together with slaves. The Romans never really bothered with Ireland, which they knew as

Hibernia, Land of Winter. Although trade with Ireland was valued in Roman times, the country was not perceived either to be a threat from its inhabitants, nor was the land and its produce sufficiently valuable to consider annexing Ireland into the spreading Roman Empire.

The Ireland of those times comprised a lot of small kingdoms, each with its own small aristocracy living well off a large population of serfs who did not own land. Warfare and raiding between the small kingdoms was common. In the early days there was a loose division of Ireland into a 'pentarchy' of five provinces; Ulster, Munster, Leinster, Connacht and Meath, each of which was governed by its own small nobility enforcing provincial laws which governed most aspects of contemporary life. An Irish script, known as Ogham, has survived from the early first millennium AD in the form of monumental inscriptions recording names.

Christianity came to Ireland in the 5th century AD and is traditionally ascribed to St Patrick. In fact a bishop named Palladius (later sanctified) was sent to Ireland by the Pope, probably in 431 AD, a few years before St Patrick, but St Patrick himself is the man remembered in many legends. He left writings which help us understand his life. Patrick grew up in Britain and was captured and taken to Ireland as a teenage slave. He spent the next six years as a shepherd, but eventually escaped and managed to return to Britain. After some years he decided to return to Ireland as a Christian missionary, and is sometimes described as the first Bishop of Armagh, which was the religious centre of Ireland at that time.

Christianity spread rapidly through Ireland and was well established by the time Patrick died at the end of the 5th century. Following Patrick's lead, and thanks to the many small monasteries that were established, Ireland's oral tradition in the Dark Ages after 400 AD gave way to written records. Bibles and other books were copied out in writing by the monks, and an Irish literary tradition was born before it appeared in Britain. The books that were produced were all on vellum and were wonderfully illuminated: the best known and preserved are the Book of Durrow, and the Book of Kells, created in the Abbey of Kells in County Meath, Central Ireland.

The Church was keen to integrate and influence Irish politics, and the first kingly coronation came about in Armagh in 574 when Aeden MacGabrain was crowned King of Dal Riata, that kingdom which spanned Ulster (including Armagh) in Northern Ireland, and the south-western corner of Scotland, north to the holy island of Iona. On Iona the monastery had been founded by the man who crowned MacGabrain, namely St Columba; MacGabrain ruled for a long time, up to 609. Monks emigrated eastward and south from Iona to spread the Christian word across Britain and Europe, and St Columba himself travelled even further, dying in Italy after founding monasteries, and teaching that private confession and penance were more appropriate than public shame and punishment. Not surprisingly, this teaching became more acceptable throughout Christian Europe than the previous customs, and it spread rapidly to become the basic Catholic approach to sin. Eventually fifty or sixty monasteries were founded across Europe in the name of St Columba, with the intent of following his teaching.

In the year 793 came the first major Viking raid on Britain with an attack at Lindisfarne (Holy Isle) on the northeast coast of England, where the monastery was plundered and burnt. This was the beginning of the Viking expansion out of Scandinavia, both westward around Britain and Ireland, and eastward into Russia and down to the Black Sea. Overpopulation combined with overuse of agricultural land and forests, seem largely to blame for the outward explosion of the Norsemen. Iona was attacked and many monks killed in 802 and again in 806.

Through the 9th century, the Vikings disrupted the sea-based communication and trade lines between the Scottish and Irish components of Dal Riata, with each half of the kingdom becoming isolated and independent. The Scottish part would join with the Picts in later years and form the early precursor of the Kingdom of Scotland. Viking settlements began to appear around Ireland, notably on the east coast where the city of Dublin has its origins in a Viking settlement established at this time, and where harbours are more sheltered.

By the end of the 10th century the O'Neill Clan reigned supreme across the north of Ireland, and produced kings who were crowned at the sacred Hill of Tara, inside an ancient iron age hillfort in County Meath. In the meantime east and south Ireland were under Viking control. In 976 the Dalcassian King of Munster, Mathgamain was assassinated, which provoked an assault on Viking Limerick by Mathgamain's brother Brian Boruma, who killed the Danish leaders in the church where they had retreated for sanctuary. From these beginnings Brian Boruma (941–1014) gradually pushed back the boundaries of his kingdom, eventually taking Dublin and coming to rule as High King of Ireland in 1002. Having effectively subdued the southern half of Ireland, Brian Boruma took an army northwards, conquering most of the north apart from Ulster, and paying tribute to the monastery and cathedral in Armagh, the ancient royal capital of Ulster and recognised as the foremost religious site in Ireland. By 1014, Brian was back in Dublin, when a large Viking force appeared and the Battle of Clondar resulted. Although the battle went largely against the Vikings, Brian was killed at the age of 70; his body was taken for burial at Armagh.

These events had all crystallised the influence of the Church, with Armagh sitting at the religious centre of a web of monasteries and abbeys. St Malachy (1094–1148) was appointed Archbishop of Armagh in 1132 by the Pope, and was able regularise church functions, services and discipline, including the Vatican Code of Morality and clerical celibacy, across the island. He was later sanctified, becoming the first native Irishman to be so honoured. Rich monasteries saw their lands and possessions come under the direction of the central Church and its bishops, and there was an increase in the influence of European monastic orders, including the Augustinians and the Cistercians. This local downgrading of the monasteries severely restricted the education and cultural activity that the monks in Ireland had previously contributed to the community.

On the other side of the Irish Sea, England finished coalescing from several smaller kingdoms into a single realm, with the accession of William the Conqueror in 1066. The same process was continuing in mainland Europe, where a patchwork of smaller princedoms and kingdoms were also being succeeded by larger more centralised realms. This was all happening at a time when the Christian church was managing to impose more conformity across Europe, and the monastic orders were helping this process, spreading ideas across the continent.

In Ireland, the struggle between small kingdoms continued, but Rory O'Connor (1116–1198) was inaugurated High King in Dublin following the example of Brian Boruma almost two centuries earlier. He had a great rival in Dermott MacMurrough (1110–1172), who had achieved some advantage by providing backing for Matilda (grand-daughter of William the Conqueror) in her struggle against her cousin Steven for the English throne. In due course, Matilda's son was crowned Henry II (1133–1189) in 1154 after some years in which MacMurrough had backed Henry. In 1166 MacMurrough was attacked by his enemies, including the Norsemen of Dublin, and eventually he fled to England, causing some Irish rejoicing at the cessation of his tyrannical and somewhat barbarous regime. In exchange for fealty to Henry II, MacMurrough was promised land in Ireland. He left with Henry's support in the form of a letter authorising him to attempt to reconquer Irish lands, this was sufficient for him to raise a supporting army with which he was able to regain his Irish position.

Henry, meantime, had started on the process of acquisition of Ireland, and managed to obtain Papal support for this, which the Vatican doubtless felt would strengthen the role of the Church, despite the fact that reforms were already being disseminated from Armagh. MacMurrough sailed from Milford Haven with the Earl of Pembroke (known as 'Strongbow') in 1167, along with a small band of Norman Welsh soldiers. Wexford was seized and fortified as their base, and thanks to their archers with longbows, the small force was able to defeat a considerably larger force of Norse and Irish.

Later that year, they besieged and sacked Waterford; the army then marched north on Dublin, coming on the city through the Wicklow Mountains rather than along the expected coastal route, whereupon the Irish and Norse forces in Dublin evaporated in front of the threat. A Norse attempt to regain the city the following year was unsuccessful, and Strongbow was able to consolidate his gains along the east coast.

As both Henry and Strongbow were descended from William the Conqueror, Henry was particularly anxious to establish his superiority. He therefore mustered a large army which sailed from Milford Haven in south Wales in the autumn of 1171, and landed at Waterford without the need for force. Dublin and other habitations offered no resistance, and a Church Synod was convened at Cashel in central Ireland in 1172, where Henry agreed Roman Church rules about all aspects of daily life, though at the end of the Synod the Irish Church came away pledging allegiance to Rome rather than to Henry.

During his subsequent stay in Dublin, Henry issued an edict making the city subservient in trade terms to Bristol, thus effectively diminishing trade links with Scandinavia and northern Europe, in favour of a more colonial relationship with southern England. The new situation was resented by a large element of Gaelic western Ireland, and low level warfare broke out almost as soon as Henry had left the country.

Henry continued to have problems with subduing his French possessions and divided his land to be ruled as four different units, of which his youngest son John, was to be King of Ireland. John finally arrived in Ireland in 1185, and treated his Irish allies and vassals in a very high handed fashion; low level rebellion was the result. After John returned to England, Henry obtained Papal permission for the establishment of Ireland as a separate Kingdom. This plan never came to pass as Henry's other sons died, and instead of becoming King of Ireland, John succeeded to the English throne in 1199, where he managed to forge a reputation as an incompetent and capricious ruler.

He did, however, achieve the construction of Dublin Council, and Ireland's first national coinage, together with implementation of English Common Law. He returned to Ireland in 1210 to suppress a rebellion by Hugh De Lacy 1176–1242), Earl of Ulster, whom he had previously appointed Viceroy over Ireland. The rebellion was quickly crushed, but once back in England John was confronted at Runnymede and compelled to signed Magna Carta by his barons in 1215, only to die the following year.

The next century saw festering resentment of the Gaelic Irish against their Anglo-Norman overlords, culminating in 1318 with King Donal O'Neill from Ulster, writing to the Pope in a document known as the 'Remonstrance of the Princes'. In this letter he argued that the Pope had awarded Ireland to the English on the understanding that the country would be governed justly and well, but that in the event government had been overbearing and unsympathetic. O'Neill wanted to bequeath his Kingdom to Edward Bruce, brother of King Robert the Bruce of Scotland. The result was invasion of Ireland by Edward with a Scottish army which started in eastern Ulster, where he conducted a particularly barbarous campaign of pacification, involving a scorched earth policy across the countryside.

Unfortunately this coincided with a downturn in European weather and consequent famine, with both the native Irish and the invading army finding survival difficult. Edward Bruce was killed in battle in 1318, and Ulster languished in the following years, only to have the Black Death arrive in 1348 to add to the woes of the population.

Through the rest of the 14th century, there remained a divide between the native Gaelic speaking Irish and the English settlers, who were often aristocratic and living off the land. English laws were introduced to try and minimise any integration, with penalties for English colonists using the Gaelic language. At the same time the sentence for killing an Englishman remained death, while the punishment for killing an Irishman was simply a fine. These types of measure were promulgated in the Statute of Labourers in England in 1351, but also applied to Ireland in the Statues of Kilkenny in 1367. The situation continued through to the end of the 15th century when the Irish Parliament met at Drogheda for some months, during which time it enacted about thirty Acts known as Poynings Law after Sir Edward Poynings (1459–1521), the King's new representative in Ireland.

Included amongst these Acts was the provision that the Irish Parliament was no longer allowed to legislate independently, and all Laws would need to be approved by the English monarch. The Laws were clearly intended to bring all the inhabitants of Ireland fully under the sway of English Law, because prior to this two imposters, Lambert Simnel and Perkin Warbeck, both pretenders to the English throne falsely claiming royal descent, had sought Irish support, thereby adding to the conflict between English and Irish communities. Simnel (1477–1525) had been used by the House of York since the age of 10 as a figurehead for rebellion against Henry VII and surprisingly was not executed but lived out his life as a menial servant in the royal household. By contrast Warbeck claimed to be the Duke of York and one of the missing princes from the Tower; he led an army against Henry and after being captured was executed.

Once Henry VIII came to the English throne, matters progressed slowly towards the rupture with Rome. By this time, the aristocratic English families in Ireland had a tradition of some three hundred years of Catholicism which they were unwilling to discard. Henry's policies continued with a formal declaration in the Irish Parliament that Henry was King of Ireland, a title which no previous English monarch had held. This was followed by the appropriation of Irish monasteries, and the inhabitants of Ireland divided into a small number of English supporting settlers in Dublin and the larger centres against the great majority of the rest of Ireland, including the clergy, who were appalled to think of the possible loss of Catholicism.

Henry instituted a policy of 'surrender and regrant', meaning that all landed citizens should give up their lands and swear allegiance to the Crown, following which the same lands would be returned to them together with English citizenship and titles after they had declared loyalty to both Crown and the new English church. This policy persisted through the Tudor years of Henry's successors, but with only partial success.

The policy continued under Elizabeth causing an uprising in Munster in 1569, which resulted in ruthless suppression. Ten years later a Papal sponsored army, including Spanish and Italian infantry, landed in the south only for the unrest to be once again ruthlessly suppressed, and a scorched earth policy pursued on behalf of England. Finally, to try and overcome the remaining rebellious population, English settlers were brought in to populate and secure the coastal ports and farm the countryside; this episode in 1585 is known as the 'Plantation of Munster'; several later plantations of English settlers would occur in the next two centuries. Similar measures were taken in Ulster where Scottish forces had been destabilising the situation and providing settlers.

Hugh O'Neill (1540–1616) is revered by the Irish as a freedom fighter. He was both Catholic and ruthless in pursuing his own interests and building up his lands. He was initially backed by Elizabeth as the local strongman, but then rejected Elizabeth's policies and gained Papal backing, being named as 'Captain General of the Catholic Army in Ireland'. Several battles were fought in 1598 with English forces which the Irish won. More rebellions occurred across Ireland following these successes, with the result that Elizabeth sent a larger and better equipped force to Ulster in 1600.

A Spanish army appeared the following year, and eventually O'Neill's Irish forces confronted the English at Kinsail in 1601. The Spanish army had not fully materialised, and an English rout followed, after which a scorched earth policy once again induced famine and destruction. Over the following decades the Gaelic population gradually declined, both in traditions and in influence. In 1607 O'Neill left Ireland with other Gaelic aristocracy but died in Rome some years later, having not been allowed to return to his native country.

Possible further reading:
The Story of Ireland by Neil Hegarty (BBC books)

Chapter 46
Early European Emigration to North America

With the early voyages of discovery, initially to North and South America, but later to the east, European spread and settlement to these previously unknown areas commenced, taking with it the Protestant Puritan philosophy to the North, and Catholic customs and systems of governance to Central and South America. The emigration of people was initially slow, but increased steadily through the years as good news returned from young colonies, and as transport across the world became easier and less dangerous. At the same time wars of religion and persecution continued in Europe, driving many to try and escape.

Spain was the dominant power in Europe at the beginning of the 16th century and the first New World Caribbean settlement was founded by Christopher Columbus in 1496 at Santo Domingo in the Dominican Republic. The city now boasts the first cathedral, castle, monastery and university of European origin in the New World but has had a chequered development, and was captured by Francis Drake for the English in 1586 and held to ransom. Rather later, Oliver Cromwell sent an expedition from Britain in 1655 to take the city, but this was unsuccessful. Over the next two hundred years the city changed hands several times between Spain and France before the country achieved independence in 1844 and started a new career of revolution and invasion by Spain and the USA amongst others.

This history perhaps encapsulates the development of many of the Central and South American countries, which all started with a parent European power in the 16th or 17th century, and then gradually grew to achieve independence, often in the early 19th century. Much of the early settlement was achieved by force in an unequal contest between invading Europeans with guns, and native Americans possessing only rudimentary early metal technology (apart from impressive gold and silver achievements in decorative and jewellery fabrication). In this way, at the beginning of the 16th century, Hernan Cortez (1485–1547) conquered the Aztec Kingdom in Central America, and Francisco Pizarro (1475–1541) conquered the Inca Empire further to the south, both with minimal military strength.

The first European to see the Pacific Ocean was the Spaniard Vasco Nunez de Balboa (1475–1519), who had founded a settlement in Panama in 1510, and crossed the Isthmus of Panama to see the Pacific Ocean on the western side in 1513. His expedition included settlers, and also Hernan Cortez, who later departed west from Cuba in 1518, landing at Vera Cruz and then marching west onto the high central plateau of Mexico, arriving in due course at the Aztec capital of Tenochtitlan (present day Mexico City), where he found an astonishing wealth of gold and jewels.

In addition the expedition also found countryside comparable to their native Spanish land on which they could cultivate European crops. The Spaniards were helped by their iron technology, horses and wheeled carts, not to mention the firearms that they brought with them. They also brought European diseases, and all of these factors helped Cortez overpower the Aztec civilisation. A little later, and in the same manner, Francisco Pizzaro conquered the Incas in Peru at the conclusion of his third expedition, capturing the Emperor Atahualpa in battle in 1532, and then taking over the Inca capital of Cusco.

Despite the payment by the Emperor of a huge ransom in gold to redeem his life, he was executed by Pizarro. Spanish settlement came a decade later, and the new colony was enormously helped by the finding of very rich silver mines at Potosi which supplied the majority of Europe's need over the next three centuries. A guerrilla resistance movement persisted for the next three or four decades, but the last Inca ruler was captured and executed in 1572. In the meantime the Inca method of farming the steep mountain hillsides was destroyed by the Spaniards, and smallpox decimated the population, such that perhaps three-quarters of the population died.

The Spanish priority remained the exploitation of the silver mines at Potosi in Bolivia, to which each Inca family was required by the Spaniards to send a family member to work in the mines. As the labour force diminished from disease the Spanish central government in Madrid allowed the importation of African slaves to work the mines. Potosi, and its exploitation of human labour, later became the focus of the Independence Movement. The Bolivian war of independence started in 1809, with independence finally being declared in 1825.

The other large island in the Caribbean is Jamaica, which was visited by Columbus in 1494. The first settlement occurred in 1509, but in due course the island was gradually populated by Spanish settlers who were eventually evicted by the English, who then ran the country from the mid-17th century as a sugar exporting colony dependent upon slave labour. Jamaica remained under British control, with a series of slave rebellions occurring, before the formal abolition of slavery in 1833. Colonial ties were gradually loosened thereafter, but Jamaica gained full independence within the British Commonwealth only in 1962.

Spain had initially claimed all of North and Central America at a time when its extent was certainly neither known nor understood. The attraction to the Spaniards was the presence of gold and silver mines which was a vital source of wealth when repatriated to Europe. The growth of sugar cane, together with other crops, initially resulted in native slave labour to do the work, but as Europeans brought smallpox and other diseases with them, much of the local population was decimated. Thus the slave trade from West Africa became necessary to provide more labourers and it flourished. It is estimated up to a million West

African slaves were transported to Mexico over the next 250 years (see slavery in chapter 59).

After the discovery of the Americas by Christopher Columbus a big change in world development started to accelerate. Through the 16th century European spread to the Americas developed at a steady rate. Much of the initial impetus was provided by Spanish colonisation and exploitation in Mexico, where the prize was seen to be the gold and silver mines. While the English and the French in North America were spurred on by trade, the Spanish in Mexico and Central America, and the Portuguese further south, were spurred on by the glittering vision of riches. The export of wealth from Mexico, together with the importation of slaves, gradually caused increasing resentment, both amongst the native population, but also among the settlers. Rebellion eventually started in several scattered places in 1811, developing slowly into the Mexican War of Independence (1810–1821, chapter 69) while Europe was preoccupied with the Napoleonic Wars, and leading to the independence of Mexico finally being declared in September 1821.

In Central and Southern America a huge mass of land was conquered by Cortez and Pizarro with small armies possessing guns, against a large native population with primitive weapons. Settlement from Spain followed over the next two or three centuries, and most of the native population was converted to Catholicism. Rule came initially from Spain with a large measure of local devolution, but when Napoleon invaded Spain, and the French and Spanish Kings abdicated in 1808 in favour of Napoleon, an independence movement rapidly grew in Mexico. Mexico declared itself a Republic in 1821: Spanish attempts at re-conquest subsequently failed, and in 1836 Spain recognised the country as an independent nation.

Centuries before, Portugal had been established in 1139 after the Muslims were driven out of the western part of the Iberian Province in the Reconquista. Much of the early exploration of the distant world was carried out by Portuguese navigators, often sponsored by the Portuguese Royal family, particularly Prince Henry the Navigator (1394–1460), the third son of the ruling Portuguese King John. The first Portuguese conquest in 1415 was that of Ceuta, the African port opposite Gibraltar at the entrance to the Mediterranean, and at the northern end of the caravan routes across the Sahara. Gold and slaves in particular, came by caravan and were then shipped from Ceuta to Europe. The Portuguese hoped to hijack the trade, but once they had occupied the territory the caravans simply moved their business along the coast.

Somewhat later, Portuguese sailors discovered the Azores, which were soon colonised from 1430 onwards. Further south, and closer to Portugal, settlement in Madeira dates from around the same time. Yet further south, the Canary Islands had also been known to the ancient Phoenicians and Greeks, and were rediscovered by the Spanish in the early 14th century, when some stone-age people were found already living there. Spanish settlement followed, and although Henry the Navigator officially bought the over-lordship of Lanzarote for Portugal, this became disputed and the Portuguese were expelled, leaving the

Canary Islands under the control of Spain since that time. Once Bartholomew Dias and Vasco da Gama had reached the Cape of Good Hope and sailed on to reach India, then Portuguese expansion to the east started.

In this way, the Portuguese were able set up the first modern European global empire, which included an enormous part of South America now known as Brazil; it also marked the beginning of the trans-Atlantic slave trade which was established to provide labour for the sugar cane plantations in Brazil, as opposed to the already long established slave trade from Africa north to Europe and the Middle East. Once passage around the Cape of Good Hope was established into the Indian Ocean, trading posts to the east sprang up around the coast of India; Mozambique and Madagascar were annexed.

Further east, the Portuguese opened up trade with Malaysia, Indonesia, and as far north as Macau in China, and even Nagasaki in Japan, where trading stations were established. The Spanish followed close behind, and intermittent disagreements, sometimes armed, engulfed some of the early settlements. An enormous earthquake in 1755, destroying most of Lisbon and killing at least a quarter of the population, put a severe brake on Portuguese trade and expansionist ambitions thereafter.

The French and the English did not manage to establish any successful colonies in the Americas during the 16th century, but in the early 17th century settlement started with Roanoke in North Carolina in 1585, and then the Pilgrim Fathers arrived further north in New England in 1620. In the early 17th century English and Dutch expansion across the Atlantic commenced with settlements further south on the east coast of America. The first English colony was founded in Virginia, already named after the Virgin Queen, and the settlement was called Jamestown after the reigning English monarch. The colony only just survived its first severe winter in 1607 with help from the native Indians, but thereafter slowly grew.

The Pilgrim Fathers came to New Plymouth in 1620, and again, around half of them perished that winter, but thereafter the colony slowly picked up and further colonies were established along the east coast of America over the next century. The Dutch also arrived, with their first colony in 1624 being named New Amsterdam, though this later became English and was renamed New York.

Other European nations provided smaller colonies from Germany, Scandinavia, Ireland and Poland. In 1670 the English Hudson's Bay Company, named after Henry Hudson (1565–1611) an early English explorer, was incorporated by Royal Charter; it had an enormous land holding, comprising the drainage area of rivers from the Canadian Shield into Hudson's Bay and amounting to about 15% of the total landmass of North America. In the 17th century the company already had a successful monopoly on the fur trade from Canada, which continue.

Meanwhile, on the other side of North America, somewhat later in time, a small amount of settlement in Alaska came from Russian emigration. It is thought that this may have happened by chance as early as 1648. A little later the coast was explored by Vitus Bering (1681–1741) who was a Danish explorer and an officer in the Russian navy. The Bering Strait, Sea, Island and Glacier, are all named to commemorate him. Summer expeditions for fur trapping continued but the first true European settlement did not happen until 1784. In due course the United States bought Alaska from Russia in 1867 at a price of seven million dollars; growth was slow: it was admitted as the 49th state of the United States of America as late as 1959.

Early Dutch emigration to North America started in the 16th century with the first Dutch settlers establishing small settlements, including New Amsterdam, around the mouth of the Hudson River from 1614 onwards. At the same time to the southeast Dutch colonists arrived in Cape Town in 1652, establishing a colony which grew very slowly to reach a population of perhaps three hundred a century later. The colony was eventually taken over by the British military as a base in 1806, afterwards surviving as a re-fuelling station for the Dutch East India Company without much interest in extending settlement inland and diversifying into farming.

Irish and Scottish contributions to populating North America are enormous and Irish emigration dates back to very early times along with conflict between Ireland and Britain from at least the time of the Roman settlement of Britain, which produced successive waves of emigrants. After the Romans left, there was emigration from Ireland to the Kingdom of Dal Riata on the Scottish west coast. Eventually these colonies merged with the Picts forming the basis of early Scotland. Irish emigration experienced an enormous upsurge during and after the English Civil War, when Cromwell commandeered Irish land to pay his soldiers and to finance his continuing invasion. Over the decade up to 1652, half of the Irish population was killed, three hundred thousand people were sold as slaves, and tens of thousands were forcibly transported to the New World, as Cromwell freed land for his 'plantations' of mainland protestants.

Scottish emigration commenced in 1628 principally to Nova Scotia, and was similarly episodic, but was increased after Scottish defeat at Culloden in 1746, and then again later with the Highland Clearances. However, it was the earlier Pilgrim Fathers who set a trend for British emigration to North America, giving it a hard-working, puritan, non-conformist and individualistic identity: this has formed the basis of subsequent growth with emphasis on enterprise, tolerance and self-sufficiency. North American Government eventually arrived in a representational form reflecting English parliamentary tradition with two chambers. This contrasts with the Central and South American experience which followed French and Spanish customs with much more authoritarian and monarchical institutions, including the organisational traditions, input and authority of the Catholic church.

Up to the 16th century, European overseas trade had mainly been from the east with superior fabrics, spices and pottery. Many of these imports to Europe came from Japan and China which had continued to develop, but were then reaching their cultural zenith through the 1600s. Settlement or colonisation in the far east was not tolerated by China and Japan or attempted by Europeans. There was a certain amount of armaments and fireworks imported after the

Chinese had developed gunpowder around 1200, but this had been seen as a means of throwing missiles a greater distance than could be achieved with simple catapults and trebuchets. The Chinese did not attempt to refine their armaments to shoot smaller and more accurate missiles, so it was left to Europeans in succeeding centuries refine small arms with the musket initially, and later the rifle.

Possible further reading:
A Short History of Migration by Massimo Livi Bacci (Polity Press)

Chapter 47
The Restoration

Charles I was beheaded in 1649, after which England was again ruled by an autocrat, though one of a different sort, the austere puritan Oliver Cromwell. In the meantime, after a Royalist defeat at the Battle of Worcester in 1651, the future Charles II had fled to France, where he spent most of the next decade. Cromwell died in 1658, and his son, Richard Cromwell (1626–1712) took up his position, but quickly proved to be an ineffective ruler.

Richard Cromwell was forced to abdicate after an unsympathetic parliament refused to back him and the country descended into civil and military unrest; General George Monck, Governor of Scotland under Cromwell, recognised the need for firm control, and marched his army to London where Parliament was re-established with members of the Long Parliament from 1640. Parliament was then persuaded to dissolve itself and call an election after defining the qualifications for voters to try and ensure a Protestant majority.

It was this Parliament which resolved, with General Monck's urging, to proclaim the exiled Charles as King, and a similar resolution came from Ireland thereby restoring the monarchy. Charles was granted a national annual income of £1.2 million to finance the realm. Unfortunately his tendencies were as spendthrift as his father and grandfather, ultimately leading to national financial problems again.

Parliament was recalled at the end of 1660, by which time it was predominantly Protestant and monarchist. The Protestants were largely Anglican, and the Parliament passed several Acts to perpetuate Anglican dominance, including the reinstatement of the Book of Common Prayer. Among the dispossessed Puritans and other non-conformists was John Bunyan (1628–1688), who wrote his famous book 'The Pilgrims Progress' in Bedford jail. Bunyan stayed in prison for twelve years as he was not ordained in the Church of England, and had been convicted of preaching without a licence.

The Restoration lifted many of the restrictions in England that had come with Puritanism. Theatres were licensed to open again, and for the first time in England, women were allowed on stage in female roles, indeed Nell Gwyn (1650–1687) on the stage captured Charles II's fancy and became one of his many notorious mistresses, while Aphra Benn (1640–1689) was able to become Britain's first woman playwright. William Shakespeare's (1564–1616) plays had already appeared on the stage along with those of Ben Johnson (1572–1637).

Christopher Wren (1632–1723) was one of the founder members of the Royal Society in 1662 and later its president who designed new theatres with movable scenery and novel facilities. The income of £1.2 million that Charles II was granted to finance the realm was also intended to build a new fleet for the navy in 1664. Several battles against the Dutch were fought with heavy losses on both sides, but with the consequence that New Amsterdam in the New World was transferred to British control and renamed New York after Charles' brother the Duke of York.

This was the time when the Royal Society, properly called the "Royal Society of London for Improving Natural Knowledge" was founded. Its founding arose out of the regular meetings of groups of physicians and natural philosophers from Oxford and Gresham College in London which was set up in 1597 as a discussion forum without students. The Royal Society received its royal support at the start of its second meeting, and a Royal Charter was signed later in 1662. The Society has been highly prestigious through the succeeding centuries and remains Britain's premier scientific organisation, still having the sovereign as its patron. Charles also founded the Royal Observatory in Greenwich Park and created the position of Astronomer Royal.

In 1665 came the first of two disasters to hit London, plague decimated the population with around one in five of London's half a million-population dying. This first disaster was followed within months by the Great Fire of London, which started in a baker's shop in the aptly named Pudding Lane. It had the effect of getting rid of remnants of the plague, and clearing a mediaeval area of wooden fire-prone buildings within the city walls. Sir Christopher Wren put forward a reconstruction plan involving wide avenue, squares, and a spacious feel to the city, but there was neither enthusiasm, nor available money for this.

Instead, London was rebuilt piecemeal, but this time brick and stone were used for most buildings, and Wren was able to design and build some fifty new churches; St Paul's cathedral had been among those destroyed and a new structure designed by Wren was rebuilt by 1710. Less than a year later a third disaster overtook the nation when a Dutch fleet sailed up the Thames estuary to the Royal Dockyard at Chatham and burnt thirteen ships, and as a final insult towed away the nation's flagship. The apportionment of blame caused a reshuffle of the King's principal advisors, and the signing of a new treaty to align England with Holland against France.

Unfortunately, in 1670, Charles himself was rash enough to sign a secret and contradictory treaty with the French to fight the Dutch in return for French cash to boost his finances; the treaty was also followed by an agreement that Charles would try and return the nation to Catholicism. But word got out about the treaty and instilled a severe mistrust of the monarchy, and in 1673 Parliament passed the Test Act in retaliation, which excluded all Catholics from any public office. The King's brother, James, Duke of York now a widower, resigned, but chose to remain Catholic: he now remarried Mary of Modena (1658–1718) from Italy, who was also Catholic.

The situation produced the possibility that James and Mary of Modena might produce a Catholic heir to the throne in due course. Suspicion caused a revival of interest and favour for William of Orange and his Protestant wife Mary. William, the grandson of Charles I, was seen as a popular leader, particularly since he had defeated a possible French invasion by flooding Dutch drainage dykes, and promising to "*die in the last ditch*": this lives on as an expression in English popular usage. Souring relations between monarch and Parliament got no better and, following an assassination plot, Charles dissolved Parliament in 1679.

One of the Parliamentary demands to which Charles would not agree was that he sign a Bill disinheriting his Catholic brother James. Parliamentary matters were becoming aligned along fairly predictable partisan lines, with the result that a large group of MPs became known as Tories, an insulting word meaning a group of Catholic Irish brigands or outlaws, while the King's pro-Dutch opponents came to be known as Whigs, a shortened and also insulting name for Whiggamor, meaning a Scottish cattle rustler.

Charles attempted to rule personally without the consent of Parliament for his last few years. He survived another failed assassination attempt in 1683, but died of a stroke in 1685, and although universally unpopular, he was interred in Westminster Abbey, but with minimal pomp or ceremony. Following his death in 1685 his brother James succeeded him, as James II (1633–1702). Once more a tactless, insensitive and autocratic Stuart had come to sit on the English throne. There was an almost instant rebellion by a pretender, the Protestant Duke of Monmouth, who was Charles II oldest illegitimate son. The rebellion was rapidly crushed, and not only was Monmouth executed, but many of his supporters were also executed and others transported into slavery, thus earning the series of trials the epithet 'The Bloody Assizes'.

James insisted on retaining the standing army and staffing it with Irish troops and Catholic officers, though not surprisingly Parliament refused money to pay for this, whereupon James dissolved it. He appointed Catholic sympathisers to both the Privy Council and the Judiciary, further alienating the majority of his Protestant subjects. As a sop James offered a Declaration of Indulgence towards Protestants, but the main Indulgence was towards Catholics. When he arrested some Protestant Bishops, they were put on trial but were acquitted.

At the same time, approaches were being made to William of Orange, grandson of Charles I, whose Protestant wife Mary was also in the line of succession line for the throne as James II daughter. Before negotiations could be completed James' wife, Catholic Mary of Modena, gave birth to a son giving rise to the possibility that Britain might again have a Catholic monarch in the future. This seemed intolerable to the majority of citizens and matters came to a head with an invitation from Protestant parliamentarians to William of Orange in Holland suggesting military intervention on behalf of the great majority of Protestant England. A fleet of ships and forty thousand soldiers were assembled in Holland and sailed along the south coast of England, finally landing in Torbay.

William marched across southern England without confrontation from James' troops. He was welcomed, both in the country and in the capital when he arrived. As Mary also had a valid claim to the throne through Charles II as her grandfather, both William and Mary were jointly crowned at Westminster. James had fled to France with the active connivance of William and his army.

The result of this further time of political intolerance and suspicion was the Toleration Act of 1689, restoring freedom of worship to Protestant minorities, but not to Catholics. The right to raise taxes for an army and to wage war was vested in Parliament alone. Later in the same year the Bill of Rights laid down that a Parliament should last for three years regardless of the wish of the sovereign, and in this legislation Parliament sealed its sovereignty over the wishes of the sovereign. The Bill of Rights predates the American Constitution by a century, and much of it was reused in the American Constitution. This was to be the last United Kingdom revolution.

Having fled the country into exile in France when William arrived, James' resolution was stiffened by his French counterpart, Louis XIV, who provided money and troops for an attempt to regain power. James landed in Ireland with an army, where he found himself opposing John Churchill, a talented military commander now elevated to the Earldom of Marlborough. After a long campaign James was finally defeated at the Battle of the Boyne in 1690 and forced to return to France. William was feted as 'King Billy', and both he and the Battle of the Boyne, have remained potent symbols of protestant sectarianism in Ireland ever since. William's wife Queen Mary was also popular, indeed she is said to have been a wise ruler at the times when her husband was away campaigning, but together she and William followed the Stuart behavioural traits of extravagance, though they had no children.

Mary died in 1694 from smallpox and William died following a fall from his horse in 1702. Mary's sister (and Charles II's grand-niece) became sovereign as Queen Anne and the last of the Stuart line. Anne was born in the reign of her uncle Charles II who had left no legitimate children. Although Charles' younger Catholic brother. James II had succeeded to the throne Charles had instructed that both Mary and Anne were brought up in the Anglican Protestant faith. It had therefore become apparent that the succession to the English throne was in question, since neither Mary, nor her Protestant sister Anne had any children. As a result Parliament passed an Act of Settlement in 1701, transferring the succession to the next nearest living relative by descent from the daughter of James, namely the House of Hanover.

A little earlier, Charles II of Spain had died leaving no heir and Louis XIV of France claimed the crown of Spain for his grandson, Philip of Anjou, thus potentially joining the Empires of France and Spain, together with some of the Low Countries and Italy, in a very large Catholic European block. About the same time in 1701, the exiled James II died in France, whereupon Louis XIV suggested his own son James as King of England. This James, who might have been James III, was rapidly named the 'Old Pretender'. Parliament united against this ambitious French manoeuvring, and voted money for William to make war against the French, alongside a coalition of Dutch, Prussian and Austrian forces: this was the start of the Hundred Years War.

In Europe, King Charles of Spain had died in 1700, the product of a consanguineous marriage he was physically disabled, backward and had no children; as he ruled nominally for thirty five years there had been political stagnation in Spain. He was the last of the Habsburg dynasty, which had provided the Holy Roman Emperor for the previous three hundred years, and had come to rule over a very large empire, including Germany, Naples, Sicily, Hungary and Portugal as well as Spain. On his deathbed he named Philip, Duke of Anjou, a grandson of Louis XIV, as his successor, which caused apprehension in other nations around Europe at the thought of the French and Spanish nations uniting to dominate Europe.

Within months of succeeding to the throne, war was declared between France and Spain on one side, and Britain, the Netherlands and Austria on the other. The war raged across the low countries initially with John Churchill. now the Duke of Marlborough defeating Bavaria in 1704 at the Battle of Blenheim, and again at the battle of Ramillies in 1706. Two years later at the Battle of Oudenarde the French were defeated. While the land campaigns were in progress the British Navy had established dominance on the sea and into the Mediterranean, emphasising the military importance of Gibraltar, which was later ceded to Britain from Spain in the final settlement treaty of Utrecht in 1713, along with Newfoundland, much of Nova Scotia, and all of the Hudson's Bay territory in Canada. John Churchill (Duke of Marlborough) was rewarded with a palace north of Oxford that bears the name of Blenheim for his consistently successful campaigning.

Portugal gave up much of its seafaring ambitions due to the British dominance in the Atlantic, and the disastrous Lisbon earthquake of 1755 cemented this trend with its costly aftermath in both human and monetary terms.

Under Anne's gentle reign at home, the Act of Union between Scotland and England was completed in 1707. On the continent, warfare had continued with a victory at Malplaquet in 1709, but with an enormous British death toll which alienated both sides in Parliament. Anne's husband had died, but she continued to chair Cabinet meetings, and the Treaty of Utrecht gave Austria control over Belgium, gave Britain Gibraltar, and extended British interests in the Mediterranean and North America. Discussions over the succession continued, with the Queen favouring the old Pretender James, who was not enthusiastic, and Parliamentary forces favouring Prince George of Hanover. The succession now became a watershed, and with Parliament and ministers in the ascendant, and the new monarch coming from foreign parts as an unknown quantity without too much interest in the minutiae of British politics, the succession passed to the House of Hanover as already decided by parliament when Anne died in 1714.

Possible further reading:
Stuart Britain by John Morrill (Oxford University Press)
What the Tudors and Stuarts Did for Us by Adam Hart-Davis (BBC Books)

Chapter 48
The Enlightenment

Although we refer to the Age of Enlightenment or the Age of Reason, it is in fact not tightly defined and is better regarded as a period in which a number of factors came together to speed the development of human thought in Europe. This development was proceeding slowly in the years before the Enlightenment and continued afterwards. Thought was able to develop more quickly because of the progressive development of both art and technology, but above all through the technology of printing, which meant that dissemination of thoughts between scholars, politicians and thinkers throughout European countries, suddenly became much easier and quicker.

Thus, although the Enlightenment may be said to start with Luther and the questioning of Catholic doctrine, Gutenberg and his invention of the printing press was a necessary pre-condition for the advancement of thought. The Enlightenment therefore emerges from the Protestant Reformation and the reaction of the Catholic Counter-Reformation, but it was also fuelled by the Renaissance and the development of philosophy, writing and art, all of which linked in together at a time when an individual could be well versed in many of these subjects simultaneously; it also leads in to the Scientific Age.

The Enlightenment was a European phenomenon and although often considered country by country, it was more a phenomenon of brilliant individual thinkers across Europe developing the progress of thought, and then writing about it. There was a concentration on the arts, and an emphasis on learning in general, together with music and writing. These were also the early days when more women started to get involved in writing, painting, composing and performing, instead of being observers on the side lines, or being generally ignored.

It was an age when people began to question the established faith, traditions and authority, and when rational thought began to take the place of blind following of tradition or the teachings of the Church, which had little in the way of rational argument to bring forward; the assumptions of previous centuries were being seriously questioned.

It was also a time when increasing travel was possible. Increasing population meant that many people now lived in towns, and flourishing merchant and professional classes were thrown together and were able to participate in discussions, both about religion and politics together with other matters of daily concern. Meeting houses, private salons, coffee houses and discussion groups were starting to appear now that this middle class was urban dwelling and no longer needed to spend time farming, fighting, hunting or managing estates.

It was however, still a time when the Church carried great sway and could impose great penalties on those who questioned the religious teaching of previous centuries which bore the authority and prejudices of the 1500 years since Christ was crucified. Nicolaus Copernicus (1473–1545) first taught that the sun rather than Earth was at the centre of our universe, and had his teaching banned by the Catholic Church as heretical. His fellow astronomer, Giordano Bruno (a Dominican monk, 1548–1600), was less fortunate and was burnt at the stake in Rome.

Tyco Brahe (1546–1601), a Danish nobleman, made astronomical observations and produced some evidence that Copernicus did not have, leading on to Johannes Kepler's (1571–1630) three laws of planetary motion after working with Brahe. Copernicus was the mathematician and astronomer who is generally recognised as providing the first understanding of the solar system with the sun at the centre, rather than Earth. He was born in Prussia and died just months after his book, *On the Revolutions of the Celestial Spheres*, was published in 1543.

After Copernicus, Galileo Galilei (1564–1642), an Italian scientist and astronomer, improved available telescopes and was able to observe sunspots, and the four moons of Jupiter, which are named after him. His championing of the theory of the sun being the centre of the universe was again rejected by the Vatican, and he was suspected of heresy and had to spend the later years of his life under house arrest, forbidden by the church to publish. His theory was not accepted universally, and relatively few scholars accepted his thinking until Isaac Newton (1642–1726) formulated the universal law of gravity and mechanics in 1687, such that the theory became generally accepted.

Francis Bacon (1561–1626) was a prominent English philosopher, statesman and scientist who wrote about the scientific method. This is sometimes known as the Baconian Method since it popularised the rational investigation of the natural world. In keeping with the life of the times, he was a precocious polymath, and became a barrister at the age of 21. A year earlier he had been elected as a member of parliament, subsequently sitting for different constituencies. His advance in political circles resulted in appointment as an Attorney General in 1613, and Lord Chancellor in 1618, but he was convicted as a debtor in 1621, and spent the last five years of his life in writing. He is credited as being one of the influential men whose ideas resulted in the founding of the Royal Society under the royal patronage of Charles II in 1660.

René Descartes (1596–1650) was a French philosopher who lived most of his life in Holland. He is also regarded as laying much of the foundations of European philosophy and made important contributions about geometry and calculus. John Locke (1632–1704), an English philosopher and physician, followed the tradition and thinking of Bacon; he wrote about political philosophy affecting both French and Scottish enlightenment thinkers, as well as the early

American revolutionaries, so that his writing and theories came to be important during the writing of the United States Declaration of Independence.

Contrary to the philosophy of Descartes, Locke felt that the human mind started with a clean slate and no preconceptions, and that knowledge resulted from experience and sensory perception. He believed in religious toleration and wrote about the mechanisms of government. He spent five years in Holland, after he was suspected of being involved in an anti-royalist plot to assassinate King Charles II, but if he was involved, his influence was minimal and he was eventually able to return to England.

Thomas Hobbes (1588–1679) was an English philosopher remembered for his thinking on political philosophy. Hobbes laid down some of the fundamentals of western thought to which we still adhere, namely the rights of the individual and the equality of all men; the difference between civil society and political state function; the view that all legitimate political power must be based on the consent of the population and be representative of that population; and an interpretation of law which allows individuals to do whatever is not explicitly forbidden by law. Hobbes also wrote about many other topics, including ethics and religion, and some early scientific thinking.

Hobbes, along with Locke, argued about the rights of the individual versus the rights of government or the state, with Locke arguing that individual rights were more important than governmental rights. This argument continues to the present day with different modern states still disagreeing over the relative rights of the individual versus the state. Later in life Hobbes, whose beliefs about God are somewhat opaque, became unable to publish his work in England due to a parliamentary bill enacted in 1666 outlawing atheism and profanity. For this reason some of his works had to be printed in Amsterdam, and others were not published until after his death.

Baruch Spinoza (1632–1677) was a Jewish Dutch philosopher recognised as providing much of the foundations of European philosophy. His writings were banned by the Jewish authorities and were also listed in the Vatican's index of forbidden books. Isaac Newton's (1643–1727) book 'Mathematical Principles of Natural Philosophy', published in 1687, provided the groundwork for much basic scientific understanding. He formulated laws of motion and gravity, and used Kepler's laws of planetary motion to develop mathematical explanations of the movement of planets, comets, equinoxes, tides and such like. This removed the remaining doubts of most intellectuals about Earth orbiting the sun. He developed the first reflecting telescope, and spent much of his life as Professor of Mathematics at the University of Cambridge.

Pierre Bayle (1647–1706) was a Protestant French philosopher who toyed briefly with Catholicism, only to return to Calvinism and seek refuge in Switzerland. He wrote extensively advocating the separation of religion and science, he also posed the question about where authority derives its own authority, and from whom. Half a century later the French philosopher Voltaire (1694–1778) was born in Paris where he grew up to be a writer. His early writings criticised both government and Church for their intolerance. He was a great exponent of the need for freedom of thought and religious toleration.

Following a disagreement in 1727, Voltaire was sentenced to imprisonment in the Bastille without trial, but took exile as an alternative punishment, then living in Covent Garden in London for three years, where he was influenced by English writers past and present, and by the difference between the English and French systems of government. He left behind writings on philosophy, some poetry and at least a dozen plays, together with historical writings; altogether he is credited with over two thousand books and pamphlets, some of which broke the censorship laws of the time.

Voltaire wrote extensively about human achievement, and the struggle between civilisation and barbarism. He suggested that there were four great or happy ages when civilisation was at a peak of perfection, namely classical Greece, then the Roman era of Caesar and Augustine, followed by the Renaissance as the home of Italy's glory, and finally the age in which he wrote, that of Louis XIV (the Sun King), which he felt eclipsed all the previous ages.

Francis Hutcheson (1694–1746) was a Scottish Protestant Presbyterian clergyman and philosopher, and contemporary of Voltaire. After an early life of writing and teaching in Dublin, he was appointed to the Chair of Moral Philosophy at Glasgow, where he taught and influenced Adam Smith among others. He also influenced David Hume (1711–1776) another extremely influential Scottish philosopher and writer. Apart from his important philosophical writings, he wrote a history of England which took fifteen years and comprised six volumes and sold many copies. He is further remembered for his influence on James Madison (1751–1836), the fourth President of the United States, who drafted much of the Constitution and the Bill of Rights, so that Hutcheson is therefore seen as having influence upon the early United States Constitution.

Immanuel Kant (1724–1804) is recognised as a central thinker in philosophy who rejected speculation and taught that reason is the underlying source of morality, with reason being related to human experience, he also felt that human experience is subjective and needs to be interpreted by reason. Cesare Beccaria (1738–1794) was an Italian philosopher and lawyer, who is remembered in his work on *Crimes and Punishments*, published in 1764, which argued against torture and the death penalty. It remains an important work in the foundations of criminology, and in particular, as the earliest advocacy for abolition of the death penalty.

In France, Denis Diderot (1713–1784) was a French philosopher and writer who is notable as the part founder and chief editor of the 'Encyclopedie'. This was published in 28 volumes containing 72,000 articles from 1751 onwards, and was unusual in including contributions from many contributors: its ambition was enormous in attempting to include all of the world's knowledge in the hopes that it would act as a reference volume for the public in general. It followed Ephraim Chambers (1680–1740) first Cyclopaedia published in London in 1728 which provided the inspiration for the Encyclopedie which followed it, although the

Chinese Emperor had attempted the same task many centuries earlier (chapter 8).

In Scotland, Adam Smith (1723–1790) was a Scottish philosopher best known for his writing on economics, and regarded as the 'Father of Economics' due to his influence. He was a collaborator of David Hume and was appointed Professor of Moral Philosophy in Glasgow. He provided the foundations of free market economic theories, and his book 'An Enquiry into the Nature and Causes of the Wealth of Nations' in 1776 sold widely and has been hugely influential, remaining in print ever since. He famously said that laws should rule, not men; and that government should not interfere in trade.

In the United States, Benjamin Franklin (1706–1790) was a remarkable polymath encompassing writing, politics and the sciences, particularly electricity, in addition to acting as ambassador for his country to Sweden and France at the time of the Revolution. He was President of Pennsylvania for three years (1785–1788). He was also a critical figure in the American Revolution providing support and arranging arms shipments. In his lifetime he changed from being a slave owner in his early years, to advocating abolition in his later years. He is remembered for inventing the lightning conductor which saved many early wooden American churches from being consumed by fire, and at the same time also saved many bell ringers from death due to being struck by lightning which could run down a wet bell rope with fatal results to the ringer in the bell tower.

The foregoing names represent only some of the headline personalities of the Enlightenment. In reality many more individuals contributed to the intellectual development of the Enlightenment, all corresponding with each other and reading each other's publications. In this way rapid development of thought occurred. Although some of these philosophers were seemingly responsible for major leaps forward in the development of thought, there were others who have not stayed in the headlines, but who contributed at the time in no small manner. As an example, one may perhaps take at random, Emilie du Châtelet (1706–1742), who had a long affair with Voltaire.

Like Voltaire, Emilie was French and a superb mathematician and physicist. She translated Newton's work and added a commentary, in addition to publishing translations of Latin and Greek plays. Among other writings, Emilie wrote and experimented about kinetic energy and derived an equation which has been regarded as a pre-cursor to Einstein's mass energy formula $E=MC^2$. It was many individuals such as Emilie who contributed much to the steady and increasing intellectual knowledge base and energy that we know as the Enlightenment.

This intellectual fever led into the questioning of monarchy and an upsurge of republicanism, which became manifest as the political ferment and revolutions of the 18th and 19th centuries, foremost among these being the American War of Independence starting in 1775, and following this the French Revolution starting in 1789; many others would follow. Standing out as a conservative brake on scientific and philosophical thought during these years, was the Catholic Church with preconceived notions of acceptable thinking and knowledge based on flimsy suppositions, which could not respond logically to the new lines of thought and discoveries.

Possible further reading:
The Day the Universe Changed by James Burke (Little Brown & Co)

Chapter 49
Early Finance and Banking

Once mankind ceased a hunter gatherer existence and started to live in fixed communities where crops were planted and animals domesticated and herded, there became a need for some form of finance. Initially, this would have been in the form of barter, but with the advent of coinage in ancient Mesopotamia there is evidence of grain loans, similar activity is known in historic Egypt, India and China, often within temples. At this time, although there is evidence of trade within Europe and the Mediterranean world in particular, most of Europe still existed on the barter system. The first European coins were possibly made in Lydia around 700 BC, but before the reign of King Croesus whose name came to be synonymous with wealth; these coins were made of electrum, an alloy made from gold and silver. Coins also exist that were made in China around the same time, though from base metals.

Coinage and finance spread from the Middle East to Ancient Greece and Rome, where temples in the cities provided market activity, together with the money changers who are mentioned in the New Testament. Aside from money changing, loans or credit (from the Latin, credo – I believe) were provided against future crops for the purchase of seed, and the money changers also accepted deposits. This money changing system persisted through the Dark Ages, particularly in Italy and around the Mediterranean, but religious problems held back the development of finance for many years.

It will be recalled that Jesus Christ drove the money changers out of the Temple because they were practicing usury, or the charging of interest. Christianity inherited this attitude to interest from the Jews, though Jewish law got around this problem by forbidding the charging of interest only between Jews, but allowing charging of interest on loans to Gentiles. Christianity in turn followed this custom by forbidding the charging of interest initially, but then gradually loosening up through medieval times; with the break between the Catholic Church and Protestantism in northern Europe, the conventions were further loosened with the Reformation. The Muslim faith also initially followed the practice of forbidding usury, but in recent years ways around this have also been found which include the charging of fees, and the practice of leasing.

In medieval times, finance continued to develop slowly. We have the expression 'merchant banking' today because much of the early lending in Europe was to merchants who speculated in the import business, bringing valuable goods from the Far East and elsewhere in the form of jewellery, pottery, cloth, silk and spices. This came to be called banking from the Italian 'banca', a bench or counter which was set up in the local market. From this in turn, we have the expression 'banca rotta', a broken bench, or the description of being bankrupt.

In Italy, where Jews were not allowed to own land, they often earned their living carrying on much of the commerce in banking. Because of the prohibition of land ownership, they frequently traded in grain, together with other lesser commodities which today would be called trading in futures. In this way, both finance and insurance gradually became available. Funds could be deposited against bills, or bills of exchange, and then used elsewhere in exchange for goods, thus obviating the need to carry bulky and valuable gold or silver around. In turn, in much later times, bills and notes spawned the introduction of cheques.

In the 10th to 14th centuries, there was a steady increase in the use of financial and banking activity. There was growth of towns with markets, particularly on trade routes, and especially at seaports. Markets were popular across Europe with rulers and their barons, since the licence fees were used as a steady source of income. At the same time, the increase in travel abroad, both on the crusades and on pilgrimage, in addition to merchant venturing, fuelled the need for a flexible financial system that would work across the whole of Europe.

Trade routes which had been largely along rivers and by sea routes, including the large European rivers Rhine, Rhone, Danube and Denier were now experiencing increased traffic, and on the roads there was also increased traffic requiring repair and construction of routes that had been largely untouched since Roman times. Overland routes through the Alpine passes were opened up.

The Hanseatic League of ports was a trading organisation around the Baltic Sea and into the North Sea, founded from the city of Lubeck in northern Germany, after its conquest in 1159 by Henry, Duke of Saxony and Bavaria (1129–1195), to promote trade and protect travelling merchants around the Baltic Sea. Hansa means a guild or convoy, and the trade guilds protected their merchant members, even raising armies to do so when necessary. Henry II of England granted the League free trading facilities through London without tolls or duties.

Other English east coast ports, including Hull, York and King's Lynn, joined the League, but failure of the League to grant reciprocal arrangements with German and Flemish cities led to problems and resentment, particularly as the Hanseatic merchants lived in walled compounds and did not interact much with local populations. Rival organisations and small states reacted by setting up their own systems, and in consequence the League declined in the face of competition, with many of the closed and privileged enclaves disappearing by the end of the 16th century. The London Royal Exchange was one such rival trading site opened in the city of London by Queen Elizabeth in 1571.

The new European wealth stimulated the growth of construction, particularly in churches and cathedrals. Milling technology, using water or wind, was adapted to power many different tasks. The technology was initially imported from the Far East and extensively used around the Mediterranean after appearing around the beginning of the first millennium and then through medieval times was adapted not just to the milling of crops, but also to other uses including the production of cloth and paper. This technology increasingly required and used credit finance for capital investment at the start of a project.

Mediaeval times were a period of steady growth in Europe as farming produced an increasing food supply, and forests were gradually cleared and turned into fields. The increase in available food was aided by the spread of the iron plough and the use of horses instead of oxen, both of which were more efficient and productive helping to increase grain yields. The population of Europe has been estimated at around 40 million souls at the millennium, increasing over the next two hundred years by 50% to 60 million. It reached a peak a hundred years later at around 80 million people before a series of calamitous harvests due to a climatic downturn led to famine in the 1320s.

No sooner had Europe started to recover from this than the Black Death decimated the population again in 1348 and subsequent years. However, trading activity and finance slowly but steadily increased again after these major setbacks, with much of Europe gradually becoming more wealthy. The Mediterranean countries, along with the eastern countries of Europe, including Russia, Poland and the Balkans, remained fairly static in their economic activity.

Italy had enjoyed a commercial revival, much of it based on the ancient trading seaports of Venice and Genoa, which had grown rich, even in ancient times, with wool and wine trading. It was in Italy that banking first separated from money changing, though both of these activities were still necessary and were given a boost by the Crusades. Gold was brought in from sub-Saharan Africa for use as capital and for exchange, particularly from what we now know as Mali, since Europe does not have a significant indigenous source of gold or silver, Mexican silver was also vitally important. Indeed, gold underpinned international trade for the next few centuries, until it finally proved insufficient when the world economy crashed in 1929 and countries left the 'gold standard'.

In those mediaeval times, Italian merchants were trading actively with China and Arabia, both importing and exporting goods to and from Europe. As an accounting system the abacus was much used in India, Babylonia and Egypt once a counting system became standardised on either a base of ten or twelve. Much of early European accountancy originated in Italy where the double entry book-keeping system was invented along with credit facilities pioneered by banking families, of which the Medicis are the best known. The Medici family rose to prominence through the first half of the 14th century in Florence and Siena thanks to trade in wool, and their bank was founded in 1397, growing steadily through the 15th century. The family became exceptionally wealthy and were generous patrons of culture and art, helping to fuel the Renaissance in addition to becoming very dominant in contemporary urban politics.

Few goods were produced in Europe at this time that were needed, or were in demand, in China or Arabia. Although early credit existed in historic China, finance was by way of conquest, plunder and taxes. Europe and its conquered countries gradually left this system of regal or military money generation for a system of credit backed trading, which often involved exploration and exploitation, as in Spain's pursuit of silver in the New World.

There was a steady slave trade from Europe, particularly to Arabia. Apart from this, gold and silver bullion was needed as a steady source of payment for imported goods to Europe from the east. Two centuries later this necessary gold and silver would start to pour into Europe, through Spain in particular, from the New World discoveries in Central and South America, including from the amazingly abundant seams of ore at Potosi in the Mexican mountains. Mexican silver crossed the Atlantic to Spain as 'pieces of eight', large silver coins known as Spanish dollars and modelled on the German thaler, later morphing into the American dollar, after becoming arguably the world's first truly international currency.

Alongside this import and export trade, the early accountancy that had originated in Italy grew together with credit facilities allowing the increase of international trade. Trade was sensitive during these times to poor harvests, but the difficulties in transport across Europe were gradually being improved with investment in shipping and roads. By the late 15th century there was little if any internal European slave trade, but black Africans were still being imported to the Iberian Peninsula, and white Europeans were still being sold to the Arabs and the Turks. The Portuguese slave trade to the Americas was increasing rapidly at the end of the 15th century, with African chiefs of coastal tribes rounding up people in the interior and selling them on to Europeans.

Throughout mediaeval times, from the Dark Ages through to the end of the 16th century, there were many little self-contained economies within Europe, but the effect of increased trading over larger distances gradually boosted financial activity, and the need for financial interchange between different regions and countries. We have seen that in early times people's needs were initially satisfied by self-sufficiency, with progression to a barter system, and then on to cash crops in early mediaeval times when markets expanded rapidly in the 12th and 13th centuries under licence in England from the King and barons.

The trade that went with these markets helped town growth if the town was on a trade route, was a seaport, or alternatively was at the centre of a large agricultural area. Growth in trade was uneven and suffered a big setback in the years following 1315 at the time of the Great Famine caused by bad weather. A much more severe downturn followed due to the Black Death in 1348 and subsequent years, with some estimates suggesting that almost half the European population died from the disease over a period of four or five years.

At the end of the 15th century, trade was picking up again at a time when Italy enjoyed primacy in banking. Unfortunately, Italy was afflicted with internal wars and great political problems in the early 16th century, so that it became a less than ideal financial centre. There was also considerable Jewish persecution in many European countries, particularly Italy, Spain and Portugal, such that many Jewish financiers were expelled and fled north to the Low Countries. Thus it was that European financial muscle leached out of Italy to northern Europe where it became centred in Amsterdam, London and Stockholm. It was in these cities that the first joint stock companies were created. This was an arrangement whereby different people could own smaller parts of companies; this comprised the beginning of the share system, an individual share in a company could be bought or sold without disrupting the functioning of the company. Initially such share dealing was carried on in a relatively informal manner in the coffee houses of London and Amsterdam.

The London Royal Exchange was opened in 1571, during the reign of Elizabeth I, for the purposes of trading these shares, following the example of its predecessor in Antwerp which was founded in 1531. The London Stock Exchange was established in 1698 to take over share dealing, rather than merchandising, and over the next two hundred years financial markets expanded enormously as trade in goods and the beginnings of manufactured goods burst upon the world alongside the onset of the Industrial Revolution. Trade was further facilitated in northern Europe by colonisation of the Americas: this provided enormous quantities of silver bullion which were needed to pay for the imported goods from the Far East. Trading companies were established, commencing with the Dutch East India Company, founded in 1602 to trade with the East Indies, and the Hudson's Bay Company trading with North America, which received its royal charter from Charles II in 1670.

Government bonds were first issued in England in 1693 to finance the Nine Years War with France in Europe and on the east coast of America, rapidly following this the Bank of England was established in 1694. In turn the founding of the London Stock Exchange in 1698, together with other institutions and companies provided a further large boost to the economy of northern Europe. Thereafter expansion in the form of colonisation by European powers would provide the overseas market for the manufactured goods that needed to be sold to keep the trade cycle rolling. Through the 17th century and at the beginning of the 18th century, trade was entirely free of taxes and duties. The system brought raw materials to England and other northern European countries, and manufactured goods were returned to be distributed for sale in the colonies and other foreign destinations.

By the early 17th century, there was regular trade, to both east and west, from Spain and Portugal as well as from northern Europe. Trade was backed up by military strength, and war if necessary, to protect and encourage merchants. All of this provided a relatively sound basis for the establishment of companies which manufactured and traded in goods. Companies were established with capital raised by joint share offers, in addition to the many privately owned companies which still flourished at that time. In order for credit to be raised and granted to individuals, some form of collateral was required, and this appeared at the end of the 17th century when it was realised that land and properties which were being bought and sold, could act as security, and in this way mortgages came into being.

Overseas trade still remained risky with shipping losses often causing substantial loss to merchant venturers; to overcome this Edward Lloyd (1648–1713) opened a coffee shop in 1686 devoted to shipping information and then insurance, which went on to grow into the first proper insurance business, Lloyds of London. Paper bills of exchange gradually replaced gold and silver bullion through the 18th century aided by the introduction of paper currency in Europe, starting properly in London in 1694, initially for individualised amounts, but later in the standardised amounts of money we have become used to. Although paper letters of credit had existed since Roman times, cheques in the form now used also came into being and were gradually refined through the 18th century.

This new and expanded capitalist system received a rude shock in 1711 when the South Sea Company became bankrupt. The Company, either wittingly or otherwise, had generated enormous expectations of vast profits from investment in its dealings, feverish speculation spread rapidly with the price of shares in the Company reaching unheard of heights, only to crash when it became clear that the Company could not realise the promised profits, indeed could not realise even a fraction of the anticipated earnings; the whole affair became known as the 'South Sea Bubble'. The resulting crash affected all of the market in shares, and the whole market was dampened down for some time, but eventually resumed with trading at a realistic level.

A similar 'bubble' occurred in the French economy only a few years later in 1719, when investors were persuaded, or deluded, into investing in the Mississippi Company which bought large tracts of land along the Mississippi River where the proposed development was difficult, expensive and very long-term; once again share prices sky-rocketed before eventually collapsing completely. Another crash occurred in the United States and is known as 'The Panic of 1837' after a similar boom of unwise over-investment.

Up to the 17th century, the aristocracy, or the wealthiest (and smallest) segment of the population, lived off the land which they held, and which was worked for them by a small army of labourers, peasants and possibly managers. Their land was effectively their capital, and in previous generations had provided the income for them to live and rule their part of the countryside, or indulge in war for the king; hunting and associated activities were seen as necessary ways of developing the required skills for the upper class leadership and management roles that this involved. With warfare becoming less frequent, and with the advent of a professional army to undertake it when required, this left the upper classes able to transfer much of their wealth generating activities involving capital to invest in shares.

In this way, upper class activity for many changed from rural and people management into shares and investment. Through the 19th century in Britain there was still the expectation that the upper classes did not 'work' in the sense that we now understand that word. Consequently the new businesses and industries that were started came about because of hard-working artisans developing their skills and scaling up their businesses. The upper classes still clung to the belief that their mission in life was to govern, either locally in the justice or voluntary systems, or nationally as members of parliament, but failing this the armed services or the church were both felt to be socially acceptable occupations.

For women, the aim in life was to achieve a 'good marriage' and then manage a large household and possibly part or all of an estate, as exemplified in the novels of Jane Austen (1785–1815) and the three Bronte sisters; these young women were all unusual in wanting to break out of the mould of life as it was available to them, and which they achieved by writing in one of the few ways in which it was then possible. These 19th century attitudes left Britain with a legacy where the arts and culture were more respected than occupations in science, engineering or business, at a time when technical universities in Europe were generating new scientists and new businesses to enrich their nations and widen their industrial bases. The divide between arts and science has persisted through the 20th century and into the present one.

Capitalist financial markets have developed into specific interests in share dealing, and indeed also in dealing in the sale and purchase of companies, but without a corresponding commitment to starting or building up new businesses, which has seen a gradual decline of British industry in the second half of the 20th century. Future financial markets from the 18th century onwards have seen a continuing cycle of 'boom and bust' up to the present day, with capital investors in shares seemingly often exaggerating either their optimism or pessimism, thus perpetuating this long and endless cycle of boom and bust, with intermittent bubbles to burst.

This cycle would be one of the reasons for 19th century financial and philosophical thinkers to search for a more rational, socially equitable, and responsible means of financing national and international trade: this has produced communism, though at the same time the capitalist system has continued to grow and develop new market adaptations each time another imperfection or problem has become apparent. A better system has yet to be devised.

Possible further reading:
The Ascent of Money by Niall Ferguson (Allen Lane)

Chapter 50
The Scientific Age

The beginning of science is conveniently held to start with Copernicus (1473–1543), who was a Prussian thinker and scientist bold enough to put forward the theory that the sun was the centre of our universe, and not Earth. Thus, he said that Earth (and indeed all the other planets), revolved around the sun, rather than the other way round. This was revolutionary thinking, since the idea that Earth, and the population upon it, were at the centre of the universe had been an article of faith for all, not least the Church, up to that time. The scientific revolution proceeded with gradual acceptance by all, except the Catholic Church, over the next 150 years.

The revolution is often recognised as complete with the publication of Sir Isaac Newton's *Principia* in 1687. The revolution runs in parallel with the Enlightenment, and throughout the years was seen as threatening by the Church. In fact most of the early scientists and ground-breaking thinkers were orthodox believers who saw no evidence for the Church's stance on insisting that Earth was at the centre of creation. In parallel with the Enlightenment, the scientific revolution was also enabled by the onset of printing, and the publication of books from the 16th century onwards. Printing was vital to the dissemination of knowledge between philosophers and scientists, so that knowledge could be spread, discussed and criticised in a way never previously possible, and then continued to grow steadily.

Some early scientific thought of a practical nature had been on-going for thousands of years; the ancient Egyptians observed and managed nature, as did the Babylonians and the ancient Chinese. Their civilisations were comprised of practical people whose observations of the natural world allowed them to make the most of crop and animal management. The Greeks, who followed them, were masters of philosophy and management at domestic and larger levels in a way that may be seen as the beginning of economics. However, at that time observation came a poor second to philosophical thought, which often resembled fantasy.

Hippocrates, and then Aristotle, collected and observed natural phenomena. The early Greek philosophers from the Ionian School in Miletus, postulated that four elements comprised the basis of all substances: thus earth, air, fire and water were thought to be the components of all matter in different proportions. This belief, for which they could assemble not a shred of evidence, persisted for two thousand years through to the beginning of the Renaissance and the scientific revolution, though Thales of Miletus (624–546 BC) broke with the mythology of the ancient Gods suggesting that everything derived from a single substance which he believed to be water. A little later in the second Ionian Revolution, Socrates (470–399 BC) left no direct writings, but was famed for his teaching through dialogue and discussions, which were recorded by his many contemporaries.

Despite this sometimes fantastical philosophy, the Greeks were astonishingly adept at arithmetic and geometry, whose foundations they laid, and which would last for the next two millennia. The name of Pythagoras is still venerated today, and indeed Pythagoras knew and wrote that Earth was spherical. Ptolemy's philosophical ideas remain respected today, including his concept that human existence was divided between body and soul, this idea has lived on into Christianity and then Islam. The thinking of Plato, and his pupil Aristotle, established lines of thought for early philosophy and scientific thinking which would persist from the 4th and 5th centuries BC for the next two thousand years.

In the Hellenistic expansion, conquered states were governed autocratically, and were not self-governing city states as understood in the Greek Federation. Early Greek ideas were transmitted and provided a strong influence on thinking. There were major libraries in Alexandria and Pergamum, which unfortunately did not survive through the turbulent times that followed. Early Greeks were familiar with this knowledge and used it to estimate the size of Earth. Reference is sometimes made to the seven sages of ancient Greece who lived between the 6th and 5th centuries BC and included Thales of Miletus, Solon of Athens and Chilon of Sparta.

The next big step forward came in Arabic thinking in the 9th and 10th centuries AD, when Islam achieved much wider literacy than across contemporary Europe. The apex of Arabic knowledge and culture was in Spain in the 11th and 12th centuries when Cordoba was renowned as a major centre of knowledge and thought, and again where a major library had been accumulated. Arabic culture was vital as a means of transmission of thought and knowledge between the Ancient World and newly emerging thought in Europe. Arabic books on medicine provided a basis for European development. The numeration system which Europe eventually adopted from India via Arabia made life a lot easier than the use of the very cumbersome Roman numbering system.

The Arabs had magnetic compasses for deep sea navigation before Europe, knowledge that had spread from China. Geographically, Arabia and Islam provided a physical block of deserts and mountains to the spread of most Chinese culture from the Far East to Europe. Thus the contribution of the Chinese discoveries to the emerging European Renaissance was limited mainly to knowledge of silk and paper, together with the use of oil-based inks, which were so vital in the success of Gutenberg's printing press.

In the 15th and 16th centuries, Europe censorship was still a considerable force. Early writings by scientists often circulated in manuscript form, rather than being publicly printed where they might attract the gaze of authority, either in the form of the Church or the state. The censorship was both official and overt, but was also present as a degree of self-censorship by those who realised that their thinking might not be acceptable to the authorities. The Church, in particular, held back scientific thinking, especially in southern Europe, where 1500 years of Catholic tradition meant that the Church tolerated changes in thought very poorly. Church doctrine was deeply rooted in authoritarianism, even if the attitudes expressed were not founded on any firm evidence.

This change in intellectual thinking was necessary to break away from the world as seen by Aristotle or the Bible, where Earth was pictured at the centre of everything. Two great thinkers were at the forefront of this change; Copernicus, the Polish mathematician and astronomer, published his observations that Earth orbited the sun rather than vice versa, shortly before his death in 1543, and Francis Bacon (1561–1626) an English philosopher and scientist in the early years of the 17th century, who advocated observation and experiment, rather than the deduction of hypotheses based on an absence of evidence or logic. In other words, the time had come when people should see the natural world as it exists, rather than make up whimsical theories about how they would like it to exist.

Copernicus was followed by Kepler (1571–1630), a younger colleague who worked with him for a while. He was also followed by Galileo (1564–1642), who again believed in experimentation, and whose book in 1632, *Dialogue on the Two Great Systems of the World*, may be seen as the first major scientific revolutionary publication with criticism of the old thinking. Johannes Kepler was a German mathematician who formulated laws of planetary motion, and confirmed the heliocentric conclusions of Copernicus.

Galileo's book began to spread around Europe, and was seen as criticism of the Aristotelian and Christian view of the world; in consequence the Church tried him for heresy. He recanted notionally, but was placed under house arrest and died without publishing any further observations. However, the mould was beginning to break and scientific thought forged on without the world at the centre of the universe.

Isaac Newton (1642–1726) was born in the year Galileo died. He was able to provide a theoretical explanation of the universe envisaged by Copernicus, and his book, *The Mathematical Principles of Natural Philosophy* (often shortened to simply *Principia*), explained how gravity was the driver behind the behaviour of the sun and its planets, together with other stars in the universe. In this way, Newton in effect opened a split between science and religion. He first went up to Cambridge as an undergraduate and then stayed becoming professor of mathematics; for the last twenty-four years of his life he was also president of the Royal Society.

The Catholic Church in particular, which was used to declaring truth on the basis of its authority, was now confronted by the thinking that its conclusions were subject to confirmation by observation or experimentation, not just simple assertion. German mathematician Gottfried Leibnitz (1646–1716), developed calculus independently of Newton, and at the same time also invented mechanical calculators and refined the binary number system, which in the fullness of time would lead to the computers that form such an essential part of our modern world. Along with Descartes (1596–1650), and Spinoza (1632–1677), Leibnitz is one of the three great advocates of rationalism of the late scientific revolution where reason, experiment and observation are regarded as the major source of knowledge.

The scientific revolution commenced with those two major developments of thought, namely that the sun was at the centre of the universe, and that the relationships of the sun and the planets to each other were predictable using the laws of gravity. In addition to these two great discoveries, other disciplines were also developing. The third area of study was that of medical discoveries with the refinement of human anatomy thanks to Vesalius (1514–1564), a Flemish physician and professor in Padua, the discovery of the circulation of the blood by William Harvey (1578–1657) an English physician, and the development of logical treatment of war wounds by Ambroise Paré (1510–1590) a French military barber-surgeon: all of these men based their writings on experimentation and observation.

In a fourth area, chemistry was developed, partly by Brahe and Newton, but also by Paracelsus (1493–1541) Swiss physician and alchemist, by Robert Boyle (1627–1691) who formulated the laws concerning the behaviour of gases, and by the English polymath, Sir Thomas Browne (1605–1682). In a fifth field, the development of optics, including the telescope and the microscope, provided vital tools for new experimentation and observation; Kepler's observations were much enhanced by the use of the new telescopes. On a sixth front, electricity became the subject of research by William Gilbert (1544–1603) who was physician first to Queen Elizabeth, and then to her successor James I, but experimented and wrote about electricity and magnetism.

It is worth mentioning that many of these early men of science (and they were all men) were of independent means, and usually protestant or non-conformist, often coming from aristocratic families; they carried with them an association of social prestige as amateurs, gentlemen without religious preconceptions but with time and money to spend upon their interests, which ranged across all, or any, fields of the new sciences. By the beginning of the 18th century such individuals were beginning to specialise more deeply in more circumscribed fields. This role of the amateur in driving forwards the frontiers of science would persist over the next two hundred years, mainly in Protestant northern Europe where the new Churches had no preconceived doctrines to be overturned, rather than in southern Europe where Catholic thinking would continue to act as a brake.

Possible further reading:
The Discoverers by Daniel J Boorstin (Vintage Books)

Chapter 51
Colonisation of North and Central America

Mankind has lived on the American continent from just before or just after the last Ice Age. The spread of humans across the Bering Strait into North America is covered in chapter 9. From the Bering Strait three broad streams of people fanned out across the American continents. The first stream spread to the east remaining in the frozen northerly regions with their descendants today called Eskimos. They are a super specialised adaptation of the human race to cope with an unusual life amid the snow and ice of high latitudes. A second band of migration ended up populating the middle prairies and east coast of temperate Canada and America, and becoming the largely hunter gatherer societies of the plains Indians.

The third broad wave of migration was down the west coast, along the mountainous spine of the North, Central and South Americas; this migration into Central and South America came later than the population of North America but there is still evidence of it occurring not long after the recent Ice Age. The migrations of humans from northern Asia across the Bering Strait is confirmed by studies of the genetics of present day inhabitants, together with research into their blood types, their language dialects, and the many different types of arrowhead, because these early American humans were essentially stone age societies.

At the time that the first Europeans discovered America, the Maya civilisation in Central America and the Inca civilisation in the South American Andes were still largely stone age societies, although metal had been smelted, and gold and silver in particular were a big draw for early Europeans, and at the same time the downfall of the native inhabitants. These early American societies had no iron, no horses and had not discovered the wheel. They were, however, expert in constructing amazing large stone buildings with precision joints between huge stones, we are still unaware of the secrets of this technology and how buildings were constructed using such huge stones. They had also domesticated both animals and plants, and in particular, had passed down to present generations the cropping of maize, squash and tomatoes.

The earliest Europeans to leave a record of their stay in the Americas were the Vikings around 1,000 years ago, but the small colony at L'Anse aux Meadows on the northern tip of Newfoundland did not last long. We do not know whether the colony failed to thrive due to difficulties of supply from the mother Scandinavian countries, or whether they were unable to produce sufficient crops or animals for their self-sufficiency. It is also possible that they were resented by the indigenous Indians and driven out. But by this time other Vikings were already settling in the Low Countries, in France (Normandy), and in Spain and Sicily, all of which must have displayed many more attractions than the northeast coast of America, particularly with the difficulties in distant travel.

European settlement in North America starts slowly at the beginning of the 16th century following the discovery of Central America by Christopher Columbus in 1492, and by John Cabot of the eastern Canadian coast in 1497. By contrast, settlement in North America, in the region we now know as New England and Canada's maritime provinces, was far less inviting than further south. It was perceived to be a rich source for fur trapping, but little else that Europeans wanted. There were no obvious metal ores available to mine, either base metals or precious metals, and the work required to clear the ground for self-sufficiency agriculture was considerable.

After Columbus' first landfall on the Bahamas, he moved on west to the islands of first Cuba and then Hispaniola, where he instigated the founding of the first European colony. Unfortunately this resulted in decimation of the native population from European diseases, which was followed by the importation of West African slaves to work the sugar plantations. By the time of Columbus' second voyage of 1493, when he arrived with a fleet of 17 ships carrying soldiers, farmers and catholic missionaries, it was apparent that Hispaniola had little by way of natural resources. By the end of the 17th century, Spain had ceded the western third of the island to France; a hundred years later the eastern two thirds became the independent Dominican Republic. The western part of the island became Haiti (after the native name Ayiti), and eventually, following a successful slave revolt inspired by the French Revolution, became the first independent nation in Latin America in 1792.

The French and the English did not manage to establish any successful colonies in the Americas during the 16th century, but in the early 17th century settlement started with Roanoke in North Carolina in 1585, and then the Pilgrim Fathers arrived further north in New England in 1620. In the early 17th century English and Dutch expansion across the Atlantic commenced with settlements further south on the east coast of America. The first English colony was founded in Virginia, already named after the Virgin Queen, and the settlement was called Jamestown after the current reigning English monarch. The colony only just survived its first severe winter in 1607 with help from the native Indians, but thereafter slowly grew.

The Pilgrim Fathers came to New Plymouth in 1620, and again, around half of them perished that winter, but thereafter the colony slowly picked up and further colonies were established along the east coast of America over the next century. The Dutch also arrived, with their first colony in 1624 being named New Amsterdam, though this later became English and was renamed New York. Other European nations provided smaller colonies from Germany, Scandinavia, Ireland and Poland.

In 1670, the English Hudson's Bay Company, named after Henry Hudson (1565–1611) an early English explorer, was incorporated by Royal Charter; it had an enormous land holding, comprising the drainage area of rivers from the Canadian Shield into Hudson's Bay and amounting to about 15% of the total landmass of North America. In the 17th century the company already had a successful monopoly on the fur trade from Canada, which continued for the next couple of centuries.

The early French did not always come to settle, and many explored the rivers of Quebec, known as Lower Canada (after the lower reaches of the St Lawrence River), and Ontario, known as Upper Canada (after the upper reaches), in large canoes where they also learnt trapping skills from the Indians. Beaver, fox and mink were all traded from the Indians for simple European goods such as blankets, axes, cookware and even guns and whisky, with these last two causing severe problems for Indian communities in subsequent years.

Samuel de Champlain (1574–1635) the French soldier, navigator and explorer who founded New France and Quebec City in 1608, was the first European to explore and map the Great Lakes, he established trading companies, sending goods back to France in the reign of King Henry IV of France. Champlain's relations with the native people had a shadow cast over them in 1609 when he got involved in an internal altercation between the Huron and Algonquin Indians who were warring with the Iroquois. Although vastly outnumbered by a large Iroquois war band, Champlain killed two of the Chiefs, whereupon the rest fled. The French company called the 'Hundred Associates' (Compagnie des Cent-Associés) was the French equivalent of the Hudson's Bay Company, though set up earlier in 1628.

Columbus had also claimed Cuba for Spain, and a settlement started in 1511, only to succumb to European diseases. Natural resources were scarce here too, but the economy struggled along with sugar plantations worked by imported slaves. The British invaded and secured Cuba in 1762, but in the Treaty of Paris a year later the island was restored to Spain in exchange for the British gaining Florida. A slave rebellion in 1812 was unsuccessful, but later rebellion in 1868 resulted in continued grumbling warfare and the abolition of slavery in the 1880s, though independence was only finally achieved in 1902.

Nearby Jamaica was visited by Columbus in 1494 with the first Spanish settlers coming in 1509; they were eventually evicted by the British in 1655, who then ran the country as a sugar exporting nation again dependent on slave labour. A series of slave rebellions culminated in the formal abolition of slavery in 1833 with colonial ties being gradually loosened over the next century, but full independence was gained within the British Commonwealth only in 1962

In this way the first successful English settlements were in the Caribbean, with their prosperity due to tobacco and sugar, and it was only later that settlement moved away from the Caribbean to the east coast of North America. At the same time the smaller Caribbean islands had become pirate bases enjoying a lucrative living which could be made off galleons returning to Spain laden with gold or silver bullion. Piracy reached its peak at the end of the 17th century and has remained popular in the public imagination ever since.

The first English settlement north of Florida and the Caribbean was at Jamestown in North Carolina, which was founded with a Charter from James 1 in 1607. The first few years were difficult, and there was a high mortality amongst the settlers, but within a couple of decades the little colony was well established. In the meantime, a year later in 1608, the French explorer Samuel De Champlain built a small French fort at the site of Quebec City. This little colony was not self-sufficient and required continual supplies of food and essentials to be sent from the mother country. Furs and fishery provided the monetary exchange that was needed to keep the little settlement going. Further south, a Dutch settlement at New Amsterdam was of dubious viability and was taken over by the English, when it became New York, named after the King's brother the Duke of York.

After these early explorations by the Frenchmen, Jacques Cartier (1491–1557) and Samuel de Champlain, early migration from France to North America followed, with initial settlements along the St Lawrence River, and to this day the Province of Quebec remains French speaking, along with some territory in the Maritime provinces which the French subsequently ceded to Britain in the Treaty of Utrecht in 1713. Somewhat later, there was a large migration of French immigrants to central North America, to an area then called Louisiana after the French Monarch, which covered many of the present central US states, and was very much larger than the present state of that name; this early Louisiana was sold to the USA by a cash-strapped France after the revolution in 1803, for fifteen million dollars.

The French Canadians in the Maritime provinces and eastern parts of Canada were subjected to a movement to Louisiana known as the 'Great Upheaval' from Acadia, (as it was then called – largely present-day Canadian Maritime provinces, New Brunswick, Nova Scotia and Prince Edward Island). While campaigning, the British army captured Acadian centres and demanded that Acadians either swear loyalty to the British crown, or be expelled. Many refused to swear loyalty, and were sent to Louisiana, where they have since become known as 'Cajuns', a corruption of the word Acadian. When French Louisiana was sold by Napoleon to the United States in 1803, it was dispersed amongst what are now fifteen of the American states.

In contrast to the English settlements which were largely composed of religious dissenters, and workers needing to escape from the mother country, the French sent nobility and grouped their farms in seigneuries. Many Catholic missionaries accompanied the settlers. France provided grants of land along the coast of the St Lawrence River measuring a mile of frontage and extending away from the river also for a mile. All transport was by river, and when the original settler died his land was divided between all his progeny, each of whom required some river frontage since this was the only means of transport available, so the original mile square grant of land rapidly became reduced to thin ribbons with narrow waterfronts extending backwards into the bush. The land itself was somewhat barren and very rocky, and this was a further factor hindering the early French settlers.

Through the 18th century, the early English in New England colonies increased steadily. They were helped in their success by the translocation of whole agricultural communities, which were well able to work the land. The land was much more easy to cultivate compared with that further north and further south, and responded to European methods of cultivation. Fishing and fur trading were added bonuses. There was no interference with transport to and from the mother country as the cargoes in each direction were of little value compared with the Spanish bullion that drew the attention of the Caribbean pirates. In addition to the favourable climate and the ability to grow European crops, the English political system and relative stability generated Protestant emigrants who wanted to avoid the continuing religious turmoil in England. The superiority of the English navy as the centuries developed also helped.

By 1700, there were twelve States along the eastern border of America with almost half a million inhabitants, many of whom were not English and included Dutch, Germans, Swiss and Scandinavians, but the Anglo-Saxon culture predominated. A degree of religious diversity was permitted, where the French settlements to the north permitted no religious liberty. In 1663 the French crown had taken over responsibility and direction of the colonies from the various trading companies that had provided the direction up to that date.

During the Seven Years War in Europe (1754–1763), the French and English colonies fought each other with support from troops sent out by the home countries. At this time the number of British colonists approached two million and was many times larger than their French counterparts. The French enlisted the help of local Indian tribes in their efforts. The British captured Acadia and deported the French settlers from what is now Nova Scotia and New Brunswick. Some were deported to Europe and some south to Louisiana. The early campaigning was much more successful for the French than the English, but as the war proceeded the British took control of Montreal in 1860 and Quebec City fell in the same year at the Battle of the Plains of Abraham.

Both the French commander, General Montcalm (1712–1759), and the British commander, General Wolfe (1727–1759), died in the battle for Quebec. Although fighting continued after this time, it was at a lower level and the Treaty of Paris was concluded in 1763, signed by Britain, France and Spain, formally ending the war. In the settlement Britain gained French Canada, the French Caribbean Islands and Louisiana was ceded to Spain.

Thus, whilst France and England had an authoritarian organisational background in their colonies with royally appointed governors, church leaders and missionaries, the early American colonies were less subservient to authority than in most European countries. Minimal church input was present from the largely Protestant settlers, and there was a greater emphasis on representative democratic bodies with assemblies talking to a London appointed governor. There was cooperation between French and English in defending against the

Indians, with the French initially recruiting the Huron Tribe, and in retaliation the English becoming allied later with the Iroquois Indians.

The American colonies cooperated in farming, and for reasons of soil and climate, competition was minimal. The new southern states produced rice and tobacco, whilst the most northerly New England states produced ships with their abundant local timber, also concentrating on fishing and maize, which were not in much demand back in the mother countries. Incidentally the first import of the hitherto unknown crop of tobacco to England from America came in 1559 and then steadily increased in quantity.

By the 1760s, more of Canada had become English, and there was very little French land left outside Louisiana. The French dreams of a New France either around Quebec, or as a large area centred around the Mississippi River and New Orleans, had died. An age of expansion from the original eastern seaboard colonies started with a push west through the mountains and into the central plains of America.

Here, the native Indians were the main hazard to settlement and farming. This led the authorities in London to impose a policy of trying to limit expansion westwards, and secondly raising taxes to pay for the military protection of settlers against the Indians. Resentment against these taxes, together with a reluctance to recognise their necessity and benefit for the settlers, started to contribute to the independence movement which would come to a climax with a demand for representation in exchange for taxation.

With French influence waning in North America, the Dutch were also eclipsed. Their eastwards expansion had been severely affected by the cost of three Anglo-Dutch wars, and by trying to hold together an empire in the Far East, which required much finance to provide military stability. Spain continued its triangular trade of gold and silver bullion to Europe, from where the ships took goods to the west coast of Africa. The ships then completed the third leg of their triangular voyage with a cargo of slaves, principally for Central and South America, for work in the cotton and sugar plantations. Further details of the slave trade are discussed in chapter 59.

By this time, the combination of the London government trying to restrict western settlement and farming, together with the increased tax to pay for forts protecting the colonists and the frontier, resulted in increasing dissatisfaction throughout the American colonies. In attempting to reform the colonial rule in America, the London based government's intentions backfired. The British government (especially George III himself) was firmly convinced that the American colonies should pay their proper share of taxes, and imposed duties on sugar together with a Stamp Act to raise revenue. Protests and even rioting followed, and the Stamp Act was withdrawn. American political leaders fanned the flames by insisting that they should not be taxed by a government in which they were not represented.

Matters came to a head at the 'Boston Tea Party' when a cargo of tea was destroyed and dumped into the harbour by rioting rebels. The choice for England was therefore between a British political retreat to accommodate the colonies, or military action to impose rule from Britain. The latter was chosen and British soldiers were first sent to Massachusetts in early 1775, where the first fighting of the War of Independence commenced. Gradually the feeling spread amongst the colonists that complete independence from Britain was necessary, both as a political act and as a means of rallying mass support from the colonists. Independence was declared in July 1776, resulting in a war between the colonists and the British government.

The colonists won this war because of the difficulties that Britain faced in fighting successfully at such a distance from the home country. Britain was not helped by the French joining the war because of their continuing resentment over the defeat and loss of lands in 1763, and also because Spain joined in helping the colonists, thereby neutralising much of the British superiority in naval forces.

A small British army of 7,000 men was trapped in 1781 between American land forces and French sea forces. The British army under General Cornwallis (1738–1805) surrendered and peace negotiations followed with a treaty being signed in 1783, recognising the independence of the United States of America, whose western border was defined by the treaty as being the Mississippi River. Divisions remained amongst the colonists between those who still felt loyalty to the crown, and others who followed the rebel philosophy. Discussions ensued between politicians from the different former colonies, particularly over the relative powers of the new central American government in relation to the newly independent states.

Finally a meeting of delegates from all the states was staged in Philadelphia in 1787 lasting for four months. Much of the hard work was done by Thomas Jefferson (1743–1826), a lawyer from Virginia who would become the third US president after Washington (1732–1799) and John Adams (1735–1826), also a lawyer. The draft constitution which they agreed was then sent to the individual states, nine of whom ratified it in 1788, bringing the constitution into force. The constitution was designed to create a federal structure of largely self-governing states as the early Americans wished to avoid the centralised government that they saw in contemporary Britain, but otherwise much of the constitution followed the British Bill of Rights of almost 100 years earlier, setting up a tripartite structure comprising a legislature with an upper and lower house (Senate and Congress), an executive (Presidency), and a judiciary.

A year later, George Washington, formerly commanding the American forces in the war against the British, was sworn in as the first President of the new republic in 1789. The date of the signing of the constitution is significant: there were few constitutional republics in the world at the time, and conventional wisdom generally did not accept that this form of democracy was a good model to be emulated. The following year, possibly aided by the news from America, and by the home coming of French troops from the conflict, the French revolution burst out.

The American constitution derived its biggest influence from previous British political and legal principles, since most of the early politicians had grown up in a British colonial system with elected assemblies. These assemblies followed the British tradition of an upper and a lower chamber on the British model, but with the monarch replaced by an elected President, subject to a limited term. Where the constitution differed from the British model was in its belief in federalism as the newly liberated colonists did not wish a central government to have the degree of power over them that they had just rejected in the form of dominance from London and King George. Thus to this day American states retain different laws and powers amongst them, with laws and attitudes which are sometimes contradictory, though overall remaining subject to the constitution and its subsequent 27 ratified amendments.

The original United States expanded to the west in 1783 with new states being formed as settlers gradually moved west and across the Mississippi River. After the early years, the population of the USA stood at about 5 million at the time of Independence, a century later in 1900 it had reached 76 million, and a century after that 281 million was recorded by 2000. Texas had been incorporated in the Union in 1845, and the western states from Arizona and California north to Washington State joined late in the 19th century.

It may be said that the initial Spanish conquest of Mexico and much of those lands to the south, is also one of those events that really changed the future course of the world, setting up Central and South America as Spanish or Portuguese (Latin America) deriving from southern and catholic European culture, and North America with its northern European culture deriving from a predominantly protestant background.

Possible further reading:
A History of the United States by Philip Jenkins (Palgrave Macmillan)

Chapter 52
Art Through the Ages

Humankind has always seemed to have an urge to express feelings in art, with evidence for this extending back through the ages, well before the invention of writing. Expressions of art have been available as cave paintings, pottery, statuary and jewellery since well before the last Ice Age, and societies have been prolific in their portrayal of topics that were clearly important to them at each period of time. Cave paintings have been found in Europe dating back more than thirty thousand years, and abundant quantities of similar paintings of people and animals have been found in African caves where the presence of warm and dry conditions has aided their preservation in the Sahara.

Similar examples of ancient cave paintings are found in Australia, where the tradition of performing such paintings has been carried on until very recent times. In Europe, the paintings that remain are on the walls of caves in southern France and northern Spain, and remarkably have survived cold and damp conditions for many millennia.

Doubtless the survival of these paintings has been helped by the complete lack of light in the caves in which they were painted, but this in turn provides us with a considerable conundrum as to the purpose of the paintings and the audience for which they were made. The puzzle is the greater since paintings have often been discovered in caves where access is difficult. Most paintings are of animals, but stick men are present, and hand stencils made by burnt pigment on a hand held pressed to the wall, are also seen.

These early paintings were often made using red or yellow ochre, which are types of iron oxide, of which several different varieties were available. Ochre can still be used as a pigment for painting as it makes a type of paint on mixing with oil which dries quickly, and can be used to cover surfaces easily. Other uses for ochre were to use it as a raddle for marking sheep, or as a waxy waterproof covering on small buildings or structures. Ochre was also probably used as a body paint, and it seems that both the ancient Picts and the Celts in the British Isles used it as such. Ochre in its various different colours was still being used for painting, particularly on walls, by the Romans, though not the Greeks before them. The practice continued through into the renaissance, when it was highly valued for painting panels and frescoes.

At the same time as cave painting started, people began making pottery containers for cooking and keeping food. Early pottery dates back at least thirty thousand years, and is found in various different locations around the world. Pots were made from clay, and the early technique was one of coiling and pinching, with the potter making a long thin sausage of clay and then building up a vessel by coiling this round and round, and pinching the coils together. The technique of producing these wares, and in later years of decorating them, produces geographically individual products which have been extensively researched. The potter's wheel seems to have been invented in Mesopotamia, and was used from the third millennium onwards.

Once wheel-made pottery became abundant, then decoration of the pottery became gradually more artistic and complex. However, at the same time as the pottery wheel appears, the pots found in Mesopotamia become duller and only minimally decorated, indicating that the invention of the potter's wheel has allowed mass production, showing that at that time early division of labour and specialisation of jobs was possible within society. This in turn indicates that agriculture had developed sufficiently to provide surpluses so that while the mass of workers was still agricultural, there was sufficient food capacity to support specialist craftsmen in towns and villages.

Clay was also used for the production of figurines, which may have been talismans or fertility symbols, or may simply have been made as decorative objects. Similar artistic creations were doubtless made in wood, and have perished with the years, but they were also made in bone or ivory, some of which have survived to be found. Much of this new technology came about in the third millennium BC in the time of Sumerians in Mesopotamia, who also invented glass and casting in bronze, most of which was used for practical purposes, but artistic objects have also survived. Trade with the cities around the Mediterranean and in the Indus Valley would rapidly have spread the new technology. Large scale glass making came late to China around 500 AD after early glass plaques found from a thousand years earlier.

Unlike the small city states of Mesopotamia, Egypt moved very rapidly from a time of early civilisation to a single state, governed centrally. Like Mesopotamia, we have good knowledge of their customs and life style from the art that has come down to us. This has been available both through statuary, and in the case of Egypt, through lavishly decorated tombs of the dead Pharaohs. Egyptian writing is also a valuable source of information, as it was used not only as a record of day to day administration and trade, but also as records on monuments and statuary intended to survive as a record for future generations. Egyptian architecture in the form of fluted columns, sphinxes and great statuary animals failed to excite succeeding generations, and in Europe it is the architecture of the Greeks and the Romans which has been emulated by succeeding generations.

During the centuries before Christ, contact between east and west was minimal. Similarly, any influences, one upon the other, were minimal until medieval times. Knowledge of Chinese culture begins with people called the Shang, somewhere around 1700 BC, who dominated much of the Yellow River Valley. The Shang have left clues to their art in ritual burials, including bronze working techniques and some decorative art. Apart from this, life was largely agricultural with the peasantry growing subsistence crops: most traces of this early civilisation and its art have not survived the passage of time. Glass making came relatively late to China with a little decorative glass found from the 5th century BC, but not then made in any quantity for another thousand years.

During the Shang years, and the rule of the Chou who followed them, writing was highly developed and prized. It was of course the preserve of only a few, the nobility and their ruling elite, but the practice of calligraphy by this small class of individuals was not only highly prized but was of great importance to hold China together as a language of both government and culture. The buildings of the Shang and the Chou were predominantly wood, and their tombs were not elaborate, so our knowledge of these times is limited. There are however, ceramic relics, together with bronzes, which show highly developed skills in the production of both useful day to day items, and also of objects of art. Under the T'ang dynasty in the 7th and 8th centuries AD, China's craftsman perfected their skills with brass and ceramics: these achievements were continued through the Sung Dynasty which followed, and many of these achievements may have resulted in part from cross-fertilisation, with skills and ideas coming from Central Asia along the Silk Road from Persia and Arabia.

Later, in the 17th century under the Manchu emperors, knowledge expanded, and was included in a massive encyclopaedia of all known topics in five thousand volumes, commissioned by the Emperor. Throughout China's history the cultural emphasis seems to have been on perfecting and refining established techniques of calligraphy, poetry, painting and artistic production, as well as pottery, brass, ceramics and enamelling.

Greece occupies an important place in the history of western classical art, which originated in the early Bronze Age culture of the Cyclades islands, and that of the Minoan civilisation on Crete, where it appears that around 1600 BC there was an enormous eruption of the volcano Thera, which destroyed the mountainous island leaving a caldera, or volcanic rim, which we now know as the Island of Santorini. Early Greek art in the first half of the first millennium BC shows relatively primitive styles of sculpture and decorated pots. This art then developed into the so-called classical era of Greek art, in which considerable realism and perfection was achieved in sculpture.

At the same time, Greek architecture came to achieve great technical and artistic excellence, exemplified by the panels originally decorating the frieze around the Parthenon in Athens, but since transferred to the British Museum by Lord Elgin (and consequently known as the Elgin Marbles). Classical Greek art was subsequently to pass both to Rome, and to have a major influence on the eastern Christian Church (also known as the Greek Orthodox Church) in Byzantine and subsequent times. The architecture and sculpture of Ancient Greece is still widely imitated, whilst painting, pottery and jewellery have moved on and developed.

Art in Ancient Rome continued the production of excellent and realistic sculptures. Wall painting has been preserved for us because of the volcanic eruptions covering Pompeii and Herculaneum, which left these towns covered in several feet of protective ash, but has now been revealed by excavation. Mosaic floors were widely used, and often pictorial, and may be seen at many excavated Roman villas. Techniques with glass continued to develop with both colouring and moulded features being found. Gold was used by sandwiching a thin layer of patterned gold leaf between two layers of glass.

Much Roman architecture has survived as temples and other buildings, together with triumphal arches carved with historical reliefs, usually celebrating military campaigns and victories. Through such celebratory sculptures we have excellent representation of both civilian and military clothes and equipment. Trajan's Column in Rome, commemorating victory in the Dacian Wars of the first few years of the 2nd century AD, is a particularly fine example, standing almost one hundred feet high, and with a spiral frieze that winds around the shaft twenty-three times; the illustrations comprise one hundred and ninety metres of pictorial representation.

Islamic art has developed from Roman, Byzantine and early Persian art, and is particularly rich in calligraphy and decorative art, both in architecture and in texts. There is a predominant school of thought in Islam that pictures of the human form, let alone Allah, are sinful, and therefore representation of people is rare, and indeed is considered idolatry under Sharia Law. Most surviving figurative art depicting people is found in illuminated manuscripts or small miniatures; the style is relatively formal rather than realistic.

Islamic carpets, also known as Turkish or Persian carpets, are again almost invariably patterned and lacking in figures. Islamic pottery, whilst well developed and containing many technical advances, tends to be patterned and free of figures, but sometimes includes stylised animals or birds. Mosaic tiling has been widely used throughout Islamic countries from the 9th century onwards especially in mosques. Islamic metalwork was made mainly in brass or bronze with decoration, sometimes with figures in enamel since Islam prohibits gold and silver vessels for eating or drinking. Much well preserved Islamic architecture is still visible in Spain as well as Iran and Central Asia. In medieval times Islamic art concentrated on refining and perfecting the various techniques of mosaic decoration of buildings, together with pottery, glass and fabrics.

The performing arts, notably theatre, came to life in Ancient Greece. Many Greek plays have survived, and portray human stories of tragedy, triumph and conflict. The theme continued to be developed in Roman times, and many ruined Roman theatres are still to be seen around the Mediterranean within the extended Roman Empire. In Islam there seems to have been little tradition of the performing arts, and there has been no Arab theatre, though poetry, singing, dancing and storytelling have left an impressive history, albeit a less persisting one, and one which has not been accessible to Europeans.

Through the Dark Ages and into mediaeval times, the exchange of objects along the Silk Road ensured a cross-fertilisation of artistic objects between China and the developing Mediterranean and European cultures, with the imported items to Europe including mainly brass, pottery and silks. Onto this bedrock of classical Mediterranean culture came the development of the Renaissance, and with the Renaissance comes innovation in art, although much of the technical abilities of previous generations had already been consolidated in sculpture, woodworking, pottery and painting. But poetry and writing continued to develop and enthral audiences in ways which can still be appreciated.

Music and drama became widely available, and continue to develop (see Chapter 55 – Music). Through mediaeval times religious subjects and the Church had a huge influence, indeed monopoly, of most aspects of culture, and this slowly breaks up through the Renaissance and into the Modern Era. These developments were greatly helped by the invention of printing, but also by the increasing concentration of people into towns and cities, where an audience and a questioning society were always eager to experience the new art forms.

Possible further reading:
Art History by Dana Arnold (A Very Short Introduction, OUP)
The Ascent of Man by Jacob Bronowski (BBC, MacDonald Futura)

Chapter 53
Literature and Theatre

Both literature and drama come onto the human scene with urbanisation. This is because the writing of literature requires a literate audience to appreciate it, and the creation of drama in theatre similarly requires a moderate sized audience to make it worthwhile. Much early work is of religious origin and may have evolved slowly from rituals staged in early conurbations when the population would have assembled at important times in the calendar year to participate in worship and spectacle. We have seen earlier that writing came relatively early in Mesopotamia by the third millennium BC, and written traditions were important both in recording and improving agricultural techniques. Although writing and scribes were present in the years before Christ, the proportion of any population achieving literacy was small.

The first literature, as opposed to records, accounts or instructions, is the Saga of Gilgamesh. This is an ancient legend first written down around 2,000 BC, and is a type of morality tale involving a struggle against the elements of nature, and eventual human mortality. It includes tales of floods, which were both common and unpredictable in Mesopotamia and the Nile valley, and which may have been the precursor to the story of the biblical flood for which Noah built his ark. Gilgamesh was a real ruler in the city of Uruk, or Erech, in modern day Iraq. Uruk grew up alongside the Euphrates from about 4,000 BC and was ruled by Gilgamesh who achieved fame for fortifying it against his enemies around 2,600 BC.

In India, along the Indus River, literature evolved as a collection of Vedic religious hymns, and is now one of the sacred texts of Hinduism. It was probably composed in the middle of the 2nd millennium BC, and amongst the hymns and prayers are included mythological and poetical accounts of the origin of the world. It was probably not written down for almost two thousand years and was initially transmitted orally through the ages. This underlines the problem with much early literature in the ages before writing had been devised, namely that accounts probably changed with repetition over the passage of time before these accounts were written down. Writing in India emerges around 700 BC when the Aryan culture became predominant in the Ganges Valley: the Aryans were nomads who migrated to India from the north, bringing with them Bronze Age technology.

In the middle of the 1st millennium BC, there is a sudden upsurge in written records available to the historian to appreciate and interpret. First Greek and then

Latin, flower with all the possibilities that writing brings, even when only a minority of the population can read and write. From this time forwards a written record is often available, though the passage of time and the degradations of war mean that much of the historical record and early literature is now lost to us.

First the Greeks, and then the Romans, offer theatre and drama to us around this time. This compensates in part for any lack of literacy in the community as a whole since illiterate citizens could still come to the local theatre and enjoy the spoken work as drama. The year 776 BC saw the first Olympic Games, which were part competition and part spectacular theatre. The stories of the *Iliad* and the *Odyssey* were written down by Homer who probably lived sometime in the 8th century BC, and are the first great writings of the classical period; the two stories appear to be consistent with what we know of the Bronze Age around the Aegean Sea.

The two works start with the *Iliad* portraying the siege of Troy and the Trojan War, over the disagreement between King Agamemnon and the warrior Achilles over Helen of Troy, a princess of exceptional beauty. The *Iliad* is followed by the *Odyssey*, which describes Odysseus' long ten year journey home after the fall of Troy and recounts many startling adventures and dangers. It is interesting to note the observations of Homer about his fellow men and the mythical beings that they meet. Relationships with the Greeks gods are also described where it is revealed that unlike the distant all powerful and infallible gods of other religions, the Greek gods of classical times appeared like human superheroes adventuring and warring amongst themselves.

The Greeks were the first to invent history as a new type of literature, including known facts as content, and criticism linked to religious belief and moral teaching. This followed the first theatre which was the ritual of religion and was therefore fostered by rulers and their priesthood. Greek theatre matured in the 4th century BC, the era of Aeschylus, Sophocles and Euripides, many of whose plays have survived and are still performed today, most of them falling into the category of either tragedy or comedy, often with political and sometimes scurrilous comment.

Roman literature and theatre that followed some five hundred to a thousand years later, is also dependent upon urbanisation. At a time when any literature had to be laboriously copied by hand, the use of theatre provided a rapid short cut for conveying stories, attitudes and morals to a large audience. Virgil (70–19 BC) is one of the greatest poets of ancient Roman times; his Aeneid is modelled after the Iliad and the Odyssey, and follows a Trojan refugee, Aeneas, who escapes after the sack of Troy, and at the end of his travels is found in Rome. Myth subsequently has Aeneas as a forebear of Romulus and Remus, who were saved and brought up as infants by a wolf. Later in life, they fell out over the exact site of the new city they wished to build, and Remus was killed by his brother, which is why Rome came to be founded by Romulus after whom it is named.

Roman theatres were built all around the Mediterranean and helped to provide the glue that bound all Romans together as they forged their large empire; when new towns were built as the empire enlarged a theatre was usually included as one of the municipal buildings. These theatres were large and semi-circular; their dimensions required that the art of diction and acting needed to be of high quality so that all the spectators could appreciate the dialogue and the action. The best preserved of all Roman theatres is at Orange, north of Avignon in France. The Romans also built amphitheatres with seating all around the central arena, but these were reserved for the spectacle of games, both contests of horsemanship and fighting, as well as animals and people fighting each other. The cultural peaks of the Roman Empire gradually declined in the 4th century and were thrown into severe disarray following the sack of Rome in 410 AD and its subsequent decline.

Later, Arabic and Muslim culture coalesced and became refined in the years after Mohammed's death in 632. Much Greek and Latin literature was translated into Arabic, and culture peaked in the 9th and 10th centuries, at which time there was a higher literacy rate in the Muslim Empire than in mediaeval Europe. A later cultural peak came in Muslim Spain in the 11th and 12th centuries when the Spanish part of the Islamic Empire became known as Al-Andalus. This Arabic culture was predominantly literary, although at the same time wonderful architecture and ceramics were being produced. Much scientific work was produced, principally as huge encyclopaedic collections. Performances of poetry and music were much appreciated, but theatre, in the sense recognised by the Greeks and Romans, was largely absent.

Arabic medical writings from those times dominated mediaeval European thinking for many centuries afterwards until the Enlightenment and the Renaissance. Initially Arabic visual art was broad, but with the development of Islamic thinking, the making of likenesses of the human form, and especially attempts to portray the likeness of the Prophet himself, generally became forbidden. Islamic art is recognised for its depiction of patterns, calligraphy and floral depictions, though it is still possible to find depictions of both Mohammed and other people in early historical Islamic art.

In Europe, the Dark Ages of the 5th to 8th centuries came to a close with the coronation of Charlemagne at the beginning of the 9th century. Although his reign cannot compare with Islam or Byzantium, he recruited large numbers of scholars and scribes, who devised a standard script now called 'Carolingian Miniscule', and many ancient textbooks were copied and made available. His accession and subsequent reign may be seen as the birth of a truly European entity.

Among his scholars was Alcuin of York (734–804), who managed Charlemagne's library in Aachen, and who wrote and taught extensively. In addition to being a great sponsor of art, Charlemagne also sponsored architecture, he standardised coinage, dividing a pound of silver into 240 denarii, or pennies, as a monetary system at about the same as King Offa of Mercia also standardised English money into a system of pounds made up of 240 pennies, this measure of currency lasted in England until the 1970s when decimal coinage was introduced. Mediaeval Europe did not develop literature and theatre much further until the early Renaissance (Chapter 39). With the spread of writing and literacy north, the Norse Sagas of the 10th and 11th centuries were written down around 200 years after they had become living oral stories: they formed a fascinating documentation of early Scandinavian times and exploration.

With the invention of printing, and the ability to produce large numbers of printed copies of books and plays from the end of the 15th century, there came an immense crescendo of expansion in European written literature and drama. Much of the early printed work in the Renaissance was sacred rather than secular, but this situation was rapidly reversed. The works of Chaucer (written just before the invention of the printing press) were printed, and there was an upsurge in poetry.

Many works from this time remain on modern reading and study lists, including those by the poet John Donne (1572–1631), the philosopher Thomas Hobbes (1588–1679), the English writer and poet John Milton (1608–1674), John Bunyan (1628–1688) who wrote *Pilgrim's Progress*, John Dryden (1631–1700), dramatist and poet, and Samuel Pepys (1633–1703), English MP and early highly formative minister for the navy, whose diary gives us a contemporary account of the great fire of London in 1666.

At the end of the 17th century in England, there was a flowering of theatre after the very repressive years of Puritan rule following the civil war, both in terms of building theatres, and in the production of works for the theatre. Initially much early theatre was performed by small travelling troupes of actors who often put on their plays in the galleried courtyards of coaching inns, or sometimes put on morality plays in churches. These players notably performed works by William Shakespeare (1565–1616), but also by his contemporaries Christopher Marlowe (1564–1593), Ben Johnson (1572–1637), and the first English woman playwright Aphra Behn (1640–1689). A little later, iconic writers in Germany included Immanuel Kant (1724–1804), Johann Goethe (1749–1832) and Johann Schiller (1759–1805), and in France Moliere (1622–1673), Voltaire (1694–1778) and Jean-Jacques Rousseau (1712–1778).

Theatre in ancient China is recorded as far back as the second millennium BC during the Shang Dynasty gradually developing into mediaeval times and including music, mime, acrobatics and puppetry, a combination of which has developed more recently including all these elements and becoming known as 'Chinese Opera'. Japanese theatre is much more recent dating from early mediaeval times with scripts surviving from the 12th and 13th centuries, often involving mime and puppetry, together with masked actors.

In India, theatre emerged at the end of the first millennium BC somewhat later than its predecessors in Greece and Rome, and was in the form of drama in Sanskrit, again often highly stylised. The theatre scene was active through the first millennium AD but was then suppressed following the Islamic conquests which arrived in India in the 10th and 11th centuries. Theatre only emerged again with the advent of British rule in the 19th century.

All of these dramatists dealt with the human condition and its problems and rewards. From this we learn that the conundrums of life and the moral problems faced by people four or five hundred years ago (and even in the Greek and Roman eras) are the same problems which continue to trouble modern populations, and that authors writing all those hundreds of years ago were little different in their attitudes and responses to human problems to those writing at the beginning of the 21st century. There has, of course, been more universal literacy, increasing emancipation of people in general and women in particular, but 16th century English literature and theatre remains both intelligible and relevant to a modern audience.

Possible further reading:
Literature and Western Man by J. B. Priestley (Penguin)

Chapter 54
Music

Musical history extends back into pre-historic times from which we have no records. The human voice is a highly versatile instrument and it is probable that from the earliest evolutionary days of homo sapiens the ability to sing and make music would have been both widely used and equally widely appreciated. Music is both ubiquitous and ancient among all human tribes and in all eras as far as we know. It is used at many gatherings from weddings to funerals and for many other celebrations. The division between performers and audience is relatively recent, and even more recent is the advent of specific buildings for the performance of music such as theatres and concert halls.

Our first historical trace is a flute made from the bone of a vulture wing, which was found in Germany and dated to around 35,000 BC. Other ancient Stone Age flutes have been found in China, India and America made from bamboo and clay. In those early days some musical inspiration may well have come from bird song.

Music may be generated in many ways apart from the singing voice. Secondly, percussion and the beating of hollow wood, or drums made from stretched animal skins, is the next simplest. The third means of generating a musical note is by blowing through a tubular structure like that early flute, with or without a vibrating reed. Thus, in early times, the horns of various animals were used, giving rise to the name as well as to other present musical instruments of the brass and woodwind sections of an orchestra, which includes modern horns, trumpets and trombones.

Woodwind instruments often use a vibrating reed, but we should note that modern wind instruments are no longer necessarily made of wood, nor do they necessarily have a reed, and a modern metal flute exemplifies this. As a variant on the blowing theme, organs have been made and used since before Roman times. The organ pipes resonate to produce a musical note because of the air blown through them. In a way this is simply a giant mechanical version of pan pipes, but with the ability to activate several pipes at the same time, using a bellows to pump air.

Fourth come instruments with taut strings or cords, where initially the strings were plucked and made a twanging sound dependent upon the length and tautness of the string. These instruments have evolved from early harps and lyres into their much more sophisticated modern counterparts, whilst also spawning instruments with several strings which are made to resonate by stroking the strings with something like a violin bow. From the static lyre or guitar to the bowed violin is thus a fairly small theoretical step, but one which took a lot of gradual practical development over many generations to produce a useful musical instrument.

Fifthly, stringed instruments can also be made in which the strings are not plucked but rather struck by small hammers, and in this way early harpsichords with keyboards evolved, and we shall return to this later. Finally, and most recently, music can now be generated electronically, and again many notes can be produced simultaneously.

In order to activate several notes at the same time a keyboard is usually necessary, by means of which the player can open several organ pipes simultaneously, or strike a variety of the strings on a zither or harpsichord. From these early beginnings came the keyboard instruments in the early Middle Ages known as spinets or virginals. Gradually human ingenuity made these instruments bigger, louder, and possessing a more extensive musical span. However, they all suffered from one problem, namely that the note once generated could not be damped or silenced, therefore the note continued to resonate as it died away, interfering with the perception of any subsequent notes that were generated. Many varieties of keyboard instruments were produced, but all suffered from this lack of damping of the notes, and from the inability of the player to regulate the volume of the sound to produce either loud or soft music.

At the beginning of the 18th century, there came together musically the two elements that often seem to be required for significant new inventions; an original thinker with significant new ideas, and a sponsor able to fund the necessary time and development. Thus came about the collaboration in Florence of the wealthy dilettante, Ferdinando de Medici (1663–1713), who had made Florence a very important musical centre, and his musical curator, Bartolomeo Cristofori (1655–1731), who was a talented harpsichord maker. Cristofori experimented with different ways of developing the harpsichord using the hammer action of the clavichord and adding a damping mechanism to produce an instrument which could be played either softly or loudly, and which, because of its soft and loud capability, became known as a pianoforte (soft-loud).

Cristofori is regarded as the inventor of the piano, but only built a few of these instruments, all of them somewhat different and experimental, but they did not catch on in Italy, and the current big-name composers of the time, including Bach, Handel and Vivaldi did not write music for them. Outside Italy however, the instruments were more widely welcomed and were further developed.

In England, in the second half of the 18th century, George III's new young queen, Charlotte of Mecklenburg (1744–1818), was extremely musical and a great patron of the arts; both Handel and an eight year old Mozart were summoned to play for her. Theatres in London were being built, including Covent Garden in 1780 seating 2,100 people, and Drury Lane in the same year seating 2,000, although the Sheldonian theatre in Oxford seating up to 1,000, built in the 1660s was the venue for the first public music concert a century earlier, and the Globe theatre for drama dates from 1599, seating (mainly standing) up to 3,000.

A German migrant cabinet maker called Johannes Zumpe (1726–1790) started making small square pianos with a range of five octaves which instantly became very popular with the general public, particularly as they cost much less than the harpsichords of the time. He was able to make about fifty of these early 'square pianos' each year. He was followed by a Scot called John Broadwood (1732–1812) who rapidly geared up to produce his much larger, more refined and sturdy grand pianos. At the same time a 21–year-old Mozart met with a Bavarian pianoforte maker called Johann Stein (1728–1792), and was captivated by the virtuosic possibilities unlocked by Stein's instrument (there is no relationship with Heinrich Steinweg who anglicised his name to Henry Steinway on emigrating to America and founding the famous piano firm that still carries his name).

Over the succeeding fifty years from 1780, popularity of the piano as a solo instrument burgeoned. As composers, including Mozart, Beethoven, Schubert and Schumann all increased both the technical virtuosity and the demands upon the instrument, so the piano became more and more sturdy and versatile, gradually resulting in the instrument which we know today. Shortly after Cristofori's first piano was made in 1700, the tuning fork was invented by British lutenist John Shore in 1711, helping to standardise equal temperament between instruments. John Broadwood took over his brother-in-law's harpsichord business in 1783 and started making pianos with added pedals and a damping action as well as extending the keyboard at both bass and treble ends; the frames of his instruments were made of very sturdy wood, but still capable of gradually being deformed leading to loss of tone.

The talented Austrian musician and composer, Ignaz Pleyel (1751–1831) came to Paris in 1797 during the French revolution where he had several close calls with the Revolutionary authorities. In 1807 he set up a music publishing business and started making pianos in what became a highly successful business, partly at least because he introduced iron frames which would not deform. He also revised and pioneered the early upright design which became very popular for domestic use during the 19th century.

At the same time as the piano was evolving, so were too the percussion, brass, woodwind and stringed instruments. Horns and trumpets, which had been confined to a single key, were provided with valves to change keys and play flats and sharps, or a slide to achieve same purpose for the trombone. The stringed instrument evolution had somewhat preceded the development of other instruments, such that the violins and other instruments of the violin family produced by craftsmen such as Antonio Stradivari (1644–1737) and Antonio Guanieri (1698–1744) in Cremona in the early 18th century have never yet been surpassed. Amazingly, many of these 300 year old instruments continue in daily use today on concert platforms with around 1,000 Stradivarius instruments still in existence and often regularly used.

Our understanding of musical tuning and the relationship of one note to another other starts with Pythagoras in the 6th century BC who was listening to a blacksmith at work one day and noted that the noise made varied with different sizes of anvil, as indeed it varied with different sizes of bell. He noted that two hammers, one weighing half as much as the other produced a musical note of a perfect octave. Intermediate weights of anvil produced intermediate notes, some of which were harmonically tuneful and some were discordant. In this way he arrived at a chromatic scale in which the octave is divided into twelve different pitches, each of which is a half tone above or below its neighbour.

Although Arab and Chinese music uses often smaller intervals, this semitone has come to be the smallest standard musical interval used in western music. The octave names the interval between one musical pitch and the next highest or lowest note with double or half its frequency; this is because the frequency of vibration of the first note will sound a perfect octave if the frequency is then doubled or halved (and this is the reason why the notation of Guido d'Arezzo repeats itself every octave upwards or downwards, of which more later). The intervals repeat on a logarithmic basis.

Attempts have been made to divide the octave into smaller fragments than the twelve semitones, and in the 20th century atonal music has been written which does not respect the chromatic scale or the idiosyncrasies of the human ear. Such music is usually difficult to understand or enjoy. Musical intervals smaller than a semitone seem somewhat discordant to western ears, and are often said to be 'out of tune'. Keyboard instruments have also been designed with more than twelve notes in an octave, again there is considerable difficulty in appreciating the music which can be played on them, and in addition, the player is confronted with enormous physical difficulties if an octave is divided into more than twelve fractions.

With wind instruments, the interval is usually predetermined by the length of tubing and the spacing of the holes bored in the instrument, but the trombone, for instance, is completely free of such problems, and so are all stringed instruments which may be played with much smaller intervals. However, if all instruments start to play with each other, then it is necessary that the same system and intervals between notes is used by each of the instruments.

Necessarily therefore, we pass to the concept of 'equal temperament'. In mediaeval times solitary minstrels, or even church choirs, could decide the starting note when commencing to make music. Today the number of players performing in unison is often considerable and it only requires a moment's thought to realise the chaos that would result if they each chose their own note on which to start. We take it for granted that at the beginning of an orchestral concert the players all tune together to a single note, usually given by the oboe. Whilst the oboe's note is fixed, it is particularly important that all the stringed instruments are tuned to match this note whereupon the playing can commence in harmony.

Equal temperament has come about thanks to Pythagoras' recognition of the mathematical basis for generating sound and organising the generation of sound by octaves. Although one may argue that this system forces music into a relative strait-jacket, the advantages the system allows, in terms of versatility, are very much greater than any disadvantage.

In earlier times, there were two predominant ways in which people made music. The first of these was usually out of doors at times of celebration or ceremony; the music needed to be loud so that the participating dancers and the audience could hear and enjoy it. It also needed to be loud because the priest, king or emperor saw it as a means of impressing the audience of subjects. The other form of music making was often indoors and much more intimate and might involve a single instrument, frequently accompanying the singing of one or possibly more voices. When church music first came inside, it was usually as unaccompanied singing. Through the 16th century, as more and more music of an often secular, rather than sacred type, came into larger buildings, there was less need for the brash, brassy instruments of previous centuries, so that softer stringed instruments were able to provide softer and more subtle tones.

During the 17th century, music developed from public spectacle, both sacred in church and secular for important occasions, to also becoming an important recreational occasion, initially in royal or wealthy salons, but then becoming a more accessible affair with the first public concert in England performed in 1672. In this way the genesis of the modern orchestra appeared and rapidly developed towards the size and sound that we recognise today.

Along the way, all the instruments have continued to develop, some changing much more than others; thus modern stringed instruments remain very similar to their ancestors of three centuries ago, while a modern grand piano is very different to its predecessors of that time, while still remaining a related and recognisable keyboard instrument. New instruments have appeared, some of which like the saxophone have found a widespread use, while others were briefly fashionable, but failed to secure a lasting place in music making.

In the same way that writing appeared and evolved slowly from about 2,000 BC onwards, music initially had no system by which it could be written down so that one musician could preserve it in a way that others could understand and reproduce it. Previously was necessary for musicians to learn by heart and by repetition, which limited the spread and availability of music. Early attempts at musical notation are known from Sumerian times soon after 2,000 BC, but such notation was primitive and inaccurate. Although, for instance, we know that the Romans indulged in music, we have no idea what it must have sounded like since there was no means of recording it in writing.

For the introduction of a universal system of notation, which has become the workhorse of western music, we have to thank a Benedictine monk and choirmaster called Guido from Arezzo in Italy who lived in the years following the millennium. Guido described a system using a central horizontal line on the paper from which notes can be placed going up or down in tone. From this has developed the present notation of treble and bass clefs, and different symbols for the notes themselves indicating their length and other characteristics. No other system of musical notation has appeared over the last thousand years and thus, unlike language, musical notation helpfully remains the same across the language barriers of speech.

When music was developing rapidly in the 17th century in Europe, the first attempt was made to produce a system of written notation for dance by Pierre Beauchamp (1631–1705), who was born into a family of French dance masters and first appeared at the Versailles court of Louis XIV at a young age, later becoming an influential member and choreographer of the royal troupe. He also taught Louis himself, who is often regarded as the father of modern dance and ballet, which he sponsored energetically, even appearing in the royal entertainments himself. Louis was a culture-loving autocrat with enormous finance at his disposal and it was for these self-publicising, opulent and glamorous activities, including personally acting the part of the sun, that he became known as the 'Sun King'.

His entertainments often contained singing and in this way he may be seen as responsible for the start of early opera as well as formal dance or ballet. In the 20th century dance notation has seen the production of further, and more sophisticated systems of notation, with computer-based recording methods being the most recent innovations. As noted, apart from dance, Louis' long reign of 72 years (1643–1715) was also seminal in laying the seeds of early opera with Jean-Baptiste Lully (1632–1681) prominent and prolific as a royal choreographer and composer; he followed the early pioneering operatic steps of Claudio Monteverdi (1567–1643) who worked initially for the Italian court in Mantua, and later at St Mark's Basilica in Venice.

Louis' extravagances and glories at court, and the contrast with the lives of ordinary people, may be seen as contributing to the causes behind the French revolution. The first purpose-built theatre for musical performance was the Sheldonian Theatre in Oxford financed and built in the 1660s by the then current Archbishop of Canterbury, Gilbert Sheldon (1598–1677), who was also Chancellor of the University at the time.

Possible further reading:
Big Bangs by Howard Goodall (Vintage UK, Random House)

Chapter 55
Russia from 1584

Following the death of Ivan the Terrible in 1584 (chapter 24), his simpleton adult son Fyodor (1557–1598) became the notional ruler of Russia. Fyodor was very religious but oblivious to politics, and a Council was appointed to rule on his behalf. Amongst the Council was Boris Godunov (1551–1605) who was of Tatar origin from a princely line of the Golden Hoard of Mongols, and was the first Russian ruler not to be a descendent of Rurik; he became a member of the Oprichniki at the age 20, gradually progressing upwards through the ranks. He emerged as the most influential member of the Regency Council running the affairs of state on Fyodor's behalf.

For the next 14 years, Boris ruled as the most prominent member of the regency council without too many problems, recovering some border towns from Sweden, and building fortresses along the north-western and south-eastern borders of Russia to keep the Finns and the Tatars under control. He encouraged many new settlements in Siberia. He is particularly remembered for a law in 1597 forbidding peasants to transfer from one landowner to a another, thus essentially making them serfs with virtually no rights.

Fyodor died in 1598 and Boris Godunov was unanimously elected by the National Assembly and then crowned Tsar. He was a relatively benign but still autocratic ruler, encouraging trade with the rest of Europe and Scandinavia. A constant cloud over his reign was the widely held perception that he had arranged the murder of Ivan's son Fyodor. After Boris' death from natural causes in 1605 his own son, Fyodor II, ruled for only a few months until he and his mother were murdered by enemies of the Godunovs.

The years that followed were characterised by political instability, and several pretenders to the throne emerged. The most serious faction was backed by a Polish-Lithuanian coalition and moved quickly to take over Moscow with an army. The chaos was not helped by the purges that had been carried out, first under Ivan the Terrible, and then under Boris Godunov, such that there was very little nobility left with any power, and most of the institutions of state, including the Church and monasteries, had been neutered and were in thrall to the central government.

An episode of climatic depression, crop failures and famine was made even worse by an outbreak of plague, with up to a third of the population dying. Pretenders to the line of succession from the Rurik dynasty appeared, including the Polish and Lithuanian one mentioned above, a monk who was supported with an army and came to occupy Moscow and proclaim himself Tsar, even marrying a Polish princess. The situation was never stable however, and in 1612, an unlikely combination of a further Polish prince and a merchant marched on Russia with an amateurish army and besieged the occupying Poles. They were remarkably successful, and the Poles surrendered on being offered a promise of safe conduct: however once they emerged from the city the promise was set aside and they were all promptly massacred.

A new National Council was convened, selected from the remaining aristocrats, church dignitaries and merchants. The Council met against a background of chaos which reinforced the perceived need for a strong and absolute ruler. From the ranks of the nobles the Romanovs put forward a 17 year old candidate, Mikhail Romanov, who claimed a tenuous link with Ivan the Terrible, as Ivan's wife Anastasia had come from one branch of the Romanov family. Mikhail, although only 17, was a grand-nephew of Ivan and was thus seen as a comforting link with the old and successful dynasty.

Mikhail would be able to satisfy the Russian need for a Tsar with unrestricted authority to promote national unity and security, and it was thought at the time that because of his youth he would be deferential and easily manipulated. Thus, the Romanov family started on a three hundred year monopoly of Tsardom, which would last until the time of the 1917 revolution, commencing initially with Mikhail and his successor, who together brought fifty years of stability.

To the west of Russia, Siberian colonisation had already started with Ivan the Terrible granting lands shortly before his death. During his reign Ivan had also annexed other land masses, considerably enlarging the area of Russia. The draw of Siberia at that time was the trapping of fox, sable and other valuable fur animals, but Siberia also started to become a penitentiary at this time, in the form of settlements into which citizens could be banished for daring to oppose the Tsar and the political elite. Russia was still a very backward country, with virtually no stone or brick buildings, and with a very static peasantry, both in terms of attitude and clothing: in addition at this time in the first half of the 17th century, the Russian economy was still purely agricultural and dependent upon serfs, where the rest of Europe was experiencing diminishing numbers of serfs and increasing industrialisation, with early population drift from the country to the cities.

To the east, Poland and Lithuania had amalgamated through the Union of Lublin in 1659, which incorporated Lithuania's Ukrainian territories into the Kingdom of Poland, and set up an aristocratic democracy with elected monarchy, in stark contrast to the hereditary autocracy of Moscow. Following the Union of Lublin, Poland and Lithuania were able to repel all Russian attempts to expand to the west, but in the Thirteen Years War (1654–1667) Polish land was lost to Moscow beyond the Dnieper River. As the Polish Lithuanian Union became weaker, Russian expansion continued under Peter the Great (1672–1725), who was able to push Russian boundaries further, and was finally able to establish Russian control over Estonia, capturing the province of Livonia with its valuable

Baltic coast to the north-east, thereby finally endowing Russia with a Baltic seaport.

Following war between Poland and Sweden (1626–1629), a large area of Livonia became Swedish with Riga becoming the second largest Swedish city. Sweden would lose this part of Livonia and Estonia, together with Ingria to the north-east, back to Russia in 1710. Following the Treaty of Nystad in 1721 between Russia and Sweden, Peter the Great made German the official language, and when Poland was partitioned in 1772 Polish Livonia became Russian. Peter founded his new capital at St Petersburg to make the most of his Baltic port acquisition (St Petersburg named incidentally after St Peter and not after the Tsar himself).

Tsar Peter I ('The Great') had come to the throne in 1681 at the age of 9, and a Council, including his mother, had ruled in his name for the next fifteen years before he assumed full power, and was able to get rid of all the factional divisions of his courtiers. He was an imposing individual of six foot seven, who was determined to reform Russia and emulate much of what was happening in western Europe. He set up Russia's first civil service on the basis of meritocratic promotion rather than the previous aristocratic cronyism. He instituted a proper army and navy, and in general westernised Russia.

At the age of 24, and just before becoming Tsar, he had travelled for a year through Europe as a merchant seaman, ending at the Royal Dockyards at Greenwich. He used the knowledge he acquired on this trip to found the Russian Navy, using imported British and other foreign expatriates he persuaded to come to Russia. By doing this he was able to achieve domination of the Baltic Sea following war with Sweden, and he was also able to gain a foothold in the Black Sea, to provide a most important southern seaport for Russia.

As part of his expansionism, he recruited a Danish map maker and explorer, Vitus Bering (1681–1741), to join the new Russian Navy and explore the northern and eastern coast of Russia. Bering is commemorated in the sea, straits and islands which bear his name. He also landed in Alaska, where a Russian expedition set up the first Polar Russian settlement on Kodiak Island. Russia never colonised Alaska, but Spanish, British and American settlements also sprang up there, all attempting to exploit the natural resources of the land. Alaska was then largely ignored by Russia over the next century until it was bought by the United States in 1867 for just over seven million dollars.

Peter's return to Russian in 1698 after his time visiting the rest of Europe was brought about by a rebellion of mutinous troops, following which hundreds were executed to restore discipline. Peter thought his sister Sophia was responsible for the mutiny and banished her to a monastery. Following his return Peter implemented the building of his new ice-free port at St Petersburg, a huge venture which turned hundreds of acres of marshland into a viable city, including a large palace for the Tsar: many serfs died in during the construction work in the appalling conditions during the land reclamation and building.

The Great Northern War (1700–1721) was fought against Sweden over an extended period of time with the decisive battle coming at Poltava in central

Ukraine in 1709. The battle marks the beginning of Sweden's decline from the status of a Great Power, and after this battle Hanover and Prussia joined Russia, Norway and Denmark in coalition against Sweden. Over the next few years continued fighting finally ended with Russia as the dominant power around the Baltic and Sweden defeated and emasculated.

In his final years, Peter the Great continued with a reformist programme and an emphasis on education for all Russians (except of the course the large majority of serfs), and at the same time continued to downgrade the Church, abolishing the position of Patriarch of Moscow and instituting instead a Holy Synod, while also retaining the power of the Tsar to appoint Bishops.

Peter died in 1725, having previously seen his second wife Katherine crowned as co-ruler ('Empress and Autocrat of all the Russias') a year previously. She only survived Peter by a couple of years, and in turn was succeeded by Peter II, grandson of Peter the Great, whose father Alexis been accused of treason and imprisoned by Peter the Great, dying in prison. Peter II was only aged 11 and died three years later. Peter the Great's niece, Anna (1693–1740), succeeded in 1730 and ruled for the next ten years with a very antipathetic attitude towards the reforms introduced by her uncle.

After Anna's death, Peter I's daughter Elizabeth (1709–1762) came to the Tsardom and started her reign promising no executions, but instead conciliation and compromise. She befriended a Prussian, Princess Catherine, who married her nephew and heir, Peter III. Elizabeth reigned for twenty years without executing a single individual.

In 1762, Peter III became Tsar having married Catherine of Prussia (1729–1796), later to be known as Catherine the Great. He concluded a peace treaty with Prussia, which angered a lot of the Russian nobility who were anti-Prussian. A year later Catherine organised a palace coup that deposed, and then murdered, her husband Peter, leaving her, a Prussian foreigner, as Empress of Russia, which she would rule for the next thirty four years. She then organised a land grab in the south to provide a neutral border, which lit up ethnic tensions that have continued ever since. In collusion with Prussia and Austria, she partitioned Poland, but on the intellectual front she acquired much great art and was greatly enamoured of Voltaire, with whom she corresponded and discussed ideas of reform. It seems initially it was her intention to reform society, and in particular the rigid caste system and nobility in Russia.

By 1774, she had invited Gregory Potemkin (1739–1791), an aristocratic military leader, both onto her Council of State, and into her bed. A Cossack revolt finally occurred which had been brewing against Catherine on the grounds that her reforms were anti-Russian. Potemkin masterminded the defeat of the rebels and execution of their leader, but afterwards Catherine turned her back on her liberal intentions and issued a defiant defence of autocracy. She granted nobles freedom of property and protection from the law in exchange for their loyalty and obedience to the monarch.

When the French Revolution burst on the world, she was horrified by the execution of Louis XVI and a similar possible prospect of revolution in Russia.

When she died in 1796 she was succeeded by her son, Paul I, who reversed many of his mother's relatively liberal actions, and increased the size and role of the secret police. He antagonised many people doing this and was murdered by palace guards only five years into his reign. In turn, he was succeeded by Alexander (1777–1825), the grandson of Catherine, whose chief advisor advocated a more European system of government and liberalism to replace the arbitrary autocracy of the previous centuries of Russian rule.

Alexander was a weak individual who followed the opinion of the most recent person he had been talking to, and in the end was unable to follow through the advice of liberalisation and constitutional reform given by his chief advisor Mikhail Speransky (1772–1839), thus leaving Russian autocracy, secret police, and backwardness unchanged. He made an informal pact with Napoleon to split Europe into French and Russian spheres of influence, but Napoleon reneged on this and then invaded Russia. Prior to this, Alexander had entertained paranoid thoughts about his military establishment becoming too powerful and he had purged seven Field Marshals and over three hundred Generals, leaving the Russian army in no fit state to confront the French.

At the Battle of Borodino, 75 miles from Moscow in 1812 Russia lost 45,000 troops to Napoleon's army, but gained a lot of confidence. Despite this the French continued to press on to Moscow which they occupied for a month. The Russians had burnt Moscow before retreating thus depriving the French of food and shelter, so that inevitably Napoleon had to retreat with his freezing and starving army. Some 300,000 soldiers are estimated to have died by the time he left Russia. France was then unable to defend itself and the allies occupied Paris. Russian troops, in particular amongst the invading force, tasted a more prosperous and libertarian society in France, stories and memories of which they subsequently brought back home to Russia.

Alexander was afraid of the liberal thinking which followed this, and his paranoia was reinforced by two failed assassination attempts. No liberalisation was permitted and autocratic enforcement was being planned when he died in 1825. He left a backward state with a poor economy, thanks to a combination of wars and an increased expenditure on secret police. His promises of reform had never materialised, and riots broke out in St Petersburg after his death, fomented by disillusioned troops who had become known as the Decembrists (who were said to be inspired by the American Revolution, and possibly also the French Revolution).

3,000 Decembrist soldiers mutinied on a military parade ground in St Petersburg and were shelled by the Tsar's artillery; those who did not die straightaway were arrested, tried and sent to Siberia or executed. The longer term response to the Decembrist revolt by his younger brother, Nikolas I who succeeded Alexander, was to increase the powers of the secret police and to increase political repression. Nikolas announced a new official state doctrine of 'orthodoxy, autocracy and nationhood', a series of values in stark contrast to the liberté, egalité and fraternité of just a few years previously in France.

Nikolas I (1796–1855) ruled all of his thirty years up to 1855 in the now traditional Russian way of autocracy, his reign was marked by severe repression, economic stagnation and an aggressive foreign policy which cost the nation dearly in economic terms, he also took Russia to war in Crimea from 1853–1856, which ended with the Russians losing.

When Nikolas died, Russia had reached the zenith of its territory at two million square kilometres. He was succeeded by his son Alexander II (1818–1881), whose 26 year reign saw the rise of revolutionaries and anarchists due to the chronic dissent and dissatisfaction in the country, and despite legislation to emancipate Russia's serfs in 1861, much of the rest of Europe was also engulfed by unrest and revolution during these central years of the 19th century. Alexander sold Alaska to the United States in 1867 for seven million dollars, or roughly two cents an acre.

He encouraged Finnish nationalism together with its language, since Finland, although autonomous at the time, was still a Russian Grand Duchy. He faced several unsuccessful assassination attempts, but was finally assassinated in a bomb attack in St Petersburg in 1881. At the time of his death Alexander was planning a more liberal future for Russia, but his assassination resulted in action by his son Alexander III to throw such plans away.

Alexander III (1845–1894) returned to the Russian historical behaviour pattern of repression and autocracy. He died of natural causes aged 49 in 1894 after a thirteen-year reign, and was in turn succeeded by his eldest son Nikolas II (1868–1918), whose reign was an inglorious one marked by economic and military decline. His reign included the revolution of 1905 when massive social unrest amongst the peasants and the military led to strikes and revolutionary demands. The strikes spread to St Petersburg, where in December 1904 striking workers paralysed the city. By early January, as a petition was being brought to the Tsar, the troops guarding the Winter Palace opened fire on demonstrators causing hundreds of deaths. The pattern was repeated across Russia, but only a minority of troops mutinied and the revolts were crushed.

Despite the suppression of the revolts, a Duma or parliament, was brought into being and a new constitution enacted in 1906 with a limited constitutional monarchy. This new constitution was enough to help quell the revolution and keep Nikolas in power, but only for twelve more years until the 1917 revolution, when the Russian Empire collapsed, Nikolas abdicated, and was eventually murdered along with his family. In the end centuries of autocracy, political suppression, and gross disparity of wealth between aristocracy and peasants made a bloody revolution inevitable, and in the October Revolution of 1917 the Bolsheviks came to power, eventually developing into the Communist Party of the Union of Soviet Socialist Republics, which in turn appeared to take on the traditional Russian ruling behaviour of autocracy and repression with a large secret police – all under a supposedly different guise.

Possible further reading:
Russia by Martin Sixsmith (BBC Books)

Chapter 56
The House of Hanover

Thanks to the Act of Settlement in 1701, and also to Queen Anne's agreement, seven years after the formal union of Scotland and England, the ruler and elector of Hanover in Germany, George (1660–1757) was invited to fill the English throne as Anne's cousin and nearest protestant relative when she died. George I came to the English throne in 1714 and ruled for the next thirteen years. He never learned to speak English, and made frequent long visits back to Hanover. He supported a Parliament controlled by the Whigs as they felt that he offered the best likelihood of preventing a return to Stuart rule; unsurprisingly he reciprocated by supporting the Whigs against the Tories.

George I was the first British Monarch appointed by his subjects and not by God. Because of his frequent absences back in his native Hanover, the position of Prime Minister suddenly became more important and diminished the role of the monarch but also increased the role of all his ministers, thus starting the transition from monarchical to cabinet government. Sir Robert Walpole (1676–1745), a most astute Whig politician, became Britain's first prime minister and stayed in that post from 1721 to 1742.

During his tenure of office, Walpole was later given a house by King George II, number 10 Downing Street, in 1731. Walpole accepted this house, which was a combination of three residences previously used for royal and other visitors, provided it was given to the nation for Prime Ministerial use, rather than to himself personally. The house has remained the centre of British politics and the residence of the Prime Minister ever since. Walpole came to power just a year after the great financial crash known as the South Sea Bubble in 1720. Shares in the South Sea Company, which had been founded nine years before to trade with South America, became the object of ridiculous speculation which could only leave it grossly overvalued and end in disaster; when this happened thousands of investors were ruined.

The Bank of England had been founded in 1694, and was able to restore financial stability in the aftermath of the many tragic personal bankruptcies. Ironically the whole situation had arisen as a consequence of the national debt reaching the then astronomical sum of £50 million; it had been a government grant of a trading monopoly to the South Sea Company which had led to ill-advised speculation in company shares. This was the first incidence of disaster where share dealings rather than property were to blame. Finances came back under control and a prudent Walpole was able to trim the military budget and reduce taxes.

Political interest and discussion flourished in the absence of a King who was uninterested in ruling. Political discussion thrived throughout his reign and satirical commentary on political matters poured from the unrestrained journalistic pens of Daniel Defoe (1660–1731), Jonathan Swift (1667–1745, famous for Gulliver's Travels), Samuel Johnson (1709–1784, 'Dr Johnson' of dictionary fame), Henry Fielding (1707–1754), who founded with his half-brother, London's earliest police force, known as the 'Bow Street Runners' in 1749, in addition to writing the classic novel Tom Jones, and Cartoonist William Hogarth (1697–1764).

It was a time when freedom of speech became prominent and autocratic government gave way to cabinet decisions and responsibility. A German import at this time was George Frederick Handel (1685–1759) who trained musically in both Germany and Italy before settling in London in 1712 where he started the production of commercial opera, and made a great impact with his oratorio 'Messiah' in 1742. His coronation anthem, 'Zadok the Priest', was composed for the coronation of George II and has been used at every subsequent British coronation.

George II (1683–1760) was crowned in 1727, at the same time also succeeding his father to become Elector of Hanover. He had grown up alienated from his father and his father's opinions thus contributing to the growth of His Majesty's Loyal Opposition. He was the last British monarch to be born in a foreign country, and also the last British monarch to lead troops into battle (at Dettingen in Germany during the War of Austrian succession against the French in 1743). At this time, there was still support for the Stuart family as possible British sovereigns, with the most support coming from the Scottish Highlands, where James Stuart, the Roman Catholic son of James VII of Scotland and II of England, still claimed the English throne.

He had been brought up in France and had landed in Scotland in 1708, but his bid to take over the throne had failed with James and his Jacobite followers fleeing, if they were not captured and executed; James was known as the Old Pretender. His son, Charles Stuart (1720–1788), followed him and became known as the Young Pretender, or Bonnie Prince Charlie. He landed in the Hebrides in 1745, won a victory at Prestonpans, near Edinburgh, with his supporters and captured Carlisle, then marching further south to Derby, where his support began to fade.

At this stage, Bonnie Prince Charlie returned to Scotland and won a battle at Falkirk, but soon afterwards he suffered a severe defeat at the Battle of Culloden in Invernesshire in 1746 at the hands of the Earl of Cumberland, George's third son (he was given the name 'Butcher Cumberland' for the severe retribution exacted on the defeated army as well as ordinary Scots after the battle). Bonnie Prince Charlie was spirited out of Scotland by supporters, including a famously patriotic woman called Flora McDonald (1722–1790) who still lives on in the collective Scottish memory; many Catholic Scots supporters did not betray him despite the offer of a massive reward, many executions and the abolition of clan rights and the wearing of tartans.

Bonnie Prince Charlie spent the rest of his life in France, apart from a visit to London anonymously in 1750, when he professed conversion to the Anglican faith, presumably with the object of keeping his claim to the throne alive. At the height of the Seven Years War he met with French ministers to discuss the possibility of joining a planned invasion of England, but he was not felt to be reliable enough, and the French plans subsequently foundered after naval defeats at Lagos in southern Portugal in August 1759, and then at Quiberon Bay in southern Brittany three months later.

No further serious attempts to claim the English throne materialised after this as these two battles had firmly established the superiority of the Royal Navy over the French Navy and eliminated the possible invasion of England planned by the French: in addition confidence in the ability of the French to trade overseas was severely damaged and the French government was forced to renege on its debts.

In the meantime, Walpole's tenure as Prime Minister ended after he had initiated war with Spain in 1742 because Spanish piracy was hurting Britain's overseas trade. The war became known as the 'War of Jenkins Ear' after a sea captain claimed to have had his ear cut off by Spanish Customs. The war only ended in 1748, after being rolled into the larger War of Austrian Succession. This larger conflict blew up over the question of the last and only female head of the House of Habsburg, Marie Theresa's eligibility to succeed to the House of Habsburg on account of her sex. It ended with the Treaty of Aix-La-Chapelle in 1748 with a compromise naming Maria Theresa (1717–1780) as Archduchess of Austria and Queen of Hungary, while Prussia retained control of Silesia (an area of present south-eastern Poland adjacent to Czechoslovakia).

The Seven Years War is generally regarded as the first truly 'world war'. Although the causes were rooted in Europe, and pitted England and Prussia against France, Spain and Russia, the war spread to the distant trading outposts of all these powers in the Americas and in India, where the Mogul Empire was already in the process of collapse. Most of Southern India was captured from French domination, and around the same time Quebec and much of French Canada was also captured by the British, along with most of the Caribbean Islands.

Following Walpole's loss of office as Prime Minister in 1742, there came the gradual rise of William Pitt the Elder (1708–1788), initially as Paymaster General of the forces, the equivalent of today's Minister of Defence. Pitt did not have an aristocratic background, but he did have a grandfather who had made a fortune as Governor of Madras with trading deals, such that he became an important political figure in the West Country. Pitt's father served as a Tory Member of Parliament for many years, as did both his uncles. Pitt himself entered Parliament as the Member for Old Sarum (Salisbury), which was one of the many 'rotten boroughs' from which MPs were returned, not by an electorate, but by the possessor of rights to return a Member of Parliament under a Royal Charter.

Pitt was a brilliant orator, and it was to this that he owed his dominance in Parliament rather than to any sponsorship by aristocratic connections. He filled many of the great offices of state between 1746 and 1768 as a member of the Whig party. During this time he had an enormous influence on Britain's war planning. During the Seven Years War Pitt sent British troops under the Duke of Marlborough, to join the Prussian army of Brunswick. In the meantime expeditions against the French trading posts in Africa, the Caribbean and North America succeeded because British control of sea power stopped the French from reinforcing their overseas possessions. Fort Du Quesne in America was captured and destroyed, and in due course replaced by Fort Pitt named after the prime minister, which in turn evolved into present day Pittsburgh. A year later. the brilliant 32 year old General James Wolfe (1727–1759) captured Quebec with an ambitious nocturnal scaling of the adjacent cliffs known as the Heights of Abraham. Although he was killed leading his troops into the battle, the action cemented British control over Canada; French parts of Canada were subsequently ceded to Britain as a colony, with Canada eventually becoming a self-governing dominion (history of Canada in chapter 70).

George II died in 1760, and as his son Frederick had already died, he was succeeded by his grandson, the 22 year old George III, who was to rule for sixty years up to 1820. George III (1738–1820) had grown up with great animosity to Pitt which had been passed on to him by his grandfather, and so Pitt retired from Prime Ministerial office to become a noisy and annoying back bencher in Parliament. In 1763 the Treaty of Paris confirmed Pitt's achievements with Britain now controlling Canada, India and most of the West Indies, but in amassing this empire Pitt had doubled the national debt, and the country was paying huge amounts each year to service this debt.

George III attempted to manage the country by using his royal patronage, and his government responded to the financial situation by introducing levies and stamp duties, followed by further import duties on corn, paper and tea. These duties were damaging to trade with the colonies, and were particularly resented in America.

Finally, in 1766, the King asked Pitt to return to office, which he did by accepting the title of Earl of Chatham and becoming Prime Minister sitting in the Lords. He was severely crippled by gout at this stage of his life, and resigned again because of ill-health two years later. At around this time two radical young MPs were elected, John Wilkes (1725–1797), a populist and rousing orator with libertarian ideals, and Edmund Burke (1730–1797), a Whig, whose name is remembered as setting many parliamentary precedents of behaviour, and who is often regarded as the philosophical founder of Whig and modern Tory thinking.

George III's imposition of taxes and duties had unfortunately stirred up argument with British colonists in America. At that time England was paying considerable sums to protect the American colonies, but the colonists did not accept the right of London to try and levy money to cover at least some of the outgoings. Most of the taxes were repealed, apart from that on tea exported from England by the East India Company. The result was the 'Boston Tea Party', where American tea merchants and tea smugglers, dressed up as native Indians and threw a cargo of tea into Boston harbour.

The London government overreacted severely, closing Boston harbour and imposing direct rule by the Governor of Massachusetts, which stimulated the calling of a Colonial Congress in Philadelphia to write the Declaration of Rights, boycotting British imports and asking for repeal of trade laws. Feelings escalated, and colonial militias took up arms with some skirmishes resulting, including the defeat of the Governor of Massachusetts when he attempted to capture militia bases at Lexington and Concorde. The Congress of Colonists met again in Philadelphia and a Declaration of Independence, mainly written by Thomas Jefferson (1743–1826, later to become the third President of the USA) was published on 4 July 1776, which declared George III to be "unfit to be the ruler of a free people".

Although the Declaration advocated freedom and liberty for all individuals, it somehow failed to recognise that this freedom should also extend to native Americans, and to southern black slaves. The low grade war continued up and down the east coast of America for the next five years with Pitt warning that America could not be subdued by military means.

The simmering war along America's east coast escalated, and the American rebels found help from Spain and France. A French fleet came to patrol the coastline and prevented both trade and the movement of British troops, who were forced to surrender at York Town in Chesapeake Bay in 1781. The ensuing treaty signed in Paris in 1783 fulfilled Pitt's forebodings and granted independence to the American colonies. Following these desperate political reverses, George III asked Pitt's son, William Pitt the Younger (1759–1806) to become Prime Minister and in an election the following year the younger Pitt won a majority that he was able to hold on to for the next seventeen years, thanks firstly to the values and common sense he had inherited from his father, and secondly, to his ability, energy and understanding of the new emerging technologies of the Industrial Revolution.

Ironically, in the newly independent America, it became necessary to raise taxes for self-protection and incomes diminished severely for the next two decades, whilst in France the legacy of the war released a revolution against the French establishment, resulting in the 1789 Parisian rebellion when the Bastille prison was overwhelmed and its prisoners released, leading into the full anarchy of the French Revolution. Many English people saw the French revolution as pursuing the same road taken by the American colonists, whilst Edmund Burke disagreed saying that the revolution had "subverted monarchy but not recovered freedom"; he predicted that the eventual result would be dictatorship. Pitt had not foreseen the chaos that the French Revolution would cause, nor had he foreseen that soon after the execution of Louis XIV in 1793 France would declare war with Britain.

Possible further reading:
A History of the United States by Philip Jenkins (Palgrave Macmillan)
Revolution by Peter Ackroyd (Pan Books)

Chapter 57
The Second Great Age of Exploration

By the end of the 15th century, Christopher Columbus had discovered the American continent, landing in the Caribbean in 1492, though believing that he had approached the East Indies by going west around the world, a fact commemorated in our reference to them even today as the West Indies. Exploration south from Spain and Portugal, reached the southern tip of Africa in 1497 and then India, in the person of Vasco da Gama, in 1498.

The 16th century saw continued consolidation and expansion of detail in the increasing knowledge and collation of world geography. Maps of the world started to become more realistic and more accurate, and in the middle 16th century Gerardus Mercator (1512–1594) in the Low Countries, aided the process by his efforts to render maps of a three dimensional spherical planet onto flat two dimensional paper or parchment. Mercator had been five years old when Martin Luther posted his theses on his church door, and grew up in a turbulent time of religious strife. He lived in a world of violent conflict and social upheaval, and in one period of his life he was imprisoned by the Inquisition on a charge of heresy, but despite this he managed a detailed lifetime of constantly improving global mapping, also contributing to the early naming and mapping of the east coast of America.

Through the 17th and 18th centuries, there was an explosion of exploration, and the years are studded with the names of intrepid early mariners who are now remembered with household familiarity, as well as being commemorated in the towns and named geographical features on our modern maps. These explorers paved the way for the opening up of the world which at the time was seen in Britain primarily as a trade opportunity, and only secondarily as a colonisation possibility.

At the beginning of this period, the Pilgrim Fathers are revered as the first significant European settlers in North America, they were Protestants escaping a troubled time of religious ferment and violence. At the end of this period, and on the other side of the world, the shipment of 717 convicts became the first major settlement, albeit involuntary, at the site of Botany Bay, by modern day Sydney.

In 1607, Henry Hudson (1565–1611) made his first voyage in the employ of the Muscovy Company of England, tasked with trying to find a northern route to the Pacific coast of Asia; the theory being that the constant day light in the northern latitudes would melt the ice and allow summer navigation. In fact Hudson was forced to return by impenetrable pack-ice after sailing as far north as about 80° and then south into Hudson's Bay. His ship was small at only 80 tonnes, and he had a crew of a mere eleven seamen. In 1608 the East India and the Muscovy Companies sent him north and east to try and find a northern passage to the north of Russia and round to the East Indies, but once again Hudson was defeated by ice.

In 1609, the Dutch East India Company despatched Hudson again, and although starting to the east Hudson ended up voyaging west past the Grand Banks fishing grounds off Newfoundland, and then sailing south down the New England coast as far as Chesapeake Bay. He also sailed up the river that now bears his name as far as present day Albany. In 1610 Hudson sailed once more for the English, passing the southern tips of Iceland and Greenland, and then sailing north round the coast of Labrador and into Hudson's Bay. Once there his ship became trapped in early pack-ice. When the ice cleared the following spring Hudson wished to explore further before turning for home, but most of his crew did not wish to extend their voyage and mutinied; Hudson and a few crewmen were set adrift in a small boat with a scanty supplies, but were never seen again.

Martin Frobisher (1535–1594) from Yorkshire first went to sea as a cabin boy at the age of nine. In 1576 the Muscovy Company in England financed three small ships for Frobisher to search again for the north-west passage around the north of Canada. Many of his crew were lost, first by shipwreck and secondly as hostages to the local Inuit during this voyage. Surprisingly in 1577 Frobisher was able to mount a second expedition with a large grant from Queen Elizabeth, but little knowledge was gained. The prospect of great mineral wealth was raised and accordingly a third expedition was mounted the following year.

This time, Frobisher brought home many tonnes of metallic ore which was thought to be gold, but subsequently turned out to be iron pyrites (iron sulphide known today as 'fool's gold'). Frobisher's life finished with fighting against the Spanish; he had been one of the commanders of the fleet which destroyed the Spanish Armada in 1588, but his later exploits should probably be called piracy, and in 1594 he was injured in an assault against a Spanish fortress in the Caribbean and died later from his wounds.

At the beginning of the 17th century, John Smith (1580–1631), a farmer's son from Lincolnshire, went to sea after his father died; he was an important figure in the early days of the establishment of the fledgling Jamestown colony. He explored the east coast of America, including Chesapeake Bay and New England further north. He provided an example in teaching farming to the early colonists, guiding them through the early days of settlement and its difficulties in achieving self-sufficiency. Smith is remembered for his relationships with the Powhatan Indians, where he was rescued from a potentially fatal Indian attack by the Chief's daughter, Pocahontas. After returning to England he became an evangelist for the potential opportunities in the New World and for the early colonists.

Samuel De Champlain (1574–1635) was a French polymath from a sea-going family who explored the east coast of North America, and is noted for establishing the French settlement that became Quebec City, and for making the first accurate maps of Eastern Canada. He was the first to explore and describe the Great Lakes for Louis XIII of France, and later governed the early French territories along the St Lawrence River. Quebec City was founded in 1608 as a small military style stockaded settlement with a moat. He is reputed to have crossed the Atlantic up to thirty times.

Going east, Abel Tasman (1603–1659) was a Dutchman in the employ of the Dutch East India Company, who made two seminal voyages in 1642 and 1644. In the first voyage he sailed past the Cape of Good Hope, stopping at Mauritius to repair his ships and refuel with food and water. From there he sailed east with the favourable winds of the Roaring Forties making landfall at Tasmania, which he named Van Diemans Land after the Governor General of the Dutch East Indies. His stay in Tasmania was brief, and after claiming it as Dutch territory, Tasman made landfall on the north-west coast of the South Island of New Zealand.

Attempts to land resulted in attacks by Maoris, and four of his crew were killed. Exploration was therefore aborted, and Tasman sailed north along the west coast of North Island and on to Fiji, then westward again back to Batavia (present day Jakarta). In his second voyage two years later Tasman made landfall on the west coast and then sailed along the north coast of Australia, which he called New Holland, before turning north back to the Dutch East Indies. Further European exploration of Australasia would wait until Captain Cook's voyages of exploration from 1768 onwards.

William Dampier (1651–1715) sailed on two early merchant voyages to Newfoundland and Java before joining the Royal Navy in his early twenties in 1673. Dampier's early nautical experience was as a crew member on buccaneering ships (otherwise known as pirates) in Central America, as a result of which he completed a circumnavigation of the globe on his home voyage. He wrote a book about his experiences on his return, which resulted in his being given command of a naval warship and instructions to explore Australia. The ship was in poor condition due to worm damage to its hull, and had to be abandoned at Ascension Island from where the crew was picked up by an East India trading vessel some weeks later.

Dampier commanded another ship in 1703, indulging in more raiding and piratical activity along the west coast of Central America. In 1708 he completed a third circumnavigation of the world, starting around Cape Horn, and once more raiding and extracting gold and silver from Spanish vessels, but he was also able to complete much exploration of coastal Australia, though a lot of this information was lost through shipwreck and in the hazards of transit back to England, but he still left an important legacy of navigational and cartographic information which was valuable to later generations including Captain Cook.

As a Danish seaman, Vitus Bering (1681–1714), joined the Russian Navy of Tsar Peter the Great in his early twenties. In 1725 he was sent by Peter the Great to explore the area of Asian eastern Russia, where he established that there was no land bridge with America. He was later sent with a much larger and better prepared expedition in 1741, when he discovered the Aleutian Islands, Alaska, and the straits and sea which now bear his name, but became severely ill, and died along with several of his company, probably from scurvy resulting from the lack of fresh fruit and vegetables in their diet. Alaska became de facto Russian territory at that time, though it would later be sold to the USA for just over seven million dollars in 1867.

Captain James Cook (1728–1779) first went to sea as a teenager, and joined the Royal Navy some ten years later. He was a superlative navigator and cartographer whose early work involved surveying and mapping the St Lawrence River estuary during the Siege of Quebec. As a result of his excellent work he was commissioned by the Navy on three exploratory voyages. His first voyage in 1768, was for the Royal Society to visit Tahiti and provide astronomical observations of the transit of Venus. The other object of this voyage was to confirm the existence of continental Australia. After leaving Tahiti Cook made landfall first in New Zealand and mapped the coastline of the whole country, He then turned west to become the first European to sight the east coast of Australia. His landfall was made at Botany Bay (modern Sydney), later to become the home of transported criminals.

Cook's second three-year voyage started in 1772, again at the behest of the Royal Society, where there was still a hypothesis that a large southern continent remained to be discovered. This voyage is notable for Cook's use of a marine chronometer made by John Harrison, which enabled the calculation of his position of longitude much more accurately (determination of longitude requires precision time-keeping for accuracy), and indeed, many of his charts were still sufficiently accurate to be in use in the 20th century. Until this time, most people had lived with their day divided by the seven time markers prescribed by the church and indicated by the tolling of the church bell; not an ideal system as the length of time periods varied with the seasons of the year as the daylight hours got longer or shorter.

John Harrison (1693–1776) was a clock and cabinet maker from Lincolnshire who obsessed over the accuracy of timepieces. In 1707 Britain had suffered a naval disaster of four returning warships simultaneously wrecked on the Scilly Islands at the approach to the English Channel because of inaccurate navigation from primitive methods of measuring and calculating a ship's position at sea. As a consequence of this disaster Parliament had offered a reward of £20,000 (almost three million pounds in today's currency) for the production of an accurate ship's chronometer, which Harrison eventually managed after many years of painstaking work, thereby instituting a great advance in the precision of marine mapping and navigation.

Sometime before this, the Italian physicist Evangelista Torricelli (1608–1647) is credited with inventing the first primitive barometer. The principle was used by the German writer Goethe to predict weather using a sealed water filled device. Such instruments remained as curiosities and were not available to Captain Cook but were later developed into a reliable mercury barometer by Captain Robert Fitzroy (1805–1865) captaining the second surveying voyage of

HMS Beagle with Charles Darwin on board. Fitzroy later continued to develop meteorology, including setting up the first meteorological service for Britain after a spell as Governor General of New Zealand.

Cook's first voyage in 1768 had included Joseph Banks as a scientific passenger. Banks (1743–1820) was the son of a wealthy Lincolnshire landowner and had displayed an unusual aptitude and enthusiasm for natural history, such that he was elected a Fellow of the Royal Society at the age of only 23, shortly after which he joined a military expedition to Newfoundland and Labrador; during a spell in port he met Cook briefly when the pair were both at St John's in Newfoundland at the same time.

It was a propitious meeting since it was on the basis of this meeting that Banks joined Cook's first voyage which was jointly sponsored by the Royal Society and the Royal Navy, with Banks able to fund privately two scientists, two artists and three servants to accompany him; this situation illustrates the role that wealthy protestant men of independent means contributed to the development of science in the 18th century. Banks did not accompany Cook on his second voyage as his demands for space and facilities for staff to journey with him were deemed unreasonably large. Instead, Banks continued his impressive intellectual life in England becoming President of the Royal Society in 1778, a post he held for more than forty years until his death, influencing the development of science; at least eighty species of plant are named after him.

Cook's third voyage for the Royal Navy in 1776–1779, was to map the American west coast from Vancouver Island north to the Bering Strait, where he was unable to find a way through to the north. Cook started to return to Britain stopping at Hawaii to replace a broken mast, but while this was being fashioned for his ship there were altercations between his crew and native Hawaiians; Cook and four of his crew were killed. Nevertheless, in his fifty years of life, and three extended voyages, he had made amazing achievements in both navigation and map making.

Louis-Antoine de Bougainville (1729–1811) was a contemporary of Cook and fought in Canada in the service of General Montcalm, participating in the defence of Quebec City. He was one of the officers involved in the general capitulation of the French in 1761. In 1766 Louis XV gave him permission to circumnavigate the globe, thus becoming the 14th European and the first Frenchman to achieve circumnavigation. His expedition arrived back in France with the loss of only seven men out of 330 crew from his two ships. Subsequently he fought for the French navy on the American east coast, but undertook no further exploration, though he was greatly honoured in France by Napoleon.

As a Scottish surgeon in the Royal Navy, James Lind (1716–1794) introduced great improvements in the hygiene and ventilation of ships together with fumigation. He thought that including acid in the diet would aid in the prevention of scurvy, responsible then for many deaths on prolonged sea voyages, and he carried out small early clinical trials on seamen with vinegar, sulphuric acid and lime juice, among other remedies. The fruit juice proved successful, though it was to be forty years before a regular ration of lime juice became compulsory for British naval seamen and led them becoming known as 'limeys'.

His discovery made a considerable difference to the health of ship's crews and the mortality of long voyages. His writing was however predated by various others, including the Portuguese Vasco da Gama who took citrus fruit on his voyage of exploration as the Portuguese already knew the value of fruit in combating disease and planted fruit and vegetables on the island of St Helena which was used as a staging and resupply post for ships passing around the Cape of Good Hope. In Canada Jacques Cartier's inland explorations in the early 16th century were threatened by scurvy, but saved when native Indians showed him how an infusion of cedar bark would prevent the disease. Cook himself took pickled cabbage on his ships, of which he insisted that his crew had a daily ration thus preventing scurvy.

Once Australia had been discovered, and Cook's mapping of the Pacific Ocean and its shores had been clarified, together with the continents and islands involved, little time was lost in putting this knowledge to early use and the first cargo of 717 convicts was transported to Botany Bay in 1788 to found Australia's first European settlement.

Captain George Vancouver (1757–1798) from a marine orientated family in King's Lynn joined the British Royal Navy at the age of 13, and served as a midshipman on Cook's second voyage to Australia in 1772. He also served on Cook's third voyage, and must have learned much from Cook, the intrepid explorer.

In 1791, Vancouver was in charge of an expedition which travelled via the Cape of Good Hope, to chart the southwest coast of Australia, then proceeding to New Zealand and China, and on to explore the northern Pacific and American mainland coast. He made accurate charts of the coast and islands of what is now British Columbia and Alaska. He undertook a polar expedition two years later in 1793, and returned home around the southern tip of South America. His maps were so accurate that they continued to be used well into the 20th century like those of Captain Cook; he is well commemorated in the city and sound which bear his name.

Possible further reading:
Captain James Cook by Alan Villiers (Charles Scribners & Sons)

Chapter 58
Early Technology

Before considering the Industrial Revolution, we must look carefully at technology and its evolution from early Stone Age times, as it is the development of technology which underpinned the Industrial Revolution. Technology is the use of tools with which humans are aided in creating things, in producing food and in travelling. In later years technology was vital in underpinning the Agricultural Revolution which allowed human settlement to become static, while at the same time increasing the production of food from ever smaller areas of land: this in turn would lead to an increase in population as people progressed from the hunter-gatherer existence of ancient Stone Age times.

In early Stone Age times, the first elements of technology involved tools made of stone, wood and bone. Baskets made from woven hazel or willow branches appeared well before the last Ice Age and at some stage the same techniques of weaving pliable wooden branches were used to build the first boats by covering a shaped framework with hide. Early in the Neolithic period came the production of stone implements, including stone arrowheads, and the production of clothing, initially from furs, to allow early people to cope with adverse climatic conditions.

We have seen that musical instruments were produced before the last Ice Age, and at the same time pottery vessels were being made some 25,000 years ago. Through the late Stone Age, the progress of technology increased, particularly with the discovery of metals leading into the Bronze Age. The invention of the plough 10,000 years ago, and the wheel 6,000 years ago, greatly enhanced human abilities in agriculture and in transport of materials.

Pottery reappeared in Europe after the Ice Age as early as 14,000 BC, probably made by baking formed clay with a fire, but proper kilns have been found dating from 5,000 BC in Mesopotamia with the potter's wheel appearing soon after, and as a development of this the lathe to shape wood appearing much later sometime probably at the beginning of the first millennium BC. Like firing clay, and also needing involving high temperature firing, glass was made in Mesopotamia in the middle of the second millennium BC, but it was not until about 100 BC that the Romans discovered how to make window glass.

In due course, the Bronze Age slowly gave way to the Iron Age at variable times across Eurasia either side of 150 BC, enhancing not only the agricultural abilities of tribes that possessed it, but also their war-making prowess. Many of these developments were pioneered initially in two centres, first in the Middle

East in Mesopotamia and Egypt, and secondly in China. In both locations, much technology was developed to harness the power of water, either by means of irrigation systems for agriculture, or by the use of watermills to replace human labour in grinding wheat and performing other tasks. Often, the introduction of a watermill required a dam to hold back water and then produce a constant flow using a leet, or channel through which the water was funnelled to the waterwheel.

Many of the earliest watermills were developed by the Romans, and the power of the wind was harnessed resulting in the many windmills that are apparent around the shores of the Mediterranean even today. Windmills multiplied across Europe, both in regions where there was no adequate water supply to power watermills, but also in areas where rivers and the water supply to drive a watermill would freeze in the winter. Most recently windmills have found a resurgence of interest as turbines, generating electricity in an environmentally friendly, non-polluting and renewable manner.

Much early technology was devised in China, where the Chinese celebrate 'the four great inventions'. These are named as gunpowder, the compass, paper making and printing. Gunpowder had been discovered in the 9th century, but was not used by the Chinese in weaponry until well after Europeans had devised guns and cannon. The first magnetic needle compasses were made in the 11th century rapidly spreading to Europe. Paper making seems to have arisen in the centuries before Christ, and had indeed reached such a level of sophistication that bank notes came into being around the beginning of the second millennium in China.

Printing in China started with wood blocks which were carved into a negative block from which the positive printed page could be produced, sometime in the middle centuries of the first millennium. Although the Chinese went on to develop movable type for book printing, this never caught on as the wooden letters deformed and wore out too rapidly, and the advent of printing had to wait until Gutenberg developed metal moveable type in Europe in the mid-15th century (chapter 36).

On the Indian subcontinent, the Indus Valley civilisation produced many innovations, particularly in measurement and in the early standardisation of weights and measures. Mathematics and astronomy were particularly strong disciplines, and the numerals that we incorrectly term 'Arabic', initially spread from the Indian subcontinent into daily use first in Arabia and then across the world, replacing the cumbersome Latin numerals of the Mediterranean towards the end of the first millennium.

During the Islamic golden age between 800 and 1200, advances were made in the production of ceramics and glassware. There was much development of music in those early years, particularly in the development of the early Arabic instrument the oud, a multi stringed instrument derived from early lutes, which in turn became the precursor of the guitar, and then the violin family; all of these instruments have several strings.

In Europe paper and printing came late to the scene, but in the years after 1500 proved a catalyst to the spread of invention and new technology across Europe. Technology was particularly vital in the evolution of sailing ships capable of long ocean passages, and their navigation. Quite early on stern rudders with central tillers were adopted from China across Europe in the first millennium replacing the ancient steering oars mounted on the side at the rear side of a ship and used by the Vikings in their explorations. Much use of European technology was devoted to the production of weapons of war, including the development of steel crossbows, ever more accurate guns, and cannons.

Early map making, necessary once long distance exploration got underway, was enabled by new thinking about latitude and longitude commencing with Mercator in the 16th century (chapter 37), and rather later by the invention of an accurate chronometer finally developed by John Harrison (chapter 57) over many years in response to a British Act of Parliament (The Longitude Act of 1714) which offered a large reward of £20,000 for production of a chronometer enabling a ship's position to be determined within one degree of longitude (60 nautical miles).

It was the invention of an effective steam engine that allowed greater useful power to be developed and formed much of the base for the Industrial Revolution. Thomas Savary (1650–1715), a military engineer from Devon in southwest England, patented an engine to condense steam creating a vacuum, and thus draw cool water up into a container and then pump it further by pressurised steam. The first industrial steam pump was that of Thomas Newcomen (1664–1729), also from Devon where there was a considerable need for pumps in tin mining at that time, who produced a commercial steam engine which used a piston and was effective in pumping unwanted water from a mine in 1712.

In agriculture, the name of English farmer Jethro Tull (1674–1741) is synonymous with the early technology revolution in agriculture. The two machines that Tull invented and pioneered were a horse drawn seed drill, which sowed the seeds more rapidly and more evenly in rows than traditional scattering could achieve, and later a horse drawn hoe for weeding between the rows of growing plants.

On the textile front, three Englishmen from Lancashire are credited with achieving big early advances in the technology of weaving and cloth production, which had originally been devised in very ancient times. James Hargreaves (1720–1778) invented the 'Spinning Jenny', which allowed a single worker to work with multiple spools of yarn after the invention of the flying shuttle some years earlier by John Kay (1704–1779). A few years after Hargreaves created the Spinning Jenny in 1764, Richard Arkwright (1732–1792) produced the spinning frame to produce yarn from wool, flax or cotton. The frame was so effective that spinning rapidly became a factory-based process rather than a cottage industry.

Because of this transition to a factory-based means of production, Arkwright became known towards the end of his life as the 'Father of the Industrial Revolution', because apart from the factory he built, he also built a village with accommodation and facilities for his workers. Somewhat later, Samuel Crompton (1753–1827) synthesised the spinning wheel from the inventions of

Hargreaves and Arkwright; the 'spinning mule', as his invention was known, spun much better thread and cloth, with a single worker being able to produce many times the amount of material that the cottage workers of the previous generation could achieve in the same time.

As agriculture developed, the population was also able to grow; numbers are somewhat inexact, but between 1750 and 1850 the population of England more than doubled from just under six million to just over fifteen million. This increase was partly the result of the Agricultural Revolution, with the country achieving the capacity to provide sufficient food for the increase in population, it was also partly brought about by the Industrial Revolution where the new factories and available employment opportunities rapidly increased.

At the same time, the mortality rate of children dying before the age of five dropped from three-quarters of new-born infants in 1740 to around a third some eighty years later in 1820, a figure which underlines the availability of a better diet and a relative increase in affluence, since this dramatic fall came before the big increases in public hygiene and health of later 19th century.

Possible further reading:
Connections by James Burke (Macmillan)

Chapter 59
Slavery

The condition in which one human being exists as the chattel, or property, of another, has been around since the mists of time. It was certainly known as far back as the first records of Babylonian society where slaves were not only vital to the Babylonian economy, but also had their rights and their conditions of treatment codified in law. They were often captives obtained during war, or by raiding, and regular slave markets were held. At different times and places over the years enslavement has also resulted from individuals falling into debt or into crime. In reality in primitive societies, the condition of servitude was probably little worse than the rest of the toiling masses who made up the majority of society in Babylon.

The word slave itself is derived from the Slavs of middle and eastern Europe, who were traded to northern Africa by the Arabs following the Islamic conquest. Slavery was on the bottom rung of human society, and in later times remained below the serfs, who formed the bulk of many medieval societies, the difference being that a serf, unlike a slave, was not free and was tied to a manor or to an overlord, but did have some rights, and was sometimes able to escape from his position in society.

Equally, slaves in some societies have been able to better their lot, and even buy their freedom as in later Roman times. Although we have no written records of slavery (or its absence) before the time of Babylon, it is clear that even in prehistoric societies slavery existed. It is evidenced in the customs and organisation of pre-literate American societies as well, including the Aztecs and the Incas, and it was also present in pre-literate Viking society.

In all of these societies, it was, in part, a solution to the disposal of prisoners captured in war. The alternative drastic solution was sometimes employed – simply to slaughter all captured soldiery, particularly if the numbers were too large for any particular society to incorporate. There was a middle road, and in some instances, women and children were taken as slaves and men of fighting age who might prove dangerous and rebellious were slaughtered.

Slavery continued under the Egyptians, and again contributed to the enormously intensive early agricultural practices required to produce enough food to keep the upper echelons of society in the relative luxury in which they lived. The Greeks had a stratified system of society, initially slaughtering male combatants captured in war, whilst taking women and children to work as slaves. This custom was eventually discontinued and male prisoners were taken back to

Greece as slaves, indeed most Greeks owned at least one or two slaves: at the high point of Greek achievement up to 25% of the population is thought to have comprised slaves.

This situation persisted through the ancient world well after the birth of Christ, but the Greek system incorporated not only slaves who did unskilled manual work, but also others who worked, for instance, as teachers and artisans, filling valuable intellectual and skilled niches in society. The Greeks used some slaves as pedagogues, initially this essentially involved child minding and escorting the child to school, but later the term evolved and pedagogues became teachers, often of considerable importance, the best known instance being that of Aristotle who tutored the young Alexander the Great.

By contrast, in Sparta on the Greek Peloponnese, slaves captured in war were known as Helots. The Spartans also had a section of society as labourers, some were bound to the land as free peasants, but not as chattels. The Helots caused considerable anxiety to Spartan society because most of these inhabitants of Sparta were not citizens, and therefore when the citizen army had to leave to fight, the Helots (who had often been enemy warriors), were left at home, leading to fears about slave revolts.

By the time of ancient Rome, the situation remained largely unchanged with some 25% of the Roman population estimated to comprise slaves. It is easy to see that this large section of society was economically vital to sustain agriculture as Rome had outgrown the ability to produce enough grain for its citizens, and to maintain well-off Romans with the standard of living to which they aspired. Equally, the fact that this large section of society was both disenfranchised and suppressed, is reflected in three large rebellions that are known as the Servile Wars.

The first and second Servile Wars occurred in 135 and 104 BC, and it took some time to suppress the rebellious slaves: the third Servile War comprised a rebellion of at least a hundred thousand slaves at its height, in 73–61 BC. Many of the men rebelling had been captured soldiers, and with little to lose, were a match even for the Roman legions. This third Servile War is associated with the name of Spartacus, and inflicted much damage on the Roman army before it was finally overcome.

In the years after the death of Mohammed, trade in slaves increased again as Arabs captured middle Europeans and exported them for sale in North Africa, where they provided many of the necessary workers to keep the fertile North African agricultural machine going. Once again, however, problems of trying to keep a whole section of society enslaved continued to prove troublesome, and we hear of the Zanj Rebellion, which extended over a number of years from 869 AD, involving up to half a million African slaves and other enslaved men imported from Muslim territories, initially to the southern Arabian Muslim territory around Basra. Tens of thousands lost their lives in the upheaval.

Through early and mediaeval Russian times, formal slavery in Russia existed alongside a very persistent state of serfdom for much of the population; serfs were entitled to protection and justice and in addition the right to cultivate (but not own) a certain amount of land for their own use. The system changed only marginally in 1723 when Tsar Peter the Great, decreed that household slaves should become serfs, allowing them more rights, but still not the right to own land. Under other jurisdictions, such as the Turks in medieval times, slaves who had often been captured soldiers, were deployed into the army as mercenaries for their hosts: although this might seem a somewhat dangerous practice, it generally seems to have worked well with the slaves thereby gaining relatively good conditions of life.

In Britain, both before and during the Roman occupation, slavery was a normal part of life, and later from 800 to 1100 the Vikings ran a large slave market in Dublin, alternately raiding coastal areas and taking captives who would subsequently be sold at the slave market. The practice, however, was undermining to society, and although the Doomsday Book census of 1086 lists 10% of England's population as slaves, this soon changed, possibly due to the attitudes of the new Norman rulers. Slavery persisted in Europe through medieval times, and was also present in both India and China. The practice was theoretically forbidden in China, and therefore slaves were traded by merchants outside the country's boundaries and jurisdiction.

By the 15th century, relatively little slavery persisted, although people from central Europe were still being enslaved and sold into slavery by both Arabs and Turks. There was still a demand for forced labour however, and Europeans had begun trading further afield, particularly south to the coastal areas of west Africa. The first black African slaves were sold in Lisbon in 1444 (and this may have been responsible for the introduction of smallpox into Europe from Africa), these slaves were rapidly recognised as a lucrative business opportunity by some merchants. For a while, the eastern Atlantic islands of the Canaries, the Cape Verde Islands and Madeira, took most of the Portuguese slaves.

The Caribbean islands had a small population of indigenous people and early Spanish immigrants, but needed additional labour for their economy. Once the islands were adequately populated, and as trans-Atlantic sailing ships became more reliable, this initial trickle of black African slaves was turned into a much larger flow of people to service the new colonies in North, Central and South America. Slaves were seen as necessary to harvest sugar cane, which was the early staple crop and source of income, and later cotton and tobacco, they were also put to work in mining, forestry and construction.

The growth of sugar cane and other crops initially relied on native slave labour to do the work, but as the Europeans brought smallpox and other diseases with them much of the local population was decimated by these diseases to which they had no immunity. Thus the slave trade from West Africa became necessary to provide more labourers. It is estimated that up to a million West African slaves were transported to Mexico over the next 250 years. The export of wealth from Mexico, together with the import of slaves gradually caused increasing resentment, both among the native population and among the settlers. Rebellion eventually broke out in several scattered places in 1811, developing slowly into the Mexican War of Independence (1810–1821) while Europe was preoccupied with the Napoleonic Wars; the rebellion led on to the Independence of Mexico being declared in 1821.

From these European Portuguese beginnings the slave trade increased; John Hawkins (1532–1595) is known as the first Englishman to become involved. Hawkins, along with his cousin Francis Drake, became heavily involved in the slave trade, and also in piracy. His first venture was the capture of a Portuguese slave ship and subsequent sale of the three hundred slaves in the Caribbean. This was effectively the start of the simmering naval conflict between Portugal and Spain, and their English adversaries. On his second trip two years later, Hawkins secured the financial backing of Queen Elizabeth. Having secured her trust, he was appointed treasurer of the Royal Navy in 1578 and used his position to upgrade the navy's fleet and its sailors. The ships he sponsored were faster and sealed below the waterline to prevent attack from the problem of tropical burrowing worms.

While the slave trade continued unabated between Africa and the Americas, there was no respite in the internal European slave market, where Europeans were sold into slavery in north Africa and Arabia; this trade continued albeit in diminishing numbers. There was at the same time a steady market in which captured individuals could be ransomed and repatriated. In the meantime, in 1542 Pope Nicholas V granted Catholics the right to enslave non-Catholics. Spanish, Dutch and English slavers continued with their human trade to the Americas. The slaves were often captured inland by African chiefs and then sold to Europeans in markets at west African ports along the coast, including Gambia, Sierra Leone, Liberia, Ghana and Nigeria.

Conditions on the slave trading ships were dire as the standards of hygiene were appalling, the food minimal and an estimated 10–20% of slaves died during their passage to the New World. Overall the trans-Atlantic slave trade is estimated to have transported 10–12 million slaves over a period of three centuries. Perhaps half of these people had been enslaved as a result of internal African wars, and as a result of internal African conflict. Thanks to British naval power, the Royal Navy was able to see that British ships dominated the trade initially, but through the 18th century opposition to the slave trade grew steadily in Britain, American and most parts of Europe.

Much of the early preaching and campaigning against slavery came from Quakers, a breakaway Protestant sect from the established English church, in the early 17th century. James Oglethorpe (1696–1785), a British MP, is among those credited with the start of the movement; he was deeply interested in prison reform and went to America as the founding governor of the new colony (or state) of Georgia; he felt it might be a suitable place to rehabilitate debtors. Later, William Wilberforce (1759–1833), also a British MP and evangelical Christian, was one of the anti-slavery movement's most ardent proponents, which culminated in Britain abolishing slavery in 1807, and then later throughout the British Empire in 1833.

Thanks to the early efforts of Thomas Jefferson (1743–1826), Virginia became the first American state in 1778 to stop importing slaves and to free those already present. Denmark, which had been active in the slave trade, was the first country to ban the slave trade in 1792, though this only came into effect a decade later. Britain's Act of Parliament followed in 1807 after the long campaign by Wilberforce and others.

As the Royal Navy was supreme in the Atlantic maritime waters, Britain was able to make trading in slaves difficult, though the slave trade across the Atlantic continued at a reduced level. The Royal Navy seized some 1600 ships over the next few decades, many of which were destined for Brazil which was the last Atlantic country to ban the slave trade. Internally however, slavery within Brazil did not end until 1888. In the meantime, the American Civil War between the northern states and the slave-using southern confederate states from 1861 to 1865, put an end to slavery within America during the presidency of Abraham Lincoln.

The seven initial southern slave states were overcome by the remaining 27 states at a cost of enormous damage to the economy and infrastructure of the southern confederate states. A total of more than half a million soldiers from the two sides died in the conflict (chapter 50). The consequences of American slavery in which slaves were transported thousands of miles across the Atlantic, and in which the slaves were all black while their owners were white, and in which the attitudes and treatment of the slaves was usually dehumanising and harsh, has left huge scars across the American nation that have still not healed today over 150 years later.

Slavery continued in many parts of the world through the 19th century. China abolished slavery in 1906 by imperial decree from the Emperor. Within Europe however the abolition movement started at the beginning of the 19th century and was completed by the end of the century. Despite this modern slavery is now well recognised and still exists underground in many modern societies in different guises, albeit in nothing like the numbers of previous times.

Possible further reading:
Slavery by Milton Meltzer (Da Capo Press)

Chapter 60
US Independence to Civil War

The original Declaration of Independence was drawn up by a young lawyer, Thomas Jefferson (1743–1826), and adopted by Congress on 4 July 1776 (now commemorated as Independence Day). The Declaration is of moderate length, but is known for the beginning of its second paragraph which states, *"We hold these truths to be self-evident, that all men are created equal; that they are endowed by their creator with certain inalienable rights; that among these are life, liberty and the pursuit of happiness. That, to secure these rights, governments are instituted among men, deriving their just powers from the consent of the governed..."*

This was written, however, some time before independence would be achieved, and it probably infuriated the governing powers, including the British monarch George III whose attitude to his colonies was very rigid. Before independence was to be granted however, much fighting would ensue. France entered the war on the American side in 1778 and two years later Spain and the Netherlands also came in to support the rebels. Nevertheless, by 1783, the Treaty of Paris recognised the new United States with its boundaries confined in the east by the Atlantic, and in the west by the Mississippi River. Benjamin Franklin (1705–1790), scientist, polymath extraordinary and diplomat, spent many of these years as ambassador to France and acting as an intermediary between the European nations aiding each side of the conflict. Royalist supporters amongst the communities on the east coast often chose to migrate north and probably 50,000 people were relocated in Canadian New Brunswick, where the British government had created the province specifically for them.

Through the last three years of the war, the new American government had been financing the conflict by printing money, which resulted in a large public debt, despite payments for the army being severely in arrears. General Washington appealed to his troops not to pursue the matter, but inflation was badly out of control and people were very short of money due to devaluation of the paper currency that had been issued. The matter was complicated by the federal system which relied on each of the individual states honouring their commitments.

The difference in size between the early States of the time did not help matters. The legal system barely worked as many courts saw the framework of Common Law as a hangover from colonial times. Merchants and creditors refused to accept the worthless printed money insisting that debts be settled in gold or silver, while the whole situation was made worse by maintenance of the contemporary imported English practice of imprisonment of a debtor until his debts were paid. A debtors rebellion broke out in Massachusetts and lingered on for a while, but served as a vital incentive to organise constitutional reform.

After much discussion, a National Constitution emerged largely representing the thoughts of James Madison (1751–1836), he was elected to the first House of Representatives and later became the fourth President. Three branches of government would be set up, namely a Legislature comprising Congress and Senate, an Executive headed by the President, and a Federal Judiciary with a Supreme Court. The length of term for which individuals would serve in the different branches of government were all staggered so that Congressmen faced election every two years, the President served for four years and Senators were appointed by state legislatures for a six-year term and not subject to popular election until the Constitution was amended in 1913 with the 17th amendment.

Although the President would serve four years, in the Judiciary Federal Justices would be appointed rather than elected. The idea behind the system was to prevent sudden overwhelming and calamitous changes in government. Three states, Delaware, Pennsylvania and New Jersey, ratified this Constitution in 1787, and eight further states followed in 1788. A Bill of Rights followed the Constitution as the first Amendment in 1791. It was modelled on the English 'Declaration of Rights of a Subject under a Just Monarch', which had been proclaimed in 1689. This Bill of Rights was intended to provide protection from oppressive government from the time of Charles II (ruled 1660–1685) onwards. Twenty seven amendments have been made over later years to the original constitution.

George Washington was unanimously elected the first President in 1789 and served two four-year terms, thus establishing a precedent for later holders of the office, he was a slave owner who freed his slaves shortly before he died. He preserved a careful balance and avoided autocratic decisions, so helping the new nation to become unified and develop a sense of nationality. Among these decisions was the creation of a new capital city rather than a choice that would favour an already existing site. The site chosen was in virgin territory on the border between Maryland and Virginia, thus promoting accessibility to both north and south. It was close to Washington's estate and became named after him.

Two broad political party groups emerged, the Federalists, mainly merchants and businessmen favouring a strong central government, and Democratic Republicans, who laid great store on the interests of farmers and individual states, and who eventually evolved into the Democratic Party. Washington appointed Alexander Hamilton (1755–1804) a close aide through the revolution, as the first Secretary of the Treasury in which post he laid solid foundations for the US banking industry as well as establishing a federal bank, sorting out the deficit left following the revolution and strengthening the military; Hamilton died in a duel with Aaron Burr (1756–1836), who was Vice-President at the time and a bitter political opponent.

Thomas Jefferson, the principal author of the Declaration of Independence, became the third President in 1800 after Washington, and John Adams (1735–1826), who was the first Vice-President became the second President. In a heavily contested election for the third president, Jefferson's enemies portrayed him as a possible dictator along Napoleonic lines. Jefferson was however a good and strong federal advocate, though he did buy the Louisiana territory from France in 1803, allowing control of the Mississippi River trade, an act for which he arguably had no mandate. This acquisition doubled the size of the United States at a stroke.

In 1804, Jefferson sponsored a ground-breaking federal expedition by two young army officers Meriwether Lewis and William Clarke to explore the new lands and this culminated in America staking claim to lands west of the Mississippi as far as the Pacific. Jefferson also proposed a national system of roads and canals, including a national road to unite the east and west of the country.

Grumbling hostilities continued through the first decade of the 19th century, particularly at sea with British and French attacks against American shipping, usually with a background of trade embargoes, which almost closed off American commerce with Europe. The French eventually agreed to respect American shipping, but Britain did not, so in the end Congress voted to declare war on Britain. In addition to trade restrictions, the war was against British support for native Indian tribes, for humiliation on the high seas, and with a view to gaining territory from Canada.

The war dragged on for two and a half years and was fought along the Atlantic coast with British blockades, and along the US Canadian border especially the Great Lakes of Ontario and Erie; it was also fought in the south including around New Orleans. British aggression was notched up in 1814 after the downfall of Napoleon released troops from continental duties. Washington with the new Capitol and the White House were burned in August 1814 by the British, but peace was finally secured in January 1815.

The peace ensured that Upper and Lower Canada (Ontario and Quebec) remained subject to the British crown, and that Canada would develop separately and not become part of the United States. The international boundary was agreed west from the Great Lakes along the 49th parallel of latitude to the Pacific Ocean.

No further warfare occurred on American soil for a few years, and in 1823 James Monroe, the fifth President proclaimed the Monroe Doctrine which looked back to the actions of France and Britain in previous years, and with reference particularly to South and Central America, declared that the United States would not tolerate European political interference in the western hemisphere at a time when the South American nations were beginning to emerge as autonomous units, and when it looked as if Spain might try and stop this trend. Monroe is also commemorated in the name of Monrovia, capital city of Liberia in West Africa, founded in 1822 and whose creation he supported as a self-governing country for any freed slaves who wished to return to Africa. Neighbouring Sierra Leone was founded as a British colony in 1808, also as a refuge for displaced or freed slaves following the American civil war.

Before the United States gained its independence, there were numerous clashes between the new settlers and the native Indians, usually over the westward creeping annexation of land by the incoming European colonists. It did not help that various groups of settlers from different European country recruited Indian tribes at various times as allies to fight alongside them in some of their colonial struggles. After independence, and with the population of settlers growing steadily, such conflicts became larger and more problematic, culminating in the War of 1812 when major alliances of Indian tribes fought unsuccessfully against the United States army.

The outcome was a number of treaties, and the passage in 1830 of the Indian Removal Act which allowed the Government to resettle Indians from their tribal lands east of the Mississippi to unsettled lands west of the river following a policy originated by Thomas Jefferson known as "Manifest Destiny", which implied that it was preordained that white settlers would spread across North America and fill the country as far as the Pacific seaboard; the result of all this was to create an enormous area where guerrilla war between settlers and Indians dragged on to the end of the century confirming the reputation of the western states as the 'wild west'.

Unfortunately some tribes were relocated on more than one occasion, overall the result was to segregate the native tribes in reservations where they were away from the settlers' attention, but also where they could not participate in government and were insulated from national education and medical and social support. North of the border in Canada equivalent moves were undertaken but on a mutually agreed basis by treaty without the wars and raiding in the western US. In retrospect it was a deeply flawed policy comparable in some respects to the later apartheid policy in South Africa and presupposing separation of the races; in both instances the indigenous peoples ended up with much smaller and less desirable parcels of land.

During the first few decades of the 19th century, partly from immigration, and partly by internal growth, the US population trebled between 1790 and 1830 to a population of almost 13,000,000. Good land along the eastern seaboard and in the south was already spoken for and developed, and therefore the later settlers pushed west initially to the region of the Louisiana purchase on both sides of the Mississippi, and somewhat later to the Pacific Coast. Around 1780 the land between the Appalachians and the Mississippi had been reserved for Indians, and under President Andrew Jackson (1767–1845), seventh President of the USA from 1829–1837, an Indian Removal Act was signed in 1830 (which was condemned by the US Supreme Court), and the Indians were relocated, often forcibly, to the new wild west lands west of the Mississippi.

To the south and west, Mexico had won its independence from Spain in 1821, but much of the northern part of this territory had already been settled by Anglo-Americans who then rebelled in 1835. They were initially defeated at the Battle of The Alamo, but later battles were won, and Texas, lying between the United

States of America and southern Mexico, became an independent republic. It applied to join the United States and was accepted as a state in 1845. Subsequently, the American government annexed further land to the south, as far as the Rio Grande River: this resulted in the US-Mexican War of 1846 in which America pushed south into the heart of Mexico and captured Mexico City for a while. At the same time America declared California a republic.

Finally, in the Treaty of Guadalupe Hidalgo in 1848, the United States acquired territories that ultimately became the states of Arizona, New Mexico, Nevada, Utah and California in addition to Texas. In the north, where Britain and America shared the Oregon territory extending along the Pacific coast from the far north to the southern border of California, peaceful division of the land was eventually settled with the border continuing along the 49th parallel, leaving British Columbia to the north in Canada, while the southern part of the Oregon territory would evolve into the American states of Washington State, Oregon, Idaho and Montana.

From the territory in the centre of the United States, native Indians were displaced, usually to lands far west of the Mississippi. Five tribes in particular were felt to be "civilised", and had similar values and customs to those of the European settlers. The Seminole tribe from Florida particularly resented their displacement after fighting with the Spanish over it in earlier years, they again fought a guerrilla campaign when threatened with displacement. Four other tribes, Cherokee, Choctaw, Muskogee and Chicksaw, all belonged to the Mississippian native cultures living in towns which were very organised, planned and built on regular patterns.

They farmed the surrounding countryside mainly for maize and beans. These were matriarchal societies established well before the advent of European colonisation, and flourishing from 800 AD onwards. All were displaced and the population of American Indians diminished by about three-quarters during the years of European settlement, partly through disease and partly through a series of running guerrilla wars with the new European settlers.

The early years in the settler frontier states were anarchic ones, fulfilling their description as the wild west. There was no real property definition, there was no law enforcement and settler communities were small. Because of their small size there was no regular police system and vigilantes often filled this gap until later in the century when police forces were established. Similarly, there was no early religious structure, apart from the Catholic Church, though most of the non-conformist churches produced itinerant preachers, who would do a circuit of many communities, stopping only for a day or two in each place.

Many new religious sects were established, and multiple small churches then grew up. The settlers would often start being self-sufficient and farming the land. Sometimes they would set up a mercantile base and make money from selling implements, clothing and other necessities. There were small banks only once communities reached a certain size. The discovery of gold in California in 1848 gave rise to a large Gold Rush in a region where many of the settlements conformed to this pattern. The Californian Gold Rush injected hundreds of millions of dollars into the US circulation, and resulted in a small number of individuals becoming very wealthy. Their wealth came not simply from gold itself, but also from ancillary activities, such as building railroads and importing vital supplies.

It all helped California to be admitted to the Union of States in 1850 as a 'free' state; free in this context meaning that slavery was not allowed. Up to that time there had been fifteen free states and fifteen non-free or slave states in the Union, and California's admission tipped the balance in Congress to a free state majority. The result was a decade of argument in Congress and the Senate and resulted in Abraham Lincoln standing in the Presidential election of 1860 on a policy of ending slavery: because of this seven states seceded from the Union to form the Confederacy before he was inaugurated. The Confederacy finally initiated war in 1861 in an attack on Fort Sumter in Charleston, South Carolina, which was then fiercely responded to by the northern alliance of free states.

The Civil War over the next four years was fought largely on southern territory causing much damage to people, property and infrastructure, resulting in poverty for many, though also freeing many slaves. In 1863, Lincoln issued a Proclamation emancipating three million slaves, but the Confederate south replied by promulgating so called 'Jim Crow Laws' (Jim Crow was a mythical southern black slave) which enforced racial segregation, and were not finally repealed until historic legal cases came before the supreme court in 1964 and 1965. The divide between north and south had been increased by the federal refusal to offer compensation to slave owners when their slaves were freed.

As the civil war was ending, and as his first term of office as the 16th President was coming to an end, Lincoln was assassinated during a theatre performance; he left a legacy of winning the war against the slaver states, strengthening the federal government and preserving the Union.

The war is remembered for General Robert E Lee who fought tenaciously on the Confederate side, and General Ulysses Grant, who was in control of all the Union army by the end of the war. The war finally ended when Lee surrendered at Appottomax Court House in Virginia on 9 April 1865. The human cost of the war is estimated as having caused the death of 8% of all white men between the ages of 13 and 43, but its legacy was also to strengthen the Federal government and to end slavery. The ending of slavery was however largely illusory since racial segregation and the treatment of African-Americans as second class citizens, would persist for a further century, with racial problems still besetting America to the present time.

The north-south divide continued to dominate United States politics through the 19th and 20th centuries due to segregation. On the religious front most of the Protestant communities lined up on the abolitionist side, but the Catholic, Episcopal and Lutheran Churches largely avoided the issue.

With the Civil War behind, however, the United States was liberated to develop its industrial and commercial base. Gold mines continued to pump capital into the economy. The transcontinental railroad would be completed through to the Pacific Coast at Sacramento in 1869, using some European immigrant labour, but a much larger number of imported Chinese labourers, not quite slaves, but definitely under privileged and exploited workers.

The ensuing decades of the next half century would see the United States industrialise and expand its commerce at an ever increasing rate. The US war of Independence is generally recognised as the first revolution in which the populace rebelled with the object of changing their form of government. The French Revolution followed soon after with much the same aims, but finished with an acceptance of the same type of autocratic rule, initially Napoleonic dictatorship and later monarchy once more.

Possible further reading:
A History of the United States by Philip Jenkins (Palgrave Macmillan)
The Penguin History of the USA by Hugh Brogan (Penguin)

Chapter 61
The French Revolution

History is full of rebellions and revolts in which oppressed minorities have risen up against injustice and oppression by their rulers. Few rebellions have been successful in the sense that usually those who were ruled continued to be the underdogs. Sometimes rebellions have resulted in a change of ruler, king or emperor, but the system of a ruling, and very rich elite usually continued after the rebellion, even if the chief, king or emperor at the top of society was changed by the rebellion. The system of societies and governments remained intact and largely autocratic through the centuries. New rulers attempting to put their nation or state onto a more benevolent course often became as autocratic as the leaders they overthrew – one only has to think of the examples of Caesar, Cromwell and Napoleon.

Magna Carta in England in 1215 perhaps represents the thin end of the first wedge in opening the door of emancipation, when the barons humbled King John, and attempted to place curbs on his power (chapter 29). Later the English Civil War in the middle of the 17th century may be seen as a harbinger of the French Revolution. King Charles I of England used his powers arbitrarily, and was seen by the majority of the nation as an authoritarian, spendthrift and feckless ruler.

He was executed in 1649 and the country then spent several years in the turmoil of civil war in which the Puritan Government over-reacted against previous excesses, only for a return to a monarchical system of rule after more than a decade. The restored king, Charles II, was less involved in day to day government, but he was still able to choose and recruit ministers to look after different aspects of the nation's affairs in his name, thereby setting the tone and direction of government and starting to change the previous autocratic system.

Somewhat later, the first of many colonial revolts started in North America in the 1760s. The American colonists and settlers resented rule from London without any representation. The British ruling elite, and King George III in particular, failed to perceive the growing disquiet and resentment in their American colonies, and the reforms that came forwards from Britain always seemed to be too late, too grudging and inadequate. The situation descended into hostilities and in an episode known as the Boston Tea Party, a cargo of tea exported from Britain to America was thrown into the harbour and destroyed (chapter 51).

The smouldering resentment of the colonists flared further after this and broke out into revolution by 1775; the Declaration of Independence was published in July 1776. After skirmishing between British and American forces the colonies agreed to a system of confederation free from Britain and under the name of the United States of America in 1781.

It was against this background that a hotbed of discontent burst into flames in France in 1789. America had followed the thinking of the English physician and philosopher John Locke (1632–1704) a century before, namely that governments hold their power in trust for the people. The American Declaration of Independence consolidated this attitude in the US Constitution. Paris, at this time, was the European centre of political thought and discussion, and it was also home to returning French soldiers who had fought with the colonists against Britain in America, imbibing anti-colonial attitudes.

France had acquired a considerable and still increasing national debt after 150 years of intermittent war, when the nation had tried to maintain its European supremacy. Louis XVI had come to the throne in 1774 and still governed as an absolute monarch. The impending financial crisis was stoked by a taxation system in which French aristocrats and upper classes were immune from much taxation as part of a system of legal and social privileges.

This system was such that effectively, the working middle classes and peasantry comprising the vast bulk of the population were bearing an unfair and much resented proportion of the needed national income generation. This privileged treatment for taxation is one of two major differences at that time compared with Britain; the other being the system of primogeniture under the British law where the eldest surviving son inherited the title and property so keeping the numbers of the aristocracy low and large estates intact; in France titles and property were divided between all surviving male heirs thus increasing the size of the aristocracy and diminishing their size of properties with the passage of time.

In 1788, in the face of mounting crisis and unrest, the Estates General was revived, This congress of individuals had last met in 1614, and although supposedly representative was once again comprised mainly of the upper classes and aristocrats. Population growth through the 18th century in France had outstripped food production, which in turn had led to inflation, and this in turn had given rise to increasing taxes, which were falling most heavily on the least well off. It did not help that through the decade leading up to 1789 there had been a succession of poor harvests caused by adverse weather conditions. Paris was a dirty, crowded and poverty-stricken city with a population density three times that of London.

Thus in 1789, elections to the Estates General took place amidst general poverty and low expectations for the future, which were shared with many other European nations. Everything suddenly changed in the summer when the Estates General, turned itself into a National Assembly and claimed sovereignty. The Estates General was made up of representatives from three categories; the First Estate comprised the clergy, from parish priests to bishops, otherwise known as the Lords Spiritual; the Second Estate was made up of the nobility and aristocracy, also known as the Lords Temporal, while the Third Estate comprised the great remaining mass of the population.

Later, writers would identify a Fourth Estate, namely the press or media. In the bargaining for powers between Louis XVI and the Estates General, Louis consistently offered concessions too late, thereby provoking an increasing crescendo of demands. This did not go down well with the Estates General, and initially, the Third Estate turned itself into a National Assembly and claimed sovereignty. The numerically much smaller First and Second Estates dithered at first, but then threw in their lot with the Third Estate. The resulting National Assembly set out to write a constitution, and over the next two years nationalised Church property, ended the feudal system, ended censorship, and did away with the old Provinces, setting up a system with fewer 'Departments' instead: the Executive Civil Service was separated from the Judiciary.

By 1791, King Louis was suspected of being anti-revolutionary, and his many grudging and drawn out concessions were seen as a continuing attempt to undermine the whole process. The Pope was dragged into the argument, since the Church had lined up against the revolution when Church property was confiscated and nationalised, and the debate continued over whether the Church or the State (i.e. the new French Constitution), should be supreme.

In 1792, France went to war with Austria, and then with Prussia. France then declared war on Britain in 1793, a state of affairs which would last with varying degrees of activity until 1815 and cause much embarrassment to the English Exchequer and even more problems to France. Feelings on each side over revolutionary arguments intensified and the King was largely discredited. Riots in Paris finally overthrew Louis, and a new Assembly was convened to draw up a new Republican Constitution. This new assembly was known as the Convention and would govern France for the next four years. At the beginning of 1793, Louis was condemned to death and executed by the guillotine. The Convention intimidated its opponents to try and preserve the revolution, and the period became known as 'The Terror'.

Many people suspected of being anti-revolutionary were convicted in a very summary system of justice and sent to the guillotine. In Paris some four thousand people died this way, and outside Paris many times more died. This had all been precipitated in August 1792 when the Paris National Guard had stormed and taken over the Royal Palace. Louis seems to have brought this disaster upon himself by trying to impose a veto on the decrees published by the National Assembly (by then called the Legislative Assembly). The monarchy was suspended, and further discussions initiated to draw up a constitution. In the meantime, France remained at war and the battles seemed to go in favour of the French with Prussia being defeated and withdrawing.

A driving force of republicanism through these years was the Society of the Friends of the Constitution, otherwise known as the Jacobins. They were behind the aggressive foreign policy and were advocates of war against Austria. The best known of the Jacobins was Maximilien Robespierre (1758–1794), a lawyer who was also a member of the Estates General and the subsequent Assembly. Robespierre advocated equality of all men and the setting up of a republic. He advocated the abolition of slavery, and felt that France should continue as a Catholic country. He was highly influential throughout 'The Terror' which in the end led to his downfall because of internal dissent and a coup within the Jacobins, who turned on their leaders, including Robespierre; following a violent struggle in which Robespierre was shot, but not killed, he was declared an outlaw shortly afterwards, and was guillotined, along with many supporters.

A second 'White Terror' followed in which many more Jacobins were executed. In this final orgy of internal fighting and executions, the revolution gradually exhausted itself. The ruling Assembly, known as the National Convention, had been put in place in September 1792 when it voted for its first motion 'that Royalty be abolished in France'. It had been the Convention which ordered the execution of Louis XVI and continued to govern France, despite the prevailing unrest.

Among the less successful aspects of the Revolution was the attempt by the National Convention in 1792 to reorganise time, by a group of mathematicians. A new decimal calendar was proposed with three ten day weeks each month, which necessitated an extra six day period to cope with the leap year problem. Days were divided into ten hours, each of one hundred minutes, and divided again into one hundred seconds; the system was not popular and only lasted thirteen years until Napoleon revoked the system when he was appointed Emperor.

By the late 1790s, France was effectively bankrupt, much of this being the result of territorial ambition with large expenditure, that had resulted in the conquest of Belgium, the Rhineland, the Netherlands, Switzerland and much of northern Italy, all of which were being highly taxed with the money returning to France to help maintain its military superiority. General Napoleon had been responsible for most of these conquests, and now carried a conqueror's aura of success about him. He was sent to campaign in Egypt with a view to undermining and reducing the Ottoman Empire and his army was successful, but Britain was still at war with France and with Napoleon; Admiral Nelson was dispatched to the Mediterranean and sank the French fleet at the battle of Aboukir Bay in 1798 by the Nile, thus isolating much of the French army in Egypt.

By 1797, 'The Terror' was over, and a recognisable parliamentary system had been instituted by the Convention, which had ended in 1796. The new governing regime, now called 'The Directory', proved to be somewhat unpredictable and capricious in its decisions. Although less bloodthirsty, the Directory still did not manage to steer a steady middle of the road political course, and generated enemies in the same way that the previous governing elite had done. By this time France had become a secular society, feudalism and legal privilege had been abolished, along with theocratic absolutism and influence over the populace.

Then ten years after the first meeting of the Estates General, some of the politicians in the Directory subverted it in a coup, headed by Napoleon Bonaparte

(1769–1821), the brilliant young general who had risen to high rank early in the revolution, and had enjoyed many military victories through the previous decade. Napoleon was largely responsible for the overthrow of the Directory, and under his subsequent leadership France held on to all the territory gained by military means. In 1802, under the Treaty of Amiens, peace came to Europe for the next fourteen months, with the French Treasury aided by the Louisiana Purchase. Because of the dire nature of the national finances, French possessions in North America, which were not deemed valuable had been sold to the United States.

This sale, the Louisiana Purchase, comprised an enormous area of over two million square kilometres with a colonial and slave population of only about 60,000 people; it could not be defended by France due both to distance, but also due to total lack of finance. The purchase price was some $15 million to America or 68 million francs (modern equivalent almost $600bn) – an effective price of 3 cents an acre, which bolstered the French treasury considerably.

Although many of the changes that had come about in the previous decade were generally welcomed by the population, persecution of the Church, and individual priests in particular, alienated people across the country, and although the Church no longer played a leading role at the heart of the nation, Church life was gradually restored at a local level: the complete abolition of religion from national life envisaged by the radical revolutionaries never came to pass. But most of the reforms envisaged by the revolutionaries had occurred early in the revolutionary process, so that feudalism and legal privilege had been abolished, and the theocratic absolutism and position of the Church at the centre of national life, had also been abolished, such that a decade after the start of the revolution France had a secular society, and as one symptom of this the great cathedral of Notre Dame had been converted to a 'Temple of Reason'.

The rest of Europe had looked on rather aghast at the idea of the revolution, and the enormous changes in the way society was governed were not welcome news to the ruling classes or monarchs across the rest of Europe who worried that their own nations might follow suit.

By the end of the decade in 1799, the monarchy had gone, the Directory had been dissolved and a triumvirate of three Consuls ruled France. These changes had been legally instituted by the remaining 'Council of the Ancients' (the Upper House of the old Directory). Napoleon Bonaparte was named First Consul and rapidly displaced the other two triumvirate consuls so that he was soon declared Emperor.

In effect, Napoleon was now a secular dictator without the considerable input of the Church, where Louis had simply been a monarchical dictator with church backing. The other difference was that unlike Louis XVI, Napoleon did not have a huge entourage of expensive aristocratic courtiers living an elaborate, highly expensive and sycophantic lifestyle at the taxpayer's expense. The new constitution was endorsed by a referendum in 1800 with the general populace feeling that stability had been restored to the country.

Napoleon did away with most of the political advisors and place men who had helped Louis to govern. On the military side he defeated the Austrians once again. He proceeded to reform the law, enshrining the principle of equality of the individual before the law, and strengthened the new Departments (provinces) with an administrative head of each Department called the Prefect. An agreement was signed with the Pope in 1801 recognising the change of status of the Church in France, but not restoring the land and property confiscated by the state during the Revolution. Although Louis XVI had been executed during the Revolution, his ten year old son had notionally become Louis XVII, but then died in prison, possibly poisoned, in 1795.

France was now the dominant country in Europe with Napoleon's campaigns extending into the Iberian Peninsula, where he had installed his brother as King of Spain. and to the east as far as Crimea. To the northeast there was a disastrous campaign when Napoleon invaded Russia in 1812, but so late in the year that when his army reached Moscow they found that the Russians had retreated after burning the city and laying waste to the surrounding countryside, leaving the French army with no shelter or food supplies; in consequence a retreat through snowy winter conditions decimated the French army, with the majority of soldiers dying of starvation or frostbite.

Napoleon remained at war with Britain where the Royal Navy had defeated French forces at the Battle of Aboukir Bay in 1798, and Trafalgar in 1805, thus neutralising the French navy and confining Napoleon. So in early 1814, Napoleon held sway over all of France, the Iberian Peninsula, much of what is now Germany, Bavaria, Italy and the Croatian coastline. This empire had all been achieved at the cost of considerable loss of troops from his armies, particularly in his unsuccessful Russian campaign. The Low Countries, Italy and Switzerland were effectively occupied and subservient.

Much of Europe up to that time had existed as small principalities, such that at the beginning of the French revolution there were more than three hundred different political entities in Europe, which were reduced by Napoleon's conquests and campaigns to only thirty-eight states by 1815. In all of these countries the new Napoleonic legal code had been imposed producing a degree of overall conformity.

Apart from the reorganisation of Europe, Napoleon had stirred up considerable nationalistic and patriotic feelings in many states which were not averse to some of the benefits brought by the French revolution, but were severely antagonised by their subservience to France including the requirement to provide troops for the French army. From before the time of the French revolution Britain had been at war with France, and the peace made in 1802 lasted less than two years.

Napoleon had intended to invade Britain, but the French and Spanish fleet sent to achieve this in 1805 had been intercepted and chased south before being defeated at the Battle of Trafalgar by Admiral Horatio Nelson (1758–1805). Napoleon's subsequent military victories kept the British alerted to his empire building intentions, which were all shattered following his invasion of Russia in 1812 when his army was decimated. Continental countries fought back and by 1814 Paris was occupied. Napoleon had overstretched himself, and was forced to abdicate and was sent into exile on the Mediterranean Island of Elba by the British and their allies.

Less than a year later, he was able to escape from Elba in March 1815, and as he journeyed north to Paris, loyal troops rallied to him, such that he had a large army by June when he was confronted at Waterloo by British, Dutch and Prussian troops under the command of the Duke of Wellington. Napoleon was defeated and under the Treaty of Vienna, he was banished to the remote Atlantic island of St Helena, where he died in 1821, having caused an estimated six million deaths in the Napoleonic wars of the preceding twenty-two years.

The combination of Napoleon's rule and the French revolution left behind enormous changes in Europe, legal, economic and social. Napoleon bequeathed to France an efficient tax system and the restoration of the church, but not church property. He kept conscription, which had started in the early revolutionary years: from then on army officers and civil servants were recruited and promoted on merit and not by their aristocratic rank. He improved higher education, where the revolution had abolished universities, and replaced them with 'écoles polytechniques'. He centralised government administration and created a system of governing France with eighty discreet 'Departments' with a centrally appointed Prefect in charge of each. He was also the moving spirit behind the Napoleonic Code of law, which, although it was largely written by one of the other Consuls, effectively ended feudalism, liberated serfs and spread throughout Europe, partly by Napoleonic conquest and partly by adoption. He perpetuated the values of the Revolution, namely Liberté, Egalité and Fraternité.

The next fifty years saw nationalism, liberalism and emancipation spread across the countries of Europe with frequent attempts at further revolution. The Treaty of Vienna in 1815 had effectively ended the French wars and much of the territorial dispositions that came out of the Treaty restored the position of two decades previously, and were aimed at containing France and avoiding revolution in other countries. Arising from the Treaty, Prussia acquired much land on the Rhine, a new Low Countries nation appeared with a Dutch King, and Austria recovered her former Italian possessions.

Revolutionary plotters were contained across Europe and borders remained relatively static for the forty years up to 1848, when a new crop of revolutions exploded onto the scene. Overall however, like the American Revolution, this was an example of people overthrowing their rulers, rather than a war of a ruler fighting another ruler for territory, although the conduct of Napoleon rather blurs the distinction.

Possible further reading:
The French Revolution by William Doyle (Oxford University Press)
The Napoleonic Wars by Mike Rapport (Oxford University Press)

Chapter 62
Britain 1760–1810

In 1760, George III came to the British throne. He was 22 years old and the grandson of George II, since his father had already died. He had been brought up with animosity towards Prime Minister William Pitt the Elder, who settled the situation by retiring. Three years later Pitt's achievements were clearly confirmed with Britain acknowledged to have control over the West Indies and India: this achievement however had been expensive and had greatly increased the national debt.

The young George III tried to pick up the reins of government personally, and attempted to address the national debt with stamp duties and import duties, particularly on corn, paper and tea. These extra taxes were resented, particularly in America, but with the Industrial Revolution now turning out large quantities of consumer goods, additional export markets were needed. George, who did not belong to a political party and therefore had no available supporting party of MPs in Parliament, was finding government difficult.

The situation lasted three years before Pitt the Elder was asked to return to office, which he did by accepting the title of Lord Chatham and moving to the Upper House as Lord Privy Seal, from where he was able to run the Cabinet and parliamentary affairs. His government gradually imposed taxes on corn, tea and paper which caused the start of alienation of the American colonies. His health improved and he lived for another ten years as a backbencher in the Lords.

During this time, he attempted to reconcile the attitudes of the American colonists with those of England in general, and George III in particular. He would later be succeeded into high office by his son William Pitt the Younger (1759–1806) who became England's youngest Prime Minister in 1783 at the age of 24.

The result of the imposed import duties was complete alienation of the American colonists. The duties had been imposed across the empire with the British cabinet counting the cost of the Seven Years War protecting Britain from French autocracy and revolution. Whilst the American colonies were unhappy about the imposition of these taxes, their main objection was that this was done without any representation of the colonies in the British Parliament, although the cost of providing protection to the American colonies amounted to far more than the new taxes could have raised.

The situation came to a head when the East India Company, alone and struggling financially, was allowed to ship tea to America, further exacerbating the resentment, and culminating in the 'Boston Tea Party' where rival tea merchants dressed up as native Indians, and threw the offending cargo of tea into Boston harbour. Government reaction was slow because of the delay of weeks for news to cross the Atlantic, but King George and the British parliament reacted by trying to reimpose direct rule on the Massachusetts colony. This all resulted in a Colonial Congress in 1774 which wrote a Declaration of Rights and instituted a boycott of British imports. Neither side appears to have been listening to the other, and the situation gradually escalated, resulting in the British governor of Massachusetts attempting to capture the colonists' militia bases in Lexington and Concord, which he failed to do.

The following year, the Declaration of Independence was produced in 1776, written mainly by a 33 year old Thomas Jefferson (1743–1826), who would later become the third President of the United States, and declaring amongst other things "that all men are created equal". Needless to say, the irony that this assertion did not apply to slaves and native Indians, let alone women, was overlooked (after decades of campaigning women finally achieved the vote in national elections in America in 1920 with passage of the 19th amendment, although some states had emancipated women earlier).

For the following five years, rebelling colonists and loyalists waged a grumbling war up and down the east coast of America, aided and abetted by the French and Spanish; a French fleet came to patrol the American coastline, and prevented both trade and the movement of British troops who could no longer be supplied and were forced to surrender at Yorktown on Chesapeake Bay in 1781 to the colonists' commander George Washington, who was to become the first American President. Britain accepted the Yorktown surrender as a final verdict on the American colonies and in the Paris Treaty of 1783 formal independence was granted to the American colonies.

Following this, a young James Madison (1751–1836) undertook much of the task of drawing up the Constitution and the Bill of Rights with Thomas Jefferson; only later was he elected to Congress and worked as a close advisor for President Washington, in time becoming the fourth President of the USA himself.

George III, who had lost the confidence of his ministers, asked William Pitt, son of William Pitt the Elder to become Prime Minister at the age of 24. William Pitt the Younger proved a capable and popular Prime Minister, remaining in office for the next 17 years, many of which were spent on combating and protecting the country against France, initially through the years of the Revolution, and later through the years of Napoleonic expansionist ambition.

A few years later, much of the philosophy of the French Revolution appeared to be an imitation of the principles of self-government which the American colonists had promulgated earlier, though with more savage violence and executions. While France was in the throes of revolution British social conditions were poor and anti-Catholic discrimination persisted following the Popery Act of 1698 which was passed into law to reinforce strict prohibition on Catholics, both lay and clergy. A new act of Parliament was intended to diminish discrimination but only served to provoke a Protestant backlash from the large Protestant Association. Following a large march by the Association to parliament, a petition was presented, but after parliamentary debate was overwhelmingly defeated. Nevertheless, days of protest and rioting followed and the army needed to be called in to restore order, which was achieved only after 285 rioters were shot and killed with many others wounded or arrested; late trials and executions followed. The riots, subsequently named the Gordon Riots after the charismatic but bizarre leader of the Protestant Association, Lord Gordon, damaged Britain's reputation and highlighted the absence of a regular police force which was already present in many other European countries.

Many English people saw the French Revolution as pursuing the same road taken by the American colonists, whilst Edmund Burke (1730–1797), an influential English MP, regarded as the founder of English conservatism, disagreed saying that the Revolution had "subverted monarchy but not recovered freedom". He predicted that the eventual result of the French Revolution would be dictatorship, as indeed it turned out. Pitt had not foreseen the chaos the French Revolution would cause, nor had he foreseen that soon after the execution of Louis XVI in 1793 France would declare war on Britain.

Other European countries besides Britain observed the French Revolution with horror and anxiety, fearful lest the revolutionary cause should spread across the rest of Europe. These fears were intensified after Louis XVI was sent to the guillotine, and the anarchy of the Terror Years resulted. They were years in which Britain was protected by its navy, with the French fleet being destroyed at the Battle of the Nile in 1798. Following this national French catastrophe Napoleon became a much more autocratic dictator.

At this stage, it is necessary to turn aside briefly and consider Ireland, where Catholic emancipation had ground to a halt. Catholic militias had come into being and the French Revolution had given hopes of emancipation to Irish Catholics whilst leading the London government to fear Irish revolution. A young Dublin lawyer called Theobald Wolfe Tone (1763–1798) produced pamphlets on behalf of the Catholics and then visited the rebellious American colonists in 1795, subsequently returning to visit the French revolutionary leaders of the Directoire in 1796. As a result, the Directoire then resolved to send an army of 15,000 men to support an Irish uprising.

A fleet of 43 ships left Brest and managed to avoid the British naval blockade, but storms drove them far out into the Atlantic before they were able to return and make landfall at Bantry Bay in southwest Ireland. At this point an invasion would have caused a very severe embarrassment to the British authorities, but French resolution crumbled, and after a week anchored offshore, the French ships returned home. Reprisals against Catholics followed, and although a rebellion broke out in Dublin in May 1798, it was suppressed within a week. Tone himself was eventually captured aboard a French ship off the Irish coast wearing a French uniform, he was tried and found guilty of treason, but frustrated the hangman by committing suicide first.

Under George IV, active union of Britain and Ireland was signed in 1800 at a time when Ireland's population amounted to 25% of the rest of the UK, and when Irish Catholics were still smarting under the veto of George III which prevented Catholics from taking up public office.

At the end of the French Revolution in 1797, Napoleon had been campaigning very successfully throughout Europe and was in Italy from where he was dispatched by the French War Minister to attack British interests in the Mediterranean. This confirmed Pitt the Younger's views in which he saw England as needing to rescue Europe from French ambitions, as his father had done during the conflict of the Seven Years War (1756–1763). Accordingly, Admiral Nelson (1758–1805) was dispatched with a fleet to the Mediterranean where he destroyed the French fleet at the Battle of the Nile in 1798.

The following year, Napoleon staged a coup declaring himself dictator; the result of this was that Pitt had to introduce Britain's first income tax (at a rate of 1%) to raise money for the continuing war. But thanks to British naval power under Nelson at the Battle of the Nile, Napoleon was contained and restricted to the continental mainland. In this way Britain spent the first years of the 19th century coping with the sequelae of the French Revolution and the subsequent dictatorship and ambitions of Napoleon.

In 1802, the British government made peace with Napoleon, only for the French to renege on the settlement in 1804. Pitt the Younger was recalled to government as Napoleon assembled an army at Boulogne to invade Britain. A considerable French fleet would be required to transport the troops, and so the Royal Navy under Admiral Nelson was sent to locate and destroy the French vessels. It took until October 1805 before the Royal Navy cornered a combined French and Spanish fleet off Cape Trafalgar in southern Spain. Nelson used innovative and unusual tactics by sailing his fleet in line astern at right angles to the spread out French and Spanish vessels. He destroyed two-thirds of the thirty-three French ships without losing one of his own, but died towards the end of the battle, shot by a French sniper in the rigging of an adjacent vessel. The battle ensured that Britain was thenceforward free of military threat from France under Napoleon.

Pitt the Younger was to die of exhaustion soon afterwards, but in May 1806 a Whig government abolished the British slave trade (though not slavery itself) following a campaign by Charles James Fox (1749–1806) MP, a prominent Whig parliamentarian, together with William Wilberforce MP (1759–1833) an evangelical Christian, and Methodist founder John Wesley (1703–1791), who died before seeing the outcome of the long campaign. It would take another 25 years for slavery in general to be abolished across the British Empire (but of course not in America where slavery continued and led eventually to the Civil War of the 1860s).

When Pitt died in 1806, a large gap was left at the top of the parliamentary system, with no obvious successor, while at the same time George III became mentally unstable. His madness included a degree of violence and aggression, necessitating his incarceration for his own and other people's protection. It appears with modern knowledge that the condition he suffered from was porphyria, and when it became apparent that recovery was unlikely, his son was declared Prince Regent.

The next few years were known for the Prince's dandyism, and the extravagant parties and balls that he sponsored; the years became known as the Regency Period, implying a time of glittering social extravagance and excess, but ignoring much general poverty and unrest. He was finally crowned George IV when his father died in 1820.

On the continent, Napoleon had been forced to change his ambitions because of British mastery of the seas. He led his large army east to fight the Austrians and the Russians, whom he defeated at the Battle of Austerlitz in the modern day Czech Republic in 1805, following which he continued to dominate Europe, invading Spain and Portugal in 1808 and making his brother Joseph, King of Spain. The British army sent to help resistance fighters in Spain suffered early setbacks with a major defeat at Corunna in northern Spain in 1809. Subsequently, however, they were able to achieve victory over Napoleon's forces in Spain at Salamanca in 1812 and Vittoria in 1814.

This was after Napoleon had invaded Russia in 1812 where he suffered a crushing defeat by the weather, as well as at the hands of the Russians. He had left his invasion too late in the year, and his supply lines on the way to Moscow became hopelessly overextended and inadequate. The Russian tactics of avoiding confrontation and drawing him ever further into their country while burning villages and crops in front of the advancing army resulted in an eventual inevitable final defeat in which the major part, perhaps three quarters, of Napoleon's very large army of around 650,000 men succumbed to disease, starvation and freezing conditions, rather than dying in battle.

Thus weakened, in April 1814, Napoleon was forced from power in a European settlement, and was banished to the Italian island of Elba. He subsequently escaped from Elba, returning to southern France in March 1815, raising an army as he marched north to Paris. At the Battle of Waterloo, in the central Netherlands, a combined Prussian, Dutch and British army under the command of the Duke of Wellington, inflicted a complete defeat. This time Napoleon was banished to the remote Atlantic island of St Helena, from which escape was not feasible, and where he died in 1821.

Throughout these years, the Industrial Revolution was forging ahead in Britain following Richard Trevithick's first use of steam power in 1804. In the period between 1821 and 1825 George Stephenson (1781–1848) built the first railway, which ran between Stockton and Darlington, and thereafter the use of steam power, both for rail transport and for water transport, rapidly multiplied. The first paddle steamer from the United States had docked at Liverpool in 1819, and the first British steamship journeyed to South America in 1821; these ships were powered by sail as well as by steam, since their steam power was insufficient for long journeys as they could not carry sufficient coal.

After the battle of Waterloo in 1815 had ended European hostilities, the Vienna Treaty had restored much of the map of Europe, but had not abolished the spirit of revolution. In Britain, Corn Laws were introduced putting an import duty on wheat to protect British farmers, and this increased the price of bread leading to riots. Industrial unrest due to the dreadful social conditions in many factories, together with unemployment and low wages, led to the rise of protestors known as Luddites who came in gangs to smash factory machinery. A peaceful demonstration in 1815 at St Peter's Field in Manchester, against lack of parliamentary representation, was broken up by troops with considerable violence, including some deaths and many injuries, and became known as the Peterloo Massacre thereby comparing it with the carnage of the Battle of Waterloo.

Transition from Regent to Monarch at the advent of George IV's reign in 1820 did not help matters as he remained both a glutton and a spendthrift, and the Regency period of social profligacy and extravagance continued. First during his period as Prince Regent, and then later as George IV, this disparity between the wealthy and the workers was emphasised by the ostentation of the upper classes compared with the crowding and poverty of workers in the newly expanding cities. The population of England had doubled from five million in 1700 to almost twice that number in 1800, and then doubled again in the next quarter of a century. The whole landscape was changing with industrialisation and the new manufacturing cities of Manchester, Birmingham, Leeds, Bradford, and Sheffield were coming to dwarf the old cathedral cities.

Possible further reading:
Pitt the Younger by Michael J Turner (Hambledon and London)

Chapter 63
Emerging Africa, Japan, China and India

Awareness of Africa was very restricted through the Middle Ages in Europe, indeed knowledge of pre-literate Africa still remains very limited. Stone Age peoples were living in a relatively temperate climate in the fourth and fifth millennia BC. They left their evidence in the form of cave paintings, which show that even at that time, goats, sheep and cattle had been domesticated, and elephants and hippopotami were living in a region which has now become the Sahara Desert. By the time of the Roman Empire, North Africa, along the shores of the Mediterranean (present Tunisia and Libya), supplied a large proportion of the grain needed in Rome that the less productive Italian estates could not manage (chapter 19).

Ancient Carthage (present day Tunis) had been founded in 814 BC as a Phoenician colony which later achieved independence about 650 BC, and became a serious rival to Rome, resulting in the Punic (meaning Phoenician) Wars between the Roman central empire and the Phoenician-descended inhabitants of North Africa and Carthage. The first Punic war erupted with much naval conflict between 264 and 241 BC. The second Punic War, lasting from 218 to 201 BC, was much more fierce, and extended as far west as Phoenician bases on the southern Iberian Peninsula. This second war included the Phoenician General Hannibal's famous march from southern Spain to northern Italy through the Alps with war elephants, and ended in impressive victories in Italy first at Lake Trasimene and later at Cannae south of Rome, where on each occasion he destroyed greatly superior Roman forces.

Hannibal never managed to occupy and defeat Rome itself and finally met his match in North Africa in 202 BC, when he was defeated by the Roman general, Scipio Africanus. After the stalemate of the first two wars, the third Punic War came with resumption of hostilities in 149 BC, when the Romans won decisively, and in their revenge Carthage itself was completely flattened and turned back to agricultural land, with all its inhabitants being massacred, or sold into slavery, under the close eye of an infuriated Rome. North Africa continued to supply Rome with much of its food stuffs, but only as part of a closely governed Roman province.

Much later in the 5th century AD, as Rome collapsed, north-eastern European tribes including Vandals, Ostrogoths and Huns rampaged across western Europe. In 410 after the Goths sacked Rome, there was further movement of tribes across the Alps, westwards along the shores of the Mediterranean, and into the Iberian

Peninsula, from where the tribes crossed to Africa, and then spread back eastwards along to the old site of Carthage. The Vandal tribe established a navy and sailed north across the Mediterranean to sack Rome in 455, in the process giving their name to mindless pillage and looting that we now call vandalism.

Following Mohammed's preaching and then death in 632, Islam was ruled by Quraysh Caliphs (leading to the Shia branch of Islam), until the last one was deposed and murdered in 661, to be succeeded by the Umayyad Caliphate (leading to Sunni Islam), which would last for the next two centuries. In the meantime Arab armies had spread both east and west, conquering the northern coast of Africa as far as the Straits of Gibraltar by 711 and then crossing into Spain. All along the southern coast of the Mediterranean Islam became the dominant force, extending southwards into Africa along trade routes, around and across what had now become the Sahara Desert.

Islam also extended down the east coast of Africa, but did not penetrate the interior and remained confined to the coastal trading routes. With the advent of aggressive trading by European nations in the 18th and 19th centuries European settlements grew up around the coast of Africa. Possession of Cape Town, on the southern tip of the continent, became important during the 16th and 17th centuries to protect and supply the increasing numbers of trading vessels passing to and from India and the Far East. Significant exploration of Africa's interior would wait until the 19th century.

---oOo---

China has remained aloof from much of the warring that occurred across Asia and Europe for most of the last four millennia, except for its own empire building by conquest of adjacent lands (chapter 7). Excellent Chinese records exist to show the determination of successive Emperors to maintain a historical record, albeit an often selective one which recorded only the ruling classes' perception of events, which is accordingly very one-sided. Although dynasties and empires changed, the elite administrative class persisted across these apparently different eras, thus keeping China on a fairly steady path of development.

A combination of distance east from Europe, Africa and India, together with barriers of mountains and deserts, meant that interchange of trade, let alone people and their attitudes, was severely limited, though there is good evidence for regular use of the Silk Roads for the purposes of trade even before the first millennium. The Ch'in Dynasty in the 3rd and 4th centuries BC unified the area and the nation which even today is recognisably close to present day China.

The teachings of Confucius from around 500 BC also provided continuity of purpose and outlook and reinforced governing principles, which survived in a relatively unchanged fashion though the first millennium AD, and up to the time of Genghis Khan in the 13th century. His Mongol armies fought their way eastwards to conquer China, as well as westward into Europe and south into Asia. On conquering China the grandson of Genghis Khan, Kublai Khan, took Peking as his capital, founding the Yuan dynasty at the end of the 13th century in 1271, though by this time, the Mongols appear to have become Chinese, rather than succeeding in changing the Chinese into Mongols. Mongol rule in China collapsed in the mid-14th century following rural rebellions which culminated in 1368 with the Mongols being driven out of Peking, and the Ming Dynasty being founded. The Ming Dynasty managed to preserve the political unity of China, along with encouraging considerable culture, and lasted for almost three centuries.

The Ming dynasty is remembered as a high point of Chinese painting and pottery. The early years of the Ming Dynasty came at a time when official China allowed some emergence from its self-imposed isolation; 1557 saw the first European trading establishment allowed to set up a base in Macao. With the traders came Roman Catholic missionaries and some early European imports. In the early 17th century the Ming Dynasty was threatened by tribes from the north living in Manchuria. Following a peasant revolt, the Manchu people invaded China in 1644; the Manchu conquest was short and brutal, with many millions dying.

A new Emperor was installed, but once again the civil service machine persisted, providing administrative continuity for this new Qing Dynasty, which then lasted to the early years of the 20th century. Chinese control was extended to include Formosa, Tibet and Mongolia, and there were some border clashes, both with Russian territory to the north, as well occupation and control being imposed on Korea to the east, and on territory to the south of China, including Burma (Myanmar). China continued under the Manchu-led Qing Dynasty with the perfection of its technological achievements, but within a culture which did not encourage technical or intellectual questioning, innovation or invention.

Further development of Chinese society and culture would await the importation of European trade and practices in the late 19th century. The notorious Opium War of 1839 was initiated by Britain to open China to British trading, and finished with European trade access to five Chinese ports and British occupation of Hong Kong on a long-term 150 year lease, which ended in 1997.

---oOo---

Japan was first populated from the northern mainland in the early centuries after the end of the last Ice Age, with further migrations, probably from Korea, around the 3rd century BC. Japan in its early days developed after civilisation on the mainland, with progression from the Stone to the Bronze Age, and in turn onto the Iron Age, somewhat later than in China. Japan was, however, blessed with a mild island climate and land which was happily able to support a relatively large population. Chinese records first mention Japan in the 3rd century AD, and then Japanese interventions in Korea resulted in closer contacts, with the teachings of Confucius and Buddha, together with Iron Age technology, coming across the sea from China.

Early Chinese writing was also brought to Japan, but despite this the cultures remained separate, and attempts to impose a Chinese type central political system in Japan all failed. Through the first millennium AD small local warlords ruled in a system of feudal anarchy in which cultural life involved participation in a family centred, and ancestor worshipping religion, called Shinto (chapter 76).

At the beginning of the 8th century, a permanent imperial capital came into being on the site of modern Kyoto, with an Emperor and subservient aristocracy. This system failed to thrive, and over the next few centuries political power gradually returned to the hands of many local warlords, with their own small armies of samurai warriors. Japan became united under a military leader known as the 'Shogun', who was theoretically subservient to the Emperor, but in practice controlled the government from the 13th century onwards (albeit with episodes of civil war as different warlords fought for the shogunate). The time from 1467–1568 was a period of considerable instability with running civil war.

Three powerful shoguns finally brought the nation together: Oda Nobunaga ruled brutally for a decade from 1576–1586 until he was overpowered and committed ritual suicide, he was followed by Toyotomi Hideyoshi whose attempted expansionist invasions of Korea both failed before his death in 1598, and he was succeeded in power by Tokugawa Ieyasu who died in 1616 leaving a largely united country. This situation then lasted to 1866; during these two and a half centuries the shoguns marginalised the Emperor to be a cultural and titular head of state with no political input or power.

An American military visit to promote trade in 1853, had been able to impose American commercial access by gunboat diplomacy on the isolationist and divided Japan. This acted as a catalyst for Japan to consider modernising itself along more modern and European lines. The 17th shogun in direct line from Tokugawa surrendered his powers to the Emperor, who was a powerless figurehead at that stage and in 1868, after both factional fighting and political infighting, the Emperor Meiji was restored to power as a means of strengthening Japan against the external threat posed by the European powers of the 19th century. Once the Emperor was restored to power, Japan embarked on a remarkably rapid conversion in the last decades of the 19th century into a modern Europeanised nation from its previous feudal state.

---oOo---

Early Korean history is covered in chapter 8.

---oOo---

Indian civilisation developed early in the Indus Valley as already noted in chapter seven. Once again, it is the writings of European visitors, Greek rather than Roman, which provide contemporary reports around the end of the first millennium BC. The different customs and foods of India surprised these early travellers, who also noted two distinct religious traditions, one Brahmin and the other Buddhist; they were also surprised by what they thought was the absence of slaves, though this was disguised within the caste system.

The Indian sub-continent is large and has always been difficult to unite and to rule. Under the rule of the Guptas in the 4th century AD, northern India was gradually united, and continued to develop a Sanskrit written culture, derived from the early Aryan Hindu religious writings. It was around the 5th century AD that the decimal system first appeared, later to be exported through Islamic Arabia and on to Christian Europe. Hinduism and Buddhism were developing in the centuries up to the arrival of Islam in the 8th century, first with trade, but soon afterwards with conquering Arab armies, who gradually established an early Muslim empire in the Ganges Valley.

In 1398, a Mongol army under Timur Lang, or Tamerlane (1346–1405) sacked Delhi in northern India, but achieved little more (chapter 28). In the 16th century Babur of Kabul (1483–1530), descendent of Timur through his father and Genghis Khan through his mother, came to colonise and rule in northern India. He kept a remarkable diary, which has survived to give a valuable insight into his cultured existence, as well as his military prowess. His reign marks the start of Mughal India, the word being a corruption of Mongol. His kingdom, when he died in 1530, stretched right across northern India, including the head waters of the River Indus in the west, and the River Ganges in the east.

Timur and his descendants built an Empire comprising most of India and Afghanistan, which was extraordinary, powerful and wealthy. Initially, Babur had conquered northern India around Delhi, but then only survived for a further four years. After his death in 1530 there was an interim period in which his son Humayun (1508–1556) lost territory to Persia, but was able to regain it some years later. This reign of Babur's son Humayun, was a time of relative instability, at least partly resulting from the claims of his several half-brothers who split up the kingdom.

When Babur's grandson, Akbar, succeeded to the throne in 1556 at the age of 14, his considerable talents meant that he was able to take on many of the royal duties as statesman and warrior within a few years, and as he reigned for almost fifty years, he had time to consolidate and extend the territorial domination of the Mughals, thus leaving to his successors more than twice the extent of empire that existed at the time of Babur's death. Although Akbar was Muslim, he incorporated both Muslims and Hindus into his government. India's rich resources, including both land and gold, were able to support a large standing army, and internal peace was furthered by a policy of toleration to all faiths, together with a taxation policy which did not penalise non-Muslims. Akbar survived to build a large empire, including much of western India, together with what is now Pakistan, in addition to the land conquered by his grandfather. He reigned for almost 50 years, dying in 1605 shortly after Queen Elizabeth I in Britain. The administrative system set up by Akbar then lasted through to the time of the British Raj in the mid-19th century.

Akbar's son, Jahangir (1569–1627), was able to extend his territorial authority further. His internal authority was somewhat challenged by two incidents: the first of these was the execution of Arjun, the ninth Guru of the Sikh religion, for subverting the Emperor's authority, the second problem came with the imprisonment of a leading Muslim theologian who criticised the Mughal policy of ignoring Sharia law. Shah Jahan (1628–1658), the fifth Mughal emperor, two generations later, built the Taj Mahal for his favourite wife who died in 1651. Shah Jahan also built several highly decorated and magnificent mosques, though his profligacy with money weakened the exchequer, in the end he was effectively overthrown and kept under house arrest for the last ten years of his reign by his children.

Shah Jahan's third son, Aurungzeb (1618–1707), ousted his three brothers and later imprisoned his elderly father to become an absolute ruler, promoting religious intolerance and suppressing the Hindu religion and its temples. His unpopularity undermined his attempts at military expansionism. When he died in 1707 instability followed, partly as a result of the other three sons disputing the succession, and partly because of increased European intervention. By the time of his death the Mughal Empire covered almost the whole of the Indian subcontinent, which in fact was close to the same size as it had been at the end of Akbar's reign, though warfare in southern and central India, and in the north-west, had weakened the Empire.

The first Europeans to reach India were the Portuguese who appeared on the west coast at the end of the 15th century, and whose traders followed, together with the inevitable catholic missionaries. The British East India Company was founded on 31 December 1600, and their first traders appeared at Babur's Court in Agra some three years later, but the British were more easily tolerated by the populace, since as Protestants, they brought fewer religious icons and missionaries than the Catholic Portuguese.

Following Babur's death, the Moghul Emperors continued in line of direct descent, initially increasing the size of the empire, but subsequently fading somewhat during the second half of the 17th century. During this period the wife of Shah Jahan died, and in her memory he erected the Taj Mahal, possibly the best known and most beautiful Islamic building in the world. Military campaigns, and the profligacy of the Indian Court exemplified in the building of the Taj Mahal, contributed to the gradual financial embarrassment and decline of the Mogul Empire. Adding to the Portuguese and the English, the French had also founded an East India Company in 1664, which then established its own trading settlement. Through the beginning of the 18th century the Mogul empire gradually crumbled under the weight of its vast military spending and court costs, and was unable to present a united front against all these European traders.

Possible further reading:
A History of China by JAG Roberts (Palgrave MacMillan)
A History of India by Peter Robb (Palgrave)

Chapter 64
The Industrial Revolution

The Industrial Revolution is understood to be a period of years in the English Midlands, notably Shropshire and Staffordshire, between about 1760 and 1840, when the mechanisation of manufacturing rapidly transformed an economy from many small craftsmen making individual products in their homes, to a much larger economy in which the same products, clothes, pottery, glass, and even weapons, for instance, were produced more rapidly, more consistently, and more cheaply with the use of machines in factories.

The Revolution required, firstly a source of power which was efficient and consistent, and secondly, machinery which would stand up to repetitive heavy use. The old use of wind and water power was at times capricious in its supply, and was also limited by its geographical situation. Coal instead of wood provided greater power instead of using timber to produce steam. Coal was known in ancient China 6,000 years ago; more recently there is evidence for its use in domestic heating during Roman times, and where easily accessed surface outcrops occurred, it had continued in use through medieval times.

The use of coal instead of wood, and of coke instead of charcoal, permitted higher temperatures and greater efficiency in the smelting of iron. Abraham Darby (1678–1717), a Quaker from the English Midlands invented an efficient blast furnace to produce iron in 1709, and his work was carried on by his son who produced further improvements in the furnaces. It was Abraham Darby's grandson, also called Abraham Darby, who built the iconic Iron Bridge in 1778 over the River Severn in Shropshire, thereby demonstrating the versatility of iron construction compared with the stone or brick methods used previously. The region around Shropshire and Staffordshire in the English Midlands spawned much of the early industrial Revolution because of its wealth of easily available coal.

Iron was needed to produce efficient steam engines, the first of which had been built by Thomas Savary in 1698 (chapter 58). Much of Savary's engine, and many other early models, used wood, but iron was more predictable and lasting. Thomas Newcomen (1664–1729), an English ironmonger supplying mining equipment in Devon, used Savary's ideas together with those of Denis Papin (1647–1713), a French physicist and inventor, to produce an improved steam engine in 1712 whose pistons drove pumps to remove water from deep mines, both the coal mines of Shropshire and the north-east of England, and the tin and copper mines of Devon and Cornwall. The use of steam engines provided an enormous step forward in efficiency and power with a diminished requirement for fuel where previous generations had used horses and wind power to pump water from wells or mines, followed by water power, until steam power became available.

Much of the early use of this power in Britain was channelled into the production of textiles from cotton imported from America. Mechanical spinning of cotton and the use of power looms increased productivity by an estimated 40–50 times. The 'Spinning Jenny' produced by Richard Arkwright, and the use of power to run the weaving looms, represented a major step forward in the production of cloth: indeed, because of this mechanisation of producing cloth, Arkwright (1732–1792), a British inventor from Lancashire, has been called the 'Father of the Industrial Revolution'. His title is further reinforced by the factory system with associated housing in which Arkwright installed his machinery and workers to produce an industrial system quite unrecognisable from fifty years previously.

This industrialisation, with the founding of factories, and often workers' villages to go with them, was typical of the way industrial development would proceed through the next century. Craft cottage industries could not compete with the new mass produced products, and the factories required large numbers of labourers, who hitherto could only have found employment on the land producing crops. It is estimated that before the Industrial Revolution about 80% of the population needed to be involved in agricultural production to feed the country; by the beginning of the 19th century this proportion had dropped to around 35%, leaving the remaining two-thirds of the population to work as craftsmen or factory hands.

At the same time, the individual working man's output had increased enormously thanks to machinery. Incomes had risen together with regular employment, and with them standards of living, though for much of the population living standards were still pretty miserable. The Industrial Revolution was not free of problems and many craftsmen resented having to move to towns and cities, and were especially suspicious of the machines which they thought would replace their jobs. It was commonly felt that the machines were a way of replacing skilled artisans with less skilled and less well paid workers.

There were riots in Birmingham in 1791 against dissenters (or non-conformists) which tied in with the revolutionary ideals coming from France. Joseph Priestley (1733–1804) was particularly singled out, both as an advocate of new ideas, and as a founding member of the new Unitarian church. Chapels, houses and businesses were burnt down and Priestley himself was forced to move, first to London, and then to the United States. A movement known as the Luddites came into being in Nottingham in 1811 which was dedicated to destroying the new machinery which people felt would replace their jobs in due course.

The Agricultural Revolution that ran side by side with the Industrial Revolution was made possible by agricultural mechanisation. Jethro Tull (1674–1741) was an Englishman from Berkshire who initially trained as a lawyer but then inherited his father's farm and pioneered agricultural technology with the production of a horse drawn seed drill in 1701, that was able to sow seeds in rows much more quickly and evenly than several agricultural labourers working at the same time. He devised similar mechanisation of ploughing and harrowing, which added further efficiency to agriculture.

The mechanisation of agriculture was also hastened by the Enclosures which was the practice of enclosing adjacent smallholdings to create a larger unit or farm, sometimes caused by the tenant or owner being forced to migrate to a factory job in the city. The process commenced at the beginning of the 17th century but rose to a peak between 1760 and 1820. In achieving enclosure by the many Enclosure Acts of Parliament in the 100 years following 1773 much common land, previously used for grazing and crops, came under the control of single individuals, so disenfranchising the peasants who had previously farmed their smallholdings and grazed their animals on common land. Many of these peasants left the land and became factory workers in the new industries in towns.

In both historic and prehistoric times, peasants and farmers rotated their crops as a way of avoiding exhaustion of the land. In Europe in medieval times this crop rotation was often a two field or a three field rotation, in which one field lay fallow in either the two or three field system. Charles Townshend (1674–1738) was a British politician and Viscount, who became known as 'Turnip Townshend', by advocating the Norfolk four crop rotation involving turnips, barley, wheat and clover, the last of these fixing nitrogen back into the soil as well as providing grazing at the end of the season and thus avoiding the need for a fallow period.

In parallel with these developments, Robert Bakewell (1725–1795) lived and worked in the Midlands of Britain and was active in selective breeding of livestock, sheep, cattle and horses. The production of sheep with longer and more profuse wool was important to supply the new factories and these sheep were also exported in large numbers to North America and Australia to become the forerunners of modern breeds. Bakewell also improved cattle breeds, increasing the size and quality of several breeds for beef yield. His work became well known to Charles Darwin, who called the process 'artificial selection' (as opposed to 'natural selection'), refining techniques of domestication and breed improvement which historic peoples had used in previous millennia.

Back on the factory front, James Watt (1736–1819) and Matthew Boulton (1728–1809) constructed a large factory in Birmingham, the Soho Manufactory, in 1767, one of the earliest examples of mass production. The Soho Foundry followed in 1795, when Watt and Boulton started building steam engines. These engines could drive machine tools and cut and make metal parts replacing the manpower previously needed for tools or lathes. The machine tools worked with an accuracy and consistency of manufacture that was a big step forward. Watt and Boulton, together with William Murdoch (1754–1839) were responsible for a considerable improvement of steam engines together with many other inventions including gas lighting to replace the candles and tallow, which had previously been necessary in the winter hours of darkness. Richard Trevithick

(1771–1833) further developed steam power, building on inventions by the American engineer and inventor Oliver Evans (1755–1819). Trevithick is remembered for his prodigious work in the Devon and Cornish copper and tin mines, but should also be remembered for building the first working railway line locomotive in 1804, which was used in a Welsh iron works for transferring the ore from the mine face back to the stamping mills.

It is noteworthy that Watt and Boulton, like many other inventors and original thinkers of the early Industrial Revolution, were non-conformists. They did not belong to the ranks of London gentry, and were not constrained by the strictures and attitudes of either the Anglican or Catholic Churches. They clustered around the Midlands of England and are notably remembered in the existence of the Lunar Society, whose members met in each other's homes in turn on the Sunday nearest to the full moon, so that they were able to find their way home safely on dark nights before street lighting. Their numbers included Josiah Wedgewood, Erasmus Darwin, and Joseph Priestley amongst others, and they shared their ideas and inventions with each other; some were early capitalists striving to manufacture quality goods for profit, but others were simply talented polymaths and inventors who called themselves natural philosophers, but whom we would recognise today as early scientists. Many of the names included in Jenny Uglow's book, cited at the end of this chapter, are now household names and include John Whitehurst, Matthew Boulton, Josiah Wedgwood, Erasmus Darwin, Joseph Priestley, William Small, James Keir, James Watt, William Withering, Richard Edgworth, Thomas Day and Samuel Galton.

The Industrial Revolution was also characterised by the early development of chemistry and chemical manufacturing. Sulphuric acid was first produced industrially in 1746 by John Roebuck from Sheffield (1718–1794), who qualified as a doctor, but then found more interest in chemistry. Other chemicals were equally important in manufacturing processes, not only in the iron and steel industries but in glass, textiles, soap and paper production. Bleaching powder, sodium hypochlorite, was extensively used in textiles after its discovery and popularisation by the Scottish chemist and industrialist Charles Tennant (1768–1838) around 1800; indeed, the company that Charles Tennant set up eventually evolved into the industrial giant ICI.

Cement has been used since historic times and is made from a basis of lime (calcium hydroxide), it was used extensively by the Ancient Greeks and then by the Romans, and continued in use through the intervening centuries. At the time of the Industrial Revolution various individuals experimented with the development of cement in the 18th century, including notably the British civil engineer John Smeaton (1724–1792), sometimes referred to as the 'Father of Civil Engineering', who built bridges, canals, harbours, and most notably, the Eddystone lighthouse on a rock off Plymouth.

Joseph Aspdin (1778–1855) from Leeds set up a manufacturing plant for producing a new and stronger cement which he called "Portland Cement", likening it to Portland stone. This production of a vital and common material was a typical product invented by many of the drivers of the Industrial Revolution.

Their products were relatively simple and straightforward, and their mass production by the new industrial methods was economically, as well as technically, successful.

Possible further reading:
Behemoth, a History of the Factory and the Making of the Modern World by Joshua B Freeman (Norton)
The Lunar Men by Jenny Uglow (Faber and Faber)

Chapter 65
Development of Scientific Thought

In early medieval times, around the beginning of the second millennium, much of the thinking and enquiry about the natural world was happening in the Muslim Empire. Alexandria in Egypt and Cordoba in southern Span had become powerhouses of Muslim thinking with universities and libraries, but as we have seen much of this changed with a radical alteration in theological attitudes at the end of the first millennium when books were burnt and enquiry into the natural world was deemed anti-Muslim, and from this moment on Cordoba lost its pre-eminence in intellectual thought.

At the time, the Muslim world had developed its lines of enquiry along writings inherited from the Greek and Roman traditions, which were available to scholars both in Muslim Al Andalus in the Iberian Peninsula, but also in geographically separate areas such as the Great Library at Alexandria in Egypt. Much of these writings and information had gradually leached through into western Europe and led into the Renaissance. Additionally, in the middle years of the second millennium, the Reformation spreading across Europe was the result of dissatisfaction with Christian thinking of previous centuries, across much of northern Europe this led directly into the Reformation.

In the Mediterranean countries of southern Europe, theological thinking appears to have been more constrained, and the Catholic and Orthodox Churches maintained their stranglehold on religious thinking and doctrine. Questioning of orthodoxy was not just discouraged, but was actively sought out and classified as heresy. Organisations, such as the Inquisition and the Jesuits, were created specifically to try and maintain religious purity and orthodoxy. Contemporary Muslim theological thinking also remained in a strait jacket with questioning attitudes discouraged.

From the middle of the millennium onwards, and contributed to in no small measure by the development of printing allowing dissemination of both the Bible and other books of philosophy and enquiry, the Enlightenment gradually picked up speed. Natural philosophy was the expression given to what we would today regard as early scientific thought; in other words the process in which the natural world was observed in an attempt to understand its workings.

Two examples are well known, the first concerning the size and orbit of Earth; the ancient Greeks, notably Aristotle and subsequently the Pythagorean School, knew that Earth was round and had made good early estimates of its size, including the writings of Eratosthenes (chapter 37), together with realising that

Earth orbited the sun, and in turn the moon orbited Earth. Somewhere over the next two millennia this information became lost, despite Arab astronomers being well aware of it and further developing astronomical science.

In Italy, Galileo Galilei (1564–1642) was investigated by the Inquisition in 1615 for his astronomical writings which included the assertion that Earth orbited the sun and not vice versa. Galileo was forced to recant his beliefs publicly, and spent the rest of his life under house arrest: he was probably lucky to avoid torture or execution aimed at making him recant his views. At the same time, Andreas Versalius (1514–1564) furthered the study of human anatomy, which up to that time had been dominated by the writings of Galen of Pergamon (129–210).

Galen's work had come to Medieval Europe through Islamic medical books, and Galen's work remained firmly at the heart of the mainstream despite European observations that did not always bear out Galen's assertions. Perhaps the most confounding experiment was that of William Harvey (1578–1657), physician to King James I, who first described the circulation of the blood in a book published in 1628. This described the interconnection between the arterial and venous systems through capillaries, and contradicted Galen's theory that blood was formed in the liver and leaked through the septum from one side of the heart to the other.

Much of Harvey's work was based on dissection and vivisection; he was one of the early thinkers to develop the method of scientific thought where observation is followed by the development of a theory to explain the observations, and further experimentation to confirm or refute the new hypothesis. Up to that time, natural philosophy had tended to dream up a theory as a means of explaining natural phenomena, and such theories as the four humours (black bile, yellow bile, phlegm and blood) each corresponding to the supposed four temperaments of individuals. There would not seem to be any observation or experiment that might have initiated, confirmed or refuted such thinking.

Thales of Miletus (624–546 BC) is the first natural philosopher whose recorded writings are known to us. His overall hypothesis of natural existence was that matter originated from a single material substance, namely water; his philosophy appears to have been derived from a position of thought and consideration uninfluenced by any observation. In mainland Greece Plato (428–348 BC) was taught by Socrates (470–399 BC) and in turn taught Aristotle, but he laid down the basis of European philosophy and science.

As a natural philosopher, he wrote broadly across all aspects of human activity. He was a firm believer in observation and experience, on which deductions could be made which today would be regarded as an early form of the scientific method. Aristotle (384–322 BC) somewhat later, studied and wrote widely across the field of human endeavour, and much of his influence did not change until the time of the Renaissance when observational findings became important. He is however a very important influence on early theology, Jewish and Christian as well as Muslim, and much of his influence was possibly due to becoming tutor to Alexander the Great, where he both influenced Alexander and also had access to considerable funds to devote to his scholarship.

Much later, in Europe, Robert Grosseteste (1175–1253) was an English scholar, theologian and early radical thinker who taught at Oxford and became Bishop of Lincoln. At around the same time Roger Bacon (1215–1292) was another English philosopher and churchman, a Franciscan friar who is remembered as an early European thinker along scientific lines. Through the 15th and 16th centuries European scientific thinking initially developed most strongly in astronomy and mathematics, with such individuals as Copernicus (1473–1543), Tycho Brahae (1546–1601), and William Gilbert (1544–1602) who first described Earth's magnetic field, Johannes Kepler who described the first two laws of planetary motion, Galileo with his astronomical observations and Anton Von Leeuwenhoek who invented the first practical microscope, Newton's (1642–1726) Laws of Gravity and Motion followed, with publication in 1687.

Into these early years of scientific enquiry and ferment was born the Royal Society which came into being around 1645 at the time of the Civil War, and following the restoration of the monarchy in 1660 held regular meetings at Gresham College in London, although initially most of its meetings were in Oxford. The Royal Society produced the first scientific journal in 1665 called 'Philosophical Transactions' which continues in uninterrupted publication to the present day. Francis Bacon (1561–1626, not to be confused with the 13th century Franciscan friar Roger Bacon) was one of the early leading lights in the Royal Society, and was highly influential in developing the scientific method. Bacon was also active in English politics and helped establish the early east coast British colonies in America.

It would be inappropriate to consider the early development of scientific thought without mentioning building and architecture where the early years of the second millennium saw a great surge in the building of huge abbeys and cathedrals, many of which have survived to the present day, though sadly many abbeys at the centre of religious movements fell victim to the Reformation in the middle years of the millennium, or to the excesses of the English Civil War and the French Revolution. Universities, initially in Muslim Cordoba, Catholic Italy, France and Spain all contributed to the mind set of learning and enquiry necessary for the evolution and introduction of scientific thought. Initially it was theology which saw these universities founded and then evolve from earlier cathedral and monastery schools.

The 17th century continued to develop as discussion and intercommunication between early thinkers and scientists became easier and more prolific. Seminal discoveries continued, aided by discussion, which has already been referred to at the Royal Society in London, and also at the Académie Royale des Sciences in Paris founded 1666 by Louis XIV: in addition to this smaller informal societies were formed between like-minded men (and they virtually were all men) about all sorts of aspects of "natural philosophy" with educated men of the times feeling able to range widely across most of the known disciplines of the era.

One such organisation already mentioned was the Lunar Society which met in Birmingham on the night of the full moon each month (chapter 64), this was so that they could find their way home by the light of the moon in the early hours. It is interesting to note that they were all non-conformists and mentally were not shackled or confined in thought by current religious or other teachings and their interests ranged widely across many different disciplines. The Lunar Society included among its members Matthew Boulton and James Watt, together with Joseph Priestley who researched gases (following the discoveries of Robert Boyle around oxygen) and Erasmus Darwin, the grandfather of Charles whose thinking presaged much of the theoretical basis of his grandson's subsequent world-shattering work on evolution.

The early development of scientific thought was further aided by the great pool of wealth and talented craftsmen working in wood, metals and engineering. Much of the basis of metallurgy and mining had been painfully discovered over the preceding centuries to provide a technological base on which scientific thought could build. Power from wind and water mills had been harnessed for millennia, and this all provided a sound base on which scientific thought could develop.

Possible further reading:
The Discoverers by Daniel Boorstin (Vintage Books)

Chapter 66
Europe After Napoleon

As Napoleon was banished to St Helena in the South Atlantic, the countries of Europe set about redrawing the map of Europe in a large and prolonged meeting known as the Congress of Vienna. Depending upon the criteria used this Congress was either successful in avoiding another major European conflict for the next century, or in releasing the revolutionary genie from the bottle. Certainly the 19th century was subsequently marked by national episodes of unrest, as revolutionary ideas, imitating the turmoil that France had been through, spread across the continent.

Agreement was finally concluded in September 1815, with the defeated France now restored to a supposedly constitutional monarchy. Much of the European map appeared unchanged, but Poland suffered badly and had been split up. A new kingdom of Belgium had been established which was envisaged as a buffer state to the north of France to check any future French ambition in that direction. Germany had coalesced from some three hundred small princedoms and kingdoms into a federation of 39 states, including Austria and Prussia.

The Congress in Venna resolved to convene future meetings and four further conventions met in the years up to 1822, during which ongoing problems, anomalies and arguments could be sorted out. Britain remained unchanged in the bargaining as an island with distinct border unequivocally delineated by the surrounding seas, however Britain did acquire a lot of foreign colonies, including Ceylon (modern Sri Lanka) and the early South Africa from the Dutch; British competitors conceded territory in India, and in addition Britain acquired some Caribbean islands and regularised its colonial lordship over Canada.

The British attitude by the Foreign Secretary Lord Castlereagh (1769–1822) was based on a reluctance to be involved in other countries' domestic affairs, even if these other countries were governed by oppressive or incompetent regimes, or indeed both. Within Europe the death of the last Habsburg ruler, and the War of Spanish Succession which finished in 1714, had weakened Spain, a state that was further damaged by the instability following the French Revolution and the Peninsular War of 1807–1814, which only ended when Napoleon was defeated.

Spain's Latin American colonies were rebelling and pursuing independence, and through the 1820s some Spanish colonies in South America gained their independence, with Britain's new Foreign Secretary, George Canning, quick to recognise them as independent republics (chapter 69). Finally, some political balance was achieved in Spain and a constitutional monarchy persisted to the end of the century and through to 1931 though civil war broke out again between royalists and republicans after an army coup in 1936. The war dragged on for three years with much input from various European nations and individuals; eventually the republican side came out best in the form of a military dictatorship under General Francisco Franco (1892–1975), which lasted until Franco's death in 1975, the war is estimated to have cost half a million lives, with the same number again lost during the following repressive dictatorship.

To the west of Spain, Portugal had built up a large empire in South America, Africa and Asia, based on the spice and slave trades, thanks to early explorations by intrepid Portuguese navigators (chapter 35). Portugal had lost the Battle of Alcacer Quibir in Morocco in 1578 over the Moroccan throne, with the King of Portugal being killed during the battle; he left no heir and large national debts so Portugal was subsumed into Spain for the next sixty years. Just ten years later and still in debt, Portugal contributed ships and men to the Armada against England which was decimated and largely destroyed by the weather costing the nation once again considerable sums of money and men.

An earthquake in 1755 destroyed most of Lisbon. Following these adverse events, Brazil rebelled and became independent in 1822 since there was little Portugal could do about it, resulting in diminished trade and cash flow. The monarchy staggered on but was deposed in 1910 in a very anti-clerical and divisive revolt; sixteen years later dictatorship was imposed following an army coup, and lasted until another bloodless coup in 1974 led to democratic reforms and constitutional monarchy.

Greece was part of the Byzantine Empire at the beginning of the second millennium and as the Empire declined it became part of the Ottoman Empire after the fall of Constantinople in 1543. Ottoman control and the rule of law was patchy and did not extend to much of inland Greece. A rebellion, known as the Orlov Revolt occurred in 1770 when Greek insurrectionists enlisted the help of Russia in the cause of liberation from the Ottoman Empire; the Russians also sent arms and agents to incite revolt in the Balkans by Orthodox Christians which Russia hoped would fortify its southern borders. However, the Russian support was inadequate and eventually the revolt was crushed. A further revolt started in 1821 and this time Russia, Britain and France all recognised Greek claims to independent statehood, so that this was finally formalised in the Treaty of Constantinople in 1832.

In Scandinavia, Denmark, Norway and Sweden had united in the uncomfortable Kalmar Union between 1397 and 1520. The Kalmar War from 1611–1613 was a failed attempt by the Danish Monarch Christian IV, to revitalise the Union by force. Subsequently the religious Thirty Years War (1618–1648) between Protestants and the Catholic Holy Roman Empire, took a huge toll on Scandinavia and the whole of Northern Europe, with an estimated total death toll of around eight million lives.

During the 17th century, Sweden expanded eastwards by military conquest, only to lose ground subsequently in the Great Northern Wars (1700–1721) with all its neighbours, including Russia, Norway, Denmark and Poland. Further ground was lost during the Napoleonic Wars when the Swedish province of Finland was ceded to Russia. Norway and Sweden were united under a single monarch in 1814 in the negotiations at the end of the Napoleonic Wars, an arrangement which lasted until full separation in 1905. Finland, which was essentially the eastern one third of Sweden, had become the Grand Duchy of Finland in Russia, and stayed as such until the 1917 October Revolution.

Throughout the first half of the 19th century, social conditions were rapidly changing in line with the expectations of the large mass of the population. Trade Unions were set up, but were regarded with suspicion by the more wealthy section of Victorian society who derived their income from investment, including buying and selling shares, and speculation. There was a great division between the wealthy, who lived off their capital in this way, and the considerable mass of workers who felt that they had generated the wealth of society through their hard labour in the first place.

Two German writers, Karl Marx (1818–1883) and Friedrich Engels (1820–1895), were expelled from Germany for their thinking and writing which described how the economies of Europe had developed through the previous two hundred years. Marx and Engels called upon workers all over the world, and not just in Europe, to combine and overthrow capitalist societies to create a new world in which class would no longer matter. This was published as the Communist Manifesto in 1848, but was largely ignored for the next half century, probably because it was felt to be too utopian.

The 19th century was portrayed in the arts by an increasing outpouring of music, literature and painting, often celebrating the defeat and downfall of dictators and tyrants. In music the opera Fidelio by Beethoven (1770–1827), and various Verdi (1813–1901) operas, including Don Carlos, resonate with this theme. In literature, Lord Byron (1788–1842) and Alfonse de Lamartine (1790–1869) not only produced stirring revolutionary poetry, but also joined the rebellions. Goethe (1749–1832) and Schiller (1759–1805) in Germany wrote strongly about socialist values, while Charles Dickens (1812–1870) in Britain and Honoré de Balzac (1799–1850) in France wrote about the negative character traits of neglect, hypocrisy and greed.

Talented painters such as Eugene Delacroix (1798–1863) in France committed the social struggles to canvas (notably a famous painting of 'Liberty Leading the People'). In Britain philosopher John Stuart Mill (1806–1873) championed women's rights, whilst at the same time Charles X in France, who ruled from 1824 to 1830, attempted to return to autocracy and his own personal form of absolutist government; he was overthrown in a July revolution and sent into exile; Louis-Philippe, Duke of Orleans, was installed in his place as King of France. Louis-Philippe abdicated in 1848 after a rule of 18 years when rioting broke out again.

Napoleon Bonaparte's nephew was elected some months later and ruled as Napoleon III (1808–1873), Napoleon Bonaparte's young son had been counted as Napoleon II although he was never old enough to be installed as Emperor.

Rebellions occurred in 1845 in Switzerland and the next year in Poland, followed by unrest in Sicily in 1847. 1848 is remembered as the year of revolutions across Europe, with France in particular suffering a second revolution, though happily not on the scale of the animosities and atrocities that occurred 60 years previously. At the end of this time Napoleon III was installed on the French throne in 1848 following which he rebuilt Paris and several other large cities.

Russia had been expansionist through the first half of the 19th century, taking in some of Poland and then Romania. In 1853 Britain, France and Turkey went to war with Russia over its attempted annexation of Crimea. The war is remembered for the Charge of the Light Brigade by a British cavalry regiment with drawn swords charging into Russian cannon fire with disastrous results, but also for the presence of Florence Nightingale (1820–1910), who was appalled by the medical facilities available to wounded soldiers. She took a contingent of 38 women and set up a hospital for the wounded at Scutari in Crimea.

This was effectively the beginning of organised nursing; she is remembered as the 'Lady of the Lamp' and returned to Britain after the war to set up a School of Nursing at St Thomas's Hospital in London. A little later in 1859 the Austrians were pushed out of northern Italy and this conflict resulted in the founding of the Red Cross movement by Henry Dunant (1828–1910), a Swiss businessman who witnessed the agonies of war, and was later awarded the first Nobel Peace Prize in 1901.

The campaign led to the unification of Italy under Giuseppe Garibaldi (1807–1882), an Italian general and politician, who ruled as a nationalistic but relatively benign dictator; he is regarded as being one of the four founding fathers of modern Italy, along with Count Camillo Cavour (1810–1861), who became the first Italian prime minister, Victor Emanuel II (1800–1878) who became the first King of Italy for 1500 years in 1861, and Giuseppe Mazzini (1805–1872), philosopher and politician. All these four men were northern Italian figures whose dream of a united Italy was finally realised in 1861 as one of the ultimate outcomes of the diplomatic process started in the 1815 Vienna Conference after the banishment of Napoleon.

Warfare at this time was transformed by two technological advances, the first being the electric telegraph which came into use in the 1840s, allowing much better communication on the battlefield, and between the front line and the organising generals; and the second rather more belligerent advance, was the invention of the breech loading rifle at around the same time; this latter advance allowed much more rapid fire and therefore much more lethal attack or defence during battle.

In 1866, Prussia fought with Austria, resulting in a big change in their respective boundaries, and following which Prussia emerged as the strongest of the still numerous German states. By 1870 Prussia was fighting France, and Paris was besieged. The French were easily overcome by Prussia to the extent that when Wilhelm I was proclaimed Prussian Emperor, the ceremony took place at Versailles. The situation rolled over into the Paris commune, or rebellion by a revolutionary government, in 1871 with a lot of fighting on the streets against the occupying Prussians in which an estimated 20,000 French citizens died.

The end result was enormous animosity and bitterness in France towards the Germans. Because France had started the war with Germany, reparations became due, and France had to pay very large damages, together with losing the partly German-speaking provinces of Alsace and Lorraine, thus leading into the first years of the French Third Republic. Warring continued in the Balkans where Austria and Hungary ruled over a number of different minorities, part Christian and part Muslim, and including Magyars, Ukrainians, Romanians, Croats, Slovenes, Poles, Moravians and Czechs. The situation mirrored that of four centuries earlier with German speakers in smaller countries still looking for independence or supremacy.

Britain and Russia on the edges of Europe were largely able to avoid taking part in this latest European restructuring, and in Russia Tsar Alexander II who enjoyed a long reign from 1855 to 1881, was slowly restructuring society and emancipating serfs. The task involved compensating owners of land which was then allocated to the newly free farmers, perhaps more correctly called peasants. Some industrious, and indeed clever peasants, prospered under the new regime, becoming rich and known as Kulaks. Their wealth would attract animosity and become one of the main targets of the 1917 Bolshevik Revolution later.

Possible further reading:
The Short Oxford History of Europe by TCW Blanning (OUP)

Chapter 67
Britain 1820–1837

Following the Battle of Waterloo in 1815, the Vienna Treaty had restored much of the map of Europe to its previous state. The Treaty itself was designed to prevent war breaking out again in Europe, and also to define national boundaries, and in both these respects it was fairly successful. The Treaty had firstly enlarged Prussia, though it was still composed of multiple small entities, it had created a United Kingdom of the Netherlands north of France to be a buffer zone which would split in 1830 into Holland, Belgium and Luxembourg, and it had allowed Austria to rule over many of the Italian states, including Venice.

Political battles in France between Left and the Right, Liberals and Conservatives, continued through the 19th century. The restoration of the Bourbon King in France did not indicate a return to pre-revolutionary values of monarchical and autocratic government. The restored monarch, Charles X, seemed somewhat unaware of this and still tried to be an autocrat at the centre of power: because of this he was deposed after a small revolution in 1830, and then replaced with a younger member of the royal Bourbon family, Louis Philippe, who had fought on the Republican side in the revolution.

Dynastic and autocratic government persisted in the multiple small Italian and German states, though the boundaries of Britain, France, Spain and Portugal were defined, and these countries were able to continue with firm constitutional government. After a local revolt and internecine conflict between Christians and Muslims in the Balkans, an autonomous Serbia emerged in Eastern Europe from a weakened and crumbling Turkish Ottoman Empire.

In Britain at this time, industrial unrest, due to dreadful social conditions in houses and factories, together with unemployment and low wages, led to the rise of protestors known as Luddites who came in gangs to smash the factory machinery they held responsible for putting them out of work. A peaceful demonstration at St Peter's Field in Manchester in 1815 had been broken up by troops with considerable violence, including some deaths and many injuries, and in the shadow of Waterloo became known as the Peterloo Massacre. The contrast between rich and poor did not help, and the advent of George IV's reign in 1820 further aggravated attitudes as he was both a glutton and a spendthrift, so the Regency Period of social profligacy continued.

The population of England had doubled from five million people in 1700 to almost twice that number in 1800, and then doubled again in the first quarter of the 19th century. The new industrial cities of Manchester, Birmingham, Leeds,

Bradford and Sheffield came to dwarf the old cathedral cities, but without representation in parliament.

During the early 19th century, the Whig party was frequently the generator of innovation, whilst the Tory party tried to suppress dissent and cling to the conservative past. Despite this, Robert Peel (1788–1850) managed to set up the first police force in London while he was Home Secretary between 1822–1827, these police became known as 'Bobbies' or 'Peelers'. Elizabeth Fry (1780–1845) who was a Quaker, campaigned to achieve improvements in prison conditions. Both during the Regency of George III, and the subsequent rule of George IV, the monarch was still involved in politics and in the passage of legislation. He still appointed the Prime Minister and other ministers, with or without advice.

George Canning (1770–1827) was Foreign Minister in the middle 1820s, and supported the Monroe Doctrine enunciated by James Monroe (1758–1831), fifth president of the United State in 1823, of non-interference from Europe in western hemisphere matters of both North and South America. He also supported the crusade of Lord Byron (1788–1924) for the realisation of Greek autonomy from the Turkish Ottoman Empire.

Matters changed abruptly when the Earl of Liverpool died whilst Prime Minister in 1827, and then George Canning, who succeeded him, died very shortly afterwards. The King next appointed the Duke of Wellington as Prime Minister who, despite being conservative, continued to pass parliamentary measures in England limiting public office to members of the Anglican Church, but promoting Catholic emancipation in Ireland.

Finally, King George IV died in 1830 without many tears being shed. He was succeeded by his 64 year old brother as William IV (1765–1837), who had not expected to accede to the throne, but who was able to rule until 1837. In 1832 the Great Reform Act passed through the Commons abolishing 60 rotten boroughs where MPs were appointed rather than elected, and re-forming 47 more, so allowing representation for the first time from the great manufacturing cities to which the parliamentary seats were re-allocated; the bill also increased the franchise somewhat among adult men. Although the Bill just managed to pass the Commons, it was subsequently defeated by the Conservatives in parliamentary committee.

This resulted in the resignation of the Prime Minister, the Whig leader Earl Grey (1764–1845), and a new General Election. The resulting new Commons was very differently coloured due to the injection of new MPs, and passed the legislation, only to have it rejected on this occasions by the House of Lords, whereupon riots occurred in Derby, Nottingham and Bristol, though not in London, where there were fears of a re-run of the French Revolution. The Bill was presented for a third time shortly afterwards, but was again rejected by the Lords, Earl Grey then demanded that the King create enough sympathetic new peers to ensure passage of the Bill, but the King refused. After much further political discussion the Lords gave in, and the Greater Reform Act became law in 1832. The Bill also increased the number of male voters, from about 500,000 to 800,000 though no women achieved the vote on this occasion.

The following year, 1833, saw slavery abolished throughout the British Empire and in South Africa after a long campaign (chapter 59), with the consequence that the Dutch Boer population, who believed they needed black slaves to run their estates, took umbrage and migrated north to found the Orange Free State and the Transvaal, as they could not accept the abolition of slavery: these attitudes would eventually lead directly to the Boer Wars at the end of the century and into the apartheid system which was to bedevil South Africa in the 20th century.

During William IV's seven-year reign, the year 1834 stands out as a year in which slavery was abolished in the West Indies, factory employment was limited to children aged 13 or over, and a Poor Law was introduced to provide welfare, albeit at a very basic level. However, the process of change proceeded only slowly, and there were setbacks along the way, such as the workers from Tolpuddle in Dorset who were sentenced to transportation to Australia in 1834 for belonging to a trade union, ten years after trade unions had been made legal. A public outcry resulted in their eventual repatriation.

Following the Great Reform Act in 1832, there had remained feelings in some quarters that the reforms achieved were insufficient, and in 1837 six members of parliament together formed a committee and in the following year published a 'People's Charter' setting out six main aims of their movement. These six objectives summarise quite well the trend in emancipation and expanding democracy and citizen involvement which were common across Europe during the 19th century.

Firstly, these Chartists demanded universal male suffrage, but without any mention of female emancipation: secondly, there was a demand that there should be annual parliaments instead of the previously erratic ad hoc arrangements with parliaments having no pre-determined length of time: thirdly, it was felt that MP's should be paid, thus allowing poorly paid individuals without private means to aspire to become an MP and represent their people: fourthly, it was felt that all electoral districts should be equal in size, although this had been very largely remedied in the Great Reform Bill with the dissolution of rotten boroughs: fifthly, voting by secret ballot was demanded, with sixth, an end to the need to be a property holder in order to qualify as a voter. The group became known as the Chartists, and despite parliament rejecting their Charter in 1840 and again in 1842, they continued to campaign, with the government needing to put down their protests using troops.

In 1844, the Cooperative Movement was set up in Rochdale, and rapidly expanded to provide mutual help amongst the working classes for both trade and housing. Following public protest the Corn Laws, which had kept the price of bread high, and had also contributed to the worsening famine in Ireland, were abolished by Sir Robert Peel who was then Prime Minister. Most of the six demands included in the original People's Charter were addressed within the decade.

During William IV's reign of seven years, an uneasy possible symbol of change occurred when the old Houses of Parliament in the Palace of Westminster burnt down in 1834: workers had been trying to burn too much rubbish in the basement furnaces with the result that the buildings' chimneys caught fire, and then the blaze rapidly spread. A competition to design and build new Houses of Parliament took place and the architects Charles Barrie (1795–1860) and Augustus Pugin (1812–1852) were selected to design and build the edifice which we now recognise at the centre of Westminster, although this took a decade to achieve.

At the end of the decade, the Whig parliamentarian Lord Melbourne (1779–1848) was Prime Minster from 1835–1841 and was in place to steer, advise and mentor an 18 year old sheltered young Queen Victoria when she inherited the throne, and to introduce her to the intricacies of statesmanship. William IV had no heirs, it was because of this that his niece Victoria came to succeed him on the throne.

The 18th century had seen the start of the Industrial Revolution in England, together with continuing sophistication and development of the Agricultural Revolution providing more food for the nation. After two centuries of fairly static population there was a rapid expansion of numbers in Britain. Europe's population probably doubled during the 19th century, though Germany, Britain and the United States all saw a much larger increase.

The Reverend Thomas Malthus (1766–1834) an English clergyman who had been appointed Professor of History at the East India Company College (now Haileybury School) wrote at this time about population, hypothesising that human population was controlled by the 'three dread horsemen' of war, famine and disease; he saw the population increase being due to the additional wealth available when he felt that this wealth should have been better directed to increasing standards of living.

The 18th century had seen the start of the Industrial Revolution in England and after two centuries of static population this had stimulated population growth so that the population of Britain had doubled through the 18th century and then doubled again in the first three decades of the 19th century. At the same time Europeans were emigrating to the New World in the Americas as well as Australasia in increasing numbers Despite this overall increase in improving conditions, and in relative wealth, many continued to emigrate from the British Isles during the 19th century, considerable numbers from other European nations, notably Germany and Scandinavia, also emigrated with the prime destination being North America, and secondary targets being Australia and New Zealand.

Possible further reading:
A History of Regency England by Carolly Erickson (Harper Paperback)

Chapter 68
Queen Victoria to 1865

King George IV died without male heirs; his father George III had four sons, but the eldest three all died without any legitimate children. Thus it was that Victoria, who was the daughter of the fourth son of George III, came to the throne at the age of 18 in 1837 after a very protected childhood. Britain had managed to escape both the revolutionary trends affecting much of Europe, and also the problems of absolutist monarchs still present across parts of Europe. Her reign is remembered as one of peace and prosperity, principally because such wars that did occur were fought a long way from the shores of the British Isles, notably the Opium Wars in China, the Crimean War and rebellions in India.

Through the century before Victoria came to the throne, Britain had aspired to a policy of mercantilism, or free trade. For this to be effective an empire of colonies was needed to produce the raw materials for the rapidly industrialised Britain, and to buy the finished manufactured products which amounted to more than home consumption could absorb.

After the loss of the American colonies British efforts were diverted elsewhere and emigration, particularly to Australia was encouraged. Since the initiation of the convict colony at Botany Bay in 1787, it had become apparent that the seaboard of Australia offered a hospitable environment for new settlers. Prior to the discovery of Australasia, penal transportation had been used in earlier years to America. Many of the early convicts who were transported were convicted of crimes which today appear minor by comparison with the punishment imposed.

Trade barriers were maintained to protect British and colonial produce. Through the first half of the 19th century the country was running a trade surplus bringing gold, silver and cash into the country. Much of this trade surplus was used for the Royal Navy, whose strength and omnipresence was necessary to protect trade routes. Industrialisation had been driving ahead in the 50 years before Victoria's accession, much of it outside London, and much of it due to the leadership of non-conformists whose thoughts and actions were not restricted by the Catholic, or less importantly, Anglican churches.

One legacy the mid-17th century Puritans bequeathed to the country was a work ethic whose importance became clear through the 17th and 18th centuries. The Scottish philosopher Adam Smith's (1723–1790) seminal economic writings from the previous century, in which he advocated free markets, was also an important factor in national thinking through Victoria's reign, though trade barriers were still frequently used as a political weapon of foreign policy through the 19th century.

At the time Victoria came to the throne, Britain had already abolished much of the autocratic behaviour of the monarchy. She was guided into office and through her initial years by Lord Melbourne (1779–1848), who had been Home Secretary for four years and then Prime Minister for the three years after Victoria came to the throne. He belonged to the Whig party, first becoming an MP in 1806. He became known for moderation, especially in the agricultural riots of 1830 in which the rioters targeted the Poor Law and tenant farmers who were introducing machinery and lowering wages.

Originally, the Poor Laws had come into being as a haphazard system of charity in mediaeval times and were then reorganised at the end of Queen Elizabeth's reign. New Poor Laws were passed in 1834 centralising the system and encouraging the building of Workhouses to replace old Parish-based charities. Social unrest had been growing for some years and came to a head in 1830. Lord Melbourne, then Home Secretary, resisted demands for emergency laws, and ensured that justice prevailed. Many of the crimes the rioters were convicted for carried the death penalty at that time, and Melbourne saw that this was often commuted to transportation.

He resigned the Prime Ministership in 1841, but left behind a lot of reform legislation concerning Poor Laws and the workhouses, together with reform of local government and reduction in the number of offences that resulted in capital punishment. The Australian city of Melbourne is named in his honour as he was Prime Minister in 1837 when it was incorporated as a Crown settlement and capital of New South Wales. He guided Victoria through the first three years of her reign in the art of statecraft as it needed to be practised by a constitutional monarch with limited powers and influence. In 1840 Victoria married Prince Albert of Saxe-Cobourg and Gotha. Soon afterwards Melbourne retired at the end of a scandal studded career, and although he continued to offer Victoria advice, much of her support came increasingly from Prince Albert after their marriage.

Through the 1830s and 1840s, Lord Palmerston (1784–1865) was Foreign Secretary for much of the time as a Whig politician, his often aggressive diplomatic policies dominated much of Britain's conduct with the rest of the world during the period especially during his two spells as Prime Minister from 1855–58 and again in 1859–65. He died in office at the age of 81 only a few months after winning a general election. Unfortunately his personal diplomatic skills were rather less than his international ones and he did not get on well with Queen Victoria. He left behind a legacy of prison reform, cleaner air, vaccination and limiting factory hours for children.

In the first half of the 19th century, the American and French revolutions with the governing powers being overthrown, were followed by revolutions in Spain and Naples in 1820, which were suppressed. In Greece, which had been under Ottoman rule since the fall of Constantinople in 1453, the successful Greek revolution, or War of Independence, began against the Ottoman Empire. Initially the Ottomans appeared to be winning, but by 1825 Britain, France and Russia all decided to intervene against the Ottoman Empire. Greece was finally recognised as an independent nation in May 1832.

Revolts in Europe continued with the overthrow of the restored Bourbon monarchy in France in 1830, and following this Belgium won independence from Holland (the United Kingdom of the Netherlands). A revolt in Poland was suppressed, and civil war broke out between liberals and the Church in Spain and Portugal. All this transpired while the British parliament was enacting reform of the Corn Laws and the Poor Laws.

The Industrial Revolution was well underway when Victoria came to the throne. Railways were starting to proliferate rapidly at the beginning of her reign. The Royal Mail, which had been established by Henry VIII in 1516, received a large boost with uniform delivery of mail across the country thanks to the railway network which replaced the mail coaches first used in 1784. The big problem of Victoria's early years as queen came in 1845 with the onset of potato blight in Ireland. London was slow to understand what was happening and slower still to respond.

Although potatoes were a widespread and vital crop across Europe, there was much more dependence upon on potatoes in Ireland for several reasons, including the religious and economic division of the population, the Corn Laws which militated against the import of grain, and uncaring or unaware absentee landlords. Over the next few years a million Irish died and a further million emigrated to the colonies, reducing the population by about a quarter. This disaster scarred Ireland badly at the time, and has been a strong formative influence on all subsequent Irish history.

Sir Robert Peel, who was Prime Minister at the time, initially failed to repeal the Corn Laws due to opposition, and although at a second attempt the Corn Laws were repealed, Peel was forced to resign in 1846: his post as Prime Minister was taken over by the Whig leader Lord Russell, but the Irish famine dragged on for several years. A coincidental gold rush in California in 1849 absorbed some of the Irish emigrants as well as attracting many from other European nations.

As previously noted, much of Britain's troubles during the 19th century occurred abroad. In 1848, rebellions and revolutions occurred across Europe, where famine caused by potato blight as in Ireland was partly to blame in France, Italy, Germany, the Ottoman Empire and even in Switzerland; there was also unrest in Spain, Denmark, and Greece. The first opium war with the Chinese, in the very early years of Victoria's reign in 1839–1842, came about because the Chinese tried to restrict the trade of British goods to China. Chinese exports, particularly silk, porcelain and tea, were widely imported into Europe and Britain without a corresponding balance of trade in other direction.

The British East India Company had a monopoly on exports to China, and began to grow opium in India for export to China. War ensued, and the superiority of the Royal Navy decided the day. In the Treaty of Nanking in 1842 five ports were finally opened to British trade and the island of Hong Kong was ceded to the British on a 150 year lease. Since the British did not achieve the diplomatic or trade improvements that were envisaged, the situation grumbled on until a second opium war broke out in 1856 and lasted, with helping interventions by France and the United States, for four years until matters were settled by the Convention of Beijing in 1860, with Britain, France and Russia. Hong Kong was confirmed on lease to Britain (it was returned to Chinese jurisdiction in 1997) and part of Manchuria was ceded to Russia.

The 19th century produced its share of towering and famous statesmen, among which must be included William Gladstone (1809–1898) who entered the House of Commons at the early age of 23, holding most of the great offices of state, including Chancellor of the Exchequer from 1855 and becoming Prime Minister for the first time in 1868. Like Palmerston his personal relationships could be difficult, provoking Queen Victoria to remark that "he speaks to me as if I were a public meeting". His first tenure in Downing Street came as leader of the new Liberal party, which had been born out of the old Whig party, and instituted a reforming programme. He increased income tax and government borrowing but cut or abolished many duties leading to lower food costs; however he failed twice in his bid to achieve home rule for Ireland at the end of the century.

The East India Company, which had received its Royal Charter from Elizabeth I in 1600, had large holdings cross the east, ruling much of India and indeed having its own private military arm. The company had frequently needed to do direct battle with its Dutch and Portuguese counterparts while expanding across India and further east. In 1856 a large Indian rebellion occurred with much of the blame being laid at the door of the East India Company, British prisoners were locked overnight in a cell only designed for two or three people, such that over 100 died of suffocation, an episode that came to be known as the 'Black Hole of Calcutta'. As a result following this rebellion the company was nationalised by the British government which took over its Indian possessions, its administrative powers and its military arm. The company continued to trade, but it was the British state that would in future govern India.

Also, in the 1850s, war broke out over Crimea when Britain and France tried to prevent Russia gaining territory and power at the expense of the Ottoman Empire. The war started in 1853 once the Ottomans felt they had the backing of Britain and France. Stalemate developed, and the conflict dragged on until peace was declared by the Treaty of Paris in 1856. As far as the British public were concerned, one of the most prominent features of the war was the contribution to wounded soldiers by Florence Nightingale (1820–1910), who took a contingent of thirty-eight women to Crimea to nurse the sick and injured, thereby laying the foundations for the modern profession of nursing. She was a tireless worker, both for nursing and on the broader social front. After her return from Crimea, she set up the first School of Nursing at St Thomas's Hospital in London.

The crowning achievement of Victoria's early reign was the Great Exhibition held in London in 1851. This was the first of a series of world fairs, and owes much of its success to Victoria's husband, Prince Albert. It had been pre-dated by the French Industrial Exposition of 1844 and some smaller local fairs; it was housed in an enormous glass-clad building that had been built on an iron frame in the space of just nine months. The building was later moved and renamed the Crystal Palace but was unfortunately destroyed by fire in 1936. Many technological and scientific innovations were shown and because of the enormous interest much export trade was generated as a result.

The advent of the American Civil War over slavery came in 1861. Palmerston and Gladstone both supported the Confederate South despite the slavery issue because significant anti-British feeling still persisted against the north since the War of Independence. Britain did not get significantly involved, but tended to favour the Confederate Union of southern states, at least partly because of the large imports of cotton which helped to keep British textile mills running; some of the lack of cotton was made up from eastern nations and some by substitution with wool.

At the end of the 1850s, John Stuart Mill (1806–1873) published his book, *On Liberty*. He was a highly influential philosopher and economist whose thinking was well ahead of his time, and was the first MP to advocate votes for women. The year before this Charles Darwin (1809–1882) had published his book, *On the Origin of Species*, in which he put forward the new idea of evolution, which explained the gradual development of plants and animals over millions of years. Darwin's thesis was put forward in conjunction with Alfred Russel Wallace (1823–1913), a fellow naturalist who was coming to the same conclusions. Some of Darwin's thinking clearly derived from his grandfather Erasmus Darwin, whose scientific thinking presages much of what his grandson subsequently published; the book generated enormous controversy at the time particularly with the church, and indeed is still rejected by some people.

In 1859, Prince Albert became ill with stomach problems: his health gradually deteriorated leading to his death in 1861. Queen Victoria wore black and remained in mourning for the rest of her life until she died forty years later. The Royal Albert Hall built in his memory was opened ten years after his death in 1871. The Industrial and Agricultural Revolutions were effectively completed in the first years of Victoria's reign, considerably assisted by the enthusiasm, energy and drive of Prince Albert.

Possible further reading:
Victorious Century by David Cannadine (Penguin)

Chapter 69
The Americas in the 19th Century

In the New World, the course of events followed those in Europe, with resentment against monarchies and autocracies turning into revolutions which were then frequently followed by internal unrest, or civil war, over power. Constitutional change with gradual evolution from monarchical power to representative control had gradually developed through the 17th century in Britain. The trend had found expression in North American demands for representation in the government which had been controlled from London. These demands were not appreciated by King George and his government at the time and resulted in the Declaration of Independence by the United States.

Not long afterwards, the French Revolution commenced in a much more autocratic society where the Louis XVI's role in government was much more authoritarian and absolute than in either Britain or the early United States. The first two years of the French Revolution were relatively peaceful, but many different factions appeared and agreement over the future proved impossible, such that violence and anarchy broke out.

In Central and South America, rigid government had been imposed, mainly from Spain, but also from Portugal, and as opposed to North America, where the United States and Canada were seen as potential future markets, in South America the new governed colonies were seen predominantly as a source of raw materials, especially gold, silver and sugar. Territories were administered by governors appointed from Madrid or Lisbon, with the flow of information being largely in one direction as instructions from a central autocratic, and still monarchical government, to the new colonies.

This central control was as true for the influence of the Catholic Church as for the more secular aspects of government. Much of the framework of both cultural and social life was provided by the Catholic Church. Some reorganisation had been attempted by the Spanish Bourbon government in the early years of the 18th century which appeared enlightened, but which were insufficient. In addition, the Spanish government's financial state was somewhat parlous because continuing expenditure on military adventures with both France and Britain was consuming much of the national budget.

This situation cost the Spanish government much territory which was ceded to other powers in order to raise desperately needed cash. Large land purchases resulted in the loss to Spain of Santo Domingo and Trinidad, and the loss to France of Louisiana (for which in 1803 the US paid 50 million francs or 11 million dollars, and cancelled some debts). The Louisiana purchase included territory from 15 present American states and two Canadian provinces (Arkansas, Missouri, Iowa, Oklahoma, Kansas, Nebraska, Minnesota, North Dakota, South Dakota, New Mexico, some of Texas, Montana, Wyoming Colorado and present day Louisiana together with some of Canadian Alberta and Saskatchewan). This massive purchase resulted in a considerable transfer of land to the new United States, comprising most of the Mississippi Basin. This had been seen as a potentially major maritime highway into the heart of North America, and its loss therefore was an especially significant blow to France.

When the South American wars of independence commenced in 1810, the capability of the Spanish navy had been overwhelmed by sea battles with the British Royal Navy, and thereafter no other European powers were able to provide transatlantic help to Central or South America. There was to emerge throughout South and Central America a series of republics, most of which were ruled by the soldiers who were the victors at the end of the various civil wars. Large thinly populated states, often with considerable natural resources, emerged from the wars of independence and were frequently in danger of splitting into smaller units as the urban minorities (predominantly European), which had led the independence movements, found it difficult to control their dispersed and largely agricultural native Indian followers.

Some racial problems were also experienced with European minorities forming uneasy alliances with what remained of native populations, and in some instances large populations of imported African slaves. The experience was different in each country, and in Argentina, for example, the relatively small native Indian population was nearly exterminated during the wars by the military, which meant that a hundred years later it more closely resembled Europe with a predominantly European population.

Close by, Brazil had a population in which the majority had been imported from Africa and was largely still composed of slaves. The resources, which were found and exported by the European overclasses, were often crops which had been introduced by those same Europeans, including sugar, coffee, chocolate, cattle and wheat. From the side-lines, but still meddling and sharing not inconsiderable influence, was the Catholic Church with grandiose plans and ambitious buildings. All the ten countries of South America ended up as republics, though Brazil lagged behind the others in not getting rid of its monarchy until 1889. Immigration had contributed to the problem with the Latin American population swelling three-fold during the 19th century.

The Portuguese King had been able to rule from Brazil for fifteen years after being forced into exile by Napoleon, until returning to Portugal in 1821, leaving his eldest son as Regent of Brazil. This son, Pedro, declared himself Emperor Pedro I, but his political aptitude was poor and instability followed his return to Portugal, where he abdicated in 1831. Brazil went through turbulent times with different rulers and different revolts until 1889 when the Republic of Brazil was initiated following a military coup.

Argentina was inhabited by a Stone Age culture for many thousands of years by early peoples who had migrated south from the Bering Straits during or after the last Ice Age. There is evidence of irrigation and crop rearing in the north-western Andean region of the country around 500 BC, and by the 1st century AD a maize based civilisation appeared in western and north-western Argentina. The Bronze Age came to Argentina around 600 AD and fortified urban settlements have been found dating from 850 AD onwards. The north-west of the country was conquered by the Incas in 1480, but their rule was to be short lived.

The Spanish explorer, Juan Diaz De Solis (1470–1516), came to the Rio De La Plata in 1516 where he was killed in battle with natives, although previous Portuguese explorers had visited successfully as early as 1502. The first colony was established in 1536 at the site of Buenos Aires only to be abandoned five years later following attacks by the natives. The colony was re-established in 1580 by settlers coming from Peru, but its viability was only slowly built up because of the lack of precious metals and other suitable products to export.

Once the status of the region was raised to that of a Spanish Vice-Royalty (which also included modern day Uruguay and Paraguay), Buenos Aires finally became a flourishing port for the export of precious metals from further north and inland. Spanish shipping found the port inaccessible after their defeat at the Battle of Trafalgar, but subsequent British attempts to invade Buenos Aires and Montevideo were both defeated.

Three great liberators are revered and commemorated in Latin America and were all influential in more than one country. Simon Bolivar (1783–1830) was born in Venezuela to an aristocratic native family, but came to Spain when he was 16, where he was enthused with the ideas of the enlightenment and imbibed an ambition to replace Spanish rulers with native born ones. The Venezuelan independence campaign started in 1808 leading to a National Congress three years later. Bolivar was elected president of Venezuela for a year between 1813 and 1814.

Venezuela had been the first of the South American countries to declare itself independent in 1811, though fighting between native and Spanish colonial forces continued for a further decade. Spanish forces attempted to control the independence movement, but Bolivar and his forces finally prevailed by 1821, leading to a fully independent Venezuela. Bolivar was also active in the founding of the first Union of Independent Countries in South America, named 'Gran Columbia', where he served as president from 1819 to 1830, he eventually resigned while president of Gran Columbia in 1830, intending to spend a peaceful exile in Europe, but died of tuberculosis before he could leave South America.

Gran Columbia subsequently split into the present nations that we recognise as Columbia, Venezuela, Ecuador, Panama, Northern Peru, Western Guyana and north-western Brazil. Bolivar's achievements did not stop with Venezuela however, and with his military leadership he also conquered Ecuador, Peru and Bolivia, which is named after him. Thus, at the end of his military career at the age of 40, he was ruling over a very large land area comprising much of northern South America and stretching from the Argentine border to the Caribbean.

Jose de San Martin (1778–1850) was of Spanish extraction, from a family who moved to Buenos Aires when he was about 4 years old, but returned to Spain a few years later, where he subsequently joined the army and participated in wars against Britain. He fought in the Peninsula War of Spain against the French, but afterwards journeyed back to Buenos Aires enthused with the enlightenment ideas of national independence, and became an important member of the new Argentine military. He was involved in the 1812 Argentine revolution, and was also active in the Chilean independence movement at that time.

Argentina underwent a week long May Revolution in 1810, but the different regions of the Vice-Royalty were not all represented. Political instability followed leading to the Argentine War of Independence, aided by the new political ideas coming from the French Revolution of 1789. Argentine independence was formally declared in 1816. The independence armies then gathered in northern Argentina and marched across the Andes in 1817 to defeat the monarchist Chilean forces, which led to the Chilean Declaration of Independence in 1818.

San Martin next became involved in the Peruvian war of independence which dragged on for a decade before he was able to announce the independence of Peru in 1821, although hostilities continued until gradually petering out by 1826. Simon Bolivar was also involved in this campaign.

The third notable name in the South American independence movement is that of Bernardo O'Higgins (1778–1842). Although his name indicates Irish ancestry, O'Higgins was born in Chile to a Spanish officer who had been born in Ireland, and later became governor of Chile. O'Higgins grew up in Chile and at the age of 17 was sent to London, where he studied and became familiar with the American independence movement and developed his ideas of independence and nationalism for Chile. He returned to Chile in 1802 to play a prominent part in political life, where an independence movement was formed following Napoleon's invasion of Spain in 1808.

In 1810, Chile declared its independence. Spain sent troops to quell the movement, but after several battles the Spanish were overcome and independence finally became a reality in 1818. Initially Jose San Martin had been offered the position of the first President of Chile, but he declined this offer in order to continue fighting for independence elsewhere in South America, and Bernardo O'Higgins took the position instead as the first leader of an independent Chile. He alienated many of his early supporters by his proposed radical reforms, including the abolition of nobility, and he also alienated the Church. He was deposed in a coup in 1823 and left to join the fighting in the Peruvian independence movement.

The national frontiers established in South America during the first half of the 19th century have largely persisted since that time, but further north large changes in North American territory came into existence through the first half of the 19th century. Florida was first encountered by the Spanish in 1513, with the object of settlement. The land was named La Florida (land of flowers), but exploration and settlement were unsuccessful, partly because of resistance from the native Indians.

In 1763, the territory of Florida was swapped by Spain with Britain for Havana in Cuba, which was a much more successful settlement. The British government gave land grants to encourage settlers to come to Florida, where sugar, fruit and indigo (which is a plant producing a blue dye with which the world is now familiar as the main colourant in jeans) was found, making the economy profitable. The Treaty of Paris in 1783 returned Florida to Spanish control, and many of the British immigrants left, but those who remained resented Spanish rule and rebellion occurred in 1810. West Florida was annexed by the USA in 1812 leading to continuing disputes with Spain. Following this, guerrilla war with the Indians continued, but finally in 1845 Florida became the 27th state in the American Union.

Spain had initially claimed all of North and Central America at a time when its extent was certainly neither known nor understood. The attraction of Mexico in particular to the Spaniards was the presence of gold and silver mines which would become a vital source of wealth when repatriated to Europe. The growth of sugar cane, together with other crops, initially needed native slave labour to do the work, but as the Europeans brought smallpox and other diseases with them much of the local population was decimated, and because of this the slave trade from West Africa became necessary to provide more labourers, after which Spanish settlements flourished.

It is estimated that up to a million West African slaves were transported to Mexico over 250 years (see slavery in chapter 59). The export of wealth from Mexico, together with the importation of slaves, gradually caused increasing resentment, both amongst the native population, but also among the settlers. Rebellion eventually started in several scattered places in 1811, developing slowly into the Mexican War of Independence which continued to 1821 while Europe was preoccupied with the Napoleonic Wars, and led to the independence of Mexico finally being declared in September 1821.

Along with the Florida and Louisiana purchases, the other great territorial realignment of the 19th century resulted from the loss of much of Mexico to the United States in the Mexican-American war of 1846 to 1848. Initially the Spanish had conquered Mexico when Cortez invaded and subdued the Aztec Empire with a minimum of troops whose superiority, thanks to the possession of guns, was overwhelming. Mexico remained under Spanish rule up to the beginning of the 19th century, but an independence movement gained great following in 1808 after the examples of the American and French revolutions.

The Spanish King abdicated in Madrid and Spain was unable to resist the war that followed through the next decade. Independence was finally agreed specifying equality between those of Spanish descent and native Indians, together with a religious monopoly for the Catholic Church. Although Spain attempted to regain control of Mexico, this did not happen, though it did cause great instability for Mexico's early years.

Emulating Napoleon, a native Indian called Agustin de Iturbide (1783–1824) eventually ruled as a dictator, and modelled himself on Napoleon, even being declared Emperor in 1822. He had to abdicate soon afterwards due to the overwhelming resistance to his rule. The Mexican government tried to populate its bare northern territories by giving land grants to families from the United States on the condition that new settlers would become Catholics and would not bring any slaves with them. The settlers came but eventually threw out these conditions and war resulted in 1835 with the result being the republic of Texas a year later.

A decade later, America went to war with Mexico after the Mexican army massacred an American army detachment in disputed territory. The outcome of this war was the transfer of huge amounts of territory from Mexico so that the states of Texas, New Mexico, Arizona, Utah, Nevada and California became incorporated into the United States at a price of $15 million. Thereafter, boundaries did not change significantly.

Possible further reading:
The Penguin History of Latin America by Edwin Williamson

Chapter 70
Development of the British Empire

In the late 16th century, war between England and Spain rumbled along with Spain trying to stop England meddling in the Netherlands, which was under Spanish control, and to try and put an end to English piracy in the Atlantic. This had been condoned by Elizabeth I, who encouraged such privateers as John Hawkins 1532–1595), Francis Drake (1540–1596) and Sir Walter Raleigh (1552–1618), who named Virginia after his sovereign, and founded the first American colony at Roanoke in 1584, though this subsequently failed.

Spain was the main power in both North and South America at that time in addition to Portugal, which had trading posts in Brazil (as well her African and Indian outposts). Matters climaxed with the Spanish Armada which was dispersed and destroyed in 1588 without landing troops on English soil, but the war grumbled on for a further sixteen years.

The Anglo-Spanish War of 1585–1604 ended thanks to the superiority of the British navy; the 'first' British Empire then came into existence, not as an exercise in colonial expansion, but rather as an unconnected string of trading posts designed to boost the British economy. This situation lasted for some two centuries up to the end of the 18th century. Although Columbus had first made landfall on the Bahamas, the Spanish had not initially colonised the area, but it was taken over by the British as a naval forward base against piracy.

English colonists joined the natives and the Bahamas became a Crown colony in 1718, increasing in importance after the American Civil War when Britain resettled American loyalists from the southern states there. In the Caribbean Jamaica and other islands were settled and thrived on the sugar plantations worked by slaves, with the sugar proving more profitable than cotton or tobacco.

The 'second' British Empire commenced in the years following the American Declaration of Independence, expanding rapidly through the subsequent Napoleonic years when Europe was inward looking and not able to pursue distant ambitions, either trading or colonial. With the loss of the thirteen American colonies after 1776, British focus turned to the rest of the world. Canada had become an important colony with the addition of loyalists from the thirteen colonies who did not wish to stay in the new American republic; and by the addition of the province of Quebec after the capture of Quebec City by General Wolfe in 1759 (formalised when France officially ceded Quebec to the British Crown in 1763).

However, Canadian history goes back much further. The first European contact with the native Indian tribes occurred with the Vikings at the end of the 10th century, and then various later explorers from the early 16th century onwards. The cod fishing off the Grand Banks of Newfoundland became important through the 16th century, and following this French explorers, including Samuel de Champlain (1574–1635) gradually penetrated the interior in search of its richness of furs, including sable (marten), beaver, fox and ermine. Also at the beginning of the 16th century Portugal started taxing the cod fisheries off the Grand Banks and establishing small coastal fishing villages, though these were to die out within decades.

Jacques Cartier (1491–1557), an explorer from Brittany landed on the Gaspé Peninsula, on the south shore of the St Lawrence River, which he was the first to describe, and claimed it in the name of France in 1534. On a second expedition he navigated up the St Lawrence as far as the first rapids, beyond which he thought that he would reach China if he continued sailing: the rapids were therefore named the Lachine Rapids. Many of his crew developed scurvy through the severe winter, but were saved by local knowledge from friendly native Indians that an extract of evergreen tree bark could cure scurvy. This knowledge then appears to have been lost to the British for the next two centuries or so.

The first permanent European settlement came in 1605, when Samuel de Champlain established Port Royal in present day Nova Scotia (it was destroyed by the British a few years later but rebuilt in 1632), and three years later he established the French settlement that became Quebec City. Champlain explored extensively, mapping the Great Lakes and describing the life of the native Indians. In the early days of Canada the settlements survived on fishing and the fur trade in contrast to the agriculture that was possible in the American colonies further south. In the same era Robert de La Salle (1643–1687), another early French explorer from Rouen, explored not only the Great Lakes of America and Canada, but also the Mississippi River, claiming the entire Mississippi Basin for France, which became known as Louisiana after the King of France.

Intermittent warfare at the end of the 17th century and the beginning of the 18th century between colonial powers continued, though the British had achieved control by 1710. From 1755 onwards Acadians from the eastern maritime coast (present day Nova Scotia and New Brunswick) of French extraction who had refused to swear allegiance to Britain were expelled and resettled, many of them in Louisiana, where they founded the Cajun culture which has remained linguistically and culturally distinct to this day.

After the battle for control of Quebec on the Plains of Abraham in 1759, France ceded its mainland Canadian territory to Britain in the Treaty of Paris in 1763. When the American colonies achieved their independence many loyalist refugees evacuated by the British were resettled in Nova Scotia and in a new colony of New Brunswick just to the north. At this time the extensive province of Quebec was divided into Lower Canada along the lower reaches of the St

Lawrence River, now the French speaking Province of Quebec, and Upper Canada, which has become the anglophone Province of Ontario.

War broke out in 1812 when the new United States tried to invade and capture some southern Canadian territory in what is today southern Ontario. The war was unsuccessful and was concluded by treaty in 1814 without any change of American or Canadian boundaries. The European revolutions against central government spread to Canada with a rebellion in 1837, which was disorganised and unsuccessful. As a result of this the British government sent Lord Durham (1792–1840), a leading Whig politician, to Canada to investigate the rebellion and make recommendations. His report in 1839, recommended a legislative union of Upper Canada, Lower Canada and the Maritime Provinces with the introduction of "responsible government".

This responsible government was taken by all concerned to be a structure which would emulate the parliamentary democracy existing at Westminster at the time. It took some years for this recommendation to be implemented, and even then Canadian government became highly partisan between the French and English populations, which in turn led to the creation of Confederation which was achieved in 1867.

Separately to the west, Vancouver Island was declared a colony in 1849, and British Columbia in 1858. British Columbia, starting as a colony, joined the Canadian Confederation in 1871. Prime Minister John Macdonald (1824–1890) created the Royal Canadian Mounted Police two years later, and by 1885 the Canadian Pacific Railway extended to the British Columbia coast to join the whole nation together. The Prairie provinces of Saskatchewan and Alberta joined the Confederation in 1905. The province of Newfoundland and Labrador rejected Confederation with Canada in the 1869 election, and again declined to join the Confederation in 1892. It therefore remained a colony, but acquired dominion status in 1907, and finally joined Canada officially in 1949 after the British North America Act.

Possible further reading:
The Path of Destiny by Thomas H Randall (Doubleday Ltd).

---oOo---

The first settlement in Australia came with the arrival of native peoples before the last Ice Age, migrating south from New Guinea at a time when the sea level was much lower and a land bridge existed. They had continued to live a primitive hunter-gatherer life, and Australia remained an unknown quantity to the rest of the world until several different Dutch explorers under the aegis of the Dutch East India Company made landfall along the northern and western shores of Australia, coming south from the East Indies in the 18th century; the first of these intrepid explorers to be documented was Willem Janszoon (1570–1630) in 1606, who was sailing for one of the predecessors of the Dutch East India Company.

Somewhat later, Abel Tasman (1603–1659), a Dutch merchant and explorer in the employ of the Dutch East India Company, sailed south from the East Indies and encountered New Zealand in 1642, returning west to discover Tasmania which now bears his name; in a second voyage in 1644 he made landfall off northern Australia and followed the coast westwards before striking across the Indian Ocean to return home past the Cape of Good Hope.

Major exploration first occurred in 1770 when Royal Naval officer Captain James Cook charted the east coast of Australia and suggested Botany Bay (present Sydney) to be a suitable site for a colony. Cook had been sent to observe the transit of Venus from Tahiti by the Royal Society, with instructions to explore further south afterwards to look for the mysterious continent that was thought to be there. Following Cook's recommendations the first penal colony was established at Botany Bay in 1788.

The Aboriginal natives were initially very friendly, but suffered badly from the advent of settlers due to a combination of imported European diseases and warring skirmishes when the settlers moved onto prized Aboriginal hunting grounds. Penal colonies were felt to be a more humane and convenient way of punishing felons than transportation to the Americas. Four thousand convicts were transported to New South Wales in the first four years of the Botany Bay colony. There were inconstant supplies from Britain to start with but the colony rapidly became self-sufficient, and by the turn of the century free settlers were coming in addition to the convicts. By 1868, when transportation for crimes ceased, 160,000 people, or 2,000 annually, had been transported of whom 15% were women.

Only finally in 1802 was the first circumnavigation of Australia achieved by Captain Matthew Flinders (1774–1814) of the Royal Navy, who stopped at the French island of Mauritius on his return journey to Britain for supplies and repairs to his ship, only to be imprisoned for the next six years as Britain and France were at war.

The mega fauna, including large flightless birds, reptiles and marsupials that had evolved in Australia were largely extinct already due to hunting by the Aboriginals, and in New Zealand by the Māori, when Europeans arrived. The early settlers however, noted that there were no mammals in Australia, and that separate development had resulted in a different class of creature, namely marsupials, though in those days before the publication of Darwin's theories, the explanation for these differences was not apparent.

In the first half of the 19th century, sheep breeding and Merino wool exports resulted in a thriving economy. The discovery of minerals, and the resulting gold rushes, stimulated immigration. English law was imported into New South Wales, which established a Legislative Council in 1825, and the State was remarkable in that the place of women in society was recognised much earlier than in European jurisdictions. The economy expanded rapidly, more settlers came from many countries other than Britain, and Australia graduated to autonomous government barely a hundred years after the first settlement at

Botany Bay, with Queen Victoria giving Royal Assent to an Australian Federation, which had spread to include the whole of the continent by 1900.

Possible further reading:
Australia in a Nutshell by Frank G Clarke (Rosenberg Publications).

---oOo---

New Zealand has the distinction of being the last region of the world to be settled, and yet it is also distinguished as the first nation to be fully democratic although its settlement is shorter than that of Australia. Māori settlement of the South Pacific islands occurred at the beginning of the last millennium, from the Polynesian Islands in the Pacific: Māori culture then was preliterate so dates and details are uncertain. Archaeological research indicates that this native culture came to New Zealand around 1300, and there is evidence of human deforestation at about the same time.

However, New Zealand's unique nature goes back many aeons before this when it was split off from the early land mass of Gondwana perhaps 80 million years ago at a time before marsupials and mammals had evolved, and as a result evolution proceeded on a separate path from much of the rest of the world so that when the first Polynesians arrived they found a land replete with huge birds, very large reptiles and insects existing nowhere else in the world. These creatures were ideal prey for the first Māori hunters and were soon decimated.

In this way, New Zealand's flora, fauna and landscape were greatly altered in a century by a process which took 20 centuries in Europe and 4 centuries in North America. The introduction of rats as predators first by the Polynesians and again later by Europeans, together with some domesticated breeds has also contributed to the transformed landscape that is now seen. Even before the advent of humans there was an enormous volcanic eruption sometime around 180 AD, which has left Lake Taupo in the North Island as its scar, and which is likely to have affected living creatures causing some possible extinctions as well as affecting the land itself.

In addition to this, the mega fauna in New Zealand was also rapidly reduced at that time, much of it to extinction. The two islands were first noted by Abel Tasman (1603–1659), the Dutch explorer supported by the Dutch East India Company. However, it was not until 1769 that Captain James Cook made landfall in New Zealand and subsequently became the first European explorer to circumnavigate the islands. Cook was a very talented and industrious map maker, and many of his maps were still in service until very recently.

Unlike Australia, penal settlements were never part of New Zealand's lot, but after Cook's explorations the islands started to open up with whaling and sealing in Antarctic waters, and for trade with the Maoris. Most of the contact with the Maoris was peaceful so European settlement occurred steadily through the first half of the 19th century. An official British Resident was appointed in 1832, and a Declaration of Independence signed with the Māori Chiefs in 1835.

The Treaty of Waitangi was signed between the British Governor and Māori Chiefs in 1840, and from then on much greater regulation of colonists and settlers was promoted by the British authorities.

In the early decades of the 19th century, the European population of New Zealand was less than a thousand or so, but by 1880 it had reached half a million. Most of these Europeans were British settlers, and about a third of them came with an assisted passage paid for by the colonial government. New Zealand was big enough to be recognised as a colony in its own right in 1841, having previously been administered from the rather larger Australian colony in New South Wales. Self-government was granted in a Constitution Act of 1852.

As in Australia, large-scale sheep farming underpinned the economy with huge quantities of wool being exported to British woollen mills. A gold rush in the 1860s to Otago in the South Island served to double the population and increased exports in general by an even larger amount. Although the Māori were aware of gold they used greenstone (a very hard rock of jade or serpentine) for their weapons, and greenstone, obsidian and bone for their jewellery.

The British writer, Edward Gibbon-Wakefield (1796–1862), had become a British politician and was a big force behind much of the early colonisation, initially of southern Australia and subsequently New Zealand. He had a rather erratic and notorious early life after first eloping with a wealthy heiress, who died young in childbirth, and subsequently trying to marry a second heiress. In 1831, believing that many of Britain's social problems were caused by overcrowding and overpopulation, he started to design a scheme for colonisation, initially influencing settlement in Australia and subsequently in New Zealand.

He was later sent to Canada by the British government alongside Lord Durham, where he was highly influential in uniting Upper and Lower Canada. He then returned to New Zealand and spent the rest of his life in colonisation projects. In the second half the 19th century, intermittent conflict between Maoris and Europeans disrupted New Zealand life somewhat, though by the end of the century the country was a stable democracy.

New Zealand was the first country in the world to give the vote to all women, followed a year later by South Australia. Both New Zealand and Australia were sufficiently strong and wealthy nations that they were able to provide men and material support on the British side when the First World War started in 1914.

Possible further reading:
Australia in a Nutshell by Frank G Clarke (Rosenberg Publications).

---oOo---

South Africa and Central Africa, including present day Kenya, Tanzania and Ethiopia, is the home of the evolution of mankind, early homo sapiens, as evidenced by archaeological discoveries dating occupation back well before the last Ice Age (chapter 2). Ancient kingdoms have left archaeological evidence of their existence around the beginning of the last millennium at a time when metal working in iron, copper and gold all bear witness to thriving civilisations.

In the drive to expand European trade, the southern route around Africa had been discovered by Bartholomew Dias (1450–1500), who had been instructed by King John II of Portugal to try and find a new sea route to the East Indies. Although he rounded the southern Cape of Africa, he did not get very far beyond this, but ten years later Vasco Da Gama (1465–1524) followed with a small fleet finally making landfall in India. At the most southerly part of Africa a Dutch trading post was set up for the Dutch East India Company, and as no native products were available for purchase by passing ships, Dutch farmers were imported, together with slaves from the Dutch far east colonies, to provide a small port which could re-vittle ships.

Britain seized this Cape Colony in 1795 to stop it falling into French hands during the Napoleonic wars, but returned it to the Dutch in 1803, only to take it over again in 1806. British sovereignty over the Cape Colony was then recognised at the Congress of Vienna in 1814 at the end of the Napoleonic Wars. By this time some twenty thousand white settlers lived in the colony with about twice that number of imported black slaves. The Dutch came into conflict with the indigenous people, who suffered badly like other native peoples, firstly from European diseases, and secondly from European superiority conferred by firearms.

More Dutch, then British settlers, arrived in South Africa in the first decades of the 19th century, but the cultures of the two nationalities proved incompatible. Initially, the English language used in schools, trade and law antagonised the white Dutch farmers, and in addition the Dutch used slave labour which the British had outlawed.

Over the next century, chronic dissatisfaction of the Dutch settlers simmered with their British rulers, and the imposition of British language. This led to Dutch migration and resettlement treks to the north in search of new land to populate and farm. These treks by covered wagon took place from 1835 to 1840, migrating northeast from Cape Colony and resulting in the founding of Transvaal, Orange Free State and Natal, but they displaced the Ndebele people and severely damaged the Zulu Empire. The impetus to move north had been given a powerful impetus by the expansionist Zulu Kingdom, established in 1709, and which, under the rule of its Chief Shaka, was also expanding to conquer new land and rival tribes.

In the early days of the century, Zulu capability in warfare was immensely improved under the under the direction of Shaka Zulu (1787–1827), an impressive warrior from one of the smaller Zulu tribes, who became king of the Zulus, but was eventually murdered by two of his half-brothers. Fighting between the British and the indigenous white population was endemic in the early years as the Dutch, German and French settlers never accepted British rule, particularly the ban on slavery, leading to the treks north to the interior to carve out their own nationalistic and cultural republics, and subsequently coalescing to become known as Afrikaners.

Because the Dutch and British settlers' cultures proved incompatible, the initial South African reply was independence and recognition in 1852 as the Orange Free State. In 1853, a colonial government was established in Cape Town with an elected assembly and council. There was a property qualification to allow voting, but this was kept low enough to encompass some of the coloured native population as voters. Continuing tensions would lead in particular to the later establishment of the system of Apartheid in South Africa in the 20th century, with the theory of separate lifestyles and separate development for white and black communities.

As previously noted, the tension between Boers and British led to the 'Great Trek' which took place in 1835 when thousands of Boers migrated north across the Orange River to form a new Afrikaner community. Animosity and violence continued to persist through most of the 19th century between Zulus, Boers and British.

By the middle of the 19th century, two independent Boer republics existed, the Orange Free State and Transvaal, whilst the original Cape Colony and Natal remained British. Diamonds were discovered in the 1870s and gold in 1880s, leading to an influx of entrepreneurs and camp followers hoping to profit. This discovery of gold and diamonds transformed the situation. Cecil Rhodes (1853–1902) traded and governed extensively though Southern Africa, he is commemorated in the name of Rhodesia, which he established, but which has since become Zimbabwe and Zambia. His ambitions for Southern Africa were transformed by the gold and diamond mines into which he had enormous input and influence, and from which he derived equally enormous financial rewards.

Cecil Rhodes had come to South Africa at the age of 17, and entered the diamond trade. He rapidly came to dominate the diamond market, and entered the parliament of Cape Colony in 1880 becoming Prime Minister ten years later. The Transvaal Boer Republic was annexed by Britain in 1877, resulting in rebellion and war between the Boers and the British in 1880. The Boers won this first war, but tensions remained between Britain and the Boers.

With mercenaries under the control of Cecil Rhodes, a second war resulted in the exclusion of largely British extraction whites from voting in the South African Republic (Transvaal). The war was declared by the South Africans (Boers), and after early British victories, turned into a guerrilla campaign in which both Europeans and Africans died. The South African Republic was finally given recognised autonomy in the London Convention of 1884, but the whole episode had destroyed any future trust or possible melding of attitudes, between the two communities.

Rhodes became Prime Minister of Cape Colony in 1890 and as such is responsible for much of the legacy of development in South Africa, but had to resign in 1896 after a disastrous military venture attacking the Transvaal went wrong. He died in 1902, but his legacy of white European supremacy is inextricably bound up with the corrosive Boer attitudes and resulting Apartheid system of the second half of the 20th century in South Africa. Rhodes remains a controversial figure and is often seen as epitomising the unacceptable face and legacy of British colonialism.

The most prominent and persistent Boer politician through this same period of the 19th century was Paul Kruger (1825–1904), who had been on the Great Trek as a child and became president in 1883, being re-elected to office until 1900. His name lives on in the national currency, the krugerrand, a town and a national park. A second Boer War lasted from 1899 to 1902 when peace was finally declared at the Treaty of Vereeniging. The South Africa Act of 1909 finally fused the four colonies into a single State which became an independent Dominion within the British Empire.

As a postscript to Rhodes seen as epitomising the unacceptable face and legacy of British colonialism: South Africa was forced to leave the British Commonwealth in 1961 when all the other Commonwealth countries felt that its apartheid policies could no longer be tolerated. Following the adoption of a new government and new multiracial policies, the country was readmitted to the Commonwealth in 1994.

Possible further reading:
A History of South Africa by Frank Welsh (Harper Collins)

Chapter 71
Physics and Chemistry

The natural or physical world has always been of intense interest to mankind. Early man was an acute observer of his surroundings and of the natural world, including the regular changes in the days over the seasons. Thales of Miletus, who lived around 1600 BC, is often given the accolade of "Father of Science"; he was a precursor of both Socrates and Aristotle. Like them, his writings survived through ancient civilisations and into the Muslim world, then spreading from the Middle East to Europe at the end of the 10th and 11th centuries.

By this time, Europe itself was beginning to wake up to the old teachings, and in most of Europe this was concentrated in religious establishments, abbeys, monasteries and cathedral schools. This gradually metamorphosed into the early universities, of which the first three are usually acknowledged as Bologna in 1088, Oxford somewhere after 1096 and Paris in 1150. The subjects studied were broad and under the four headings of theology, philosophy, law and medicine. The way in which these three institutions grew up and were financed exemplifies the different patterns of enquiry and learning for the next three centuries. The University of Bologna was founded in 1088 with the students getting together and hiring teachers, there was thus a high premium on the ability to engage with the students and provide stimulating lecture content; by contrast in Paris the lecturers were recruited, chosen and paid for by the Catholic Church; differently again, Oxford in the 12th century was supported by the Crown and the state, thus in later centuries, the Reformation of the Church did not upset the University or the organisation of teaching. By contrast, in many continental universities, founded and supported by the Catholic Church, the ecclesiastical upheavals of the 16th and 17th centuries were often considerable. In Paris in particular, the university was suspended during the French Revolution in 1793 and its buildings sold (along with many other clerical foundations) and then refounded in 1806.

In Spain in the 12th century, there was excellent access to teachings from ancient times, and many translations and transcriptions of old knowledge were undertaken before first, Muslim attitudes, and second Catholic Church attitudes, were to impose a heavy straitjacket on much of the learning about the natural world. Knowledge in those times was initially confined to a small number of centres, and books were all produced laboriously by hand and were therefore exceedingly precious, but with the invention of the printing press at the end of the 15th century the dissemination and expansion of knowledge expanded exponentially. Early scientific enquiry really commenced with the

Enlightenment, and increased steadily until the 18th and 19th centuries revolutionised the way the European world understood the workings of nature.

Through the 17th century, much of the foundation for subsequent scientific discoveries had commenced. Galileo, Kepler and Newton had all applied their thinking to the known universe and to matters of gravity. Free-thinking individuals had realised that our universe was centred on the sun, although this opinion was unacceptable to the Catholic Church. Evangelista Torricelli (1608–1647) in Rome had demonstrated the existence of a vacuum above a column of water or mercury, thereby producing an early barometer; while in Magdeburg in Germany, Otto von Guericke (1602–1686) harnessed horses to opposite sides of a pair of brass hemispheres held together only by a vacuum to demonstrate that the vacuum would not allow them to be pulled apart.

Von Guericke also made early experiments with static electricity, which in turn led to Benjamin Franklin's experiments in 1750 and the observation that lightning would be attracted to, and conducted down, a metal lightning conductor. Benjamin Franklin (1706–1790) was a non-conformist American polymath who travelled extensively in Europe and whose advice was sought by officialdom and by the Royal Society, of which he had been made a member.

From the discovery of a vacuum and the realisation that creatures could not survive in a vacuum, thoughts led on to the discovery of oxygen by Joseph Priestley (1733–1804; a non-conformist, anti-monarchist and founder member of Unitarianism), and the fact that oxygen itself was only a minor component of the air we breathe. David Rutherford (1749–1819), Scottish chemist, physician and founder member of the Royal Society of Edinburgh isolated nitrogen in 1772 and Lavoisier recognised oxygen in Paris.

Lavoisier also worked on improving the manufacture of gunpowder from saltpetre (KNO_3) when he became head of the French Grand Arsenal, from where one of his fellow researchers emigrated to the United States, setting up the du Pont Corporation and gunpowder factory which eventually provided much of the firepower for the American Civil War. It became known that air expanded when heated, and with this knowledge the first hot air balloon flight was made by the Montgolfier brothers in France in 1783 after initial unmanned tests. Not too much later in Hamburg a hot air balloon flew to a height of over 6,000 metres.

The compass, and finding magnetic north using a magnetised iron needle, had been known for many years, knowledge initially propagated from China. In 1600 Queen Elizabeth's personal physician William Gilbert (1544–1603) published a book on magnetism summarising many years work and theorising that Earth was essentially a giant magnet with north and south poles of attraction. By the end of the 18th century Charles De Coulomb (1736–1806) a French military engineer and physicist found and quantified electricity using a magnetised needle. At the same time, Luigi Galvani (1737–1798), an Italian physician and scientist, discovered the presence of small electric currents in animal bodies.

Another Italian scientist, Allesandro Volta (1745–1827), was able to show that electricity was produced from the reaction between two different metals, and was able to make the first battery to produce regular electric current by stacking alternate discs of silver and zinc with wet paper between them. Out of these experiments came the production by electrolysis, of chlorine and minerals, and in turn the process of electro-plating, which involved plating metal objects with a thin surface layer of a different metal, usually silver or gold. Other names that have remained current in our present usage, apart from the volt, is the conductivity or resistance of a metal assessed by the German physicist Georg Ohm (1789–1854), the ampere after the French physicist André-Marie Ampere (1775–1836), and the watt named much later after James Watt (chapter 73).

By 1821, Michael Faraday (1791–1867) at the Royal Institution had come to the conclusion that magnetism and electricity were interchangeable. Faraday was able to produce electricity by rotating a magnet within an iron wrapped sphere, and this basic insight would lead to the development of electric motors, in turn he is remembered in the farad, a measure of a unit of capacitance. Faraday's work, and the relationship and similarity between light and electric current, was pursued further by a Scottish scientist called James Clerk Maxwell (1831–1879), who was able to propose a common theory of wave propagation, which is seen as the vital link between the work of Newton and the later research of Albert Einstein.

The French Academy of Sciences recommended adoption of the decimal system in 1790, and a few months later defined the metre as one ten millionth of the distance from the pole to Earth's equator based on a fraction of a one minute angle of Earth's latitude: this was not easy to measure and soon afterwards a standard length bar of metal was substituted as the standard. The zero meridian of longitude stayed centred at Greenwich despite a French attempt to switch it to Paris.

Samuel Morse (1791–1872) in America produced the telegraph in 1844 and started with the ability to switch on and off a small magnet a hundred miles away. Morse is, of course, also remembered for developing the use of this into the telegraph by developing Morse Code by which messages could be sent down the wires. Thomas Edison (1847–1931) was an extremely prolific American inventor producing the light bulb in 1879; up till that time household lighting had only progressed from candles in the 16th and 17th centuries to coal gas lighting early in the 19th century.

The Lunar Society has already been mentioned in chapter 64, but among its members were Matthew Boulton and James Watt. Boulton and Watt are well known for their pumping engines that aided the exploitation of mines by keeping them clear of water. In conjunction with a third young colleague, William Murdoch, they also took out a patent for the manufacture of the gas and other products from the distillation of coal. Two gas burners were installed initially in the Boulton and Watt factory in Birmingham's Soho, and the new invention was rapidly taken up by other factory owners, as the new lighting was cheaper, brighter and safer than the previous use of candles and whale oil lamps.

It was only a short time before the gas was being produced in sufficient quantity to supply houses through a distribution network rather than relying on individual installations. By the middle of the 19th century all major British towns were lit by gas, with an extensive network of mains gas piping.

Another product from the distillation of coal was naphtha which was rapidly discovered to be an excellent organic solvent, in particular naphtha would dissolve rubber, which could be them used to rubberise sheets of cotton. In 1823 Charles Mackintosh (1766–1843) obtained a patent for this product and rapidly built up an extensive business in waterproof sheeting and garments in Glasgow. An English inventor called Thomas Hancock (1786–1865) also experimented with rubber, which he used to make waterproof items of clothing, including shoes, gloves and garters, and then use of the material spread rapidly.

The importation and use of rubber soared, especially when Hancock and Mackintosh produced their new raincoat together. Hancock's brother Walter was also an enterprising inventor who made and ran steam buses in London. Wellington boots, first made for the Duke of Wellington in leather began to be made of rubber after 1854 following a fruitful meeting between Charles Goodyear (1800–1860) of tyre fame and Hiram Hutchison (1808–1869), an American industrial entrepreneur, who set up a rubber and vulcanising factory in France.

Another early chemical of great benefit was quinine, derived from the bark of the cinchona tree. This was imported from Peru, and became fashionable for its antipyretic properties. The use of quinine for malaria prophylaxis with the British army in India was especially important. From other coal tar distillation products came an organic chemical compound named aniline, which was initially black, but after washing and treatment became purple; it went on sale in 1857 as the first of a new line of aniline dyes synthesised by a very young London chemistry student called William Perkin (1838–1907). These dyes were exploited by the German chemical industry where technical expertise in the new chemistry was excellent.

By this time, Britain had become rich with its early lead in the industrial revolution and had a very strong industrial base with a large import capacity of cheap commodities from its colonies. By contrast, German schooling in the technical side of chemistry and other sciences now allowed Germany to take a rapid lead in the new dyes. The use of gaslight resulted in large quantities of by-products from the distillation of coal, and the new industry producing organic distillates from coal tar found the perfect breeding ground in the German industrial culture.

Germany had founded technical high schools early and standardised its universities by the end of the 19th century, so that in the last years of the century Germany went from being a largely agricultural country in 1870 to a very powerful industrial nation by the beginning of the First World War less than fifty years later. With much of Germany's rural population migrating to the cities to work in factories, this was encouraged by the importation of large quantities of sodium nitrate fertiliser imported from Chile. The other great agricultural advance was the invention of a mechanical reaper by several engineers including American inventor Cyrus McCormick (1809–1884), able to harvest crops at many times the rate of agricultural labourers. As the supplies of sodium nitrate from Chile gradually dwindled, German chemists found a method of producing ammonia and sodium nitrate industrially. Acetylene was also discovered and purified; it is a gas given off when calcium carbide and water combine, and produces a very intense white light when burnt. It was much cheaper than coal gas and electricity, and was also a very practical means of welding metal. In later years work on acetylene after the first World War would produce polyvinyl chloride (PVC) the forerunner of plastics, which dominate many of our industrial products today.

Possible further reading:
Physical Chemistry by Peter Atkins (Oxford University Press)

Chapter 72
Development of Biology and Medicine

In ancient times, explanations of how the natural world functioned were mainly theoretical and to our modern understanding, often bizarre. The regimes for treatment of diseases and injuries were sometimes very practical but at other times alarmingly inconsistent and theoretical. Despite the prevalence of war and its constant production of injuries, there were very few attempts to collect a series of similar observations, conditions or injuries and analyse their outcomes: this would have to wait until the Enlightenment and the gradual development of the scientific method in much more recent times.

The Edwin Smith papyrus found in a Cairo pawn shop in 1862, and written around 3,000 BC, appears to have been a collection of medical cases, possibly written by Imhotep (chapter 6). It seems to be a distillation of suggested treatments, possibly from even earlier centuries, and is concerned predominantly with injuries, including fractures and dislocations. In the document, the physician is instructed to triage the injured patient into one of three categories; the first category is where treatment is deemed possible, the second type where an attempt to treat and cure may be undertaken, and a final category suggests the injuries that should not be treated as chances of survival are felt to be minimal.

Treatment is concerned with bandaging, splinting fractures, and the various ointments and products useful to apply to open wounds. Surprisingly around the same time Ayurvedic medicine in early India concentrated not just on herbal remedies, but also gives details of early surgical operations, including those for cataracts or bladder stones, and even early plastic surgery, as in rhinoplasty for patients who had lost their noses either to disease or as legal punishment. In ancient China emphasis was placed on herbal medicine, but in addition the ancient practice of acupuncture was used with special placement of needles for almost all known sorts of disease.

Hippocrates (460–370 BC) is usually hailed as the 'Father of Medicine'; he lived, worked and taught on the Greek island of Kos. He was the first person to regard disease as originating from natural causes, rather than being the result of divine punishment or some other superstition. In those far off times much of how the human body worked, and how disease was caused, were the product of philosophical hypotheses rather than any scientific extrapolation from facts. Thus one of the common theories about the workings of nature attributed good health to a correct balance of the four 'humours' that were supposed to be balanced within the body, namely black bile, yellow bile, phlegm and blood.

In many ways, this thinking seems to us today as unlikely as the similar biological thinking of the time which suggested that all living matter was made from varying combinations of earth, air, fire and water. These theories were perpetuated in the writings of the time two millennia ago, and the Roman physician Galen of Pergamum (129–216 AD) set them down in his writings. Galen was an experienced physician, and in his early years as a physician treated many gladiators, giving him an excellent grounding in the treatment of injuries. Unfortunately his knowledge of anatomy was largely theoretical and was not questioned for the next 1500 years. Galen had never dissected the human body, but his works were translated and underpinned the Islamic understanding of anatomy, physiology and disease.

In medieval times, his teachings were translated into Greek from Arabic, and then into European vernacular, or were rediscovered in Latin by medieval physicians so that he came to embody the theoretical basis of European medical beliefs until after the Enlightenment and Reformation started to take hold. Avicenna (980–1037) was an important Arabic thinker on both medical and other matters in Islamic Persia. He was an extensive writer on many subjects, and thus an intermediate in transmitting medieval learning to later Europeans.

A Swiss physician known to us as Paracelsus (1493–1541) studied science and physiology as well as medicine and natural philosophy. His practical experience led him to reject the teachings of Galen and Avicenna, but he was an abrasive man and only survived a short period as a professor at the University of Basle where he taught that experience and practical knowledge were far more important than theoretical considerations. Paracelsus' teaching began to strike a chord at the beginning of the 16th century, as did the thinking of his contemporaries Copernicus, Leonardo da Vinci and Martin Luther.

At the same time, Andreas Vesalius (1514–1564) started dissecting the human body at Padua where he was professor. Up to that time the theories of Galen ruled supreme and there was no hands-on experience of anatomy due to Islamic and Catholic prohibitions on dissection. Vesalius' contemporary, Ambroise Paré (1510–1590), a French barber surgeon with considerable experience gleaned from the battlefield injuries of the French army, pioneered several general early advances, and is best remembered for stopping the use of boiling oil to cauterise wounds, instead using ligatures to seal blood vessels when doing an amputation. He is also remembered for advocating manual turning of the unborn child within the womb if the child was lying in the dangerous transverse position.

Understanding how living creatures and plants are composed and work took a big step forward with the making of an early microscope by Robert Hooke (1635–1703), polymath, astronomer and natural philosopher in London, who first described individual cells in 1665 and named them 'cells' after the similarity he saw with the very small institutional rooms in which monks lived. It was however Antonie von Leeuwenhoek (1632–1723) from Holland who developed an ability to grind glass lenses and was then able to magnify material up to 200 times. In this way, Von Leeuwenhoek was able to show different parts of cells, bacteria, single-celled organisms and spermatozoa. He was also able to see the minute capillaries in the tissues allowing the blood to circulate from the arterial to the venous side of the circulation. This completed the important work started by William Harvey (1578–1657) physician to James I and then Charles I. By means of dissections Harvey had been able to disprove the Galenic theory that the blood was formed in the liver. Harvey showed that blood circulated through the lungs to be oxygenated and then through the rest of the body to distribute oxygen, and was in fact generated in the bone marrow and spleen.

Living well before von Leeuwenhoek, and without the benefit of magnification, Harvey had not been able to discover how the blood got from the arterial to the venous side of the circulation, and thought it must simply have percolated through the tissues. The question was solved by Marcello Malphigi (1628–1694), an Italian physician from Bologna who demonstrated capillaries in the lungs and other organs. With these important basic discoveries the scene was set for progressively greater understanding of the working of human and animal bodies.

Antoine Lavoisier (1743–1794) was born and educated in Paris, taking a law degree but never practising law, as he became inspired with the French Enlightenment and the science of chemistry. He published his first scientific paper in his mid-twenties, and then experimented on combustion and chemicals. Lavoisier was visited in 1774 by Joseph Priestley (1733–1804) who was an English non-conformist and founder Unitarian clergyman.

From this start, Priestley was able to isolate oxygen and demonstrate its properties and its necessity for life. Lavoisier's chemical experiments continued and he was involved in drawing up a scheme for the naming of chemical compounds for the French Academy in 1787. Unfortunately Lavoisier, who was a wealthy aristocrat, had bought into the Ferme Generale, a company which collected taxes in France: as such he was arrested and convicted as a traitor during the Revolution, and went to the guillotine in 1794.

During the Enlightenment years of the 17th and 18th centuries, there was an upsurge in independent and radical thinking about the biological, physical and chemical sciences which would come together in the 19th century to provide a coherent and logical explanation of the natural world. Carl Linnaeus (1707–1778), Swedish physician and biologist, commenced the modern system of naming plants and animals and putting their groupings together; he is known as the 'Father of Modern Taxonomy' meaning the naming and classification of organisms. Jean-Baptiste Lamarck (1744–1829) wrote and taught as professor in Paris and promoted early thinking along the lines of possible evolution to produce species: he felt that inheritance was mediated by each generation inheriting the acquired characteristics of the previous generation (which was later disproved).

Erasmus Darwin (1731–1802) grew up in the English Midlands, where he was a seminal thinker and member of the Lunar Society. Apart from being a physician, he was also influential in early biological thought, and his thinking on evolution pre-date those of his grandson, Charles Darwin: a visit to his house in

Lichfield which is now a museum is both stimulating and enlightening about contemporary thought.

James Hutton (1726–1797) contributed to the understanding of the natural world through his work as a geologist and naturalist; he is known as the 'Father of Geology'. Alexander von Humboldt (1769–1859) grew up in Prussia, becoming a naturalist and an explorer of the world. His travels in South America later took him over twenty years to organise and write up from his travel notes; he was one of the first people to suggest that the coasts of South America and Africa had once been contiguous, and had somehow drifted apart. Georges Cuvier (1769–1832) grew up in France, training as a naturalist and zoologist. He was fascinated by fossils; his career was distinguished by proposing the extinction of species thus explaining the presence of fossils.

Gideon Mantell (1790–1852) grew up on the south coast of England with an intense interest in natural history; he qualified as a doctor and like many early natural philosophers his interests and understanding of the relationship between natural history and medicine cross-fertilised each other. His interest in fossils and their place in the life history of Earth was another step in furthering understanding of the workings of the natural world.

Commencing with Robert Hooke's microbiological observations, and continuing with the findings of von Leeuwenhoek, the theory of cells as the basic components of all life developed so that cell theory was finally fully formulated around 1838. Mathias Schleiden (1804–1881) used his background in botany in Germany to postulate that all plants are made of cells, arising in the first place from a single cell. Theodor Schwann (1810–1882) helped to develop cell theory and is remembered today in the cells which sheath nerve conducting fibres and are known as Schwann cells.

Another German doctor, Rudolph Virchow (1821–1902), was a polymath in addition to his medical interests. He is often known as the 'Father of Modern Pathology', and is remembered for his work in public medicine and hygiene. He completed the third rule of modern cell theory; the rules are very simple as follows, firstly, all living organisms are composed of one or more cells, secondly, the cell is the basic unit of structure and organisation of living organisms, and thirdly, all cells come from pre-existing cells.

Charles Lyell (1797–1875) was an important Scottish geologist who developed the work of James Hutton and was also a close friend of Charles Darwin (1809–1882). He contributed to Darwin's thinking about evolution and helped to arrange the publication of Darwin's 'Origin of Species' alongside that of Alfred Russel Wallace (1823–1913) in 1858. Charles Darwin grew up in the English Midlands in Shrewsbury with a physician father and grandfather. He did not enjoy his early medical student years, and was therefore sent to Cambridge to study natural history, and after he graduated was offered a place on an exploratory expedition to chart the coast of South America.

This voyage of HMS Beagle, which was supposed to last two years, stretched out to five years. Darwin was able to study many fossils in Patagonia, together with geological features showing evidence of different sea levels in historic times. On the Galapagos Islands he noted many variations, both in the famous finches which he studied, and in the shape of tortoise shells. After his return home Darwin slowly wrote up his results with the help of others, which was necessary because of the considerable number of specimens that he had brought home. He became friends with Charles Lyell, the pioneering Scottish geologist, discussing his results with him, but was diffident about publishing his theories on evolution as he realised the enormously controversial effect this would have on current and past theological thinking. Eventually, Darwin and Alfred Russel Wallace became aware of each other's thinking about evolution, and after the intervention of Charles Lyell, their papers were presented at the same meeting of the Linnean Society in 1858.

Alongside cell theory, it was clearly important that the means of perpetuating cells and organisms should be understood, together with the factors allowing such organisms to thrive. The Reverend Thomas Malthus (1776–1834) was a foremost early thinker in this field, noting that populations, of people, plants or animals, would be subject to both famine and disease. His writings emphasise firstly, that any increase of population is limited by available food, secondly that if available food increases so will population, and thirdly, that as far as people are concerned, population may also be checked by the contemporary conditions including crime, misery, vice and warfare: his thinking were greatly influenced at the time by both the Poor Laws and the Corn Laws at a time when Britain was no longer producing enough indigenous food for its population.

Contemporary with Charles Darwin, Gregor Mendel (1822–1884) grew up in Moravia in eastern Europe on a farm. He became a monk after a scientific education, and was able to continue his studies on inherited characteristics using pea plants. He formulated laws of inheritance, defining dominant and recessive characteristics, but his findings were published in an obscure journal with the result that they were ignored until a couple of decades after his death.

Cell theory developed further with improvements in optics, particularly by the optical manufacturing firm of Carl Zeiss (1816–1888) producing microscopes in particular designed by physicist Ernst Abbé (1840–1905). The German theory of disease had been put forward by Girolamo Fracastoro (1476–1553), an Italian physician and natural philosopher who proposed in 1546 that epidemic diseases were caused by 'spores', transferred either by direct contact or indirectly. It would be three centuries before Louis Pasteur and Robert Koch could fill in the details of the theory and identify the bacteria that corresponded to Fracastoro's 'spores' and caused many infectious diseases.

Louis Pasteur (1822–1895) initially worked and taught as a chemist in Paris and is remembered today in the term 'pasteurisation' in which heat treatment of milk and other products kills bacteria, prolonging the useful life of natural products; he is often given the designation 'Father of Microbiology'. Robert Koch (1843–1910) grew up in Hanover, graduating in medicine and working as a microbiologist with infectious diseases, discovering the specific bacteria causing tuberculosis, cholera and anthrax. Koch's postulates for the confirmation of a specific agent as causing a disease require firstly that the micro-organism must always be present in each case of the disease, secondly that it must be isolated from any patient with the disease and grown in pure culture, thirdly, that specimens taken from the culture must cause the disease when inoculated into a healthy animal or person, and fourth, that it must be isolated from the inoculated animal and identified as the same as the original organism.

With this background knowledge, the way was open for Joseph Lister (1827–1912), a Glasgow surgeon, to apply the principals involved for the prevention of infection and to pioneer antiseptic surgery. His practical means of achieving this was to use a fine spray of carbolic acid to sterilise surgical instruments and wounds. These advances led to a rapid reduction in sepsis in surgical cases. It is tragic that the earlier work of Ignaz Semelweis (1818–1865) in Hungary, working with puerperal fever at the Vienna General Hospital, and Oliver Wendell-Holmes (1809–1894) in Boston, also working with sepsis on maternity wards was disregarded by their contemporary colleagues, and control of infection had to wait until Lister was able to persuade the world of the cause of infections and the principles necessary to combat the problem.

Away from medicine, but armed with the scientific knowledge of bacteria and with their mode of life now understood with regard to infections and the rotting of dead tissues, advances in the preservation of food followed (although the ancient Peruvians had first frozen and then produced powdered and dried potatoes for long term storage). Although the freezing of food was rediscovered as a means of inactivating bacteria the 1860s, it was Clarence Birdseye (1886–1956), an American naturalist and entrepreneur, who really made the process viable with 'flash freezing' in the 1930s. Much earlier, and before decay was properly understood, a Parisian chef, Nicholas Appert (1749–1841) had used the principle of excluding air from cooked food to preserve it, by storing food in airtight jars or cans.

Two profound advances in medicine occurred in the 19th century, the first of these was when a Boston dentist William Morton (1819–1868) first demonstrated the use of ether as an anaesthetic in 1846. The second was the discovery of x-rays by Marie Curie (1867–1934), who was both the first woman to become a professor at the University of Paris, and also the first woman to win a Nobel Prize. Amazingly she won a second Nobel prize for the discovery of the elements radium and polonium. Unhappily the effects of radiation were not fully appreciated for many decades, and she eventually died from aplastic anaemia (failure to produce red blood cells), when years of causal radiation had destroyed her bone marrow. The practical outcome of her research was the use of x-rays by Wilhelm Röentgen (1845–1923), a German mechanical engineer and professor of physics who produced the first x-ray in 1895 for which he won the first Nobel Prize in physics.

Nobel prizes are named for the Swedish chemist Alfred Nobel (1833–1896), who invented dynamite and was also a highly successful businessman, making a fortune from the sales of armaments; he left his fortune in his will for the prizes, only four people have won the prize twice, of whom Marie Curie was the first. The prizes are given annually under five headings; chemistry, physics, medicine, literature and peace. Only six laureates have won more than one prize, the International Committee of the Red Cross on three occasions, and twice each for the United Nations High Commissioner for Refugees, Marie Curie, Linus Pauling (1901–1994) an American chemist in quantum chemistry, John Bardeen (1908–1993) an American physicist for transistors and semi-conductors, and Frederick Sanger (1918–2013) a British biochemist for elucidating the structure of proteins.

With all these great leaps forward in the 19th century, a further and very practical leap forward was made by the English nurse and social reformer Florence Nightingale (1820–1910). Nightingale herself was not a nurse, but her contribution to the Crimean War in terms of compassion, technical organisation and nursing were immensely important. She returned from Crimea and founded the first nursing school at St Thomas's Hospital in London, but was also a pioneer in statistical analysis and sanitation, both in England and in India; she effectively created the profession of nursing.

Possible further reading:
The Invention of Nature, the Adventures of Alexander von Humboldt by Andrea Wulf (John Murray, publisher)
Physician Extraordinary, a Novel of the Life and Times of William Harvey by David Weiss (Dell Paperback)
Florence Nightingale by Cecil Woodham Smith (Constable)
The Private Life of Florence Nightingale by Richard Gordon (Penguin)

Chapter 73
Civil Engineering – Roads, Buildings and Canals

Through the 19th and early 20th centuries, four broad categories of engineering were recognised – civil, mechanical, chemical and electrical. Since then these disciplines have split and subdivided into for example aeronautical, acoustic and electronic engineering being added to the four basic divisions. Civil engineering is concerned with structures which we recognise today, and society's infrastructure of roads, bridges, canals, railways and buildings.

In Stone Age times, ancient man was frequently nomadic. Settlements would have been semi-permanent and the occasion for transport of objects between villages would have been small. There would have been a need for small and valuable items, such as jewels and weapons, to be carried for the purposes of trade between villages and even further. Heavier items, principally for building, would have needed the cooperation of many people to move them, one of the most interesting examples is the transport of the enormous stones that comprise Stonehenge from the mountains of South Wales to build the monument in rural Wiltshire over 110km away.

It is suggested that this might well have been achieved by floating the stones on rafts down rivers to the River Severn and then up the River Avon close to Stonehenge. About the same time in Mesopotamia the wheel had been invented and carts had become ubiquitous as a means of transporting heavy objects, but had not appeared in Britain by then. A single pack horse, or similar beast of burden, can carry a load of perhaps 100kg. When pulling a wagon with two or four wheels, the load can be increased by a factor of four, although the wheeled wagon is more limited in its access to areas of difficult terrain; however, even a very large cart would not be capable of transporting the 25–ton stones to Stonehenge.

Once people settled in villages and some towns began to grow, then local supplies of wood and stone would rapidly become exhausted and there would have been a need for such commodities to be transported some distance: this was the incentive for the building of the first roads so that a level and reasonably durable surface could be constructed for the frequent use of wagons. As wealth increased and an upper class appeared, there became a requirement for more sophisticated transport, eventually in terms of coaches to carry people and couriers or Royal Mail and messages.

The first road systems came into existence as small centres of settlement gradually became kingdoms and then even empires. In order to provide durability, paving stones followed soon afterwards, once the wealth of the state was able to afford this. Roads paved with stone are found in the city of Ur in Mesopotamia dating around 4,000 BC, and a paved road in Egypt has been dated from around 1,500 years later between urban centres. Also around 3,000 BC, streets paved with bricks have been excavated from early Indian cities. In England at the same time on the marshy Somerset Levels roads, or perhaps more accurately laid hurdles of woven hazel branches, sufficed as pathways or primitive roads across boggy areas. Because these early Somerset highways were buried in the wet acidic peat they have decayed only very slowly, and have subsequently been found during recent peat cutting.

Once the Roman Empire became wealthy and started extending its borders and conquests, a system of roads was gradually developed, mainly with military usage in mind, but also available for traders and other travellers. The Romans made extensive use of level roads without surfacing or simply with gravel laid on top. These roads would not stand up to heavy wear, and certainly not to the use of marching legions. So the major Roman roads were constructed with a well impacted base of hard-core and a top surface of granite blocks, like large cobbles. By the reign of Diocletian between 285–305 AD, when the Roman Empire reached close to its maximum extent, there were 372 paved roads recorded in the Empire with a total mileage of 85,000 kilometres.

After the western Roman empire collapsed in 410 AD, and then through the Dark Ages into the time of early expansion of early Islam, little further road building took place. Along with other remains of the Roman Empire the highways continued to offer benefits to travellers, but without imperial maintenance roads gradually crumbled with no central imperium to look after their upkeep. Once the Romans and their centralised structures of government left both England and other parts of Europe the road infrastructure gradually deteriorated and no significant change in the transport network occurred during the next millennium or so.

In England, much of the traffic used roads like the Ridgeway, these were particularly sited along the top of hill escarpments to avoid marshy and boggy areas, and their associated streams and rivers: all had been well trodden highways by men and beasts since the Stone Age. Similar courses were taken by long distance routes in central Germany.

With the Enlightenment and the Industrial Revolution, supplies of commodities needed to be transported, and finished products then taken to market. In 1663 the English Parliament had ordered that Justices of the Peace should improve their roads, set up turnpikes (toll roads), and pay for these improvements. In places this resulted in serious upgrading, but in other places local responsibility was evaded. By contrast, in France press gangs of peasant labourers were used to widen and maintain roads. These roads became wider as travellers attempted to skirt around the ruined areas and travel times lengthened as a consequence. Merchants trying to convey their newly imported cargoes of sugar, coffee, spices, tobacco and such like became frustrated, even with the use of pack animals for transportation.

The pressure for improvement was considerable and John Louden McAdam (1756–1836) devised a new process for building roads with a replaceable and durable surface. Whilst still in his twenties McAdam was a trustee of the Ayrshire Turnpike in Scotland and displayed increasing interest and involvement with road construction. His method of construction used a base of large stones on which an upper layer of crushed stone and gravel provided a hard smooth top (note the similarity with Roman construction). This method spread rapidly, both through Britain and also to America and the rest of Europe: it is still the basis of road construction today.

Turnpikes or toll roads existed throughout the Middle Ages, and indeed since very early times; they represented a mechanism for landowners to raise money from travellers passing through and along their lands. Tolls tended to vary with the size of the load, and Turnpike Trusts were set up initially to maintain the principal roads in Britain from the 17th century onwards. Toll houses are still frequently seen by the sides of British main roads, usually small octagonal buildings facing each way along the road to spot approaching traffic; in the 17th to 19th centuries they would have had an adjacent gate to stop the traffic for payment. The system declined in the second half of the 19th century as railways were built in competition to the roads, and then in 1888 a Parliamentary Act made County Councils responsible for maintenance of the road system.

Despite these improvements in road building, McAdam's construction methods still left roads liable to potholing and rutting in winter, and dust generation in summer. Various attempts were made through the 19th century to seal the surface by spreading tar on the upper layers, but it was not until an English inventor, Edgar Hooley (1860–1942), patented a method of stabilising the upper surface of roads that matters improved. Hooley was inspired by noticing an area of tar spill which had been covered with gravel mixed into the tar to improve matters. His method of improved road construction was rapidly adopted, especially since his invention coincided with the early years of the motor car and motor truck transport. Subsequent development of road networks has merely been detailed improvements on the process started by the Romans, continued by McAdam and refined by Hooley.

---oOo---

Engineering in early times was often associated with architecture. Many features and monuments have survived down the ages so that we can admire the principles of design and construction to this day. In Europe the Ancient Greeks built temples and theatres which have often survived remarkably intact. The Romans also built temples and other big buildings, but in addition have left us roads, bridges, viaducts and dams. By the 19th century civil engineers were busy through the second half of the century with evermore ambitious buildings.

In England, the home of the British Parliament, the Palace of Westminster, was destroyed by fire in 1834 when careless incineration of waste materials caused chimney fires in the flues which spread to the rest of the building. After a competition in which 97 entries were submitted, the architect Charles Barrie (1795–1860) was selected to rebuild the Palace of Westminster. Work started in 1837, and went massively over budget and over the time estimate for its completion. The Victoria Tower, completed in 1860, is 323 feet tall, housing the famous Big Ben clock: it was the tallest building in the world for many years. Barry was aided in his work redesigning the Houses of Parliament by the architect and designer Augustus Pugin (1812–1852), who was responsible for much of the interior design, he was also responsible for the design of many other churches throughout the United Kingdom in the 19th century.

As a side branch of civil engineering, through medieval times and into the Middle Ages, much engineering was the result of military efforts, and as so often in the past war has acted an urgent incentive to develop and improve technologies. In ancient times the Romans built fortifications and maps with interconnecting roads to allow their legions access to far flung parts of the Empire which needed defending. There was also great ingenuity put into the construction of engines of war, thus giving rise to the title of "engineer" for a person who constructed not only defensive structures but such engines of war as catapults, rams and siege towers. As castles became bigger, engineers were required to undermine their walls in order to breach the defences, and they brought to their work the hard won techniques and skills of miners of previous generations. Military engineers found their epitome in the great French military engineer Sebastian De Vauban (1633–1707), who later became Baron Vauban under Louis XIV. He built many fortifications throughout France and indeed in North America, and upgraded many more, which still survive as monuments to static warfare and military tactics in the 17th and 18th centuries.

---oOo---

Water transport has been equally as important as road transport in human history. River transport became vital when people were trying to move large loads over long distances, particularly if the loads were heavy. It is about ten times more efficient in energy terms to move loads by water than by land. However, not all rivers are suitable for navigational crafts and the oceans are not always kind to travellers. Canals came into being to make up for the lengths of non-navigable rivers, or alternatively to go to destinations not visited by rivers.

The first and one of the largest canal schemes ever devised commenced around 600 BC in China, where several lakes were linked together by having canals dug between them. This grand scheme would eventually link the northern Yellow and southern Yangtze Rivers through a total of 1776 km of waterway. The canal became fully viable only once locks of the sort that we see on all canals today allowed water borne traffic to move in either direction from about the 11th century onwards in China. The canal was started as long ago as 485 BC and was finally completed in 600 AD.

Intentional breaches were sometimes used to defeat advancing armies by flooding the countryside. Up to five million labourers were reputed to be employed in the last years of construction. A system of post offices and routes for couriers existed alongside the canal. However, it was not until the 10th century that the Chinese invented locks as a means of changing the level at which the canals could run. Early Chinese engineers were also responsible for construction of the Great Wall of China, and again early sections of the wall were built us early as 7th century BC, but the wall was only completed and finished during the Ming Dynasty around 1500 AD. Many sections were built and rebuilt through time, all with the intention of providing defence against invading Mongols form the north. The wall also acted as a conduit for communications along the northern boundary of China, and its protection for one section of the Silk Road to the west.

Other less sophisticated early engineering was present in the Indus Valley civilisation where Holy Stoups were built and irrigation systems were also constructed, though most of these have disintegrated due to lack of maintenance through the passage of time. There is also some evidence for irrigation systems in the New World around the beginning of the 2nd millennium, principally in South America. North American Indian tribes have left no evidence of significant irrigation systems.

Canal building in Europe came somewhat later and perhaps the knowledge of lock building was one of many inventions which spread from east to west, or vice versa along the old Silk Routes. As might be expected, canals and locks first came into use in the Low Countries, notably in Belgium and Holland at the end of the 14th century, but in addition a little later a series of locks were constructed on the Milan canal system in Italy. In France the Canal du Midi which connects the Atlantic, via the Garonne River and then through 240km of canal, to the Mediterranean, was started in 1666 under the direction of Jean Baptiste Colbert (1619–1683), who was Minster of Finance to Louis XIV, and engineer Pierre Paul Riquet (1609–1680). Many people at the time felt that the project was not feasible, but it was completed after 15 years in 1681, with the canal rising and falling through 189 metres along its course.

The first of the great civil engineers and the first person to so designate himself was John Smeaton (1724–1792) who was associated with the Lunar Society of Birmingham, and also became a Fellow of the Royal Society at the age of 29. He designed canals, harbours and bridges with his most high profile construction being the Eddystone Lighthouse off Plymouth around 1759. This was possible because Smeaton finally had the use of "hydraulic lime" which set under water. This invention led to the development of Portland cement, which is manufactured from limestone and which in turn led to the development of modern cement and concrete, widely used in construction projects today. Portland cement is so called because of its similarity in strength to the Portland stone quarried from the limestone peninsula of Portland in Dorset.

James Brindley (1716–1772) grew up in Derbyshire and Staffordshire in England, displaying a remarkable talent for machinery. He designed the Bridgewater Canal, which opened in 1761, and which is usually regarded as the first modern British canal. It is 66km in length, now opening into the Manchester Ship Canal, which was opened much later in 1894. A little later, Thomas Telford (1757–1834) grew up in Scotland, becoming an apprentice stonemason at the age of 14, but his talents rapidly expanded as there were so few civil engineers able to design projects at the time. Telford designed the Caledonian Canal connecting the east and west coasts of Scotland, together with numerous others in Shropshire and western England, and the bridges and viaducts associated with them. He became the first President of the new Institution of Civil Engineers in 1818. He built roads, canals and bridges in the English Midlands as well as in his native Scotland, and including the Pontcysyllte Aqueduct over the River Dee, which is a more remarkable structure carrying the Ellesmere Canal 38 metres above the river for a distance of 300 metres.

English canal building had started with the construction of the Bridgewater Canal. which opened in 1761 allowing the price of coal in Manchester to halve within a year. Compared with more benign and level countryside through which other canals have been built Brindley (1716–1772), designed an aqueduct to carry the Bridgewater Canal 12 metres above the River Irwell as part of his solution

The English canal system was narrow gauge compared to most of the continental European canals, and took specially designed "narrowboats" whose dimensions are limited by the size of the locks rather than the size of the canals. A standard narrowboat is less than 7 feet wide (2.13m) and up to 72 feet (22m) in length and was drawn by a horse. By transferring heavy bulk cargoes around the Midlands of England canals contributed greatly to the early years of the Industrial Revolution. Canal trade was fairly steady from around 1850 to 1950, but the new railway network which came into being at the beginning of this period gradually took away much of the canal trade. Following 1950, canal usage became largely a leisure and holiday activity.

Possible further reading:
Engineering by David Blockley (Oxford University Press)

Chapter 74
Mechanical and Transport Engineering

In ancient times, most transport was provided by beasts of burden with horses being the animal of choice for either simple transport, or into battle, which is why horses were domesticated early and fairly easily and are still favoured as modern day mounts. In contrast to this it is notable that human powered transport only first appeared in the shape of a primitive scooter or bicycle in 1818 to a design by the German born inventor Baron Karl von Drais (1785–1851). Sometimes called a velocipede or 'dandy horse', the machine was propelled along by the rider sitting astride it like a bicycle and propelling it forwards with his two feet.

It was not until two decades had passed that Kirkpatrick Macmillan (1812–1878), a Scottish blacksmith, produced pedals to power the rear wheels through connecting rods in 1839. Although Macmillan's machines initially used the pedals to drive the rear wheel, subsequent designs used the pedals directly connected to the front wheel axle for propulsion. Later still the front wheel was enlarged and the rear wheel diminished in size to become a much smaller stabiliser, producing a bicycle known as a 'penny farthing', which must have been both difficult to mount and to ride. The design did however increase possible speeds, and other improvements included ball-bearing movements in the wheel axles, together with solid rubber tyres and a hollow steel frame to cut down weight. The main advantage of these early bicycles was low cost, while their disadvantage of relatively limited range was not a problem for people simply travelling to and from work; exposure to the weather was sometimes more of a disadvantage.

Once the idea of the bicycle had become accepted, it was a small step to envisage the addition of a motor instead of using human power. Many attempts were made towards the end of the 19th century to find a suitable complementary small sized unit and there was even a trial of a small coal-fired steam boiler used, but by the last decade of the century a multiplicity of early motorcycles appeared powered by petrol; designs continued to proliferate and the technology became steadily more reliable.

Inventive mechanical engineers underpinned the Industrial Revolution. Machinery of all sorts was invented and manufactured to harness the power of steam, though where machinery was static the available power of water or wind was still often used. Through the 19th century new means of power came from two sources, electric motors and the first internal combustion engines. Electric motors were steadily developed becoming reliable enough by the final decade of the century to be used for the London Underground system, but it was only in 1859 that Etienne Lenoir (1822–1900), a Belgian engineer, was able to demonstrate his first internal combustion engine which ran on coal gas.

Previous engines had been produced, but not in significant numbers and not of commercial viability. Although Lenoir did build a small powered carriage and also put one of his engines in a boat; most of the engines he produced were static and used as factory machinery, he eventually sold around 700 altogether. Petrol was first used by German engineer Nicholas Otto (1832–1891) in a four-stroke internal combustion engine in 1861 and within fifteen years was selling over 600 a year.

In the meantime, Thomas Rickett, manager of a firm producing steam-powered agricultural machinery in Buckingham, made a few steam road carriages. In France, Amadée-Ernest Bollée produced his first steam vehicle in 1873. A German engineer and motor car designer, Karl Benz (1844–1929), is credited with the first production of a satisfactory working automobile. It was in fact an open carriage with a single steerable front wheel and two driven rear wheels; by the end of the century Benz's vehicles had four wheels and were selling well, with almost 600 produced in 1899. At the same time, Benz was producing similar small trucks and buses with modified bodywork.

By 1909, Benz had been able to build a special vehicle which set the world land speed record at Brooklands of 142mph (227km/h). Across the Atlantic Henry Ford (1863–1947) founded the Ford Motor Company using the now tried and tested method of a manufacturing assembly line; the first Ford was called a Quadricycle and had been built in 1896. The Ford Motor Company was founded in 1903 and rapidly expanded, mass-producing early cars, including the popular 'Model T' which cost around $800 in 1908 ($32,000 at today's prices or £25,000). Sales reached a quarter of a million by 1914, with the price effectively half that of a decade earlier.

In Europe, early motor vehicles powered by internal combustion engines would be designed and armoured as tanks for the First World War which, as is usual with war, produced a huge flood of research money into everything from weapons to transport and communications to surgery.

---oOo---

Commencing several decades, and even centuries after the early canals, the rail system in many countries now provides vital communication links, sharing passengers and commercial traffic with road transport. A wagonway is the term applied to a system of tracks, usually of gentle gradient, in which carts full of heavy material can easily be pulled by a horse or mule. Some of these trackways existed in ancient times with the tracks cut into stone or made of wood; they include the Diolkos at the Isthmus of Corinth during ancient Greek times, where it seems that ships were loaded onto a wheeled carrier and then hauled across the Isthmus. In wartime small ships were transported, but in peacetime commercial vessels or their cargos were pulled across. No earlier examples are known to be preserved.

In medieval times, and later in the Middle Ages, smaller versions were often found, particularly in mines where the ore and spoil were most easily transported back along the mine shaft. In the Middle Ages such systems evolved into early railways as rails were attached to underlying wooden boards, and in turn the rails, or the wheels of the carts, became flanged so that the carts were kept running more easily in the direction required. Such a system permitted a horse to haul a much heavier load than using an ordinary cart over rough ground. Iron rails were brought in during the middle of the 18th century in Coalbrookdale at the heart of the early Industrial Revolution.

Over the next fifty years, it became apparent that for coping with heavy loads and bulk materials, wagonways had many of the advantages of canals, but with lesser initial construction time and capital outlay. Richard Trevithick (1771–1833) was a Cornish mining engineer who harnessed steam power to mechanise these wagonways, or tramways as they were often known once the iron rails came into general use. Trevithick installed a steam engine in the iron works in Merthyr Tydfil in Wales using the steam engine invented by Newcomen and further developed by Watt and Boulton. He also built early steam engines which were able to carry passengers, but did not concentrate particularly on mobile steam engines though he consulted across the world on the use of static steam engines and their use in mines.

Following these initial evolutionary steps from wagonways in the early part of the 19th century, steam engines for use on rails were increasingly produced and George Stephenson, also known as the 'Father of Railways' was the early pioneer who built the first functioning public railway; this was the Liverpool and Manchester Railway which opened which opened in 1830 using steam engines to pull carriages. Stephenson had already built an eight-mile colliery railway in 1820, and the Stockton and Darlington Railway running 25 miles (40km) between collieries in 1821. He standardised on a gauge of 4ft 8in (125cm), still used on British railways today, and a maximum gradient of 1 in 100, or 1%, both to make engine ascents easy, but also to keep braking requirements to a sensible level.

Following the success of the Stockton and Darlington Railway and then the Liverpool and Manchester Railway, companies were founded to join cities and towns across Britain and in many other countries. Thus twenty years later in 1850 Europe and America boasted 40,000km of railway, and after a further thirty years in 1880 this number had multiplied by a factor of ten. In the meantime where land was precious, or simply not available, underground railways were being constructed in tunnels with the first such one being opened in London in 1863. The underground network in London has continued to expand steadily, now comprising eleven different lines, mostly crossing in the centre of the city with many interconnecting stations.

The initial tunnels were made by excavating a deep trench, laying the rails, and then covering the top with a strong roof. As these tunnels were near to the surface and often short, the system was able to cope with the early steam engines, but electrification followed in 1890. Following these first 'cut and cover' lines, the second generation of underground railways were constructed by tunnelling, which is more expensive but avoids problems with buildings on the surface. The alternative solution, New York's overhead elevated railways (the 'el') which first opened in 1868 was generally noisy and oppressive and degraded life above ground so it was phased out in the 1950s. Today some 150 cities worldwide have underground passenger railways networks.

In the middle years of the 19th century, a Bristol engineer of genius, inspiration and perseverance appeared, called Isambard Kingdom Brunel (1806–1859). He worked with his engineer father on the first tunnel under the Thames which was the first tunnel under a navigable river; it was dangerous and suffered early disastrous accidents. At the age of 33 he was appointed Chief Engineer for the Great Western Railway running from London to the western tip of Britain in Cornwall, and was responsible for the design and construction of tunnels and bridges as well as the line itself. H advocated a gauge of 7ft (2.13m), but later as the railways all connected up the GWR had to standardise with the rest of the British rail network on Stephenson's preferred gauge of 4ft 8in.

Brunel wanted the GWR to be able to sell tickets from London to New York and therefore turned his hand to designing the SS Great Britain, the first iron-built passenger steamship to cross the Atlantic in 1845. After a working lifetime she was left to rust in the Falkland Islands, but has recently been salvaged and brought back to a dry dock in Bristol. Brunel continued to build ships, including the SS Great Eastern which was 705ft long and able to carry 4,000 passengers from Britain to Australia without refuelling.

Railways were much slower to come to Asia, Africa and Latin America where the perceived need, and the production of commodities, was slower to appear so that the relevance of railways, and indeed roads, developed more slowly. In the USA rail networks were initially built on the east and west coasts, and finally linked in 1869 to give the first transcontinental rail link. To the north in America's smaller cousin nation the Canadian Pacific Railway Company completed a transcontinental route in 1885.

---oOo---

In the air, the history of flight is often felt to start at the beginning of the 20th century with early aircraft; however, for the full history it is necessary to go back to the 18th century when the Montgolfier brothers, Joseph-Michel (1740–1810), and Jacques-Etienne (1745–1799), pioneered hot-air balloon flight in the Ardeche Department of France in 1783. Balloon flight relies on the observation that hot air expands, thus becoming lighter and able to lift a balloon if the gas is contained within the balloon.

A little later, Sir George Cayley (1773–1857), a prolific British inventor and engineer, set out the principles of flight for a fixed wing machine. He designed the first flying model aeroplane and then the first glider; he identified the four forces controlling flight (weight, lift, thrust and drag) and predicted that significant flight would not be possible until a lightweight engine could be produced. His first flight in 1853 was of short duration, and perhaps significantly Cayley delegated the actual flying to his coachman! A replica of the machine lives in the Yorkshire Air Museum and was flown successfully for television.

The history of powered flight starts with the Wright brothers once a light and reliable engine became available. Wilbur Wright (1867–1912) and Orville Wright (1871–1948) were competent inventors and machinists and made the first reasonable distance fight in Kittyhawk, North Carolina in 1903. This ability to produce the first flight in a fixed wing aircraft depended on being able to control the aircraft in ascending or descending and being able to steer it: they used a small petrol engine and propellors located behind the main wings so as not to disturb airflow over the wings.

Development of the Wright brother's planes proceeded by trial and error and with several crashes. Louis Blériot (1872–1936) a French engineer and inventor ran a successful business making vehicle headlights, and on the profits was able to develop an early plane in which he crossed the English Channel in 1909. The 36 minute flight ended with a final crash landing near Dover due to difficult wind conditions, but still won him the £1,000 prize offered by a British newspaper.

Following the first flight by the Wright Brothers in 1903, the years up to the start of the First World War were filled with a lot of pioneering aeroplane development, which then became available for use in the conflict, and were steadily improved through the four war years, giving another example of the way war acts as a stimulus to research and development. Aviation continued to develop rapidly, and in a converted bomber just after the war John Alcock (1892–1919, who died in a plane crash just a few months later) and Arthur Brown (1886–1948) crossed the Atlantic non-stop from Newfoundland to Ireland, a distance of 1980 miles (3168 km).

Eight years later in 1927, Charles Lindberg (1902–1974), a US Army Air Corps pilot finally achieved a solo Atlantic crossing from New York to Le Bourget airfield, a distance of 3,600 miles (5,800 km) in just over thirty-three hours, representing an average speed of 109 mph.

Possible further reading:
Canals by Liz McIvor (BBC Books/Penguin)
The World's Railroads by Christopher Chant (Chartwell Books)

Chapter 75
Astronomy and Navigation

The 16th and 17th centuries saw mapping of the world completed, often with great accuracy (chapter 37). All the world came to be measured using agreed standards of latitude and longitude. The invention of the sextant replaced astrolabes, then accurate time chronometers were produced allowing much greater precision of navigation at sea. By the middle of the 19th century the Greenwich Meridian and Greenwich Meantime (GMT) were in place, permitting a degree of accuracy and common understanding of time and place which had not previously been possible, even though the magnetic compass had been used for several centuries. In addition, the invention of the log by the Portuguese at the beginning of the 16th century had allowed sailors to make a rough estimate of speed and distance travelled. The log was a simple piece of wood thrown over the side of the ship attached to a rope with knots at fixed intervals; by counting the number of knots paid out in a certain time the distance travelled could be calculated, and this is why sailors still express speed in knots.

Although sea routes around the southern tips of Africa and South America had been discovered and were coming into commercial use in the 16th century, the possibility of a further sea route around the north of Canada from the Atlantic into the Pacific remained an enticing challenge for explorers. The first and unsuccessful attempt to find the northwest passage was by a Venetian called John Cabot (1450–1500), financed by King Henry VII of England. Further English explorers followed as it was valuable to a northern European country to discover a shorter route to the Pacific. Somewhat later other British explorers took up the challenge, first Martin Frobisher (1535–1594), and then Henry Hudson (1565–1611), both of whose names are still prominent on modern maps of northern Canada.

Sir John Franklin (1786–1847) led a naval expedition which got trapped in winter ice and resulted in him perishing with all his crew. It was only finally in 1903–1906 that an expedition by the Norwegian explorer Roald Amundsen (1872–1928) managed to navigate the passage. Amundsen also became the first man to reach the South Pole in 1911 in a friendly contest, with the English Captain Robert Scott (1868–1912) following a few weeks later.

A Dutch cartographer, Gerardus Mercator (1512–1594), had published a highly accurate map of Europe, and then later in 1569, a world map with his revolutionary projection of the curved surface of Earth onto a flat two-dimensional sheet of paper. Europe, Africa and Asia were reasonably well presented, but the information available to Mercator about China and the Americas was rudimentary (chapter 37). The astrolabe and the quadrant were still similarly primitive instruments and difficult to use at sea in anything but the calmest waters.

John Hadley (1682–1744), an English mathematician and a member of the Royal Society, together with Thomas Godfrey (1704–1749), an American optician, both devised the principle for the octant about 1730. Following this came the sextant, which is a sophisticated optical device which allows measurement of the angle between the horizon and a fixed celestial point (usually a star). The sextant is built and named on a frame comprising one-sixth of a circle or 60°, and evolved steadily from the octant which had a frame of one-eighth of a circle (45°), and the quadrant which had a frame comprising 90° or a quarter of a circle.

A naval disaster in the Scilly Islands off the southwest tip of Britain in 1707 resulted in the loss of a returning fleet of four British warships and over 1500 crewmen. The disaster brought home the need for better navigation as it had been caused by the ships' captains wrongly estimating their position off southwest England. To have accurate measurements of latitude and longitude, it is necessary to have highly accurate measurement of time once out of sight of land. As a result of this disaster in 1707 the British Parliament offered the huge financial reward of £20,000 (almost £1 million at current values) for production of an accurate chronometer.

The Act of Parliament had established the Board of Longitude which offered this large reward. Further rewards were offered through the years for increasing standards of accuracy and for some navigational achievements. A clockmaker from Lincolnshire, John Harrison (1693–1776) who was the son of a carpenter used his skills to make clocks, gradually refining the degree of accuracy and producing a timepiece that was unaffected by temperature, humidity or pressure over long periods.

By 1736, Harrison had produced a clock which performed well, but over the next two decades he worked tirelessly to perfect his clock, eventually producing a chronometer for maritime use which performed to an accuracy of a few seconds over a period of several days. After political arguments and machinations, Harrison was finally awarded a very large amount of money from Parliament, but not the full prize.

Captain James Cook (1728–1779) was one of the early maritime explorers and map makers to benefit from Harrison's chronometer. Cook went to sea as a teenager and saw active service in the Seven Years War between Britain and France. He surveyed and mapped much of the coast of eastern Canada and the St Lawrence River during the Siege of Quebec. As a result of the excellence of the charts that he produced he was commissioned into the Royal Navy and despatched on three subsequent voyages to the Pacific Ocean, to survey and chart both maritime and coastal features.

The first of these voyages in 1768 was a joint venture between the Royal Navy and the Royal Society to record the transit of Venus from Tahiti. After the astronomical observations Cook's instructions took him south to investigate the reports of 'Terra Australis'. The presence of land in the southern hemisphere south of Asia had been known since the voyages of the Dutch merchant and explorer, Abel Tasman (1603–1659) and others, who had explored the area in the services of the Dutch East India Company.

On his first voyage east from the Cape of Good Hope, Abel Tasman had made landfall on the coast of Tasmania, and then carried on eastwards to New Zealand. The presence of land was known to him from the writings of Marco Polo much earlier, and speculations about the presence of land in the south Pacific were also present on the maps of Heinrich Hammer, a German cartographer working in Florence at the end of the 15th century. On his second journey a few years later Tasman sailed south from the East Indies and then along the north-west coast of Australia: his findings of uninhabited land unsuitable for trade disappointed his employers, the Dutch East India Company.

No further explorations in the region were undertaken until Cook came south from Tahiti on his first voyage over a hundred years later. He made landfall on the south-east coast of Australia and recorded the presence of dark skinned natives, but his vessel ran onto the Great Barrier Reef and had to be beached for several weeks while repairs were made.

Sir Joseph Banks (1743–1820) acted as naturalist and botanist to Cook's expedition. He had been elected as a member of the Royal Society at the precocious age of 23, and thanks to his private income was able to join an expedition to Newfoundland and Labrador to study the natural history there. He was subsequently appointed to join Cook's voyage to Tahiti and on to Australia, and later in 1778 as a distinguished botanist he was elected President of the Royal Society, a post which he then held until his death in 1820.

Cook's second voyage from 1772–75 was commissioned by the Royal Society to investigate the presence of land in the southern hemisphere since it was still thought possible that a large land mass was present to the south of Australia and New Zealand. On his first voyage Cook had circumnavigated New Zealand showing that it was not part of any southern larger land mass, and on his second voyage he circumnavigated the globe within the Antarctic Circle at 66° 33' south and managed to make landfall on the mainland of Antarctica. He also made landfall at several Pacific islands, including the Friendly Islands, Easter Island, Norfolk Island, New Caledonia and Vanuatu. Cook's second voyage is notable for his use of Harrison's marine chronometer, and the accuracy of his charts of the southern Pacific Ocean. He was elected to Fellowship of the Royal Society on his return, and also awarded the Society's Gold Medal for completing the voyage of three years without losing any sailors as a result of scurvy. Cook's third voyage in 1876–79, was commissioned to try and locate a north-west passage around the American continent. He explored the western coast of British Columbia, tracking the coast up to the Bering Strait, finally becoming blocked by sea ice. From there the expedition turned south to Hawaii where Cook was killed in an altercation with native villagers.

Alexander Von Humboldt (1769–1859) was born in Prussia and left a significant mark on early exploration and understanding of the world. He was a naturalist and explorer, and spent five years at the age of 30 in exploration of Latin America, making both botanical and geological observations. Humboldt wrote up his findings in great detail and his extensive publications were widely read at a time when the public appetite for the study of natural history was considerable. Humboldt contributed to climatology as well as meteorology and geology, and he also discovered a decrease in the intensity in Earth's magnetic field approaching the equator.

Humboldt was the first person to recognise the similarities of the opposing coasts of South America and Africa, and suggested that they might once have been conjoined: the 20th century recognition of plate tectonics has confirmed this, along with much of his other thinking, including the prescient early observation of global warming due to human activity. It is an appropriate measure of Humboldt's importance and originality that there are hundreds of plants and animals named after him, together with dozens of places and geographical features

To complete the mapping and navigation of the planet, a zero meridian known as the Greenwich Meridian was established in 1851. In due course, this meridian has allowed the position of satellites to support a global positioning system (GPS) so that by the end of the 20th century travellers could establish their position on the globe through GPS satellites. The meridian, or longitude of zero, passes through Greenwich as an imaginary line from the north to the south poles, and acts as the basis for all longitudinal measurement. Latitudinal measurements are taken at the Equator going north or south through 90° from equator to pole. Each degree is further subdivided into 60 minutes, and each minute in turn has been designated as the standard measurement of a nautical mile, now agreed as 1852 metres. The land measurement of a land mile is now standardised as 1609 metres.

Possible further reading:
Longitude by Dava Sobel (about John Harrison) (Harper Perennial)
For the book recommendation on Captain Cook, see chapter 57
For the book recommendation on Humboldt, see chapter 72

Chapter 76
The Far East

As we saw in chapter 28, the Mongols invaded and subdued the whole of China by the end of the 13th century. This conquest is estimated to have cost the lives of over a quarter of the population – a figure approaching thirty million people. However, in a rather reverse version of conquest the Mongols then became Chinese rather than the other way round. Kublai Khan, the grandson of Genghis Khan, adopted Chinese customs and the remaining years of the Mongol Era are recorded as the Yuan Dynasty. The Mongols discarded their nomadic and conservative customs from the steppes, and the large Chinese civil service continued to rule and impose Chinese customs on the populace.

The Chinese people were forbidden to learn the Mongol language or to marry Mongols, and they were not allowed to carry weapons. Foreigners, rather than Chinese, were employed in the civil service (including Marco Polo for a period of three years). Kublai Khan, increased the size of his army and extended his conquest south into Vietnam, Burma and Java, but failed to conquer Japan. Distant maritime trade with India and Arabia increased. Mongol rule declined in the 14th century because of opposition to oppressive laws and some adverse natural disasters.

A number of rebellions broke out and one of the leaders of a rebel faction called the Red Turbans, Chu Yuan-Chang, was able to seize Nanking in 1356. Twelve years later, he had driven the Mongols out of Peking and founded the Ming Dynasty. Although the Ming Dynasty, declared in 1388, became a period of great cultural achievement, which remains synonymous with superb Chinese ceramic production, the background politics and unity continued through to the 20th century, during which time China remained conservative and isolated. The great fleets of exploration mentioned in chapter 7 came to an end in the early 15th century as China withdrew in upon itself. Rather later, the Ming Dynasty gradually became dissolute and divorced from the population at large, while areas previously subdued by conquest to the south and west, including Burma and Tibet, were lost to the Chinese Empire.

European traders, and Jesuit missionaries in particular, appeared in China in the 16th century, and then in the 1640s there was a large peasant revolt which resulted in the Manchu people invading China from the north. Once again many millions of peasants died as the new dynasty was established under the long lived Manchu Emperor Kangxi, who stayed in power for sixty years up to 1722. During his reign military campaigns were plentiful, including the imperial conquest of Formosa (Taiwan) and Tibet, and subjugation of the Mongols. Border clashes with Russia to the north resulted in a common land boundary finally being declared.

Later in the 18th century, Manchu conquest continued to include Korea, Vietnam and Burma, together with full subjugation of Tibet. As a nation China remained extremely conservative in cultural matters, as well as social and political organisation. Technical advances in ceramics, painting and textiles were considerable, but the culture itself barely changed. Although the Chinese had developed gunpowder and maritime mapping long before Europe, these inventions were not implemented for use either in war or for the benefit of the population in civilian uses.

By the year 1800, Chinese society had not changed significantly from a millennium previously and the population had reached at least three hundred million. Trade from Europe had been minimal, since up to that time there were no European products, apart from silver bullion, which the Chinese were interested in buying. The trade was predominantly from the East to Europe in the form of textiles, ceramics and spices. The Silk Roads continued to be busy throughout the centuries.

In the early decades of the 19th century, the Industrial Revolution began to offer products which the Chinese welcomed, but over the 18th and 19th centuries a big balance of payments deficit built up with Europe, since the Chinese were unwilling to allow significant quantities of imports except opium where British merchants found that the Chinese would buy large quantities of opium produced in India. This prompted Britain to send a naval expedition to force China to allow a more equitable balance of trade; the Qing Dynasty which followed the Ming Dynasty and lasted from 1644 to 1911, was unable to resist the superior fire power of the British Navy sent to break the Chinese trade restrictions by military action.

This first Opium War lasted three years, until in the Treaty of Nanking in 1842, opium was officially allowed into China, trade restrictions were lifted to the extent of naming five treaty ports for external trade, and Hong Kong was ceded to Britain (on a 150 year lease, an arrangement which lasted until 1997 when the island of Hong Kong was returned to the government of China). Trade matters continued to be contentious and a second Opium War resulted in 1856–1860, with France joining Britain.

The second half of the 19th century saw increasing internal unrest in China. Much of this was sparked by the opium trade wars, but internal uprisings, including the Taiping Rebellion of 1851–1864 which was really a civil war, weakened the central Chinese government. This rebellion broke out because the evangelical Taiping under Hong Xiuquan (1814–1864) sought to convert the Chinese to Christianity and in consequence were persecuted by the government, which in turn resulted in the chronic rebellion of the Taiping over more than a decade. Hong Xiuquan believed he was the son of God and a brother of Jesus Christ.

Although the Taiping rebellions between 1850 and 1864 were all eventually put down, the casualty count was very high, possibly of the order of 50 million people, and the central government in Peking suffered severely. This was just the latest of hundreds of rebellions through the centuries, usually put down more or less easily, and more or less ruthlessly. Mao Zedong later described these as "peasant revolutionary wars", and said that "they alone formed the real motive force of Chinese historical evolution".

In 1860, European forces who had been present because of the opium or trade wars were approaching Beijing and a peace delegation was sent to parlay with the Imperial troops, but the delegation was imprisoned, tortured and about twenty men were killed; in retaliation the British and French troops sacked and burnt the Summer Palace. The Chinese Qing government was weakened and under much pressure at that stage and in November was forced into ceding a huge expanse of northern land east of the Wusuli River to Russia which allowed the Russians to build a new naval base at Vladivostok on the Pacific Ocean.

War with Japan in 1894 and 1895 over Chinese control of Korea ended with the more technologically advanced Japan firmly in the ascendent and provoked Chinese government reforms a couple of years later, at a time when the central government was effectively controlled by the conservative Chinese Empress Cixi (1835–1908), ruling as regent for her son (who was five years old when she first assumed power); she ruled altogether for a period of 47 years until she died in 1908.

---oOo---

Japan has been inhabited since pre-historic times, but the many small tribes and kingdoms were finally united, and an Imperial Dynasty was established with a new capital city at Kyoto in 794. Internal warring continued, but over the centuries the power of the Emperor and his court gradually passed to military chiefdoms with their private armies of samurai warriors in a country which remained fragmented for several hundred years Different chiefs, or Shoguns, then ruled Japan after reunification was achieved in the 16th century issuing in an era of peace and prosperity known as the Edo period (1603 to 1868). This time was a stable one with an emphasis on arts and culture, and like China, an isolationist policy with the outside world, indeed, in 1635 the Japanese were forbidden from travelling outside Japan.

Christian missionaries were executed and Christianity eradicated from the islands by 1660. A strict class system below the Emperor and aristocrats grew up, with samurai, peasants, craftsmen and merchants in descending social order. In 1845 an emissary from the United States was refused the ability to trade with Japan (shortly after China had capitulated and accepted trade with the west). Some years later an American squadron of four ships came to Tokyo (then known as Edo) and a trading agreement was signed under duress, thus ending Japan's policy of isolation from the rest of the world (chapter 63).

The Dutch had long traded with the Japanese, though at a defined port, but Dutch books brought into Japan during the 19th century stimulated interest and knowledge in European culture and learning. After the agreement of 1854 with America, which was regarded by the Japanese as a very unequal treaty, there was internal disquiet and disagreement which resulted in the Emperor Meiji (1852–1912) being persuaded to modernise the country once he came to the throne in 1868, and after a battle with the Shogun's army, victory for the new Emperor allowed modernisation of Japan to proceed.

Over the next three or four decades, industrialisation and modernisation of the armed forces transformed Japan and the caste system of four divisions of society was officially abolished. All these changes had the result that in the first Sino-Japanese war of 1894–95, fought for control of Korea, the Japanese were victorious. Success was also achieved in the Russo-Japanese war of 1904–05 between an expansionist Russia and a Japan which wished to see Russia contained. During these years Japan's political structures were reorganised along western lines, with a prime minister and cabinet in position by 1885, and a two-chamber parliament. The Emperor Meiji died in 1912, and a new Emperor presided over the growth of increasing democracy and increasing importance on the international stage.

Japan joined the First World War on the side of the Allies, from which she gained new colonies in the South Pacific that had previously been German. These small islands were not of any economic significance, but were strategically located for passing ships, and were also valuable to Japan at the beginning of the Second World War which Japan joined on the German side.

---oOo---

Korea forms a peninsula from the Chinese mainland, with Japan just a short distance away across the sea. The country has had a somewhat chequered past; small tribal kingdoms existed initially, and a written record is present from around 1700 BC. By the 1st century AD, three kingdoms only controlled the peninsula, with the whole country being united under the single Kingdom of Silla by the late 7th century AD. Warfare and shifting boundaries continued over the centuries, but the peninsula was subdued by the Mongols in the 13th century. The Mongol military campaigns across the Korean peninsula decimated the civilian population, and Mongol rule only lasted for about 80 years.

Thereafter, a Joseon Dynasty was established by King Yi Seonggye which lasted from 1392 up to 1910, albeit with Japanese and Manchu invasions which each resulted in several decades of turmoil. Manchu influence diminished and the Joseon Dynasty prospered again, the peninsula becoming peaceful and life remaining easier for the Koreans until disagreement with China caused the First Sino-Japanese war in 1894. After Japan's victory over China, Korea enjoyed a brief period of independence from 1897 to 1910, but this situation was not to last, and in 1910, after defeating Russia, the Japanese annexed Korea by treaty in 1910.

The Japanese thought that Korea would be easily integrated into Japan's political and social structures, but through the next decade there was a large non-violent resistance movement with organisations in exile up until the end of the Second World War, when Japan was defeated in 1945. At this time after the Second World War Korea became partitioned into a northern half controlled by the Soviet and Chinese Communist Parties, and a southern half controlled by America.

War between these two halves of the peninsula was fought by the two proxies until an eventual truce and demarcation line was agreed in 1952, which still persists at the 38th Parallel, dividing the old single country into two very unequal halves; a formal peace treaty has still not been signed and the two halves of Korea are still technically at war. South Korea has progressed to become a successful capitalist democracy along American lines, while North Korea has remained reclusive, shut off, poor and under the control of a supreme communist autocrat, with the dictatorship passed down within the same family from the founder for the past three generations during the past seven decades.

Possible further reading:
A History of China by JAG Roberts (Palgrave MacMillan)
The Walled Kingdom by Witold Rodzinski (Fontana Paperbacks)
A History of Korea by Kyung Moon Hwang (Palgrave Macmillan)

Chapter 77
Britain 1865–1901

The second half of the 19th century, and indeed the second half of Queen Victoria's reign, represented the zenith of British achievements, both nationally and internationally This compares with the Far East where India, China and Japan had all peaked culturally in the 16th and 17th centuries. At the end of the 19th century Britain was still reaping the benefits of the Industrial Revolution which it had pioneered, while other western countries, including Germany and America, were lagging behind although rapidly catching up. It was already a time when the superiority of Europe as a whole was clearly evident in both industrial machinery and the weaponry of war. At the same time, there was a superiority, and indeed arrogance, about Christian missionary activity towards the rest of the world.

In addition to this, and perhaps because of the dividends of the Industrial Revolution, it was generally a period in which Britain in particular enjoyed peace, and a time in which there were no distractions for the nation, and no need to fight wars close to home, though some arose in South Africa, India, Crimea and in other far off places. British achievement had been showcased at Prince Albert's suggestion, in the Great Exhibition of 1851, an exhibition to which all countries were invited to demonstrate their mechanical and cultural strengths. Previous fairs had frequently been held by individual nations to show their own products since the initial fair in Prague in 1791, but British industry continued to lead the way internationally through the years leading up to the Great War.

Electoral reform and social reform, which had started at the beginning of the 19th century, continued to evolve. British democracy evolved with it, although in the early years of the 19th century the word reform carried a different connotation to the meaning we attach to it today, in particular the difference was felt to be exemplified by the violence of the French Revolution and subsequent military dictatorship, which was a road down which the British population did not wish to proceed.

The first big electoral act had occurred in 1832 with regularisation of parliamentary constituencies and the first extensions of the electoral roll. A further extension of the franchise came with an electoral act in 1867 and again in 1872, together with the institution of secret balloting. The process was to be continued with pressure for votes for women that appeared toward the end of the century. The Women's League was founded in 1889 to further the voting rights of women and included such figures as Emeline Pankhurst (1857–1928), although it was New Zealand that claimed the honour of being the first to emancipate women with the vote in 1893. British women would not achieve this until the end of the Great War when the vote was given to women over 30, doubtless in part due to the large increase in the number of women working to aid the war effort while the men of the families were away fighting. It was only in 1929 that the voting age for men and women was equalised at 21, and has since been reduced to 18.

The second half of the 19th century also saw the introduction of a new Poor Law, together with further Factory and Mining Laws (the first Factory Law had been introduced much earlier at the beginning of the century). The legal system itself was rebuilt, and the restrictions on Roman Catholics, Jews and Non-Conformists were removed. Universal public education was at last taken seriously. All of these measures came about thanks to the overall increase in the wealth of the nation, quite apart from the reforming zeal of many politicians. Much reform came to be centralised through different parliamentary acts which imposed uniform standards and expectations across the country.

The development of major British colonies through the years up to the Great War was less fraught with problems. The local difficulty in Canada was the tensions between the English and French communities, but this was at least partially resolved and Canada became a Dominion in 1867. French-English tensions have however continued to the present day, with a referendum on possible secession of Quebec in the 1970s being defeated, leaving Canada intact as a nation.

Australia became a Commonwealth or Dominion in 1901. The local difficulty here in achieving confederation was in part due to transportation of convicts which continued up to 1867, and caused tension between the voluntary immigrant community and the convicts and their descendants. It has to be said however that the sentence of transportation in the early years of the 19th century was often arbitrary, and frequently imposed for minor or dubious transgressions, so that it gradually came to be seen as inappropriate.

New Zealand achieved Dominion status in 1907. The delays here were partly due to wars with the indigenous Maoris, who had arrived in New Zealand from Polynesia around 1300. As with other colonies, when the first white settlers first came to New Zealand they brought with them some of the evils of European civilisation, including alcohol, disease and fire-arms, which the Maoris acquired and then used against each other initially, and subsequently against the settlers. It took a while for the nation to bed down before independence could occur.

Politically, the second half of the 19th century was notable for two dominant politicians who alternated in power as Prime Minister. Benjamin Disraeli (1804–1881) is remembered as the founder of the modern Conservative Party. He became a trusted confidante of Queen Victoria, but before becoming Prime Minister had spent time as Chancellor of the Exchequer with an emphasis on balancing the budget. He became Prime Minister for less than a year in 1868, but his administration failed with disagreements between Protestants and Catholics over Ireland and disestablishment of the small Anglican Church in Ireland, and proposals for a Catholic University in Dublin.

Despite this, Disraeli's first government passed useful legislation, including nationalising telegraph companies, ending public executions, and passing a Corrupt Practices Act. Disraeli was again Prime Minister from 1874 to 1880, although by this time he was in poor health and was granted a peerage so that he could rule from the less fevered precincts of the House of Lords. His administration passed many reforms on housing, public health and education, together with a new Factory Act.

His great opponent, the Liberal party leader William Gladstone (1809–1898), was also a reformer whose achievements included the Reform Act of 1884 giving the vote to farm labourers. He tried unsuccessfully to get bills passed in 1886 and again in 1893 on Home Rule for Ireland, though this would not be achieved until after the end of the Great War. The Irish population at this time had halved from an initial high total of 8 million (one-third of the total for the British Isles) to half that figure, whilst at the same time mainland British population had been increasing steadily.

Despite this, the Irish Parliamentary Party was much reduced due to the depopulation persisting since the potato famines in the 1840s. It is hard to overstate the influence of Irish affairs on British politics as a whole through the last years of the 19th century, where they combined the passions and interests of the opposing sides of Catholicism, landlords and colonialism; indeed the tensions and antagonisms had started in Cromwell's time two centuries previously with plantations of Protestant settlers being pitted against Catholics and casting a deep and continuing shadow over Irish-English affairs (chapter 42).

In matters of health, the 19th century saw enormous advances. The importance of clean water and appropriate disposal of sewage was recognised and measures to provide both were implemented – lessons first learnt in Roman times, but vital with the growth of crowded urban dwelling where disease was rife. The principles of causation of infectious diseases were recognised by Koch and Pasteur, and partly as a result, but partly from empirical observations, measures to control infection were instituted, notably by Semmelweis in Vienna, Wendell-Holmes in Boston and Lister in Glasgow (chapter 72).

Vaccination had been put on a scientific footing by Edward Jenner (1749–1823), a Gloucestershire physician and surgeon, to control smallpox, a disease which has been estimated to have killed around 10% of the population at the time, as it was endemic and uncontrolled. Widespread philanthropy saw the establishment of voluntary charitable hospitals in English towns.

A multitude of Factory Acts were passed by parliament commencing in the early years of the century to improve conditions in the cotton mills in 1819 and 1825. Acts in 1833 limited hours of work and protected the welfare of children who had previously little restrictions on how they were employed and exploited up to that time, and at the same time a factory inspectorate was established to enforce the law. In 1844 the limitation of hours was extended to women and set at ten hours a day. In 1891 women were not allowed back to work for at least four weeks after childbirth, and at the same time the age for children being permitted to work was raised from ten to eleven, and they were only allowed to work for half days.

Education was accorded major importance and it is interesting to note that from the time of Alfred through to Henry I, who came to the throne in 1154, England probably did not have a literate king. Through the Middle Ages education had been provided on a sporadic and haphazard basis by religious foundations, but had remained mainly the benefit of the upper echelons of society, but with the advent of printing and the appearance of printed bibles, first in Latin, and then in the vernacular thanks to Tyndale, there became much more incentive to learn to read.

Thomas Paine (1737–1809), philosopher and political thinker, grew up in England and emigrated to America at the age of 36 where he was highly influential in the thinking behind the Revolution and produced two widely read pamphlets, including 'The Rights of Man'. Among many things he suggested were that it was the natural right of all citizens to an education, an old age pension and other social welfare. Similar views were expressed by William Wilberforce (1759–1833) an English MP who also campaigned for schools, civil rights, and prison reform, as well as being a force against slavery.

Unlike in the United States where the self-made man was recognised for his ability, in 19th century Britain, it was still believed that inherited ownership of land was the mark of a gentleman and that the highest pursuit for such a gentleman was in government rather than in commerce; this attitude is reflected in the literature of the time. The middle classes expanded with an immediate spread of attitudes and occupations, namely the professions such as law, medicine, accountancy and the military, rather than simply occupying the central ground between upper and lower classes.

Victoria's reign is also noted for the work of Walter Bagehot (1826–1877), a West Country journalist and businessman and qualified barrister who published "The English Constitution" in 1867, a work which is still seen as the authoritative parliamentary reference book. 1871 saw the founding of the Trades Union Congress which finally brought together representatives of most British Trade Unions, though these had existed since the early years of the century. It had finally become apparent that much more could be achieved by unions working in concert, than by small individual efforts, but there was still a severe ban on picketing.

By the turn of the century, England had changed enormously compared to the situation one hundred years previously in 1800. The majority of the population now lived in towns or cities in brick or stone houses, and with an infrastructure comprising paved streets and the provision of mains water and sewers. Household supplies of gas and electricity were becoming more common, with the provision of state or charity education, and hospitals; it was also a time when individual philanthropy fuelled by fortunes built on industrial processes and inventions, burst on the scene eclipsing the charity of the church and the monarch from previous times.

London had an early underground rail system, and both railways and tarmac roads extended nationally to all corners of the British Isles (chapter 73). The changes through the 19th century were as profound as those of the previous thousand years, and were the somewhat delayed consequences of the Enlightenment and the ensuing Industrial Revolution, followed by its agricultural counterpart. Much of this had been achieved in the reign of a single monarch, with Victoria on the throne for almost the last two-thirds of the century, before she died in 1901.

Possible further reading:
Victorious Century by David Cannadine (Penguin)

Chapter 78
The United Kingdom

After James VI of Scotland was crowned simultaneously James I of England, the national affairs of both countries interlaced intimately through the turmoil of the 17th century with its two central decades of civil war and republican government under Cromwell. The English monarchy also acquired the Irish crown during this time, and many Scots were resettled to the Province of Ulster in Northern Ireland in so-called 'plantations'. After the failure of the Jacobite Rising in 1745, and the certainty that the Stuarts would not return to the Scottish or English thrones, there was a gradual settling of the turbulence in Scotland. The Highlands were now garrisoned and highland culture was repressed. The battle of Culloden in 1745, when the forces of Bonnie Prince Charlie were overcome by the English was the last pitched battle to be fought on English soil. Bonny Prince Charlie was to die in exile.

By the end of the 18th century, it became clear that most Scottish agriculture was of marginal profitability, though new hardier breeds of sheep were more profitable and required much less intensive attention and care. This realisation ushered in a period at the end of the 18th century known as the Highland Clearances, when the large tenant population on many highland estates were no longer required to work the land and were evicted. 1792 became known as the 'Year of the Sheep', because sheep had become more profitable than the rent from tenant farmers, and this resulted in a huge wave of mass emigration.

Some purpose-built settlements were created for the displaced Highlanders, but many were simply put on ships to the North American colonies, or left without visible means of support. This coincided with a failure in the potato crop, the consequences of which were devastating. Thirty years later a second phase of clearances took place, effectively wiping out the Highland population and culture. The changes were supported in parliament because of a view that the ancient Scottish clan system was a threat to the British establishment, and in consequence the Scottish ruling class acted to preserve its wealth and social status.

Ironically, sheep farming proved to be less than a quick panacea, since cheaper and better quality meat and wool from Australian and New Zealand farms soon became available as new fast refrigerated clippers were able to bring it from the southern hemisphere. William Cullen (1710–1790) in Scotland is credited with the first experiments to induce cooling, but commercially ice was used initially, though it was 1882 when the first commercially viable and artificially refrigerated cargo came from Australia to Britain.

Scottish Clan tartans had been in existence since Roman times and were all but eliminated after the battle of Culloden in 1746 until a visit by King George IV in 1822 spurred a revival of Scottish national identity alongside the romantic poetry writings of Robert Burns (1759–1796), and the popular novels of Walter Scott (1771–1832). Scotland had a further boost when Queen Victoria came to the throne and bought Balmoral Castle; highland games that originally dated back at least to the 11th century were resurrected, but all this was too late to have any effect on the Highland Clearances and the enormous depopulation and national resentment which it left behind.

While agriculture was being destroyed in Scotland, the Industrial Revolution spread into Scotland's four great cities, Edinburgh, Glasgow, Dundee and Aberdeen to fill the gap, with textiles, iron and shipbuilding bringing employment and wealth to Glasgow, fishing to Aberdeen, commerce to Edinburgh and a large jute processing industry in Dundee from raw materials shipped in from the distant Empire. The advent of coal mining in Scotland speeded industrial development. Despite this, and in large measure as a consequence of the upheavals caused by the Highland Clearances, the 19th century was a time of disruption and protest. Political protest started early in the century and led to some electoral reform and parliamentary representation.

In 1843, the Church of Scotland suffered a major crisis known as 'The Disruption' when large numbers of people left the established Anglican Church which was felt to be too closely tied to the State and involved in both education and welfare which appeared unsatisfactory: those who left set up their own Free Church without affiliations. This religious fragmentation followed a century of discord with the Church of Scotland dividing into evangelical and moderate wings; the moderate side of the Church providing a lot of support for the early Enlightenment in Scotland.

In literature, James MacPherson (1736–1796) published an ancient epic poem by Ossian, Son of Fingal, or Finn McCool, a legendary character in Irish mythology dating back to the Dark Ages. Although MacPherson claimed simply to have translated the document, it is not clear where the manuscript came from, and it has been suggested that much of the story was invented. It did however, act as a classical epic poem for Scotland, influencing both Robert Burns and Sir Walter Scott. Scotland's other internationally popular author of the time, Robert Louis Stevenson (1850–1894), the author of 'Treasure Island' and 'Kidnapped', wrote in relative isolation, often writing travelogues, not always about Scotland.

The end of the century saw a continuation of strife between landowners and their impoverished tenants. The Highland Laird League was founded in 1884 to protect the interests of landowners, the Crofters Act followed two years later in which crofting was officially recognised and protected. Crofting was a system of land usage in which the crofter farmed a few acres of reasonable land for crops and then grazed sheep on a much larger acreage of common land. This parliamentary act reduced rents, guaranteed crofters security of tenure, and even broke up some large estates to provide crofts for the homeless; three crofters were also elected to Parliament. The rights of crofters were looked after by a Commission to arbitrate in disputes between landlords and their small tenants.

In 1892, Keir Hardie (1856–1915), a Glasgow socialist union organiser, was elected to parliament in London. He had been given a good education by his parents, and after working in the mines in Ayrshire became the first labour member of the British Parliament, where he then formed the socialist Independent Labour Party (ILP) in 1893. At this time there was a groundswell of support for working class representation in parliament for which the Liberal Party had been the best means of achieving this until the founding of the ILP. The British Trade Union movement had come together to form the Trades Union Congress in 1886 with similar objectives.

The Party was not supported by the Marxists who believed in a much more ferocious class struggle and had founded their own Social Democratic Federation in 1881. The Social Democratic Federation was supported by William Morris (1834–1896), George Lansbury (1859–1940) and Eleanor Marx (1855–1898), the youngest daughter of Karl Marx (1818–1883), but not by Friedrich Engels (1820–1895), Marx's long-term collaborator who subsequently died in 1895.

The 19th century saw the population of Scotland almost double in the first fifty years and grow at a similar rate in the second half of the century. During this time agriculture had become much less important and the cotton industry had never recovered following the cessation of supplies at the time of the American Civil War; instead Scotland became important in engineering, shipbuilding and the production of steam engines for the railways. Coal mining underpinned much of this and was an enormously important employer into the 20th century.

Railways were important in the Scottish economy with expansion following the opening of the first commercial railway line in 1831, though Scottish geography prohibited significant construction of canals. Urbanisation and industry brought continuing relative wealth to Scotland through the early years of the 20th century. The Labour Party, founded from the Trade Union Movement and other socialist organisations in 1900, continued to grow through the first two decades of the 20th century affiliating with the ILP from 1906 and overtaking the Liberal Party as the main parliamentary opposition soon after the First World War, and then forming minority governments in 1924 and again in 1929.

---oOo---

Wales had effectively been incorporated into the mainstream of English life under Henry VIII when the nation remained Anglican and Royalist. Wales supported the Monarchy through the Civil War of the 1640s, though most military activity took place in England and there were no major battles in Wales. The Welsh Methodist Movement began with John Wesley (1703–1791), an Oxford educated minister who felt that his beliefs and teachings were still compatible with a Church of England which had split off from Rome two centuries previously.

Wesley, together with his brother Charles (1707–1788), and a fellow student, George Whitefield (1714–1770), became evangelical and felt a need to travel throughout the country preaching. Much of their thinking derived from the Dutch Reform Church of Jacobus Arminius (1560–1609) and was distinct from the thinking of other protestant thinkers including Luther, Zwingli and Calvin. There was a belief in Christian salvation and forgiveness, and in the ability of the individual to resist sin with the help of God. Wesley's Methodist Movement did not break away from the established Church of England and much of his energies and attitudes were directed towards social undertakings and bettering the lives of the poor, including establishing hospitals, schools and orphanages. Other non-conformist Churches became popular in Wales, and the Church Sunday Schools were a big force in achieving literacy throughout the country.

The Industrial Revolution and the availability of extensive coal deposits in South Wales helped Wales to industrialise at the beginning of the Industrial Revolution. Coal mining expanded to feed the iron works in the southern Welsh valleys and other English towns moving into the industrial age, but the process was often an unhappy one. After years of tension and unrest, 1831 saw the Merthyr Rising in which coal miners rioted against having their wages and jobs cut. The army was deployed to restore order which made the situation worse, both soldiers and rioters were injured, some fatally. It took several days for the authorities to regain control.

Low-level protest continued but in 1839, the Rebekah Riots occurred (the name may refer to a verse in the Bible concerning Rebekah), involving a series of protests by local farmers taking action against unfair taxation and toll gates on the highways, which put up the costs for farmers taking their produce to market.

Also at this time, involvement of the Chartists, a national protest movement in England, extended to the South Wales valleys (chapter 67). The Chartists were making six demands, firstly a vote for every man over 21, secondly, secrecy of the ballot, thirdly, no need for ownership of property to become a Member of Parliament, fourth, pay for Members of Parliament, fifth, equal sized constituencies, and sixth, annual parliamentary elections. The Movement was started by six members of Parliament in 1838, and resulted in large gatherings and several riots, including one armed protest in Newport Monmouthshire where several Chartists were killed.

By 1842 a petition with over three million signatures was submitted to parliament, but was rejected, resulting in a wave of strikes. Many Chartists were imprisoned and some were transported. One Chartist was elected to Parliament in 1847, but over the following decade the movement lost momentum and fizzled out, though it must be noted that soon five of the six reform demands had been implemented, leaving only the call for annual parliamentary elections unfulfilled.

In 1855, the first coal mine had opened in the Rhondda Valley, considerably increasing the size of the coal industry in South Wales. It was not until 1858 that the ancient cultural legacy of Wales was revived in the form of a national Eisteddfod, or cultural festival, which also spawned many smaller such Eisteddfods over coming years. 1872 saw the birth of University College Wales in Aberystwyth which became one of the three campuses of a Federal University of Wales (including Bangor and Cardiff) and was incorporated by Royal Charter subsequently in 1893.

----oOo---

In Ireland, the English Reformation of 1536, when Henry VIII established the Anglican Church, has left a legacy of chronic animosity, and at times outright warfare. Over the succeeding years after Henry's action most of the governing authorities and aristocrats in Ireland became Protestant, whilst the mass of the population remained Catholic. The situation was not helped as many large Irish estates belonged to English Anglican landowners who were often absentee landlords and unsympathetic to their rent paying tenants. Ireland's persistence as a Catholic nation instead of converting to Protestantism, as much of the rest of northern Europe did, may also be blamed on the education and missionary work of Catholic priests educated in mainland Europe, together with a lack of available printing presses and literature, and poor literacy amongst much of the Irish population at the time, although the first Irish university, Trinity College Dublin, was established in 1592.

From 1607, Irish Catholics were barred from public office and the Irish constituencies were changed to conserve a Protestant majority in the Irish House of Commons (although the Irish House of Lords had a Catholic majority up to the end of the 17th century). Large numbers of Protestant immigrants were sent to Ireland, principally in the north-east and south-west counties of Ireland by the Crown, which confiscated land and gave land grants to settlers ('planters') who were Protestants. This migratory process began under Henry VIII and then continued through successive reigns up to the time of Cromwell, when thousands of Parliamentary soldiers were granted land in Ireland. Some English Catholics migrated to Ireland to avoid persecution at a time when Puritanism and Protestantism were rife in England.

In 1641, after a poor harvest, an Irish nobleman, Felim O'Neill, led a rebellion in which Irish Catholics attacked the various 'plantations' around Ireland, and particularly in Ulster. The rebellion failed and O'Neill was later captured and executed by Cromwell's troops in 1653. In general however, following the uprising the rebels had achieved control over most of Ireland and ruled briefly during the remainder of the reign of Charles I. After Charles was executed, Oliver Cromwell reasserted control over Ireland in a particularly brutal campaign, which included not only massacres, but also a scorched earth policy, thus causing famine throughout the country. Catholic lands were confiscated and laws passed forbidding Catholics from living in towns, marrying Protestants, or being members of the Irish parliament.

The overall effect was to leave a strong sense of bitterness and resentment which continues to plague Ireland up to present times. A further brief episode of Catholic repression occurred in 1678. In the Glorious Revolution of 1688 James II was deposed in England and replaced by William of Orange. Irish Catholics at this time were backing the catholic King James to try and reverse oppressive laws and confiscation of land, whilst British Protestants were strongly behind William of Orange. Williams' success at the Battle of the Boyne in Ireland in 1690, which was essentially a Catholic versus Protestant confrontation, lives on very strongly in Irish folklore and attitudes.

Through the 17th century, the period is known as the Protestant Ascendancy. At this time, some three-quarters of the Irish population were Catholic with the remaining quarter of Protestants being equally split between Presbyterians and Anglicans. Ireland was theoretically a self-governing kingdom with its own parliament, and since this parliament was almost entirely filled with Anglican supporters it was clearly deeply in thrall to the British parliament. Although Ireland gained a constitution in 1782, the situation basically remained unchanged and led to a republican rebellion in 1798, with the rebels inspired by the earlier revolutions in America and France.

A French fleet with 14,000 troops was sent as an invasion force to support the Irish Catholics but was unable to land due to storms, and as in the case of the Spanish Armada, Ireland was spared a foreign invasion. Atrocities and executions without trial were common, further reinforcing the divide between Catholics and Protestants. Finally, after passage through the British and Irish parliaments, Acts of Union were passed in 1800 effectively incorporating both states into a single union within the United Kingdom of Great Britain and Ireland.

Initially, the early years of the 19th century achieved little change in Ireland as George III believed that Catholic emancipation would endanger the Anglican Church. However, by 1829 the Duke of Wellington was able to persuade George IV to sign a Catholic Relief Act allowing Catholic MPs. Some local government reforms were also introduced, but a retrograde step followed with a Reform Act in 1832 removing the vote from freeholders below a certain income level. Some intermittent small rebellions and unrest occurred with particular resentment that the Catholic population was obliged to pay tithes to the Anglican Church of Ireland.

Ireland was overtaken by the Great Irish Famine lasting from 1845–1849 when the potato crop failed. Enclosures of land and the Irish tradition of inheritance which divided estates between all the surviving male heirs, meant that many farms had become too small to support the families owning them. The disaster was compounded by the English Corn Laws, and by the Westminster based parliament failure to provide food, particularly wheat, for support to the population of Ireland. It is estimated that from a population of around 8 million before the famine perhaps one million died and one million more emigrated.

It took many decades for Ireland to recover, but by the time of a census in 1911, the population was only just over 4 million indicating continuing emigration alongside deaths from other causes. In the same period, the population of England and Wales doubled from 32 to 62 million. It is clear that the British government failed to provide adequate economic or food support to Ireland during the famines, either because the crisis was severely underestimated, or because of sheer governmental incompetence and procrastination. The resentment in Ireland over the famine has left a persisting attitude in favour of Irish independence, which has been fuelled both economically and emotionally by many of the emigrants in the wider Irish diaspora of British colonies and dependencies, not forgetting the large American numbers with Irish roots.

Over the succeeding decades, this all led to continuing unrest, though eventually several Irish Land Acts, beginning in 1881, restored rights to tenant farmers and gave more power to Irish Catholics at the expense of the landed Anglican gentry. The effect was to create a large number of small property owners in the Irish countryside thereby diluting the power of the old Anglo-Irish property owning class. A Local Government Act in 1898 delegated the running of rural affairs to local level, but it did not end the fast-running tide of nationalism that was still aiming for an independent Ireland.

This was personified in the Home Rule League founded in the 1870s and continued by a Protestant Irish landowner Charles Parnell, whose Irish parliamentary party came to dominate Irish politics at the end of the 19th century. Two Home Rule Bills were brought before parliament by Gladstone, first in 1886 and again in 1893, but neither passed the House of Commons. Finally however, Home Rule should have been achieved with the Parliament Act of 1911 when the Commons passed the legislation after the House of Lords lost its power to veto legislation; a year later the Bill passed, to be delayed but not completely killed, by the House of Lords which still possessed power to delay a Bill for two years.

Further debate continued in the Commons over the minutiae of Home Rule, and in particular over the Protestant Ulster Unionists' resistance. The Bill was therefore due to pass in 1914 at the beginning of the First World War, but because of the War was put on ice, as the fighting was not expected to last for more than a few months.

The First World War did, of course, drag on for four years, and tens of thousands of Irishmen fought for Britain against Germany. A small number of Irish citizens remaining at home staged a rebellion known as the Easter Rising in Dublin in 1916, which was brutally put down and the leaders executed. At the time the Rising was felt to be inappropriate while fellow Irishmen were dying abroad, and with Home Rule already through parliament and in sight on the horizon. At the end of the war in elections for the Irish parliament there was a battle between the Irish Parliamentary Party and the Nationalist Sinn Fein party, but when it became known that the British government intended to implement conscription the public mood turned against Britain and the Irish Parliamentary Party withdrew its MPs.

Sinn Fein won three-quarters of the seats and for the next two years Ireland was enveloped by civil war. Finally, after much delay and further consideration the British government granted Home Rule to two separate parts of Ireland, namely the largely protestant north-eastern six counties of Ulster, and the remaining largely catholic 26 counties which now form the nation of Eire. Initially the 26 countries refused to cooperate, and therefore in 1921 the Anglo-Irish Treaty was finally implemented with Eire, or the Irish Free State, finally coming into being in 1925.

Possible further reading:
The Four Nations by Frank Welsh (Harper Collins)

Chapter 79
19th Century France

The last decade of the 18th century and the first decade of the 19th century were a time of memorable unrest and uncertainty in France. The Revolution (chapter 61) had seen a massive populist uprising with summary executions of many notable French citizens, culminating in the execution of the King, Louis XVI. Up to that time, France had been governed by an autocratic monarch with a privileged upper class and a complacent and acquiescent Catholic Church. The King had been an absolute ruler, using as his advisors those whose outlook fitted his own view point. All this was brought into question and changed by the Revolution. Ironically, by the end of the Revolution, France had reverted to government by another autocratic monarch, albeit one not styled as a king, but known as the Emperor Napoleon. He was seen much more as a man of the people than the previous royal line, and although he suffered with a certain amount of megalomania, he did not project the personal excesses of France's 18th century monarchs. France felt safe with his autocracy, although Napoleon overstretched himself at the end, and was lucky to be treated in a more sympathetic and civilised manner than his guillotined predecessor Louis XVI, and was simply exiled.

The boundaries of France were little different from those of Gaul as it was found by the Romans two millennia earlier. Boundaries had moved through the intervening years, but the northward invasion of Muslim armies in the 8th century had been stopped by Charles Martel (chapter 22), and turned back south fairly rapidly. France had then been consolidated under Charlemagne, but although a notional monarch ruled France through the next millennium, there was considerable independence of the many different provinces under Counts and Princes. The French custom of inheritance, dividing lands and property between all male heirs, made for instability and episodic fighting as princedoms grew smaller, and it had also resulted in a very large and privileged aristocracy supported financially by taxes from the rest of the population.

Part of Napoleon's legacy was to reform this situation with the abolition of feudalism, and the centralisation of power in Paris. He set up eighty Departments, each governed by a Prefect appointed from Paris. The effect of this was to diminish regional differences, with central decisions from Paris promoting a more homogenous application of the law. The Church had suffered badly, and many clergy had been killed in the Revolution, but Church life was returning to normal in the early years of the 19th century, although Church land and property was not restored.

The Napoleonic Code which he had instituted provided the best system of Law that Napoleon's legal advisors could devise. The Code recognised the revolutionary principles of Liberté, Egalité and Fraternité without reference to the Catholic Church. New inheritance laws required that property and land be divided amongst all children of a marriage, and not just the male ones, but perpetuating the problems of an ever widening aristocracy with ever diminishing shares of land.

Despite the years of instability, there was still a movement in France at the end of Napoleon's reign to restore the monarchy; it seemed that France was happiest under an autocrat. The royal family of Bourbon was restored to the throne in 1814 in the person of Louis XVIII, brother of Louis XVI, after the defeat of Napoleon, and ruled for the next ten years with a short period of exile when Napoleon temporarily returned. The nephew of Louis XVI had been notional Head of State following the execution of his uncle, Louis XVI, but he had subsequently died as a child and had never been crowned: he would have been Louis XVII.

Louis XVIII governed following the Declaration of Saint-Ouen in 1814 in which he undertook that the Constitution would allow representative government with a two-chamber parliament, protect freedom of the press, of opinion, of worship, and protect public liberty. He also undertook that Napoleon's legal innovations would remain in force, along with Napoleon's changes to the educational system. Although the feudal system had been abolished, only one percent of the population were given a vote. Louis's early days as monarch were greeted with popular enthusiasm, but as he tried to reverse some of the changes that had come with the Revolution, he rapidly lost support amongst the population.

Meanwhile, Napoleon escaped from Elba, and on his march from the south coast of France to Paris, rapidly gathered an army from amongst the disillusioned population. Louis fled northwards, and was only able to return once Napoleon was defeated at the Battle of Waterloo, and banished to St Helena in the South Atlantic, from where he could not escape, nor could he influence any further developments in French politics.

In the early years of Louis XVIII's rule, there was considerable disagreement between the liberals and the rather reactionary conservative elements who wished to return to a society more closely resembling that which had existed before the Revolution. Even with the changes that still persisted from the Revolution, French government had not been liberalised to the degree which England had achieved a hundred years earlier. Louis XVIII died in 1824 to be succeeded by his brother who became Charles X, and was crowned in Rheims in a very extravagant ceremony that some saw as harking back to the pre-revolutionary grandeur of the monarchy.

Disagreement persisted between the modernisers, and the conservative elements who wished to return to the customs of the olden days (the 'Ancien

Regime'). Charles delivered a very threatening and reactionary speech early in 1830, known as the Ordinances of St Cloud, where amongst other measures he suspended the liberty of the press and dissolved the elected lower chamber of parliament as well as diminishing the numbers and powers of elected members; this all produced a parliamentary revolt and a majority against the government. The dissolution of parliament was done in a manner reminiscent of his namesake in Britain two hundred years earlier.

Charles felt that the majority of the population still supported him, which was a massive miscalculation, and resulted a few months later in the July Revolution of 1830; he was forced to abdicate and left for sanctuary in England while nominating his grandson to be the next ruler. The French parliament refused to recognise this and proclaimed Louis Philippe, the leader of Orleanist Party, as monarch. Although his father had supported the Revolution, he had gone to the guillotine during the Reign of Terror and in consequence Louis Philippe had spent twenty-one years in exile, mainly in Switzerland. He came to the throne promising to pursue moderate policies and to avoid the extremes of both conservative and radical ends of the political spectrum.

His eighteen-year reign was marked by continuing political battles between conservative and radical elements in France, and as the country continued to see-saw between liberalism and radicalism, the public mood remained unstable and volatile until a further revolution in 1848, when the population of Paris rebelled against the conservative tendencies of the government. Unrest was probably fomented by the estimated one third of the population of Paris who could not find work at this time.

The result of deposing Louis Philippe was to bring into effect the Second Republic, which would last for the next four years. The two major reforms during this time were firstly the provision of unemployment relief, and secondly the enlargement of the franchise to all adult men, thus enormously increasing the numbers of those entitled to vote. Louis Napoleon, nephew and heir of the Great Napoleon Bonaparte was elected President.

Louis Napoleon, known as Napoleon III, is remembered for his great remodelling of Paris, but also of other major French cities, including Marseilles and Lyons. He promoted the extension of the French railway system and the merchant navy. He modernised the French banking system which financed the building of the Suez Canal among other projects. Multiple social reforms were made, including expanding education in public schools, and increasing the importance of educating women.

Abroad, Napoleon sought to increase French influence so that he joined with Britain to defeat Russia in the Crimean War of 1854–56. He assisted Italian unification, whilst at the same time annexing the areas of Savoy and Nice, and also defending the Vatican State against incorporation by Italy. In his last years of power through the late 1860s, Prussia under Otto Von Bismarck, was aiming for German unification, unwisely Napoleon went to war with Prussia, but with a French army that was inferior in numbers, training and leadership. A series of battles were lost by the French, culminating in a resounding defeat at the Battle of Sedan on the River Meuse in north-eastern France.

Napoleon was captured along with most of his army. The overall result was to end Napoleon's reign and push France into its Third Republic, whilst French opponents coalesced into a unified Germany under Bismarck. Napoleon himself, who was in poor and deteriorating health, was exiled to England where he died early in 1873. Paris itself was surrounded and had to surrender in early 1871, after which the Treaty of Frankfurt was signed, with the province of Alsace-Lorraine being transferred to Germany.

The next few decades, up to the beginning of the First World War, saw the modernisation of France and the completion of its industrialisation. Government was centralised in Paris. Schools were supervised by the central government, and military conscription for all young men was introduced. The railways were extended, and the road network was also brought up to date.

Initially, the government of the new Third Republic was placed in Versailles because of continuing unrest in Paris, which gradually escalated until the rebellious and radical Paris Commune came into being and controlled Paris for two months in the spring of 1878. At the end of this time with the rebels refusing to recognise the French government at Versailles, French troops moved in to suppress the revolt. Several thousand citizen soldiers of the Commune were killed. After the new President and Prime Minister designate failed to form a government, a new President was elected and a government finally formed. France continued to try and expand its empire, but had to cede control of Egypt to the British.

Algeria was already in the French orbit and colonies had been founded in Asia, including Vietnam. With memories of war with Germany haunting the French, alliances were made, first with Russia in 1894, and then with Britain in 1904 known as the Entente Cordiale: this all led in due course to Britain and Russia joining the First World War as allies of France. In 1889 France put on the Exposition Universale with the crowning glory being the newly completed Eiffel Tower, designed to showcase the nation's industrial capability.

When war broke out in the summer of 1914, Germany quickly captured Belgium, which was ostensibly neutral, and the German forces continued through Belgium towards Paris, but were stopped some 40 miles short of the city. Over the next four years the Western Front, as it was called, was fought over a long but narrow strip of land between the opposing forces in trenches on each side. There was great loss of life and little movement of the front line. In 1917 Germany had defeated Russia and was preparing to concentrate all its forces along the Western Front, but by this time America had entered the war and in the summer of 1918 the combined Allied Western Front proved impregnable, so that the Allies, now including America, went on the offensive.

Germany had no reserves left, and its allies, Austria and Turkey, both collapsed. The German government fell and signed the Armistice ending the fighting on the 11th of November 1918. During the war the French had lost 1.4 million dead, both military and civilians. The Peace Treaty involved Germany admitting guilt in starting the war, and very large war reparations being paid to the Allies. France also regained Alsace Lorraine from Germany as French territory.

The French republics:
First republic 1792–1804,
Second Republic 1848–1852,
Third republic 1870–1940,
Fourth Republic 1946–1958,
Fifth Republic 1958 onwards.

Possible further reading:
A History of France by Jonathan Fenby (Simon & Schuster)

Chapter 80
Germany

The known history of Germany starts with Julius Caesar and writings in his diaries. Two millennia ago, there were many inter-related tribes living in eastern Europe, they were not literate, and the history they left has been discovered mainly by archaeology. Gaul had been conquered by the Romans and served as a springboard to Europe east of Roman Gaul and across the River Rhine. At one time the Romans felt that they could subdue these Germanic tribes and annex them into the Roman Empire. This plan went terribly wrong when the tribes cooperated together and ambushed the Roman legions at Teutoburg (some 60 miles north-east of Cologne) in AD 9. Three legions, comprising 15,000–20,000 troops, were massacred in the worst battlefield disaster the Romans had ever experienced. The result of this was a decision by the Romans to halt their advance and to use the Rhine as the outermost limit of the Empire.

The tribes were then left were undisturbed for the next few hundred years, they included Franks, Goths, Alemanni and Vandals: we hear little of them in their native surroundings, but they earned their place in the history books when they broke out of eastern Europe, possibly due to poor harvests and famine, and rampaged across the Roman Empire, sometimes sacking cities, sometimes simply searching for better land in which to settle (chapter 16). The Vandals crossed the Rhine into the Roman Empire in 406, and later sacked Rome in 455.

Even before this, the Visigoths had sacked Rome in 410 (leading to withdrawal of Roman forces from Britain and other frontier regions), and subsequently faced Attila the Hun (406–453) in 451 at a disputed battle of the Catalaunion Fields. In due course. the Huns withered, or were incorporated into the population of Gaul, they were a large tribe from the Caucasus and Central Asia who were prominent in the 1st to 7th centuries following their migration, but were last heard of when they were defeated by the Goths in 451. The Alemanni were another tribe living around the Upper Rhine who were conquered by Clovis at the end of the 5th century, and finally it was Clovis, King of the Franks (466–511), who united all the Frankish tribes together, establishing a line of kings that would lead to Charlemagne (chapter 22).

Charlemagne (742–814), grandson of Charles Martel (chapter 20), united much of western Europe, thereby laying the foundations for what we know today as France and Germany. He was crowned Holy Roman Emperor on Christmas Day 800 by the Pope, and this Papal coronation added great legitimacy to his conquests and authority. Of distinction in the lineage from Charlemagne through to present Germany is Otto I (912–973), who conquered the Magyars of Hungary in 955, and following this conquered the King of Italy a few years later.

In the story that would become the line to modern Germany, two great figures of the Middle Ages become very important later. First, Gutenberg invented the printing press enabling the wide and much more rapid dissemination of information (chapter 36), and second, Martin Luther, whose objections to Catholicism and written religious tracts and the selling of indulgences underpinned the conversion of much of northern Europe from Catholicism to Protestantism (chapter 39). At the time of Luther, the German speaking world was one of many dialects and petty kingdoms, numbering over three hundred. Luther's legacy is two-fold, clearly the first is the establishment of Protestantism which broke away from the Catholic Church.

Unlike similar religious protestors in England and other nations, who were executed or burnt at the stake, Luther was protected by the protestant ruler of one of the small German states, since each of these states followed either the Protestant or Catholic religion chosen by the ruler. In this respect Luther was lucky to be protected by Frederick III after being declared a heretic; he was then kept in protective custody at Frederick's castle of Wartburg. But Luther's second and somewhat incidental legacy is that of rationalising the many German dialects of the time into the language in which he himself wrote, simply by virtue of his Bible translation being the most widely read book in Germany, so that in this way the German language became standardised.

In the Thirty Years War, between 1618 and 1648, Germany was fought over as a consequence of its division into Catholic and Protestant enclaves. The Catholic Emperor of the Holy Roman Empire was trying to achieve unity, both religious and political, by conflict and war was broadened in its later years by the intervention of Denmark, Sweden and France. The Emperors and Kings of the Holy Roman Empire came from the Austrian Hapsburg dynasty for a three hundred year period through this time and up to 1740, including the Thirty Years War.

Social disruption in central Europe was enormous, with soldiers rampaging across the different small kingdoms of Germany, living off the land, and causing fear and starvation for most of the population: the net effect was a drop in population of many millions of people. The War finally ended in 1648 with the Treaty of Westphalia, which involved many of the other European powers apart from the warring combatants.

In the early years of the peace, one of those kingdoms, Prussia under the Hapsburgs, grew significantly in power. In Prussia Frederick II, whose long reign extended from 1740 to 1786, was a very cultured man, and in addition to being a military genius, he reorganised the Prussian army to make the country a great power within Europe.

Germany saw the Enlightenment take off under Frederick's patronage, in an era which saw literature from Goethe (1742–1832) and Schiller (1759–1805): music in Germany flourished with amazing works produced by Bach (1685–1750), Haydn (1730–1809), Mozart (1759–1791) and later Beethoven (1770–

1827). All these great composers sit in an evolutionary line each developing music afresh in a clear progression.

The American Revolution, leading to peace and independence in the 1780s, together with the much less controlled and more vicious French Revolution of 1790s, were watched from Germany with apprehension; the two decades either side of 1800 were ones in which Europe became a very uncertain and dangerous place. Frederick II died in 1786, just before the majority of these evils, and although he is often seen as a unifying German precursor of Bismarck, the European problems with Napoleon's immense ambitions after the Revolution were considerable. France occupied the Rhineland imposing Napoleonic reforms, which included feudalism and forcing the aristocracy to share power with the up and coming middle classes; a constitution was established, freedom of religion, including the Jews, was also established.

Napoleon created the Kingdom of Westphalia in 1807 and many of his reforms became permanent, although when he tried to impose the French language this proved a step too far for the German states. After the Rhineland Napoleon occupied Berlin in 1806 after defeating the Prussian army, and by the beginning of 1812 he controlled much of Europe, but his subsequent ill-judged invasion of Russia undid most of his conquests. By 1813 the other European nations were beginning to cut Napoleon down to size in Wars of Liberation. In the remaining years of the first half of the 19th century Germany was free to develop both its industry and its culture in the enlightenment.

Like several other countries however, 1848 saw revolution in Germany, but after a period of uncertainty and military suppression of revolutionaries, the German Confederation was re-established by 1850. German rule was still autocratic at that time, but in 1857 the Kaiser had a stroke, and his brother, acting as Regent, named Otto Von Bismarck (1815–1898), who came from an aristocratic family in Saxony and had trained as a lawyer, as Chancellor in 1862.

Over the next decade, Bismarck's diplomacy united the many German states under Prussia, but excluding Austria. He engineered war against an ill-equipped Denmark in 1864, and against Austria in 1866, vanquishing both countries. He then provoked the French to war which lasted almost a year, once again the French were ill-prepared and inferior in numbers, and the war ended with their defeat at the Battle of Sedan in 1870 following which Napoleon III was exiled to England where he died three years later. This end result created a strong and unified German Empire in a Europe where the balance had changed radically from the peace agreement of 1815, which had seen the end of Napoleon I.

Bismarck remained in power as German Chancellor until 1890, during which time he not only remained a master of diplomatic foreign policy, but also worked hard on the home front, creating the first welfare state amongst other achievements; the welfare included provision for citizens in the form of accident insurance, medical care, and old age pensions. He built up Germany's armaments and armed forces, and the development of the nation was such that by 1900 Germany had passed Britain as the leading industrial nation, and had also passed Britain in terms of its armaments.

Bismarck was dismissed from office in 1890 by the new Kaiser, Wilhelm II (1851–1941), grandson of Queen Victoria and a rather immature and bombastic individual who then took control of Germany's foreign policy as well as trying to supervise most other government policies and functions like an autocrat from previous centuries. Much later, he was finally forced to abdicate after accepting the terms of Germany's surrender in 1918 after which he lived out the rest of his life in exile in Holland. The armaments race with Britain gradually soured relations between the two countries, although in terms of naval power Britain managed to remain ahead of its German rival.

Increasing differences in attitudes between the various European powers, particularly Russia, France and Britain ranged against Italy, Germany and Austria-Hungary, gradually built up tensions and mistrust, until in July 1914, Archduke Ferdinand of Austria was assassinated in Serbia. Serbia had been caught between the two big power blocks without being significantly aligned to either side, but the murder of the Archduke, which was an individual act without any governmental connivance, acted as the kindling to light the fire of the First World War, with Germany unfairly holding Serbia responsible.

Possible further reading:
Germany by Neil MacGregor (BBC Books)
A History of Germany by Peter Wende (Palgrave Macmillan)

Chapter 81
USA 1865–1918

Considering that the first permanent American colony was only established in 1607, the new country progressed rapidly. Independence was achieved at the end of the Civil War in the early 1780s when the country was a very sparsely populated agricultural land along the east coast. Expansion westwards followed with each successive wave of immigrants moving further west to find virgin land for farming. In the first half of the 19th century the original eastern colonies had continued to expand, first with the Louisiana purchase from France in 1803, and then the purchase of Florida from Spain in 1819.

Much of northern Mexico was annexed in 1848 by war, and the western seaboard territories also came to be part of the USA in that year. The frontier border with Canada was fixed on the 49th Parallel, resulting in the United States of the shape and size that persists today (apart from the additional purchase of Alaska in 1867). The California Gold Rush in 1848 brought further migration to the west coast.

Unsurprisingly, the European population of America grew rapidly following the founding of the first settlement in Virginia to just under four million souls in 1790 at the time of the first census. Immigration was proceeding rapidly and another million people were added in the next decade. By 1850 the population had grown to 23 million, and the second half of the 19th century saw this figure rise to 76 million. Before 1850 Britain was the only industrialised country in the world, but this changed rapidly through the second half of the 19th century, and American industrial expansion in particular, grew to equal that of Britain by 1900. Part of this was due to the exploitation of the previously untapped resources of the new continent, including its coal, gold and mineral wealth: oil would contribute later.

The Civil War was fought from 1861 to 1865 between the Union States of the north-eastern seaboard that were both agricultural and manufacturing for their livelihood, and the Confederate, or Southern states, whose riches lay in the production of cotton thanks to a large slave population working the plantations and estimated at around four million African Americans at the start of the Civil War. The Northern Union states were led through the war by Abraham Lincoln, lawyer and 16th President (1809–1865), who managed to steer a narrow path with great skill, preserving the Union and abolishing slavery while also strengthening the economy and the Federal Government. He was assassinated just five days after peace was signed between the two sides.

Cotton was an extremely important resource: its production doubled in the 1820s, and doubled again in the 1830s. By 1860 it was accounting for two-thirds of all American exports, mainly to Britain. The early United States was a lawless place, subsequently immortalised in countless 'western' films. The early Americans were cavalier with their treatment of the native Indians who were progressively moved further west from their original homelands onto reservations, which in turn were revised downwards in size, particularly when the discovery of minerals or forests became ripe for exploitation. The treatment of the native population resulted in chronic grumbling warfare which the Indians almost invariably lost due to the European superiority in weaponry. Early America was also oblivious to the damage to flora and fauna inflicted in the rush to settle the country, for instance almost driving the native herds of buffalo to extinction.

The picture was no different in the eastern states where manufacturing was getting underway. America refused to recognise English and other European patents, and became adept at pirating ideas, machinery and even individuals from British manufacturers, the same was also true of the emerging German industrial base at this time (later, in the 20th century, the same criticism would be levelled first at Japanese, and then Chinese, industry). However, although the early US industrial expansion involved cartels, political corruption, bribery and very poor workers' rights, the United States did have the foresight to set up technical colleges for the production of trained engineers and technicians who would be needed to continue industrial expansion.

Another big difference between the British Industrial Revolution early on, and that later in America, is that the British advances were made entirely by private individual entrepreneurs who set up private companies when possible to exploit their inventions or innovations. This private capitalist system extended not just to industry, but also to the provision of public services, such as roads, railways and canals. By contrast, in America government money and government engineers assisted in the early strategic building of this necessary public infrastructure.

The railway system responded to commerce and industry, building lines to towns and sites where the provision of transport was vital. The transcontinental railroad was finally completed in 1869, from the east to the west coast. The first canal in North America pre-dates this by a considerable time and was a much more impressive venture than the equivalent smaller British canals; the Erie Canal was built to join the Great Lakes system with the east coast maritime transport; it covered 363 miles from Buffalo on Lake Erie through to Albany on the Hudson River, thus avoiding the Niagara River and Falls, and the St Lawrence Rapids downstream of Lake Ontario. The canal was dug between 1817 and 1825, it was much wider and deeper than standard English canals, and opened up the mid-west of America to provide agricultural and manufactured goods to the eastern states, and to the larger world beyond.

The second half of the 19th century was a time when industrialists and bankers made huge fortunes. Even before this, John Harvard 1607–1638), an

English minister and Cambridge graduate, left sufficient money in his will (despite dying young from tuberculosis) to found the first American university, which bears his name. Francis Cabot Lowell (1775–1817) is often credited with laying some of the basis for the early mercantile and industrial revolution, while also making a huge fortune from shipping and trading. Johns Hopkins (1795–1873) was a very wealthy philanthropic Quaker merchant and a shrewd investor from Baltimore whose gifts founded the University, Hospital, Medical and Nursing Schools which bear his name.

Thomas Mellon (1813–1908) emigrated to America from Ireland with his family in childhood; he founded both a highly successful bank and also invested in large tracts land around Pittsburgh; his offspring were all successful in business and became influential philanthropists. Also included in the roll call of men (and they were all men) who were highly successful entrepreneurs, and subsequently philanthropists, are JD Rockefeller (1839–1937) who established Standard Oil, Andrew Carnegie (1835–1919) who also emigrated to America from Scotland as a child, establishing much of the early steel industry in Pittsburgh, and JP Morgan (1837–1913), American banker, financier and industrialist.

Henry Ford (1863–1947) founded the Ford Motor Company in 1903 producing the famous mass-produced 'Model T' in 1908, and implementing a philosophy of mass production and generous pay for workers. The car was a runaway success with an annual output of a quarter of a million by 1914. Ford also left a large philanthropic foundation, giving grants not only to education and arts in America, but also towards Third World development. These men have all left a huge legacy to their country, both in terms of industry and organisations, but also in terms of their later huge philanthropic foundations which continue to pour money into educational and scientific foundations across America.

Different, but no less important legacies, have been left by early American thinkers, including Benjamin Franklin (1706–1790) from an earlier era, and Henry George (1839–1897), political economist, philosopher and journalist, who wrote extensively about the divide between private and public land, facilities and wealth. He felt it wrong that private profit could be gained by restricting access to natural resources, whilst those who engaged in productive activity such as farming or factory work, were taxed on their work.

During the second half of the 19th century, reforms and expansion of education occurred with government encouragement, and political, business and social reforms also advanced rapidly. Between 1865 and 1918 over 27 million new immigrants arrived from Europe fuelling the expansion of both industry and agriculture, such that the US population by the end of the first World War was around 100 million. By 1950, the population had risen to over 150 million with 85% of the population being of European stock, while most recently this figure has become a population of 325 million with approximately 60% of European heritage.

At the end of the Civil War in 1865, millions of black slaves were suddenly free, but the myth of freedom was a distant mirage for most of them, since they were uneducated and untrained. Their choices seemed to lie between remaining in the south and continuing to work on cotton plantations or in other menial jobs for poor rewards, or alternatively migrating to the north to find jobs in the new mid-western industrial belt. Many chose this second option and bolstered the rapidly developing American industrial base, though their rewards and family situations did not alter greatly, except in so far as they changed from a rural to an urban setting. It would take at least another century for this problem to start working out, while at the same time the racial divisions had been exported from the south to the north of the United States, with continuing repercussions throughout the 20th century and even on into the present time.

On the land, American agriculture was expanding rapidly, thanks to both the large supply of available labour, and to the rapid introduction of farm machinery pioneered in the industrial mid-west. At the same time continuing guerrilla warfare between European settlers and native Indians persisted, with the Indians chronically losing and being gradually pushed back onto smaller reservations on less desirable and less productive, agricultural land. The contrast with the relative peace and integration north of the border in Canada is a sobering one.

The 25th president, William McKinley (1843–1901), was assassinated shortly after the beginning of his second four year term of office in 1901. He had led America into war with Spain in 1898 which ended with the independence of Cuba, he had kept America on the Gold Standard, and he had used protective import tariffs to defend American agriculture and industry. These measures were put in place during his first term of office, following his election in the midst of a deep recession in 1896. The economy rapidly turned around with the protective tariffs and the economic reliance on gold. Also during his first term of office, the United States deposed the Queen of Hawaii and annexed the country following a request for American troops to stabilise the island after an extensive period of unrest.

McKinley was assassinated in 1901 and this may be traced back to the economic recession when a young man of Polish immigrant parentage lost his job in the mid-west and was slowly converted to anarchism; this was a fashionable contemporary political belief that had also been popular in Europe where some royalty and high officials had been targeted during the late 19th century. Assassination was not unknown to the citizens of America since Abraham Lincoln (1809–1865) had been assassinated by a southern confederate supporter in 1865 and less than twenty years after that the 20th President, James Garfield (1831–1881), had been assassinated in 1881 by an embittered protestor whom Garfield was not prepared to promote to federal officialdom. Garfield was only six months into his presidency, but during that time he had achieved a surprising amount of reforming legislation in addition to continuing as a consistent supporter of black emancipation.

Earlier in the century, James Monroe, fifth president of the United States (1758–1831), had enunciated the doctrine in 1832 that bears his name, and which later came to be formalised in 1850. The Monroe Doctrine was intended to deter any European efforts to colonise, or interfere with existing nations in North or

South America, and laid down that if such aggression or interference occurred, then the United States would side with any of the nations in the American hemisphere. Importantly, the Monroe Doctrine, when first propounded, indicated an acceptance by most Americans that conquest and annexation of Canada to the north would not be pursued, but the United States itself was not above acquiring further territory later in the 19th century starting with the annexation of territory from Mexico that would ultimately become the states of Utah, Nevada, California and most of Arizona. The United States was also happy to get involved in many of the wars of independence in South America.

Following unrest in Hawaii, and on the pretext of protecting American citizens and property, Hawaii had been annexed in 1898. Puerto Rico in the Caribbean, and Guam in the Pacific, were also ceded to the United States from Spain in 1898 under the terms of the Treaty of Paris, but even in the 21st century have not yet been admitted to full statehood. Cuba was ceded to the United States by Spain following the Spanish-American War in 1898, but was granted nominal independence four years later as a United States Protectorate, a situation which lasted until a coup in 1933.

The United States facilitated the secession of a narrow piece of land in Central America from Colombia in 1903 during the time of the 26th President, Theodore Roosevelt (1858–1919), thus allowing the construction of the Panama Canal to be built by the US army. The canal is a 51 mile (82 km) ship canal allowing passage for large ships between the Pacific and Atlantic Oceans which was begun under construction in 1881 by France, but was discontinued due to engineering difficulties and a high rate of tropical diseases among the workers. The United States took over the project in 1904 and opened the canal ten years later.

For most of the 20th century, the United States continued to control and oversee the canal, but in 1999, canal management was finally transferred to the Panamanian government. Most recently, the canal has been enlarged and diverted through new bigger locks to take much larger cargo vessels when the new locks opened in 2016. During this period, Roosevelt was awarded the Nobel Peace Prize for his efforts in ending the Russo-Japanese war of 1904/05.

The opening years of the 20th century saw increasing advances and social reforms in America. Education improved, corporate behaviour by "robber barons" was reigned in, and political gerrymandering and corruption were diminished. In keeping with the isolationist ideology of the Monroe Doctrine, America initially abstained from participation in the First World War only declaring war on Germany in April 1917 claiming that Germany had violated America's neutrality by attacking American shipping.

By this time however, Britain and Germany had almost bankrupted each other in the arms race that had become stalemated in northern Europe: in addition the war had greatly enriched the United States which was able to provide vast amounts of agricultural and armament exports, without committing itself to the costs of troops or arms. The eventual American intervention tipped the balance of hostilities against Germany which surrendered, with peace being declared on the 11th of November 1918, 18 months after the United States joined the conflict.

Possible further reading:
A History of the United States by Philip Jenkins (Palgrave Macmillan)

Chapter 82
Urbanisation

Early man lived a spartan hunter gatherer existence living off the bounties of the natural world. Life was hard and there was no spare time for what would be recognised today as rest or recreation. It was with the coming of agriculture that the process of urbanisation would finally start. The first step was the domestication of plants and animals, so that the small bands of hunter gatherers no longer needed to be constantly on the move in search of food. This led to fixed communities which could then grow gradually through time. The process happened at different times in different places across the world and was at least partly due to the location of communities in areas where the soil, geography and climate were favourable for the transition to farming.

The next phase occurred with the gradual improvement of plants and animals that had been domesticated using selective breeding, so that small communities were able to generate surpluses of produce, and therefore wealth. Only once a community produces more food than is required by its members, can that community afford to have some members whose working hours can be devoted to non-farming pursuits. Initially, at this level of development, the production of clothing, weapons and jewellery may become delegated to members of the community whose working hours can then be devoted to their new activity rather than to the production of food.

Because at this stage of development, the land is often populated with many small village communities, some of which have more of a surplus than others, there is the early appearance of a trading system between communities. The trade will not be limited to food or other items, but will include artisan items produced by members of a community supporting different crafts including tools, weapons and jewellery, and trade will also result in an interchange of ideas which can spread rapidly. The process would have been accelerated by the transport of goods by water, or using carts and horses.

In this way, villages may come to agglomerate together and result in what would then be recognised initially as a town, and in turn gradually develop into a city. In this context the city is probably defined as an area in which several thousand people live and work together. They will be surrounded by agricultural fields, where isolated communities, or individual workers, live and grow crops, but the farming may also involve workers from the city going out to surrounding areas to toil in agricultural pursuits each day.

Once the city has grown large enough, it will provide a critical mass for the development of further human endeavours, including the development of a priesthood and a ruling caste, or a system in which both functions are performed by one set of people. This in turn leads to the elaboration of religion, and with the growth of religion comes bigger and better civic buildings devoted to this communal religious activity. Writing and the keeping of records soon follow.

Cities with these characteristics have arisen in all the continents across the world except Australasia, thus early cities are known in China around 2,000 BC, and in the Indus Valley, Mesopotamia and Turkey at about the same time; such cities also arose in Central and Southern Asia, often in the former instance, due to the trade along the Silk Routes. Cities emerged in the Americas under the Olmec civilisation prior to 1,000 BC; the capital city of the Aztec civilisation before the Spanish conquest was Tenochtitlan, which is thought to have had a population of around a quarter of a million, greater than any contemporary European city.

In Africa, Great Zimbabwe was a flourishing city in the 12th to 15th century AD. Although many of these prehistoric cities were sizeable and boasted many artisans spread amongst a wide variety of trades, they were often overtaken by war or pestilence, and only some have survived on their original sites. They coexisted with a large surrounding hinterland of agricultural workers to support them.

Although most of these ancient cities were thriving concerns, the next phase of urbanisation had to wait until the onset of the Industrial Revolution. The early part of the Industrial Revolution produced machinery and factories where goods could be manufactured more rapidly, more accurately, and more economically than previously. The cities multiplied in size as poor workers migrated from their agricultural jobs, or self-sufficiency, in the surrounding countryside to become factory workers, or to run small artisan businesses in the new urban environment.

As part of the Industrial Revolution, the whole activity of farming became mechanised and much more efficient. On one side the science of breeding bigger and better crops and livestock gradually became well understood, and alongside this farming implements became mechanised and capable of dealing with much larger quantities of crops. The early combine harvesters, threshers and carts were initially all horse-drawn, but through the 19th century, first steam power, and finally the internal combustion engine, aided the process of bringing in the crops. Although the plough first appeared in the fourth millennium BC, it was not until about the beginning of the second millennium AD that a plough was devised with two wheels, a mould-board and a coulter: this plough was able to invert the soil creating a true furrow, and thus making a better seed bed. In addition, a collar to replace the old harness was devised which no longer pressed against the windpipe of the draft animal. Ploughs were still being pulled by oxen, which were much cheaper to keep than horses.

Jethro Tull (1674–1741), an English landowner from Berkshire, invented the horse-drawn seed drill around 1701, and several years later developed a horse, or oxen drawn, hoe. Farming had also been improved with the enclosures creating more easily managed fields. However, a different consequence of the enclosures and the industrialisation of farming was the resulting poverty caused amongst smallholders who were thrown off their land to become labourers, a process formalised in Scotland and known as the Highland Clearances.

William Cobbett (1763–1835), a reforming farmer, journalist and MP, remarked at this time that "when farmers became gentlemen their labourers became slaves". Many of these labourers migrated to the cities as part of the process of urbanisation, where they found jobs in factories and homes in overcrowded, poverty stricken and disease-ridden streets.

In previous generations, labourers had been scattered across the countryside in their agricultural jobs. Britain, at the beginning of the 19th century, passed Combination Acts, which made it illegal for labourers to combine together to achieve better working conditions, but these Acts were repealed in 1825. Some years later in 1832, six labourers from Tolpuddle in Dorset, formed the 'Friendly Society of Agricultural Labourers' in protest against diminishing wages due to the introduction of agricultural machinery. The labourers were prosecuted and sentenced to seven years transportation to Australia, however in due course, and after a public outcry, the judgement and banishment was overturned, and the Tolpuddle Martyrs returned to England after several years of exile.

With the concentration of workers together in towns and cities and larger factories, ease of organisation and association rapidly promoted trade unions. Initially, such unions were illegal, but eventually the whole Trade Union Movement, working for better conditions for workers, was legalised in 1871. Unions were formed amongst similar workers in different trades and crafts, and at the end of the 19th century they were instrumental in the election of MPs to represent workers. In 1900 the Labour Party was formed, rapidly overtaking the Liberal Party in Britain as the main opposition to the ruling Conservatives in the early 20th century.

At the same time as urbanisation was increasing rapidly in Britain through the 19th century, there was also increasing job specialisation. Most workers were adequately fed, housed and clothed, though conditions were still very basic by modern day standards. Social reformers worked through the 19th century to improve conditions both at work and at home. Public health gradually improved so lowering infant and childhood mortality and bringing greater longevity. In addition urbanisation brought with it a need for better transport: initially this was above ground, but as streets grew increasingly clogged up with people, horses, carts and carriages, London had come up with the solution of an underground railway, of which the first line was opened in 1863 (chapter 74).

As well as a transport need to move people around the city, there was also a need for citywide development of other services, notably the provision of water, sewage, gas and electricity. These services were put in place by the Victorians across British cities, with a consequent improvement in living standards and general quality of life. The availability of mass audiences gave rise to expansion of cultural activities, including theatre and music on a scale not seen since the spectacles of the Greek and Roman amphitheatres.

Unfortunately, expansion of human activity on this scale through the second half of the 19th century inevitably resulted in unforeseen additional consequences, apart from the original simple intentions: the result is known as pollution. In Victorian British cities the pollution was largely of air and water in rivers, but we have now come to recognise that pollution can be just as bad in terms of litter, noise, light or heat. Matters came to a head in the summer of 1858 in London which was known as 'the Great Stink', and the River Thames in particular was affected. Not only was the air foul and smog-like, due to the burning of enormous amounts of wood and coal for both domestic and industrial purposes, but there was also no organised system for the disposal of human, industrial or chemical waste.

The construction of an adequate sewer system was commenced under the direction of Sir Joseph Bazalgette (1819–1891), London's Chief Engineer, and took almost two decades to complete after starting in 1859. Although many sewers had been constructed before this time, their ability to cope had been overtaken by the speed of urbanisation and increasing population. London water supply through the Middle Ages had been largely by means of wooden water pipes, which were replaced with iron ones.

Daily living for many of the population was made easier by refrigeration and by the introduction of canned food, a process devised by the French confectioner Nicholas Appert (1749–1841) in France in the years after 1795, after observing that food cooked in sealed containers did not spoil provided the seal remained unbroken. The process was commercialised by another Frenchman in London with two British businessmen; it was initially time-consuming, cumbersome and expensive, but invaluable to explorers and armies.

It was rapidly taken up though and the first canning factory is reported in New York City in 1812. Refrigeration appeared somewhat later, and for the first half of the 19th century had only been feasible where ice could be harvested in winter and stored in ice-houses until the summer. Early refrigeration research was carried out by Benjamin Franklin amongst others, but the first practical method was devised in the 1850s by James Harrison (1816–1893), an English printer who had emigrated to Australia, and his method rapidly spread through the European nations and the Americas.

Fertilisers helped agricultural yields as part of the process to feed the new urban populations. Enormous amounts of seabird guano were mined from Pacific islands and atolls for use as agricultural fertiliser toward the end of the 19th century and between the two world wars, but at the same time chemists were discovering how to synthesise ammonia and phosphates through the 19th century and these processes were rapidly industrialised.

In ancient times, the population of the world some three or four millennia ago, was probably less than one hundred million. By the beginning of the first millennium AD this had only increased slightly to an estimated 130 million. Small areas of urbanisation had occurred bringing with them slums and ghettoes.

In the small village culture of those ancient times, common bloodlines and consanguinity was frequent, and close relationships between neighbours and families were also common. This contrasts with urban cultures today where bloodlines tend to be distant and familiarity with neighbours is often limited.

On a different plane, in small villages communal behaviour and cooperation tend to be the rule, whilst in urban communities behaviour becomes much more competitive and crime tends to increase as it is cloaked by the anonymity of a large conurbation. The urban population of the United Kingdom was about 10% of the country's total in 1800, but due to the Industrial Revolution had increased to 75% by 1900.

Today, the concept of a megacity is often discussed; interestingly one area where this is occurring is the Po River delta in China, where trade and commerce commenced with the founding of the Dutch centre of Macau, and the British centre of Hong Kong. Today the Po River delta in China houses seven cities of more than 10 million inhabitants, all of which appear to be rapidly running together to form an indisputable megacity. Elsewhere the world now boasts the cities of Delhi and Tokyo both approaching 40 million inhabitants, and there are several cities of over twenty million inhabitants, mainly in China and South-East Asia, but also further afield; Mexico City, Sao Paolo in Brazil, New York City, Lagos, and Cairo have all expanded to unwieldy sizes.

Sheer size of numbers however is insufficient to indicate the possible accompanying problems, the density of the population, recorded as the number of people living in each square kilometre, is a more meaningful, and indeed alarming, concept. Present day London houses about five and a half thousand inhabitants per square kilometre, whilst New York City manages double this number, but these figures pale into insignificance against some of the cities of South-East Asia including Macao, Calcutta, Rawalpindi and Peshawar with well over twenty thousand inhabitants per square kilometre.

The slums, ghettos and overcrowding that this situation produces has frequently been documented as resulting in social deprivation, poverty and crime statistics. Some of the answers to this problem must include population control (chapter 99), reversal of the drift to urbanisation, and better planning of our cities of the future.

Possible further reading:
The Great Cities in History by John Julius Norwich (Thames & Hudson)

Chapter 83
Edwardian England 1901–14

When Edward VII came to the throne after his mother, Queen Victoria, died in 1901, Europe was gradually becoming less stable. Many European states were grappling with internal problems, perhaps not unexpectedly since their coalescence into our modern version of Europe was still young. British Government at the end of Victoria's reign had been solidly Tory under Lord Salisbury (1830–1903), the last Prime Minister to head a government from the Lords, who in turn passed it on to his nephew, Arthur Balfour (1838–1930). The Tories lost to the Liberals in the 1904 General Election, presaging a crumbling of the recognisable edifice and party divisions which had ruled the country for much of Victoria's reign.

Germany had only been brought together by a canny statesman in 1871 (chapter 80). Otto Von Bismarck (1815–1898) had been able to use victory in war over France in 1870, to create Germany as a Federal State, and in 1871 the King of Prussia, Wilhelm I accepted the crown as German Emperor over the state which became known as the Second Reich, since it replaced a previous medieval German Federation which now became known as the First Reich (or Holy Roman Empire, lasting from 962–1806). The period from 1933 under Hitler to the end of the second World War is known as the Third Reich.

Through the same period of time, Italy had also been progressing towards agglomeration as a single entity from its previous existence as a multiplicity of smaller states. Italian coalescence came about in part because of the manoeuvring of the Kingdoms of Sardinia and Prussia, each of which had pursued a path of expansion at the expense of Austria. France was ruled at the time by another Napoleon; this one called himself the Third, although Napoleon II really only existed in fantasy because he was a child and had never ruled.

Napoleon III was the nephew of Bonaparte, and had been elected President of the Second Republic, only to overrule the constitution in a coup d'état. He was able to throw his weight behind the Prime Minster of Sardinia and Northern Italy, the Count of Cavour (1810–1861), and also behind Otto Von Bismarck, the Prime Minister of Prussia. Cavour died in 1861 having seen Italy's first War of Independence fail in 1848/49. However, Italy's second War of Independence in 1859, in which Sardinia and France under Napoleon III defeated Austria, resulted in the gradual acceptance of Italy as a nation. In this way the country became largely united in 1871 with Rome as its capital, though with the Vatican State remaining as a tiny independent entity within the city.

Giuseppe Garibaldi (1807–1882) also played a large part in the foundation of Italy. He is recognised as a towering figure in the 'Risorgimento' (resurgence, or resurrection, and reunification), a process of bringing Italy together under a single rule following the 1815 Treaty of Vienna and achieving completion in 1871. Garibaldi gained his military experience in the South American Wars of Independence in Brazil and Uruguay and returned from South America to join the first Italian War of Independence in 1848.

When the war was over, Garibaldi spent some years in exile, returning to Europe in 1854, initially staying in the north of England before returning to Italy to join the second Italian War of Independence between France and Sardinia against Prussia. After victory in this war, Garibaldi continued to the south of Italy, leading an expedition to take over Sicily, which was then incorporated into the newly unified Italy.

As an aside, it is interesting to note that the final battle in which France and Sardinia defeated Austria in 1859, the Battle of Solferino, was the occasion which led a Swiss observer of the battle, Henri Dunant (1828–1910), to lay the foundations for the Red Cross and the Geneva Convention on the rules of war. He was so appalled by the atrocities and treatment of the wounded and prisoners that the organisation was founded with the object of protecting civilians, and providing a code of conduct for the combatants. The Red Cross, and its Islamic cousin the Red Crescent, organised somewhat later in 1876, have steadily increased their work to help both civilians and combatants in wars, both official and unofficial, ever since that time.

The Red Cross symbol is a colour reversal of the Swiss flag, and similarly the Red Crescent is a colour reversal of the symbol of the Ottoman Empire. The Geneva Convention, a code of conduct for war and prisoners, was signed by twelve European nations in 1864, but again has continued to develop and was most recently updated after the Second World War in 1949, with 196 countries across the globe becoming signatories.

During all this turmoil in continental Europe, Britain was becoming internally more prosperous at all levels of society. The British Empire had by this time grown to a considerable size, comprising over 400 million people, or 23% of the world population at the beginning of the first World War. The Royal Navy required to defend the Empire had been built up to a large size, and a similar size of merchant navy was also thriving and carrying the majority of maritime trade around the world. However, by the end of the century, the newly reorganised Europe was catching up.

France and Germany were pioneering the manufacture of cars in a fledgling industry which had not taken root in Britain. The United States was also forging ahead with new industries, and in particular would move into the new century beginning to manufacture both cars and planes. Britain was feeling threatened by Germany, which was envious of the British Royal Navy and Merchant Navy, and was building up its own maritime power. The situation resulted in a treaty, the Entente Cordiale, signed between Britain and France in 1904 with the express purpose of trying to contain German expansion and aggression.

At the same time, the British government was spending just over half its total budget on defence and only 10% on education, with the other 35% devoted to general public works, including National Insurance which was started in 1911. There was still a national reliance on the great natural reserves within the British Isles of coal and iron ore. As the perception of German aggression continued to increase, a second Entente Cordiale was signed in 1907 which included Russia, a nation which also had a considerable interest in containing German territorial ambitions.

The political landscape changed abruptly in 1904 in Britain when Henry Campbell Bannerman came into office with his Liberal Party following a landslide victory after which he could rely on 400 MPs against the Tories 157, the administration also included 29 Labour MPs. Campbell Bannerman (1836–1908) was Prime Minister for three years, but did not enjoy good health and died very shortly after resigning office. Herbert Asquith (1852–1928) had already served as Chancellor of the Exchequer under Campbell Bannerman and replaced him as Prime Minister until midway through the Great War when he could no longer hold his cabinet together.

He was succeeded as Chancellor by David Lloyd George (1863–1945), a fiery Welshman who had been Secretary for War under Asquith. Under Asquith and Lloyd George, apart from war matters, a great reforming period was ushered in which laid the foundations of an early welfare state, provided the first old age pensions, and also started free school meals and clinics, to add to National Insurance which had started in 1911. This was all made possible by diminishing spending on defence and by increasing income tax, so that by 1909 income tax for those earning less than £5,000 was set at 1 shilling and 6 pence in the pound (7½ pence), whilst it was 2 shillings (10 pence) for those with earned incomes over £5,000.

Taxation was introduced for the first time on land, tobacco, alcohol and petrol. The earliest precursor of the Health Service would not follow until 1918 when the Ministry of Health was established and took the first steps towards the present National Health Service under (Lord) Christopher Addison (1869–1951), a qualified doctor and Minister of Health.

There was considerable difference in attitude between the two parliamentary chambers, with the House of Lords refusing to pass budgets and welfare measures proposed by the Commons in 1910, and therefore an election was called specifically to restrict the power of the Lords to revise Parliamentary Bills initiated in the Commons. Asquith was returned but with a minority government from this election, though by now the House of Commons included 40 Labour MPs and 82 Irish MPs. To overcome the impasse imposed by his minority government Asquith requested that 250 extra Liberal peers be appointed to the Upper House which the old King, George V, initially hesitated to do, but George died in 1910 to be succeeded by his son Edward VIII, who then agreed to the request for additional Liberal peers.

Although Asquith had been returned in the election of 1910, he remained dependent for his majority on those 40 Labour and 82 Irish MPs, but welfare spending was saved. In those turbulent times social unrest continued with railway workers, dock workers and seamen all participating in disruptive strikes. Suffragettes and suffragists (who campaigned within the law) were campaigning for the vote for women (chapter 88).

The three smaller members of the United Kingdom – Wales, Scotland and Ireland – continued to be represented by MPs at Westminster, but the Irish in particular were demanding Home Rule, and in view of their strength in parliamentary numbers, a new Home Rule Bill for Ireland was put forward by the Commons, but again opposed by the Lords. The Bill was therefore delayed until 1914, but by that time the First World War was starting and the Bill's implementation was suspended for the duration of the war. Talks also continued to find a solution to the great conundrum with the majority of southern Roman Catholic Ireland wishing for Home Rule, and the six northern Protestant counties of Ulster set firmly against it (these were the descendants of Cromwell's plantations).

Despite British parliamentary action to grant home rule to Ireland, which had only been delayed because of the war, a small number of Irish Republicans rebelled in an armed Easter Rising in April 1916. Almost 500 people died, half unarmed civilians, one third British soldiers and some 66 Irish Republicans, while the British army, which included tens of thousands of Irish volunteers, put down the rebellion. Independence was granted in the aftermath of the war.

In June 1914, a train of events had led into the First World War. The heir to the Austro-Hungarian throne, Archduke Franz Ferdinand of Austria, was assassinated in Sarajevo in Serbia by a Serbian nationalist, which set in the motion the various alliances and ententes that nations had signed in the previous decade. Despite the fact that this was murder by an individual anarchist, Austria felt obliged to punish Serbia, whereupon Russia in turn mobilised in support of Serbia, thus activating Austria's alliance with Germany. The German Kaiser decided this was the moment to test the Entente Cordiale between France, Britain and Russia, and declared war on Russia and France.

These moves were all unexpected, and Germany then invaded Belgium before France or Russia could mobilise their armies, and before Britain could either mobilise or move troops across the Channel. Britain had been one of the signatories at the creation of Belgium in 1831, guaranteeing its neutrality, and was now confronted by the German army and navy in control of the North Sea and Channel ports and able to block British trade, imports and exports, so that when the Kaiser's armies invaded Belgium Britain finally responded by declaring war on Germany, a war that would become largely static, but would last for four years before all parties could find a suitable way out of it.

Thus, by the beginning of the First World War in 1914, Europe had become the pre-eminent part of the globe. The Americas, North and South, with Australasia were essentially European, with their native populations decimated and hardly contributing to the new era. In addition, across the world, the effect of the British dominions, including South Africa, India, Australia and New Zealand, had all added to the Europeanisation of the planet. China was locked on the margin and trying to avoid integration into world affairs, including trade. Africa was divided into many states which did not cooperate with each other, and did not contribute significantly to world trade or affairs. By contrast European populations across the globe were now accustomed to change, and were a great driver of what was seen as progress. At the same time in terms of world affairs, the United States had not yet consolidated, and was not greatly involved in world affairs until 1917 when it joined in the First World War against Germany.

Up to this point, Europe had been a great driver of world history for several centuries, with an unmatched achievement of material and industrial development over the previous century. Following the end of the First World War European culture then blurred into that of the rest of the world. European political structures and national boundaries had been largely settled following the Congress of Vienna in 1815, and subsequent manoeuvrings over the next 50 years.

Two great empires, Austro-Hungary and the Ottoman Empire, did not accept the new identity of states, and partly as a consequence, collapsed after First World War. Some western nations within Europe enjoyed good geographical definition; namely: Portugal, Spain, France, the United Kingdom and Scandinavia, which aided their integrity and preservation through the centuries (see chapter 86).

Once peace, prosperity, and the new industrialisation and public health, ushered in the prosperous 19th century for Europe it is interesting to note that in 1880 only three European cities, London, Paris and Berlin had over one million inhabitants. Twenty years later, at the turn of the century, four more had been added with Glasgow, Vienna, Moscow and St Petersburg all greatly expanded. The improvement in transport and electrification would continue this great increase in building suburbs. It is also perhaps important to note that one-third of the world's benign agricultural land lies in Europe, while the importance of the early raw mineral resources of the Industrial Revolution, namely coal and iron, were additional vital early beneficent features of European expansion and advancement.

Possible further reading:
The Edwardians by JB Priestley (Heinemann)

Chapter 84
Empires

The known history of the civilised world is replete with examples of empires, which have existed since the early days of civilisation, and since prominent and successful rulers tried to extend their territorial ambitions. Where a group of nations or states is ruled over by one state from among them, this becomes known as an empire. Such an entity may include either loose or tight control from the centre, and may include differing nationalities or ethnic groups within it. Empires have been set up either by force, or by coercion in some way, such as the need for standardisation of politics, religion or culture: more recently empires have been formed to promote trade, either in the form the export of manufactured items from the central nation, as in the British Empire in the 19th century, or for the purposes of exploitation of natural resources from the peripheral nations.

A further, and almost accidental, founding of an empire may occur due to colonisation when the mother nation exports colonists to another part of the world which is relatively under populated: in these circumstances the colonists may depart of their own accord to escape a religious or political system in which they feel unable to continue to live, or they may be unwilling convicts, as in the case of Australia; in later times colonists may have been attracted by what were perceived to be better opportunities.

The justification for the founding of an empire in the past has been varied and often due to multiple reasons. Early man, like many other animals, was undoubtedly territorial. This has carried over into more modern times as a feeling for the need for more territory, particularly as population increased. Sometimes the driving ambition seems to be a simple quest for more power, but often the quest for territory and power seem to blend together, especially where the territory will bring either desirable natural resources, including gold and silver which the Spanish saw as the benefit from the New World, or a perception that the extra territory would simply bring in increased tithes or taxes thereby further enriching the emperor or the central state.

Security has often been cited in the valuing of an empire, particularly where the original nation state was surrounded by hostile adjacent states and justified the takeover of the surrounding states to provide peace of mind. Such acquisition of the additional territory by force sometimes backfired, and not only failed to confer security but actually resulted in the overthrow of the central state itself. Promotion of trade has also been the driving force, as in the case of Britain where the Industrial Revolution had thrown up the ability to mass manufacture many goods, so that expansion of the market for those goods was necessary.

Colonisation has already been mentioned, and once the ability to explore the world was opened up by exploration to the Americas and to the Far East, colonists followed (chapters 31–33). The early colonists or settlers sometimes returned to the mother country after exploration, possibly after generating a lot of wealth, and sometimes stayed to settle if they found that the new climate and opportunities were to their liking. Sometimes also the early settlers were woefully ill-equipped for life in their new surroundings, and history is again full of records of settled communities that were decimated or sometimes wiped out by starvation or disease.

The political organisation of an empire can be either loose or much more strict. Loose political alliances, which are often voluntary, have often proved more satisfactory, but it must be the case that exploitation of the satellite nations cannot be too overt and the satellite nations must continue to derive some form of benefit from the central nation. The alternative way to maintain an empire is by military occupation and subjugation, which can sometimes be relatively discreet and not too oppressive. Military subjugation does however require permanent occupation and a large standing army. This in turn drains resources from the central nation, and raises the cost of empire. Eventually, the difficulties of finding the sheer number of troops required become very high. Even if the satellite nations have provided some of the troops, there is always a concern about mutiny and desertion, and all these factors led to the Roman Empire over-extending itself and finally being unable to protect its borders and its citizens. Military superiority is highly advantageous at the start of a conquest, but such technologies will gradually diffuse down through the conquered nations resulting in difficulties maintaining a subjugated population.

The length of time for Ih empires have lasted is highly variable. It often depends on the charisma and authority of the emperor himself, or at least the political and military elite who surround him at the centre. Empires have extended for many generations, particularly where the ethos and individual family members have subordinated their roles to that of the emperor. Within an emperor's family however two scenarios have been common in the past, the first of these is where more than one individual in the next generation feels that he or she should assume the emperor's mantel on his demise, and the second is where the emperor himself decides to try and distribute his responsibilities and his position between several of his children. Charlemagne did this at the beginning of the 9th century, but appears to have assessed his sons incorrectly as they set to squabbling after he died and were responsible for the breakup of his empire. Empires have fallen because of coups by either members of the emperor's inner circle, or by more distant and ambitious followers. Some emperors have failed to produce an heir leaving the empire to internal strife, and sometimes those inheriting the mantel of an autocratic emperor possessed neither the charisma, the ruthlessness, nor the military ability or ruthlessness to keep the empire on track.

In ancient times, Upper and Lower Egypt were united by King Narmer in an early empire which led into the Egyptian dynasties following 3,000 BC. Later, around 2,400 BC, the Akkadian Empire came together under Sargon of Akkat in an empire which included much of Mesopotamia. Although Sargon fused many of the Sumerian city states together, his Empire lapsed into revolt after his death and then disintegrated. Somewhat later King Hammurabi again managed to unite all of Mesopotamia under his control, he is remembered by his Code of Laws (chapter 4).

In another part of the world, the Chinese civilisation gradually came together, and the first empire that is well documented is that of the Shang dynasty commencing around 1500 BC. That was succeeded by the Chau Empire around 1100 BC, before disintegrating into many small states which comprised China for the next 500 years.

The Persian Empire was established by Cyrus the Great in 550 BC when he conquered the adjacent states of Media, Lydia and Babylonia (chapter 10). This first Persian or Achaemenid empire grew out of the smaller empire of the Medes and extended across the Middle East to include North Africa, Egypt, and Turkey together with what we now recognise as Pakistan and Afghanistan. The Achaemenid Empire was conquered by Alexander the Great, commencing in 334 BC when he conquered all of the Achaemenid territory, but then died at the early age of 32, possibly of infection or malaria (though some accounts suggest that he was poisoned). He had no heirs, and the Empire then split up into warring factions ruled by Alexander's various provincial governors, who fought each other in the same way as siblings might.

In India, after Alexander, Chandragupta Maurya established an empire in 322 BC that subsequently expanded enormously to take in most of what is today India, Bangladesh, Pakistan, and Afghanistan. The Empire included north-western provinces ruled by some of Alexander's governors after he died. After Chandragupta Maurya's death in 297 BC the empire continued under Ashoka, and after his death in 232 BC the Empire continued for another 50 years before succumbing to a rival Indian dynasty who established the Shunga Empire (chapter 7). The Shunga Empire was followed by two other dynasties, that of Karva and then the Guptas, with this last dynasty being finally over run by the Huns coming from the north in the middle of the 6th century AD.

Probably the best-known empire of ancient times was that of the Romans. Although much of our European intellectual and cultural heritage comes to us from the Greeks through the Romans, the Greeks themselves did not build an empire, and existed as a consortium of city states. The Roman Empire grew out of the previous Roman Republic which had been gradually developing and growing through the previous 500 years. The Empire was at its maximum geographical extent under the rule of Trajan who died in 117 AD. Thereafter, the Empire slowly declined, partly due to the difficulty and expense of maintaining a large standing army to keep the empire under control with its frequent rebellions and uprisings. The process of collapse was accelerated by the sacking of Rome in 410 by the Visigoths, and again in 455 by the Vandals, when Roman military power was declining and dispersed over a large geographical area. The Empire limped on thereafter as the Eastern Roman Empire eventually succumbing to conquest by the Ottoman Turks in 1415.

On the other side of the world, totally unknown to Europe, India or China at the time, civilisation was steadily developing in the Americas. The Olmec civilisation, indeed Empire, appears to have come into existence around the 1st century BC existing in much of Central America and Mexico. An Aztec Empire appears much later around 1250 AD with remarkable central control and organisation, together with transport throughout the Andes considering that this geographical area is not particularly suited for being able to support a large population from its agriculture, the climate is also adverse. The Incas appear in an Empire based on much of the northern Andes, taking over from the Aztecs, and incorporating many of their beliefs. In this instance these empires disappeared as the conquistadors of Spain overran native populations in the 15th and 16th centuries. It was an unequal battle between an advanced European civilisation with firearms, and a sophisticated stone age people who stood no chance of avoiding defeat.

In Europe, the Eastern Roman Empire, which continued the customs of Rome once the Western Empire was lost after the sacking of Rome, was centred on Constantinople as its capital city and existed as a very powerful economic and cultural grouping based around the eastern Mediterranean including Greece, Turkey, the Middle Eastern states, Egypt and some of the coast of North Africa. It was at its maximum geographical extent in the middle of the 6th century and had Christianity as its official state religion which gradually morphed into what we know today as the Greek Orthodox version of Christianity with an eastern Pope enthroned in Constantinople.

The sacking of Constantinople during the fourth crusade in 1204 signalled the beginning of the end, and Constantinople finally fell to the Ottoman or Turkish Empire in 1453. The Ottoman Empire had been founded at the end of the 13th century and gradually expanded militarily, culminating in the defeat of Constantinople in 1453. The Empire continued to expand both east of Turkey and south along the sides of the Red Sea and along the coast of North Africa, reaching its maximum extent at the end of the 17th century.

Following this, the Empire gradually declined as a consequence of many battles against European powers. The Empire became allies of Germany at the time of the First World War hoping to recover lost territory, but during the war several episodes of genocide against Armenians, Greeks and Syrians resulted in dissolution of the Empire at the end of the First War and the formation of the new secular state of Turkey.

While the Ottoman Empire was involved in internal European struggles, the western nations of Europe entered a colonial period in the 19th century. The process was given momentum by the earlier discovery of the Americas with Spain, Portugal, France, the Netherlands and Britain all joining a rush to colonise the New World. Exploration east was also a prominent feature of this colonial period with British and Dutch settlements extending into South-East Asia, and with the British continuing on to Australia and New Zealand. Most of these Empires have now disappeared as former colonies reached the size where independence and nationhood became appropriate, though it was often only achieved through bitter rebellion and warfare.

The American colonies were the first to go after a period of discord over taxation by the central government in London. More recently enlightenment has changed colonies into self-governing nations, the largest of which, Canada, South Africa, India, Australia and New Zealand, all initially became members of what was rechristened the British Commonwealth of Nations. India in particular had been taken over and administered with the East India Company first controlling the region, but the British government then took over in 1857. The main object was trade and Britain put in infrastructure in the form of railways, roads, schools and hospitals, but without significant colonisation, though with a central core of expatriate civil servants, most of whom returned to Britain at the end of their careers.

India was unusual in that it was incorporated into the British Empire, not to settle colonists, but as a source of raw material and a recipient market for trade; few Britons came as colonists and even fewer stayed in the long term. Only a few very small colonies remain as British protectorates due to their size, though in most respects they are now self-governing. In the 20th century the Russian Empire was short lived, while the Chinese Empire is still young and trying to expand.

One of the difficulties with empires is the differences in distribution of resources, natural, agricultural and climatic, so that when the empire splits up or disbands the new countries are often left with very unequal resources following a time when the central empire had tended to even out such matters. Empires have usually split into smaller more viable units, politically and economically, especially since different nations within the empire may not share much in common either in terms of culture or commerce and their subsequent future may depend on the number of residual colonists planted during the period of empire, as in South America where some modern countries have a population with a very high level of European ancestry. In the long term however an empire seems to be an inherently unstable construct which is often highly dependent on a charismatic individual at the top.

Possible further reading:
Empire by Niall Ferguson (Penguin)

Chapter 85
Emancipation

The word emancipation is probably most often used in a political context. The more broad definition implies release from restraint, bondage or disability of any description. In ancient, and indeed medieval times, emancipation simply did not exist; government was promulgated according to the whims of a single individual, Emperor, King, Queen or someone similar and no one was emancipated. In the first instance, we will discuss political emancipation, but later in this chapter the discussion will be extended to emancipation from religious discrimination and from racial discrimination or slavery, together with emancipation for women; it is also necessary to consider finally the subject of human rights.

Emancipation, particularly in the political sense, is often traced back to Magna Carta (chapter 29). This 'Great Charter' was signed by King John in 1215 when he had been brought by his barons to sign a proclamation of protection against unfair justice, and to provide a promise of a fair trial to an accused individual. In the years following the signing both King John and the Barons failed to honour their respective promises.

However, subsequent British monarchs have repeated the pledge through the years and the benefits of Magna Carta have steadily been extended to the less privileged and less affluent sections of society. In its time it was a giant step forward both in fact and in thinking, since the monarch had finally conceded that those who ruled should do so honestly and justly and not be above the laws which applied to everyone else.

It was to be over four and a half centuries before a further attempt to deal with the relationships between a monarch and his subjects came up again. In the Declaration of Rights the British Parliament presented a document to William and Mary in 1689 inviting them to become joint rulers of England. The Declaration lays down the limits of the powers of the monarchy and also sets out the rights of parliament, including the principle of free elections and freedom of speech. The Declaration came about following the overthrow of King James II, and invasion by William of Orange with a Dutch fleet and military backing. The Bill outlined very specifically the privileges of the monarchy and similarly the authority and rights of parliament. In turn this Bill of Rights led on one hundred years later to the American Bill of Rights and the Declaration of Independence in 1789.

At the same time in 1789, in France, the National Constituent Assembly passed the Declaration of the Rights of Man and of the Citizen at the beginning of the Revolution (chapter 60). Much of this document owes its genesis to the American Thomas Jefferson working with the French General Lafayette (1757–1834). Jefferson used much of the material from the Virginia Declaration of Rights a decade earlier. Despite the high-minded principles of the Declaration, France descended into the anarchy of revolution over the next few years, but the Declaration of Rights has remained intact and has been used each time the French nation has re-established itself, so it is included in the constitution of the Fourth French Republic, promulgated after the Second World War in 1946, and again later in 1958, at the start of Fifth Republic.

The process of securing and perpetuating political and individual emancipation has continued since that time, but only after a long interval and two world wars, has it been found necessary to expand the Declaration. Following the Second World War the United Nations issued a 'Universal Declaration' in 1948, which was followed in 1953 by a European Convention on Human Rights, which also established the European Court of Human Rights.

Most recently, an 'International Covenant' was declared by the United Nations in 1966 and this was further updated in the Vienna Declaration of 1993. In this context, some people have recognised increasing development and refinement of human rights. This has been developed largely since the Second World War and owes its importance both to the general atrocities of war that occurred, but also in particular to the aftermath of details of the Holocaust, which only became fully apparent once the conflict was over.

Three stages of development of human rights have been recognised: the first of these applies mainly to civil and political rights. Two names are important here, that of John Locke (1632–1704) who was an English physician and philosopher whose thinking was influential with both the American Revolutionaries and the contemporary French thinkers, including Voltaire and Rousseau; and secondly that of Francis Hutcheson (1694–1746), an Irish clergyman who moved to become one of the early Fathers of the Scottish Enlightenment teaching philosophy at the University of Glasgow. The second generation of human rights is about equality in the economic, social and cultural context. The third generation of human rights has been debated much more and is by no means universally agreed; it relates to lesser "rights" such as peace and the environment: it may perhaps be recognised more as a wish list for an ideal society than as an entitlement for individual humans. It will be noted that this three generation concept corresponds loosely to the three demands of the French Revolutionaries in 1789, namely liberté, égalité, fraternité. More recently than the French Revolution, Karl Marx in the second half of the 19th century, had advocated the equal status of all individual citizens before the law, regardless of religion, property or other private characteristics (which we would now recognise as including race and gender).

Back in time, a second type of emancipation is release from slavery. Many cultures through time have practised slavery and indeed some still do (chapter

59). A system of slavery was in existence throughout much of the early civilisation that arose in the Fertile Crescent and continued through and into classical antiquity under both Greek and Roman civilisations. For these latter two, some redeeming features may be discerned, particularly the fact that slaves were not necessarily demeaned and confined to menial tasks, the Greeks in particular recognised the intellectual and teaching contributions of many who were technically slaves: the Romans promoted a system where slaves could at least earn or buy their freedom under certain circumstances.

In the Middle Ages, in the African world, there was considerable slave trading internally and to the outside world; additionally and less widely recognised, there was a white slave trade from Europe southwards (hence the name "Slav" given to middle Europeans captured and trafficked south). It was the first part of the 19th century before a campaign in Britain and other parts of Europe finally condemned slavery as outrageous and impermissible. Also during the 19th century the gradual emancipation and spread of voting rights came to a slowly increasing number of individuals, men it is to be noted and not women.

Serfdom in Russia was abolished in 1861, two years before Lincoln introduced a similar measure in America. Gradually the necessary qualifications for a political vote were extended, and the early qualifications, which required substantial ownership of property, were gradually reduced, until by the early 20th century all adult males had achieved the vote.

However, the extension of voting rights was slow to be extended to women. In the English-speaking world, the vote was first extended to women who owned property, who could vote in the Isle of Man elections in 1881. New Zealand followed by giving the vote to all women in 1893. After the prominent contribution of women in the First World War in Britain, women over 30 achieved a vote if they owned property in 1918, and ten years later the vote was extended to all women over the age of 21. Initially, in Britain, the campaign had been pursued energetically, and at times violently, by women suffragettes before the First World War, with Emmeline Pankhurst (1858–1928) being the most prominent protester in those early years.

Female emancipation has been chronically slow, with women being admitted to universities and to the professions in Europe only towards the end of the 19th century, and with female numbers only matching those of men by the end of the 20th century. In many other parts of the world, female emancipation still lags far behind this, with Islamic societies in particular still proving slow at the turn of the 20th century to educate, let alone emancipate, women. Japan made a good start emancipating women in the 1860s following the Meiji restoration of 1868, but by the beginning of the 20th century, China was still not schooling its girls. At this time, the urge to educate and emancipate women was still largely a middle class European movement.

Since alterations in the law, and public protest and enlightenment, most western nations now have full electoral emancipation for women. The age at which men and women can vote is invariably the same, but can vary between 16 and 21, and can also depend on whether the vote is for local or national elections.

In Second and Third World countries, the level of female emancipation at the beginning of the 21st century remains very variable and often incomplete. It still seems curious that throughout history, at different times and in different places and societies, when no appropriate man was available, then women as widows, sisters or daughters, have succeeded to the highest offices and been successful and unquestioned (though not in Greek or Roman times). While the great mass of women remained unemancipated; no one through the years has noted or disagreed with this inconsistency.

Religious emancipation has been extremely variable throughout the world. In Britain King Henry VIII took the country away from Roman Catholicism and Papal jurisdiction at the time of the Reformation in the mid-1500s. Not everyone was anxious to become protestant and the catholic religion went underground for several decades with Catholics being subject to numerous restrictions, in particular being forbidden to purchase land, to hold civil office, to hold seats in parliament or to join the military. The Gunpowder Plot in 1605 reinforced the perception of Catholics existing as a dangerous and subversive entity within the country, and it took a long while for such attitudes to subside.

The Relief Act of 1778 finally allowed Catholics in Britain to acquire land officially and to practice their religion without penalty. The Act of Union in 1801 uniting Great Britain with Ireland failed to emancipate Catholics due to a combination of powerful Irish and British protestants, and the equally powerful and anti-Catholic George III. Finally however, after energetic campaigning by the Irish lawyer Daniel O'Donnell (1775–1847), parliament under the British Prime Minister, the Duke of Wellington, passed the Emancipation Act of 1829. Following this Catholic freedoms in England were complete, except that Catholics were still barred from ascending the throne.

In contemporary terms, the French state became officially both anti-monarchist and anti-Christian during the last decade of the 18th century during the Revolution. Similar changes in Germany in the struggle between the Catholic Church and the state continued into the beginning of the 20th century alongside many other European countries, including Belgium, Holland, Spain and Italy. Across the Atlantic in North America the same considerations did not apply since many of the early settlers had left Britain or elsewhere in Europe to avoid religious persecution and were often of Protestant faiths, but in most South American countries, Catholicism has remained a bastion of resistance against female emancipation, especially within the catholic church.

The Jews in Europe have a highly disturbing history of persecutions and restrictions. They were often forced to live in small enclaves, finding work as financiers, bankers and merchants. Jews were often blamed for the political and financial disasters in various countries and as a consequence were subject to massacres; then in the 13th to 15th centuries there were massive expulsions of Jews from France, Germany, England and Spain, and many moved to eastern Europe, to Poland in particular.

With the Enlightenment, gradual emancipation of Jews followed, and in the early years of the Revolution France became the first European country to emancipate its Jewish population, following Poland some four centuries earlier. Other European nations were slower to emancipate their Jewish population but this followed in the middle years of the 19th century. Unfortunately this record of emancipation was to be completely negated in the Holocaust later in the 20th century under Hitler.

In other parts of the world, emancipation or the lack of it, has been reflected in the continuing divide in some national populations, notably between Muslims of Shia and Sunni persuasions, and between the Hindu and Muslim populations in India which necessitated the division into the separate countries of India and Pakistan after the Second World War, and also in the caste system in India itself.

In USA, emancipation has been a long time coming, given the divide between the voluntary white emigrants from Europe and the black captured slaves from Africa. An abrupt change occurred at the end of the Civil War when Abraham Lincoln issued a Presidential Proclamation on the 1st of January 1863 legally freeing slaves. This Presidential order did not pass through the US Congress and did not apply in the southern Confederate states who were still fighting the northern states.

Discrimination and segregation persisted for a further century, and the legal segregation of schools was only stopped by a Supreme Court decision in 1954, with all public segregation finally abolished by the Civil Rights Act of 1964 following extensive protests and demonstrations, with Martin Luther King (1929–1968) being the most prominent campaigner. Even this has not yet managed to abolish all the problems between the races in America.

In South Africa the separation of black and white races was legally enforced under the name of 'apartheid' by the governing National Party from 1948 to 1991, when finally, after years of protest, rapprochement between the white national party and the African National congress was agreed and South Africa had its first black president in Nelson Mandela (1918–2013), elected in 1994. In other countries the emancipation of native communities, particularly in the Americas and Australasia has only come about lately during the 20th century.

In many countries of the world the concepts of emancipation and segregation have now been subsumed into a larger understanding of acceptable patterns of behaviour, known as Human Rights. These Rights have been enumerated from ancient times as we have seen, starting with the Legal Code of Hammurabi some 4,000 years ago, and often reiterated in different forms, and with different emphasis, through succeeding generations. More recently matters were grossly simplified and articulated in the French Revolution as "liberté, égalité, fraternité". This simplification made an excellent revolutionary sound bite 200 years ago that followed the thinking of some early Christian philosophers, and the subsequent Enlightenment thinking of such individuals as Sir Francis Bacon (1561–1626), John Locke (1632–1704), Francis Hutcheson (1694–1746), and John Stuart Mill (1806–1873), who was the first to call for women's suffrage in Britain, Jean-Jacques Burlemaqui (1694–1748) from Switzerland, and Voltaire (1694–1778) and Rousseau (1712–1778) in France.

As noted earlier recently human rights have been divided into First, Second and Third Generation Rights reflecting the progression of society and the order in which such Rights have been defined and introduced. First Generation Rights are generally those of civil and political privileges. Second Generation Rights are somewhat lesser, and are defined as equality of opportunities, economic, social and cultural, while Third Generation Rights are largely a wish list for the future development of Western Society. Such proclamations of Rights usually omit to emphasise that rights in any context also bring responsibilities, which also need to be defined.

Possible further reading:
Lincoln's Hundred Days by Louis P Masur (OUP)

Chapter 86
Legal Systems

Human societies have always required a code of conduct to promote people living together in harmony, which by extension places restrictions on certain activities, together with mediating between individuals. The need for such formal rules probably only became apparent when humans had to give up the erratic and nomadic lifestyle and settle into small communities. Once these communities became bigger the ruler, chief or king often seems to have felt obliged to set down laws in writing. As societies and communities became larger, the rules often became more extensive and more complicated covering more aspects of each individual's life. The reverse of such rules laid down in legal systems is that the individual also has rights with respect to the society in which he or she lives.

Today, it is felt that certain human rights are inherent for all people; in medieval times these were called 'natural rights' which then gradually became more developed through the time of the Enlightenment. By the same token, the thinkers and philosophers of the Enlightenment period speculated on whether there were fundamental rules or laws which should govern the behaviour of all individuals.

The rights of the individual first rose to prominence with Magna Carta in Britain in 1215, which was articulated as a protest against the arbitrary behaviour and decisions of King John (chapter 29). By contrast, the laying down of laws is apparent very much earlier. The first and oldest legal code so far discovered is that of Ur-Nammu around 2100 BC in which the ruler of Ancient Babylon set down his principles of conduct: these included some rights for women, including divorce. Somewhat later, another Babylonian ruler, Hammurabi, set out his code of laws.

Each time a new code appeared, it not only varied slightly, but it also seemed to have grown in size. Hammurabi's rules comprised some 282 separate articles which have survived for us because they were engraved on stone steles. It is clear that the code itself implies limits on an individual's behaviour and power, but also it implies the delegation of power to the ruler (chapter 4). Later, also in the Middle East, a further set of rules has come to us through the Cyrus Cylinder which records on a cylindrical stone the code of laws laid down by Cyrus the Great of Persia in the middle of the first millennium BC (chapter 10).

Around the same time as Cyrus was laying down his rules, religious laws started to appear; the first of which were the Jewish laws recorded in the Halakha, which were also said to be unalterable: this last condition was obviously put in to bind the hands and minds of future generations, and whilst this may have seemed reasonable, it has considerably hampered the development of the Jewish religion and led to divisions and sub-sects developing over succeeding years and generations. Later the same problem came to affect the Muslim religion, where there is no mechanism or permission to reconsider or develop the laws of Mohammed in the light of developing knowledge through the centuries. The thinking must have been in each case that as the laws were given directly by God there could be no case for change or rethinking with the passage of time.

Following the Jews, and indeed as an offshoot therefrom, Christianity developed its own code of laws. Mercifully this was small and is succinctly expressed in the Ten Commandments. As with many other things in life, simplicity is usually a blessing, and as a simple means of guiding personal morality, the Ten Commandments are successful, and are easily understood. Unfortunately however, they have not prevented Christianity also from splitting into many different and smaller sects; although the differences are more usually about matters of belief; within Christianity the Ten Commandments are largely accepted as the basis for morality.

In the 8th century, after Mohammed had died, the Caliph Uthman became aware of differences that existed between different recitations of Koranic verses which were all supposed to be identical and to echo what Mohammed had been told by God and then conveyed to his followers. Accordingly he appointed five Imams to record and correct existing accounts of what the Prophet had said; the result sets out the rules for a morally acceptable life for Muslims; Al-Risalah Al-Huquq, the fourth Shia Imam finally set this down in writing.

On the other side of the world, in China, in the centuries before Christ, the period known as the 'Hundred Schools' (Chapter 8) was a time of intense speculation and developing philosophy about the foundations of government, ethics and morality. The 'legalists' emerged urging law-making power over the previously important well developed rituals. The Chinese also developed the idea that a single statement of the law should be sufficient to encompass all individuals, from the ruler at the top to the peasant at the bottom (compare with Magna Carta). The thinking behind these rules was aimed at the creation of a wealthy and powerful state, which the legalists propounded in a long and drawn out argument.

Against this point of view, the main opponents of the thinking of the legalists were the followers of China's best known ancient philosopher, Confucius, who lived in the 6th century BC. Confucius was a conservative reformer who aimed to teach the essential truths of the ancient ways (Tao) which had become tarnished by routine and familiarity. Confucius believed in the preservation of order, whether within the family, government, army, or any other institution, and his thinking underpinned much of Chinese behaviour for the next two millennia, until he was paid the ultimate compliment of criticism by the first post-Confucian Chinese state, namely the 20th century Communist Republic.

His thinking was developed over the years, and his name was given to the text known as the Thirteen Classics, but in fact these were not published and finalised until the 13th century AD, long after his death. Confucius was a practical man and his teachings were not religious in the sense that we understand it, but they were a stabilising influence on Chinese society. Following Confucius, a little later in time, other eastern religions developed their codes of behaviour according to the perceived wisdom of Buddha, and within the melange which gives rise to Hindu teachings.

In France, the Roman Emperor Justinian's code of laws was used, but in addition early laws were written down by Clovis, King of the Franks, who had united the Franks in what was previously Roman Gaul, by the time he died in 511 AD. Known as Salic Law as it was promulgated for the Salians or Wester Franks, it is usually quoted for its association with monarchical and property inheritance, and indeed when Clovis died his kingdom was split amongst his four sons. Two features of Salic Law are often quoted, firstly the principle that succession and property should be divided amongst all male heirs equally, and secondly, that women are excluded from the succession.

This is in contrast to the Anglo-Saxon system where a single individual would succeed to a kingdom or property, promoting continuity and preservation of the kingdom, and not excluding women, though the addition of the concept of primogeniture was added, in other words female succession is allowed, but only once the search has excluded all possible male heirs. After Clovis the next time succession became problematic was with the death of Charlemagne in 814, when his kingdom was divided between his four sons. On each occasion, following both Clovis and Charlemagne, the division of the kingdom contributed to weakness and instability as a number of ruling sons competed to achieve primacy.

The Salic Code prohibition on women succeeding to a throne, was to cause succession problems on several occasions in France in later centuries. English monarchical succession did not have this written specified female prohibition, and consequently Matilda was able to fight for her right to the throne in the 12th century, whilst somewhat later, first Elizabeth and then Mary succeeded to the English throne, followed in due course by Queen Anne, Queen Victoria and Queen Elizabeth II. Much later in France the legal system was radically overhauled and codified by Napoleon at the beginning of the 19th century, mainly using the Code of Justinian from the 6th century.

In Europe, the English legal system developed along with ancient Scandinavian and Germanic law. In England as the country emerged from the Dark Ages, a set of Shire Courts had been instituted well before the Norman Conquest. Alfred the Great was the main driving force in setting up the English legal system, his son Edward the Elder spent more time pursuing war than promulgating peaceful activities, but his grandson Athelstan continued to build on the organisational basis first set up by Alfred, which had divided the country into many semi-autonomous shires which owed allegiance to the king. There was relatively little alteration of this system by the Normans after the invasion of 1066.

William the Conqueror continued with the shire system, and indeed found it of great benefit when he set out to compile his register of all the national assets, known as the Domesday Book, because on the basis of this he was able to determine taxation levels across the country. The shire courts were reinforced and indeed have continued to function up to the present time. Alfred in his lifetime had continued to emphasise the importance of literacy, education and the use of the vernacular rather than the Latin language. A certain amount of his legal organisation was borrowed from Charlemagne and in turn, before that, from the Salic Law propounded under Clovis in the 6th century.

Much European law of the current century derives from Roman Law, especially as it was codified by the Emperor Justinian in 529 AD, and European law has become divided into two major branches – Civil Law and Common Law. In addition to this, religious law of each of each of the major religions also plays a part in determining people's conduct, though in most societies today religious law takes second place to the law of the state in either its civil or common form. The main exception to this is Muslim religious law, Sharia, which is not separate from civil law, notably in some countries in the Middle East, such as Iran and Saudi Arabia.

Following the Norman invasion, the first Plantagenet King, Henry II, codified what has become known as Common Law, because the law was common throughout the country, and he also reinforced the jury system, where citizens who have been sworn on oath, decide the case. Henry delegated judges from London to preside over cases across the country, who could then discuss their decisions together later, and in this way a common understanding together with the precedence of previous decisions could be used in making future decisions.

This system contrasts with Civil Law, derived from statutes passed by governments, and under which the decisions of judges play only a minor role since Civil Law systems rely on laws written down in statute and decided by a jury. Common Law, on the other hand, tends to emphasise the separation of powers between the judiciary and the executive branch of government. The other major difference is that Common Law uses an adversarial system, in which each side in a legal case presents their side of the case to a neutral judge and jury to decide. Under Civil Law, however, criminal proceedings in particular, go forward under an inquisitorial system, where an examining magistrate, advocate or the police develop the evidence and the arguments for each side before presenting these findings to a judge.

In this way, the judge in Civil Law (or the President of the Bench) is not simply a neutral umpire, but is allowed to directly interview witnesses or complainants. In the English speaking world the system of Common Law is most often used, since the law spread with colonisation and development of the British Empire. By comparison, most of the rest of Europe uses a Civil Law system derived from the Napoleonic Code, which also spread to former colonies or countries which had been occupied or associated with France through Napoleonic times (chapter 61).

The English Bill of rights in 1689 propounded the supremacy of parliament over the king, but also listed a number of fundamental rights and liberties. Many similar bills in other countries have either preceded, or more usually followed this, starting with Magna Carta in 1215, and including the Twelve Articles, which came out of the German Peasants War of 1525 in Germany. The United States Declaration of Independence includes the Rights, and was followed by the American Bill of Rights which was completed in 1789, one hundred years later than in England. At the same time, during the French Revolution, the Declaration of the Rights of Man and of the Citizen, was promulgated, and briefly summarised in the spirit of the French Revolution as "Liberté, Egalité et Fraternité", though this of course is a gross oversimplification. The United Nations Universal Declaration of Human Rights eventually followed in 1948, with the European Convention on Human Rights in 1950.

Thus, we see that the Civil Law comprises that which is promulgated by rulers, kings or parliaments, and which co-exists in the English-speaking world with Common Law. Common Law applies to both criminal and civil cases and relies on precedent and previous similar decisions by judges and juries, criminal cases in common law systems are therefore tried before a jury where the verdict has to be given as being "beyond reasonable doubt"; in other words the jury is asked to decide, not between a verdict of guilty or not guilty, but whether or not the defendant is guilty 'beyond reasonable doubt'. Juries were previously also used in non-criminal cases, but this is now less common and unusual in Britain, except in libel and slander cases, though some other jurisdictions do still use juries in civil cases.

In modern times, we are familiar with the jury system where a selection of citizens, usually twelve, is asked to determine, after hearing the evidence, whether or not the accused is guilty. Although justice in ancient times was often quite arbitrary and frequently depended on the individual assessment or whim of a chief or ruler, the involvement of the greater public, or society, appears quite early and existed in Ancient Greece, though Greek and Roman 'juries' could consist of several hundred people. More recently the system has evolved from Germanic tribal systems in the early centuries AD and was present in Anglo-Saxon culture before the Norman Conquest. Modern English juries came in with the Assize of Clarendon in 1166 under Henry II (the word derives from the Norman French 'juré' meaning sworn).

The intention was to end trial by ordeal, combat, duel or compurgation (oath-taking on behalf of the accused by his fellow citizens), these means of determining guilt still took several centuries to die out, and for the full use of the jury system to take effect by the 19th century. Until very recently, and in keeping with many other aspects of life, women were excluded from the judicial system in Britain and were excluded from juries until 1919; even then there was a requirement to own property which was not lifted until 1974.

All this while in Christian Europe, a system of Canon or religious law existed alongside the national law in which the church was responsible for judging and dispensing justice to members of its organisation. There have been frequent disputes between churches, and the states in which they were established, about who should be responsible for errant churchmen; such disputes continue and are sometimes acrimonious, but recent years have seen it firmly established that national laws take precedence, as originally set out in Magna Carta.

Possible further reading:
The Law by Raymond Wacks (Oxford University Press)

Chapter 87
Electrical and Chemical Engineering

Electricity first started to interest the new scientists and engineers in the early 17th century. William Gilbert (1544–1603) is remembered as the 'father of electrical engineering' since he described both electricity and magnetism. His work was done from the basis of a medical degree; in the last two years of his life he was physician to Queen Elizabeth I and subsequently to the newly crowned King James I. Johan Carl Wilcke (1732–1796) in Sweden was a clergyman who experimented in physics at the Royal Swedish Academy of Sciences. He invented an electrostatic generator which was later improved by Alexandro Volta whose name is immortalised in the measure of electrical current, and who also pioneered the electric battery. George Ohm (1789–1854) from Bavaria is commemorated in the name of the unit of resistance of electrical currents, while André-Marie Ampère (1775–1836), French physicist and academic, is another name we honour as a measure of electrical current.

In 1831, Michael Faraday (1791–1867) discovered electro-magnetic induction and electrolysis; his work established the basis on which electric motor technology became practical. The first electric motor followed, built in 1832 by William Sturgeon (1783–1850), an English physicist who worked for the East India Company. Faraday's early work on electricity and magnetism led on to that of James Clerk Maxwell (1831–1879), an academic who worked at Edinburgh, Cambridge, Aberdeen and London on theoretical mathematical physics and whose calculations explained the theory of electromagnetic radiation, interpreting electricity, magnetism and light as wave phenomena, and this in turn led to the prediction of the existence of radio waves.

Maxwell's work built upon that of Isaac Newton, and he forms a necessary and vital link between Newton's theories and those of Einstein (1879–1955), who published his paper on the Special Theory of Relativity in 1905. Maxwell's contributions to physics are generally placed on a par with those of Newton and Einstein.

After the early electrical discoveries in the 18th century and first part of the 19th century, the second half of the 19th century saw a blossoming of work in electrical engineering. Electricity was first used in communication by Sir Francis Ronalds (1788–1873), an English inventor, and was the beginning of an ability to convey messages over distance which obviated the need for messengers to convey the information by hand either in civilian life or in battle. Several inventors gradually improved this 'telegraph' (literally 'distance writing'), with the first commercial system being developed in London by William Cooke (1806–1879) and Sir Charles Wheatstone (1802–1875). Wheatstone was a very prolific English inventor in communications technology, who was also active in developing musical instruments (including the concertina) and early experiments in spectroscopy. Cooke produced the first proper and useful means of telegraph communication when he installed several miles of a system out of Paddington station in London for the use of the Great Western Railway and later founded the world's first public telegraph company in 1846.

Samuel Morse (1791–1872) was a noted American portrait painter and inventor who continued to develop the telegraph using a single wire rather than the multiple wires used previously. His interest and resolve to develop a means of rapid communication had been stimulated when he received a letter telling him that his wife had been ill, and then on the next day a further letter telling him that she had died. This was followed by his development of Morse Code in which letters are represented by different combinations of short and long signals known as dots and dashes, and which gradually came into widespread use through the second half of the 19th century.

The first underwater cable to convey telegraph messages became functional between England and France in 1850 with similar cables to Ireland, Holland and Belgium very soon afterwards. After considerable technical and maritime problems the first trans-Atlantic cable became functional in 1866 between the west coast of Ireland and Newfoundland. Many cables were laid from the end of the 19th century and into the 20th century forming direct links between most of the countries of the world. Early messages were sent by telegraph with the first phone call across trans-continental America, and the first trans-Atlantic phone call coming in 1915.

The development of the telegraph system and later the radio telephone system brought the opportunity for the rapid dissemination of news. This opportunity was grasped by Paul Reuter (1816–1899) a German telegraph pioneer and inventor who moved to London in 1845 where he founded the news agency which, in much larger form, still carries his name today. Guglielmo Marconi (1874–1937) from Bologna invented radio and a resulting radio-telegraph system. Radio waves, otherwise known as electromagnetic radiation, had been discovered by Heinrich Hertz (1857–1894), thus proving James Clerk Maxwell's theoretical predictions.

Marconi's radio experiments initially fell on deaf ears in his native Italy, and aged 21 he came to England where the government, in the form of the Admiralty and Post Office, were interested in facilitating further development. Cross channel radio messages were sent in the last year of the century and the first transatlantic radio messages were sent between Cornwall and Newfoundland in 1901, a distance of over 2,200 miles (3,500 km). Radio continued to develop steadily and Marconi was awarded a Nobel prize in physics in 1909.

Unlike the telegraph carrying electrically coded messages, the acoustic phone – familiar to children as two tin cans joined by a tight length of string – is recorded by Robert Hooke at the end of the 17th century, and is still sometimes seen in the form of 'speaking tubes', but the telephone as we understand it, with the facility of direct speech, was developed by Alexander Graham Bell (1847–1922) who was the Scottish son of a prominent Edinburgh elocutionist and speech therapist. His family emigrated to Canada in 1870 with Bell being able to develop and patent the first recognisable telephone in the following years; the Bell Telephone Company was founded in 1877 and Bell went on to make and patent many further inventions from laboratories he set up further south in America.

The other great burgeoning development of the second half of the 19th century was the increasing use of electric motors for both industrial and domestic purposes. Mortiz Von Jacobi (1801–1874) was an academic at the Russian Academy of Sciences who developed the first practical electric motor which he used for demonstration purposes to propel a 28 foot boat in 1839. He was also active in researching and developing the electric telegraph. Although gas lighting became commonplace through the first half of the 19th century, the use of electricity to produce light lagged considerably behind this.

Carbon arc lights produce an intense light by means of an electric arc between two carbon electrodes and were invented by Humphrey Davy (1778–1829), a Cornish chemist, later knighted and made President of the Royal Society, who also discovered several elements, including the alkaline earth metals (potassium, sodium, calcium, strontium, barium, magnesium and boron), but is probably best remembered for his invention of the miners' safety lamp.

Through the first decade of the 19th century, he produced ever better arc lights, and these were used particularly for bright light sources in theatres and other public spaces, but were not suitable for domestic use. This had to wait for the invention of the light bulb by Thomas Edison (1847–1931) who set up the first industrial research laboratory in New Jersey when he was only 29. Edison experimented with many different types of filament before settling on carbon filaments which became incandescent when an electric current was passed through them. His experiments were contemporary with those of Sir Joseph Swan (1828–1914) in England who also devised a system of electric lighting dependent on rendering an electric wire incandescent; after some patent arguments over the precedence of Swan's patents the two men formed a joint company to market light bulbs.

It was however not until after the First World War that light bulbs became sufficiently dependable for everyday domestic use and for general use in public spaces, including street lighting, although the first experimental electric street lighting had been installed in London as early as 1878, prior to which gas had been used for public lighting.

Electronic engineering, so widespread in all our modern gadgetry, really only came into being in the second half of the 20th century. However, its roots extend well back into the 19th century to Charles Babbage (1791–1871) whose machines were among the first mechanical computers, although they were never completed due to lack of funds and Babbage's difficulty in interacting with fellow scientists. He did however manage to interact with Ada Lovelace (1815–1852), the daughter of Lord Byron, who is credited with writing algorithms for Babbage's machine which are often seen as the first computer programmes. However, it was not until the 1950s and the miniaturisation of electronic components that followed that the subject would develop further.

Ada Lovelace not only wrote notes about the calculating machine that Babbage had designed, she understood the significance of this: she foresaw the laptop computer and the smart phone, and that these were universal machines that in future generations could be programmed to do almost anything. Unfortunately her work was not picked up for the next hundred years, until suddenly the electronic age commenced. The first machine that could really be called a computer appeared after the Second World War in the form of the American ENIAC machine (Electronic Numeral Integrator and Computer) developed by the US Army.

Thereafter, the computer developed rapidly thanks to silicon chip engineering, which led into the early appearance of the first personal computers in the 1970's, and which in turn was followed by the invention of the world-wide web by Tim Berners-Lee in the 1980s.

---oOo---

At the same time as electricity was becoming understood and developed for both industrial and domestic purposes, chemistry and its industrial counterpart chemical engineering, were becoming important branches of engineering study, especially since chemical engineering became very important on an industrial basis in the years leading up to the First World War. Its science is devoted to the production or modification of raw materials into modern consumer goods either for the use of manufacturers (industries, farmers, distributors and so forth) or directly for individual consumers themselves.

George Davis (1850–1906) is an important early figure and regarded as a founding father; he moved into academia after a broad industrial experience: and wrote a handbook of chemical engineering and gave the first ever series of university lectures on the subject in 1888 at the Manchester Technical School, which brought together both his own industrial experience and that of other pioneers. The Society of Chemical Industry was founded in 1881 with Davis as its first secretary. It took some time for the subject to be established as a fully separate discipline with the American Institute of Chemical Engineers being founded in 1908 and the British Institution of Chemical Engineers in 1922.

Much of the early chemical work was concerned with dyes and plastics. The first man-made aniline dye was synthesized by William Henry Perkins (1838–1907) who was admitted to the London School of Chemistry at the unusually early age of 15, and in adult life was knighted for his impressive lifetime of research in 1908. The use of dyes expanded rapidly since at the time of his discovery in the 1850s the British Industrial Revolution was producing immense quantities of textiles and clothing, much of it for export. Gradually however the research in aniline products passed to Germany, where a very strong chemical industry was growing up in the second half of the 19th century.

Synthetic plastics, as opposed to natural rubbers and gums, were also developed during the second half of the 19th century. The process of vulcanising rubber was discovered by an American chemist and engineer, Charles Goodyear (1800–1860), but it was the man-made materials which really opened the era of plastics. Parkescine, based on nitrocellulose, was the first synthetic material and was named after its inventor Alexander Parkes (1813–1890), an English metallurgist who worked in Birmingham and showed his new product at the Great International Exhibition in London and at the World Fair, both in 1862.

All of the early plastics tended to be developed from naturally occurring products which were treated and hardened by varying chemicals. The first widely used plastic, Bakelite, was a pure chemically derived product, valuable as an insulator and also fireproof, and developed in New York in 1907 by Belgian chemist Leo Baekeland (1863–1944); it became the basis for many early plastic products.

Since the beginning of the 20th century, chemical engineering has also extended into biochemical fields, notably with the production of drugs and other plastics. Aspirin (acetyl salicylic acid) was first synthesised in 1853 by the German chemist Charles Frédéric Gerhardt (1815–1856) and then came to the market produced as the first product of the drug company Bayer in 1899. Later, Bayer company scientists produce the first anti-bacterial agent prontosil in 1932.

Penicillin, the first true antibiotic, was discovered by Sir Alexander Fleming (1881–1955) in 1928, but not produced in any significant quantities until the early war years of the 1940s when the Oxford team of Sir Howard Florey (1898–1968), a pathologist originally from Melbourne in Australia, and Ernst Chain (1906–1979), a Jewish refugee from Hitler's Germany, developed mass production, which became ready just in time for the treatment of wounded troops in 1944 when the allies invaded German occupied France. Florey and Chain shared the 1945 Nobel Prize with Fleming. The structure of penicillin was elucidated by Dorothy Hodgkin (1910–1994), working in Oxford, and followed later by the structures of first vitamin B12, and then insulin, for all of which she became only the third woman to receive the Nobel chemistry prize in 1964.

Possible further reading:
Connections by James Burke (Macmillan)

Chapter 88
Culture, 1600–1914

Once Johannes Gutenberg had printed and distributed his first Bible in 1455, there was a gradual widening of the pool of literature available to readers (chapter 36). Gutenberg himself did not stray significantly from the religious theme, but in England William Caxton (1422–1491) published his first English language books in the years after 1476. Unlike Gutenberg, the first books he produced were not religiously inspired, but were aimed at an increasing number of wealthy literate readers: the best known publications in this genre are the books of Geoffrey Chaucer, including the *Canterbury Tales*, and the *Tales of King Arthur* by Sir Thomas Mallory (1415–1471). It is noteworthy that Chaucer, who died in 1400, produced his works almost a century before Caxton printed them, but their circulation would have been miniscule until printed copies became available.

Much early printed work became available either as poetry or as drama. Poetry often appeared as epic poems and Edmund Spenser's (1553–1599) masterpiece *the Faerie Queene* was published in two parts in the 1590s: it is a heroic allegory often seen to be celebrating the Tudors and Elizabeth I in particular, who was on the throne at the time. Further epic poetry was produced in the next century, including *Pilgrim's Progress* by John Bunyan (1628–1688), and *Paradise Lost* by John Milton (1608–1674). In Spain, around the same time, Miguel de Cervantes (1547–1616) wrote *Don Quixote De La Mancha*.

The 17th century in England saw a profuse flowering of metaphysical poets whose intellectual output discussed spiritual matters; their numbers included John Donne, George Herbert, Henry Vaughan, Andrew Marvel and Thomas Traherne. Literature and drama were considerably disrupted both by the Civil War and by the period of subsequent Puritan rule under Oliver Cromwell from 1649 to 1660. Theatres were banned, and much literature went underground for this time, but returned rapidly once the monarchy was restored with Charles II.

The 18th century in Europe saw intellectual writing blossom with such writers as Montesquieu (1689–1755) who influenced the American Founding Fathers, Voltaire (1694–1778) who influenced and corresponded with Catherine the Great of Russia, Rousseau (1712–1778) whose thoughts were important to the French revolutionaries, Kant (1724–1804) the German philosopher, and Goethe (1749–1832), German writer and statesman.

In England the emergence of the novel is seen with the story of Robinson Crusoe by Daniel Defoe (1660–1731), but also including Samuel Richardson

(1689–1761), Henry Fielding (1707–1754) and his sister Sarah Fielding (1710–1768), who wrote the first children's book. Samuel Johnson (usually known as Dr Johnson, 1709–1784) ranged widely across the whole range of writing from poetry, essays and criticism to biography and his famous dictionary of the English language.

The 19th century saw a considerable expansion in literature, both poetry and novels. In poetry the early years of the century saw a great blossoming of English romantic poets including William Wordsworth (1770–1850), Lord Byron (1788–1824), and Samuel Taylor Coleridge (1772–1834), whilst the novel developed rapidly with the writings of exponents such as Jane Austen (1775–1817), Charles Dickens (1812–18700 and Charlotte Bronte (1816–1855).

This early period in the 19th century provides the first occasion when many women started writing, though not all were comfortable using their own names so that some such as Mary Ann Evans (1819–1880) wrote in the pen name of George Eliot, whilst in France Amantine Dupin lived for a period with pianist Frederick Chopin and wrote under the name of George Sand (1804–1876). In Russia literature flourished with the works of Dostoyevsky (1821–1881), Tolstoy (1828–1910) and Chekov (1860–1904). In Germany romanticism grew from an earlier date with Goethe (1749–1832) and Schiller (1759–1805) writing predominantly at the end of the 18th century and into the early 19th century.

---oOo---

Early music has been discussed in chapter 54. Through the first millennium AD most music was played either by individuals such as minstrels, or it was church and choral music of a restricted nature. At the beginning of the second millennium the invention of a practical system of music notation allowed the gradual expansion and exploration of music across previously difficult barriers. With the coming of the Renaissance music blossomed through the 14th and 15th centuries in Europe. Music was composed, sung and played for both religious and secular occasions including dancing. Little has survived from the period before 1600, but after this time Giovanni Gabrieli (1554–1612) and Claudio Monteverdi (1567–1643) were composing in Venice, Dieterich Buxtehude (1637–1707) in Germany, whilst in England Thomas Tallis (1505–1585) and William Byrd (1539–1623) were prominent composers.

In Germany, much music was composed for the organ, and many excellent instruments were made for even quite small churches. Germany fostered a musical tradition where rich and aristocratic patrons employed not only individually talented performers and composers, but even small orchestras. At this time the organ was an excellent accompanying instrument at a time when the small percussive keyboard instruments had yet to evolve into something stronger and more versatile.

The German musical tradition developed rapidly in what is known as the Baroque Era from around 1600 to 1750. It reached its zenith with Johann Sebastian Bach (1685–1750,) but included George Frederick Handel (1685–

1759) who settled in London in 1721, and his predecessor Henry Purcell (1659–1695). In Italy, composers included Claudio Monteverdi, a most important musical pioneer developing from the renaissance into the baroque period, Antonio Vivaldi (1678–1741), Domenico Scarlatti (1685–1757) and Musio Clementi (1752–1832), who was based in London after growing up in Rome, and who taught and gave recitals in addition to becoming an important music publisher and manufacturer of the newly developing pianos.

During this period, the use of tonality and the formalisation of different keys became part of accepted musical use: to this day most western music remains tonal in both classical and popular music. The Baroque Era also saw the rapid evolution of musical instruments, with the stringed instruments of the viol family developing into instruments that we still recognise and use today. Antonio Stradivari (1644–1737) became particularly famous in subsequent years with his production of stringed violins and larger instruments of the viol family.

Amazingly, it is estimated that at least half of Stradivari's output of 900 violins and 200 other instruments still exist and are highly prized and played in concerts to this day. Early keyboard instruments, including the harpsichord and clavichord, evolved equally rapidly into the early fortepiano and pianoforte (chapter 54). The advent of these iconic instruments allowed the composers of the 19th century to explore and develop music in a way that had not previously been possible.

Musical composition continued to develop from the Baroque into a period now regarded as classical music, comprising the second half of the 18th century and the early 19th century. The sonata, symphony and concerto arrived at a standard form with Wolfgang Amadeus Mozart (1756–1791) standing out as its arch exponent. Despite his early death at the age of 35, he composed over 600 works, including nearly 50 symphonies, over 20 piano concertos, and nearly 20 operas.

The classical period of musical composition shades into the Romantic era equated roughly with the 19th century, and with Ludwig van Beethoven (1770–1827) being a seminal transitional figure between the two eras. Beethoven became gradually deaf starting in his late 20's and causing him much misery, but despite this his genius was such that he was able to continue composing and produced many of his most impressive works during the final years of his life. Through the 19th century, Romantic music continued to expand and delight audiences, particularly with the construction of theatres and halls which allowed its performance in front of much larger audiences.

In the early years of the century, Franz Schubert (1797–1828), Hector Berlioz (1803–1869), Felix Mendelssohn (1809–1847), Frédéric Chopin (1810–1849), and Robert Schumann (1810–1856) produced exciting and inspiring music and were followed through the second half of the century by further musical giants including Franz Liszt (1811–1886), Johannes Brahms (1833–1897) and Pyotr Tchaikovsky (1840–1893).

Opera became a spectacular development arising from the combination of human voice and choruses with stirring music and dramatic presentations. From the early compositions of Monteverdi through the operas of Mozart and the single opera of Beethoven, the 19th century produced Giaochino Rossini (1792–1868), Vicenzo Bellini (1801–1835), Hector Berlioz, Giuseppe Verdi (1813–1901), and finally Richard Wagner (1813–1883), who all transfixed audiences with their operatic creations.

At the turn of the 19th century, composers started to experiment more liberally with traditional forms of composition being stretched by such composers as Anton Bruckner (1824–1896), Gustav Mahler (1860–1911), Debussy (1862–1918), Scriabin (1872–1915), and Stravinsky (1882–1971). Schoenberg (1874–1951), Webern (1883–1945) and Berg (1885–1935) followed with new music that was often atonal and theoretical rather than melodic.

---oOo---

After the Greek and Roman periods, public entertainment in Europe became much more sparse through the Dark Ages and into Medieval times. Itinerant bands of actors might tour and produce small plays or scenes from liturgical religious texts, but it was not until late medieval times in the 12th and 13th centuries that the role of theatre in communal life began to increase again when medieval mystery plays were performed in towns across England, France and Germany.

In the 15th century, small companies of professional actors appeared and would tour their plays around the castles and great homes of the times. The Reformation led to the banning of religious plays in many countries with Elizabeth I following the Papal states and France in banning all religious plays in 1558. The result of this was to drive public entertainment towards secular productions and away from the sacred.

At the end of the 16th century, theatres began to be built and plays were seen both in these purpose built buildings, and also in such places as coaching inns where a large courtyard, usually with surrounding balconies, could be easily adapted. One such theatre was the Globe Theatre in England purposely built south of the river Thames to escape some of the control and censorship of the London authorities north of the river. The theatre was open to the elements in the centre, but with sheltered seating round the outside separate from the cheapest standing area in the unsheltered centre.

The Globe was built in 1599 by a company of actors known as the Lord Chamberlain's Men, one of whose number was William Shakespeare (1564–1616). It burnt down some fourteen years later but was rebuilt only to be closed at the beginning of the Puritan era in 1642. The theatre flourished again once King Charles II had been restored to the throne in 1660, and in the restoration plays after 1660 in England women were finally permitted on the stage to take female parts which hitherto had not been allowed and had been played by boys.

By the middle of the 18th century, theatres were being built in central London, and because of satire denigrating established religion, political and anti-royal attitudes, censorship by the King's Lord Chamberlain was introduced in 1737.

In Europe, particularly in France and Russia, professional dancers acted out stories to music, and in this way ballet came into being as a highly stylised and technical mode of dance with a French vocabulary reflecting its early roots. These roots were given a large impetus during the reign of Louis XIV, the Sun King (1638–1715), who enjoyed participating in dance and who founded the Académie Royale de Danse in 1661. Some years later the first professional ballet company, the Paris Opera Ballet, came into being as a branch of the Paris Opera.

---oOo---

Sculpture is probably the most enduring of all the arts. Small carved figurines have been found dating back before the last Ice Age: such figurines have survived well if made of ivory or hard wood, but stone carvings are the most enduring. Pottery figurines are equally well preserved. From the time of Ancient Greece realistic and exquisitely carved figures survive in profusion carved during the first millennium BC. Throughout medieval times sculpture became an important component of Church art, both as free-standing statues and as carved friezes and altar pieces. Cast bronze statues which were made in ancient times were absent from the Dark Ages, but around the last millennium started to reappear once the complicated and expensive process of bronze casting was again mastered.

The explosion of cathedral building in Western Europe from the 11th century onwards under the Normans gave a great boost to sculpture with effigies of Christ and the saints filling many decorative porticoes on both the external and internal walls of the new cathedrals despite the third commandment to make no graven images of God. In renaissance 15th and 16th century Italy an extraordinary quartet of supremely talented men have all left wonderful and enduring paintings and sculptures; metal sculptor Lorenzo Ghibert (1381–1455), Filippo Brunelleschi (1377–1446) who built the dome of the cathedral in Florence and pioneered perspective, Leonardo da Vinci (1452–1519) genius and polymath, and Michelangelo (1475–1564) painter, sculptor and architect have all left us superb examples of their work.

The increasing wealth of some families in the Middle Ages, in particular the Italian banking community, continued to produce wonderful sculpture with Bernini (1598–1680) from Naples being both the leading sculptor in his age as well as the architect of many churches and public monuments. This cultural blossoming in Italy was undoubtedly due to the affluence of contemporary bankers and wealthy nobles who patronised art.

The tradition was continued in the 18th century by Antonio Canova (1757–1822). Through the ages the wish of great men, and occasionally women, or their families, to immortalise and perpetuate themselves has ensured a steady stream of commission for busts of such individuals. Most other countries from Asia to Africa to ancient America have similarly left us busts of their contemporary heroes, sometimes in stylised fashion, sometimes wonderfully realistic. At the end of the 19th century and into the early 20th century realism often gave way to attempts to produce stylised beautiful sculptures, and this in turn would give rise to modernism through the 20th century where abstract concepts come to the fore and realism has retreated.

---oOo---

The history of painting parallels that of sculpture. Early cave paintings are present in Europe and in Africa and Australia dating back up to 40,000 years before the last Ice Age. In more recent times much of our knowledge about the ancient Egyptians comes from their many excavated tombs containing profuse wall paintings. Greek painting has not survived except for portrayals of life and people on ceramic vases. Roman painting survives as wall paintings in villas, particularly thanks to volcanic eruptions which have buried and preserved buildings and their wall decorations until recent excavations at Pompeii and Herculaneum have brought them back to view again.

In the Far East, painting has survived from the last century BC; such painting is usually stylised, but again provides valuable commentaries on the social and working practices of the time. Japanese painting is not known before the 6th century, compared with Chinese painting which still survives from a millennium earlier. Korean painting, once again highly stylised, has also survived from the 1st century BC.

Painting in Europe was stylised through the first millennium, and usually devoted to sacred subjects, with separate styles developing in the eastern and western Holy Roman Empires. The Greek and Russian Orthodox tradition of stylised icon painting persists to this day. With the coming of the Renaissance painting became steadily more realistic and in addition to sacred subjects, portraiture began to assume a large proportion of the output, reaching its apogee in such Italian painters as Leonardo da Vinci, Michelangelo, Durer (1471–1528) and Titian (1488–1576). Through the 17th and 18th centuries, much more painting was devoted to realistic subjects and portraiture as a means of preserving and enhancing the history of great families.

Painting continued in this vein through the first part of the 19th century, when several break-away interpretive movements of painting occurred. The Pre-Raphaelite painters in England and the Impressionists in France were followed by the Symbolists in Russia and France, and the Romantic School which followed the French Revolution with many of its heady aspirations cloaked in heroic terms.

Islamic art was produced across the Islamic world commencing soon after the death of the Prophet. Painting tends to concentrate on patterns, calligraphy and the use of geometric designs of flowers and plants. Some painting has included the human figure, but in general Islam has disapproved of depictions of people and of portraiture in general. Depicting God or the Prophet is thought to be idolatrous and is therefore forbidden by Islamic Law, as it is by the third commandment given to Moses.

By the end of the 19th century, painters turned to what has become known as Modern Art. This has included many different schools, all of which departed from the previous depiction of realistic images. The topics chosen were usually secular and seldom religious; at the turn of the 19th century striking new concepts were unveiled by artists such as Henri Matisse (1889–1954) in France and Pablo Picasso (1881–1973) in Spain. Vassily Kandinsky (1886–1984) moved from Russia to Germany and then had to move again when his art was deemed politically incorrect, even 'degenerate', by the Nazis, Paul Klee (1879–1940) evoked similar disapproval in Germany and had to move to Switzerland. Gradually through the 20th century many painters would pursue much more abstract concepts on canvas in parallel with similar changes in direction for sculpture and other creative projects.

Possible further reading:
Art History by Dana Arnold (Oxford University Press)

Chapter 89
La Belle Epoque – Development of Science

The development of science and industry through the last half of the 19th century and up to the beginning of the Great War moved at a steadily accelerating pace; the period is known as la Belle Epoque, or the Edwardian Era after Edward VII who came to the British throne in 1901 at the age of 60, following the death of his mother, Queen Victoria. Most of the change was happening in Europe and North America as much of the rest of the world had yet to wake up to the changes that were happening, and the speed with which this would continue, and indeed the extent to which it would expand and alter lives. Change was occurring, not just in the way of life and the growing substitution of urban for rural life, but also in attitudes and beliefs.

Europe was at the centre of all this, and was providing the tools of change which were spreading outwards like ripples in a pond, to the rest of the world, in some places more welcomed than in others. Hand in hand with all this change wealth had come to Europe, which was not only transforming lives, but was gradually spreading wealth more evenly than in previous centuries. It must be said however that the percolation of wealth from the top of European society down to the labouring masses at the bottom, was a very slow process. European influence was now guiding world progress, partly because Europeans had colonised, and were running so many countries, also partly because for those other parts of the world without European colonisation, the future dictated by trade and international relations were becoming dominated by European rules.

In the sciences, the achievements and advances of the 17th and 18th centuries had been immense and were transferring the beliefs in the divine guidance of nature to a growing realisation of scientific principles which controlled nature, and life in general. The debate between divinity and scientific principles controlling everyday life had come to a head with the publication of Charles Darwin's theory of evolution in 1856, and the realisation of the enormous length of time it had taken for the world to produce life, and for that life to become intelligent and purposeful.

Through the 19th century, the dawn of modern physics progressed steadily. Julius Robert Von Mayer (1814–1878), a German doctor and physicist, and James Prescott Joule (1818–1889), an English brewer and physicist, are credited with the simultaneous exposition of what is now called the First Law of Thermodynamics, namely that there is a constant relationship between mechanical work and heat, with the one being convertible into the other at a predictable rate. This led in turn to the Second Law of Thermodynamics about the dissipation of energy, such that heat always flows spontaneously from a hotter to a colder body.

This law is attributed to Nicholas Carnot (1796–1832) who was a French physicist and military engineer who died young in a cholera epidemic; because of the disease his belongings and writings were buried with him so that much of his output remains unknown. This early work was followed by that of James Clerk Maxwell (1831–1879) who first published theories of electromagnetic radiation, proposing that electricity, magnetism and light were all manifestations of the same source of energy, and travelled similarly as waves. Maxwell's thinking is seen to span the development of physics between Newton and Einstein, and he incidentally also devised a method for producing the first colour photograph in 1855, a discovery which lay unused in obscurity for the next four decades.

Work on radiation continued with Wilhelm Roentgen (1845–1923), a German engineer and physicist discovering electromagnetic radiation in 1895, now known as x-rays, for which he received a Nobel Prize. Henri Becquerel (1852–1908) working in Paris at the same time discovered rays resembling x-rays emitted from uranium salts. This research on radioactivity was followed up by Marie Curie (1867–1934); she was born in Poland but started work in Paris as an adult because of the exclusion of women from academic life in Poland at the time. She won the 1903 Nobel Prize in Physics with her husband, Pierre, and with Henri Becquerel, whose name is commemorated in the measurement of units of radioactivity. Marie Curie subsequently undertook the first studies into the treatment of cancer by radioactive radiation; she also discovered the element Polonium in 1898, atomic number 84, named after her native country.

John Dalton (1766–1844), an English chemist and physicist from Cumberland, had propounded an atomic theory as far back as 1803. Dalton's theory postulated that elements are made of extremely small particles which he called atoms, which are all identical in size and mass in one element, and which cannot be subdivided, created or destroyed. He felt that atoms of different elements could be combined together forming chemical compounds, and that in a chemical reaction atoms are combined, separated or rearranged.

These discoveries, together with the acceptance of atomic theory expounding the concept of atoms and molecules, was firmly accepted by the end of the 19th century when Max Planck (1858–1947), a German theoretical physicist published his quantum theory explaining the behaviour of atomic structures in 1900 for which he later received the Nobel Prize.

The late 19th century saw the appearance of the earliest mechanical device for recording sound, which was invented in 1877 by Thomas Edison (1848–1931) who was a very prolific inventor, including amongst his ideas the electric light bulb in 1879 (chapter 88). In the last decade of the century Guglielmo Marconi (1874–1937) built the first successful wireless telegraph or radio, which earned him a Nobel Prize. The first radio news programme was broadcast in 1920 in Detroit to a very small audience. In England broadcast entertainment was put out from the Marconi Research Centre for the first time in 1922, with the British Broadcasting Corporation (BBC) being founded in the same year.

Recording of images, as opposed to sound, starts with Thomas Wedgwood (1771–1805), the son of the master potter Josiah Wedgwood. He died at the early age of 34 and the torch passed to Nicephore Niepce (1765–1833), a French inventor who used papers coated with silver chloride initially. It was, however, his colleague, Louis Daguerre (1787–1851) who made the process a practical proposition, again using silver salts and 'fixing' the image by removing the unaltered silver salts.

Henry Fox Talbot (1800–1877), a British scientist and inventor, simultaneously devised a very similar method of making early photographs in the 1830s, and through the rest of his life became a pioneering photographer as well as maintaining his interest in other fields. It was much later in the century before the first motion picture was made by Louis Le Prince (1841–1890) a French inventor, in Leeds in England. Edison was amongst those involved in the early motion picture scene, and in 1886 theatres showing moving pictures opened in major cities across Europe. The first colour film was produced in 1908 with Technicolor following in 1917.

---oOo---

In biology, the impressive achievements in microscopic magnification had led to the general acceptance of Roberts Hooke's (1635–1703) demonstration of the cellular nature of matter, and the work of the German physician and microbiologist Robert Koch (1843–1910) led to the confirmation of the germ theory of disease for which he received a Nobel Prize. Koch's four Postulates state that first, the causative organism must be present in every case of disease, second, the organism must be grown and isolated from a diseased person, third, when the organism is inoculated back into a healthy animal it must cause the disease, and fourth, the organism must again be isolated from the inoculated animal and match the original disease organism.

Louis Pasteur (1822–1895) was a French microbiologist who advanced the understanding of bacterial disease: his name is commemorated in the process which aids preservation of food, particularly milk, which used to be a potent transmitter of tuberculosis; by heating milk to a temperature of 72°C the tubercle bacteria are killed, and although some other bacteria remain, the shelf life of the product is extended and passage of the disease is stopped.

Acceptance of the theory of bacterial infection led rapidly to much safer surgery, starting with a Viennese obstetrician, Ignaz Semmelweis (1818–1865), who instituted hand washing by doctors on the obstetric wards, which cut post-partum infection rates considerably. This practice of eliminating bacteria from hands and instruments was not well accepted at the time, but gradually became incorporated into routine surgical practice when Joseph Lister (1827–1912) in Glasgow introduced carbolic acid as an antiseptic in 1867.

It was then but a small step from this practice of antisepsis in surgery to the practice of asepsis, in other words the performance of surgical treatment with sterilised instruments and sterile conditions of the operator and the surgical site. Synthesis of antibiotics had to wait until the middle of the 20th century when penicillin was discovered by Alexander Fleming (1881–1955) in 1928, but its commercial synthesis was not achieved until the press^{ur}es of war made the investment of time and money urgent and its manufacture was devised after further research by Howard Florey and Ernst Chain in 1942 – all three men shared the Nobel Prize in 1945.

Along with the development of aseptic technique came the introduction of effective inhalational general anaesthesia, first used in Boston by dentist William Morton (1819–1868) in the form of ether. Chloroform was similarly used by Sir James Simpson (1811–1870), an Edinburgh physician, a year later, though the flammability of chloroform proved a hazard in general use. However, the maximum health impact on the general population through the second half of the 19th century came with the basic twin innovations of firstly providing clean water, and secondly the safe piped closed disposal of sewage.

Although both of these elements had been present in Roman cities two millennia previously, its importance had been neglected and fallen into disuse through the intervening years in Europe. The process of purifying sewage was devised in 1913 in the Manchester Corporation Works, rapidly spreading across Europe and North America in the next few years as a process involving "activated sludge".

---oOo---

In the larger natural world, the science of geology gradually began to gel when some early naturalists thought beyond the creation myth, with ideas that rock formations and fossils had formed by sedimenting out from an ocean which once covered most or all of Earth. A Scottish physician and chemist called James Hutton (1726–1797) had suggested in 1780 that Earth's formation had involved heat, with a molten rock mass gradually cooling and solidifying. Another Scot, Charles Lyell (1797–1875), developed and popularised Hutton's work, also explaining earthquakes and volcanoes; in addition he was a friend of Charles Darwin and helped persuade Darwin to publish his work alongside the work of Alfred Russel Wallace in 1858.

These geological theories were reinforced by the findings of William Smith (1769–1839), a mining surveyor who noted that different geological strata always occurred in the same sequence with the same constant fossils to identify them. At the same time in France the naturalist Georges Cuvier (1769–1832, later Baron Cuvier) classified species in living and fossil forms; he is often known as the 'Father of Palaeontology' and established the fact of extinctions, believing in a cycle of life forms with alternating episodes of creation and extinction He rejected the idea of evolution of creatures, and it was to be another fifty years before Darwin's ground-breaking publication.

Alexander von Humboldt, a scientific polymath from Prussia who explored the Americas for five years (as well as Russia), and then needed a further twenty years to write up all his detailed findings in a huge number of volumes, first proposed that South America and Africa had once been joined together eons ago and had slowly drifted apart; he was also the first person to describe human effects on climate. The full exposition of the theory of continental drift was eventually set out by Alfred Wegener (1880–1930), a German polar researcher in 1912.

---oOo---

The science of economics, and the study of wealth in general, has attracted many philosophers through the ages. Much has been written, but the Scottish philosopher and economist Adam Smith (1723–1790) is often cited as the starting point for modern economic theory with his book *"An Enquiry into the Nature and Causes of the Wealth of Nations"* which he wrote in 1776 discussing the growth of wealth and the division of labour. He felt that society was best served by each worker looking after his or her own interests as efficiently as possible rather than trying to work in the interests of society as a whole.

Through the subsequent century, much was written on the subject, and economists came to analyse the production and distribution of both manufactured goods and services. The wide approach was necessitated by the Industrial Revolution which allowed workers and individual capitalists to generate more wealth than previously. Adam Smith believed that by means of each worker labouring with his best efforts, society as a whole would benefit when the individual workers efforts were subject to a competitive market where the competition would automatically act to adjust values and prices to their correct levels.

This concept of competition led into the further advocacy of free trade between individuals and countries which was invoked politically in the first half of the 19th century. Another of its advocates was Jeremy Bentham (1748–1832), a radical thinker, philosopher and social activist whose interests ranged across many other scientific subjects as well as economics. British philosopher and economist John Stewart Mill (1806–1873) became a member of Parliament and wrote a book entitled *"Principles of Political Economy"* in 1848, which was seen as the orthodox view at the time. He tried to steer a middle line between Adam Smith's view of increasing opportunities for trade and manufacture, and those of Thomas Malthus (1766–1834) an Anglican clergyman who wrote about populations. Malthus hypothesised that populations would increase in good times with plentiful food and opportunity, and that the reverse would occur in hard times, his theory applied to both animal and human populations and he noted that war and disease were also potent forces acting on populations.

Karl Marx (1818–1883) was born in Prussia but because of his radical politics and generalist writing was expelled first from Germany and then from France, and therefore moved to London where he continued to write. In collaboration with Friedrich Engels (1820–1895), a wealthy German philosopher and social scientist, their thinking eventually led to the publication of the Communist Manifesto and the book entitled *Das Kapital*, published in 1867. This was a highly researched exercise analysing the process by which capitalism generated wealth, and in which Marx and Engels theorised that revolution would lead to the overthrow of both monarchy and establishment, leaving power in the hands of the workers.

This entirely theoretical concept would come to underlie both the Russian Revolution in 1917, and the Chinese Civil War between the Nationalist government and the Communists, which started in 1927 and ended in 1949 with the Communist Party in power after the deaths of many millions through war and starvation. In the meantime western economic thought has fragmented with different European countries following different strands of economic thought, including both free market and social market economies, along with other variants of thought.

The workings of the mind have fascinated philosophers through the ages, but the science of psychology arose in Germany and Prussia with the thinking of Emanuel Kant (1724–1804), together with the philosophers Georg Hegel (1770–1831) and Johann Herbart (1776–1841). By the middle of the 19th century psychological experimentation was being undertaken both in Europe and America, with psychological thinkers dividing into different schools of thought, including the biological, behavioural, cognitive and social branches. Best known at this time was Sigmund Freud (1856–1937), an Austrian neurologist who advocated psychoanalysis, or the use of discussion and understanding of past experiences between patient and analyst.

He was followed by Carl Jung (1875–1961), a Swiss psychiatrist who wrote and talked extensively about the unconscious and its relationship with conscious thought. Much of Freud's thinking has now been superseded with the criticism that it was largely based on theorising without any significant experimental basis; some critics even group it with communism as a belief or religion, free of any supporting evidence or fact base.

In recent years, the use and understanding of statistics has become increasingly important with the realisation that few deductions can be made from one person's single limited experience, and that multiple aggregated experiences are the only way to arrive at valid conclusions; in other words it is not appropriate to generalise from a particular happening or experience.

Sociology and the study of social science grew up after the Enlightenment thinking, and studies the interaction of both individuals and groups of individuals. The subject involves the study of both conflict and change within society. The discipline follows the thinking of the French businessman and thinker Henri de Saint-Simon (1760–1825), the first person to define a working class as opposed to what he called the 'idling class'; many wealthy individuals in those days did not have a 'job' as we now recognise it, but instead lived on the income of their estates and invested wealth. The French philosopher Auguste Comte (1798–1857) is often felt to be the 'Father of Sociology'; he hoped the

French mindset following the Revolution could be improved by thinking based on scientific reasoning. This led him to advocate a new 'religion of humanity' which he hoped would replace contemporary organised religion.

The English scientist and philosopher Herbert Spencer (1820–1903) wrote extensively adopting Darwin's theory to the social context, in particular coining the phrase "survival of the fittest" to indicate that the most effective social cultures would persist to develop (only later did Darwin himself come to use the term in a biological sense as well as a social one; this phrase has been used in more recent times to apply to other fields of human activity including businesses and universities). Modern social science is credited largely to Emile Durkheim (1858–1917), French sociologist and academic, Max Weber (1864–1920) German sociologist and economist, and Karl Marx (1818–1883).

Possible further reading:
Das Kapital by Karl Marx (Atlantic Books)

Chapter 90
Sleeping Eastern Giants – India and China

Early Indian history is covered in chapter 7. Through the Middle Ages, India expanded as a Mogul Empire under three decisive and talented emperors, of which the first was Babur (1483–1530), who ruled for 24 years. The second important Emperor was Babur's grandson Akbar (1542–1615) with a 49 year reign, the third impressive Emperor was Shah Jahan (1592–1666), the grandson of Akbar, who ruled for 30 years. These three Emperors stand out as talented and successful individuals from a line of 21 Emperors from the early 16th century to the middle of the 19th century, their long reigns helping them to fulfil their ambitions.

The early Indian Empires had been Muslim, and the initial three great Mogul Emperors were also Muslim, but were tolerant of other faiths, especially the majority Hindu community to whom Babur in particular allowed freedom of worship and culture. India was initially stable under this gradually enlarging empire which started with Babur, who conquered the city of Samarkand on the Silk Route (in modern Uzbekistan) at the tender age of 14 after only two years on the throne. His empire finally comprised Northern India and much of what we know as Pakistan.

His grandson, Akbar, also ruled from the young age of 14, enlarging the empire again to include most of northern and middle India into a stable state. Shah Jahan, once again the grandson, expanded the empire southwards to include most of southern India. He spent his last eight years as an invalid, and after his death successive Emperors gradually lost control of the unwieldy empire. After Mogul power diminished from the middle of the 17th century to the middle of the 19th century, British rule, or 'The Raj', was established in 1857 at the end of a long period of feuding between traders from Portugal, France, Holland and England.

As Mogul stability and control diminished in the 17th century, a Sikh Empire started to appear in north-west India. Muslims and Hindus became less tolerant, and each reinforced their own religious practices in response to hard-line activists. At this time, the British only wished to pursue commerce and finance, whilst the Portuguese, Dutch and French sent a lot of zealous missionaries. The British East India Company expanded and gradually took over both the administration and daily running of the state, including organising and equipping the Company's own private army: the aim of this was to preserve trade, rather than to conquer or subjugate the population, and in this respect deserves comparison with what was happening in the Americas at the same time. By the turn of the 20th century an expatriate British population of around 100,000 civil servants were employed ruling and administering the country of three hundred million Indians.

1857 saw an Indian rebellion or mutiny against the East India Company army. Up till then, the army had been punctilious in respecting Hindu and Muslim beliefs and customs separately, though this observance sometimes failed. A crisis came because financial compensation for armed service away from army bases on campaign, and promotion for Indian sepoys, was perceived to be too slow. Matters came to a head over the grease used in new ammunition, with a rumour being spread amongst the Hindu community that the grease was derived from beef fat, with the cow being sacred to Hindus; and spread amongst the Muslim community that it was pork fat, with pork meat being forbidden to Muslims.

In response to this rebellion, the rule of the British East India Company was taken over by the British Crown and persisted until independence in 1947, when the country was partitioned into separate Indian, largely Hindu, and Pakistani, largely Muslim, states. The word Raj means rule in Hindustani, and under the British Raj 175 large states and 500 smaller ones were reorganised after 1857 under the British Secretary of State with a ruling Council of 15 British and Indian civil servants. The Indian army was reorganised. No further social reforms were undertaken as it was felt that India and its caste system was too rigid to reform. Literacy, health, transport and the legal system were all improved along the British model. The rights of women were still very poor, but attempts were made to abolish two glaring problems – the first being the Hindu practice of sati, in which a widow was expected to immolate herself on her dead husband's funeral pyre, and the second, that of female infanticide of unwanted children, was not changed either.

The University of Calcutta was established, and provided an educated middle class from 1857 onwards, with Bombay and Madras following shortly after. The railways were expanded, such that by 1880 there were 25,000 km of track. The last years of the 19th century, and the years leading up to the First World War, saw a further bout of social reform. Conflict between Hindu and Muslim communities was proving difficult, and as a consequence the State of Bengal was divided or 'partitioned' in 1905, only to be reorganised again some seven years later. This antagonism between Hindu and Muslim communities resulted in the formation of the Muslim League during this time. In the early years of the 20th century Indian Councillors were increasingly recruited onto District and Municipal Boards to represent the communities.

During the Great War, Indian troops fought with other troops, both from Britain and from other British Territories, and clearly through the years there became an expectation that India was a mature enough country to govern itself. A Home League Rule was formed by Mahatma Gandhi (1869–1948) in 1915 after he had returned from working in South Africa to live in India, which emphasised his major guiding principle of non-violence. Indian independence was discussed through the inter-war years, and almost came to fruition but, like Ireland earlier, was shelved because of the onset of war.

Ultimately, India was partitioned into Muslim and Hindu nations in 1947, but unfortunately, as this needed to be done in a hurry, not only were there many unsettled features, but also there was an enormous amount of violence between the followers of the two religions. Some 14 million people were displaced and estimates of the number of deaths in the associated violence range as high as two million.

---oOo---

Chinese history up to the 19th century has been outlined in chapter 76, where it was noted that for at least three millennia China was a very closed society. Outside relationships, both intellectual and in trade, were minimised. This remained the situation at the beginning of the 19th century, at a time when European powers were expanding and wishing to trade across the world, including with China and India. Historically the Chinese had exported large quantities of silks and pottery to the west, but taken very little in return, except hard currency in the form of silver bullion.

By 1840, however, British merchants had discovered that the Chinese were willing to buy large quantities of Indian opium, and the Opium Wars broke out with British merchants demanding access to the Chinese market to sell the very lucrative opium that could be produced in India. Considering British naval and military weaponry, the Opium Wars were very one-sided but in the Treaty of Nanking in 1842 Chinese trade restrictions were greatly relaxed while at the same time Hong Kong was ceded to Britain as a trading base on lease, under an agreement which lasted until 1997 (with a short period under Japanese occupation during the Second World War).

The second half of the 19th century saw increasing internal unrest in China. Much of this was sparked by the opium trade wars, but internal uprisings, including the Taiping Rebellion, or civil war, fought between the Qing Dynasty and the Taiping Christian 'Heavenly Kingdom' between 1851–1864, weakened the central Chinese government; the war had ranged across all of China resulting in a horrific death toll among both civilians and soldiers estimated at up to 100 million people. Although the rebellions were all eventually put down, the very high number of deaths caused enormous hardship as well and the central Chinese government in Peking was severely weakened.

In contrast to China, Japan had westernised and modernised since 1865 so that when war between the two countries came in 1894 and 1895 this provoked central reforms in China a couple of years later, at a time when the central government was effectively controlled by the Chinese Empress Cixi, who ruled as regent for her son over a period of 47 years until she died in 1908. In 1898 a process known as the 'Hundred Days Reform' was initiated bringing political, legal and social changes, but these reforms were too radical for many civil service arms of the government, and in 1899 the Boxer Rebellion resulted in northern China. The rebel philosophy was both anti-Christian and anti-foreigner with a large anti-colonial feeling.

The Empress supported the rebels and their cause and declared war on the foreign powers that were supporting them, including Russia, Japan, the United States and the United Kingdom. The rebellion ended in chaotic circumstances with diplomats, foreigners and Chinese Christians being besieged in the Legation Quarter of Beijing. The troops of the eight foreign nations (which also included France, Germany, Italy and Austro-Hungary) finally overcame the Boxer rebels in Peking after enormous numbers of people had died, many after torture and major atrocities. To add to the instability while central China was feeling threatened by Christian missionaries, there were large Muslim uprisings in the north-west and south-west.

The overall effect of this, together with the well-armed troops of eight foreign nations fighting against the rebels within China, destroyed the conviction of millennia past that China possessed infallible supremacy over the rest of the world, known as the 'Mandate of Heaven'. Additional Treaty Ports were opened by other nations on the coast of China, while Russia acquired the opening of the northern border of China to Russian trade, together with annexation of land which would include the site of the future port-city of Vladivostok, thus allowing Russia direct access to a warm-water Pacific port. The Japanese took Formosa, while other islands, and Korea which had paid tribute to China since the 18th century, became independent.

In the intentions of the Hundred Days of Reform in 1898, the reformers had looked toward the achievement of Peter the Great in Russia and contemporary reformers in Japan, whilst still hoping that they could usher in a new era rooted in the tradition of Confucius. In the end the Boxer Rebellion had been put down by military intervention of all the great powers under a German commander, but unfortunately the result had left China more unstable. The reforms were aimed at improving the educational system and modernising the civil service entry exams; the military were to be reorganised, and industrialisation promoted, and perhaps most importantly China was to be encouraged towards a constitutional monarchy with widespread democracy. The reforms were however too radical for many in government, and in particular for the conservative dowager Empress Cixi under whose direction a coup took place with execution of the reformist leaders.

Many students were still planning and plotting reform, including a young doctor and philosopher called Sun Yat-sen (1866–1925). Inspiration was also drawn from western thinkers, including the British philosopher John Stuart Mill (1866–1925), and the American journalist and political thinker Henry George (1839–1897). Eventually this movement would become the party that emerged as the dominant one in the New Chinese Republic. Chinese students had brought home radical ideas from the western world, and in addition a modernised army derived a lot of new thinking and attitudes from the foreign troops that had fought across China.

Finally, the Dowager Empress and her puppet child Emperor died in 1908. The event raised new hopes of reform, but over the next three years change was very slow: the situation changed when military commanders defected from the central government. Clearly at this stage the dynasty was lost, the Mandate of Heaven had ceased, and in 1912 the last Manchu Emperor (aged only six) was forced to abdicate. A new Republic was proclaimed with Sun Yat-sen as its President, though he soon resigned this position to the influential General Yuan Shih-K'ai. Unfortunately Yuan displayed increasingly autocratic tendencies, abolishing the national and provincial assemblies and declaring himself Emperor in 1915. His colleagues in government resented all this and he was forced to abdicate within the year and died only a few months later.

Once more, the radicals returned to conflict, and Sun Yat-sen set out anew to unite China. Help was given from the Soviet Union in the early years after the Russian Communist revolution of 1917, and the next three or four decades continued to see internal conflict, initially with General Chiang Kai-shek (1887–1975) controlling most of south and central China, until Mao Zedong (1893–1976) emerged as a guerrilla Communist leader in 1934. The civil war continued but Chiang Kai-shek purged many of the communist leaders in the years leading up to the Second World War and then led China's fight against the Japanese who had invaded and occupied much of China.

Civil war resumed after Japan surrendered and Chiang was elected president for a brief period in 1948 but corruption and a very weakened state and army made his position untenable, so he retreated with his supporters to Formosa (now Taiwan), staying as president until his death until his death in 1975. Mao Zedong continued as Chairman of the communist party and ruler of mainland China after winning the civil war until he too died in 1976.

A single centre of government, often disputed and fought over, but embodying a constant cultural climate, has allowed China to weather the millennia with remarkable constancy even through changes in dynasties. This unchanging internal social milieu, despite the enormous purges and internal massacres of the second half of the 20th century, combined with equally unchanging external geographical constraints has given the Chinese a reassuring and steady national tale persisting even through the Communist revolution and up to the present time when the Chinese Communist Party is effectively an organisation practising autocracy which clamps down on dissent as severely and effectively as any past emperor or mediaeval monarch.

Possible further reading:
A History of India by JAG Roberts (Palgrave MacMillan)
The Walled Kingdom by Witold Rodzinski (Fontana Paperback)

Chapter 91
World War 1

The 19th century saw much redrawing of European boundaries. Boundaries had also appeared and then been redrawn in the Americas. The newly autonomous United States of America had acquired much extra land with the Louisiana purchase, annexed Texas after a two year war, and bought Alaska from Russia. In addition the USA had participated in various South American wars of independence between 1810 and 1826, with individual South American countries being liberated and becoming self-governing republics – Brazil from Portugal in 1822, Paraguay in 1811, Argentina in 1816, Chile and Ecuador in 1820, Peru in 1821, Bolivia in 1825, and Uruguay in 1828, all from Spain.

The lessons of the United States independence forty years earlier had not been lost on these young countries, though it would appear that Spain and Portugal had failed to take note of a popular trend, even need, for self-determination. The USA itself, despite being an equally large agglomeration of land and people was held together as a federal structure, in which people's primary allegiance was often to an individual state, and only secondarily to the larger nation.

Back in Europe, the Congress of Vienna at the end of the Napoleonic era in 1815 had resulted in considerable redrawing of European boundaries. These persisted for the rest of the first half of the 19th century, but in 1848 revolution erupted across Europe again, though it was largely quelled without boundary changes. Prussia defeated Austria in 1866, only to have war between France and Prussia erupt in 1870. The Austro-Hungarian Empire had come into being between the two countries in 1867 with a realisation of common aims and conditions between them, and remained a force to be reckoned with. Within the Empire, Croatia-Slavonia was incorporated as an autonomous region, while Bosnia and Herzegovina were under direct civil and military rule. Somewhat earlier, Russia's territorial ambitions had seen her annex the Caucasus and Crimea in 1859.

In 1885, a conference in Berlin showed the European nations in their "scramble for Africa". Most European countries made a bid to acquire different areas of Africa as colonies. At the same time, the French also expanded into Indo-China, principally trying to control the nations of south-eastern Asia lying between China and India. A little later in 1902 the British brought the Second Boer War against Dutch settlers to a close, which led to the formation of the Union of South Africa (incorporating Cape Colony, Natal, Transvaal, and Orange

River State) under nominal British rule in 1910, with transition to fully independent autonomy as a Dominion in 1931.

By 1900, Britain was facing a growing challenge from German, American and Austro-Hungarian industry. Each of those countries already had technical institutes of education producing the engineers and artisans required by their country's growing industries. In America, the early automobile industry and young aviation industry were both forging ahead, together with the new cinema industry to cater for people's leisure hours. In Europe, the automobile industry was represented by Mercedes in Germany and Renault in France as the largest producers.

In 1904, the Entente Cordiale was signed between Britain and France, and then extended in 1907 to include Russia, all for the purpose of trying to contain a future militaristic threat from Germany, including a German bid to build a navy to rival that of Britain. In 1902 British manufacturing was beginning to slip down the league tables and Foreign Minister Joseph Chamberlain (1836–1914) advocated an end to free trade and an introduction of protectionism: this was not a popular suggestion as it would have meant more expensive imports, particularly affecting food. In 1908, under Prime Minister Henry Asquith (1852–1928), a reforming Liberal government with David Lloyd George (1863–1945) at the Treasury, enacted several welfare measures, including the first payment of pensions to those over 70, free school meals and clinics.

In an economy that was spending 10% of its budget on education, income tax was increased to one shilling and twopence (6p in modern currency or 6% of income), with petrol, alcohol and tobacco taxes in addition; the defence spending on the army and navy still accounted for more than 50% of the total government expenditure. In 1909 the budget, including new welfare measures, was initially refused and delayed by the House of Lords. After new elections, but with the Liberals in a minority and supported by 42 Irish and 40 Labour MPs, the extra votes allowed an Irish Home Rule Bill to be passed, though again it was held up in the Lords; it became law in 1914, but was then suspended, first because of the unresolved question about the six northern Protestant counties in Ulster, and secondly because of the outbreak of the War.

In the Far East, Japan and China were at war in 1894–95 for the control of Korea, with the newly industrialised and powerful Japan overcoming China, which had failed to modernise and industrialise. After the Emperor and his regent, the Empress Cixi, died in 1908, the remaining Manchu Court continued to resist attempts at modernisation, and this in turn led to a period of rebellion eventually resulting in the Xinhai Revolution and the abdication of the new child Emperor, thus ending the Qing dynasty, with China becoming a republic under its first president, Sun Yat-Sen in 1911. In 1904–05 Japan's territorial ambitions had taken it to war with Russia over control of Manchuria, with Russia seeking a warm water pacific port since Vladivostok ices up in winter. Japan was also seeking control over North Korea as a territorial buffer against Russia and China.

Back in Europe, continued fomenting of nationalist sentiments was generating tides that would lead to boundary disputes. In Scandinavia, Norway achieved independence from Sweden in 1905, and Finland continued its campaign against Russian dominance, winning its own parliament in 1906. The small Baltic States of Estonia, Latvia and Lithuania continued to struggle against the territorial and linguistic ambitions of both Russia and Germany.

However, it was in the Balkan countries, Serbia, Bulgaria, Romania, Greece and Montenegro, where the European tinder box finally burst into flames. The area was surrounded on its three aspects by the Austro-Hungarian Hapsburg Empire and the Russian Empire to the north and east, with the Turkish Empire to the south and east. Bulgaria declared independence from Turkey, and Austria annexed Bosnia Herzegovina (also notionally Turkish) in 1908. Serbia was thus encircled and felt besieged, while Russia and Turkey both felt insulted and severely aggrieved. The Turkish Sultan was deposed in 1911 and the Greeks, who had been defeated in their previous war with Turkey in 1897, had a new government with territorial ambitions to the north.

Thus it was in 1912 that the first Balkan War, between the Balkan League (Bulgaria, Serbia, Greece and Montenegro) and the Ottoman Empire broke out, culminating some six months later in a decisive defeat of Ottoman Turkey, only to have a further war break out almost immediately between Serbia and Greece. By 1913 the three warring parties comprised Russia, with Serbia as her main proxy, Greece and Romania were backed by Britain and France, while the third faction in this triangular contest comprised Bulgaria and Ottoman Turkey facing off against Austro-Hungary.

In this febrile atmosphere, a state visit to Bosnia by the heir to the Austrian throne, Archduke Ferdinand, was inevitably risky. The Archduke was assassinated by a Bosnian Serb student, and Austria launched a retaliatory strike on Serbia as punishment, although the student was clearly not acting under official instructions, nor as an agent of the Serbian Government.

At the time Germany was simmering with territorial ambitions, and expected to be able to invade France to the west, while Austria provided a block to any Russian help that might come from the east. The problem with this was that the German plan, which had been years in the making, and which had been designed to shatter the Entente Cordiale between Britain, France and Russia, required that invasion of France start with a rapid military advance through Belgium. Britain felt very strongly that the invasion of neutral Belgium had crossed a non-negotiable red line, and in the event the German advance through Belgium was not swift enough to prevent deployment of British and French troops. It was this sequence of events which started the Great War.

The German armies were stopped two days march north of Paris, along the River Marne, where the troops of both sides dug trenches and bombarded each other for the next three years. Minimal territory was exchanged, and the two armies were locked in a deadly and muddy stalemate which claimed hundreds of thousands of lives in useless assaults against each other's front lines. Britain opened a second front fighting Germany's Turkish allies in Mesopotamia and the Middle East, together with an unsuccessful attempt to land a substantial force at Gallipoli in Crimea, in an attempt to divert men and resources from the stalemate in France.

The stalemate continued for two years until the Battle of Jutland in 1916 between the English and German navies, which had been largely avoiding each other up to that point. Finally on this occasion the two great battle fleets met, a total of 250 ships overall. At Jutland the British losses were greater, but resulted nonetheless in victory, with the German fleet forced back to port, and the Germans relying on sinking merchant ships using submarines for the rest of the war. The following year a further major blow to Germanys' ambitions was struck, firstly by the Russian Revolution, which resulted in Russia leaving the war and losing much territory (the Tsar abdicated in early 1917 and was murdered with his family in October that year).

Secondly, and far to the west, the neutral Americans, who had been punctilious about remaining out of the conflict, were being angered by German attacks on American merchant shipping, when it became public that the German Foreign Minister had promised Mexico help in recovering the Texan lands which had become part of the United States some 70 years earlier. A modest initial contingent of American soldiers came into the war in early 1918 and by September a massive US army of nearly a million men had joined the war against Germany.

Within a couple of months, the German Kaiser, who had been orchestrating and encouraging his country's war-time ambitions, accepted that his territorial ambitions had failed, and abdicated. A new German government accepted a peace agreement which came into force on the eleventh hour of the eleventh day of the eleventh month, a date in time since commemorated every year by the victors.

Britain and France extracted massive war reparations from Germany, together with an admission of guilt for commencing hostilities, but unfortunately not requiring German disarmament, and not including a formal surrender. The German government signed the Treaty of Versailles on 28th June 1918 and then resigned. Latvia and Lithuania were able to declare their independence from Germany as part of the Peace Treaty, and Estonia secured its separation from Russia two years later. Poland, which had been fought over during conflict Cossack Germany and Russia, was resurrected as a sovereign country in its own right. Further south on the eastern front, the Turkish Ottoman Empire was dismantled, and Greece recovered territory and reparations from Turkey.

New boundaries were drawn up to form new countries in the Middle East following the Sykes-Picot agreement, which had been drawn up by two British and French diplomats under a secret action plan in 1917 Between Russia and Turkey, a border was settled, but at the expense of Armenians and Kurds living along the disputed line, who became divided communities across the boundaries between Turkey, Russia and Iran, giving rise to discontent and problems which persist to the present day. Episodes of mutual ethnic cleansing also occurred between minority communities in Greece and Turkey.

Throughout this First World War, Britain had much support from its dominions and colonies, both in terms of finance and military personnel. Seven hundred thousand British troops had died, though the total deaths across all participating nations was some 15 times higher than this. Military deaths in France were almost 1.5 million, in Russia over 2 million; German military deaths are estimated at 2 million and a further 1.25 million from Austro-Hungary; civilian deaths across all European nations are estimated to have been over 6 million people.

The financial cost was also high, and the British national debt of £40 million in 1914 had swollen to almost ten times that amount by the end of the war. The wholehearted participation of all segments of British society was reflected in a national coming together at the end of the war, with all men over 21 and all women over 30 being granted the vote.

Possible further reading:
Catastrophe by Max Hastings (William Collins)

Chapter 92
Russian and Chinese Revolutions

We have already seen that Russia has a long history of autocracy commencing with Rurik and continuing through the Tsars of the Middle Ages on a direct blood line until the line ran out after Ivan the Terrible. Boris Godunov came to power and was a relatively benign autocrat until he was overthrown and Tsardom was restored in the form of the Romanov Dynasty at the request of the aristocracy. In a continuing line of Tsars Peter the Great came to the throne at the age of 9 in 1682, coming to rule in his own right at the age of 24. He was a reforming Tsar, but like others before him and since his time, attempts to reform were retracted early on at the first sight of protest by Russia's small aristocracy.

There were many attempts at reform and an equal number of rebellions through Russian history. These include a Cossack and peasant revolt in 1670 of 'The Old Believers' under a leader called Stenka Razin, who had split from the politically motivated Orthodox Church also in the 17th century, the Decembrist Revolt against Nicolas I in 1825, and more recently the revolt against Alexander II at the end of the 19th century, who also ended up murdered by an assassin. Peter the Great's daughter Anna was presented with a list of demands emulating the Bill of Rights but refused to sign it.

After she died young in childbirth, Peter's second daughter Elizabeth seized power with the aid of troops and was active in suppressing the reforms that had been demanded. Peter's granddaughter, Catherine the Great, who was a German Princess trapped in a loveless marriage but resorting to many affairs, arranged that her husband be murdered only months after becoming the Tsar. Catherine took up the reins of power and initially seemed to be very progressive starting her rule as a reformer, but when she faced rebellions and protest, she retrenched.

It was a recurring theme that successive Tsars appeared to have acknowledged a need for reform and progressive liberation, only to retreat on their views once opposition was apparent, or indeed when militant protestors suggested that the reforms did not go far enough. Nicolas II (1868–1916) who came to power in 1894 became very repressive as demonstrated by the manner in which rebellions were put down and subsequent pogroms pursued. He was also held responsible for Russia being defeated by the Japanese during the 1905 Russo-Japanese War fought by the two imperial powers with ambitions over Manchuria and Korea, and with Russia seeking to acquire a warm water all year Pacific port.

Nicholas' father Alexander III (1845–1894) had, during his reign, revoked his own father's plans for reform in a document entitled "The Tsar's Manifesto On Unshakeable Autocracy": the title speaks for itself. Alexander's attitudes and those of his chosen advisors reflected the view that in the world's largest nation, encompassing many ethnic minorities and religions, government could only succeed if there was a single central autocratic authority: this attitude and thinking was passed to his son Nicolas II.

Thus, after the failure of many revolts and the withdrawal of several planned attempts at liberalisation, the Russian intelligentsia concluded that popular revolution would not occur until the peasant masses supported it. Needless to say the large peasant population was illiterate, and largely ignorant of the political issues of the day, and was also mistrustful and suspicious about any proposed changes which they often felt were simply designed to increase repression. It did not help that many would-be revolutionaries, particularly at the end of the 19th and into the 20th century, were intellectual members of the aristocracy.

These armchair revolutionaries concluded that as the peasant masses would never be sound supporters for a revolution it would therefore be necessary that a dedicated small group of individuals would need to act on behalf of the people. These self-appointed revolutionaries who contemplated action on behalf of the peasant masses did not see the need to make provision for the general peoples' opinion of what was planned in their name. Indeed it is reputed that on their return to Russia from exile, Lenin told Stalin "…first we seize power, then we decide what to do with it".

No doubt this quotation when given without context sounds remarkable and indicates an activist politician who is more interested in achieving power than in pursuing an unspecified political agenda once power is achieved. Power is only a step on the way to achieving a desired or stated outcome, and Lenin and Stalin both saw it as a step on the way to achieving the perfect communist state in which equality would be foremost, there would be no aristocracy, and the will of the great mass of citizens would control the future of the country, even if they were not consulted; matters did not this utopian plan.

Thus, as Lenin (1870–1924), Stalin (1878–1953) and Trotsky (1879–1940), together with their revolutionary colleagues, while mainly in exile, had come to the conclusion that the mass of the Russian people would never be reliable supporters for a revolution, they decided that a dedicated small group of individuals would need to act. This small group would act on behalf of the people, the peasants and masses, nowhere did the revolutionaries see the need to make provision for the people's opinion of what was planned in their name and for their future.

Meanwhile, the young Tsar Nicholas had called reform "senseless dreams" and was at pains to reinforce "the principle of absolute autocracy". Disturbances had taken place in Russian universities and several senior government ministers were murdered in the early years of the 20th century. By the end of 1904 turmoil had ensued with an increase in political violence and a coincidental failure of the harvest leading to hard times for most Russian peasants. In 1905 a peaceful unarmed protest parade was fired on by troops with up to 4,000 deaths, earning the epithet "Bloody Sunday".

Lenin, whose brother had been hanged in 1887 for a plot against the State, had been jailed in 1900 for plotting against the Tsar, afterwards being exiled to Switzerland, where he welcomed the news of early rebellious activity and political violence in 1905 as something which would hasten the onset of an impending revolution. Trotsky had been living in exile in Britain after being arrested in 1905 by troops who stormed the St Petersburg Soviet (meaning Council), afterwards he was sentenced to exile in Siberia but managed to escape. The whole revolution collapsed in 1906.

A communist party congress in London in 1903 had previously ended up divided up into Trotsky's supporters, known as Mensheviks, and Lenin's supporters, known as Bolsheviks, who felt a small but dedicated group of professionals should be in charge. After the first revolution a Dumas, or parliament, was offered in 1905, but only to provide consultation and advice to the Tsar, without any power or commitment to implement this advice.

An interesting character appears on the scene a little later called Rasputin, as an advisor to Tsar Nicholas and the Tsarina Alexandra. He was a drunken lecherous monk, who achieved considerable sway over the opinions of the Tsarina by acting as a healer to her son who suffered from haemophilia (a condition which even today has no cure). His attitudes and advice were bizarre and included a tendency to call upon the supernatural. He was eventually murdered by aristocrats who felt he had become far too dangerous in his influence over the Tsarina.

Russia entered the First World War against Germany, but by 1917, with the war in stalemate, there were considerable food shortages in Russia and local rebellions as well. Troops were recalled from the front to control the rebellions, and early in the year unrest got out of hand. Tsar Nicholas was persuaded to abdicate, which he did believing that his brother could still become the next Tsar. A moderate provincial government took overruling the country. Once this unrest and revolution appeared to be underway Lenin, who was in exile in Switzerland, decided that he needed to return to Russia.

Germany, still at war with Russia, decided that Lenin's presence in Russia could only add to Russian instability and therefore could help lift some of the pressure on Germany's eastern front. The German government therefore arranged for money and a train to cross Germany to Russia from Switzerland carrying Lenin and some two or three dozen of his fellow activists. The Germans hoped that Russia would withdraw from the war if the internal problems got worse, and indeed in due course this happened.

Lenin predicted that the worldwide socialist revolution that he expected was underway, while in Russia no one was really in control, and there was no overarching plan for the future, but a provisional government had been installed which was planning elections and liberal reforms. Lenin at this time was advocating abolition of police, army and bureaucracy, confiscation and nationalisation of land, together with nationalisation of banks and the assumption of all power by the soviets (communist committees). With these stirring promises, which the peasants wanted to hear, the Bolsheviks became the standard bearers of the people with other factions being brushed aside.

A few months later, the provisional government was failing. There was a mass up-rising in Petrograd of protesting peasants, as a result of which many troops deserted. Lenin himself fled, and lived first in the countryside, and then in Finland. The provisional government attempted to discredit Lenin, portraying him as a German agent, and while he was in hiding Trotsky organised a Revolutionary Committee and was elected chairman in September 1917.

The Winter Palace In Petrograd was stormed at the end of October, though it seems there was little resistance from those inside. Following this the Bolsheviks set up a new government which was unelected, and created a new secret police. Lenin returned from his hideaway in Finland, and was effectively translated into a Tsar with different clothes and different policies, but equally implacable attitudes to controlling the peasant masses and prescribing future policies; he clearly felt he was acting alongside a tide of history and is reputed to have claimed that "just as Darwin discovered the law of evolution as it applies to organic matter, so Marx discovered the law of evolution as it applies to human history". Although a constituent assembly was elected, it only met once: the Bolsheviks who were in a minority somehow rode roughshod over the other parties and elected members, despite the Socialist Revolutionary Party at this stage having twice as many seats in the provisional parliament as the Bolsheviks.

As Germany had hoped, Russia made peace and withdrew from the war in March 1918, accepting Russian loss of land in Poland, Finland, the Baltic States and Ukraine in order that they could devote their efforts to concentrating on government at home. The Tsar and his family had been kept in secret confinement in the country, and were finally murdered in July 1918, probably on Lenin's direct orders. Lenin, Trotsky and Stalin were now firmly in control of Russian internal politics, and much infighting would ensue as the contest for absolute power and autocracy returned to Russia.

---oOo---

The Chinese Revolution in many ways seems to have been a replay of many of the changes that occurred in Russia. China also had been ruled with considerable repression by a small self-serving autocracy through previous millennia. Between 1815 and 1873 a succession of rebellions came close to overthrowing the Qing Dynasty starting with the Taiping Revolt, or Civil War, from 1850–1864 which resulted in a death toll of around twenty million people before it ended.

There was a Confucian belief that the Chinese dynasties started with virtuous rulers who enjoyed the "mandate of heaven". The theory continued that at some stage later dynastic rulers would be unable to maintain the early standards, so that government would gradually decline leading in due course to rebellion, and leading on eventually to a new dynasty: in this way the cycle would continue. At the end of the cycle, said the theory, the Chinese Court often seemed to have become extravagant and the bureaucracy corrupt, and the army towards the end of this cycle would lose its ethos and be unable to defend the central government. To cover the extravagances and to improve military performance taxes would be increased leading to rebellion.

Looking back through history, Mao Zedong saw the history of Chinese uprisings as an expression of class struggle. The Tongzhi Emperor between 1861 and 1875 was a child, coming to the throne at the age of 5, so that a regency ruled under his mother, the Dowager Empress Cixi (1835–1908) with improving fortunes through to the end of the 19th century. The emperor only ruled for two years before dying without any heirs and Cixi's 4–year-old nephew was named as emperor, so that in this way Cixi was able to continue as a very powerful regent right up to the time of her death in 1908. Attempts at westernisation had been defeated by the very conservative Empress, which explains how Japan, which had westernised, was able to win the Sino-Japanese War of 1894–95, a conflict which was fought between the two countries over establishing influence on Korea and Manchuria which had been tributary states to China until then. A series of international incidents led up to the war with contemporary observers expecting the Japanese to be defeated.

In 1898, a Reform Agenda was introduced following the disastrous Sino-Japanese War, but at the same time some individuals began to plot revolution, including a young Chinese called Sun Yat-Sen (1866–1925). It initially appeared that modernisation along the lines of the Japanese reforms since the Meiji Restoration in 1865 might follow in China. However, the Empress Cixi was extremely conservative and overturned the Hundred Days Reform Agenda in a military coup and executed many of the progressive elements, she continued to oversee China with a very controlling and conservative outlook until her death in 1908.

Finally, in the Wuchang Uprising in 1911, the ruling dynasty was overthrown and another child Emperor forced to abdicate. A provisional government was installed after political agreement between Sun Yat-Sen and the Qing military leadership. A provisional government was agreed with Sun Yat-Sen as the first President, which took over in 1912. He only stayed in the presidency for a couple of months before handing the post to Yuan Shikai (1859–1916), the army chief, who tried to preserve the central bureaucracy and control of the nation. Internal struggles within various nationalist and communist Chinese factions would continue for the rest of the first half of the 20th century.

This Civil War became a contest between the Chinese Nationalist Party and the Communist Party, with the various Communist armies escaping and retreating through 1934–35 in a military retreat known as 'The Long March' under the direction of Mao Zedong (1893–1976) and Zhou Enlai (1898–1976). It is reputed that only ten percent of the military force that set out on the Long March completed the journey. Mao Zedong came to rule China at the beginning of the second half of the 20th century by which time China was fully under the control of the Communist Party in a regime which ruled by repression, secret police, arbitrary justice and a policy of exile and executions.

Possible further reading:
The Russian Revolution by Geoffrey Hosking (Oxford University Press)
A History of China by JAG Roberts (Palgrave Macmillan)
See also suggestions in chapter 93

Chapter 93
Brief World Overview of the 20th Century

The events of the second decade of the 20th century determined the path that the world would follow for the next fifty years and beyond into the 21st century. At the conclusion of the First World War Germany had been defeated and severe reparations and penalties were imposed which would have an enormous effect on the economic conditions of the next two decades. Russia and China were dissolving into civil wars which would end with the establishment of the world's first communist regimes.

Towards the end of the War in 1917, revolution in Russia had seen the abdication of Tsar Nicholas II and the installation of provisional government. Within months the provisional government was removed and replaced with a Communist Bolshevik government. Internal power struggles continued with the Bolsheviks led by Vladimir Lenin (1870–1924). Lenin developed Marxist theories, and the early Russian Communist Party followed his thinking, which was now known as Marxist Leninism. The Imperial family were all executed surreptitiously in 1918, and thereafter Russian society tended to lawlessness under its new dictator; terror, secret trials and executions formed a large part of the means of controlling the Russian populace, just as the Tsars had done for centuries before.

The League of Nations came about due to the diplomatic efforts of the winning powers of the Great War in 1920. It was a toothless organisation throughout its lifetime, and its effectiveness was severely limited by the absence of the United States, where President Woodrow Wilson had been one of the driving forces behind its formation, but the US Senate subsequently voted not to join, and as the richest nation in the world, and one of the least affected by the war, America then abdicated its leadership role. Many other nations also failed to join or left after a short period, severely limiting the effectiveness of the League.

Several areas of the map of the world were redrawn; in Central Europe Finland achieved autonomy from Russia, as did Estonia, Latvia and Lithuania notionally. Poland was restored as a nation between Germany and Russia after two hundred years of absence from the European map. In the Middle East the map was redrawn by the victors after much discussion but with little regard for ancient tribal and religious loyalties and alliances, so Iraq, Iran, Palestine and Syria all appeared as new nations.

Within the United Kingdom, an Anglo-Irish Treaty was agreed in 1921 giving the majority of Ireland complete independence in Home Rule, but allowing Northern Ireland (the 'Six Counties' – predominantly protestant) to remain within the United Kingdom. The Treaty ended three years of war for independence between the Irish Republican Army and British forces. The Irish Free State, Eire, which is predominantly catholic and which resulted from the Treaty comprised the twenty six southern counties of Ireland, and was initially a Dominion of the British Commonwealth of Nations, the six northern protestant counties remained within the United Kingdom.

However, political manoeuvring continued because the King of Britain remained notionally King of Ireland and appointing a Governor General was rejected. The status of Dominion, identical to that of Canada, Australia and the other Dominions, was resented and Ireland wished the pursue its own policies in foreign affairs, rather than allow Westminster continuing authority in this role. A new constitution was the subject of a referendum in 1937, and was approved by 56% of voters (just over 38% of the electorate).

The new constitution included the words that "a united Ireland shall be brought about only by peaceful means with the consent of the majority of the people, democratically expressed, in both jurisdictions in the island". Unfortunately, despite this the Irish Republican Movement south of the dividing border has continued to pursue a policy of insurgency to unite all of Ireland together, while the Protestant Six Counties in the north have resisted strongly, thus regardless of the peaceful intention in the new constitution, intermittent guerrilla warfare has persisted ever since.

At Westminster, the three parties, Labour, Liberal and Tory, continued as adversaries, but were fairly united about implementing new social policies. The Conservative Party had won the 1922 General Election after withdrawing from the coalition government with Liberal Prime Minister Lloyd George. Activist Conservative MPs formed a backbench discussion and pressure group, which still exists, known as the 1922 Committee. A further election a year later had resulted in the Conservatives losing MPs, but remaining the largest party, although in a minority. The election had been fought over "food taxes" or tariffs on imported foods. It was argued that as the Labour party was the largest anti-tariff party it should form the government, so in 1924 Ramsey MacDonald (1866–1937), one of the three main founders of the Labour Party was sworn as the first Labour Prime Minister.

His government was not a success due to its minority status, and due to fears that its socialist thinking might represent the extension of Communism from Russia. A letter from a Soviet leader, Gregory Zinoviev, advocating "a successful rising in the working districts of England" to bring the revolution to Britain and its colonies, turned out to be a forgery or an early example of fake news, but played badly with the electorate, so at a further election in 1929 Labour only managed to win 151 seats compared to the Conservative's 419 seats (the Liberals were reduced to just 40 seats).

One of the agreed measures that came into being during MacDonald's social legislation was the Balfour Declaration in 1926, at which Britain and its dominions agreed that they were all equal in status within the British Commonwealth. After the Second World War in 1949 the designation 'British' would be dropped allowing the organisation to become simply The Commonwealth.

Within Britain, radio broadcasting had started in 1920 from the Marconi factory, under licence from the General Post Office (GPO). Two years later almost one hundred other requests for licences had been received, and the GPO suggested that a single broadcasting licence should be awarded to a consortium of companies and known as the British Broadcasting Company. The money raised by the licence system was inadequate, particularly as advertising was not allowed. With a General Strike in 1926 over worsening pay and conditions for coal miners, newspaper publication also ceased and the BBC became the primary source of news for most people. Following this, the Company was nationalised and became a state owned utility with a duty of impartiality as far as the news was concerned, and financed by a licence fee.

In 1929, the US stock market ("Wall Street") suffered a severe crash losing approximately one-third of the total value of its shares. Recovery followed only very slowly, and the resulting Depression persisted into the middle of the 1930s in most countries. During this time unemployment rose and incomes dropped, further compounding the economic situation. It was a decade before share prices returned to their pre-depression level in the United States, and for working people through the decade unemployment was as high as 25%.

As a result, US President Franklin Roosevelt (1882–1945) put in place social programmes funded with public money at the beginning of his first term of office in 1933. The programmes comprised major spending on public infrastructure in an attempt to diminish unemployment. In addition to public spending, Roosevelt initiated suspension of the Gold Standard for the value of money, together with social relief programmes and a reform of banking and securities regulations. Redistribution of income by income tax was also one of the measures which gradually pulled the USA out of depression with other countries following.

Through the 1930s, the severe economic conditions caused profound dissatisfaction amongst voters with their governments in all countries. Fascism, embracing economic rectitude and a generally right-wing political attitude, saw a surge during these difficult economic years. Benito Mussolini (1883–1945) was the leader of Italy's National Fascist Party coming to power in 1922. He remained as legitimate Prime Minister for three years, but thereafter ruled as a dictator, becoming known as 'Il Duce'.

In this way, Italy essentially became a police state up to the outbreak of the Second World War. Mussolini was deposed and imprisoned by the King in 1943, but was then rescued by German commandos. After being taken to meet Hitler he was put at the head of a puppet regime in Northern Italy, but with the war going against Germany, and with Italy being liberated by the allies, he attempted to escape to neutral Switzerland, but was captured and executed by Italian partisan communists in 1945.

In Russia, a seven-man Politburo committee was elected following the revolution to run the country. Amongst these seven men were Trotsky (1879–1940), Lenin (1870–1924) and Stalin (1878–1953). Lenin died in 1924. Trotsky's concept of communism, and the way Marxism should develop, was somewhat different from the rest of the committee, and he was expelled from the Communist Party in 1927 and exiled to Alma-Ata in modern Kazakhstan two years later. He continued to write and be a thorn in the flesh of the regime from a distance, and was eventually assassinated on Stalin's orders in 1940.

In this way, Stalin essentially became the single individual controlling the Soviet Union following the death of Lenin and remained as an absolute dictator for the succeeding three decades up to his death in 1953. During this time his economic management of the Soviet Union produced famines in 1932, and again during the War, as a result of a policy of 'collectivisation' (agglomeration of peasant farms or communes). In the late 1930s, fearing intellectual and political opposition, he directed a massive purge of officials, government and party, as well as the armed forces and intellectuals: it is estimated that up to 20 million people were executed or perished in the Siberian gulags (concentration camps) during this time.

Stalin did however manage to halt the progress of German armies in the Second World War by a policy reminiscent of the Russian opposition to Napoleon using sheer force of numbers and destroying the countryside and crops as troops retreated, thus denying the invading Germans shelter and food (an uncanny resemblance to Napoleon's retreat from Moscow in 1812). The Russian retreat from Stalingrad in 1943 marked the turning point of the war on the Eastern Front against the Germans, leaving an over-extended and vulnerable German army to retreat back westwards. Stalin finally died in 1953 with a reputation not only as a brutal and ruthless dictator, but also as an unreliable ally and statesman who frequently went back on his word and agreements which he had made earlier.

Like Mussolini and Stalin, Adolf Hitler (1889–1945) came to power in a constitutional fashion only to subvert the constitution and gradually become a brutal and intolerant dictator. Hitler's Nazi party had a commitment firstly to the destruction of Communism to the east, secondly to the expansion of German settlement in eastern Europe ('lebensraum' or living room) where the regime regarded the Slavs as an inferior race, and thirdly to exterminate Jews in Europe, believing that the German Nordic Aryan race was superior and that Jews needed to be purged or purified from German society, since the regime accused the Jews of monetary crimes against the state, enriching themselves thereby.

Hitler's first years in power resulted in rapid economic recovery from the depression after Hitler became Chancellor (Prime Minister) in 1933. Large amounts of money were spent on infrastructure and on re-arming the German nation in defiance of the post-war settlement of 1919. The Second World War started because of Hitler's unprovoked aggression in invading first

Czechoslovakia in 1938 and then Poland in 1939 in search of 'lebensraum'; Britain and France as treaty allies of both countries, declared war on the first of September 1939 following Germany's invasion of Poland.

After a titanic struggle, which came to involve most of the countries across the world, Germany was finally defeated in the Second World War, and as Russian, British and American troops closed in on Berlin, Hitler committed suicide. The Nazi regime is calculated to have been responsible for the genocide of around 6 million Jews, 20 million civilians and prisoners of war, and a further 29 million people who died across the world, both as soldiers and civilians fighting Germany.

A fourth European dictatorship emerged in the years before the Second World War in Spain, when a group of generals attempted a fascist coup against the democratic government which had socialist leanings, although it comprised individuals from the liberal side of the spectrum through to revolutionary anarchists. The resulting Spanish Civil War lasted for three years from 1936, and attracted support in the form of weaponry and soldiers from Nazi Germany and Fascist Italy. Most of Europe remained neutral, but individuals from European countries rallied to fight with the Spanish Republicans.

Ultimately, and despite outside support, the Nationalist General Franco (1892–1975) won the war after three years of fighting, and then ruled for the next four decades until his death in 1975. During his time as dictator, Franco called himself 'El Caudillo' (comparable to 'Il Duce' in Italy and 'Die Führer' in Germany) and Spain became a one-party state including the Monarchists and Fascists, but outlawing all other political parties. As in other dictatorships, arbitrary imprisonment and executions took place and concentration camps were set up. Spain sided with Germany and Italy through the Second World War. Finally on Franco's death in 1975 Spain was able to revert to being a constitutional monarchy, though political division between supporters and opponents of the dictator have persisted to present times.

Japan had westernised rapidly towards the end of the 19th century, and after participating in the First World War alongside the Allies had enjoyed excellent economic growth, but in the years leading up to the Second World War had become very nationalistic and embarked upon a series of wars, notably attacking China in 1937, an episode which ended in the Nanking Massacre with widespread rape, looting and the death of probably 250,000 Chinese civilians. The USA imposed sanctions against Japan in consequence, but this tipped Japan into the war in alliance with Germany and Italy.

On 7 December 1941, Japan launched a surprise attack and sank much of the American Pacific fleet at Pearl Harbour in Hawaii, the result of which was to bring previously neutral America into the war on the side of the Allies. Although Japan occupied the Philippines, Malaysia, Hong Kong, Singapore, Burma and the Dutch East Indies in their military campaign following Pearl Harbour, allied troops, principally American, subsequently drove the Japanese back out of their attempted Pacific Empire into the Japanese islands.

After Germany had surrendered and the war in Europe had officially ended on 8 May, the Japanese continued to fight. In consequence, and in an attempt to hasten the end of the war, an atomic bomb was dropped for the first time, on Hiroshima on 6 August 1945, killing up to 100,000 people. As this first bomb did not achieve Japanese surrender, a second atomic bomb was dropped on Nagasaki three days later, following which Japan surrendered on 15 August. Japan was occupied by the United States up to 1952, during which time a new constitution was introduced, guaranteeing civil and worker rights, together with women's suffrage, in addition to prohibiting the existence of an army or navy. Throughout the war years, and then when occupied and into the 1950s, Japan concentrated on economic and industrial growth very successfully.

Following the end of the Second World War, the ineffective League of Nations was replaced in late 1945 by the United Nations, which possessed strengthened military peace-keeping capability using troops drawn from the member nations. The first big test of the United Nations came in 1950 when North Korea, with Chinese and Russian backing, invaded South Korea. The nation had been divided as part of the peace settlement into a communist north and an American protected south.

Very soon, Chinese forces were fighting alongside beleaguered North Korean troops, and the United Nations intervened with 21 countries supporting and fighting for South Korea, though the majority of the troops were American. An armistice was signed to end the war, but an official peace treaty has never yet been signed and the two nations are still technically at war and separated by a demilitarised zone with a hereditary communist dictatorship in the north.

Following the end of the war, the North Atlantic Treaty Organisation (NATO) came into being in 1949 with a system of collective responsibility for defence, with all member states agreeing to support other members in the event of an attack: it is generally regarded as one of the pillars ensuring peace in Europe since 1945. At this time, Stalin wished to have a significant barrier between the communist countries of Russia and occupied eastern Europe and democratic western Europe. What was described by Winston Churchill as an 'Iron Curtain' divided the east from the west with the division separating two halves of Germany under Soviet and Western occupation, including Poland and the eastern European countries in the Soviet sphere of influence.

Berlin, as the capital of Germany, was occupied by the three conquering powers, Russia, America and Britain, but was a small enclave in the middle of Soviet occupied East Germany, and gradually came to be seen as an affront to Russia by Stalin. A blockade on rail and road supplies was instituted by the Russians in the summer of 1948 hoping to starve the British and Americans out of Berlin, but Britain and America continued to supply Berlin by air. The blockade lasted for almost a year with massive amounts of supplies being flown in, but with the eastern and western sectors of Berlin becoming autonomous as communist and democratic entities.

The blockade, in defiance of previous agreements signed by Russia, further consolidated the antagonism between east and west and confirmed the British and American mistrust of Soviet politics and policies in reliability and trustworthiness between the two adversarial sides and led into the Cold War, which then lasted until a wave of eastern European revolutions liberated most European nations from Russian domination in 1989.

Following the Second World War, America, which had benefitted rather than suffered economically through the war years, instituted an economic aid plan to Europe. This was named Marshall Aid after George Marshall, the United States Army Chief of Staff through the war and Secretary of State from 1947 to 1949. This far-seeing plan worth $12 billion ($120 billion at today's prices) was a vital aid to economic recovery across Europe where many countries had been fought over and incurred severe damage to their industrial and domestic stock, and to Britain in particular, which had incurred enormous debts (mainly to America) in commissioning the necessary personnel and weaponry to fight the war.

In Britain, William Beveridge (1879–1963), a noted economist and public servant, had written widely about social security and unemployment even before the war, and produced a report in 1942. Prior to the war he had been able to implement national insurance to fight poverty and unemployment and organise a national system of labour exchanges. In the post-war general election of 1945 the Tory party, under Winston Churchill (1874–1965), who had been prime minister for the last five years of the war, lost the election to Labour's Clement Atlee (1883–1967), who proceeded to introduce the welfare proposals recommended in Beveridge's 1942 report.

At the same time, plans were worked up for the introduction of a National Health Service in which primary and secondary medical care was provided for all citizens from general taxation. The Health Service commenced in 1948 and was revolutionary in covering all citizens, including visitors to the country, and in being financed from central taxation. The system included provision of public health measures and organisations, the whole service mirrored a recommendation made by the British Medical Association just before the war but not implemented due to hostilities.

In Britain, the nation was saddened by the death of King George VI in 1952. He and Queen Elizabeth had helped maintain morale for the nation by refusing to leave London during the blitz of 1940, and by their prominence in support of both troops and ordinary citizens. He was succeeded by his eldest daughter, Elizabeth, who was also prominent in serving the nation in the Auxiliary Territorial Services in the war years. She had married Prince Philip of Greece (later Duke of Edinburgh) in 1947 who had a distinguished war record serving in the navy, both in the Mediterranean and in the Pacific. Elizabeth's coronation took place in 1953 on the same day that news reached London that a British expedition to climb Mount Everest for the first time had succeeded: the occasion provided a great boost to national morale.

Soon after, in 1955, war broke out between North and South Vietnam. As in Korea The conflict was a classic cold war proxy war with the Soviet Union and China supporting the north, and the Americans becoming increasingly involved on behalf of South Vietnam. America saw the need for the war as buttressing the nations of south-east Asia against a domino style political collapse into communist rule.

By 1968, stalemate had been achieved and the American public was getting increasingly disillusioned with the costs that the nation was incurring, both economic and in terms of American lives, at a time when neighbouring Cambodia and Laos had also been dragged into the conflict. America withdrew from the conflict in 1975, and North and South Vietnam were reunited under communist rule. The conflict has become notorious for the amount of genocide involved and for the use of torture and summary executions, principally by the communist North Vietnamese, although American investigations have shown that US forces were not blame-free either in this conflict.

The Cold War, lasting from the end of the Second World War up to the time of the collapse of the Berlin Wall in 1989, was an extensive period of confrontation between the communist east, financed and directed by the Soviet Union and China, and the capitalist west comprising the western European countries and North America. Physically the Cold War was symbolised by the 'Iron Curtain', comprising a reinforced, militarised and rigidly policed border extending from the Arctic Ocean almost to the Mediterranean, fencing in the communist countries so that their citizens should not escape and nor should they learn what activities and standards of living were possible outside the Soviet system, though first broadcasting, and later limited travel and then the internet brought comparisons of conditions either side of the Iron Curtain to Soviet citizens.

During this time, small conflicts broke out through the rest of the world with the Cold War adversaries often lining up to support opposite sides, and thus perpetuate the conflicts. Both sides had nuclear weapons that acted as a deterrent under a scenario that postulated mutually assured destruction should one side attack the other. The contrast between the two opposing sides was stark, with the Soviet Union and China subject to dictatorship, severe press restrictions and secret police, while on the other side, democratic states were predominantly capitalist with an unfettered press and independent organisations, which included those protesting against the possession of nuclear weapons and refusing to criticise communist behaviour.

The height of the Cold War is possibly best represented by the Cuban Missile crisis in 1962 when Russia attempted to place missile bases in Cuba less than 100 miles from American shores; after a protracted stand-off the missiles were eventually withdrawn.

A Chinese Civil War between the government of China and communist party rebels had begun in 1927 but continued through the intervening years. The communist forces under Mao Zedong negotiated a secret truce with the Japanese army in China, which weakened the Chinese Nationalist army. Mao Zedong (1893–1976) was a founder member of the Communist Party in China and also helped to found the Red Army. He was prominent in the 'Long March' in 1934/5 when the communist army under Mao and Chou Enlai retreated about 9,000km in a year to avoid annihilation by the pursuing Nationalist army, but around 90% of the marching soldiers died.

Mao then became leader of the Communist Party of China. Following the Long March, hostilities between the Nationalists and the Communists ceased until the end of the Second World War when the Communist Army was resurrected to drive the Nationalists out of mainland China to the island of Taiwan, where it has continued to maintain an adversarial stance against mainland China ever since. The People's Republic of China continued with its implementation of communist ideology, including Mao's epic plans of the 'Great Leap Forward' from 1958–62 and the 'Cultural Revolution' over the years following 1966.

The Great Leap Forward was intended to achieve rapid industrialisation for China, while the Cultural Revolution was aimed at purging traditional Chinese and intellectual thinking and capitalist ideas. These two ideas of Mao caused immense misery to much of the population and much persecution of intellectuals and professionals. Up to 45 million deaths have been estimated resulting from the Great Leap Forward and the Cultural Revolution, which Mao saw as a necessary violent class struggle to bring ordinary workers to power.

In Europe, the Cold War ended and the 'Iron Curtain' came down. In 1991, in a series of mass peaceful protests which started in Poland with a trade Union reform movement called 'Solidarity', and spread inexorably to East Germany, Hungary, Bulgaria and Czechoslovakia, with only Romania succumbing to two years of violence in its transition from communist dictatorship. After electoral fraud in Soviet East Germany was followed by mass protests the communist regime collapsed, leading to the breaching and demolition of the Berlin Wall (the physical Iron Curtain through Berlin). In subsequent months reintegration between East and West Germany was achieved with the prosperous West gradually restoring equality to the downtrodden and poorer East.

Additional notable events through the 20th century:
1920: World-wide flu epidemic kills up to 100M or 5% of the world population. Prohibition of alcohol starts in USA and lasts till 1933. Estonia and Latvia achieve independence from Russia. Earthquake at Haiyuan, Central China, kills 180,000.
1921: Coup in Persia installs the new Shah.
1922: Insulin first used in Toronto. Egypt gains self-government from Britain. BBC formed. Tomb of Tutankhamen discovered in Egypt.
1923: Germany faces bankruptcy and defaults on reparations leading to economic crisis. Turkey become a republic after dissolution of the Ottoman Empire.
1924: Lenin dies, Stalin purges his rivals.
1925: Mongolian People's republic founded.
1925: Mussolini becomes dictator in Italy. John Logie Baird (1888–1946) demonstrates first TV transmission. The first small format Leica 35mm camera is introduced in Germany.

1926: UK General Strike against reductions in wages.
1927: First non-stop solo trans-Atlantic flight by Charles Lindbergh. A League of Nations Treaty abolishes all slavery across the world. Iraq gains independence from the UK.
1928: First Iron lung. First colour TV Broadcast. Alexander Fleming (1881–1955) discovers penicillin, later awarded Nobel Prize.
1929: Wall Street Crash, start of Great Depression.
1930: Frank Whittle (1907–1996) develops first jet engine. Brazilian Revolution ends in dictatorship.
1931: Catalonia achieves autonomy within Spain. Japan invades and occupies Manchuria.
1932: First splitting of the atom by Sir John Cockcroft in Cambridge.
1933: Hitler appointed German Chancellor, Dachau concentration camp opened. US President Roosevelt declares New Deal in Germany. Prohibition repealed. USA leaves gold standard.
1934: Third Reich declared, Hitler becomes 'Fuhrer' after President von Hindenburg dies.
1935: Mussolini invades Ethiopia. Radar first used in Britain. Germany rearms and introduces conscription.
1936: Coup by General Franco in Spain starts civil war. Start of Stalin's great purge. George V dies, Edward VIII abdicates, George VI ascends throne in UK.
1937: Second Sino-Japanese war – 25M combatants and up to 50M civilians die. Frank Whittle in UK tests first jet engine. Baird mounts first colour broadcast in UK.
1938: Germany occupies Austria. Oil discovered in Saudi Arabia. Germany invades Czechoslovakia. Nylon first available commercially. Lazslo Biro patents his ballpoint pen.
1939: Kristalnacht in Germany, many Jews killed, others sent to concentration camps. World War II starts – 25M combatants and up to 50M civilians die.
1940: British troops evacuated from Dunkirk. Denmark and Norway occupied. Battle of Britain prevents Hitler from invading UK. Italy joins Germany. Japan invades Indochina.
1941: Japanese raid on Pearl Harbour, Hawaii, brings USA into the war.
1943: World's first electronic computer analyses German radio transmissions. Gloster Meteor jet fighter's first flight. First use of LSD.
1944: Italy surrenders. June 6th D Day invasion by US and UK. August 25 Paris liberated.
1945: American President Roosevelt dies on April 12th. Hitler commits suicide 30 April. 4 May, Netherlands and Denmark liberated. Germany surrenders (8 May designated VE, victory in Europe, Day). 6 August, world's first atomic bomb dropped on Hiroshima; Japan fails to surrender and therefore, a second bomb is dropped on Nagasaki three days later. 15 August becomes VJ, victory in Japan Day.
1947: World's first peaceful atomic reactor at Harwell, Oxfordshire.

Possible further reading:
Penguin History of the 20th Century by JM Roberts (Penguin)
All Hell Let Loose by Max Hastings (Harper Press)
The Gulag Archipelago by Alexander Solzhenitsyn (Harper & Row)
Wild Swans by Jung Chang (Harper Collins)

Chapter 94
Energy

Humankind harnessed fire many millennia ago. It was used in a variety of ways, most notably for heating and cooking, but also as a quick means of deforestation so that land could be cleared for agricultural use. A combination of wood as a fuel and as a building material resulted in areas of the British Isles being deforested never to recover. The south-west moors of Exmoor, Dartmoor and Bodmin Moor remain bare to this day and without productive use, supporting only a few grazing animals, sheep and ponies. In a similar way much of the Scottish moors and the Irish countryside have also been deforested and left as wide unproductive spaces. Once people settled down in villages, fire continued to be vital to the advancement of humankind through its use domestically, in construction and in agriculture.

The Bronze Age (chapter 4) was ushered in once people discovered the ability to smelt metal ores and produce metal implements. At the same time in hot climates solar power was also used, particularly in brick making where mud or clay, once formed into regular shapes, could be left to dry and harden in the sun before use. Early man was also very ingenious with the renewable energy sources available so both wind and water mills appear very early in the timeline of civilisation. They have the great advantage of providing a more continuous and unsupervised supply of energy than fire. Mill ponds, dams and leets to channel water to where its latent energy could be used, persist from the earliest of days.

Later, it was discovered that in various places around the world, dead vegetable matter, including wood, had been converted by pressure and huge amounts of time into compact sources of available energy. The production of these so-called 'fossil fuels' relies on the exclusion of oxygen so that the plant matter does not decay, and can be dug up for use in which the fuel is oxidised in the process we recognise as fire. Thus decaying vegetable matter left to rot under pressure will gradually progress to peat in thousands of years, coal in millions of years, and oil or natural gas in hundreds of millions of years.

Peat is the least compact fuel formed from dead organic matter, and peat bogs are found across the world. Peat is also the least efficient form of fossil fuel, and produces the least heat, but it is formed in only thousands of years as demonstrated by its presence in areas from which the ice sheets of the last Ice Age have retreated. In many parts of the world it remains a valuable domestic source of energy. It has other uses and quite apart from being used as a soil conditioner, has provided valuable insights into the customs and habits of ancient people.

Just as the vegetation is preserved in the anoxic depths of a peat bog, so too are any creatures, human or other, who die and fall into the bog. In this way some preserved human bodies have provided a fascinating insight into early civilisation. Peat is also a very good means of carbon capture, preventing carbon dioxide from being released into the atmosphere as a greenhouse gas, although once the peat is dug up and burnt it does then give up its carbon as gaseous carbon dioxide to build up in the atmosphere. The uncontrolled burning of peat was responsible for the 1997 'South-east Asian Haze' which was due to massive forest burning in Indonesia. In this way peat contributes to global warming, as well as to deforestation and loss of habitat. In Indonesia, and in the Brazilian jungle, 'slash and burn' agriculture has also contributed to global warming.

Peatlands as a whole comprise some two or three percent of the world land area. If peat is undisturbed and remains protected from oxygen, it will gradually turn into lignite coal, the first stage of its conversion by pressure and time, into a more compact energy form. Lignite is also known as 'brown coal', and in some settings, notably around the Baltic Sea and the North Sea, it is found as small pieces which are known to jewellers as 'jet'. It has a carbon content of somewhere around two-thirds, and is relatively high in moisture with a relatively low energy density.

It has been used by later generations of people for power generation, but because of its relative inefficiency and density, power stations that have been designed to run on lignite have had to be built adjacent to lignite deposits. By contrast with peat which forms in thousands of years, lignite is formed much more slowly over millions of years.

If the process of transformation of dead organic matter (both vegetable and animal) continues to be subjected to time and pressure, the result is coal. The water content has markedly diminished and coal is approximately 90% carbon. Because of its concentration it also contains a relatively high content of impurities, especially sulphur compounds, which become dangerous as sulphuric acid and add to pollution and to global warming. When coal is burnt, it leads to a large release of carbon dioxide which previously was bound and captured.

Coal was probably first used in China around 4,000 BC, and initial deposits of coal were found as surface seams, from which open cast mining could be used to recover the coal. The use of coal probably occurred in western Europe also from about 4,000 BC, often coinciding with the onset of the Bronze Age, since the heat that burning coal releases was necessary for the smelting and casting of bronze. Later in time the intense heat provided by burning coal was necessary for the smelting of iron, and progress into the Iron Age.

Coal was a vital component to power the early Industrial Revolution. The combination of easily available iron ore and coal together in the Welsh valleys explains why the early Industrial Revolution came about in this location. From early open cast mining in Britain the 19th century progressed to produce vast quantities of deep mined coal, which is a much more expensive process, both in terms of time and effort, but also in the human cost of mining hazards and accidents.

In parts of the world, particularly America and China, coal deposits lie very much closer to the surface and are still exploited by open cast mining techniques, albeit on a much more massive scale today now that large sophisticated machinery is available. Under some conditions coal continues to be transformed by the combination of time and pressure into deposits of oil and natural gas. These deposits were increasingly exploited through the 19th century, not only for lighting and heating purposes, but also contributing to the explosive development of the internal combustion engine for land, sea and air transport, together with a mass of other petrochemical-derived products, commencing at the end of the century.

It is salutary to recall that electricity generated from coal or gas which we now take for granted as a power source for mankind, was only discovered some 200 years ago, and has only been substantially developed for everyday use in the last 100 years; it is also necessary to explain its relatively slow uptake owing to difficulty in storage, but as battery technology has developed recently this has helped. Commercial production of electricity in most countries is now centred in power stations using coal, oil or natural gas with a resulting huge burden of carbon dioxide being added to the planet's atmosphere.

Domestic use of electricity came later than the use of gas and first occurred in England as recently as the end of the 19th century, only becoming widespread by the middle of the 20th century. Electricity to power vehicles was first used in milk delivery floats after the first world war for vehicles which had a short range and a considerable weight and volume of lead acid batteries to carry around; it took almost the next hundred years before early models of electric cars became seriously practical.

Storage of electricity remains a problem although battery technology has steadily improved since Alessandro Volta produced his first primitive pile of alternating copper and zinc plates in 1800 (chapter 87). Battery technology is now recognised as a high priority and considerable improvements have been researched and introduced in the early 21st century.

Renewable energy was harnessed early on in human history, particularly in terms of wind and water power. In the last few decades there has been an increasing realisation that humankind is gradually using up the non-renewable fuels and minerals of the planet particularly fossil fuels, whilst at the same time these fossil fuels are contributing severely to problems of global warming and pollution. The need to return to clean renewable sources of energy has been increasing steadily since the beginning of the Industrial Revolution, and with the population of the planet and energy usage ballooning at the same time, the need to switch energy use into renewable sources has become vital.

This explains why, at the end of the 20th century, there has been an upsurge in provision of hydroelectric and wind power, but it also accounts for many small renewable systems for the production of electricity by wind, water or solar power. In addition, bio-fuels produced by anaerobic digestion of bio-mass, are increasingly being investigated, albeit on a relatively small scale. In appropriate areas of the world tapping into geothermal energy through heat exchangers is a rapidly developing technology, and indeed the natural use of volcanic hot springs has powered much of Icelandic heating needs for some time.

Wave power and tidal barriers can produce hydroelectric power in steady amounts, and the science of generating electricity from dams or falls on rivers is being increasingly used. The Niagara Falls power station came on-line in 1879, and has been steadily up-rated to produce a large commercially available electric supply ever since. The first generation of electricity generating stations came online in New York and London in the 1880s. Tidal power is also constant, readily available and non-polluting. Wind power is unpredictable, though off-shore wind farms provide rather more constant generation than land-based systems. Solar power is only available during the hours of daylight, but is rapidly developing, and along with wind power, is becoming increasingly viable as new methods of electricity storage are developed.

In the early 21st century, electricity storage has progressed from simple throwaway batteries to systems which can store and then discharge their electric load much more reliably, repeatedly, and for much more extended periods of time. The 21st century is going to see steady improvement in both the generation of renewable electricity, and more particularly in its storage for later release at times of demand.

As world population continues to increase, and as affluence increases expectations, the need for energy generation will undoubtedly increase with it. The only other present source of electricity not so far mentioned is that of nuclear power, where the fission of naturally radioactive elements, usually uranium, is used to produce a controlled amount of heat as steam, which in turn is fed into turbines to produce electricity. The first nuclear power station to feed electricity into the national grid came online in Russia in 1954 with an output of 5 megawatts; it was followed a year later in Britain by Calder Hall with an output ten times greater at 50 megawatts, and then in 1956 by the Shipping port reactor in USA with an output of 60 megawatts.

Nuclear power suffers from very high capital costs, together with the problem of long-term disposal or storage of nuclear material which is spent as far as electricity generation is concerned, but which is still radioactive and dangerous. The public is fearful of radiation problems, both from the disposal of nuclear waste and from the consequences of nuclear power station accidents. Three or four major nuclear disasters, including Three Mile Island (USA), Chernobyl (USSR) and most recently, Fukushima (Japan) have all turned public sentiment away from nuclear power, which as a result re-emphasises the need to develop non-nuclear renewable sources of electricity. In all nuclear accidents so far however, investigation has shown distressing departures from protocols and over-riding of safety procedures which should allow nuclear power to provide clean and constant electricity when correctly used in the future.

It is possible to draw up a rough balance sheet comparing different methods of energy:

- Wind power is cheap, capital costs low, reliability variable and pollution minimal.
- Water power is also cheap, capital costs low, reliability good and pollution minimal.
- Solar power is also cheap, low capital cost, reliable but only works in daylight.
- Coal power is costly and can be dangerous, the capital costs are moderate, reliability is good, but pollution is high and a lot of carbon dioxide is produced.
- Oil and gas are similar to coal, but have the added expense of needing to be moved around the world, pollution is high and much carbon dioxide is produced.
- Nuclear power is very costly with high capital costs, reliability is good and pollution is low except for the problem of disposal of still radio-active, but spent, fuel.

In terms of providing an assured electricity supply in the future, it seems likely that future methods of generation will need to include all different types of renewable supply, including particularly nuclear power. Different areas of the world and different countries have inherited differing potential energy sources, for instance coal, oil and gas are all highly localised in their occurrence; similarly hydro power is only available in large amounts to some lucky countries which have won in this particular geographic lottery. It also seems clear that in acknowledgment of both pollution and the dire future consequences of global warming, non-polluting technology, including nuclear generating capacity, must continue to develop rapidly, even if this means that electricity will cost more for future generations.

However, these future populations will be more affluent and more easily able to pay an appropriate price for their energy generation. The alternative is to accept increasing pollution and global warming, which would be both foolish and highly undesirable, and would, even in the medium term, lead to deterioration in Earth's resources and a very compromised future for the generations that will follow us (chapter 100).

Possible further reading:
Energy, a Human History by Richard Rhodes (Simon & Schuster)

Chapter 95
Evolving Politics

In the early years of human civilisation, we have seen that tribes gradually enlarged, particularly with the introduction of farming and a more static and ordered life. Even at that time the archaeological evidence is that within any given tribe or village there was a hierarchy of people, with a chief at the top of the pyramid who would set the agenda for the village, and when the time came would be buried with honours above and beyond the majority of his or her fellows. By the time records become available, there is often evidence of a monarch or tribal chief, together with a priestly class, all over and above the rest of the people.

Tribes and villages seem often to have been at war with each other from the earliest times, and the chief or monarch would have usually been the commander-in-chief in time of battle. In this way one person would have been in charge and responsible for all the major decisions, and the future of the tribe would have been dependent upon the wisdom of his, or occasionally her, decisions. In this way politics became group discussions and decisions, and the first duty of the group (government) is to protect its people, members or citizens.

Thus, the state comes into being, principally as a defensive, but sometimes as an offensive, organisation dedicated to preserving the way of life of its people, and sometimes to enlarging its boundaries, or indeed defending those boundaries against threats from outside. As the state got larger, advisors and administrators would aid the head of state, chief, king, queen or emperor in their decisions, because once beyond a certain size it would no longer be possible for a single individual to possess all the necessary knowledge, or indeed administer all the obligations of the state.

Later, the state would become involved in property where two models evolved: in the first of these individuals were allowed to own property and to buy and sell it, but in the second model, all property belonged to the state, or indeed to the king or emperor, who would possess the power to allocate property to favoured individuals and confiscate it from others. This second system was a common one through intermediate times when states were developing, and still exists today under various communist regimes.

As the city or state grew in size, it took on various other responsibilities, some of which were solely the prerogative of the ruler, and others were devolved in one way or another. As we have seen, allocation or confiscation of property rapidly became a function of some early states. The second function, which appeared early, was the administration of justice, which was often a prerogative of the ruler in small states, but once the nation grew in size justice was usually delegated in most routine instances to other aristocrats. The third function of the young nation was that of taxation, since the ruler needed to raise wealth for two specific reasons, the first of these being to finance his own, sometimes lavish lifestyle, and secondly, to provide for defence of the nation by way of providing weaponry, and raising and paying an army, which might only be done in times of need and until the need had disappeared.

Those who were ruled would gradually come to recognise the existence of a public interest or greater good than that of the ruling aristocracy, and as necessary for the good of the whole nation, and also for the protection of individual citizens. Thus the fourth and fifth duties of the state were to provide legislation ordering the patterns of daily life with sanctioned customs and behaviour, and prohibitions against other behaviours. Finally, it would be necessary for the state to appoint an executive or administrative system to ensure that the population abided by the rules which had been laid down.

In the middle of the first millennium BC, there was, for intermittent periods, democratic government in the city state of Athens, though this was not democracy as we understand it, but rather in the sense that basic decisions were taken, almost like a referendum, by all the assembled population after being addressed by the protagonists for each side of the argument. The Greek word derives from demos (people) and kratia (rule or power). It was far from what we would feel today to be democratic, since in order to attend the assemblies and vote you had to be over thirty, own property and be male; women and slaves did not have a voice, but even this was better than aristocracy or autocracy, rule by an elite few.

This was interrupted from time to time by what would be called today a coup d'état, but in the periods of democracy the intent was to give all citizens a voice to participate in government. The Greeks used the name tyranny for intervals in democracy when an absolute ruler, known as a tyrant, ruled without observance of law or a constitution. (We can note that even today Switzerland has a democracy in which all major proposals are put to a referendum of all citizens entitled to vote.)

By the time of the Romans, democracy had become modified, and although there were still occasions in which all eligible citizens could vote, most of the government of Rome was carried out by elected officials, including praetors, tribunes and consuls, and through the medium of the senate, where elected senators voted on legislative proposals. In practice, it was difficult to become a senator or a high official without coming from a privileged or patrician background and without 'sponsoring' (some would say bribing) a proportion of the electorate. Rome eventually became a dictatorship under Julius Caesar, and persisted in this form of government with an absolute emperor for many centuries.

The rest of the world through those ancient times was largely governed by kings or emperors, who sometimes succeeded to the position, as in a hereditary monarchy, and sometimes emerged following either a coup d'état or assassination of the previous ruler. All the variants of this type of autocracy were prone to abuse, not only by greed and cheating, but also by cronyism, where the ruler appoints his close friends and cronies to lucrative positions, or rewards them with grants of property, rather than choosing the most appropriate and best qualified people.

Most of the world was governed by some variation of this system with an autocrat and a small subservient aristocracy at the top, and the great mass of the population having to decide either to obey the system, or to elect for full blown rebellion. The status quo often seems preferable to major change, and not all members of a tribe or nation will agree to rebel, so therefore rebellions were often unsuccessful and were put down, although. sometimes the rulers changed but not the system. At various times a governing elite has been unrepresentative of the country it ruled and names have been coined to describe the attitudes and philosophy of the ruling class; in this way aristocracy usually coexists with monarchy or autocracy, while oligarchy also implies a small ruling elite though not one associated with nobility. Kleptocracy is a term of recent origin often directed at dictators and autocrats appropriating and sequestering the nation's riches at the expense of their citizens, while theocracy is applied to government by a religious minority. The only benign description is meritocracy which may be applied to systems of government where the elite is chosen for ability rather than family connections, wealth or other reasons.

Heredity is not a good system for political stability and has often led to wars in past times. Autocrats' and dictators' children are seldom as single-minded, ruthless and well educated as their parents, nor do they have the same formative childhood experiences, such as hardship, rebellion or revolution, indeed the children may well have grown up in a very sheltered atmosphere. History is littered with examples of children succeeding to a throne or leadership position and then turning out not to have the comprehension, tact, ability or dedication of their parent. The situation was even worse where the inheriting child had been brought up to believe that he had come to the position by divine right. One needs look no further than present day Africa, South America or the Middle East for examples.

One of the reasons that there were so many dynasties in ancient Egypt and China was that often a weak individual would lead to a break in the chain and then either internal civil war, or external forces and war, would lead to a new dynasty. Only Russia and China have avoided this in recent times by severe repression in a backward country with a ruthless policy resulting in the deaths of millions, and it is ironic that this should occur in countries supposedly dedicated to government for the greater good by the mass of the population.

It is curious that autocrats and dictators have seemed unable to recognise that innate human ability varies considerably and that not all offspring will possess their parents' ability to govern the nation that they have been able to do; not all children wish to take over the mantle that their parents have worn.

England celebrates Magna Carta, when in 1215 King John, a domineering and autocratic monarch, was brought to heel by a rebellion of all his aristocrats and barons, whom he had alienated by his capricious and arbitrary rule. King John was brought to Runnymede, an island in the River Thames by his aggrieved barons, but he had virtually no support. He was made to sign Magna Carta in which he agreed to practice less arbitrary and unsupported government.

Although King John went back on some of his proposals and died only a year later, the precedent had been set, and over the next three or four centuries there was gradually increasing involvement of barons and nobles in government. Quite apart from anything else, it was easy to recognise that the nation and its population was now too large for one individual to rule without help in the form of advisors, backed up by a small army of administrators.

English parliamentary life evolved into a two-party system after the civil war when attitudes threw up two basically different approaches; the Tories first emerged in 1678 against the Whigs when they opposed the Exclusion Bill which sought to disinherit the catholic presumptive heir to the throne, James Duke of York, who would become James II despite this. The Whigs believed in constitutional monarchy, but opposed absolute monarchy and the catholic church. The system continued to evolve over the next three hundred years to present times, where we recognise the important post of Prime Minster as an individual who recruits, and then delegates to today's other ministers various duties, thus forming a Cabinet of around two dozen individuals.

These cabinet ministers possess not only individual responsibility for a particular function of state (e.g., defence, education, health, etc) but all cabinet ministers attend the cabinet meetings where subjects are discussed and policies are decided by all those ministers present arriving at a consensus, which is then referred back to the individual ministers to implement, partly because his colleagues have participated in the consensus decision and partly because each minister has support in the shape of a large body of civil servants who can implement the details of agreed policies.

In many other countries, a political party system has also grown up in which two or more opposing political attitudes are represented. These divisions were reinforced at the time of French Revolution, when Republican leaning delegates sat on the left hand side of the Chamber, and the supporters of the Monarch and aristocracy sat on the right hand side, thus giving the title left wing politics to radical and socialist attitudes, whilst right wing attitudes imply support for the status quo and an unwillingness to change.

These two attitudes sat in opposition and often alternated through the 19th century years of European government, but in some countries, many more shades of political opinion existed than the two extremes, and some modern parliaments have been built with a parliamentary chamber in the form of a semi-circle as a means of indicating variation of opinion on a gradient from left, socialist or communist, through to the right wing, monarchist or conservative. The French and American revolutions were relatively unusual in that they were really civil wars pitting one segment of the population against another rather than one part of the population against their ruler.

Revolutions polarise attitudes and brutalise people, but seldom usher in better conditions for most citizens. Political extremism, which often precedes revolution, tends to feed on cultural pessimism, which in turn is often exaggerated and unrepresentative of the real situation; the average citizen is usually better served by stability of culture and governmental institutions than by periods of wild upheaval, even civil war, where the majority of the casualties and the losers are the ordinary citizens. Civilian death tolls and family disruption in past revolutions have usually been enormous.

Communist revolutions in the 20th century have been particularly disruptive and oblivious to the value of human life. Much of man's evolution as societies has been through warfare. Even now that the means of warfare have become so lethal after the invention and use of the atomic bomb at Hiroshima, that global war has been held in check between super-powers for the past 75 years (albeit with many smaller local wars still breaking out), relationships between nations still often seem to be conducted on a confrontational basis.

In step with these changes leading to democracy of various sorts, has come a gradual increase in universal suffrage, which implies the privilege of each individual citizen to comment and vote in all the issues of the day. It also implies that the individual citizen has the ability to understand those issues coming before parliament, together with a willingness to vote thereon with objectivity in seeing the best course of action for the town, city or state as a whole. It has always been the case that some individuals either for reasons of personal greed or selfishness, or indeed for the wish to see developments located elsewhere and not adjacent to their own properties or interests must be subordinated to the nation's good as a whole.

Indeed, politicians will often offer sweeteners in the form of such things as tax cuts to various sectors of the economy or electorate without considering the overall picture; these are often referred to as bribes and may be wholly inappropriate at a state or larger level. The average citizen in a democracy will vote for the measures that favour himself or herself without considering the overall picture. Senators and Congressmen in America are subject to a lot of heavy paid lobbying and may be induced to vote for certain measures by cash or other incentives for their own district or state, thus overriding any intent or pretence of providing the same level of services and opportunities to all citizens equally across the nation. The word 'nimby' ("not in my back yard") has been coined to denote some of these attitudes.

There is also an implication in arriving at decisions of this nature that all voters have sufficient information and available facts, preferably supplied by government and objective media, to understand such information, and then to make an informed decision. Unfortunately, in our modern state, such information usually gets conveyed to the public by means of press, television or other media, which is not always controlled by individuals renowned for their objectivity. Partisan and one sided reporting of current affairs and government policies is therefore a considerable danger in the modern state, complex matters are abbreviated and often reduced to trite and insufficient soundbites, but at least this is better than in many autocratic and totalitarian states where the news itself is heavily censored, controlled or slanted.

There is also the presumption that all citizens in a democracy should vote, and that all votes from the poorly educated and ill-informed to the highly qualified and well informed, carry an equal value – a proposition which is difficult to argue in favour of. Subjective opinions on social media with partisan and biased postings by individuals or special interest groups have made the problem worse in recent years, quite apart from the recent advent of deliberately fake news or the reduction of advocated policies to mere meaningless soundbites.

A further danger is the distance that has come today between rulers and those who are governed. It is often said that many politicians do not live in the real world, and this reflects firstly their experience of life in their upbringing and in different past jobs, but also their relative insulation from the public as a whole, as they can easily be out of touch with the majority feeling of voters. It is difficult to devise a system where this can be remedied, but the English system of representative MPs, each of whom represents a number of constituent citizens who can approach the MP and air their views directly, is one way of doing it, though as most constituencies now have a population of over 100,000 it is extremely difficult for an MP to represent all shades of opinion.

A House of Commons of more than the present 650 MPs would also be dysfunctional and unwieldy. The autocrat, or even the disdainful and disconnected parliamentarian, can ignore the general feeling and attitudes of those he or she represents only if oblivious to the danger of being voted out, overthrown, or even in some countries assassinated. There is clearly a difference between the autocrat who forges ahead in steam roller fashion against advice and public feeling, and the more consensual politician who considers all sides of the question and solicits advice from all sides of society before making decisions.

Most recently, there has been much publicity given to feminists who believe that our gender balance in parliament is wrong and that women should account for 50% of the total of MPs and ministers. Matters are changing and representation of women has been slowly moving closer towards this 50% mark, and since women tend to be less aggressive and less confrontational there are grounds for hoping that as women account for greater numbers of our rulers our politics might become more considered, less strident and command more respect from greater numbers of voters.

General scepticism with politicians has been present through the ages, leading to the comment by Lord Acton (1834–1902, English MP and politician) that "power tends to corrupt, and absolute power corrupts absolutely. Great men are almost always bad men". It is perhaps the second sentence here, the sting in the tail, which is often overlooked or omitted, but which needs to be present in the consciousness of those elected to power and taking decisions for communities. Charismatic leaders with a mission to change a nation's system of government (to communism, for instance) are often totally oblivious to alternative viewpoints, and arrogant to the point of assuming that the 'silent majority' of citizens not only share their views but will benefit if the system is changed.

Communism is a political and socio-economic system in which common ownership exists of the means of production of goods and food with an absence of social class. This was all advocated in a book called Utopia by Thomas More (1478–1535), from which we get the adjective utopian referring to a state of perfection which is unlikely to be achieved. Marx and Engels believed that proletarian revolution would overthrow the bourgeois class society and abolish private property resulting in a classless and stateless society, but even in societies where communism has come, the system still appears stratified with a layer of oligarchs at the top showing little resemblance to what Marx believed and hoped would result. Like most religions communism has fragmented into different interpretations or sects with differing viewpoints and ways of organising society.

In the same way that nations devise rules and laws for the governance and behaviour of their citizens, so it has also become clear that many of the same principles should apply to the relationships between nations. This was first addressed with the creation of the League of Nations after the First World War, but despite this the 1920s and 1930s were turbulent times, both in national politics and in world financial problems, and the League of Nations was not helped by the refusal of the United States to join the organisation.

Despite the League of Nations, Europe still lapsed into the Second World War because of three autocrats or dictators, namely Mussolini, Hitler and Stalin. At the conclusion of the Second World War, a much stronger United Nations was created, hopefully to try and police the contact of nations with each other, though the historical record of the last seventy years indicates only limited success towards these objectives. There is still great reluctance for other states to comment on, or interfere with, events in other countries, even when gross abuses may be seen to be occurring, though as responsible members of the world community states should be prepared to call out, or even intervene, in cases of manifestly unacceptable behaviour; today this is sometimes done in the name of the United Nations, though on other occasions no action is taken because a large nation mistakenly shelters the offending smaller one.

Several conclusions emerge at the end of this chapter; namely: first, that autocracy is bad, that power corrupts, and that great and powerful men must make great efforts to avoid becoming bad men, divorced from the public. Second, if democracy is to be successful, then minimum secrecy and maximum information must be available to the voting public. Third, in pursuit of a well-informed public, there must be press freedom, and the press itself must not be concentrated in the hands of only a few individuals who usually have very defined attitudes and objects, and the press must certainly not be subject to government control.

Fourth, it follows that government must work hard to achieve full public literacy, numeracy, understanding of science and statistics and the issues brought forward. Sixth, procrastination is never a good government policy, and bold decisions may require to be taken, even in the presence of adverse attitudes, with politicians leading opinion rather than following public attitudes. Seventh, it is necessary for rulers to assess the attitude of their nation as accurately as possible; US President Richard Nixon's reference to the 'silent majority' (which he felt represented the course of moderation) must be balanced against the vociferous minorities, who may well be unrepresentative.

Finally, it must be said that progress is usually best achieved by evolution and not by revolution, especially when the birth pangs of modern Russia and China, not to mention other smaller countries, are seen as examples and when the appalling death tolls are recalled.

Perhaps we should finally recall Churchill's words: "No one pretends that democracy is perfect or all-wise. Indeed, it has been said that democracy is the worst form of government except all those other forms that have been tried from time to time." It is also salutary to remember that he also said: "…the best argument against democracy is a five-minute conversation with the average voter."

The possible further reading for this chapter is wide and the reader may wish to choose from the following slim volumes of 'Very Short Introductions' published by Oxford University Press:
American Politics by Richard M Valelly
British Politics by Anthony Wright
Communism by Leslie Holmes
Democracy by Bernard Crick
European Union by John Pinder and Simon Usherwood
Fascism by Kevin Passmore
Politics by Kenneth Minogue
Revolutions by Jack A Goldstone
Utopianism by Lyman Tower Sargent.

Chapter 96
Climates and People

Early man, homo sapiens, spread from Africa over all areas of the globe in a way no other individual animal in the wild has managed, so today homo sapiens can be found from the Arctic to the desert, and in each region of the world he has adapted to different habitats and climates. Other early species of homo also spread across the globe and their remains and traces have been found at various global sites, but not in as widespread distribution as homo sapiens. It is possible that even more subspecies of homo evolved at different times and in different places of which we are unaware, but our direct ancestors appear to have come from Africa (chapter 2).

As early man fanned out across the globe from Africa, along sea shores and up rivers, small pockets of early settlers stayed in some locations to settle where food and shelter seemed propitious, while others pushed on. The end result is a planet populated from the inclement Arctic by Eskimos, to desert-dwelling Tuareg. The only uninhabited and inhospitable continent is Antarctica, where other species have adapted sufficiently to claw a living from its inhospitable shores. Many locations have been benign and welcoming to human habitation, and indeed some may have been settled initially, only for its population of people to move on eventually, or die out. Climate has not been static through the last million years, of which the Ice Ages are the best testament.

Thus, although people were probably present in northern Europe thirty thousand years ago before the last Ice Age, they would all have had to migrate southwards before the advancing ice cap, since we know that most of northern Europe, including Britain and Ireland was covered for thousands of years by a layer of ice thousands of metres thick. Once the Ice Age started to warm up again, melting the icecap, then people, plants and animals could again gradually spread north. The land once again started greening, and the prey of game animals was available for carnivores who could migrate northwards.

It is interesting to note that since the Ice Age the mega-species of animals have all died out, including woolly mammoths, aurochs and similar animals, buffalo barely survived the coming of Europeans to North America. These extinctions coincided with the surge in hunting ability of Stone Age humans. The last continent on which this occurred was Australasia, where the mega-fauna and flightless birds, such as the dodo, have all become extinct since human hunting started and then increased. In some areas, humans themselves have been a prey animal, particularly to members of the cat family, such as lions and tigers across South America, Africa and Asia.

Of equal importance to humans for the choice of settlement areas has been the availability of fertile land. Each band of migrating humans that settled somewhere would have made the best of their choice, but could not have foreseen what future directions or changes in climate might appear. It would have been important to avoid areas where natural disasters, including volcanic eruptions and floods, were likely. In the early hunter gatherer stage of civilisation people would simply have avoided those areas where food and game were sparse.

Once the hunter gatherer era had passed, people became settled in villages and farming became their most important means of subsistence. As civilisation developed from the Stone Age to the Bronze Age and on to the Iron Age, man's ingenuity played an important part in shaping lives and civilisation.

At around this stage, the adverse problems faced by people changed from accidents and attacks by wild animals, to the problems of famine, plague and disease. Sometimes famine would have been a man-made disaster due to over cropping or soil exhaustion, but living in close proximity to one another in villages or towns brought with it an increase in disease, and ease of spread of disease within a community. Natural disasters also contributed to decimate populations in the form of droughts causing famines, and floods destroying crops, together with other occasional disasters such as tsunamis, forest fires and volcanic eruptions.

Only very recently has it been possible for individual humans to develop lives of specialisation with trades or professions; in the past most people would still have needed to work on the land until the Industrial Revolution, which revolutionised not only the production of goods, but also farming itself. However, disease would erupt as if from nowhere and spread rapidly, like the Plague, or the Black Death, in the Middle Ages in Europe.

Large communities of people were prone to the risk of rapidly spreading infectious diseases, whilst the old killer, famine, still stalked the land. Wikipedia carries a startling list of famines and floods (mainly from the last millennium where adequate records are present to inform us), and documents the areas across the globe where considerable numbers of population died. There is a similar list of epidemics available, which demonstrates the galaxy of different diseases which have caused millions of deaths through the centuries.

Not to be forgotten amongst the causes of human death is that of warfare. The size of wars has increased steadily as the size of settlements increased, and as nations and states increased in size. Some regimes and empires have been particularly active in perpetrating massacres, either in battles, sieges or afterwards when the populations of whole cities have been massacred and the cities razed to the ground by their conquerors at various times. The Romans were not averse to putting settlements to the sword, and similar massacres occurred in the Middle East under the Persians. The Mongol campaign as they spread across Europe is estimated to have caused 30–40 million deaths, and the death toll of conquest by Timur across the Middle East and Asia is put at around 17 million, or 5% of the world population at the time.

Purges in China in the 20th century under Chairman Mao Zedong is thought to have sustained a death roll of the same order. Stalin's policies, including purges and the exiling of many to Siberia, are again of the same order of tens of millions. The Second World War across the globe is estimated to have caused up to 85 million deaths compared with about a quarter of that number in the First World War. In earlier times the world was more sparsely populated and against these large numbers the Punic Wars in the early centuries BC are thought to have caused a death toll of up to 2 million, and the Crusades in Medieval Europe a death toll of up to 3 million. The Holocaust, Nazi attempts to exterminate the Jews together with gypsies and homosexuals during the Second World War, is recorded as killing up to 6 million Jews and a total of at least twice that many people altogether.

The importance of good and fertile soil for farming is vital. One-third of the world's good agricultural land is located in Europe. Another large area of agricultural land is in North America. The favourable conditions available in these areas enhance the ability of the population to reach their maximum potential. No one area is ideal, and early trade between small communities was mainly between areas gifted with resources to other areas without such benefits. Many areas had some distinctive and tradable products or resources, whether the surplus that they came to trade was for basic food, for warfare and its weapons, or simply for jewellery.

In some areas, use of irrigation and water resources have been vital in maximising the potential of the land. Systems for irrigating the land in dry climates were first used in Mesopotamia, Arabia and Ancient Egypt, often to fall into disrepair with the passage of time, due to subsequent generations having less commitment to maintaining their assets than their ancestors. Irrigation has also been used extensively in China from very early times to produce good crops of rice. Most recently, irrigation has been used on an ever increasing scale as a means ensuring consistent cropping, and indeed adequate crops in dry zones where growth would otherwise be unreliable, though in places this practice has so reduced and damaged the level of the water table that the future of agriculture has been put at risk, as in the American Dust Bowl of the 1930s.

In this way, we can see that geography shapes nations. The early clusters of population that have grown together are shaped by their surrounding geography, including the importance of fertile farming land, but also paying attention to natural boundaries, such as mountains and deserts, and raising crops appropriate to the natural capacity of the land. Some island populations have been particularly blessed both in constancy of climate and in protection from disease predators. Some nations have been lucky, or indeed unlucky, in their planetary situation which has conferred suitable land for living and farming, or alternatively unsuitable land.

Saudi Arabia, which is largely desert, has been unlucky in the land lottery, in that its climate and soils are unsuitable for farming and crop rearing, but although unlucky in the land stakes, the country has been lucky in the oil reserves that lie underneath the land, which have made the country rich. By contrast, America has been doubly lucky in having excellent land for farming together with natural resources of forests and abundant mineral and oil deposits, the USA has also been particularly lucky in starting afresh with an almost clean sheet for habitation since the native Indians had hardly made an impression on the lands' bounties and were living a life which respected the continent's ecosystem, although everything changed markedly with the coming of Europeans who almost eliminated the natives and took over the land.

If we put aside the Indians and their near extermination, North America is geographically defensible with oceans on both sides. Much of the continent possesses a relatively stable climate, although it varies from the severe extremes in the mountains in the west in particular, to the central Mississippi Basin where agriculture finds highly favourable conditions. It has profuse natural resources from oil and coal to iron ore, and realisation of these advantages have assisted American development through the last two hundred years. This contrasts with older settled areas of the world, such as the Middle East, India and China, where the land has been cropped for thousands of years, and where the climate is now only suitable for certain restricted types of farming. Other natural resources across these last three areas are also spread thinly, apart from oil in the Middle East.

Thus, when thinking of countries and their potentials, it is vital to note both the climate and the natural resources available. Natural disasters often relate to both climate and the geography of the land. All of these factors may in turn add up to a picture of a well-endowed country in a situation, although playing a lesser and more localised role. Any of these factors may render a state desirable to its neighbours and therefore prone to take over bids, either peacefully, or by war. The grass often seems greener on the other side of the fence, and in human history it has not taken too much enticement for adjacent countries to lust after their neighbours' perceived advantages and benefits.

There is a moral conundrum here since clearly human settlements have happened in a somewhat random distribution across the globe with some populations being blessed with a temperate climate while others have to live with extremes: some are endowed with mineral wealth in a very uneven fashion – diamonds, gold or oil versus an abundance of jungle, forest or wildlife: some have productive areas of fresh water or adjacent ocean yielding crops of fish, while others have none.

Should there be an obligation for humankind to share these natural bounties, or is it right that one nation can enjoy extreme wealth as a result of a naturally gifted oil bonanza, while another nation with very little resources has a population which has to live on a per capita income of less than $2 a day? Is it realistic to expect altruistic behaviour and sharing of the world's resources given our human history of competition and war for the world's valuable assets of climatic benevolence, and geographical gifts of ores, oil and natural gas? There is perhaps an analogy here in the way many nations look after all their citizens and apply both differential taxation and welfare benefits to try to lessen (not equalise) the gap between rich and poor.

The gap remains large, even in communist states where the political intention is to minimise or even eliminate both poverty and extreme wealth. If this were ever to happen it would be a big step towards diminishing warfare and migration from poor to rich countries. Inequalities within and between countries are getting wider and are reminders that climate change and melting glaciers are observable aspects of over production and over consumption by humans, and indeed that over-population by humans is the largest and most direct cause of the problem.

One problem is that personal self-denial and responsible use of the world's resources does not have sufficient impact to stop global warming or pollution, and therefore action will only be effective when nations act, and of course they need to act in concert since individual nations' failures will negate the ultimate aim in the same way that individual citizens can destroy or impede their community's aims.

Possible further reading:
Prisoners of Geography by Tim Marshall (Elliott and Thompson)

Chapter 97
Religion

Religion is important to society because through the ages it has been a vital scaffold in forming the laws of nations and their moral codes, together with shaping, not only social structures, but also the art forms of different cultures. From early times religion has been used to justify the central authority of tribes and nations, and has also been used to maintain peace between unrelated individuals, although on occasions it has also been a cause of war in the past.

Religion has been a great unifier of people, whilst on occasions also causing great divisions between peoples: the other great unifiers of society through the ages have been firstly money, and secondly, nationality or empires. There is a view that as sentient animals humans have an innate need for religion to explain and justify their existence, but without any hard evidence or pointers each person may come up with his own explanation for the meaning of life.

Western religions have tended to concentrate on monotheism since the time of the early Jews who were the first to worship a single god, whilst in the east there has been tendency towards personal beliefs and philosophies. Like trade, where there has been contact and influence between cultures since very early times, the same also holds true for religion, and throughout history different religions, and new religions, have all borrowed from contemporary neighbouring practices, and from the beliefs of previous generations.

Early peoples believed in the laws of nature, often feeling that specific local gods were behind the actions and events of nature, and of both plant and animal life. Formal religion may have started when nomads ceased to be hunter gatherers and settled forming villages and societies. Archaeology has indicated early deities were often female, perhaps because of the association of fertility, in both plants and animals, with the female gender. The earliest known religious thinking was in Sumeria in Mesopotamia. Early temples there have been dated to between 5,000 and 3,000 BC, with early writings referring to the creation of the world out of a great flood.

The earliest human story is recorded about 2,000 BC in the epic of Gilgamesh, who was a ruler in Uruk (Erech in the Bible) where the flood is a dramatic start to the story. The flood theme is an important one in the start of recognised religion, and is understandable coming from Mesopotamia where the Tigris and Euphrates rivers were subject to frequent flooding, while further south and west the Egyptian civilisation also grew up depending upon annual flooding, in this case of the River Nile. The Nile valley was never more than 20 or 30 km wide but approaches 2,000km in length; the Babylonian Empire in Mesopotamia, which evolved from Sumeria, was also long and thin, at up to 125km wide and 1,200km from north to south, along the Tigris and Euphrates rivers. Although the Yangtze River is also subject to major flooding along its 6,300km course the hinterland is much broader than the Nile, Tigris or Euphrates and much of the flooding has now been controlled by the building of the largest hydroelectric dam in the world – the Three Gorges Dam.

In Babylon, as in Sumeria, a large spectrum of gods was worshipped, representing both the elements and the natural forces, and in addition individual cities also boasted specific gods. Babylon had three great male gods and one place or destination sat above them all granting life and prosperity in return for obedience and elaborate rituals. Anu was the father of the Gods, Enlil was the lord of the air, Enki the God of wisdom, while Sheol was the place of darkness, the modern equivalent of hell.

Natural disasters, bountiful harvests and the fortunes of war were all felt to be subject to the whims of the gods, and sometimes resulted from the disregard or disobedience of people or nations – a situation not infrequently related in the Old Testament. These three chief gods of Babylon endorsed the civic order of people in three classes, firstly royalty and aristocracy, secondly administrators or priests, and thirdly, the remaining great bulk of the population comprising workers or slaves.

There are similarities both of geography and of religion with Egypt, where religious beliefs supported a large priesthood and bolstered the social framework of the nation, which was also reinforced by the elevation of the Pharaoh to the status of a god. There were many temples and monuments concerned with the rituals of religion, but in addition serving an economic function. A profound belief in the afterlife is demonstrated by the extensive funerary practices, and it is through these burial rituals of important individuals that we know so much about the ancient Egyptians.

Those of high caste were buried with sufficient goods and chattels to see them through to the afterlife, and the walls of their tombs were decorated with wonderful murals illustrating ancient Egyptian life, which have often survived thanks to being extremely well hidden from tomb robbers, and thanks also to the dry and desiccating climate of Egypt. The beliefs of the great majority of the population are unclear, and it must be uncertain whether they aspired to, or indeed were even promised, an afterlife along the lines of their superiors.

Contemporaneously with Ancient Egypt, the small pastoral tribe of Hebrews developed a religion in response to the frequent pressures of drought and famine; the word Jew means wanderer. The Jews have an early presence in Egypt around 1,700 BC, with a documented history of Jacob's family serving the Pharaohs, and recorded for us centuries later in the Torah and the Old Testament of the Bible, written down around one thousand years later in the 7th century BC. The Jews were the first to profess a monotheistic belief, which in due course would give rise initially to Christianity, and later to Islam. Their God was a jealous one named Yahweh, and the Jewish religion adopted the early story of the flood.

The Jews were cemented together by Moses and the flight to the Promised Land, during which Moses received from God the Ten Commandments for human conduct, which remain perhaps the simplest and best overall moral guidance for humanity. Contemporary archaeological finds agree with the story of the destruction of Canaanite cities in the 13th century BC. Saul reigned, as told in the Old Testament, to be followed by David and then Solomon, who died in 935 BC. These three kings remained a model for monarchy for many years, and much of their morality and law giving would later be adopted by Christianity, and then by Islam.

In keeping with the times, and the problems of famine and other natural disasters, the Jews have had a particular susceptibility to human disasters, deportations and ethnic cleansing. Israel was wiped out by the Assyrians in 722 BC, and its people were deported as slaves. Judah, including Jerusalem, was conquered by Babylon in 587 BC by Nebuchadnezzar and once again massive deportations ensued. Purges of the Jews have continued through the millennia, often because they were suspected and despised as money lenders and bankers. Persecution continued even up to the Holocaust of the 1940s perpetrated by the Nazis.

Somewhat further east, Persian religion is notable both for its diversity and its tolerance. It took influences from Vedic India and from Persian mystics believing in fire and sacrifice. The latter gradually evolved into the mysticism of Zoroastrianism, which in turn has bequeathed to Christianity both benign angels and malignant hellfire.

At the same time, India was being infiltrated from the north by Aryans, a Bronze Age people who had many gods. They too believed in sacrifice, and many of their beliefs were consolidated and written down as the Rig-Veda about 1,000 BC. Many of these beliefs were subsequently consolidated into Hinduism after evolution from Vedic beliefs. Texts known as the Upanishads, dating from about 700 BC, comprise a mixture of short items, the reflections of holy men, hymns, aphorisms and devotional utterances, and are a development of the Rig-Veda.

Within India, other cults also arose, including Jainism, a non-violent belief in the sanctity of life, both animal and human. This belief in non-violence resulted in five ethical values, the first of which was not to eat meat, the second committed the believer to Satya or truth, the third principal prohibited stealing, the fourth was that of chastity, and the fifth was a belief in non-materialism and the renunciation of property by monks and nuns. Alongside these principles of Jainism came the teachings of Buddha, a warrior prince named Siddhartha Gautama who lived in the 5th century BC.

The Buddha was unfulfilled by life so for seven years practiced asceticism, which also failed to satisfy him. He therefore put forward an austere ethical doctrine, part of which was yoga, and was intended to achieve truth by perfect control of mind and body. No rituals and no gods were involved, and as a personal religion its popularity gradually grew, becoming the first world religion to spread beyond the society in which it arose.

Further to the east, religion evolved in China along two parallel lines; the great mass of peasants believed in the spirits of nature from plants and animals to rivers and mountains, whilst the aristocracy, existing as about a hundred special or noble families, believed that each family or clan had been founded by a god. Rituals were developed and the supreme family, that of the Emperor, spent considerable time in ritual and worship.

To the Chinese, prediction of the future was important, and the Emperor in particular was responsible for consulting oracles. This was done by engraving the shells of turtles, or the shoulder blades of animals, with written characters, and then heating the shell or shoulder blade to produce cracks in it. The direction and length of these cracks was then read, especially by the Emperor, to determine the most propitious time for such activities as ploughing, planting and harvesting. Such practices evolved with time but remained in active use up to the early 20th century and the re-ordering of Chinese society under communism.

Buddhism came to China at the end of the first millennium BC from the Indian subcontinent, while Confucianism and Taoism both originated within China taking their relative philosophies from often itinerant teachers a few centuries earlier. Today those who practise religion in China are mainly Buddhists, though the following of Confucius still finds favour with quite a sizeable group; the Chinese Government is officially communist and atheist with any religious practice or membership formally declared incompatible with membership of the Communist Party.

During the early first millennium BC, Greek society coalesced into city states around the Aegean Sea sometime after 776 BC, a date which is remembered as the year of the first Olympic games. Even prior to this the Greeks had been literate, but their writing came initially from the Phoenicians, allowing the early appearance of records. The founding myths of the Greeks and their gods helped to cement Greece as a culture. Although the Greeks borrowed gods from other cultures, the Greek gods and goddesses seem remarkably human, in both their virtues and their vices. Multiple gods were still held responsible for much of humankind's victories and woes.

The Greek gods were not instantly predictable, as is apparent from Homer's writing, where the gods are noted to take sides in the Trojan War, and later Poseidon the Sea God causes problems for Ulysses in his Odyssey. The two books, the *Iliad* and the *Odyssey*, with their gathering together of the Greek gods and heroes, were written down about the 7th century BC when the Greeks developed their own writing. Once again the giving of oracles became important, and the shrines of these oracles, such as Delphi and Olympia, were places of great pilgrimage.

Roman religion was a public affair enhanced by ritual. There was no religious creed or dogma, and Romans tended to have household and nature gods who varied throughout society. Greek mythology persisted, and various festivals and rites were derived from the Roman customs of the early days, again paying due importance to fertility and agricultural seasons. One religious festival still with us is Saturnalia in December, which has now morphed into Christmas. The

Roman Emperor held the office of Chief Priest (Pontifex Maximus), and the practice of sacrifice was limited to special occasions when it was felt necessary to determine the auguries for the future and the cult of the Emperor as Chief Priest gradually increased.

The Romans allowed a large minority of Jewish communities to act as money lenders and tax collectors. Into this mix of Roman law and customs, with its little enclaves of Jewish money-lenders, came a preacher whose teaching took much from the Jewish faith, and who was a more orthodox Jew than many; he said that to love God and to love your neighbour encapsulated all the law and the prophets of Judaism. Jesus was arrested at the insistence of the Jewish High Priests, and was tried for blasphemy and sentenced to death in front of the Roman governor, Pontius Pilate.

The occasion was one of the Roman days of festival and games where the governor was allowed to please the crowds and offer pardon or execution for certain prisoners. The story of Jesus' confirmation of execution and his subsequent crucifixion, is well recorded in the New Testament gospels written soon after his death. The two remarkable things about Christ's crucifixion are firstly the New Testament recording Jesus' resurrection, and secondly, the empowerment of his twelve disciples to go out into the Roman world and preach Jesus' message.

The resurrection and the tasking of the disciples to teach has no religious precedent. Over the next couple of decades, the disciples, particularly Paul, succeeded in disseminating the idea and ideals of Christianity around the Mediterranean world. The message was one of forgiveness to all people, Jews and Gentiles alike, together with a promise of an afterlife; these attitudes were incompatible with most contemporary Jewish thought, and indeed with the Old Testament.

Confrontation between the Roman authorities and the early Jewish Christians was frequent; 66 AD saw a great Jewish rising resulting in storming of the Temple in Jerusalem by Roman troops; later came the suicidal massacre of almost 1,000 Jews at Masada in 73 AD when they were confronted by besieging Roman troops. Persecution and rebellions continued for the next 250 years with Christianity gradually becoming stronger, until in 312 AD the Emperor Constantine saw a vision of Christ before battle. He ordered his troops to put the Christian cross on their shields, and when the battle was won, belief in the Christian God was heavily reinforced.

Constantine formally declared himself Christian in 324, and then presided personally over the Council of Nicaea which was called to consider the question of Jesus' divinity in particular. Thereafter Constantine ruled over an officially Christian Empire, and supposedly at God's command he founded a new city on the site of the old Greek colony of Byzantium at the entrance to the Black Sea: this was dedicated in 330, notably in his name not that of God's, as Constantinople. The Roman Empire went into slow decline after Constantine's death in 337, eventually splitting in two, an eastern Church centred on Constantinople, and a western Church with its centre still in Rome.

War between the Roman Empire and its more eastern neighbours in Persia and India, where cults and religions were rife, suddenly changes in the early 7th century. Mohammed appears in Arabia preaching a message of one God who is just, but who will judge all men, and teaching that individual salvation is guaranteed by following God's will in religious observance and in personal and social behaviour. The essence of this message is little changed from the God of Abraham and the Jews, and the later message of Jesus, but the many prohibitions laid down by Mohammed compared with the much looser ten commandments of the bible is striking.

Mecca, close to the western coast of Arabia on the Red Sea, where it was both an important stop on the caravan routes and the home of a holy meteoric black stone, the Kaaba, provided a home for Mohammed to preach. Mohammed's dreams over the next two decades formed what was to become the religion of Islam, and at the same time bound the Arabs together by virtue of its writing, in a way that Luther's Bible did the same for Protestantism almost a millennium later in Europe (chapter 20). However, where the bible, and the Old Testament or the Torah in particular, offer many stories giving examples of both good and bad behaviour, the Koran exists as a shopping list of conduct which is deemed unalterable and unable to evolve with time and understanding since it was given directly to Mohammed by an infallible deity. In the same way that Mohammed's dreams are believed to have been directly caused by God and therefore cannot be altered or changed in the future, so the doctrine of Papal Infallibility makes it very difficult for the Catholic Church today to question, modify, or alter previous doctrinal teachings set down by earlier popes, even though some modern situations were never envisaged or even possible in early Christian times.

Islam spread rapidly throughout Arabia, then to the east through Persia and into Northern India, to the west along the north coast of Africa, and across the Straits of Gibraltar and then north through Spain to the Pyrenees by war. In contrast with Christianity, Islam developed rapidly without division between the religious and secular authorities (although many sects splintered off within the faith), while Christianity divides authority between Church and State. These two great monotheistic religions, Christianity and Islam, now dominate the globe with relatively few polytheistic religions remaining, except in more isolated countries.

At the end of this account, one is compelled by the profusion of religions and the differences between them, to consider whether any or all of them are either logical or valid. In the final analysis all are belief systems, usually fixed and incapable of change with time or circumstances, except by splitting off daughter sects with new or altered beliefs. The basic idea of religion means different things to different people and at different times; one only has to consider the early Christian convocations with disagreements over what many would consider unnecessarily trivial matters of belief that illustrate this.

Many would also consider that communism is also a belief system or religion, it is equally incapable of proof and equally promises a rosy distant, but unachievable future. Like other religions communism has also splintered into different factions or sects under different charismatic leaders in the brief century since it first burst onto the world, and also like many religions communism is very intolerant of dissent or freedom of expression with harsh penalties for those unwilling to toe the party line. At the same time since the advent of science and objectivity with the Enlightenment, thinking has become gradually more secular and less deferential to religion.

Possible further reading:
The Great Transformation by Karen Armstrong (Atlantic Books)

Chapter 98
Warfare

It would seem that fighting and war has been a very frequent human activity at least as far back as history allows us to trace. Indeed, of the 100 chapters in this book war is an important component in over half of them. It was the Reverend Thomas Malthus (1766–1834) who wrote an important essay on population in 1798, he saw that national populations would increase if food production improved, and that this was a big limiting factor in improving the human condition. Similarly, in times of famine populations would diminish. In addition to famine, Malthus saw disease and war as the three big scourges of humanity.

Through the ages, war has been such a regular human activity that one has to ask whether there is a human gene for aggression, and indeed whether it might be linked to male sex; if so it could have been useful to early man in his hunting pursuit of prey for food. Even today hunting, shooting and fishing are usually male pastimes reminiscent of past ages. From a Darwinian perspective, one can see the importance of such competition, physical and intellectual, as important survival attributes in early societies. (Around the world in 2020 there were two major and fourteen or more minor wars in progress).

Initially, warfare was a hand-to-hand affair with primitive man using clubs or axes. Although bows and arrows were early weapons in the Stone Age, the evidence for their use in human contact is relatively small, and they seem to have been used largely for hunting. As an improvement on bows and arrows the crossbow was invented in China in 500 BC, but although more accurate, it has never become a very useful weapon of war as it takes a relatively long time to reload, and thus the bow and arrow, with its capacity for much more rapid fire, became a staple of warfare in early years. The bow and arrow reached its apogee at the Battle of Agincourt in 1415, where a small British army defeated the larger French army because of the ability to saturate the air with arrows.

There have been long periods throughout human history when warfare seems to have been largely static, with minimal development of technology. Thus there were several millennia in which developments in war were small. Both Rome and China failed to develop their weaponry much, in each case for over a thousand years. Over time however there has been a steady increase in the lethal capacity of weapons.

With the coming of the Bronze Age, shields and armour became more important, but it was not until the Iron Age that a really tough sword was developed with iron being much harder than bronze. The use of horses and the development of cavalry probably came from the great Asian steppes and was adopted by the Romans among others. Horses were previously deployed in chariot warfare in early Mesopotamia and Egypt, but this was only applicable where nations could afford a standing army which could be trained and kept in readiness. Smaller conflicts were limited to the raising of a scratch army of unwilling peasants or slaves, with little or no training, who would just be pressed into service and frontline hand-to-hand fighting.

Defence works were often minimal, and at a time of hand-to-hand combat, inevitably so. The Roman Legions could throw up an earth fortification in a matter of days, and if it was intended for longer use, then a wooden stockade would surmount the banks, providing both protection and a high vantage point for the use of bows and arrows and other weapons. Castles were a development of this theme but developed somewhat later and were far more costly and time consuming to construct. Along with the development of castles came siege engines designed to throw large missiles, either into castles or to demolish the walls. Siege warfare was slow and time consuming, and often the deciding factor was the provision of food and water within the castle, and how long it would last the defenders.

Although gunpowder was discovered and used in fireworks in China from quite early times, it was never developed into firearms by the Chinese. Gunpowder came to Europe in early medieval times when it was initially used in muskets and then in cannons or mortars. The precursor of the musket and the first effective firearm was the arquebus which was large and heavy and appeared in the 15th century; because of its size and weight it had a projection underneath to steady it on a battlement or a special rest. It fired lead balls of about 100g and was very slow to reload limiting its usefulness, it gradually evolved into the lighter and more manageable musket, which is a smoothbore long gun, but both of these weapon, like crossbows before them, are time consuming to reload, and during the period of reloading the soldier is unprotected and not contributing to defeating the enemy.

It was therefore not until the rifle came in that firearms became really useful in battle. Firearms were used in single combat as pistols, but little more. Once the rifle was developed with precision bullets and a longer and more accurate range, then firearms developed much more rapidly, and became much more useful. The rifle is so called because of the rifling helical grooves cut in the barrel which give the missile a spin as it leaves the gun, this makes for accuracy and stability in its flight though the air; the first rifle appears to have been developed by Benjamin Henry (1821–1898), a New England gunsmith, in 1860.

The Winchester repeating rifle first appeared in 1866, and was known after its New England developer Oliver Winchester (1810–1880); it made a considerable difference as it was then possible to have a magazine and much more rapid firing. From this base, it was inevitable that the development of machine guns would appear: these are weapons able to fire several hundred rounds a minute, with the Gatling Gun, patented by its American inventor Richard Gatling (1818–1903) in 1861, being the first of its kind to offer high speed repeated firing, and also appearing in the 1860s in time to be used occasionally in the civil war.

The effect was devastating and contributed both to the high casualty rate of the First World War, and to the static nature of the warfare, where troops became stuck in opposing trenches unable to get close enough to each other because of the indiscriminate machine gun fire. The stalemate would only be broken when armoured vehicles, known as tanks, first appeared on the battlefield towards the end of the first World War.

War has always been a great driver of invention with bigger and better weapons being produced. Clearly if your enemy is able to develop better technology to defeat your present weapons, then the only logical response is to research and develop something to counter it, or something better. This has been the history of warfare, particularly through the 19th and 20th centuries, culminating of course in the development of the atomic bombs dropped on Hiroshima and Nagasaki to end Japanese involvement in the Second World War in 1945. Chemical and biological weapons have been produced, and the use of chlorine as poison gas during the First World War is notable but these weapons have been agreed by most nations to be totally inappropriate, and are now banned under the Geneva Convention.

In the same way that war has resulted in the more rapid development of weaponry as an arms race, it has also acted as a spur for technical development in non-weapon improvement, involving the technology of communications (radio and radar), medicine (surgery and antibiotics), transport (vehicles, ships and planes), as well as provoking governments to greater efforts in the discipline and efficiency of their peoples. Naval warfare, which started as ships carrying waterborne soldiers, progressed through means of effective ramming as practiced by the Greeks and Romans, either to sink the opposing ships, or to board them for hand-to-hand combat.

The mounting of cannons on ships first appeared in mediaeval times but still boarding and hand-to-hand combat was often employed. The first submarine was tested in the River Thames and built by a Dutchman called Cornelius van Drebbel in 1620, who also devised contact mines to try and sink shipping. Aerial warfare was first used in the Great War, only a few years after the first proper aeroplanes took to the skies, and has been used ever since in the form of fighter aircraft and bombers, in addition to the mundane work of ferrying troops and supplies. In some types of war, sophistication of weaponry may be neither necessary nor advantageous as in guerrilla war or in asymmetric war with big differences between the size and capability of the combatants.

The involvement in war of civilians has been deplored, though massacres of non-combatants have been used throughout history to terrify and subdue a nations' population. Rome was quick to exact reprisals against civilian populations on many occasions. As an instrument of policy the Mongol armies were notorious in massacring the whole population of cities as an instrument of terror in their conquests. In the 20th century Stalin in Russia through the 1920s and 1930s conducted overt war against his own population with purges and massacres.

Hitler, through the same decades of the 1920s and 1930s, came increasingly to target civilians, intellectuals, and those whose opinions he simply did not like, quite apart from the initiation of the holocaust. Chairman Mao in China is also responsible for the death of tens of millions in the civil war that grumbled through three decades of Chinese history. On a more disturbing basis women civilians have frequently been subject to rape by conquering armies while at the same time their husbands and children have either been killed or taken into slavery; the resulting harrowing mental trauma is usually long in persistence and immensely disabling.

The concept of war against civilians resulted in the actions of Henry Dunant (1828–1910) who was witness to the aftermath of the Battle of Solferino in 1859 between Austria and Napoleon III of France. Many thousands of dead and wounded soldiers were left on the battlefield and Dunant was appalled at the callousness of the scene and became involved in organising aid and treatment for the injured. He wrote a book on his experience, and this eventually led to the founding of the International Committee of the Red Cross in 1863. Dunant later became the first recipient of the Nobel Peace prize in 1901. His actions also led to the enactment of the initial Geneva Convention in 1864, which laid down basic rules of warfare regarding civilians, captured prisoners, and the wounded. Indirectly his actions also led to the establishment of the League of Nations in 1920 following the First World War, and subsequently the United Nations after the Second World War.

All these organisations and treaties were aimed at promoting the civilised pursuit of warfare and the treatment of wounded and captured soldiers, together with the protection of civilians. It may seem curiously inappropriate to have rules for warfare, but most nations now subscribe, at least in theory, to the overall aims laid down in these treaties.

The causes of war are relatively few, but often result from a misjudgement on the part of one nation about the possible reaction of their enemy under certain circumstances. In early times possibly the most frequent cause of war was a desire for power. The Emperor in China, Alexander the Great, the Romans and Genghis Khan all went to war to build an empire; conquest itself appears to have been sufficient incentive. Once human civilisation had spread around the globe, then the desire for territory, especially other nations' territory, was a very large factor in the initiation of war. Some nations are poor and relatively poorly endowed with natural resources, either in terms of agricultural land or in terms of mineral or other resources, so this represents a second frequent cause for war.

For a large nation envious of its smaller neighbour's assets, it is a small step in thinking to combine the two. A third cause of war is differences in ideology or religion between nations. Thus, the dramatic and enormous expansion of the Muslim world in the 7th and 8th centuries came about because of the Arab determination to extend Islam by conquest. Similarly, the Crusades in the 12th century came about because of European ambitions to reverse the Islamic conquests and restore Christianity to the Middle East. Much more recently, as religions have fragmented, we have seen a fifth cause for war originate within religious groups, such as Catholic and Protestant followers, and between Sunni and Shia Muslims. Finally, it must not be forgotten that retaliation by a nation insulted, assaulted or invaded will form a ready excuse for war.

The successful prosecution of war requires several pre-existing conditions. Firstly, there must be a nation united in its determination to pursue the cause of the war, and a civilian population that regards the cause as just. Secondly, there must be present an available militia or army, so that most nations now maintain standing armies. Thirdly, the militia or army in question must be trained and well disciplined: ill-disciplined rabbles do not fight successful wars. Fourth, the overall strategy and the day to day tactics must be clear and achievable. Perhaps finally, it also helps if the nation has a charismatic leader or leaders to pursue the conflict, indeed it is possible that an autocratic leader will feel able to initiate war without consulting others.

Legally, two concepts have been advocated in the pursuit of war, the first being that the war should be "just", a legal concept known as 'jus ad bellum'. This concept is subject to six criteria, namely first, that the war should be declared by a lawful authority (usually a nation), secondly, the cause must be just and righteous, thirdly, the aggressor must be seeking to advance good and to curtail evil, fourthly the war must have a reasonable chance of success, fifth war must be a last resort after diplomatic and political contact, and finally, the ends of the war must be proportionate to the means used in conflict. Needless to say the justification for a war is usually very differently portrayed by the two opposing sides.

During the conflict, the second legal principle is of rights in war, 'jus in bello'; this basically means that the conflict must be proportionate and the means used in war must not be excessive; the involvement of civilians and genocide are clearly both out of proportion here. Secondly, there must be discriminatory action which avoids non-combatants, particularly women and children, and indeed all civilians. Humanitarian treatment of the wounded and of prisoners is also vital. As already noted, Henry Dunant's Red Cross, followed by the Geneva Convention, were the first steps in trying to regularise the actions of war.

Civil war may result from protracted revolutions as in Russia and China. Within a nation civil war may come about because of the commitment of a section of the population, often quite small, but vociferous and devoted with unwavering certainty to the pursuance of societal change without the necessary backing of the mass of the population, the 'silent majority'. Such political movements are often justified by an unreasoning assumption that the costs of any ensuing war are justified by the possible end result. Guerrilla wars and terrorist civil wars are often justified in this way by small, frequently unrepresentative minorities with the arrogance of moral certitude. It is also necessary to remember the forgotten costs of rebuilding shattered lives and countries in the aftermath of war which may exceed the cost of war itself.

In conclusion, it is salutary to recall the Four Horsemen of the Apocalypse who appear in the New Testament book of Revelation, namely four riders who symbolise pestilence, war, famine and death. Through the ages these four have been a constant threat to humanity. Although pestilence (disease) and famine have been major determinants of human fortunes, war has been an ever present problem. Aside from smaller conflicts, it is salutary to recall some numbers involved: the Mongol conquests in the 13th century, all under Genghis Khan, are thought to have been responsible for at least 60 million deaths, Tamerlane's Mongol rule in the 14th century is estimated to have caused 17 million deaths, the Taiping Rebellion in China from 1850–1864 some 40 million deaths, the first World War 39 million deaths, and the Second World War up to 80 million deaths.

These figures are gross estimates of both combatant and civilian casualties, and may well be underestimates. They represent the best case for trying to ensure an effective United Nations and Red Cross. With world population increasing, resources becoming more scarce and climate change bringing more adverse conditions to some countries, it would be foolhardy to forecast that nations will be able to curb their warlike tendencies in the future. With regard to war (as with other matters), it is often said that those who forget the lessons of history are condemned to repeat the mistakes of history, but it is equally important in this context to note that those who cannot put history aside to forgive and forget are condemned not to live in peace and to be imprisoned by their history as can often happen after a civil war.

Possible further reading:
Three more 'Very Short Introductions' from Oxford University Press:
Hobbes by Richard Tuck
Rousseau by Robert Wokler
Clausewitz by Michael Howard

Chapter 99
World Population

At the time of the last Ice Age, the total population of humankind is estimated to have been around three million people. These were individuals living in very small communities, often on coasts or beside rivers, whose sustenance came from hunting and gathering fruit, nuts and berries. Inter-tribal disputes must have occurred, but it is assumed that these were relatively few and far between since there was enough space for hunting game and gathering natural crops to go around without competition or conflict between groups. Evidence for interpersonal or inter-tribal fighting between humans in those early days is minimal.

The first big jump in population came with the development of agriculture and farming. The spectre of famine was gradually being subdued, though episodic famines would continue to the present day due to intermittent droughts, climatic changes, and occasional natural disasters resulting in localised crop failures. Although scientific advancement has had major benefits for humankind, both at an individual level and for populations generally, the limiting factors for populations remain the four great categories of death, famine, war and disease.

The first great natural disaster affecting human population was probably the eruption of Toba, some 75,000 years ago. The volcanic fall-out from the eruption of Toba in the Philippines, led to a lowering of global temperatures and crop failures, and this in turn has been blamed for a severe diminution in the numbers of humans, together with other animals. There is some genetic evidence to suggest that the number of humans in the world may have been diminished to as little as 10,000 individuals, with the subsequent recovery of numbers as the climate was restored after a long period of cold weather with poor crops. By the time of the early introduction of agriculture after the last ice age numbers of humans had climbed back into the low millions. Further natural disasters of the magnitude of the Toba volcanic explosion have been mercifully fewer and smaller.

The advent of agriculture (chapter 11) occurring roughly simultaneously in the Middle East, China and the Americas, resulted in the gradual growth of human numbers once more, such that by the beginning of the first millennium AD the total world population may have approximated to three or four hundred million people. Better estimates are available for some localised areas as population records were beginning to be kept for the purposes of taxation. Thus, in China, the population at the time of Christ is estimated at over 50 million people, whilst the same amount is estimated for the Roman Empire rather later at the time of the 4th century AD. A population total of one billion worldwide is estimated to have been achieved around the year 1800, with two billion being achieved in 1927. Due to continuing exponential growth present world population of just of seven billion was reached less than a century later in 2012.

Natural disasters have made relatively much lesser impact since the time of the Agricultural Revolution. However, different parts of the world have grown at different rates, partly because agricultural technology has always been spread unevenly across the world, and partly because natural disasters of drought and famine have been episodic and localised to different areas. Similarly, disease has been a variable factor affecting different countries at different times. Plagues were recorded in Egypt and set down in the Bible and in the Torah of ancient times. A plague of unidentified nature struck Ancient Greece in 430 BC, but stayed localised to the country; many different bacterial diseases have been suggested for this epidemic including typhus, smallpox and anthrax. The plague of Justinian, named after the reigning Roman Emperor of the time in 541 AD, was probably bubonic plague or the black death, which killed about half the population of the Roman Empire at the time.

Disease has been increasingly better understood since the Enlightenment when 19th century research discovered bacteria as the cause of infections. Better hygiene, better public health, clean water and sewage treatment, have all gradually spread during the last two centuries, with a consequent fall in the number of people dying from infectious diseases. Infectious diseases and plagues or epidemics, which are their worst large manifestations, have been a constant, feared and unpredictable killer in the past, especially when people became crowded together in an urban setting with no real understanding of the causes of diseases and their transmission. This knowledge permeated outwards from Europe and was aided by colonisation, so that in this way the knowledge spread into other areas of the world. However, the chances of calamitous epidemics of uncontrollable diseases, such as smallpox, anthrax and Ebola are still not beyond the realms of possibility.

The provision of clean water is one of the most effective ways of diminishing diarrhoeal diseases and other epidemics in both adults and susceptible young children. The work of John Snow (1813–1858) an English doctor, in tracing the water pump which was the source of a cholera outbreak in London's Soho in 1854 led to a re-evaluation of the need for clean water and the effective provision of waste systems; incidentally Snow was also responsible for supporting the early use of ether and chloroform as surgical anaesthetics and gave chloroform to Queen Victoria for the birth of her last two children in 1853 and 1857.

The two measures of the provision of clean drinking water and the disposal of sewage have contributed probably more than any other measures to the steadily diminishing infant and maternal mortality through the 19th century, not forgetting the contribution also played by the understanding of childhood disease. It is salutary to recall that in 1740 up to three-quarters of children died before the age of 5, and that in 1820 less than a century later, this figure had reduced to one-third of children dying before the age of 5.

A second Agricultural Revolution took place alongside the Industrial Revolution of the 18th and 19th centuries thanks to technology. Mechanisation of arable farming, together with selective breeding of domesticated animals, provided enormous increases in productivity for the production of food, together with a general lowering of the price of food, and this should not be overlooked as a contributor to ensuring better nutrition, and therefore better resistance to disease, through the 19th century. The 18th century had seen a great change in the way people lived in northern European countries; in 1800 just 3% of the population led an urban life, but by 1900 the figure had risen to 47% with 50% being achieved by 1910.

At the same time, through the 19th century, the combination of better understanding of disease and better nutrition also went hand in hand with an upsurge in welfare, initially seen in the institution in Britain of workhouses and then alms-houses, together with a steadily climbing rate of literacy, and then later in the century the beginnings of government welfare, in terms of unemployment and sickness insurance: all of these factors combined to increase longevity, and by doing so also increased the size of the population. This was reflected in a fourfold increase in European population from 100 to 400 million occurring between 1700 and 1900, with a similar fourfold increase in the UK population from 10 to 40 million. Malthus (chapter 89), who linked population size and growth to the availability of food, also emphasised that times of plentiful food would not only lead to healthier animals, but that as a result spare nutrition would result in increased breeding and animal numbers so that paradoxically increased food results in increase in populations rather than being reflected mainly in healthier animals.

However fast population may have grown, and its rate of increase has been exponential since very early times, this increase has been interrupted by disease and famine. Natural disasters cause significant knocks to the population locally, but do little to affect the overall trend of growth. Similarly, war may dent the growth rate for a period, but the European population grew from 400 million to 550 million between 1900 and 1950, even through the two world wars, indicating that despite the war time carnage, overall population growth continued. War will undoubtedly continue as a form of human behaviour, as recently exemplified in the early 20th century by the Japanese attempt to expand into China, and the German expansionist policy of 'Lebensraum' (room for living).

This attitude was initially brought about by a shortage of food in Germany through the First World War and the years following the war. The thinking was then extended to justify the annexation of lands neighbouring Germany in order to provide space and agricultural produce. Lebensraum also came to be justified on the grounds of German superiority as members of the Aryan race.

This aspect of thinking then logically implied inferiority of the neighbouring countries and their Slavic races, which in turn justified not only the expansion of Germany, but also the subjugation and ethnic cleansing of non-Germans, including Romanies, Gypsies and Jews. It was of course the Nazi German solution to exterminate the Jews which resulted in the Holocaust and the murder of some six million Jews across Europe by the Nazi regime during the Second World War.

Of the four great influences affecting population size we can see that the two most dramatic ones, warfare and natural disasters have been the two smaller factors affecting growth, while famine and disease have played the larger part. Among the factors promoting rapid population growth in the last century (and in rough order of importance) are:

1. Better clean water supplies and public health,
2. Discovery of the causes of diseases and the ways to combat them, especially with smallpox, polio and tuberculosis,
3. Diminished deaths in childbirth and lower neonatal and infant mortality,
4. Increased longevity and greater numbers of elderly people,
5. Improved nutrition and fewer episodes of famine thanks to better agriculture.
6. Modern medicines, including antibiotics (since the 1940s),
7. A failure to promote birth control now that the means to do so are well established ('the pill' became generally available in the 1960s), and now that the spectres of famine and disease are controlled in much of the world the pressure to have large families has lessened. With better education and literacy family sizes have been diminishing, but despite this the 20th century has seen enormous increases in population in Africa and Asia. China's 'one child policy' helped keep the country's growth to a minimum, but at the expense of distorting the population demographics, so that now there is concern that there may not be enough young adults to care for the increasing numbers of the elderly in future,
8. The under-populated countries of the world have provided a safety valve and absorbed a lot of excess growth since they were discovered by Europeans in the last four centuries, particularly from Europe into the Americas and Australasia, though now this safety valve has been used there will not be further help to humanity in the future.

Increasing world population has brought with it an increased need for food and farming together with environmental degradation and pollution, and with considerable damage not just to man's terrestrial environment, but also to the oceans, where we are only just beginning to realise the considerable and accumulating problem of plastic debris which was not foreseen when plastics were welcomed by consumers as a wonderful addition to manufacturing possibilities. Future generations are going to have a steadily increasing problem, not only in cleaning up the lands and seas after their parents, but also in making sure that future pollution is minimised or ideally abolished.

In addition to this, addressing carbon dioxide build-up and global warming is an equally major problem for future generations: it remains to be seen whether nations can cooperate together to solve all these massive problems, particularly as many people do not yet realise or accept that there is a problem with population size, pollution and global warming which are all inter-twined.

Possible further reading:
A Concise History of World Population by Massimo Livi-Bacci (Blackwell Publications)

Chapter 100
Global Warming

The last two centuries have seen a steady increase in the planet's temperature, which has been accelerating and has really come to light and to be noticeable and measurable over the last few decades. Good records are available for more than a hundred years now, and show a steady baseline increase in Earth's temperature, the pace of which is accelerating. Through the 19th century it was not really appreciated that the increase in population and the rise in the use of fossil fuels which have both come about because of the Industrial Revolution, were changing Earth's balance so adversely. The production of carbon dioxide has been implicated as the biggest single factor, since this accumulates in the atmosphere and prevents heat dissipation. Inevitably a large increase in population has generated much more carbon dioxide from heating and cooking, but possibly most of all through the 20th century from internal combustion engines using oil products to power vehicles, boats and planes. Increased manufacturing uses many resources and also causes the release of carbon dioxide as well as often causing overlooked or ignored pollution.

Carbon dioxide is normally used and kept in balance in the atmosphere by vegetation, notably trees, but the concomitant deforestation of the world's jungles and forests (which take up and fix carbon dioxide) since the end of the Ice Age, for agriculture, at the same time as increased production of carbon dioxide, has led to a steady increase in climatic temperatures, which has become irrefutably marked over the last two decades and into the 21st century; indeed half of all greenhouse gases emitted since the last Ice Age have been released in the last three decades from 1990 onwards.

Other factors have also contributed to global warming, including the increased production of methane resulting from increased farming of meat; grazing animals produce large quantities of the gas which is more powerful at global warming than carbon dioxide, but happily has a shorter life span in the atmosphere. The production of nitrous oxide and the release of chlorofluorocarbons (refrigerants) into the atmosphere have also played their part, not just with altered CO2 levels, but also by damaging the ozone layer. At the same time as this, the increased human population buys increased quantities of food and consumer goods, thus depleting some of Earth's less abundant commodities, particularly minerals and metals.

From the time of Christ through to the year 1800, there was very little change in most people's standards of living, but in the last 200 years there has been an exponential increase in wealth and the goods on which people have spent their incomes. Despite this, we have now reached a situation where the world's eight richest people (all men) possess more wealth than the poorest half of humanity. One must observe firstly that this seems both grossly unfair and obscene, and secondly it is necessary to wonder whether the eight individuals can possibly use or control such wealth in any meaningful way; it is certainly far more than any one person can possibly use. It is also possibly appropriate to ask if it is morally justifiable for a single individual to exploit his fellow humans in this way.

If global warming continues, as it surely must do until adequate counter measures are effectively instituted, then these trends will get worse. It now seems likely that the average temperature on the planet is likely to rise by between 1° and 4°C by 2100, and this has major implications for all of humankind and especially those living in marginal land areas, such as Bangladesh and some Pacific islands. Glaciers will diminish, releasing much water into the oceans, which will then rise inundating low lying areas, including some modern nations such as Bangladesh and some Indian Ocean islands.

If all of the Greenland ice sheet were to melt, it has been calculated that global sea levels would rise by about 6m. At the same time, the consequences of a larger population using more of the planet's resources and failing to recycle consumer goods, can only lead to massive further increases in pollution, both on land and at sea. These effects are quite separate from, but will contribute to, the overcrowding of the planet and the struggle for food and resources between nations and populations in all the different parts of the world.

Warming of the seas is already starting to cause the death of coral reefs, notably the Great Barrier Reef, and the fish and other creatures that live on them; acidification of the oceans from absorbed carbon dioxide forming carbonic acid is a further threat to marine life. It may also be noted that while a 10m rise in sea level would only flood 2% of the present Earth's land mass; some 10% of the world population presently live in this area of land.

The advent of agriculture and man's expansion in the past few millennia, has caused the extinction of most species of mega fauna, but many other animal and plant species are coming perilously close to extinction if present trends continue. As agriculture expands to feed a growing population, wildlife habitat, both fauna and flora, inevitably diminishes. In the second half of the 20th century many chemicals, including antibiotics and other drugs, together with weedkillers, have been discovered through research based on the planet's wildlife: if these resources are diminished then future scientific research, and production of valuable compounds including antibiotics, for mankind will become ever more difficult, but in the meantime release of these chemicals into the seas and onto the land are also gradually damaging wildlife.

There are remedies, but the human race has in the past shown itself to be poor in terms of cooperating for the general good of mankind, particularly between nations, instead history tells us that countries are prone to resort to warfare to achieve selfish ends. The two main remedies that would enable humans to continue to co-exist with its planet are firstly, to stabilise, or even diminish, the population of the world, and secondly to switch from using fossil fuels and instead promote renewable energy. These two very simple, but difficult measures, would if implemented, guarantee the continuing and relatively cooperative symbiosis between planet Earth and humankind.

21st century technology and science has progressed sufficiently for this to be achievable, though whether people and nations are sufficiently receptive, firstly to recognise the problem, and secondly to agree the remedies, seems rather dubious. There are those who say that agriculture can be developed and refined sufficiently to feed billions more people, but if this were to be implemented it would be likely to result in much further degradation of the planet.

Unfortunately, failure to proceed along these lines will result inevitably in increasing population pressures and conflict between nations, but at the same time failure will continue to cause general warming of the planet, which is likely to make life more difficult, and eventually even impossible for those remaining in the world. This all amounts to a rather depressing vicious circle for the future of humanity unless education of humans can lead to a reasoned solution. A further possible scenario remains, namely a huge world disaster, but this time a nuclear war causing depopulation on a massive scale rather than a more localised natural catastrophe; with the human propensity to solve problems by war apparent in the previous chapters, this clearly remains one possible future for the planet.

Possible further reading:
Climate Change by Mark Maslin (Oxford University Press)